STATE OF WASHINGTON

2023
Washington State
Adult Sentencing Guidelines
Manual

Washington State
Caseload Forecast Council

State of Washington
Caseload Forecast Council

Sen. Derek Stanford, Chair
Washington State Senator

David Schumacher, Vice Chair
Director, Office of Financial Management

Rep. Steve Bergquist
Washington State Representative

Chris Corry
Washington State Representative

Jilma Meneses
Secretary, Department of Social and Health Services

Sen. Lynda Wilson
Washington State Senator

Council Staff

Erik Cornellier, JD, MPA
Executive Director

Elaine Deschamps, PhD
Deputy Director

Kathleen Turnbow
Confidential Secretary

Clela Steelhammer
Senior Criminal Justice Policy Analyst

Alex Ge, PhD
Senior Caseload Forecaster

Jennifer Jones
Senior Research Analyst

Duc Luu
Database and Sentencing Administration Manager

Paula Moore, MPA
Senior Caseload Forecaster

Van Nguyen
Research Analyst

Webb Sprague, PhD
Senior Caseload Forecaster

Erik Sund, MPA
Senior Caseload Forecaster

Shidong Zhang, PhD
Senior Caseload Forecaster

ACKNOWLEDGMENTS

The Caseload Forecast Council acknowledges the work of Duc Luu, Jennifer Jones, Clela Steelhammer, and all the criminal justice participants that assisted in updating, reviewing, proofing, and offering language and formatting suggestions for revisions in the current manual.

We also acknowledge The Honorable Ronald Kessler (Ret.) for providing the update for the Sentencing Reform Act portion of the Criminal Caselaw Notebook©. Electronic versions of the Criminal Caselaw Notebook may be obtained at no charge by e-mailing a request to caselawnotebook@gmail.com

The Council also appreciates the suggestions for improvements and additions to the manual received from users.

We always welcome suggestions for making the manual easier to use.

TABLE OF CONTENTS

DISCLAIMER

The Caseload Forecast Council is not liable for errors or omissions in the manual, for sentences that may be inappropriately calculated as a result of a practitioner's or court's reliance on the manual, or for any other written or verbal information provided by the Caseload Forecast Council or its staff related to adult or juvenile sentencing, per RCW 43.88C.040(3). The scoring sheets are intended to provide assistance in most cases but do not cover all permutations of the scoring rules. If you find any errors or omissions, we encourage you to report them to the Caseload Forecast Council (CFC).

If errors are identified, staff at the CFC will make necessary corrections and issue an errata sheet. The errata sheets are maintained on the CFC website under the Publications link.

USE OF THIS MANUAL

The Adult Sentencing Guidelines Manual provides comprehensive information on adult felony sentencing in the state of Washington. This manual offers specific guidance on how to determine the appropriate standard sentence range for an offense by identifying the seriousness level of the offense and by "scoring" the person's criminal history. This manual also addresses reviews, modifications, and discharges of sentences, as well as vacating conviction records. As an aid to judges, prosecutors, defense attorneys and other criminal justice professionals, this manual also includes forms for use in "scoring" criminal history.

Adult felony sentencing in Washington is governed by the Sentencing Reform Act (SRA) of 1981, Chapter 9.94A RCW, as amended. This manual includes a digest of recent appellate and Supreme Court decisions interpreting and affecting the SRA and is excerpted from the *Criminal Caselaw Notebook©* courtesy of The Honorable Ronald Kessler (Ret.). Electronic versions of the *Criminal Caselaw Notebook* may be obtained at no charge by e-mailing a request to caselawnotebook@gmail.com.

Persons interested in a comprehensive legal analysis of the SRA are advised to read *Sentencing in Washington*, by David Boerner (Butterworth Legal Publishers) and the 2011-2012 supplement to *Washington Practice Volume 13A: Criminal Law*, by Seth Aaron Fine (West Publishing Co).

This edition of the manual has been updated to reflect amendments to the SRA enacted during the 2023 Legislative Session. Earlier editions of this manual should be retained for reference on offenses committed prior to the effective dates of the recently enacted legislation.

Copies of the 1984 through 2023 Adult Sentencing Guidelines Manuals and supplements are available electronically on the Council's website.

http://www.cfc.wa.gov

Bound copies of the 2011 through 2023 Adult Sentencing Guidelines Manuals are available for purchase through the web site as well.

Comments or suggestions related to this manual should be directed to:

Clela Steelhammer, Senior Criminal Justice Policy Analyst
Washington State Caseload Forecast Council
P.O. Box 40962
Olympia, WA 98504-0962
Telephone: (360) 664-9381
E-mail: Clela.Steelhammer@cfc.wa.gov

INTRODUCTION

Individuals meeting the definition of "offender" in RCW 9.94A.030 who committed felonies on or after July 1, 1984, are subject to the provisions of the Sentencing Reform Act of 1981, as amended (SRA). The goal of Washington's sentencing system, which is based on a determinate sentencing model and eliminates parole and probation, is to ensure that individuals who commit similar crimes and have similar criminal histories receive equivalent sentences. The enabling legislation, RCW Section 9.94A *et seq.*, contains guidelines and procedures used by courts to impose sentences that apply equally in all parts of the state, without discrimination as to any element that does not relate to the crime or to a defendant's previous criminal record. The SRA guides judicial discretion by providing presumptive sentencing ranges for the courts to follow. The ranges are structured so that offenses involving greater harm to a victim and to society result in greater punishment. Sentences that depart from the standard presumptive ranges must be based upon substantial and compelling reasons and may be appealed by either the prosecutor or the defendant.

The Sentencing Guidelines Commission (Commission) developed the initial guidelines and continues to advise the legislature on necessary adjustments. The Commission is composed of twenty-five voting members. Twenty are appointed by the Governor and include four Superior Court judges; two defense attorneys; two elected county prosecutors; five citizens (one of whom is a victim of crime or a crime victims' advocate and one who was formerly incarcerated in the state correctional system); one juvenile court administrator; one elected city official; one elected county official; one person representing the interests of tribes; one behavioral health professional; one person with knowledge of and expertise in academic research in the field of criminology or sociology; and the chief of a local law enforcement agency. Five voting members serve in an *ex-officio* capacity to their state positions: the Secretary of the Department of Corrections; the Director of the Office of Financial Management; the Assistant Secretary of the Department of Children, Youth, and Families' Juvenile Rehabilitation Administration; the Chair of the State Supreme Court Minority and Justice Commission; and the Chair of the Indeterminate Sentence Review Board. The Speaker of the House of Representatives and the President of the Senate each appoint two nonvoting members from their respective chambers, one from each of the two largest caucuses in each body.

The SRA mandated that the Commission develop and maintain computerized databases of adult felony sentences and juvenile dispositions and conduct research related to adult and juvenile sentencing. In addition, the Commission has traditionally assessed the prison, jail, and community corrections impacts of proposed sentencing policy changes as part of the state's fiscal note process.

The state legislature, in ESSB 5891 passed during the 2011 Legislative Session, transferred responsibility for the sentencing databases, sentencing manuals, and statistical summaries from the Commission to the Caseload Forecast Council (Council), effective August 24, 2011.

In order to carry out its mandate, the Council will continue to rely upon the cooperation and assistance of the superior court clerks of all thirty-nine counties in the state. The clerks transmit copies of Judgment and Sentence forms issued in all adult felony convictions to the Council. The Council's staff extracts data from the forms relating to the crime, the person sentenced, the sentencing judge, the sentence imposed, and alternatives to incarceration, where applicable, and enters the information into a computerized database. Using this database, the Council produces and distributes descriptive reports on actual sentences and analyzes the effects of changes in the law on prison, jail, and community corrections populations.

The Council database is also the source of information used in preparation of annual statistical summaries of sentencing practices and other reports and studies related to felony sentencing in the state. Please direct questions about the sentencing manuals, databases, and sentencing research to the Council's office.

SECTION 1

FELONY OFFENSES AFFECTED

BY 2023 SESSION LAW

RCW	RCW Title	Effective Date	Summary	Session Law	Sect.	Bill Number
28B.10.901	Hazing prohibited—Penalty.	7/23/2023	Amends the definition of Hazing and raises the offense from a misdemeanor to a gross misdemeanor. In cases resulting in substantial bodily harm, establishes the new Class C felony of Hazing.	Ch. 196	§1	HB 1002
9.94A.411	Evidentiary sufficiency.	7/23/2023	Adds the felony offense of Hazing to the list of offenses classified as a Crime Against a Person.	Ch. 196	§2	HB 1002
9.94A.515	Table 2- Crimes included within each seriousness level.	7/23/2023	Ranks felony Hazing at Seriousness Level (SL) 3 on the Adult Felony Sentencing Grid. Additionally makes technical corrections by removing the previously repealed offenses of Willful Failure to Return from Furlough at SL 4, Willful Failure to Return from Work Release at SL 3, and Unlawful Use of Prohibited Aquatic Animal Species at SL 1 and corrects RCW references for Domestic Violence Court Order Violation at SL 5.	Ch. 196	§3	HB 1002
9A.04.080	Limitation of actions.	7/23/2023	Extends the statute of limitations for sex offenses that applies to suspect identification from DNA testing or photograph from two to four years.	Ch. 197	§8	2SHB 1028
69.50.418	Tableting and encapsulating machines prohibited—Penalties.	7/23/2023	Establishes a new Class C felony of Possess, Purchase, Deliver, Sell, or Possess with Intent to Sell a Tableting Machine or Encapsulating Machine on the Adult Felony Sentencing Drug Grid.	Ch. 66	§1	EHB 1209
9.94A.518	Table 4—Drug offenses seriousness level.	7/23/2023	Ranks the offense established in RCW 69.50.418 at SL 2 on the Adult Felony Sentencing Drug Grid.	Ch. 66	§2	EHB 1209
9.94A.525	Offender score.	7/23/2023	Eliminates certain juvenile adjudications, (other than Murder 1,	Ch. 415	§2	EHB 1324

RCW	RCW Title	Effective Date	Summary	Session Law	Sect.	Bill Number
			Murder 2, and Class A sex offenses) from the offender score calculations in an adult conviction.			
9.41.010	Definitions (as amended by 2022 c 104).	7/23/2023	Amends the definition of "Firearm" to include frames and receivers and the definition of "Serious Offense" by adding felony DUI and Physical Control to the definition. Additionally adds definitions for the terms "Conviction or Convicted," "Domestic Violence," and "Sex Offense."	Ch. 295	§2	SHB 1562
9.41.040	Unlawful possession of firearms— Ownership, possession by certain persons— Restoration of right to possess— Penalties.	7/23/2023	Expands the definition for the offenses of Unlawful Possession of a Firearm 1 or 2 and moves the language regarding the right to petition to restore the right to possess a firearm to a new section.	Ch. 295	§3	SHB 1562
9A.46.110	Stalking.	7/23/2023	Expands and amends the definition of the Class B felony offense of Stalking. Adds the prohibited behaviors codified in Cyberstalking.	Ch. 461	§1	HB 1696
9A.90.130	Cyberstalking	7/23/2023	Repeals RCW 9A.90.130 which codifies the offense of Cyberstalking.	Ch. 461	§2	HB 1696
10.99.040	Duties of court— No-contact order.	7/23/2023	Prohibits the denial of a non-contact order based on the existence of a civil protection order. This expands the definition of the offense, punished as Domestic Violence Court Order Violation ranked at SL 5 on the Adult Felony Sentencing Grid.	Ch. 462	§302	E2SSB 1715
9A.44.160	Custodial sexual misconduct in the first degree.	7/23/2023	Elevates Custodial Sexual Misconduct 1 from a Class C felony to a Class B.	Ch. 7	§1	SSB 5033
9A.44.170	Custodial sexual misconduct in the second degree.	7/23/2023	Elevates Custodial Sexual Misconduct 2 from a gross misdemeanor to a Class C felony.	Ch. 7	§2	SSB 5033

RCW	RCW Title	Effective Date	Summary	Session Law	Sect.	Bill Number
9.94A.515	Table 2- Crimes included within each seriousness level.	7/23/2023	Raises Custodial Sexual Misconduct 1 from SL 5 to SL 7 and ranks Custodial Sexual Misconduct 2 at SL 5 on the Adult Felony Sentencing Grid.	Ch. 7	§3	SSB 5033
69.50.4011 & 69.50.4013	Counterfeit substances— Penalties & Possession of controlled substance— Penalty	7/1/2023	SB 5476 passed during the 2021 session expired on June 30, 2023. The expiration of the changes resulted in the offenses of Possession of a Controlled Substance and Possession of a Counterfeit Substance becoming unconstitutional (as ruled in *St. v. Blake.*) 2E2SSB 5536 addresses the unconstitutionality of the statutes and codifies the offenses as gross misdemeanor offenses, effective July 1, 2023.	Ch. 1, 2023 1st Special Session	§1 & §2	2E2SSB 5536
9A.36.080	Hate crime offense— Definition and criminal penalty.	7/23/2023	Expands the definition of the Class C felony Hate Crime, ranked at SL 4 on the Adult Felony Sentencing Grid.	Ch. 52	§1	ESB 5623
9.94A.411	Evidentiary sufficiency.	7/23/2023	Adds the felony offense Hate Crime to the list of offenses classified as a Crime Against a Person.	Ch. 52	§2	ESB 5623

SECTION 2

CASELAW RELATED TO THE

SENTENCING REFORM ACT

Excerpted from the *Criminal Caselaw Notebook©*, with permission, by The Honorable Ronald Kessler (Ret.). The selection for inclusion in the summary below is Calendar Years 2022 and 2023 to date. Electronic versions of the *Criminal Caselaw Notebook* may be obtained at no charge by e-mailing a request to the following.

caselawnotebook@gmail.com

ASSAULT

Matter of Mulamba, ___ Wn.2d ___, 2022WL1256426 (2022)
 Assault of a child 1° and 2° are alternative means crimes that do not require an unanimity instruction, *State v. Kiser,* 87 Wn. App. 126 (1997); 8-1.

DEADLY WEAPON/FIREARM

State v. Kelly, 25 Wn.App.2d 879 (2023)
 Deadly weapon enhancements must run consecutively, may not be mitigated at least for adults, State v. Mandefero, 14 Wn.App.2d 825 (2020), State v. Wright, 19 Wn.App.2d 37 (2021), but see: State v. McFarland, 189 Wn.2d 47 (2017); II.

State v. Wade, ___ Wn.App.2d ___, 534 P.3d 1221 (2023)
 Defendant is convicted of three crimes with a firearm enhancement on each, argues he cannot be sentenced to consecutive firearms enhancements as he possessed but one gun; held: RCW 9.94A.533(3) (2020) requires consecutive sentences for firearm enhancements, does not violate double jeopardy clause, *State v. DeSantiago, 149 Wn.2d 402,* 421 (2003); I.

State v. Senior, ___ Wn.App.2d ___, 533 P.3d 442 (2023)
 Felony firearm registration requirement, RCW 9.41.330(3) (2016), only applies to convictions after June 9, 2016; I.

DOMESTIC VIOLENCE

State v. Rivers, ___ Wn.2d ___, 533 P.3d 410 (2023)
 Trial court's qualifying sexual assault nurse examiner as an expert to testify to a correlation between strangulation and memory loss is within court's discretion, *State v. Flett,* 40 Wn.App. 277 (1985); 8-0.

State v. Abdi-Issa, ___ Wn.2d ___, 504 P.3d 223 (2022)
 Defendant kills his date's dog, is convicted of animal cruelty with a domestic violence aggravator; held: domestic violence statute, RCW 10.99.020(4), "includes, but is not limited to" specific crimes as domestic violence offenses, while the dog is the direct victim, the statutory definition of victim includes any person who has sustained injury as a direct result of the crime charged, RCW 9.94A.030(54), domestic violence aggravator was properly applied; 7-2.

GUILTY PLEAS

State v. Olsen, ___ Wn.App.2d ___, 530 P.3d 249 (2023)
 In 2003 defendant pleads guilty to VUCSA and other crimes, seeks to withdraw all pleas because VUCSA is invalid, *State v. Blake,* 197 Wn.2d 170 (2021), and pleas were indivisible; held: guilty plea to VUCSA was not invalid at the time, *Pers. Restraint of Newlun,* 158 Wn.App. 28, 35 (2010), *United States v. Broce,* 488

U.S. 563, 572, 109 S. Ct. 757, 102 L. Ed. 2d 927 (1989), thus plea agreement was not indivisible, distinguishing *State v. Turley,* 149 Wn.2d 395 (2003) ; II.

MURDER/MANSLAUGHTER

Cruz v. Arizona, 598 U.S. 17, 143 S.Ct. 650, 214 L.Ed.2d 391 (2023)

    In capital case defendant has a due process right, when future dangerousness is at issue, to an instruction that he is not eligible for parole if sentenced to life in prison despite possibility of executive clemency, *Lynch v. Arizona,* 578 U.S. 613, 136 S.Ct. 1818, 195 L.Ed.2d 99 (2016), *Simmons v. South Carolina,* 512 U.S. 154, 161–162, 114 S.Ct. 2187, 129 L.Ed.2d 133 (1994); 5-4.

State v. Avington, ___ Wn.2d ___, 2023WL6302339 (2023)

    Defendant is charged with murder by extreme indifference, evidence shows that he and others fired shots, one of which, not from defendant's gun, killed victim, defendant testifies he fired but wasn't aiming, trial court declines manslaughter lesser instruction; held: where there is some evidence, from any source, that presents a question of fact for the jury and that affirmatively establishes defendant's theory, court should give a lesser included instruction, *State v. Coryell,* 197 Wn.2d 397 (2021); here, defendant's testimony did not point to affirmative evidence supporting the lesser of manslaughter as there was no evidence that victim was killed recklessly or that shooter knew of and disregarded a substantial risk that a homicide may occur, RCW 9A.32.060(1); affirms *State v. Avington,* 23 Wn.App.2d 847 (2022); 8-1.

State v. Canela, ___ Wn.2d ___, 2022WL803396 (2022)

    Attempted murder 1° information alleges that defendant did an act that was a substantial step toward the commission of murder 1° and that the act was done with intent to commit murder 1°, jury also instructed on the definition of murder 1° including premeditation, defense argues for the first time on appeal that premeditation is an essential element that must be included in the charging document; held: premeditation is not an essential element that must be included in the charging document for attempted first degree murder, *State v. Orn,* 197 Wn.2d 343 (2021), *overruling, in part, State v. Murry,* 13 Wn. App.2d 542 (2020); 9-0.

PERSISTENT OFFENDER

Cruz v. Arizona, 598 U.S. 17, 143 S.Ct. 650, 214 L.Ed.2d 391 (2023)

    In capital case defendant has a due process right, when future dangerousness is at issue, to an instruction that he is not eligible for parole if sentenced to life in prison despite possibility of executive clemency, *Lynch v. Arizona,* 578 U.S. 613, 136 S.Ct. 1818, 195 L.Ed.2d 99 (2016), *Simmons v. South Carolina,* 512 U.S. 154, 161–162, 114 S.Ct. 2187, 129 L.Ed.2d 133 (1994); 5-4.

State v. Rivers, ___ Wn.2d ___, 533 P.3d 410 (2023)

    POAA defendant is entitled to resentencing if past conviction for robbery 2° was used as a basis of finding that offender was a persistent offender, RCW 9.94A.647 (2021), *State v. Caril,* 23 Wn.App.2d 416 (2022); 8-0.

State v. Reynolds, ___ Wn. App.2d ___, 505 P.3d 1174 (2022)

Prior strike occurred when defendant was a juvenile and was declined; certified copy of decline order plus other documents showing he was represented by counsel is sufficient to establish the prior strike, *cf.: State v. Knippling,* 166 Wn.2d 93 (2009); life without parole is not precluded by a prior committed when the defendant was a juvenile, *State v. Teas,* 10 Wn. App.2d 111 (2019), does not iolate equal protection or constitute cruel and unusual punishment; I.

PROBATION, PAROLE, COMMUNITY CUSTODY

State v. Hubbard, 1 Wn.2d 439 (2023)

Once a SSOSA is revoked trial court cannot modify community custody provisions, *State v. Petterson,* 190 Wn.2d 92, 103 (2018); reverses *State v. Hubbard,* 21 Wn.App. 834 (2022); 9-0.

Pers. Restraint of Ansell, ___ Wn.2d ___, 533 P.3d 875 (2023)

ISRB-imposed condition that child sex offender not possess sexually explicit materials that further defines sexually explicit is not vague, *cf.: State v. Sansone,* 127 Wn.App. 630 (2005), *State v. Nguyen,* 191 Wn.2d 671 (2018), *State v. Irwin,* 191 Wn.App. 644 (2015); prohibiting dating persons with children without approval is not vague, *State v. Nguyen, supra.* at 682; requirement that defendant not form relationships with persons with minor children unless he discloses sex offender status is not vague or improper; prohibiting use of cannabis where marijuana was not related to the crime is not authorized; 8-1.

Pers. Restraint of Campbell, ___ Wn.App.2d ___, 533 P.3d 144 (2023)

Defendant is on community custody, is charged with new crimes, at revocation hearing ISRB declines to dismiss violations based on new crimes that had not been adjudicated, DOC serves defendant's lawyer with discovery; held: DOC policy calling for dismissal without prejudice when a new charge is pending is discretionary not mandatory; discovery may be served upon counsel, need not be given directly to defendant; II.

State v. Frederick, 20 Wn. App. 1081, 506 P.3d 690 (2022)

Condition that defendant not engage in "sexual communication" with minors is not vague; condition that defendant obtain CCO's permission before entering a "romantic relationship" is vague; Indeterminate Sentencing Review Board can impose conditions that are reasonably related to the offender's risk of reoffending, condition that defendant submit to drug monitoring in sex offense is proper where defendant was under the influence of marijuana at time of sex offense; condition that defendant not access the internet without a monitoring device at defendant's expense is proper where defendant used the internet to contact victim, *State v. Johnson,* 197 Wn.2d 740 (2021), *cf.: Packingham v. North Carolina,* —— U.S. ——, 137 S. Ct. 1730, 198 L. Ed. 2d 273 (2017); condition that defendant not possess "sexually explicit material" is not vague, *State v. Nguyen,* 191 Wn.2d 671 (2018); condition that defendant not engage in a romantic or dating or sexual relationship with anyone with minor children without CCO permission is not vague, *but see: State v. Geyer,* 19 Wn. App.2d 321 (2021); condition that defendant inform potential partners of his sexual offense history does not violate his Fifth Amendment rights; condition that defendant not remain overnight in a residence (as opposed to "premises") without CCO approval is not vague, *State v. Breidt,* 187 Wn. App. 534 (2015); III.

Matter of Rodriguez, ___ Wn. App.2d ___, 506 P.3d 1256 (2022)

Court cannot impose 12 months community custody for first time offender waiver if no treatment is ordered, RCW 9.94A.650; III.

RESTITUTION/LFO

State v. Griepsma, 25 Wn.App.2d 814 (2023)

Victim penalty assessment does not violate excessive fine clauses of Eighth Amendment of CONST. art. I, §14; I.

State v. Ellis, ___ Wn.App.2d ___, 530 P.3d 1048 (2023)

Court has discretion to waive restitution, RCW 9.94A.753(3) (2022), VPA, RCW 7.68.035(4) (2023), filing fee, RCW 36.18.020(2)(h), retroactive to cases on direct appeal; community custody supervision fees are no longer authorized, RCW 9.94A.703(2) (2022); II.

State v. Long, ___ Wn. App.2d ___, 505 P.3d 550 (2022)

Restitution for vacation and sick leave taken by the victim due to her injuries is proper; I.

ROBBERY

State v. Derri, ___ Wn.2d ___, 2022WL2252282 (2022)

That portion of robbery statute that states "[s]uch force or fear must be used to obtain or retain possession of the property, or to prevent or overcome resistance to the taking, RCW 9A.56.190, is an essential element of the crime, *disapproving, in part, State v. Phillips,* 9 Wn. App.2d 368 (2019), but, where challenged after trial the element can be fairly implied by inclusion of the language "take…by…inmediate force…and fear; affirms *State v. Derri,* 17 Wn. App.2d 376 (2021); 9-0.

SENTENCING

Pers. Restraint of Dean, ___ Wn.App.2d ___, 2023WL4783545 (2023)

Defendant is convicted of possession of drugs and robbery, receives consecutive sentences, drug charge is vacated per *Blake,* defendant seeks credit for time served on the VUCSA to apply to the robbery; held: defendant is entitled to credit for time served on a vacated conviction when serving time for another offense; III.

SRA: MITIGATING FACTORS

State v. Kelly, 25 Wn.App.2d 879 (2023)

Where the offender score is reduced, *State v. Blake,* 197 Wn.2d 170 (2021), but the standard range remains the same as the reduction is from 10 to 9, the judgment is not facially invalid and resentencing may be time barred, *In re Pers. Restraint of Richardson,* 200 Wn.2d 845 (2022); deadly weapon enhancements must run consecutively, may not be mitigated at least for adults, *State v. Mandefero,* 14 Wn.App.2d 825 (2020), *State v. Wright,* 19 Wn.App.2d 37 (2021), *but see: State v. McFarland,* 189 Wn.2d 47 (2017); II.

State v. Ellis, ___ Wn.App.2d ___, 530 P.3d 1048 (2023)

At resentencing pursuant to *State v. Blake, 197 Wn.2d 170 (2021)* defendant who committed murder at age 18 seeks mitigated sentence for youthfulness, trial court declines stating it lacked authority, follows defense counsel's standard range sentence; held: while a court has discretion to impose a sentence below the standard range due to an 18-year old's youthfulness, *State v. Nevarez, 24 Wn.App. 2d 56, 60 (2022) State v. Mandefero,* 14 Wn.App.2d 825 (2020), *State v. Meza,* 22 Wn.App.2d 514 (2022), here error was harmless as court-imposed sentence requested by defense counsel; II.

State v. Stewart, ___ Wn.App.2d ___, 532 P.3d 211 (2023)

Defendant who is resentenced as he was a juvenile at time of offense, *State v. Houston-Sconiers*, 188 Wash.2d 1, 8 (2017), cannot appeal the resentencing if sentencing court meaningfully considers his youth and sentences within the standard range; II.

SRA: PROCEDURE

State v. Royal, ___ Wn.App.2d ___, 530 P.3d 573 (2023)

In presentence report defense counsel lists defendant's priors, excluding two, on appeal defense argues that none of the priors were proved; held: a defendant's assertion of his criminal history amounts to an affirmative acknowledgment, relieving state of burden to prove priors, *cf.: State v. Lucero, 168 Wn.2d 785 (2010)*; while state failed to prove the priors that were not acknowledged, because defendant's offender score was 9+ and thus recalculated score would not impact standard range matter need not be remanded for resentencing unless record showed that trial court wanted to sentence defendant to low end, *but cf.: State v. McCorkle, 88 Wn.App. 485 (1997), aff'd*, 137 Wn.2d 490 (1999); I.

State v. Conaway, ___ Wn. 2d ___, 512 P.3d 526 (2022)

A misdemeanor deferred sentence that was dismissed after successfully completion is a conviction for purposes of the SRA, *State v. Haggard,* 195 Wn.2d 544, 551 (2020), *cf.: Pers. Restraint of Carrier,* 173 Wn.2d 791 (2012); 5-4

State v. Barnett, ___ Wn. App.2d ___, 506 P.3d 714 (2022)

Firearm enhancement, RCW 9.94A.533(3), must run consecutive to all offenses, including unlawful possession of a firearm; I.

Matter of Rodriguez, ___ Wn. App.2d ___, 506 P.3d 1256 (2022)

Court cannot impose 12 months community custody for first time offender waiver if no treatment is ordered, RCW 9.94A.650; III.

SRA: SAME CRIMINAL CONDUCT

State v. Westwood, ___ Wn.2d ___, 534 P.3d 1162 (2023)

Defendant enters victim's house, pushes her into her room, orders her to get undressed, threatens to kill her, victim is nicked with defendant's knife, defendant is convicted of attempted rape, assault 1°, argues same criminal conduct; held: court looks to the statutory intent of the crimes, here separate and distinct charges were brought, jury found that statutory intent for each was proved, objective analysis is that the crimes did not have the same objective criminal intent, crimes did not further the other crimes thus did not encompass the same criminal conduct, *State v. Dunaway,* *109 Wn.2d 207 (1987), State v. Chenoweth, 185 Wn.2d 218 (2016)* ; *reverses State v. Westwood,* 20 Wn.App. 582 (2021); 5-4.

State v. Bell, ___ Wn.App.2d ___, 523 P.3d 847 (2023)
Defendant shoots victim from a car, is convicted of assault 1°, RCW 9A.36.011(1)(a) and drive-by shooting, RCW 9A.36.045, argues same criminal conduct; held; because assault involves a specific named victim and drive-by shooting involves only that defendant created a risk to an unnamed other person the crimes do not involve the same victim and thus do not encompass the same criminal conduct, *State v. Haddock, 141 Wn.2d 103 (2000)*; I.

SRA: WASH
State v. Green, 26 Wn.App.2d 517 (2023)
Sentencing court includes two prior convictions in offender score where state was unable to prove the date defendant was released to establish that more than five years had passed, RCW 9.94A.525(2)(c) (2017, 2023); held: the court may rely on a judgment and sentence to establish the impossibility that an offense has washed and thus the state need to prove the actual release date, *cf.: State v. Havens,* 171 Wn.App. 220 (2012); III.

SEX OFFENSES
State v. Hubbard, 1 Wn.3d 439 (2023)
Once a SSOSA is revoked trial court cannot modify community custody provisions, *State v. Petterson*, 190 Wn.2d 92, 103 (2018); reverses *State v. Hubbard,* 21 Wn.App. 834 (2022); 9-0.

Pers. Restraint of Ansell, ___ Wn.2d ___, 533 P.3d 875 (2023)
ISRB-imposed condition that child sex offender not possess sexually explicit materials that further defines sexually explicit is not vague, *cf.: State v. Sansone, 127* *Wn.App. 630 (2005), State v. Nguyen,* 191 Wn.2d 671 (2018), *State v. Irwin,* 191 Wn.App. 644 (2015); prohibiting dating persons with children without approval is not vague, *State v. Nguyen, supra.* at 682; requirement that defendant not form relationships with persons with minor children unless he discloses sex offender status is not vague or improper; prohibiting use of cannabis where marijuana was not related to the crime is not authorized; 8-1.

In re Glant, 25 Wn.App.2d 567 (2023)
Detective poses on Craigslist as the mother of two children seeking sex, defendant responds, is arrested at the place he was to meet the mother and children, is convicted of two counts of attempted child molestation, argues same criminal conduct; held: crimes affecting more than one victim cannot encompass the same criminal conduct, *State v. Canter,* 17 Wn.App.2d 728 (2021), *State v. Lessley, 118 Wn.2d 773,* *777 (1992)*; I.

State v. Reedy, 26 Wn.App.2d 379 (2023)
In multiple count sexual assault case trial court does not give "separate and distinct" instruction but prosecutor's closing argument describes each incident as

separate and that, to convict, jury must be convinced beyond a reasonable doubt that three separate incidents occurred; held: where it is manifestly apparent from evidence, arguments and instructions that state is not seeking to impose multiple punishments for the same offense and that each count is based on a separate act there is no double jeopardy violation, *State v. Mutch,* 171 Wn.2d 646, 661-66 (2011), *State v. Land,* 172 Wn.App. 593, 598-603 (2013); I.

State v. Domingo-Cornelio, 26 Wn.App.2d 187 (2023)
Mandatory sex offender registration for juveniles, RCW 9A.44.130 (2017) [amended, LAWS OF 2023, CH. 150, §5], is not punishment and thus does not violate Eighth Amendment, disposition court did not have discretion to waive registration; II.

State v. Aguilar, ___ Wn.App.2d ___, 534 P.3d 360 (2023)
Defendant is convicted of **rape 1°**, information alleges, as an alternative means, that complainant was "situated" in the building, RCW 9A.44.040(1)(d), evidence establishes she was not in the building, no unanimity instruction was given thus reversed; evidence described two distinct instances of rape but jury was not instructed that it had to unanimously agree as to which act constituted the single rape offense, thus reversed; if state chooses to retry rape case upon remand court may not instruct jury on the insufficiently proven alternative means, felonious entry, prohibited by double jeopardy clause; I.

State v. Crossguns, ___ Wn.2d ___, 505 P.3d 529 (2022)
While evidence of collateral misconduct relating to a specific victim, including prior uncharged acts of sexual conduct, remains admissible under ER 404(b), "lustful disposition" is not a separate purpose for admitting evidence; the phrase "lustful disposition" is "incorrect and harmful" even though the evidence that has come in under the doctrine remains admissible; overrules or modifies *State v. Medcalf,* 58 Wn. App. 817 (1990), *State v. Guzman,* 119 Wn. App. 176 (2003), *State v. Ferguson,* 100 Wn.2d 131 (1983), *State v. Dawkins,* 71 Wn. App. 902, 908-10 (1993); 8-1.

State v. Braun, ___ Wn. App.2d ___, 502 P.3d 884 (2022)
For purposes of human trafficking, RCW 9A.40.100 (2017), physical assaults constitute "force;" even if defendant didn't personally use "force, fraud or coercion" evidence is sufficient as long as he knew someone would use such means; defendant may be both perpetrator of the force, fraud or coercion and the beneficiary of the sexual act; withholding drugs from an addict to get her to commit prostitution is coercion; promises of marriage if victim commits prostitution constitutes fraud; III.

State v. Frederick, 20 Wn. App. 1081, 506 P.3d 690 (2022)
Condition that defendant not engage in "sexual communication" with minors is not vague; condition that defendant obtain CCO's permission before entering a "romantic relationship" is vague; Indeterminate Sentencing Review Board can impose conditions that are reasonably related to the offender's risk of reoffending, condition that defendant submit to drug monitoring in sex offense is proper where defendant was under the influence of marijuana at time of sex offense; condition that defendant not access the internet without a monitoring device at defendant's expense is proper where defendant used the internet to contact victim, *State v. Johnson,* 197 Wn.2d 740 (2021), *cf.: Packingham v. North Carolina,* —— U.S. ——, 137 S. Ct. 1730, 198 L. Ed. 2d 273

(2017); condition that defendant not possess "sexually explicit material" is not vague, *State v. Nguyen,* 191 Wn.2d 671 (2018); condition that defendant not engage in a romantic or dating or sexual relationship with anyone with minor children without CCO permission is not vague, *but see: State v. Geyer,* 19 Wn. App.2d 321 (2021); condition that defendant inform potential partners of his sexual offense history does not violate his Fifth Amendment rights; condition that defendant not remain overnight in a residence (as opposed to "premises") without CCO approval is not vague, *State v. Breidt,* 187 Wn. App. 534 (2015); III.

SECTION 3

SENTENCING GUIDELINES

This section explains the rules for applying the sentencing guidelines to **felony crimes committed after June 30, 1984,** including changes enacted by the 2023 legislative session.

DETERMINING FELONY CLASS

Felonies defined in Title 9A and Title 9 of the Revised Code of Washington (RCW) fall into one of three classes: Class A, Class B or Class C. The class of these felonies is either defined explicitly as part of the definition of the offense, or implicitly, based on the statutory maximum period of incarceration. The felony class is used to determine the washout period (RCW 9.94A.525(2)), vacation of conviction record (RCW 9.94A.640), status as a violent offense (RCW 9.94A.030(58)), length of certain enhancements, statutory maximum period of incarceration, along with other determinations.

Felonies Defined in Title 9A RCW

Felonies defined by Title 9A RCW have an A, B or C class designation explicitly stated. These felonies carry the following maximum penalties (RCW 9A.20.021):

Class A   Life in prison, $50,000 fine

Class B   Ten years in prison, $20,000 fine

Class C   Five years in prison, $10,000 fine

Felonies Defined outside Title 9A RCW

Some felonies are defined outside Title 9A RCW without an explicit felony class. The 1996 Legislature[1] enacted RCW 9.94A.035, establishing the classes of such offenses for SRA purposes. The class is based on the maximum period of incarceration provided for the first conviction of violating the statute creating the offense:

Class A   20 years or more

Class B   Eight or more, less than 20 years

Class C   Less than eight years

Therefore, statutes increasing the maximum sentence for subsequent convictions do not affect the classification of the offense for SRA purposes, even though they increase the maximum sentence that may be imposed.

Felonies for which no maximum punishment is specifically prescribed are punished by confinement for not more than ten years and a fine not to exceed $20,000 or both and are classified as Class B felonies (RCW 9.92.010).

DETERMINING THE OFFENSE SERIOUSNESS LEVEL

The offense of *conviction* determines the offense seriousness level.

---

[1] Historically, RCW 9A.20.040 was used to determine the class of these "unclassed" offenses for SRA sentencing purposes, based on the same relationship between the offense and the maximum sentence as shown. A 1995 decision of the Court of Appeals, Division II (*State v. Kelley*, 77 Wn. App. 66) held that RCW 9A.20.040 should not be used to determine the class of crimes defined outside Title 9A, or where the statutory maximum has been doubled as a result of sentencing enhancements. The 1996 legislation was intended to be consistent with the *Kelley* decision.

General Felony Crimes

The seriousness level is measured on the vertical axis of the sentencing guidelines grid (Section 4, page 85). Offenses are divided into 16 seriousness levels ranging from low (Level I) to high (Level XVI). RCW 9.94A.515 lists the crimes within each seriousness level (Section 4, page 87).

This edition of the Sentencing Manual includes the grids applicable to offenses committed after July 24, 1999, as well as the 2023 changes to the list of offenses ranked on the adult felony sentencing grid. Previous versions of the grid can be found in Section 4.

On the grid, numbers in the first horizontal row of each seriousness category represent sentencing midpoints in months (m). Numbers in the second and third rows represent standard sentencing ranges in months, or in days if so designated. 12+ represents one year and one day.

Drug Crimes

Drug offenses committed on or after July 1, 2003, are divided into three seriousness levels and sentenced according to the drug grid (Section 4, page 94). RCW 9.94A.518 lists the crimes within each seriousness level (Section 4, page 95).

Unranked Felony Crimes

Some felonies are not included in the Seriousness Level table and are referred to as "unranked". Sentences for unranked felonies are entered without reference to a standard sentence range and do not require sentence calculations. The sentencing options for unranked felonies are described in Section 3, page 58.

DETERMINING THE OFFENDER SCORE

The offender score (RCW 9.94A.525), which is one factor affecting a felony sentence, is measured on the horizontal axis of the sentencing guidelines grid. An individual may receive from 0 to 9+ points on that axis. In general, the number of points received depends on five factors: (1) the number of prior criminal convictions or juvenile dispositions for countable offenses; (2) the relationship between any prior offense(s) and the current offense of conviction; (3) the presence of other current convictions; (4) the person's community custody status at the time the crime was committed; and (5) the length of crime-free behavior between offenses.

CRIMINAL HISTORY COLLECTION

Pursuant to RCW 9.94A.030(11), criminal history includes the defendant's prior adult convictions and juvenile court dispositions, whether in this state, in federal court, or elsewhere, and any issued certificates of restoration of opportunity. Although criminal history consists almost exclusively of *felony* convictions, in some instances, it also includes misdemeanors. The effect of criminal history also relates to the felony class of the crime (Class A, Class B or Class C), and the type (i.e., serious violent, violent, nonviolent, sex, etc.) of the offense. Lists of such felony offenses can be found in Section 4.

Adult Criminal History

The Criminal Justice Information Act (Chapter 10.98 RCW) established the Washington State Patrol Identification and Criminal History Section (the Section) as the primary source of information on state felony conviction histories. The Act directs judges to ensure that felony defendants are fingerprinted, and that arrest and fingerprint forms are transmitted to the Washington State Patrol (RCW 10.98.050(2)). After filing charges, prosecutors contact the Section for a person's Washington criminal history. Prosecutors also obtain out-of-state or federal criminal history information from the Federal Bureau of Investigation or other appropriate sources.

A conviction is defined as a verdict of guilty, a finding of guilty, or an acceptance of a plea of guilty. RCW 9.94A.525(1) defines a prior conviction as one existing before the date of the sentencing for the offense for which the offender score is being computed. Convictions entered or sentenced on the same date as the conviction for which the offender score is being computed are deemed "other current offenses" within the meaning of RCW 9.94A.589.

Prior adult convictions should be counted as criminal history unless:

"Wash out" provisions apply; or

A court has previously determined that they constituted "same criminal conduct" as defined by RCW 9.94A.589; or

They were not previously deemed "same criminal conduct", but their sentences were served concurrently, and a court now determines that they were committed at the same time, in the same place, and involved the same victim; or

The sentences were served concurrently, and they were committed before July 1, 1986.

RCW 9.94A.030(11) provides that, when the information is available, criminal history should include the length and terms of any probation and/or incarceration. This information is often collected as part of the Pre-sentence Investigation Report that may be ordered by the court in certain sentences (RCW 9.94A.500 and 9.94A.695).

Juvenile Criminal History

Felony dispositions in juvenile court for any Class A sex offense, Murder 1, or Murder 2, are the only offenses to be counted as criminal history for purposes of scoring adult offenses committed after July 22, 2023. For offenses committed prior to July 23, 2023, all felony dispositions in juvenile court must be counted as criminal history for purposes of adult sentencing except under the general "wash-out" provisions. Juvenile offenses sentenced on the same day must be counted separately unless they constitute the "same criminal conduct" as defined in RCW 9.94A.589(1)(a) or unless the date(s) of the offenses were prior to July 1, 1986.

Although juvenile records generally are sealed, RCW 13.50.050(10) provides that after a charge has been filed, juvenile offense records of an adult criminal defendant or witness in an adult criminal proceeding shall be released upon request to the prosecution and defense counsel, subject to the rules of discovery. A charging of an adult felony subsequent to the sealing has the effect of nullifying the sealing order of a juvenile record.

"Wash Out" of Certain Prior Felonies

The rules governing which prior convictions are included in the offender score can be found in RCW 9.94A.525 and are summarized as follows:

Prior Class A and felony sex convictions are always included in the offender score.

Prior Class B felony convictions, other than sex offenses, are *not* included in the offender score if, since the last date of release from confinement (including full-time residential treatment) pursuant to a felony conviction, if any, or since the entry of judgment and sentence, the person had spent ten consecutive years in the community without committing *any* crime that subsequently results in a conviction.*

Prior Class C felony convictions, other than sex offenses, are *not* included in the offender score if, since the last date of release from confinement (including full-time residential treatment) pursuant to a felony conviction, if any, or since the entry of judgment and sentence, the person had spent five consecutive years in the community without committing *any* crime that subsequently results in a conviction.*

Prior serious traffic convictions are *not* included in the offender score if, since the last date of release from confinement (including full-time residential treatment) pursuant to a conviction, if any, or since the entry of judgment and sentence, the person had spent five years in the community without committing *any* crime that subsequently results in a conviction.

Prior convictions for repetitive domestic violence offense, as defined in RCW 9.94A.030, are *not* included in the offender score if the person has spent ten consecutive years in the community without committing any crime resulting in a conviction since the last date of release.

If the present conviction is felony driving while under the influence of intoxicating liquor or any drug (RCW 46.61.502(6)) or felony physical control of a vehicle while under the influence of intoxicating liquor or any drug (RCW 46.61.504(6)), all predicate crimes for the offense as defined by RCW 46.61.5055(14) shall be included in the offender score, and prior convictions for felony driving while under the influence of intoxicating liquor or any drug (RCW 46.61.502(6)) or felony physical control of a vehicle while under the influence of intoxicating liquor or any drug (RCW 46.61.504(6)) shall always be included in the offender score.

The Sentencing Reform Act permits vacating records of conviction under certain conditions and provides that vacated convictions "shall not be included in the offender's criminal history for purposes of determining a sentence in any subsequent conviction." RCW 9.94A.640. Vacation of the conviction record does not affect or prevent the use of a person's prior conviction in a later criminal prosecution.

The eligibility rules for vacation of conviction record are similar to the "wash-out" rules. Because the "wash-out" rules are automatic and do not require court action, an offense will "wash out" before formal record vacation occurs. The main distinction between vacation of record of conviction and "wash-out" is that, after vacation, a person may indicate on employment forms that he or she was not convicted of that crime.

Federal, Out-of-State or Foreign Convictions

In order for a prior federal, out-of-state, or foreign conviction to be included in criminal history, and thereby affect the offender score, the elements of the offense in other jurisdictions must be compared with Washington State laws (RCW 9.94A.525(3)). In instances where the foreign conviction is not clearly comparable to an offense under Washington State law, or where the offense is usually considered a felony subject to exclusive federal jurisdiction, the offense is scored as a Class C felony equivalent.

SCORING CRIMINAL HISTORY

Once relevant prior convictions are identified, the portion of the offender score may be calculated. The rules for scoring prior convictions are contained in RCW 9.94A.525. It should be noted that the scoring rules for some offenses are calculated differently, depending upon the category of the offense. Offense scoring forms can be found in Section 7 of this manual and specify the correct number of points for prior convictions depending on the current offense. The forms are intended to provide assistance in most cases but do not cover all permutations of the scoring rules or are provided for all offenses. A thorough understanding of the criminal history rules is important in order to use these forms correctly and to perform calculations not covered by the forms.

General consideration should also be given to often-applicable exceptions to general scoring rules. For instance, misdemeanors generally are not included in score calculations. Exceptions exists in certain circumstances. Where the current conviction is for a felony traffic offense, serious traffic offenses are included in the score[2]; and for felony domestic violence where domestic violence was plead and proven[3], misdemeanor offenses of repetitive domestic violence are included in the score. In addition, if the present conviction is for Theft of a Motor Vehicle, Possession of a Stolen Vehicle, Taking a Motor Vehicle without Permission 1° or 2°, prior convictions for Vehicular Prowl 2° are also included in the offender score.

Additionally, with present convictions of anticipatory offenses (criminal attempt, solicitation, or conspiracy) prior convictions of felony anticipatory offenses count the same and are scored as if they were convictions for completed offenses.[4] Exceptions to the general scoring rules also exist for Burglary 1°[5], Burglary 2° and Residential Burglary,[6] for Manufacturing Methamphetamine and other drug offenses,[7] for Escape offenses,[8] for Failure to Register as a Sex Offender,[9] or for crimes involving the taking, theft, or possession of a stolen motor vehicle[10, 11].

Prior convictions for felony anticipatory offenses (attempts, solicitations, and conspiracies) are scored as if they were convictions for completed offenses. RCW 9.94A.525(4).

Finally, an exception should also be noted for convictions with a finding of sexual motivation. A finding of sexual motivation changes the underlying offense to a sex offense as defined in

---

[2] See RCW 9.94A.525(2)(e), (11) and (12).
[3] See RCW 9.94A.525(21).
[4] See RCW 9.94A.525(4)-(6).
[5] See RCW 9.94A.525(10).
[6] See RCW 9.94A.525 (16).
[7] See RCW 9.94A.525(13).
[8] See RCW 9.94A.525 (14) and (15).
[9] See RCW 9.94A.525(18).
[10] See RCW 9.94A.525 (20).
[11] See RCW 9.94A.525(21).

RCW 9.94A.030(47), changing the scoring rules and impacting the sentence options. This scoring rule only applies to crimes committed on or after July 1, 1990 (RCW 9.94A.525(17)).

SCORING MULTIPLE CURRENT CONVICTIONS

Multiple convictions may also affect the offender score. For multiple current offenses, separate sentence calculations are necessary for *each* offense because the law requires that each receive a separate sentence unless the offenses are ruled the same criminal conduct (RCW 9.94A.589).

Multiple Offense Scoring Steps

If the current offenses do *not* include two or more serious violent offenses arising from separate and distinct criminal conduct, apply RCW 9.94A.589(1)(a):

Calculate the score for each offense.

For each offense, score the prior adult and countable juvenile convictions.

For each offense, score the other current offenses on the scoring form line entitled "Other Current Offenses."

The court may find that some or all of the current offenses encompass the same criminal conduct and are to be counted as one crime.

In cases of Vehicular Homicide or Vehicular Assault with multiple victims, offenses against each victim may be charged as separate offenses, even if the victims occupied the same vehicle. The resulting multiple convictions need not be scored as constituting the same criminal conduct.

Convictions entered or sentenced on the same date as the conviction for which the offender score is being computed are scored as "Other Current Offenses."

Example: Assume that a person is convicted of one count of Theft in the First Degree and one count of Forgery, with both offenses arising from separate and distinct criminal conduct, and that the person had criminal history consisting of one conviction for Burglary in the Second Degree. In this case, the rules in RCW 9.94A.589(1)(a) apply, and the theft and forgery must be separately scored. The prior burglary and the current forgery are included in the offender score for the theft, resulting in a score of two and a sentence range of 3 to 9 months. The prior burglary and the current theft are included in the offender score for the forgery, resulting in a score of two and a sentence range of 2 to 5 months. The sentence for each offense will run concurrently.

Example: Assume that a person is convicted of one count of Theft in the Second Degree and one count of Possession of Stolen Property in the Second Degree in a circumstance where both counts encompassed the same criminal conduct, and that the person had no criminal history. In this case, the other current offense is not counted in the offender score because under RCW 9.94A.589(1)(a) where current offenses are found to encompass the same criminal conduct, those current offenses shall be counted as one crime. Therefore, the theft and possession would both be scored with scores of zero, with a sentence range for each crime of 0 to 60 days. The sentence for each offense will run concurrently.

Example: Assume that a person is convicted on one count of Assault in the Third Degree, with a criminal history consisting of adult convictions for Theft in the Second Degree and Forgery and a single adjudication of Murder in the Second Degree as a juvenile. Pursuant to RCW 9.94A.589(1)(a), the prior Theft in the Second Degree and Forgery are included in the offender score as one point each, and the juvenile Murder in the Second Degree also scores as one point, resulting in a score of three points. The sentence range is 9 to 12 months.

If the current offenses include two or more serious violent offenses arising from separate and distinct conduct, apply RCW 9.94A.589(1)(b):

Calculate the score for each offense.

Identify the serious violent offense with the highest seriousness level. Calculate the sentence for that crime using the person's prior adult and countable juvenile convictions. Do not include any other current serious violent offenses as part of the offender score but do include other current offenses that are not serious violent offenses.

Score all remaining serious violent current offenses, calculating the sentence for the crime using an offender score of zero.

For any current offenses that are not serious violent offenses, score according to the rules in (A) above.

Example: Assume that a person is convicted of two counts of Kidnapping in the First Degree and one count of Assault in the First Degree. These offenses are classified as serious violent offenses. Assume further that these offenses arose from separate and distinct criminal conduct and that the person's criminal history consists of one Assault in the Third Degree conviction. The scoring for these offenses follows the rules in RCW 9.94A.589(1)(b). First, the crime with the highest seriousness level must be identified and scored. Since Assault in the First Degree is more serious (Level XII) than Kidnapping in the First Degree (Level X), that offense is scored by counting the prior Assault in the Third Degree as part of the adult criminal history. This calculation results in a score of one and a sentence range of 102 to 136 months. The Kidnapping in the First Degree convictions are scored using a criminal history of zero. These calculations result in two sentence ranges of 51 to 68 months. The three sentences will run consecutively.

If the current offenses include Unlawful Possession of a Firearm in the First or Second Degree and one, or both, of the felony crimes of Theft of a Firearm or Possession of a Stolen Firearm, score according to the rules in RCW 9.94A.589(1)(c).

SCORING STATUS WHILE ON COMMUNITY CUSTODY

The offender score also reflects whether the offense was committed while the person was under community custody. An additional point is added to the offender score for crimes committed on or after July 1, 1988, while the person was on community custody. RCW 9.94A.525(19). Community custody includes community placement and post-release supervision as defined in RCW 9.94A.030.

DETERMINING THE STANDARD RANGE USING THE SENTENCING GRID

Once the offense seriousness level has been determined and the offender score has been calculated, the presumptive standard sentence range may be identified on the appropriate sentencing grid.

The standard sentence range for any ranked offense *not* covered under Chapter 69.50 RCW (controlled substances) is established by referring to the standard sentencing grid (RCW 9.94A.510). For each current offense, the intersection of the column defined by the offender score and the row defined by the offense seriousness level determines the standard sentence range. Alternatively, the same range is identified on the individual offense scoring forms provided in this manual. In those cases where the presumptive sentence duration exceeds the statutory maximum sentence for the offense, the statutory maximum sentence is the presumptive sentence unless the person has been sentenced as a persistent offender. If the addition of a firearm or other deadly weapon enhancement increases the sentence so that it would exceed the statutory maximum for the offense, the portion of the sentence representing the enhancement may not be reduced (See RCW 9.94A.599).

Sentences **Imposed for Aggravated First Degree Murder on or after June 1, 2014, REGARDLESS OF THE DATE OF THE OFFENSE**, should be calculated and entered in accordance with the sentencing grid in Section 4, page 85 of this manual and as set forth in RCW 9.94A.510.

Sentences **Imposed on or after July 1, 2013,** for **Drug Crimes, REGARDLESS OF THE DATE OF THE OFFENSE**, should be calculated and entered in accordance with the drug sentencing grid in Section 4, page 94 of this manual and as set forth in RCW 9.94A.517.

Sentences **Imposed before July 1, 2013, for Drug Crimes committed on or after July 1, 2003,** should be calculated and entered in accordance with the drug sentencing grid in Section 4, page 101 of this manual.

Sentences for **crimes committed on or after July 25, 1999**, and not affected by the 2002 amendments to the SRA, should be determined according to the sentencing grid in Section 4, page 85.

Sentences for **crimes committed on or after July 27, 1997, and before July 25, 1999,** should be determined according to the sentencing grid in Section 4, page 97.

Sentences for **crimes committed on or after July 1, 1990, and before July 27, 1997,** should be determined according to the sentencing grid in Section 4, page 98.

Sentences for **crimes committed prior to July 1, 1990,** should be determined according to the sentencing grid in Section 4, page 99.

Anticipatory of Non-Violation of the Uniform Controlled Substances Act (VUCSA) Offenses (Attempts, Conspiracies, and Solicitations)

The standard sentence range for persons convicted of an anticipatory felony offense (criminal attempt, solicitation, or conspiracy) is 75% of the standard sentence range of the completed offense, determined by using the offender score and offense seriousness level (RCW 9.94A.595). For aid in calculating the range, refer to the anticipatory offense grids in Section 4.

Criminal Attempt (RCW 9A.28.020)

A person is guilty of an attempt to commit a crime if, with intent to commit a specific crime, he or she does any act which is a substantial step toward the commission of that crime.

If the conduct in which a person engages otherwise constitutes an attempt to commit a crime, it is no defense to a prosecution of such attempt that the crime charged to have been attempted was, under the attendant circumstances, factually or legally impossible of commission.

An attempt to commit a crime is a Class A felony when the crime is:

Murder in the First Degree,

Murder in the Second Degree,

Arson in the First Degree,

Child Molestation in the First Degree,

Indecent Liberties by Forcible Compulsion,

Rape in the First Degree,

Rape in the Second Degree,

Rape of a Child in the First Degree, or

Rape of a Child in the Second Degree;

Class B felony when the crime attempted is a Class A felony other than an offense listed above;

Class C felony when the crime attempted is a Class B felony;

Gross misdemeanor when the crime attempted is a Class C felony;

Misdemeanor when the crime attempted is a gross misdemeanor or misdemeanor.

Criminal Solicitation (RCW 9A.28.030)

A person is guilty of criminal solicitation when, with intent to promote or facilitate the commission of a crime, he or she offers to give or gives money or other thing of value to another to engage in specific conduct which would constitute such crime, or which would establish complicity of such other person in its commission or attempted commission had such crime been attempted or committed.

Criminal solicitation shall be punished in the same manner as criminal attempt under RCW 9A.28.020.

Criminal Conspiracy (RCW 9A.28.040)

A person is guilty of criminal conspiracy when, with intent that conduct constituting a crime be performed, he or she agrees with one or more persons to engage in or cause the performance of such conduct, and any one of them takes a substantial step in pursuance of such agreement.

It shall not be a defense to criminal conspiracy that the person or persons with whom the accused is alleged to have conspired:

Has not been prosecuted or convicted; or

Has been convicted of a different offense; or

Is not amenable to justice; or

Has been acquitted; or

Lacked the capacity to commit an offense; or

Is a law enforcement officer or other government agent who did not intend that a crime be committed.

Criminal conspiracy is a:

Class A felony when an object of the conspiratorial agreement is Murder in the First Degree;

Class B felony when an object of the conspiratorial agreement is a Class A felony other than Murder in the First Degree;

Class C felony when an object of the conspiratorial agreement is a Class B felony;

Gross misdemeanor when an object of the conspiratorial agreement is a Class C felony;

Misdemeanor when an object of the conspiratorial agreement is a gross misdemeanor or misdemeanor.

Anticipatory Offenses (RCW 9.94A.595)

For persons convicted of the anticipatory felony offenses of criminal attempt, solicitation, or conspiracy under Chapter 9A.28 RCW, the presumptive sentence is determined by locating the sentencing grid sentence range defined by the appropriate offender score and the seriousness level of the crime and multiplying the upper and lower range values by 75% to produce the anticipatory sentencing range.

In calculating an offender score, count each prior conviction as if the present conviction were for the completed offense. When these convictions are used as criminal history, score the same as a completed offense.

Anticipatory VUCSA Offenses (Attempts, Conspiracies, and Solicitations)

The calculation of sentences stemming from anticipatory VUCSA offenses (Chapter 69.50 RCW) presents different challenges than calculating sentences for anticipatory offenses arising under the criminal code.

An attempt or conspiracy to commit a VUCSA offense is specifically addressed in RCW 69.50.407, which provides that such offenses are punishable by "...imprisonment or fine or both which may not exceed the maximum punishment prescribed for the offense..." The appellate courts have consistently held that for VUCSA offenses, RCW 69.50.407 takes precedence over Chapter 9A.28 RCW. Although current statute and caselaw should be reviewed for definitive guidance in this area, the following summarizes current sentencing practices.

An attempt or conspiracy to commit a VUCSA offense is typically sentenced as an "unranked" offense (0-12 months). In *State v. Mendoza*, the Court of Appeals held that as "a conspiracy conviction under RCW 69.50.407 has no sentencing directions from the Legislature, it is punished under the unspecified crimes provisions of RCW 9.94A.505(2)(b)." 63 Wn. App. 373 (1991).

A *solicitation* to commit a VUCSA offense is not specifically addressed in Chapter 69.50 RCW. It is usually charged under Chapter 9A.28 RCW and sentenced under

RCW 9.94A.517 at 75% of the standard range. Solicitations to commit VUCSA offenses are not considered "drug offenses" but do score as such and are subject to the multiple "scoring" requirement. See RCW 9.94A.525(4), (6) and *State v. Howell*, 102 Wn. App. 288, 6 P. 3d 1201 (2000).

Table 1 presents the current status of statute and caselaw on appropriate sentence ranges for anticipatory VUCSA offenses.

Table 1. Sentence Ranges for Anticipatory VUCSA Offenses

Offense Type	Sentence Range	Statute
Attempt [*]	Unranked (0 to 12)	RCW 69.50.407
Conspiracy [*]	Unranked (0 to 12)	RCW 69.50.407
Solicitation [**]	75% of Standard Range	RCW 9A.28.030

Delivery Definition (RCW 69.50.101(i))

"Deliver" or "delivery" means the actual or constructive transfer from one person to another of a substance, whether or not there is an agency relationship.

Criminal Conspiracy (RCW 69.50.407)

Any person who attempts or conspires to commit any offense defined in this chapter is punishable by imprisonment or fine or both which may not exceed the maximum punishment prescribed for the offense, the commission of which was the object of the attempt or conspiracy.

Criminal Solicitation (RCW 9A.28.030)

A person is guilty of criminal solicitation when, with intent to promote or facilitate the commission of a crime, he or she offers to give or gives money or other thing of value to another to engage in specific conduct which would constitute such crime, or which would establish complicity of such other person in its commission or attempted commission had such crime been attempted or committed.

Criminal solicitation shall be punished in the same manner as criminal attempt under RCW 9A.28.020.

The Washington State Court of Appeals ruled that although VUCSA offenses are not considered drug offenses as defined in 9.94A.030, they do score as a drug offense. See *State v. Howell*, 102 Wn. App. 288, 6 P.3d 1201 (2000).

The Supreme Court clarified that solicitations to commit VUCSA offenses are not "drug offenses" and are not subject to the community custody requirement for drug offenses, under RCW 9.94A.701 and 9.94A.702. See In re *Hopkins*, 137 Wn.2d 897 (1999).

---

[*] If a standard sentence range has not been established for the offender's crime, the court shall impose a determinate sentence which may include not more than one year of confinement; community restitution work; a term of community custody under RCW 9.94A.702 not to exceed one year; and/or other legal financial obligations. The court may impose a sentence which provides more than one year of confinement and a community custody term under 9.94A.701 if the court finds reasons justifying an exceptional sentence as provided in RCW 9.94A.535.

[**] Solicitations drop one class from the underlying offense (e.g., a solicitation to commit a Class B felony is a Class C felony). Solicitations to commit Class C felonies are gross misdemeanors.

SECOND OR SUBSEQUENT DRUG OFFENSE (RCW 69.50.408)

Any person convicted of a second or subsequent offense under this chapter may be imprisoned for a term up to twice the term otherwise authorized, fined an amount up to twice that otherwise authorized, or both.

For purposes of this section, an offense is considered a second or subsequent offense, if, prior to his or her conviction of the offense, the individual has at any time been convicted under this chapter or under any statute of the United States or of any state relating to narcotic drugs, cannabis, depressant, stimulant, or hallucinogenic drugs.

This section does not apply to offenses under RCW 69.50.4013.

TERMS OF CONFINEMENT
Standard Range Sentence

The sentencing grid prescribes the standard sentence range for most of the commonly charged felonies. RCW 9.94A.599 provides that if the presumptive sentence duration given in the sentencing grid exceeds the statutory maximum sentence for the offense, the statutory maximum sentence shall be the presumptive sentence.

The ranges in the sentencing grid are expressed in terms of total confinement. A court may convert total confinement sentences to partial confinement or community service in some sentences.

Location Where Sentenced is Served (RCW 9.94A.190)

Sentences are served at a state facility or institution when the sentence imposed is:

A term of confinement is at least one year and one day (12+),

A Drug Offender Sentencing Alternative which has a standard range of over one year,

Any sex offense sentenced under RCW 9.94A.507, or

A felony with a term of confinement of one year or less and the person sentenced is committed or returned to confinement in a state facility on another felony conviction with confinement greater than one year.

Sentences are served at a local facility or institution when the sentence imposed is a term of one year or less (other than those described above).

"Unranked" Crimes

Convictions for "unranked crimes," crimes without an assigned seriousness level, are not subject to standard sentence ranges. In such cases, courts are required to impose a determinate sentence which may include zero to 365 days of confinement and may also include community service, legal financial obligations, a term of community custody not to exceed one year, and/or a fine. Orders of confinement longer than one year constitute exceptional sentences, which must be justified in writing (RCW 9.94A.505(2)(b); RCW 9.94A.535).

Persistent Offenders

Voters approved Initiative 593 ("Three Strikes and You're Out") in 1993. The law, which became effective on December 2, 1993, established the penalty of life in prison without the possibility of release for "persistent offenders." The life sentence applies to individuals sentenced under the "Three Strike" and "Two Strike" laws.

"Three Strikes"

The original "Three Strikes" legislation defined a "persistent offender" as a person who is convicted of a "most serious offense" and who has at least two prior convictions for most serious offenses that would be included in the offender score under 9.94A.525. Adjudications in juvenile court are not counted as strikes. In order to be applicable to the three strikes statute, the first prior conviction must have occurred before the second prior conviction offense was committed. See Section 5, page 111 for a list of the "most serious offenses" as defined by RCW 9.94A.030(32).

"Two Strikes"

The definition of persistent offender also includes life without parole sentences for individuals sentenced under the "Two Strike" sex offense law. To qualify as a persistent sex offender, an individual must have two separate convictions of specified sex offenses. Adjudications in juvenile court are not counted as strikes. The 1997 Legislature broadened the list of offenses that qualify as strikes under the "Two Strikes" law. The specific offenses qualifying as "Two Strikes" are enumerated in the "persistent offender" definition in RCW 9.94A.030(37)(b) and can be found in Section 5, page 111.

A person convicted of one of these offenses, who has at least one previous conviction for one of these offenses, must be sentenced to life in prison without the possibility of release.

Non-Persistent Sex Offenders (Determinate-Plus)

During the 2001 Second Special Session, the Legislature enacted 3ESSB 6151 – The Management of Sex Offenders in the Civil Commitment and Criminal Justice Systems. The resulting "non-persistent offender" system is also called "determinate-plus", but it is an indeterminate sentence (RCW 9.94A.507). A person must be sentenced to an indeterminate term if he or she is not a persistent offender but:

Is convicted of:

(i) Rape in the first degree, rape in the second degree, rape of a child in the first degree, child molestation in the first degree, rape of a child in the second degree, or indecent liberties by forcible compulsion; or

(ii) Any of the following offenses with a finding of sexual motivation: murder in the first degree, murder in the second degree, homicide by abuse, kidnapping in the first degree, kidnapping in the second degree, assault in the first degree, assault in the second degree, assault of a child in the first degree, assault of a child in the second degree, or burglary in the first degree; or

(iii) An attempt to commit any crime listed in (i) or (ii); or

Has a prior conviction for an offense listed in RCW 9.94A.030(37)(b), and is convicted of any sex offense, other than failure to register.

This sentencing rule does not apply to individuals seventeen years old or younger at the time of the offense and who have been convicted of Rape of a Child in the First Degree, Rape of a Child in the Second Degree or Child Molestation in the First Degree.

A "determinate-plus" sentence must contain a minimum term of confinement that falls within the standard range, according to the seriousness level of the offense and the offender score, and a maximum term equaling the statutory maximum sentence for the offense. The minimum term may also constitute an exceptional sentence as provided by RCW 9.94A.535.

The following offenses have a minimum term that is either the maximum of the standard sentence range for the offense or twenty-five years, whichever is greater, if the certain criteria exist:

- Rape of a Child in the First or Second Degree or Child Molestation in the First Degree, when there has been a finding under RCW 9.94A.836 that the offense was predatory; or

- Rape in the First Degree or Second Degree, Indecent Liberties with Forcible Compulsion, or Kidnapping in the First Degree with Sexual Motivation, when there has been a finding under RCW 9.94A.837 that the victim was under the age of fifteen at the time of the offense; or

- Rape in the First Degree, Rape in Second Degree with Forcible Compulsion, Indecent Liberties with Forcible Compulsion, or Kidnapping in the First Degree with Sexual Motivation, when there has been a finding under RCW 9.94A.838 that the victim was, at the time of the offense, a person with a developmental disability or mental disorder, or a frail elder or vulnerable adult.

A person sentenced as "determinate-plus" is eligible for earned release pursuant to RCW 9.94A.729 and is given the opportunity to receive sex offender treatment while incarcerated. Some individuals sentenced as "determinate-plus" are eligible for the Special Sex Offender Sentencing Alternative as provided in RCW 9.94A.670, unless they have committed Rape in the First Degree, Rape in the Second Degree or any of the following offenses with sexual motivation: Murder in the First Degree, Murder in the Second Degree, Homicide by Abuse, Kidnapping in the First Degree, Kidnapping in the Second Degree, Assault in the First Degree, Assault in the Second Degree, Assault of a Child in the First Degree, Assault of a Child in the Second Degree or Burglary in the First Degree. Additionally, all sentences under this provision must be served in prison, regardless of the sentence length.

Individuals receiving "determinate plus" sentences fall under the purview of the Indeterminate Sentence Review Board through the maximum term of the sentence.

Those released from prison will be supervised by the Department of Corrections (Department) and will remain on community custody through the maximum term of the sentence and are not eligible for the Supervision Compliance Credit established in RCW 9.94A.717.

EXCEPTIONAL SENTENCES

The standard sentence range is presumed to be appropriate for the *typical* felony case. The SRA, per RCW 9.94A.535, however, provides that the court "may impose a sentence outside the standard sentence range for that offense if it finds, considering the purpose of this chapter, that there are substantial and compelling reasons justifying an exceptional sentence."

An exceptional sentence must be for a determinate term and cannot exceed the statutory maximum for the crime. An exceptional sentence cannot include a term less than a mandatory minimum term of confinement if one exists. RCW 9.94A.540 sets a mandatory minimum term of confinement for certain offenses. Per terms specified in RCW 9.94A.570, persistent offenders sentenced to life in prison are not eligible for exceptional sentences.

Pursuant to the United States Supreme Court, before a court is permitted to impose sentences above the standard range, "[o]ther than the fact of a prior conviction, any fact that increases the penalty for a crime beyond the prescribed statutory maximum must be submitted to a jury and proved beyond a reasonable doubt." *Blakely v. Washington*, 542 U.S. 296, 124 S.Ct. 2531, 159 L.Ed.2d 403 (2004).

If an exceptional sentence is given, the sentencing court is required to set forth the reasons for the departure from the standard range (RCW 9.94A.535) or from the consecutive/concurrent policy (RCW 9.94A.589(1) and (2)) in written Findings of Fact and Conclusions of Law. Exceptional sentences may be appealed by the individual or by the state.

RCW 9.94A.535 provides a list of factors that the court may consider in deciding whether to impose an exceptional sentence.

Mitigating Circumstances for Exceptional Sentences

Mitigating circumstances justifying a sentence below the standard range can found in RCW 9.94A.535(1). The circumstances on this list are provided as examples only. It is not intended to be an exclusive list of reasons for a departure below the standard range.

Aggravating Circumstances for Exceptional Sentences

Unlike mitigating circumstances, an exceptional sentence that is aggravated must be based on one or more of the circumstances listed in the statute. The list is not illustrative.

The court may impose an aggravated exceptional sentence *without* a finding of fact by a jury if the defendant and state both stipulate that justice is best served by an exceptional sentence and the court agrees that the stipulation is in the interest of justice and consistent with the Sentencing Reform Act under RCW 9.94A.535(2).

The court may also impose an exceptional sentence above the standard range if the procedures specified in RCW 9.94A.537 are followed and a jury makes findings of fact supporting any of the aggravating circumstances found in RCW 9.94A.535(3).

CONSECUTIVE AND CONCURRENT SENTENCES

RCW 9.94A.589 sets forth the rules regarding consecutive and concurrent sentences. Generally, sentences for multiple offenses set at one sentencing hearing are served concurrently unless there are two or more separate serious violent offenses, driving under the influence offenses, or weapon offenses. In those cases, the sentences are served consecutively, unless an exceptional sentence is entered (RCW 9.94A.589(1)(a-c)). The exceptions to this general rule are as follows:

Offenses that Constitute Same Criminal Conduct

If the court enters a finding that some or all of the current offenses required the same criminal intent, were committed at the same time and place, and involved the same victim, the offenses are treated as one offense (RCW 9.94A.589(1)(a)). A departure from this rule requires an exceptional sentence (RCW 9.94A.535).

Multiple Serious Violent Offenses

In the case of two or more serious violent offenses arising from separate and distinct criminal conduct, the sentences for these serious violent offenses are served consecutively to each other and concurrently with any other sentences imposed for current offenses (RCW 9.94A.589(1)(b)). A departure from this rule requires an exceptional sentence (RCW 9.94A.535).

Certain Firearm-Related Offenses

In the case of sentences that include Unlawful Possession of a Firearm in the First or Second Degree *and* one or both of the crimes of Theft of a Firearm or Possession of a Stolen Firearm, the sentences for these crimes are served consecutively for each conviction of the felony crimes listed and for each firearm unlawfully possessed[12]. (RCW 9.94A.589(1)(c)). A departure from this rule requires an exceptional sentence. (RCW 9.94A.535).

Felony Driving while under the Influence (DUI) /Felony Actual Physical Control of a Vehicle while under the Influence

All sentences imposed under RCW 46.61.502(6), RCW 46.61.504(6) and RCW 46.61.5055(4) shall be served consecutively to any sentences imposed under RCW 46.20.740 and RCW 46.20.750 (RCW 9.94A.589(1)(d)). Additionally, under RCW 46.20.740 and RCW 46.20.750, any sentences imposed under RCW 46.20.740 and RCW 46.20.750 shall be served consecutively to each other, as well as consecutively to RCW 46.61.502(6), RCW 46.61.504(6), or RCW 46.61.5055(4).

Under RCW 46.20.750, any sentences imposed under RCW 46.20.750 shall be served consecutively with any sentence imposed under RCW 46.61.520(1)(a) or RCW 46.61.522(1)(b). However, this is not codified under RCW 9.94A.589.

Enhancements

For sentences involving the following enhancements, the enhancement portion of the sentence is served consecutively to all other sentencing provisions:

- Firearm or other deadly weapon enhancements for offenses committed after July 23, 1995 (RCW 9.94A.533(3) and (4)).

- Impaired driving enhancements (RCW 9.94A.533(7) and (13)).

- Sexual motivation enhancement for offenses committed on or after July 1, 2006 (RCW 9.94A.533(8)).

Felony Committed while under Sentence for Another Felony

Whenever a current offense is committed while the person is under sentence for a previous felony and the person was also sentenced for another term of imprisonment,

---

[12] Part of Initiative 159. Effective for offenses committed after July 23, 1995 (RCW 9.41.040(6)).

the latter term may not begin until expiration of all prior terms (RCW 9.94A.589(2)). A departure from this rule requires an exceptional sentence (RCW 9.94A.535).

Felonies Committed while under Sentence for Another Felony

This rule applies when individuals face multiple charges or have multiple convictions from different jurisdictions. Subject to the above policies, whenever a person is sentenced under a felony that was committed while the person was *not* under sentence for a felony, the sentence runs concurrently with felony sentences previously imposed by any court in this or another state or by a federal court, unless the court pronouncing the subsequent sentence expressly orders that they be served consecutively (RCW 9.94A.589(3)).

Probation Revocation

Whenever any person granted probation under RCW 9.95.210 or RCW 9.92.060, or both, has a probationary sentence revoked and a prison sentence imposed, this sentence runs consecutively to any sentence imposed, unless the court pronouncing the subsequent sentence expressly orders that they be served concurrently (RCW 9.94A.589(4)). This rule applies when a pre-SRA case probation is revoked and he or she is also sentenced on a conviction for a crime committed after June 30, 1984, the inception date of the SRA.

Serving Total Confinement with Consecutive Sentences

In the case of consecutive sentences, all periods of total confinement must be served before any periods of partial confinement, community service, community supervision or any other requirement or condition of a sentence (RCW 9.94A.589(5)). This rule applies to individuals who have not completed their sentence requirements from a previous conviction and are sentenced to total confinement on a new offense. A departure from this rule requires an exceptional sentence (RCW 9.94A.535).

LIMITS ON EARNED RELEASE

RCW 9.94A.729 provides that a person's sentence may be reduced by "earned release time." This time is earned through good behavior and good performance, as determined by the correctional agency that has jurisdiction over the individual. A person can be credited for "earned release time" for time served on a sentence and during pre-sentence incarceration.

Earned release time of up to 50% for certain non-violent, non-sex offenses was effective July 1, 2003, and applied to individuals convicted prior to July 2, 2010.

Earned release time of up to 15% is allowed for an offense categorized as a serious violent or Class A sex offense committed on or after July 1, 1990, and before July 1, 2003.

Earned release time of up to 10% is allowed for an offense categorized as a serious violent or Class A sex offense committed on or after July 1, 2003.

For sentences pursuant to RCW 10.95.030(3) or RCW 10.95.035, the time served during the minimum term of confinement imposed by the court is not eligible for earned release time; for any remaining portion of the sentence served, the aggregate earned release time may not exceed 10% of the sentence.

For sentences under the Special Sex Offender Sentencing Alternative, the time served for a suspended sentence is not eligible to accrue any earned release time.

For the portion of a sentence that results from any firearm and/or deadly weapon enhancements, sexual motivation enhancement, or impaired driving enhancements, earned release time is not allowed.

For all other offenses, the aggregate earned release time shall not exceed one-third of the total sentence.

Finally, no matter how much release time has been earned under RCW 9.94A.729, a person sentenced for a crime that has a mandatory minimum sentence shall not be released from total confinement before the completion of the mandatory minimum for that crime unless allowable under RCW 9.94A.540.

REVIEW OF SENTENCES

Sentences within the standard range cannot be appealed (RCW 9.94A.585). These include sentences imposed pursuant to the First-time Offender Waiver provisions found in RCW 9.94A.650. Sentences outside the standard range may be appealed by the defendant or by the prosecutor.

Review is limited to the record made before the sentencing court. Pending review, the sentencing court or the Court of Appeals may order the defendant confined or placed on conditional release, including bond.

Before reversing a sentence that is outside the sentence range, the Court of Appeals must find that:

> The reasons supplied by the sentencing judge were not supported by the record;
>
> They do not justify a sentence outside the range; or
>
> The sentence imposed was clearly excessive or clearly too lenient.

The Department may request a review of a sentence committing a person to the custody or jurisdiction of the Department. This review must be limited to errors of law and must be filed with the Court of Appeals no later than 90 days after the Department has actual knowledge of the term of the sentence. The Department must certify that all reasonable efforts to resolve the dispute at the Superior Court level have been exhausted.

A person convicted of one or more crimes committed prior to the person's eighteenth birthday may petition the Indeterminate Sentence Review Board for early release after serving no less than 20 years of total confinement (RCW 9.94A.730(1)), provided the person has not been convicted for any crime committed subsequent to the person's eighteenth birthday, the person has not committed a major violation in the twelve months prior to filing the petition for early release, and the current sentence was not imposed under RCW 10.95.030 or RCW 9.94A.507.

RCW 10.95.030 mandates that any person who was sentenced prior to June 1, 2014, to a term of life without the possibility of parole for an offense committed prior to their eighteenth birthday, shall be returned to the sentencing court or the sentencing court's successor for sentencing consistent with RCW 10.95.030.

VIOLATION OF COMMUNITY CUSTODY CONDITIONS

A person under the supervision of the Department who violates any condition or requirement of a sentence may be sanctioned by the court with up to sixty days' confinement for each violation or by the Department with up to thirty days confinement as provided in RCW 9.94A.737.

Any time served in confinement awaiting the violation hearing must be credited against any confinement order. If a court finds that a violation was not willful, the court may dismiss the violation and regarding payment of legal financial obligations and community service obligations or modify its previous order. In all cases of community custody escape, escape charges may also be filed, if appropriate.

These rules and procedures apply retroactively and prospectively regardless of the date of the underlying offense.

Arrest and Confinement (RCW 9.94A.631)

If a violation of any condition or requirement of a sentence occurs, a community corrections officer may arrest or cause the arrest of the person without a warrant, pending a determination by the court or by the Department. If there is reasonable cause to believe that a violation of a condition or requirement of the sentence has occurred, a community corrections officer may require the individual to submit to a search and seizure of his or her person, residence, automobile, or other personal property.

For the safety and security of Department staff, individuals under the Department's jurisdiction may be required to submit to pat searches, or other limited security searches, by community corrections officers, correctional officers, and other agency approved staff, without reasonable cause, when in or on Department premises, grounds, or facilities, or while preparing to enter Department premises, grounds, facilities, or vehicles. Pat searches shall be conducted only by staff who are the same gender as the individual, except in emergency situations.

A community corrections officer may also arrest a person under the Department's jurisdiction for any crime committed in his or her presence. The facts and circumstances of the conduct of the individual shall be reported by the community corrections officer, with recommendations, to the court, local law enforcement, or local prosecution for consideration of new charges. The community corrections officer's report shall serve as the notice that the Department will hold the person for not more than three days from the time of such notice for the new crime, except if the underlying offense is a felony offense listed in RCW 9.94A.737(5), in which case the Department will hold the person for thirty days from the time of arrest, until a prosecuting attorney charges the person with a crime, or until the prosecuting attorney notifies the Department that new charges will not be filed, whichever occurs first. This does not affect the Department's authority under RCW 9.94A.737.

If a community corrections officer arrests or causes the arrest of an individual under this section, the person shall be confined and detained in the county jail of the county in which he or she was taken into custody, and the sheriff of that county shall receive and keep in the county jail, where room is available, all prisoners delivered to the jail by the community corrections officer, and the person shall not be released from custody on bail or personal recognizance, except upon approval of the court or authorized Department staff, pursuant to a written order.

Sanctions and Procedures (RCW 9.94A.633)

A person who violates any condition or requirement of a sentence may be sanctioned by the court with up to sixty days' confinement for each violation or by the Department with up to thirty days' confinement as provided in RCW 9.94A.737.

In lieu of confinement, the sanction imposed may include work release, home detention with electronic monitoring, work crew, community restitution, inpatient treatment, daily reporting, curfew, educational or counseling sessions, supervision enhanced through electronic monitoring, or any other community-based sanctions.

If the person was under community custody pursuant to one of the following statutes, the sanction may be sanctioned as follows:

> If the person was transferred to community custody in lieu of earned early release in accordance with RCW 9.94A.728, he or she may be transferred to a more restrictive confinement status to serve up to the remaining portion of the sentence, less credit for any period actually spent in community custody or in detention awaiting disposition of an alleged violation.

> If the person was sentenced under the Drug Offender Sentencing Alternative (RCW 9.94A.660), he or she may be sanctioned in accordance with that section.

> If the person was sentenced under the Parenting Sentencing Alternative (RCW 9.94A.655), he or she may be sanctioned in accordance with that section.

> If the person was sentenced under the Special Sex Offender Sentencing Alternative (RCW 9.94A.670), the suspended sentence may be revoked, and the person committed to serve the original sentence of confinement.

> If the person was sentenced to a Work Ethic Camp (RCW 9.94A.690), he or she may be reclassified to serve the unexpired term of his or her sentence in total confinement.

> If a person was sentenced to a sex offense pursuant to RCW 9.94A.507, he or she may be transferred to a more restrictive confinement status to serve up to the remaining portion of the sentence, less credit for any period actually spent in community custody or in detention awaiting disposition of an alleged violation.

> If a person was sentenced under the Mental Health Sentencing Alternative (RCW 9.94A.695), he or she may be sanctioned in accordance with that section.

If a probationer is being supervised by the Department pursuant to RCW 9.92.060, 9.95.204, or 9.95.210, the probationer may be sanctioned pursuant to subsection (1) of this section. The Department shall have authority to issue a warrant for the arrest of an individual who violates a condition of community custody, as provided in RCW 9.94A.716. Any sanctions shall be imposed by the Department pursuant to RCW 9.94A.737. Nothing in this subsection is intended to limit the power of the sentencing court to respond to a probationer's violation of conditions.

The parole or probation of a person who is charged with a new felony offense may be suspended and the person placed in total confinement pending disposition of the new criminal charges if he or she:

Is on parole pursuant to RCW 9.95.110(1); or

Is being supervised pursuant to RCW 9.94A.745 and is on parole or probation pursuant to the laws of another state.

Sanctions – Where Served (RCW 9.94A.6331)

If a sanction of confinement is imposed by the court, the following applies:

If the sanction was imposed pursuant to RCW 9.94A.633(1), the sanction shall be served in a county facility.

If the sanction was imposed pursuant to RCW 9.94A.633(2), the sanction shall be served in a state facility.

If a sanction of confinement is imposed by the Department, and if the person is an inmate as defined by RCW 72.09.015, no more than eight days of the sanction, including any credit for time served, may be served in a county facility. The balance of the sanction shall be served in a state facility. In computing the eight-day period, weekends and holidays shall be excluded. The Department may negotiate with local correctional authorities for an additional period of detention.

If a sanction of confinement is imposed by the Indeterminate Sentence Review Board (Board), it shall be served in a state facility.

Sanctions imposed pursuant to RCW 9.94A.670(3) shall be served in a county facility.

As used in this section, "county facility" means a facility operated, licensed, or utilized under contract by the county, and "state facility" means a facility operated, licensed, or utilized under contract by the state.

Sanctions – Which Entity Imposes (RCW 9.94A.6332)

The procedure for imposing sanctions for violations of sentence conditions or requirements is as follows:

Sanctions shall be imposed by the Department or the court for the following sentences:

Drug Offender Sentencing Alternative (RCW 9.94A.660),

Sex Offender Sentencing Alternative (RCW 9.94A.670),

Parenting Sentencing Alternative (RCW 9.94A.655), or

Mental Health Sentencing Alternative (RCW 9.94A.695).

Sanctions shall be imposed pursuant to RCW 9.95.435 by the Board for the following sentences:

Sex offenses sentenced under RCW 9.94A.507,

Individuals released pursuant to RCW 9.94A.730, or

Sentences imposed pursuant to RCW 10.95.030(3) or 10.95.035.

In any other case, if the person is being supervised by the Department, any sanctions shall be imposed by the Department pursuant to RCW 9.94A.737.

If a probationer is being supervised by the Department pursuant to RCW 9.92.060, 9.95.204, or 9.95.210, upon receipt of a violation hearing report from the Department, the court retains any authority that those statutes provide to respond to a probationer's violation of conditions.

If the person is not being supervised by the Department, any sanctions shall be imposed by the court pursuant to RCW 9.94A.6333.

Sanctions – Modification of Sentence (RCW 9.94A.6333)

If a person violates any condition or requirement of a sentence, and is not being supervised by the Department, the court may modify its order of judgment and sentence and impose further punishment in accordance with this section.

If a person fails to comply with any of the nonfinancial conditions or requirements of a sentence the following provisions apply:

- a. The court, upon the motion of the state, or upon its own motion, shall require the person to show cause why the he or she should not be punished for the noncompliance. The court may issue a summons or a warrant of arrest for the person's appearance;

- b. The state has the burden of showing noncompliance by a preponderance of the evidence;

- c. If the court finds that a violation has been proved,

    - i. It may impose the sanctions specified in RCW 9.94A.633(1).

    - ii. Alternatively, the court may:

        - Convert a term of partial confinement to total confinement; or

        - Convert community restitution obligation to total or partial confinement.

If the court finds that the violation was not willful, the court may modify its previous order regarding community restitution obligations; and

If the violation involves a failure to undergo or comply with a mental health status evaluation and/or outpatient mental health treatment, the court shall seek a recommendation from the treatment provider or proposed treatment provider.

Enforcement of orders concerning outpatient mental health treatment must reflect the availability of treatment and must pursue the least restrictive means of promoting participation in treatment. If the failure to receive care essential for health and safety presents a risk of serious physical harm or probable harmful consequences, the civil detention and commitment procedures of chapter 71.05 RCW shall be considered in preference to incarceration in a local or state correctional facility.

If a person fails to pay legal financial obligations as a requirement of a sentence, the following provisions apply:

- The court shall require the person to show just cause why no punishment should be imposed for noncompliance;

- The state has the burden of showing noncompliance by a preponderance of the evidence;

- The court may not sanction for failure to pay, unless the court finds that the failure to pay is willful;

- If the court determines that the person is homeless or a person who is mentally ill, failure to pay is not willful noncompliance and shall not subject the person to penalties;

- If the court finds that a failure to pay is willful noncompliance, it may impose sanctions as specified in RCW 9.94A.633(1); and

- If the court finds the violation was not willful, the court may, and if the court finds that the defendant is indigent, the court shall modify the terms of payment, reduce, or waive nonrestitution legal financial obligations, or convert to community restitution if the jurisdiction operates a community restitution program.

- The crime victim penalty assessment shall be waived by the court if the defendant is indigent at the time of sentencing.

Any time served in confinement awaiting a hearing on noncompliance shall be credited against any confinement ordered by the court.

Nothing in this section prohibits the filing of escape charges if appropriate.

Department Structured Violation Process (RCW 9.94A.737)

If an individual is accused of violating any condition or requirement of community custody, the Department shall address the violation behavior. The Department may hold disciplinary proceedings not subject to chapter 34.05 RCW. The Department shall notify the person in writing of the violation process.

The violation behavior shall determine the sanction the Department imposes:

- The Department shall adopt rules creating a structured violation process that includes presumptive sanctions, aggravating and mitigating factors, and definitions for low level violations and high-level violations.

- After a person has committed and been sanctioned for five low level violations, subsequent violations committed *may be* considered high level violations, provided that any decision to elevate a violation complies with policies and rules established by the Department.

- The Department must define aggravating factors that indicate the person may present a current and ongoing foreseeable risk, which elevates the behavior to a high-level violation process.

- The state and its officers, agents, and employees may not be held criminally or civilly liable for a decision to elevate or not to elevate a person's behavior to a high-level violation process under this subsection unless the state or its officers, agents, and employees acted with reckless disregard.

The Department may intervene as follows when a low-level violation is committed:

- For a low-level violation, the Department may impose sanctions to include one or more nonconfinement sanctions or not more than three days in total confinement.

- The Department shall develop rules to ensure that each person subject to a short-term confinement sanction is provided the opportunity to respond to the alleged violation prior to imposition of total confinement.

- Individuals may appeal their short-term confinement sanction to a panel of three reviewing officers designated by the secretary or by the secretary's designee. The appeal must be in writing and hand-delivered to Department staff or postmarked within seven days after the sanction is imposed.

If a person is accused of committing a high-level violation, the Department may impose a sanction of not more than thirty days in total confinement per hearing.

- An individual is entitled to a hearing prior to the imposition of sanctions and may be held in total confinement pending a sanction hearing. Prehearing time served must be credited to the sanction time.

- If the underlying offense is one of the following felonies and the violation behavior constitutes a new misdemeanor, gross misdemeanor, or felony, the person shall be held in total confinement pending a sanction hearing, and until the earlier of: the date the sanction expires; the date a prosecuting attorney files new charges against the person; or the date a prosecuting attorney provides the Department with written notice that new charges will not be filed. The following underlying offenses apply to these restrictions:

    a. Assault in the First Degree, as defined in RCW 9A.36.011;
    b. Assault of a Child in the First Degree, as defined in RCW 9A.36.120;
    c. Assault of a Child in the Second Degree, as defined in RCW 9A.36.130;
    d. Burglary in the First Degree, as defined in RCW 9A.52.020;
    e. Child Molestation in the First Degree, as defined in RCW 9A.44.083;
    f. Commercial Sexual Abuse of a Minor, as defined in RCW 9.68A.100;
    g. Dealing in Depictions of a Minor Engaged in Sexually Explicit Conduct, as defined in RCW 9.68A.050;
    h. Homicide by Abuse, as defined in RCW 9A.32.055;
    i. Indecent liberties with Forcible Compulsion, as defined in RCW 9A.44.100(1)(a);
    j. Indecent Liberties with a Person Capable of Consent, as defined in RCW 9A.44.100(1)(b);
    k. Kidnapping in the First Degree, as defined in RCW 9A.40.020;
    l. Murder in the First Degree, as defined in RCW 9A.32.030;
    m. Murder in the Second Degree, as defined in RCW 9A.32.050;

n. Promoting Commercial Sexual Abuse of a Minor, as defined in RCW 9.68A.101;

o. Rape in the First Degree, as defined in RCW 9A.44.040;

p. Rape in the Second Degree, as defined in RCW 9A.44.050;

q. Rape of a Child in the First Degree, as defined in RCW 9A.44.073;

r. Rape of a Child in the Second Degree, as defined in RCW 9A.44.076;

s. Robbery in the First Degree, as defined in RCW 9A.56.200;

t. Sexual Exploitation of a Minor, as defined in RCW 9.68A.040; or

u. Vehicular Homicide while under the Influence of Intoxicating Liquor or any Drug, as defined in RCW 46.61.520(1)(a).

The Department shall adopt rules creating hearing procedures for high-level violations. The hearings are disciplinary proceedings and are not subject to chapter 34.05 RCW.

The procedures shall include the following:

- The Department shall provide the person with written notice of the alleged violation and the evidence supporting it. The notice must include a statement of the rights specified in this subsection, and the person's right to file a personal restraint petition under court rules after the final decision.

- Unless the person waives the right to a hearing, the Department shall hold a hearing, and shall record it electronically. For individuals not in total confinement, the Department shall hold a hearing within fifteen business days, but not less than twenty-four hours, after written notice of the alleged violation. For individuals in total confinement, the Department shall hold a hearing within five business days, but not less than twenty-four hours, after written notice of the alleged violation.

- The person alleged to have committed the violation shall have the right to:

    a. Be present at the hearing;

    b. Have the assistance of a person qualified to assist the person in the hearing; appointed by the hearing officer if there is a language or communications barrier;

    c. Testify or remain silent;

    d. Call witnesses and present documentary evidence;

    e. Question witnesses who appear and testify; and

    f. Receive a written summary of the reasons for the hearing officer's decision.

The hearings officer may not rely on unconfirmed or unconfirmable allegations to find that a violation of a condition occurred.

DISCHARGE AND VACATION OF CONVICTION RECORD
Discharge

When a person reaches the end of supervision with the Department, and all of the requirements of sentence except payment of legal financial obligations have been completed, the Department shall notify the county clerk who will then supervise payment of legal financial obligations.

When a person completes all of his or her sentence requirements, the Department (or the county clerk, if the clerk has been supervising payment of legal financial obligations) must notify the sentencing court in accordance with RCW 9.94A.637.

If a person is not subject to supervision by the Department or does not complete all of his or her sentence requirements while under Department supervision, he or she may file a motion with the sentencing court for a certificate of discharge when completion of all sentencing conditions, including payment of legal financial obligations, has occurred.

A person may also file a motion with the sentencing court if all conditions are completed other than legal financial obligations. He or she must provide verification of completion of conditions. A certificate of discharge issued under these circumstances is effective either five years after completion of community custody, or if no community custody was required, after completion of full/partial confinement; or the date all legal financial obligations were satisfied, whichever is later.

When the court has adequate notice from the Department, the court clerk, and/or the individual, the court then discharges the person and provides him or her with a certificate of discharge. This certificate restores all civil rights lost upon conviction. It is not, however, based on a finding of rehabilitation.

Every signed certificate and order of discharge shall be filed with the county clerk of the sentencing county. The court shall also send a copy of the certificate and order to the Department. The county clerk shall also enter the person's name, date of discharge and date of conviction and offense, into the database maintained by the Administrative Office of the Courts.

Following discharge, the person's prior record may be used to determine the sentence for any later convictions and may also be used in later criminal prosecution as an element of an offense or for impeachment purposes. Unless specifically ordered by the sentencing court, the certificate of discharge will not terminate the person's obligation to comply with an order issued under Chapter 10.99 RCW that excludes or prohibits he or she from having contact with a specified person or coming within a set distance of any specified location that was contained in the judgment and sentence. Individuals may still be prosecuted for violating any such provisions.

A person who is not convicted of a violent offense or a sex offense and is sentenced to a term of community supervision may be considered for a discharge of sentence by the sentencing court prior to the completion of community supervision, provided that at least one-half of the term of community supervision has been completed and all other sentence requirements have been met.

Upon release from custody, individuals may apply to the Department for counseling and help in adjusting to the community. The voluntary help may be provided for up to one year following the release from custody.

Vacation of Conviction Record

Everyone discharged under RCW 9.94A.637 may apply to the sentencing court for a vacation of the conviction record as provided in RCW 9.94A.640. A person's record cannot be cleared if:

Any criminal charges are pending against him or her in any court in this state, another state, or federal court;

The offense was a violent offense (as defined in RCW 9.94A.030);

The offense was a crime against persons (as defined in RCW 43.43.830) other than the following offenses that do not include a firearm, deadly weapon, or sexual motivation finding: Assault in the second degree (RCW 9A.36.021) Assault in the third degree when not committed against a law enforcement officer or peace officer (RCW 9A.36.031) or Robbery in the second degree (RCW 9A.56.210).

The offense was a Class B felony and the person has been convicted of a new crime in this state, another state, or federal court in the 10 years prior to the application for vacation;

The offense was a Class C felony and the person has been convicted of a new crime in this state, another state, or federal court in the five years prior to the application for vacation;

The offense was a Class B felony, and less than ten years have passed since the later of: (a) the applicant's release from community custody, (b) the applicant's release from full/partial confinement, or (c) the applicant's sentencing date;

The offense was a Class C felony, other than felony Driving under the Influence of Intoxicating Liquor or any Drug or felony Physical Control while under the Influence of Intoxicating Liquor or any Drug and less than five years have passed since the later of: (a) the applicant's release from community custody, (b) the applicant's release from full/partial confinement, or (c) the applicant's sentencing date; or

The offense was felony Driving under the Influence of Intoxicating Liquor or any Drug or felony Physical Control while under the Influence of Intoxicating Liquor or any Drug.

If these tests are met, the court may clear the record of conviction by:

Permitting the person to withdraw his/her guilty plea and to enter a plea of not guilty; or

Setting aside the guilty verdict, if the person was convicted after a plea of not guilty; and

Dismissing the information or indictment against the person.

Once the court vacates a record of conviction, the person's conviction may not be included in the person's criminal history for purposes of determining a sentence in any subsequent conviction, and the person must be released from all penalties and disabilities resulting from the offenses. For all purposes, including responding to questions on employment applications, a person whose record of conviction has been vacated may state that he or she has never been convicted of that crime. However, a vacated conviction record may be used as an element of a crime in a later criminal prosecution. A vacated conviction does qualify as a prior conviction for the purposes of charging a present recidivist offense and may be used to establish an ongoing pattern of abuse for the purposes an aggravated exceptional sentence (RCW 9.94A.535).

The sentencing guidelines allow automatic "wash-out" of prior convictions that meet the requirements of vacation of conviction. This policy allows individuals who do not formally apply to the court to have eligible offenses excluded from their criminal history in subsequent convictions. (See Determining Offender Score, Criminal History Collection in this section for further discussion of this policy.)

In addition, a victim of sex trafficking, prostitution, or commercial sex abuse of a minor; sexual assault; or domestic violence, may apply directly to the sentencing court to vacate the victim's record of conviction for a Class B or C felony offense. See RCW 9.94A.648 for further description of the process to vacate such offenses.

ALTERNATIVES TO CONFINEMENT
Alternative Conversions

The sentencing grid ranges are expressed in terms of total confinement (RCW 9.94A.530). For certain sentences, a court may convert terms of total confinement to partial confinement or to community service. This provision allows courts to take advantage of available alternatives to confinement in cases where it is deemed appropriate. If the court does not use an alternative conversion for a nonviolent offense with a sentence range of one year or less, the reason why must be stated on the Judgment and Sentence form (RCW 9.94A.680).

The 1999 Legislature modified the requirements for convictions of *non-violent or non-sex* offenses with a sentence of one year or less. Where a court finds that a chemical dependency contributed to the crime, the court may authorize the county jail to convert jail confinement to an available county-supervised community option. The court may require the person to perform affirmative conditions, such as rehabilitative treatment, which are reasonably related to the circumstances of the crime and are reasonably necessary or beneficial to the individual and to the community (RCW 9.94A.680).

For sentences of one year or less, one day of total confinement may be converted to one day of partial confinement. Individuals with convictions of non-violent offenses with sentences of one year or less, conversion of total confinement to community service (one day of confinement equals eight hours of service) is allowed. This community service conversion, however, is limited to 30 days or 240 hours. If a community service conversion is ordered and the determinate sentence is greater than 30 days, the balance of the term is to be served in total or partial confinement (RCW 9.94A.680).

Partial confinement sentences may allow a person to serve the sentence in work release, home detention, work crew, or a combination of work crew and home detention. If the person violates the rules of the work release facility, work crew, or home detention program, or fails to remain employed or enrolled in school, the facility director may transfer the individual to the county detention facility. The person may then request an administrative hearing. Pending the hearing, or in the absence of a request for such a hearing, the remainder of the term of confinement shall be served in total confinement (RCW 9.94A.731).

Work Crew

Work crew is a partial confinement option created by the 1991 Legislature. Those who qualify must have committed the offense on or after July 28, 1991. The offense must not be a sex offense. For offenses committed before July 25, 1993, the person must be sentenced to a facility operated or utilized under contract by a county (*i.e.*, the sentence must be one year or less in length); this restriction does not apply to offenses committed after that date. If the sentence is nine months or more, at least 30 days of total confinement must be served before becoming eligible for work crew. Work crew may be simultaneously imposed with electronic home detention. Work crew hours served may include work on civic improvement tasks, substance abuse counseling, job skills training or a maximum of 24 hours per week at approved, verified work.

To be eligible to receive credit for approved, verified work, a person must first successfully complete four weeks of work crew, each week comprised of 35 hours of service. Work crew projects specified by the work crew supervisor must be completed in coordination with approved, verified work. Unless exempted by the court, individuals using approved, verified employment as part of their work crew hours must pay a monthly supervision assessment (RCW 9.94A.725).

Home Detention

Home detention is a subset of electronic monitoring and means a program of partial confinement that may be available. In home detention, an individual is confined in a private residence 24-hours a day, unless an absence from the residence is approved, authorized, or otherwise permitted in the order by the court or other supervising agency that ordered home detention. The option was created by the 1988 Legislature and is available for individuals convicted of nonviolent or non-sex offenses committed on or after June 9, 1988. Because partial confinement programs are limited to sentences of one year or less, home detention is not an option for individuals with prison sentences unless imposed as part of the Parenting Program under RCW 9.94A.6551 or the Graduated Reentry Program under RCW 9.94A.733.

Eligibility for home detention is generally conditioned upon (a) employment or school attendance, performance of parental duties to minors normally in the custody of the individual; (b) program rules adherence; and (c) compliance with court-ordered legal financial obligations (RCW 9.94A.734(4)).

Convictions for any of the following offenses result in ineligibility for home detention unless imposed as partial confinement in the Parenting Program or the Graduated Reentry Program:

> A violent offense;
>
> A sex offense;
>
> A drug offense;
>
> Reckless Burning in the First or Second Degree;
>
> Assault in the Third Degree;
>
> Assault of a Child in the Third Degree;
>
> Unlawful Imprisonment; or
>
> Harassment.

Home detention may be imposed for individuals convicted of Possession of a Controlled Substance (RCW 69.50.4013) or Forged Prescription for a Controlled Substance (RCW 69.50.403), providing the person fulfills the participation conditions set forth in this section and is monitored for drug use *(2E2SSB 5536 passed in the special session of 2023 amended Possession of a Controlled Substance laws by classifying such offenses as gross misdemeanors; however, RCW 9.94A.734 was not amended to reflect the change.)*

Individuals convicted of Burglary in the Second Degree or Residential Burglary must meet the following eligibility conditions for home detention: (a) successful completion of a twenty-one day work release program; (b) no convictions for Burglary in the Second Degree or Residential Burglary during the preceding two years and not more than two prior convictions for Burglary or Residential Burglary; (c) no convictions for a violent felony offense during the preceding two years and not more than two prior convictions for a violent felony offense; (d) no prior charges of escape; and (e) fulfillment of the other conditions of the home detention program.

Individuals convicted of Theft of a Motor Vehicle without Permission in the Second Degree, Theft of a Motor Vehicle, or Possession of a Stolen Motor Vehicle must meet the following eligibility conditions for home detention: (a) no convictions for any of these crimes during the preceding five years and not more than two prior convictions for any of these offenses; (b) no prior convictions of a violent felony offense during the preceding two years and not more than two prior convictions for a violent felony offense; (c) no prior charges of escape; and (d) fulfillment of the other conditions of the home detention program.

Home detention may also be ordered for a person with medical or health-related conditions, concerns, or treatment that would be better addressed under the home detention program, or where the health and welfare of the individual, other incarcerated individuals, or staff would be jeopardized by the person's incarceration. Participation in the home detention program for medical or health-related reasons is conditioned on the person abiding by the rules of the home detention program and complying with court-ordered legal financial obligations.

A sentencing court shall deny the imposition of home detention if the court finds that (1) the person has previously and knowingly violated the terms of a home detention program and (2) the previous violation is not a technical, minor, or nonsubstantive violation.

A sentencing court may deny the imposition of home detention if the court finds that (1) the person has previously and knowingly violated the terms of a home detention program and (2) the previous violation or violations were technical, minor, or nonsubstantive violation.

A home detention program must be administered by a monitoring agency that meets the conditions described in RCW 9.94A.736.

Community Parenting Program

For individuals not sentenced under the Parenting Sentencing Alternative (RCW 9.94A.655), but otherwise eligible under this section, no more than the final twelve months of the term of confinement may be served in partial confinement as home detention as part of the parenting program developed by the Department.

Eligibility requirements - The secretary may transfer a person from a correctional facility to home detention in the community if it is determined that the parenting program is an appropriate placement and when all of the following conditions exist:

The sentencing be served has a high end of the range is greater than one year;

The current conviction is not for a felony that is a sex offense or a serious violent offense;

The individual has no current conviction for a violent offense; or where the individual has a current conviction for a violent offense, he or she has not been determined to be a high risk to reoffend;

The individual signs any release of information waivers required to allow information regarding current or prior child welfare cases to be shared with the Department and the court;

The person must be:

- A parent with guardianship or legal custody of a minor child;
- An expectant parent;
- A biological parent, adoptive parent, custodian, or stepparent with a proven, established, ongoing, and substantial relationship with a minor child that existed at the time of the current offense; and
- The Department determines that participation in the parenting program.is in the best interests of the child.

Prior juvenile adjudications are not considered offenses when considering eligibility, expect for any sex offense, serious violent offense, or felony offense where the individual was armed with a firearm or deadly weapon in the commission of the offense.

When the Department is considering partial confinement as part of the parenting program for an individual, the Department shall inquire of the individual and with the Department of Children, Youth and Families (DCYF) as to whether the agency has an open child welfare case or prior substantiated referral for abuse or neglect involving the individual being considered for the program. If DCYF or a tribal jurisdiction has an open child welfare case, the Department will seek input from DCYF or the involved tribal jurisdiction as to: (a) The status of the child welfare case; and (b) recommendations regarding placement of the individual and services required of the Department and the court governing the individual's child welfare case. The Department and its officers, agents, and employees are not liable for the acts of individuals participating in the parenting program unless the Department or its officers, agents, and employees acted with willful and wanton disregard.

All individuals placed on home detention as part of the parenting program shall provide an approved residence and living arrangement prior to transfer to home detention.

While in the community on home detention as part of the parenting program, the Department shall:

Require placement in electronic home monitoring;

Require participation in programming and treatment that the Department determines is needed;

Assign a community corrections officer who will monitor compliance with conditions of partial confinement and programming requirements; and

Collaborate and communicate with DCYF's social worker in provision of services if there is an open child welfare case.

The Department has the authority to return any person serving partial confinement in the parenting program to total confinement if he or she is not complying with sentence requirements.

Graduated Reentry Program

An individual serving a term of total confinement in a state correctional facility may have a portion of his or her sentence transferred to home detention through the Graduated Reentry (GRE) program operated by the Department (RCW 9.94A.733). Program eligibility and length of time that may be served in the program is based on the categorization of the current offense.

If the current offense is a sex offense, a violent offense, or a crime against a person as defined in RCW 9.9A.411, the person may be transferred to the community to serve up to the last five months of the sentence in the GRE program, after completing a minimum term of six months in total confinement. Individuals subject to a deportation order, civil commitment order, or the interstate compact for adult supervision under 9.94A.745 may not be placed in the program.

The Department may not transfer an individual to participate in the GRE Program until the Department has conducted an assessment for substance use disorder (SUD) and must assist those assessed as having a SUD enrollment in SUD services.

For individuals not serving a sentence for an offense described above, he or she may be transferred to the community to serve up to the last 18 months of the sentence in the GRE program, after completing a minimum term of four months in total confinement. Individuals subject to a deportation order or to the jurisdiction of the Board may not be placed in the program.

Individuals in the GRE program must:

- Provide an approved release residence,

- Be placed on electronic home monitoring,

- Participate in required programming and treatment based on assessed need, and

- Be monitored by a community corrections officer.

RESTITUTION

Restitution is generally governed by RCW 9.94A.750 (for offenses committed on or before July 1, 1985) and 9.94A.753 (for offenses committed after July 1, 1985). Pursuant to RCW 9.94A.753, restitution must be ordered whenever a person is convicted of an offense which results in injury to any person or damage to or loss of property, unless extraordinary circumstances exist. If such reasons exist and restitution is not ordered, the court must indicate the extraordinary reasons on the record.

Restitution may also be ordered to pay for an injury, loss, or damage if the person pleads guilty to a lesser offense or fewer offenses and agrees with the prosecutor's recommendation that he or she pay restitution for any offenses not prosecuted pursuant to a plea agreement.

Restitution is based on three factors:

Easily ascertainable damages for injury to or loss of property;

Actual expenses incurred in treatment for injury to persons; and

Lost wages resulting from injury.

Restitution for the crimes of Rape of a Child in the First, Second, or Third Degree, in which the victim becomes pregnant, must include:

Victim's medical expenses associated with the rape and resulting pregnancy; and

Support for any child born as a result of the rape if child support is ordered.

Restitution shall *not* include reimbursement for damages for mental anguish, pain and suffering and other intangible losses, but may include reimbursement for counseling reasonably related to the offense. The amount of restitution may not exceed double the amount of the perpetrator's gain or the victim's loss from the commission of the crime.

Restitution is to be determined at the sentencing hearing or within 180 days. As part of the sentence, the court must set the terms and conditions under which the defendant makes restitution. It is required that the court be specific about the payment schedule for restitution, so that these sentence conditions may be appropriately monitored by the community corrections officer. The court may not reduce the total amount of restitution ordered because of the person's lack of ability to pay the total amount.

The court shall not issue any order that postpones the commencement of restitution payments until after a person is released from total confinement. A person's inability to make restitution payments while in total confinement may not be the basis for a violation of his or her sentence unless his or her inability to make payments resulted from a refusal to accept an employment offer to a Class I or Class II job or a termination for cause from such a job.

For offenses committed prior to July 1, 2000, a person's compliance with the restitution requirement may be supervised for ten years after the date of sentence or release from confinement. The restitution portion of a sentence may be modified as to amount, terms, and conditions during this period regardless of the community supervision term and the statutory maximum of the crime. A court may extend the restitution requirement for a second ten-year period.

For offenses committed on or after July 1, 2000, RCW 9.94A.760(4) states: "For an offense committed on or after July 1, 2000, the Court shall retain jurisdiction over the offender, for purposes of the offender's compliance with payment of the legal financial obligations, until the obligation is completely satisfied, regardless of the statutory maximum for the crime. The Department may only supervise the offender's compliance with payment of the legal financial obligations during any period in which the Department is authorized to supervise the offender in the community under RCW 9.4A.728, 9.94A.501, or in which the offender is confined in a state correctional institution or a correctional facility pursuant to a transfer agreement with the Department, and the Department shall supervise the offender's compliance during any such period. The Department is not responsible for supervision of the offender during any subsequent period of time the offender remains under the court's jurisdiction. The county clerk is authorized to collect unpaid legal financial obligations at any time the offender remains under the jurisdiction of the court for purposes of his or her legal financial obligations."

Restitution for victims is the first priority for payment.

Effective January 1, 2023, at any time, including at sentencing, the court may determine that the individual is not required to pay, or may relieve the person of the requirement to pay, full or partial restitution and accrued interest on restitution where the entity to whom restitution is owed is an insurer or state agency (except for restitution owed to the Department of Labor and Industries), if the court finds that the individual does not have the current or likely future ability to pay. A person does not have the current ability to pay if the person is indigent.

Restitution in Cases involving Fraud or Deceptive Practice

If a person or organization is found guilty of an offense involving fraud or other deceptive practice, a court may require that notice be given to the class of persons or sector of the public affected by the conviction or financially interested in the subject matter of the offense. The notice may be accomplished by mail, by advertising through designated media, or by other appropriate means (RCW 9.94A.753(8), RCW 9.94A.750(7)).

Restitution in Cases involving a Fraudulent Filing of a Vehicle Report of Sale

If a person has caused a victim to lose money or property through the filing of a vehicle report of sale in which the designated buyer had no knowledge of the vehicle transfer or the fraudulent filing of the report of sale, upon conviction or when the person pleads guilty and agrees with the prosecutor's recommendation that he or she be required to pay restitution to a victim, the court may order the defendant to pay an amount, fixed by the court, not to exceed double the amount of the defendant's gain or victim's loss from the filing of the vehicle report of sale in which the designated buyer had no knowledge of the vehicle transfer or the fraudulent filing of the report of sale (RCW 9.94A.753(10)).

FINES

Unless otherwise provided by a statute of this state, on all adult sentences under this chapter the court may impose fines on according to the following ranges (RCW 9.94A.550):

Class A felonies	$0 - $50,000
Class B felonies	$0 - $20,000
Class C felonies	$0 - $10,000

Unless the court finds a person to be indigent, every conviction of certain VUCSA violations (RCW 69.50.401 through 69.50.4013, 69.50.4015, 69.50.402, 69.50.403, 69.50.406, 69.50.407, 69.50.410, 69.50.415) shall result in a fine of $1,000, in addition to any other fine or penalty imposed. The fine increases to $2,000 if the violation is a second or subsequent violation of one of the laws specified (RCW 69.50.430).

When a fine is imposed for Manufacture, Delivery or Possession with Intent to Manufacture or Deliver Methamphetamine, or for Possession of Ephedrine or Pseudo Ephedrine with Intent to Manufacture Methamphetamine, the first $3,000 may not be suspended and must be provided to the law enforcement entity responsible for cleaning up the methamphetamine lab site. The fines in this section only apply to individuals convicted as an adult (RCW 69.50.401).

Other Legal Financial Obligations

The Sentencing Reform Act allows a court to impose several additional monetary obligations. These include:

Court costs (RCW 9.94A.030(31));

Defense attorney's fees and defense costs (RCW 9.94A.030(31));

Contributions to a county or local drug fund (RCW 9.94A.030(31));

Crime victims' compensation assessment (RCW 9.94A.030(31) and (RCW 7.68.035));

Recoupments to the victim for the cost of counseling as a result of the crime, in cases where the Special Sex Offender Sentencing Alternative is exercised (RCW 9.94A.670(6)(g));

Payment for the cost of incarceration, at the rate of up to $100 per day if incarcerated in a prison or for the actual cost of incarceration if incarcerated in a county jail (RCW 9.94A.760(3));

Payment of up to $2,500 in costs incurred by public agencies in an emergency response to the incident that resulted in conviction for Vehicular Assault or Vehicular Homicide while under the Influence of Intoxicating Liquor or any Drug, Driving or Physical Control of a Vehicle while under the Influence of Intoxicating Liquor or any Drug, Operating an Aircraft under the Influence of Intoxicants or Liquor, or Use of a Vessel while under the Influence of Alcohol or Drugs (RCW 9.94A.030(31) and (RCW 38.52.430)); and/or

A fine of $15, in addition to any penalty or fine imposed, for a violation of a domestic violence protection order issued under the chapter (RCW 7.105.410(1)(b)(ii)).

All other legal financial obligations for an offense committed prior to July 1, 2000, may be enforced at any time during the ten-year period following the person's release from total confinement or within ten years of entry of the judgment and sentence, whichever period ends later. Prior to the expiration of the initial ten-year period, the superior court may extend the criminal judgment an additional ten years for payment of legal financial obligations including crime victims' assessments. All other legal financial obligations for an offense committed on or after July 1, 2000, may be enforced at any time the person remains under the court's jurisdiction. For an offense committed on or after July 1, 2000, the court shall retain jurisdiction over the person, for purposes of compliance with payment of the legal financial obligations, until the obligation is completely satisfied, regardless of the statutory maximum for the crime.

The Department may only supervise a person's compliance with payment of the legal financial obligations during any period in which the Department is authorized to supervise the person in the community under RCW 9.94A.728, 9.94A.501, or in which the person is confined in a state correctional institution or a correctional facility pursuant to a transfer agreement with the Department, and the Department shall supervise compliance during any such period. The Department is not responsible for supervision of the person during any subsequent period of time the person remains under the court's jurisdiction. The county clerk is authorized to collect unpaid legal financial obligations at any time the person remains under the jurisdiction of the court for purposes of his or her legal financial obligations.

In order to assist the court in setting the monthly payment sum, the individual must truthfully report to the Department regarding earnings, property, and assets, and must supply requested documentation.

The Department may recommend to the court modifications in the payment schedule if the person's financial circumstances change during the period of supervision. In cases where the Department sets the monthly assessment amount, the Department may modify the monthly assessment without consulting the court.

Independent of the Department or the county clerk, the party or entity to whom the legal financial obligation is owed shall have the authority to use any other remedies available to the party or entity to collect the legal financial obligation. These remedies include enforcement in the same manner as a judgment in a civil action by the party or entity to whom the legal financial obligation is owed.

Contact with Individuals

A court may prohibit contact with specified individuals or a specific class of individuals for a period not to exceed the maximum allowable sentence for the crime, regardless of the expiration of the community supervision or community placement term. The order prohibiting contact must relate directly to the circumstances of the crime of conviction.

SECTION 4

SENTENCING GRIDS

AND FELONY OFFENSES

SENTENCING GRID D: CRIMES COMMITTED AFTER JULY 24, 1999
"CURRENT"

Seriousness Level	Offender Score									
	0	**1**	**2**	**3**	**4**	**5**	**6**	**7**	**8**	**9+**
LEVEL XVI	Life sentence without parole/death penalty for offenders at or over the age of eighteen. For offenders under the age of eighteen, a term of twenty-five years to life.									
LEVEL XV	280m 240 - 320	291.5m 250 - 333	304m 261 - 347	316m 271 - 361	327.5m 281 - 374	339.5m 291 - 388	364m 312 - 416	394m 338 - 450	431.5m 370 - 493	479.5m 411 - 548
LEVEL XIV	171.5m 123 - 220	184m 134 - 234	194m 144 - 244	204m 154 - 254	215m 165 - 265	225m 175 - 275	245m 195 - 295	266m 216 - 316	307m 257 - 357	347.5m 298 - 397
LEVEL XIII	143.5m 123 - 164	156m 134 - 178	168m 144 - 192	179.5m 154 - 205	192m 165 - 219	204m 175 - 233	227.5m 195 - 260	252m 216 - 288	299.5m 257 - 342	347.5m 298 - 397
LEVEL XII	108m 93 - 123	119m 102 - 136	129m 111 - 147	140m 120 - 160	150m 129 - 171	161m 138 - 184	189m 162 - 216	207m 178 - 236	243m 209 - 277	279m 240 - 318
LEVEL XI	90m 78 - 102	100m 86 - 114	110m 95 - 125	119m 102 - 136	129m 111 - 147	139m 120 - 158	170m 146 - 194	185m 159 - 211	215m 185 - 245	245m 210 - 280
LEVEL X	59.5m 51 - 68	66m 57 - 75	72m 62 - 82	78m 67 - 89	84m 72 - 96	89.5m 77 - 102	114m 98 - 130	126m 108 - 144	150m 129 - 171	230.5m 149 - 198
LEVEL IX	36m 31 - 41	42m 36 - 48	47.5m 41 - 54	53.5m 46 - 61	59.5m 51 - 68	66m 57 - 75	89.5m 77 - 102	101.5m 87 - 116	126m 108 - 144	150m 129 - 171
LEVEL VIII	24m 21 - 27	30m 26 - 34	36m 31 - 41	42m 36 - 48	47.5m 41 - 54	53.5m 46 - 61	78m 67 - 89	89.5m 77 - 102	101.5m 87 - 116	126m 108 - 144
LEVEL VII	17.5m 15 - 20	24m 21 - 27	30m 26 - 34	36m 31 - 41	42m 36 - 48	47.5m 41 - 54	66m 57 - 75	78m 67 - 89	89.5m 77 - 102	101.5m 87 - 116
LEVEL VI	13m 12+ - 14	17.5m 15 - 20	24m 21 - 27	30m 26 - 34	36m 31 - 41	42m 36 - 48	53.5m 46 - 61	66m 57 - 75	78m 67 - 89	89.5m 77 - 102
LEVEL V	9m 6 - 12	13m 12+ - 14	15m 13 - 17	17.5m 15 - 20	25.5m 22 - 29	38m 33 - 43	47.5m 41 - 54	59.5m 51 - 68	72m 62 - 82	84m 72 - 96
LEVEL IV	6m 3 - 9	9m 6 - 12	13m 12+ - 14	15m 13 - 17	17.5m 15 - 20	25.5m 22 - 29	38m 33 - 43	50m 43 - 57	61.5m 53 - 70	73.5m 63 - 84
LEVEL III	2m 1 - 3	5m 3 - 8	8m 4 - 12	11m 9 - 12	14m 12+ - 16	19.5m 17 - 22	25.5m 22 - 29	38m 33 - 43	50m 43 - 57	59.5m 51 - 68
LEVEL II	0-90 days	4m 2 - 6	6m 3 - 9	8m 4 - 12	13m 12+ - 14	16m 14 - 18	19.5m 17 - 22	25.5m 22 - 29	38m 33 - 43	50m 43 - 57
LEVEL I	0-60 days	0-90 days	3m 2 - 5	4m 2 - 6	5.5m 3 - 8	8m 4 - 12	13m 12+ - 14	16m 14 - 18	19.5m 17 - 22	25.5m 22 - 29

NOTES:

SSB 5087, passed in the 2023 Legislative Session, eliminated language in RCW 10.95.030 authorizing the death penalty, but did not amend Seriousness Level XVI to remove language referencing the death penalty.

2SSB 5064, passed during the 2014 Legislative Session, amended the mandatory minimum term for aggravated first degree murder committed before the offender's 18th birthday. The changes were made retroactive and, therefore, apply regardless of the date of offense. Refer to RCW 9.94A.510, RCW 9.94A540, RCW 9.94A.729, RCW 10.95.030, and RCW 10.95.035.

"CURRENT"

		Offender Score									
		0	1	2	3	4	5	6	7	8	9+
S e r i o u s n e s s L e v e l	LEVEL XVI	Life sentence without parole/death penalty for offenders at or over the age of eighteen. For offenders under the age of eighteen, a term of twenty-five years to life.*									
	LEVEL XV	180 - 240	187.5 - 249.75	195.75 - 260.25	203.25 - 270.75	210.75 - 280.5	218.25 - 291	234 - 312	253.5 - 337.5	277.5 - 369.75	308.25 - 411
	LEVEL XIV	92.25 - 165	100.5 - 175.5	108 - 183	115.5 - 190.5	123.75 - 198.75	131.25 - 206.25	146.25 - 221.25	162 - 237	192.75 - 267.75	223.5 - 297.75
	LEVEL XIII	92.25 - 123	100.5 - 133.5	108 - 144	115.5 - 153.75	123.75 - 164.25	131.25 - 174.75	146.25 - 195	162 - 216	192.75 - 256.5	223.5 - 297.75
	LEVEL XII	69.75 - 92.25	76.5 - 102	83.25 - 110.25	90 - 120	96.75 - 128.25	103.5 - 138	121.5 - 162	133.5 - 177	156.75 - 207.75	180 - 238.5
	LEVEL XI	58.5 - 76.5	64.5 - 85.5	71.25 - 93.75	76.5 - 102	83.25 - 110.25	90 - 118.5	109.5 - 145.5	119.25 - 158.25	138.75 - 183.75	157.5 - 210
	LEVEL X	38.25 - 51	42.75 - 56.25	46.5 - 61.5	50.25 - 66.75	54 - 72	57.75 - 76.5	73.5 - 97.5	81 - 108	96.75 - 128.25	111.75 - 148.5
	LEVEL IX	23.25 - 30.75	27 - 36	30.75 - 40.5	34.5 - 45.75	38.25 - 51	42.75 - 56.25	57.75 - 76.5	65.25 - 87	81 - 108	96.75 - 128.25
	LEVEL VIII	15.75 - 20.25	19.5 - 25.5	23.25 - 30.75	27 - 36	30.75 - 40.5	34.5 - 45.75	50.25 - 66.75	57.75 - 76.5	65.25 - 87	81 - 108
	LEVEL VII	11.25 - 15	15.75 - 20.25	19.5 - 25.5	23.25 - 30.75	27 - 36	30.75 - 40.5	42.75 - 56.25	50.25 - 66.75	57.75 - 76.5	65.25 - 87
	LEVEL VI	9 - 10.5	11.25 - 15	15.75 - 20.25	19.5 - 25.5	23.25 - 30.75	27 - 36	34.5 - 45.75	42.75 - 56.25	50.25 - 66.75	57.75 - 76.5
	LEVEL V	4.5 - 9	9 - 10.5	9.75 - 12.75	11.25 - 15	16.5 - 21.75	24.75 - 32.25	30.75 - 40.5	38.25 - 51	46.5 - 61.5	54 - 72
	LEVEL IV	2.25 - 6.75	4.5 - 9	9 - 10.5	9.75 - 12.75	11.25 - 15	16.5 - 21.75	24.75 - 32.25	32.25 - 42.75	39.75 - 52.5	47.25 - 63
	LEVEL III	0.75 - 2.25	2.25 - 6	3 - 9	6.75 - 9	9 - 12	12.75 - 16.5	16.5 - 21.75	24.75 - 32.25	32.25 - 42.75	38.25 - 51
	LEVEL II	0 - 67.5 days	1.5 - 4.5	2.25 - 6.75	3 - 9	9 - 10.5	10.5 - 13.5	12.75 - 16.5	16.5 - 21.75	24.75 - 32.25	32.25 - 42.75
	LEVEL I	0 - 45 days	0 - 67.5 days	1.5 - 3.75	1.5 - 4.5	2.25 - 6	3 - 9	9 - 10.5	10.5 - 13.5	12.75 - 16.5	16.5 - 21.75

NOTES:

SSB 5087, passed in the 2023 Legislative Session, eliminated language in RCW 10.95.030 authorizing the death penalty, but did not amend Seriousness Level XVI to remove language referencing the death penalty.

2SSB 5064, passed during the 2014 Legislative Session, amended the mandatory minimum term for aggravated first degree murder committed before the offender's 18th birthday. The changes were made retroactive and, therefore, apply regardless of the date of offense. Refer to RCW 9.94A.510, RCW 9.94A540, RCW 9.94A.729, RCW 10.95.030, and RCW 10.95.035.

OFFENSE SERIOUSNESS LEVELS FOR STANDARD GRID (RCW 9.94A.515)

Seriousness Level	Statute (RCW)	Offense	Class
XVI	10.95.020	Aggravated Murder 1	A
XV	9A.32.055	Homicide by Abuse	A
	70.74.280(1)	Malicious Explosion of a Substance 1	A
	9A.32.030	Murder 1	A
XIV	9A.32.050	Murder 2	A
	9A.40.100(1)	Trafficking 1	A
XIII	70.74.280(2)	Malicious Explosion of a Substance 2	A
	70.74.270(1)	Malicious Placement of an Explosive 1	A
XII	9A.36.011	Assault 1	A
	9A.36.120	Assault of a Child 1	A
	70.74.272(1)(a)	Malicious Placement of an Imitation Device 1	B
	9.68A.101	Promoting Commercial Sexual Abuse of a Minor	A
	9A.44.040	Rape 1	A
	9A.44.073	Rape of a Child 1	A
	9A.40.100(3)	Trafficking 2	A
XI	9A.32.060	Manslaughter 1	A
	9A.44.050	Rape 2	A
	9A.44.076	Rape of a Child 2	A
	46.61.520(1)(b)	Vehicular Homicide – in a Reckless Manner	A
	46.61.520(1)(a)	Vehicular Homicide – while under the Influence of Intoxicating Liquor or any Drug	A
X	9A.44.083	Child Molestation 1	A
	9A.42.020	Criminal Mistreatment 1	B
	9A.44.100(1)(a)	Indecent Liberties - with Forcible Compulsion	A
	9A.40.020	Kidnapping 1	A
	9A.82.060(1)(a)	Leading Organized Crime – Organizing Criminal Profiteering	A
	70.74.280(3)	Malicious Explosion of a Substance 3	B
	9A.76.115	Sexually Violent Predator Escape	A
IX	9A.42.060	Abandonment of a Dependent Person 1	B
	9A.36.130	Assault of a Child 2	B
	70.74.180	Explosive Devices Prohibited	A
	46.52.020(4)(a)	Hit and Run - Death	B
	79A.60.050(1)(a)	Homicide by Watercraft – while under the Influence of Intoxicating Liquor or any Drug	A
	9A.82.060(1)(b)	Leading Organized Crime - Inciting Criminal Profiteering	B
	70.74.270(2)	Malicious Placement of an Explosive 2	B
	9A.56.200	Robbery 1	A
	9.68A.040	Sexual Exploitation of a Minor	B
VIII	9A.48.020	Arson 1	A
	9.68A.100	Commercial Sexual Abuse of a Minor	B
	79A.60.050(1)(b)	Homicide by Watercraft – in a Reckless Manner	A
	9A.32.070	Manslaughter 2	B
	9A.88.070	Promoting Prostitution 1	B
	69.55.010	Theft of Ammonia	C
VII	46.37.660(2)(b)	Air Bag Diagnostic Systems (Causing Bodily Injury or Death)	C

Seriousness Level	Statute (RCW)	Offense	Class
	46.37.660(1)(b)	Air Bag Replacement Requirements (Causing Bodily Injury or Death)	C
	9A.52.020	Burglary 1	A
	9A.44.086	Child Molestation 2	B
	9A.48.120	Civil Disorder Training	B
	9A.44.160	Custodial Sexual Misconduct 1	B
	9.68A.050(1)	Dealing in Depictions of Minor Engaged in Sexually Explicit Conduct 1	B
	9A.36.045	Drive-by Shooting	B
	9A.84.040(2)(a)	False Reporting 1	B
	79A.60.050(1)(c)	Homicide by Watercraft - Disregard for the Safety of Others	A
	9A.44.100(1)(b-c)	Indecent Liberties - without Forcible Compulsion	B
	9A.76.140	Introducing Contraband 1	B
	70.74.270(3)	Malicious Placement of an Explosive 3	B
	46.37.650(1)(b)	Manufacture or Import Counterfeit, Nonfunctional, Damaged, or Previously Deployed Air Bag (Causing Bodily Injury or Death)	C
	46.37.675	Negligently Causing Death by Use of a Signal Preemption Device	B
	46.37.650(2)(b)	Sell, Install, or Reinstall Counterfeit, Nonfunctional, Damaged, or Previously Deployed Airbag	C
	9.68A.060(1)	Sending, Bringing into the State Depictions of Minor Engaged in Sexually Explicit Conduct 1	B
	9.41.040(1)	Unlawful Possession of a Firearm 1	B
	9.41.225	Use of a Machine Gun or Bump-fire Stock in Commission of a Felony	A
	46.61.520(1)(c)	Vehicular Homicide - Disregard for the Safety of Others	A
VI	9A.76.170(3)(a)	Bail Jumping with Murder 1	A
	9A.68.010	Bribery	B
	9A.64.020(1)	Incest 1	B
	9A.72.160	Intimidating a Judge	B
	9A.72.130	Intimidating a Juror	B
	9A.72.110	Intimidating a Witness	B
	70.74.272(1)(b)	Malicious Placement of an Imitation Device 2	C
	9.68A.070(1)	Possession of Depictions of Minor Engaged in Sexually Explicit Conduct 1	B
	9A.44.079	Rape of a Child 3	C
	9A.56.400(1)	Theft from a Vulnerable Adult 1	B
	9A.56.300	Theft of a Firearm	B
	69.55.020	Unlawful Storage of Ammonia	C
V	9A.42.070	Abandonment of a Dependent Person 2	C
	9A.82.030	Advancing Money or Property for Extortionate Extension of Credit	B
	46.37.660(2)(c)	Air Bag Diagnostic Systems	C
	46.37.660(1)(c)	Air Bag Replacement Requirements	C
	9A.76.170(3)(b)	Bail Jumping with Class A Felony	B
	9A.44.089	Child Molestation 3	C
	9A.42.030	Criminal Mistreatment 2	C
	9A.44.170	Custodial Sexual Misconduct 2	C

Seriousness Level	Statute (RCW)	Offense	Class
	9.68A.050(2)	Dealing in Depictions of Minor Engaged in Sexually Explicit Conduct 2	B
	7.105.450, 10.99.040, 10.99.050, 26.09.300, 26.26B.050, or 26.52.070	Domestic Violence Court Order Violation	C
	9A.56.120	Extortion 1	B
	9A.82.020	Extortionate Extension of Credit	B
	9A.82.040	Extortionate Means to Collect Extensions of Credit	B
	9A.64.020(2)	Incest 2	C
	9A.40.030(3)(a)	Kidnapping 2	B
	9A.40.030(3)(b)	Kidnapping 2 with a Finding of Sexual Motivation	A
	46.37.650(1)(c)	Manufacture or Import Counterfeit, Nonfunctional, Damaged, or Previously Deployed Air Bag	C
	9A.72.020	Perjury 1	B
	9.94.070	Persistent Prison Misbehavior	C
	9A.56.310	Possession of a Stolen Firearm	B
	9A.44.060	Rape 3	C
	9A.76.070(2)(a)	Rendering Criminal Assistance 1	B
	46.37.650(2)(c)	Sell, Install, or Reinstall Counterfeit, Nonfunctional, Damaged, or Previously Deployed Airbag	C
	9.68A.060(2)	Sending, Bringing into the State Depictions of Minor Engaged in Sexually Explicit Conduct 2	B
	9A.44.093	Sexual Misconduct with a Minor 1	C
	9A.44.105	Sexually Violating Human Remains	C
	9A.46.110	Stalking	B
	9A.56.070	Taking Motor Vehicle without Permission 1	B
IV	9A.48.030	Arson 2	B
	9A.36.021(2)(a)	Assault 2	B
	9A.36.021(2)(b)	Assault 2 with a Finding of Sexual Motivation	A
	9A.36.031(1)(h)	Assault 3 - of a Peace Officer with a Projectile Stun Gun	C
	9A.36.041(3)	Assault 4 (Third Domestic Violence Offense)	C
	79A.60.060	Assault by Watercraft	B
	9A.72.100	Bribe Received by Witness	B
	9A.72.090	Bribing a Witness	B
	9.46.1961	Cheating 1	C
	9A.68.060	Commercial Bribery	B
	9.16.035(4)	Counterfeiting - Endanger Public Health or Safety	C
	46.61.502(6)	Driving while under the Influence of Intoxicating Liquor or any Drug	B
	9A.42.100	Endangerment with a Controlled Substance	B
	9A.76.110	Escape 1	B
	9A.36.080	Hate Crime Offense	C
	46.52.020(4)(b)	Hit and Run - Injury	C
	79A.60.200(3)	Hit and Run with Vessel - Injury Accident	C
	9.35.020(2)	Identity Theft 1	B
	9A.88.010(2)(c)	Indecent Exposure to a Person under Age 14 (Subsequent Sex Offense)	C
	9A.82.070	Influencing Outcome of Sporting Event	C
	46.61.504(6)	Physical Control of a Vehicle while under the Influence of Intoxicating Liquor or any Drug	C

Seriousness Level	Statute (RCW)	Offense	Class
	9.68A.070(2)	Possession of Depictions of Minor Engaged in Sexually Explicit Conduct 2	B
	9A.52.025	Residential Burglary	B
	9A.56.210	Robbery 2	B
	9A.56.080	Theft of Livestock 1	B
	9.61.160	Threats to Bomb	B
	9A.82.050	Trafficking in Stolen Property 1	B
	9A.56.290(4)(b)	Unlawful Factoring of a Credit or Payment Card Transaction (Subsequent Violation)	B
	48.44.016(3)	Unlawful Transaction of Health Coverage as Health Care Service Contractor	B
	48.46.033(3)	Unlawful Transaction of Health Coverage as Health Maintenance Organization	B
	48.15.023(3)	Unlawful Transaction of Insurance Business	B
	48.17.063(2)	Unlicensed Practice as an Insurance Professional	B
	9A.82.080(1),(2)	Use of Proceeds of Criminal Profiteering	B
	9A.52.100(3)	Vehicle Prowling 2 (Third or Subsequent Offense)	C
	46.61.522(1)(a-b)	Vehicular Assault – in a Reckless Manner or while under the Influence of Intoxicating Liquor or any Drug	B
	9.68A.075(1)	Viewing Depictions of Minor Engaged in Sexually Explicit Conduct 1	B
III	16.52.205(3)	Animal Cruelty 1 - Sexual Conduct or Contact	C
	9A.36.031(1)(a-g) & (i-j)	Assault 3 – Excluding Assault 3 of a Peace Officer with a Projectile Stun Gun	C
	9A.36.140	Assault of a Child 3	C
	9A.76.170(3)(c)	Bail Jumping with Class B or C Felony	C
	9A.52.030	Burglary 2	B
	9.68A.090(2)	Communication with Minor for Immoral Purposes (Subsequent Violation or Prior Sex Offense Conviction)	C
	9A.46.120	Criminal Gang Intimidation	C
	9A.36.100	Custodial Assault	C
	9A.90.120(2)(b)	Cyber Harassment	C
	9A.76.120	Escape 2	C
	9A.56.130	Extortion 2	C
	9A.84.040(2)(b)	False Reporting 2	C
	9A.46.020(2)(b)	Harassment	C
	28B.10.901(2)(b)	Hazing	C
	9A.76.180	Intimidating a Public Servant	B
	9A.76.150	Introducing Contraband 2	C
	81.60.070	Malicious Injury to Railroad Property	B
	9.41.190	Manufacture of Untraceable Firearm with Intent to Sell	C
	9.41.325	Manufacture or Assembly of an Undetectable Firearm or Untraceable Firearm	C
	19.144.080	Mortgage Fraud	B
	46.37.674	Negligently Causing Substantial Bodily Harm by Use of a Signal Preemption Device	B
	9A.56.350(2)	Organized Retail Theft 1	B
	9A.72.030	Perjury 2	C
	9.40.120	Possession of Incendiary Device	B

Seriousness Level	Statute (RCW)	Offense	Class
	9.41.190	Possession of Machine Gun, Bump-fire Stock, Undetectable Firearm, or Short-Barreled Shotgun or Rifle	C
	9A.88.080	Promoting Prostitution 2	C
	9A.56.360(2)	Retail Theft with Special Circumstances 1	B
	21.20.400	Securities Act Violation	B
	9A.72.120	Tampering with a Witness	C
	9.61.230(2)	Telephone Harassment (with Prior Harassment Conviction or Threat of Death)	C
	9A.56.083	Theft of Livestock 2	C
	9A.56.340(2)	Theft with Intent to Resell 1	B
	9A.82.055	Trafficking in Stolen Property 2	C
	77.15.410(3)(b)	Unlawful Hunting of Big Game 1	C
	9A.40.040	Unlawful Imprisonment	C
	77.140.060(3)	Unlawful Misbranding of Fish or Shellfish 1	C
	9.41.040(2)	Unlawful Possession of a Firearm 2	C
	77.15.120(3)(b)	Unlawful Taking of Endangered Fish or Wildlife 1	C
	77.15.260(3)(b)	Unlawful Trafficking in Fish, Shellfish or Wildlife 1	B
	77.15.530(4)	Unlawful Use of a Nondesignated Vessel	C
	46.61.522(1)(c)	Vehicular Assault - Disregard for the Safety of Others	B
II	77.15.500(3)(b)	Commercial Fishing without a License 1	C
	9A.90.040	Computer Trespass 1	C
	9.16.035(3)	Counterfeiting – 3 Conviction and Value $10,000 or more	C
	9A.90.060	Electronic Data Service Interference	C
	9A.90.080	Electronic Data Tampering 1	C
	9A.90.100	Electronic Data Theft	C
	77.15.620(3)(b)	Engaging in Fish Dealing Activity Unlicensed 1	C
	72.09.310	Escape from Community Custody	C
	61.34.030	Equity Skimming*	B
	9A.44.132(1)(a)	Failure to Register as a Sex Offender (Second Violation Committed on or after 6/10/2010)	C
	9A.44.132(1)(a)	Failure to Register as a Sex Offender (Subsequent Violation Committed on or after 6/7/2006 but before 6/10/2010)	C
	9A.44.132(1)(b)	Failure to Register as a Sex Offender (Third or Subsequent Violation Committed on or after 6/10/2010)	B
	48.80.030	Health Care False Claims	C
	9.35.020(3)	Identity Theft 2	C
	9.35.010	Improperly Obtaining Financial Information	C
	9A.48.070	Malicious Mischief 1	B
	9A.56.350(3)	Organized Retail Theft 2	C
	9A.56.068	Possession of a Stolen Vehicle	B
	9A.56.150	Possession of Stolen Property 1 (other than Firearm or Motor Vehicle)	B

* While Equity Skimming is not found on the offense list under RCW 9.94A.515. RCW 61.34.030 language states "Equity skimming shall be classified as a level II offense under chapter 9.94A RCW, . . ." so it was included in this list.

Seriousness Level	Statute (RCW)	Offense	Class
	9A.56.360(3)	Retail Theft with Special Circumstances 2	C
	19.290.100	Scrap Processing, Recycling, or Supplying without a License (Second or Subsequent Offense)	C
	9A.56.030	Theft 1 (Excluding Firearm and Motor Vehicle)	B
	9A.56.065	Theft of a Motor Vehicle	B
	9A.56.096(5)(a)	Theft of Rental, Leased, Lease-purchased or Loaned Property (Valued at $5,000 or more)	B
	9A.56.340(3)	Theft with Intent to Resell 2	C
	48.30A.015	Trafficking in Insurance Claims (Subsequent Violation)	C
	9A.56.290(4)(a)	Unlawful Factoring of a Credit or Payment Card Transaction	C
	77.15.570(2)	Unlawful Participation of Non-Indians in Indian Fishery	C
	2.48.180	Unlawful Practice of Law (Subsequent Violation)	C
	77.15.650(3)(b)	Unlawful Purchase or Use of a License 1	C
	77.15.260(3)(a)	Unlawful Trafficking in Fish, Shellfish or Wildlife 2	C
	18.130.190(7)(b)	Unlicensed Practice of a Profession or Business (Subsequent Violation)	C
	9A.44.115	Voyeurism 1	C
I	46.61.024	Attempting to Elude Pursuing Police Vehicle	C
	74.08.055(2)	False Verification for Welfare	B
	9A.60.020	Forgery	C
	9A.60.060	Fraudulent Creation or Revocation of Mental Health Advance Directive	C
	9A.48.080	Malicious Mischief 2	C
	78.44.330	Mineral Trespass	C
	9A.56.160	Possession of Stolen Property 2 (other than Firearm or Motor Vehicle)	C
	9A.48.040	Reckless Burning 1	C
	77.15.450(3)(b)	Spotlighting Big Game 1	C
	77.15.670(3)(b)	Suspension of Department Privileges 1	C
	9A.56.075	Taking Motor Vehicle without Permission 2	C
	9A.56.040	Theft 2 (Excluding Firearm and Motor Vehicle)	C
	9A.56.400(2)	Theft from a Vulnerable Adult 2	C
	9A.56.096(5)(b)	Theft of Rental, Leased, Lease-purchased or Loaned Property (Valued at $750 or more but less than $5,000)	C
	48.17.063	Transaction of Insurance Business Beyond the Scope of Licensure (Violation of RCW 48.17.060)	B
	77.15.630(3)(b)	Unlawful Fish and Shellfish Catch Accounting 1	C
	9A.56.060(4)	Unlawful Issuance of Checks or Drafts (Value greater than $750)	C
	9A.56.320(3)	Unlawful Possession of a Personal Identification Device	C
	9A.56.320(4)	Unlawful Possession of Fictitious Identification	C
	9A.56.320(5)	Unlawful Possession of Instruments of Financial Fraud	C
	9A.56.320(2)	Unlawful Possession of Payment Instruments	C
	9A.56.320(1)	Unlawful Production of Payment Instruments	C
	9.91.144	Unlawful Redemption of Food Stamps	C

Seriousness Level	Statute (RCW)	Offense	Class
	77.15.250(2)(b)	Unlawful Releasing, Planting, Possessing or Placing Deleterious Exotic Wildlife	C
	9.91.142(1)	Unlawful Trafficking in Food Stamps	C
	77.15.580(3)(b)	Unlawful Use of Net to Take Fish 1	C
	9A.52.095	Vehicle Prowl 1	C
	77.15.550(3)(b)	Violating Commercial Fishing Area or Time 1	C

DRUG OFFENSE SENTENCING GRID C: OFFENSES COMMITTED ON OR AFTER JULY 1, 2018

Seriousness Level	Offender Score		
	0 to 2	3 to 5	6 to 9+
LEVEL III	59.5m 51 - 68	84m 68+ - 100	110m 100+ - 120
LEVEL II	16m 12+ - 20	40m 20+ - 60	90m 60+ - 120
LEVEL I	3m 0 - 6	12m 6+ - 18	18m 12+ - 24

DRUG OFFENSE SENTENCING GRID C: OFFENSES COMMITTED ON OR AFTER JULY 1, 2018
(SOLICITATIONS FOR OFFENSES UNDER CHAPTER 69.50 RCW, ANTICIPATORIES FOR OFFENSES NOT UNDER CHAPTER 69.50 RCW)

Seriousness Level	Offender Score		
	0 to 2	3 to 5	6 to 9+
LEVEL III	38.25 - 51	51.02 - 75	75.02 - 90
LEVEL II	9.02 - 15	15.02 - 45	45.02 - 90
LEVEL I	0 - 4.5	4.52 - 13.5	9.02 - 18

OFFENSE SERIOUSNESS LEVELS FOR DRUG SENTENCING GRID (RCW 9.94A.518)

This list includes most statutory drug offenses as well as drug-related offenses not defined as drug offenses under RCW 9.94A.030(22).

Seriousness Level	Statute (RCW)	Offense	Class
III	9.94A.602	Any felony offense under Chapter 69.50 RCW with a Deadly Weapon Special Verdict under RCW 9.94A.825	
	69.50.415	Controlled Substance Homicide	B
	69.52.030(2)	Delivery of Imitation Controlled Substance by Person 18 or over to Person under 18	B
	69.50.4015	Involving a Minor in Drug Dealing	C
	69.50.401(2)(b)	Manufacture of Methamphetamine	B
	69.50.406(1)	Over 18 and Deliver Heroin, Methamphetamine, a Narcotic from Schedule I or II, or Flunitrazepam from Schedule IV to Someone under 18	A
	69.50.406(2)	Over 18 and Deliver Narcotic from Schedule III, IV or V, or a Nonnarcotic, Except Flunitrazepam or Methamphetamine, from Schedule I-V to Someone under 18 and 3 Years Junior	B
	69.50.440	Possession of Ephedrine, Pseudoephedrine or Anhydrous Ammonia with Intent to Manufacture Methamphetamine	B
	69.50.410	Selling for Profit (Controlled or Counterfeit) any Controlled Substance in Schedule I	C
II	69.50.4011(2)(a-b)	Create or Deliver a Counterfeit Controlled Substance – Schedule I or II Narcotic or Flunitrazepam or Methamphetamine	B
	69.50.4011(2)(c-e)	Create or Deliver a Counterfeit Controlled Substance – Schedule I-II Nonnarcotic, Schedule III-V Except Flunitrazepam or Methamphetamine	C
	69.50.401(2)(b)	Deliver or Possess with Intent to Deliver - Methamphetamine	B
	69.50.4012	Delivery of a Material in Lieu of a Controlled Substance	C
	69.50.402(1)(f)	Maintaining a Dwelling or Place for Controlled Substances	C
	69.50.401(2)(a)	Manufacture, Deliver or Possess with Intent to Deliver - Narcotics from Schedule I or II or Flunitrazepam from Schedule IV	B
	69.50.401(2)(b)	Manufacture, Deliver or Possess with Intent to Deliver - Amphetamine	B
	69.50.401(2)(c-e)	Manufacture, Deliver or Possess with Intent to Deliver - Narcotics from Schedule III, IV, or V or Nonnarcotics from Schedule I-V (except Cannabis, Amphetamine, Methamphetamine, or Flunitrazepam)	C
	69.52.030(1)	Manufacture, Distribute or Possess with Intent to Distribute an Imitation Controlled Substance	C
	69.50.418	Possess, Purchase, Deliver, Sell, or Possess with Intent to Sell a Tableting Machine or Encapsulating Machine	C
I	69.41.020	Forged Prescription - Legend Drug	B
	69.50.403	Forged Prescription for a Controlled Substance	C
	69.50.401(2)(c)	Manufacture, Deliver or Possess with Intent to Deliver - Cannabis	C
	69.53.010	Unlawful Use of Building for Drug Purposes	C

SENTENCING GRID C: CRIMES COMMITTED JULY 27, 1997, THROUGH JULY 24, 1999

	Offender Score									
	0	1	2	3	4	5	6	7	8	9+
LEVEL XV	LIFE SENTENCE WITHOUT PAROLE/DEATH PENALTY									
LEVEL XIV	23y 4m	24y 4m	25y 4m	26y 4m	27y 4m	28y 4m	30y 4m	32y 10m	36y	40y
	240 - 320	250 - 333	261 - 347	271 - 361	281 - 374	291 - 388	312 - 416	338 - 450	370 - 493	411 - 548
LEVEL XIII	14y 4m	15y 4m	16y 2m	17y	17y 11m	18y 9m	20y 5m	22y 2m	25y 7m	29y
	123 - 220	134 - 234	144 - 244	154 - 254	165 - 265	175 - 275	195 - 295	216 - 316	257 - 357	298 - 397
LEVEL XII	9y	9y 11m	10y 9m	11y 8m	12y 6m	13y 5m	15y 9m	17y 3m	20y 3m	23y 3m
	93 - 123	102 - 136	111 - 147	120 - 160	129 - 171	138 - 184	162 - 216	178 - 236	209 - 277	240 - 318
LEVEL XI	7y 6m	8y 4m	9y 2m	9y 11m	10y 9m	11y 7m	14y 2m	15y 5m	17y 11m	20y 5m
	78 - 102	86 - 114	95 - 125	102 - 136	111 - 147	120 - 158	146 - 194	159 - 211	185 - 245	210 - 280
LEVEL X	5y	5y 6m	6y	6y 6m	7y	7y 6m	9y 6m	10y 6m	12y 6m	14y 6m
	51 - 68	57 - 75	62 - 82	67 - 89	72 - 96	77 - 102	98 - 130	108 - 144	129 - 171	149 - 198
LEVEL IX	3y	3y 6m	4y	4y 6m	5y	5y 6m	7y 6m	8y 6m	10y 6m	12y 6m
	31 - 41	36 - 48	41 - 54	46 - 61	51 - 68	57 - 75	77 - 102	87 - 116	108 - 144	129 - 171
LEVEL VIII	2y	2y 6m	3y	3y 6m	4y	4y 6m	6y 6m	7y 6m	8y 6m	10y 6m
	21 - 27	26 - 34	31 - 41	36 - 48	41 - 54	46 - 61	67 - 89	77 - 102	87 - 116	108 - 144
LEVEL VII	18m	2y	2y 6m	3y	3y 6m	4y	5y 6m	6y 6m	7y 6m	8y 6m
	15 - 20	21 - 27	26 - 34	31 - 41	36 - 48	41 - 54	57 - 75	67 - 89	77 - 102	87 - 116
LEVEL VI	13m	18m	2y	2y 6m	3y	3y 6m	4y 6m	5y 6m	6y 6m	7y 6m
	12+ - 14	15 - 20	21 - 27	26 - 34	31 - 41	36 - 48	46 - 61	57 - 75	67 - 89	77 - 102
LEVEL V	9m	13m	15m	18m	2y 2m	3y 2m	4y	5y	6y	7y
	6 - 12	12+ - 14	13 - 17	15 - 20	22 - 29	33 - 43	41 - 54	51 - 68	62 - 82	72 - 96
LEVEL IV	6m	9m	13m	15m	18m	2y 2m	3y 2m	4y 2m	5y 2m	6y 2m
	3 - 9	6 - 12	12+ - 14	13 - 17	15 - 20	22 - 29	33 - 43	43 - 57	53 - 70	63 - 84
LEVEL III	2m	5m	8m	11m	14m	20m	2y 2m	3y 2m	4y 2m	5y
	1 - 3	3 - 8	4 - 12	9 - 12	12+ - 16	17 - 22	22 - 29	33 - 43	43 - 57	51 - 68
LEVEL II		4m	6m	8m	13m	16m	20m	2y 2m	3y 2m	4y 2m
	0-90 days	2 - 6	3 - 9	4 - 12	12+ - 14	14 - 18	17 - 22	22 - 29	33 - 43	43 - 57
LEVEL I			3m	4m	5m	8m	13m	16m	20m	2y 2m
	0-60 days	0-90 days	2 - 5	2 - 6	3 - 8	4 - 12	12+ - 14	14 - 18	17 - 22	22 - 29

Seriousness Level (vertical axis label)

NOTES:

SSB 5087, passed in the 2023 Legislative Session, eliminated language in RCW 10.95.030 authorizing the death penalty, but did not amend Seriousness Level XVI to remove language referencing the death penalty.

2SSB 5064, passed during the 2014 legislative session, amended the mandatory minimum term for Aggravated First Degree Murder committed before the offender's 18th birthday. The changes were made retroactive and, therefore, apply regardless of the date of offense. Refer to RCW 9.94A.510, RCW 9.94A.540, RCW 9.94A.729, RCW 10.95.030, and RCW 10.95.035.

SENTENCING GRID B: CRIMES COMMITTED JULY 1, 1990, THROUGH JULY 26, 1997

Seriousness Level	Offender Score									
	0	**1**	**2**	**3**	**4**	**5**	**6**	**7**	**8**	**9+**
LEVEL XV	LIFE SENTENCE WITHOUT PAROLE/DEATH PENALTY									
LEVEL XIV	23y 4m 240 - 320	24y 4m 250 - 333	25y 4m 261 - 347	26y 4m 271 - 361	27y 4m 281 - 374	28y 4m 291 - 388	30y 4m 312 - 416	32y 10m 338 - 450	36y 370 - 493	40y 411 - 548
LEVEL XIII	12y 123 - 164	13y 134 - 178	14y 144 - 192	15y 154 - 205	16y 165 - 219	17y 175 - 233	19y 195 - 260	21y 216 - 288	25y 257 - 342	29y 298 - 397
LEVEL XII	9y 93 - 123	9y 11m 102 - 136	10y 9m 111 - 147	11y 8m 120 - 160	12y 6m 129 - 171	13y 5m 138 - 184	15y 9m 162 - 216	17y 3m 178 - 236	20y 3m 209 - 277	23y 3m 240 - 318
LEVEL XI	7y 6m 78 - 102	8y 4m 86 - 114	9y 2m 95 - 125	9y 11m 102 - 136	10y 9m 111 - 147	11y 7m 120 - 158	14y 2m 146 - 194	15y 5m 159 - 211	17y 11m 185 - 245	20y 5m 210 - 280
LEVEL X	5y 51 - 68	5y 6m 57 - 75	6y 62 - 82	6y 6m 67 - 89	7y 72 - 96	7y 6m 77 - 102	9y 6m 98 - 130	10y 6m 108 - 144	12y 6m 129 - 171	14y 6m 149 - 198
LEVEL IX	3y 31 - 41	3y 6m 36 - 48	4y 41 - 54	4y 6m 46 - 61	5y 51 - 68	5y 6m 57 - 75	7y 6m 77 - 102	8y 6m 87 - 116	10y 6m 108 - 144	12y 6m 129 - 171
LEVEL VIII	2y 21 - 27	2y 6m 26 - 34	3y 31 - 41	3y 6m 36 - 48	4y 41 - 54	4y 6m 46 - 61	6y 6m 67 - 89	7y 6m 77 - 102	8y 6m 87 - 116	10y 6m 108 - 144
LEVEL VII	18m 15 - 20	2y 21 - 27	2y 6m 26 - 34	3y 31 - 41	3y 6m 36 - 48	4y 41 - 54	5y 6m 57 - 75	6y 6m 67 - 89	7y 6m 77 - 102	8y 6m 87 - 116
LEVEL VI	13m 12+ - 14	18m 15 - 20	2y 21 - 27	2y 6m 26 - 34	3y 31 - 41	3y 6m 36 - 48	4y 6m 46 - 61	5y 6m 57 - 75	6y 6m 67 - 89	7y 6m 77 - 102
LEVEL V	9m 6 - 12	13m 12+ - 14	15m 13 - 17	18m 15 - 20	2y 2m 22 - 29	3y 2m 33 - 43	4y 41 - 54	5y 51 - 68	6y 62 - 82	7y 72 - 96
LEVEL IV	6m 3 - 9	9m 6 - 12	13m 12+ - 14	15m 13 - 17	18m 15 - 20	2y 2m 22 - 29	3y 2m 33 - 43	4y 2m 43 - 57	5y 2m 53 - 70	6y 2m 63 - 84
LEVEL III	2m 1 - 3	5m 3 - 8	8m 4 - 12	11m 9 - 12	14m 12+ - 16	20m 17 - 22	2y 2m 22 - 29	3y 2m 33 - 43	4y 2m 43 - 57	5y 51 - 68
LEVEL II	0-90 days	4m 2 - 6	6m 3 - 9	8m 4 - 12	13m 12+ - 14	16m 14 - 18	20m 17 - 22	2y 2m 22 - 29	3y 2m 33 - 43	4y 2m 43 - 57
LEVEL I	0-60 days	0-90 days	3m 2 - 5	4m 2 - 6	5m 3 - 8	8m 4 - 12	13m 12+ - 14	16m 14 - 18	20m 17 - 22	2y 2m 22 - 29

NOTES:

SSB 5087, passed in the 2023 Legislative Session, eliminated language in RCW 10.95.030 authorizing the death penalty, but did not amend Seriousness Level XVI to remove language referencing the death penalty.

2SSB 5064, passed during the 2014 legislative session, amended the standard range of "Life Sentence without Parole/Death Penalty" (i.e., the mandatory minimum term for Aggravated First Degree Murder), where the offense was committed before the offender's 18th birthday to a minimum term of "25 years to life." The changes were made retroactive and, therefore, apply regardless of the date of offense. Refer to RCW 9.94A.510, RCW 9.94A.540, RCW 9.94A.729, RCW 10.95.030, and RCW 10.95.035

SENTENCING GRID A: CRIMES COMMITTED BEFORE JULY 1, 1990

	Offender Score									
	0	**1**	**2**	**3**	**4**	**5**	**6**	**7**	**8**	**9+**
LEVEL XIV	LIFE SENTENCE WITHOUT PAROLE/DEATH PENALTY									
LEVEL XIII	23y 4m 240 - 320	24y 4m 250 - 333	25y 4m 261 - 347	26y 4m 271 - 361	27y 4m 281 - 374	28y 4m 291 - 388	30y 4m 312 - 416	32y 10m 338 - 450	36y 370 - 493	40y 411 - 548
LEVEL XII	12y 123 - 164	13y 134 - 178	14y 144 - 192	15y 154 - 205	16y 165 - 219	17y 175 - 233	19y 195 - 260	21y 216 - 288	25y 257 - 342	29y 298 - 397
LEVEL XI	6y 62 - 82	6y 9m 69 - 92	7y 6m 77 - 102	8y 3m 85 - 113	9y 93 - 123	9y 9m 100 - 133	12y 6m 129 - 171	13y 6m 139 - 185	15y 6m 159 - 212	17y 6m 180 - 240
LEVEL X	5y 51 - 68	5y 6m 57 - 75	6y 62 - 82	6y 6m 67 - 89	7y 72 - 96	7y 6m 77 - 102	9y 6m 98 - 130	10y 6m 108 - 144	12y 6m 129 - 171	14y 6m 149 - 198
LEVEL IX	3y 31 - 41	3y 6m 36 - 48	4y 41 - 54	4y 6m 46 - 61	5y 51 - 68	5y 6m 57 - 75	7y 6m 77 - 102	8y 6m 87 - 116	10y 6m 108 - 144	12y 6m 129 - 171
LEVEL VIII	2y 21 - 27	2y 6m 26 - 34	3y 31 - 41	3y 6m 36 - 48	4y 41 - 54	4y 6m 46 - 61	6y 6m 67 - 89	7y 6m 77 - 102	8y 6m 87 - 116	10y 6m 108 - 144
LEVEL VII	18m 15 - 20	2y 21 - 27	2y 6m 26 - 34	3y 31 - 41	3y 6m 36 - 48	4y 41 - 54	5y 6m 57 - 75	6y 6m 67 - 89	7y 6m 77 - 102	8y 6m 87 - 116
LEVEL VI	13m 12+ - 14	18m 15 - 20	2y 21 - 27	2y 6m 26 - 34	3y 31 - 41	3y 6m 36 - 48	4y 6m 46 - 61	5y 6m 57 - 75	6y 6m 67 - 89	7y 6m 77 - 102
LEVEL V	9m 6 - 12	13m 12+ - 14	15m 13 - 17	18m 15 - 20	2y 2m 22 - 29	3y 2m 33 - 43	4y 41 - 54	5y 51 - 68	6y 62 - 82	7y 72 - 96
LEVEL IV	6m 3 - 9	9m 6 - 12	13m 12+ - 14	15m 13 - 17	18m 15 - 20	2y 2m 22 - 29	3y 2m 33 - 43	4y 2m 43 - 57	5y 2m 53 - 70	6y 2m 63 - 84
LEVEL III	2m 1 - 3	5m 3 - 8	8m 4 - 12	11m 9 - 12	14m 12+ - 16	20m 17 - 22	2y 2m 22 - 29	3y 2m 33 - 43	4y 2m 43 - 57	5y 51 - 68
LEVEL II	0-90 days	4m 2 - 6	6m 3 - 9	8m 4 - 12	13m 12+ - 14	16m 14 - 18	20m 17 - 22	2y 2m 22 - 29	3y 2m 33 - 43	4y 2m 43 - 57
LEVEL I	0-60 days	0-90 days	3m 2 - 5	4m 2 - 6	5m 3 - 8	8m 4 - 12	13m 12+ - 14	16m 14 - 18	20m 17 - 22	2y 2m 22 - 29

Seriousness Level (vertical label on left side)

NOTES:

SSB 5087, passed in the 2023 Legislative Session, eliminated language in RCW 10.95.030 authorizing the death penalty, but did not amend Seriousness Level XVI to remove language referencing the death penalty.

2SSB 5064, passed during the 2014 legislative session, amended the standard range of "Life Sentence without Parole/Death Penalty" (i.e., the mandatory minimum term for Aggravated First Degree Murder), where the offense was committed before the offender's 18th birthday to a minimum term of "25 years to life." The changes were made retroactive and, therefore, apply regardless of the date of offense. Refer to RCW 9.94A.510, RCW 9.94A.540, RCW 9.94A.729, RCW 10.95.030, and RCW 10.95.035

DRUG OFFENSE SENTENCING GRID B: <u>SENTENCES IMPOSED</u> ON OR AFTER JULY 1, 2013, AND FOR OFFENSES COMMITTED ON OR BEFORE JUNE 30, 2018

Seriousness Level		Offender Score		
		0 to 2	**3 to 5**	**6 to 9+**
	LEVEL III	59.5m 51 - 68	84m 68+ - 100	110m 100+ - 120
	LEVEL II	16m 12+ - 20	40m 20+ - 60	90m 60+ - 120
	LEVEL I	3m 0 - 6	9m 6+ - 12	18m 12+ - 24

DRUG OFFENSE SENTENCING GRID A: <u>OFFENSES COMMITTED</u> ON OR AFTER JULY 1, 2003, AND SENTENCED BEFORE JULY 1, 2013

Seriousness Level	Offender Score		
	0 to 2	**3 to 5**	**6 to 9+**
LEVEL III	59.5m 51 - 68	84m 68+ - 100	110m 100+ - 120
LEVEL II	16m 12+ - 20	40m 20+ - 60	90m 60+ - 120
LEVEL I	3m 0 - 6	12m 6+ - 18	18m 12+ - 24

SERIOUS VIOLENT OFFENSES

RCW 9.94A.030(46)

Statute (RCW)	Offense	Class	Seriousness Level
10.95.020	Aggravated Murder 1	A	XVI
9A.36.011	Assault 1	A	XII
9A.36.120	Assault of a Child 1	A	XII
9A.32.055	Homicide by Abuse	A	XV
9A.40.020	Kidnapping 1	A	X
9A.32.060	Manslaughter 1	A	XI
9A.32.030	Murder 1	A	XV
9A.32.050	Murder 2	A	XIV
9A.44.040	Rape 1	A	XII

Attempt, Solicitation or Conspiracy to commit one of these felonies.

Any federal or out-of-state conviction for an offense that, under the laws of this state, would be a felony classified as a serious violent offense.

VIOLENT OFFENSES

RCW 9.94A.030(55)

Statute (RCW)	Offense	Class	Seriousness Level
9A.48.020	Arson 1	A	VIII
9A.48.030	Arson 2	B	IV
9A.36.021(2)(a)	Assault 2	B	IV
9A.36.021(2)(b)	Assault 2 with a Finding of Sexual Motivation	A	IV
9A.36.130	Assault of a Child 2	B	IX
9A.76.170(3)(a)	Bail Jumping with Murder 1	A	VI
9A.52.020	Burglary 1	A	VII
9A.44.083	Child Molestation 1	A	X
70.245.200(2)	Coerce Patient to Request Life-ending Medication	A	Unranked
9A.36.045	Drive-by Shooting	B	VII
70.74.180	Explosive Devices Prohibited	A	IX
9A.56.120	Extortion 1	B	V
70.245.200(1)	Forging Request for Medication	A	Unranked
79A.60.050(1)(c)	Homicide by Watercraft - Disregard for the Safety of Others	A	VII
79A.60.050(1)(b)	Homicide by Watercraft – in a Reckless Manner	A	VIII
79A.60.050(1)(a)	Homicide by Watercraft – while under the Influence of Intoxicating Liquor or any Drug	A	IX
9A.44.100(1)(a)	Indecent Liberties - with Forcible Compulsion	A	X
9A.40.030(3)(a)	Kidnapping 2	B	V
9A.40.030(3)(b)	Kidnapping 2 with a Finding of Sexual Motivation	A	V
9A.82.060(1)(a)	Leading Organized Crime – Organizing Criminal Profiteering	A	X
70.74.280(1)	Malicious Explosion of a Substance 1	A	XV
70.74.280(2)	Malicious Explosion of a Substance 2	A	XIII
70.74.270(1)	Malicious Placement of an Explosive 1	A	XIII
9A.32.070	Manslaughter 2	B	VIII
69.50.406(1)	Over 18 and Deliver Heroin, Methamphetamine, a Narcotic from Schedule I or II, or Flunitrazepam from Schedule IV to Someone under 18	A	DG-III
9.68A.101	Promoting Commercial Sexual Abuse of a Minor	A	XII
9A.44.050	Rape 2	A	XI
9A.44.073	Rape of a Child 1	A	XII
9A.44.076	Rape of a Child 2	A	XI
9A.56.200	Robbery 1	A	IX
9A.56.210	Robbery 2	B	IV
9A.76.115	Sexually Violent Predator Escape	A	X
9A.40.100(1)	Trafficking 1	A	XIV
9A.40.100(3)	Trafficking 2	A	XII
9.82.010	Treason	A	Unranked

Statute (RCW)	Offense	Class	Seriousness Level
9.41.225	Use of a Machine Gun or Bump-fire Stock in Commission of a Felony	A	VII
46.61.522(1)(a-b)	Vehicular Assault – in a Reckless Manner or while under the Influence of Intoxicating Liquor or any Drug	B	IV
46.61.520(1)(b)	Vehicular Homicide – in a Reckless Manner	A	XI
46.61.520(1)(a)	Vehicular Homicide – while under the Influence of Intoxicating Liquor or any Drug	A	XI

Any conviction for a felony offense in effect at any time prior to July 1, 1976, that is comparable to a felony classified as a violent offense.

Any federal or out-of-state conviction for an offense that under the laws of this state would be a felony classified as a violent offense.

Criminal solicitation of or criminal conspiracy to commit a Class A felony.

Any felony defined under any law as a Class A felony or an attempt to commit a Class A felony.

Any offense defined as a Serious Violent offense.

Note: Vehicular Homicide – Disregard for the Safety of Others is defined as a Class A felony offense and appears to be a violent offense under RCW 9.94A.030. However, under *State v. Stately*, 152 Wn. App. 604, 216 P.3d 1102 (2009), it is not to be considered a violent offense.

SEX OFFENSES

RCW 9.94A.030(47)

Statute (RCW)	Offense	Class	Seriousness Level
9A.36.021(2)(b)	Assault 2 with a Finding of Sexual Motivation	A	IV
9A.44.083	Child Molestation 1	A	X
9A.44.086	Child Molestation 2	B	VII
9A.44.089	Child Molestation 3	C	V
9.68A.100	Commercial Sexual Abuse of a Minor	B	VIII
9.68A.090(2)	Communication with Minor for Immoral Purposes (Subsequent Violation or Prior Sex Offense Conviction)	C	III
9A.44.196	Criminal Trespass Against Children	C	Unranked
9A.44.160	Custodial Sexual Misconduct 1	B	VII
9A.44.170	Custodial Sexual Misconduct 2	C	V
9.68A.050(1)	Dealing in Depictions of Minor Engaged in Sexually Explicit Conduct 1	B	VII
9.68A.050(2)	Dealing in Depictions of Minor Engaged in Sexually Explicit Conduct 2	B	V
9A.44.132(1)(a)	Failure to Register as a Sex Offender (Second Violation Committed on or after 6/10/2010)	C	II
9A.44.132(1)(b)	Failure to Register as a Sex Offender (Third or Subsequent Violation Committed on or after 6/10/2010)	B	II
9A.64.020(1)	Incest 1	B	VI
9A.64.020(2)	Incest 2	C	V
9A.44.100(1)(a)	Indecent Liberties - with Forcible Compulsion	A	X
9A.44.100(1)(b-c)	Indecent Liberties - without Forcible Compulsion	B	VII
9A.44.100(1)(d-f)	Indecent Liberties - without Forcible Compulsion	B	Unranked
9A.40.030(3)(b)	Kidnapping 2 with a Finding of Sexual Motivation	A	V
9.68A.053(2)	Minor Dealing in Depictions of Another Minor Twelve Years or Younger Engaged in Sexually Explicit Conduct 1	B	Unranked
9.68A.053(3)	Minor Dealing in Depictions of Another Minor Twelve Years or Younger Engaged in Sexually Explicit Conduct 2	B	Unranked
9.68A.053(4)	Minor Financing or Selling Depictions of Another Minor Engaged in Sexually Explicit Conduct	B	Unranked
9.68A.070(1)	Possession of Depictions of Minor Engaged in Sexually Explicit Conduct 1	B	VI
9.68A.070(2)	Possession of Depictions of Minor Engaged in Sexually Explicit Conduct 2	B	IV
9.68A.101	Promoting Commercial Sexual Abuse of a Minor	A	XII
9.68A.102	Promoting Travel for Commercial Sexual Abuse of a Minor	C	Unranked
9A.44.040	Rape 1	A	XII
9A.44.050	Rape 2	A	XI
9A.44.060	Rape 3	C	V
9A.44.073	Rape of a Child 1	A	XII

Statute (RCW)	Offense	Class	Seriousness Level
9A.44.076	Rape of a Child 2	A	XI
9A.44.079	Rape of a Child 3	C	VI
9.68A.060(1)	Sending, Bringing into the State Depictions of Minor Engaged in Sexually Explicit Conduct 1	B	VII
9.68A.060(2)	Sending, Bringing into the State Depictions of Minor Engaged in Sexually Explicit Conduct 2	B	V
9.68A.040	Sexual Exploitation of a Minor	B	IX
9A.44.093	Sexual Misconduct with a Minor 1	C	V
9A.44.105	Sexually Violating Human Remains	C	V
9.68A.075(1)	Viewing Depictions of Minor Engaged in Sexually Explicit Conduct 1 (Effective 6/10/2010)	B	IV
9.68A.075(2)	Viewing Depictions of Minor Engaged in Sexually Explicit Conduct 2 (Effective 6/10/2010)	C	Unranked
9A.44.115	Voyeurism 1	C	II

Any conviction for a felony offense in effect at any time prior to July 1, 1976, that is comparable to a felony classified as a sex offense in RCW 9.94A.030(47)(a).

Any federal or out-of-state conviction for an offense that, under the laws of this state, would be a felony classified as a sex offense under 9A.44 other than 9A.44.132.

Any felony with a finding of sexual motivation under RCW 9.94A.835 or 13.40.135.

Attempt, solicitation, or conspiracy to commit any Class A or B felony listed above. An attempt, solicitation, or conspiracy to commit a Class C felony above is a gross misdemeanor (RCW 9A.28.020-040) and, therefore, not a sex offense [RCW 9.94A.030(47) requires a crime to be a felony in order to be a sex offense.]

DRUG OFFENSES

RCW 9.94A.030(22)

The offenses contained in this list are based on the statutory definition of a "drug" offense per RCW 9.94A.030(22). It may not include all "drug-related" offenses.

Statute (RCW)	Offense	Class	Seriousness Level
69.50.465	Conducting or Maintaining a Cannabis Club	C	Unranked
69.50.415	Controlled Substance Homicide	B	DG-III
69.50.416	Controlled Substance Label Violation	C	Unranked
69.50.4011(2)(a-b)	Create or Deliver a Counterfeit Controlled Substance – Schedule I or II Narcotic or Flunitrazepam or Methamphetamine	B	DG-II
69.50.4011(2)(c-e)	Create or Deliver a Counterfeit Controlled Substance – Schedule I-II Nonnarcotic, Schedule III-V Except Flunitrazepam or Methamphetamine	C	DG-II
69.50.401(2)(b)	Deliver or Possess with Intent to Deliver – Methamphetamine	B	DG-II
69.50.4012	Delivery of a Material in Lieu of a Controlled Substance	C	DG-II
69.50.402	Dispensing Violation (VUCSA)	C	Unranked
69.50.4015	Involving a Minor in Drug Dealing	C	DG-III
69.50.402(1)(f)	Maintaining a Dwelling or Place for Controlled Substances	C	DG-II
69.50.401(2)(b)	Manufacture Methamphetamine	B	DG-III
69.50.401(2)(b)	Manufacture, Deliver or Possess with Intent to Deliver – Amphetamine	B	DG-II
69.50.401(2)(c)	Manufacture, Deliver or Possess with Intent to Deliver – Cannabis	C	DG-I
69.50.401(2)(a)	Manufacture, Deliver or Possess with Intent to Deliver - Narcotics from Schedule I or II or Flunitrazepam from Schedule IV	B	DG-II
69.50.401(2)(c-e)	Manufacture, Deliver or Possess with Intent to Deliver - Narcotics from Schedule III, IV, or V or Nonnarcotics from Schedule I-V (except Cannabis, Amphetamine, Methamphetamine, or Flunitrazepam)	C	DG-II
69.50.406(1)	Over 18 and Deliver Heroin, Methamphetamine, a Narcotic from Schedule I or II, or Flunitrazepam from Schedule IV to Someone under 18	A	DG-III
69.50.406(2)	Over 18 and Deliver Narcotic from Schedule III, IV or V, or a Nonnarcotic, Except Flunitrazepam or Methamphetamine, from Schedule I-V to Someone under 18 and 3 Years Junior	B	DG-III
69.50.418	Possess, Purchase, Deliver, Sell, or Possess with Intent to Sell a Tableting Machine or Encapsulating Machine	C	DG-II
69.50.440	Possession of Ephedrine, Pseudoephedrine or Anhydrous Ammonia with Intent to Manufacture Methamphetamine	B	DG-III
69.50.410	Selling for Profit (Controlled or Counterfeit) any Controlled Substance in Schedule I	C	DG-III

MOST SERIOUS OFFENSES (PERSISTENT OFFENDER "THREE STRIKES")

RCW 9.94A.030(32)

Statute (RCW)	Offense	Class	Seriousness Level
10.95.020	Aggravated Murder 1	A	XVI
9A.48.020	Arson 1	A	VIII
9A.36.011	Assault 1	A	XII
9A.36.021(2)(a)	Assault 2	B	IV
9A.36.021(2)(b)	Assault 2 with a Finding of Sexual Motivation	A	IV
9A.36.120	Assault of a Child 1	A	XII
9A.36.130	Assault of a Child 2	B	IX
9A.76.170(3)(a)	Bail Jumping with Murder 1	A	VI
9A.52.020	Burglary 1	A	VII
9A.44.083	Child Molestation 1	A	X
9A.44.086	Child Molestation 2	B	VII
70.245.200(2)	Coerce Patient to Request Life-ending Medication	A	Unranked
69.50.415	Controlled Substance Homicide	B	DG-III
70.74.180	Explosive Devices Prohibited	A	IX
9A.56.120	Extortion 1	B	V
70.245.200(1)	Forging Request for Medication	A	Unranked
9A.32.055	Homicide by Abuse	A	XV
79A.60.050(1)(c)	Homicide by Watercraft - Disregard for the Safety of Others	A	VII
79A.60.050(1)(b)	Homicide by Watercraft – in a Reckless Manner	A	VIII
79A.60.050(1)(a)	Homicide by Watercraft – while under the Influence of Intoxicating Liquor or any Drug	A	IX
9A.64.020(1)	Incest 1 (When Committed Against a Child under 14)	B	VI
9A.64.020(2)	Incest 2 (When Committed Against a Child under 14)	C	V
9A.44.100(1)(a)	Indecent Liberties - with Forcible Compulsion	A	X
9A.44.100(1)(b-c)	Indecent Liberties - without Forcible Compulsion	B	VII
9A.44.100(1)(d-f)	Indecent Liberties - without Forcible Compulsion	B	Unranked
9A.40.020	Kidnapping 1	A	X
9A.40.030(3)(a)	Kidnapping 2	B	V
9A.40.030(3)(b)	Kidnapping 2 with a Finding of Sexual Motivation	A	V
9A.82.060(1)(b)	Leading Organized Crime - Inciting Criminal Profiteering	B	IX
9A.82.060(1)(a)	Leading Organized Crime – Organizing Criminal Profiteering	A	X
70.74.280(1)	Malicious Explosion of a Substance 1	A	XV
70.74.280(2)	Malicious Explosion of a Substance 2	A	XIII
70.74.270(1)	Malicious Placement of an Explosive 1	A	XIII
9A.32.060	Manslaughter 1	A	XI
9A.32.070	Manslaughter 2	B	VIII

Statute (RCW)	Offense	Class	Seriousness Level
9A.32.030	Murder 1	A	XV
9A.32.050	Murder 2	A	XIV
69.50.406(1)	Over 18 and Deliver Heroin, Methamphetamine, a Narcotic from Schedule I or II, or Flunitrazepam from Schedule IV to Someone under 18	A	DG-III
9.68A.101	Promoting Commercial Sexual Abuse of a Minor	A	XII
9A.88.070	Promoting Prostitution 1	B	VIII
9A.44.040	Rape 1	A	XII
9A.44.050	Rape 2	A	XI
9A.44.060	Rape 3	C	V
9A.44.073	Rape of a Child 1	A	XII
9A.44.076	Rape of a Child 2	A	XI
9A.56.200	Robbery 1	A	IX
9.68A.040	Sexual Exploitation of a Minor	B	IX
9A.76.115	Sexually Violent Predator Escape	A	X
9A.40.100(1)	Trafficking 1	A	XIV
9A.40.100(3)	Trafficking 2	A	XII
9.82.010	Treason	A	Unranked
9.41.225	Use of a Machine Gun or Bump-fire Stock in Commission of a Felony	A	VII
46.61.522(1)(a-b)	Vehicular Assault – in a Reckless Manner or while under the Influence of Intoxicating Liquor or any Drug	B	IV
46.61.520(1)(c)	Vehicular Homicide - Disregard for the Safety of Others	A	VII
46.61.520(1)(b)	Vehicular Homicide – in a Reckless Manner	A	XI
46.61.520(1)(a)	Vehicular Homicide – while under the Influence of Intoxicating Liquor or any Drug	A	XI

Attempt to commit one of these felonies.

Any Class A felony or criminal solicitation or criminal conspiracy to commit a Class A felony.

Any felony offense in effect at any time prior to December 2, 1993, that is comparable to a most serious offense under this subsection, or any federal or out-of-state conviction for an offense that under the laws of this state would be a felony classified as a most serious offense under this subsection.

Any other Class B felony offense with a finding of sexual motivation.

Any other felony with a deadly weapon verdict under RCW 9.94A.825.

Any out-of-state conviction for a felony offense with a finding of sexual motivation if the minimum sentence imposed was ten years or more; provided that the out-of-state felony offense must be comparable to a felony offense under Title 9 or 9A RCW and the out-of-state definition of sexual motivation must be comparable to the definition of sexual motivation contained in this section.

A prior conviction for indecent liberties under RCW 9A.88.100(1) (a), (b), and (c), chapter 260, Laws of 1975 1st ex. sess. as it existed until July 1, 1979, RCW 9A.44.100(1) (a), (b), and (c) as it existed from July 1, 1979, until June 11, 1986, and RCW 9A.44.100(1) (a), (b), and (d) as it existed from June 11, 1986, until July 1, 1988.

A prior conviction for indecent liberties under RCW 9A.44.100(1)(c) as it existed from June 11, 1986, until July 1, 1988, if: (A) The crime was committed against a child under the age of fourteen; or (B) the relationship between the victim and perpetrator is included in the definition of indecent liberties under

Most Serious Offenses (PERSISTENT OFFENDER "THREE STRIKES")

Statute (RCW)	Offense	Class	Seriousness Level
RCW 9A.44.100(1)(c) as it existed from July 1, 1988, through July 27, 1997, or RCW 9A.44.100(1) (d) or (e) as it existed from July 25, 1993, through July 27, 1997.			

PERSISTENT OFFENDER OFFENSES ("TWO STRIKES")

RCW 9.94A.030(37)(b)

Statute (RCW)	Offense	Class	Seriousness Level
9A.36.011	Assault 1 with a Finding of Sexual Motivation	A	XII
9A.36.021(2)(b)	Assault 2 with a Finding of Sexual Motivation	A	IV
9A.36.120	Assault of a Child 1 with a Finding of Sexual Motivation	A	XII
9A.36.130	Assault of a Child 2 with a Finding of Sexual Motivation	B	IX
9A.52.020	Burglary 1 with a Finding of Sexual Motivation	A	VII
9A.44.083	Child Molestation 1	A	X
9A.32.055	Homicide by Abuse with a Finding of Sexual Motivation	A	XV
9A.44.100(1)(a)	Indecent Liberties - with Forcible Compulsion	A	X
9A.40.020	Kidnapping 1 with a Finding of Sexual Motivation	A	X
9A.40.030(3)(b)	Kidnapping 2 with a Finding of Sexual Motivation	A	V
9A.32.030	Murder 1 with a Finding of Sexual Motivation	A	XV
9A.32.050	Murder 2 with a Finding of Sexual Motivation	A	XIV
9A.44.040	Rape 1	A	XII
9A.44.050	Rape 2	A	XI
9A.44.073	Rape of a Child 1 (Where the Offender was Age 16 or Older at the Time of the Offense)	A	XII
9A.44.076	Rape of a Child 2 (Where the Offender was Age 18 or Older at the Time of the Offense)	A	XI
Attempt to commit one of these felonies.			

CRIME AGAINST PERSONS OFFENSES
RCW 9.94A.411(2)

Statute (RCW)	Offense	Class	Seriousness Level
10.95.020	Aggravated Murder 1	A	XVI
9A.48.020	Arson 1	A	VIII
9A.36.011	Assault 1	A	XII
9A.36.021(2)(a)	Assault 2	B	IV
9A.36.031(1)(h)	Assault 3 of a Peace Officer with a Projectile Stun Gun	C	IV
9A.36.031(1)(a-g) & (i-j)	Assault 3, excluding Assault 3 of a Peace Officer with a Projectile Stun Gun	C	III
9A.36.041(3)	Assault 4 (Third Domestic Violence Offense)	C	IV
9A.36.120	Assault of a Child 1	A	XII
9A.36.130	Assault of a Child 2	B	IX
9A.36.140	Assault of a Child 3	C	III
9A.52.020	Burglary 1	A	VII
9A.44.083	Child Molestation 1	A	X
9A.44.086	Child Molestation 2	B	VII
9A.44.089	Child Molestation 3	C	V
9.68A.090(2)	Communication with Minor for Immoral Purposes (Subsequent Violation or Prior Sex Offense Conviction)	C	III
9.16.035(4)	Counterfeiting - Endanger Public Health or Safety	C	IV
9A.84.010(2)(b)	Criminal Mischief (if against a person)	C	Unranked
9A.42.020	Criminal Mistreatment 1	B	X
9A.42.030	Criminal Mistreatment 2	C	V
9A.36.100	Custodial Assault	C	III
7.105.450, 10.99.040, 10.99.050, 26.09.300, 26.26B.050, or 26.52.070	Domestic Violence Court Order Violation	C	V
46.61.502(6)	Driving while under the Influence of Intoxicating Liquor or any Drug	B	IV
9A.56.120	Extortion 1	B	V
9A.56.130	Extortion 2	C	III
9A.36.080	Hate Crime	C	IV
28B.10.910(2)(b)	Hazing	C	III
9.35.020(2)	Identity Theft 1	B	IV
9.35.020(3)	Identity Theft 2	C	II
9A.64.020(1)	Incest 1	B	VI
9A.64.020(2)	Incest 2	C	V

Statute (RCW)	Offense	Class	Seriousness Level
9A.44.100(1)(a)	Indecent Liberties - with Forcible Compulsion	A	X
9A.44.100(1)(b-c)	Indecent Liberties - without Forcible Compulsion	B	VII
9A.44.100(1)(d-f)	Indecent Liberties - without Forcible Compulsion	B	Unranked
9A.72.130	Intimidating a Juror	B	VI
9A.76.180	Intimidating a Public Servant	B	III
9A.72.110	Intimidating a Witness	B	VI
9A.40.020	Kidnapping 1	A	X
9A.40.030(3)(a)	Kidnapping 2	B	V
9A.32.060	Manslaughter 1	A	XI
9A.32.070	Manslaughter 2	B	VIII
9A.32.030	Murder 1	A	XV
9A.32.050	Murder 2	A	XIV
46.61.504(6)	Physical Control of a Vehicle while under the Influence of Intoxicating Liquor or any Drug	C	IV
9A.36.060	Promoting a Suicide Attempt	C	Unranked
9A.88.070	Promoting Prostitution 1	B	VIII
9A.44.040	Rape 1	A	XII
9A.44.050	Rape 2	A	XI
9A.44.060	Rape 3	C	V
9A.44.073	Rape of a Child 1	A	XII
9A.44.076	Rape of a Child 2	A	XI
9A.44.079	Rape of a Child 3	C	VI
9A.56.200	Robbery 1	A	IX
9A.56.210	Robbery 2	B	IV
9A.46.110	Stalking	B	V
9A.56.400(1)	Theft from a Vulnerable Adult 1	B	VI
9A.56.400(2)	Theft from a Vulnerable Adult 2	C	I
9.61.160	Threats to Bomb (if against a person)	B	IV
9A.40.040	Unlawful Imprisonment	C	III
46.61.522(1)(c)	Vehicular Assault - Disregard for the Safety of Others	B	III
46.61.522(1)(a-b)	Vehicular Assault – in a Reckless Manner or while under the Influence of Intoxicating Liquor or any Drug	B	IV
46.61.520(1)(c)	Vehicular Homicide - Disregard for the Safety of Others	A	VII
46.61.520(1)(b)	Vehicular Homicide – in a Reckless Manner	A	XI
46.61.520(1)(a)	Vehicular Homicide – while under the Influence of Intoxicating Liquor or any Drug	A	XI

PATTERN OF CRIMINAL STREET GANG ACTIVITY OFFENSES
RCW 9.94A.030(36)

Defined as:

The commission, attempt, conspiracy, or solicitation of, or any prior juvenile adjudication of or adult conviction of, two or more of the following criminal street gang-related offenses;

That at least one of the offenses listed shall have occurred after July 1, 2008;

That the most recent committed offense listed occurred within three years of a prior offense listed; and

Of the offenses that were committed in this list, the offenses occurred on separate occasions or were committed by two or more persons.

Statute (RCW)	Offense	Class	Seriousness Level
10.95.020	Aggravated Murder 1	A	XVI
9.41.171	Alien Possession of a Firearm	C	Unranked
9A.48.020	Arson 1	A	VIII
9A.48.030	Arson 2	B	IV
9A.36.011	Assault 1	A	XII
9A.36.021(2)(a)	Assault 2	B	IV
9A.36.021(2)(b)	Assault 2 with a Finding of Sexual Motivation	A	IV
9A.76.170(3)(a)	Bail Jumping with Murder 1	A	VI
9A.52.020	Burglary 1	A	VII
9A.52.030	Burglary 2	B	III
9A.44.083	Child Molestation 1	A	X
70.245.200(2)	Coerce Patient to Request Life-ending Medication	A	Unranked
9A.36.070	Coercion (gross misdemeanor*)	n/a	n/a
9A.46.120	Criminal Gang Intimidation	C	III
Chapter 69.50 RCW	Deliver or Possess with Intent to Deliver a Controlled Substance		
9.41.110(8)	Delivery of Firearm by Dealer to Ineligible Person	C	Unranked
9.41.080	Delivery of Firearms to Ineligible Person	C	Unranked
9A.36.045	Drive-by Shooting	B	VII
70.74.180	Explosive Devices Prohibited	A	IX
9A.56.120	Extortion 1	B	V
9A.56.130	Extortion 2	C	III
70.245.200(1)	Forging Request for Medication	A	Unranked
9A.46.020(1)	Harassment (gross misdemeanor*)	n/a	n/a
9A.46.020(2)(b)	Harassment	C	III
9A.36.080	Hate Crime Offense	C	IV
79A.60.050(1)(c)	Homicide by Watercraft - Disregard for the Safety of Others	A	VII

Statute (RCW)	Offense	Class	Seriousness Level
79A.60.050(1)(b)	Homicide by Watercraft – in a Reckless Manner	A	VIII
79A.60.050(1)(a)	Homicide by Watercraft – while under the Influence of Intoxicating Liquor or any Drug	A	IX
9A.44.100(1)(a)	Indecent Liberties - with Forcible Compulsion	A	X
9A.72.110	Intimidating a Witness	B	VI
9A.40.020	Kidnapping 1	A	X
9A.40.030(3)(a)	Kidnapping 2	B	V
9A.40.030(3)(b)	Kidnapping 2 with a Finding of Sexual Motivation	A	V
9A.82.060(1)(a)	Leading Organized Crime – Organizing Criminal Profiteering	A	X
70.74.280(1)	Malicious Explosion of a Substance 1	A	XV
70.74.280(2)	Malicious Explosion of a Substance 2	A	XIII
9A.48.070	Malicious Mischief 1	B	II
9A.48.080	Malicious Mischief 2	C	I
9A.48.090	Malicious Mischief 3 (gross misdemeanor*)	n/a	n/a
70.74.270(1)	Malicious Placement of an Explosive 1	A	XIII
9A.32.060	Manslaughter 1	A	XI
9A.32.070	Manslaughter 2	B	VIII
9.41.190	Manufacture of Untraceable Firearm with Intent to Sell	C	III
9.41.325	Manufacture or Assembly of an Undetectable Firearm or Untraceable Firearm	C	III
9A.32.030	Murder 1	A	XV
9A.32.050	Murder 2	A	XIV
69.50.406(1)	Over 18 and Deliver Heroin, Methamphetamine, a Narcotic from Schedule I or II, or Flunitrazepam from Schedule IV to Someone under 18	A	DG-III
9A.56.310	Possession of a Stolen Firearm	B	V
9A.56.068	Possession of a Stolen Vehicle	B	II
9.41.190	Possession of Machine Gun, Bump-fire Stock, Undetectable Firearm, or Short-Barreled Shotgun or Rifle	C	III
9.68A.101	Promoting Commercial Sexual Abuse of a Minor	A	XII
9A.44.040	Rape 1	A	XII
9A.44.050	Rape 2	A	XI
9A.44.073	Rape of a Child 1	A	XII
9A.44.076	Rape of a Child 2	A	XI
9A.36.050	Reckless Endangerment (gross misdemeanor*)	n/a	n/a
9A.52.025	Residential Burglary	B	IV
9A.56.200	Robbery 1	A	IX
9A.56.210	Robbery 2	B	IV
9A.76.115	Sexually Violent Predator Escape	A	X
9A.56.070	Taking Motor Vehicle without Permission 1	B	V

Pattern of Criminal Street Gang Activity Offenses

Statute (RCW)	Offense	Class	Seriousness Level
9A.56.075	Taking Motor Vehicle without Permission 2	C	I
9A.72.120	Tampering with a Witness	C	III
9A.56.300	Theft of a Firearm	B	VI
9A.56.065	Theft of a Motor Vehicle	B	II
9A.40.100(1)	Trafficking 1	A	XIV
9A.40.100(3)	Trafficking 2	A	XII
9.82.010	Treason	A	Unranked
9.41.040(1)	Unlawful Possession of a Firearm 1	B	VII
9.41.040(2)	Unlawful Possession of a Firearm 2	C	III
9.41.115	Unlawful Private Transfer of a Firearm (Subsequent Offense)	C	Unranked
9.41.360	Unlawful Storage of a Firearm	C	Unranked
9.41.225	Use of a Machine Gun or Bump-fire Stock in Commission of a Felony	A	VII
46.61.522(1)(a-b)	Vehicular Assault – in a Reckless Manner or while under the Influence of Intoxicating Liquor or any Drug	B	IV
46.61.520(1)(b)	Vehicular Homicide – in a Reckless Manner	A	XI
46.61.520(1)(a)	Vehicular Homicide – while under the Influence of Intoxicating Liquor or any Drug	A	XI
Any felony conviction by a person eighteen years of age or older with a special finding of involving a juvenile in a felony offense under RCW 9.94A.833.			

Gross misdemeanor offenses listed count as predicate offenses.

FELONY OFFENSES REQUIRING SEX OFFENDER REGISTRATION
Sex Offender Registration (9A.44.140)

For further information on duration of registration and relief from registration, refer to RCW 9A.44.140 through RCW 9A.44.143. If the person is required to register for a federal, tribal, or out-of-state conviction, when the person has spent 15 consecutive years in the community without being convicted of a disqualifying offense during that time, the person may petition the court for relief from registration.

	LIFETIME REGISTRATION		
Statute (RCW)	Offense	Class	Seriousness Level
Chapter 71.09 RCW	Determined to be a Sexually Violent Predator	n/a	n/a
9A.44.100(1)(a)	Indecent Liberties - with Forcible Compulsion (If convicted as an adult for an offense committed on or after 6/8/2000)	A	X
9A.28.020(3)(a)	Indecent Liberties - with Forcible Compulsion – Criminal Attempt (if convicted as an adult for an offense committed on or after 6/8/2000)	A	X
9A.28.030(2)	Indecent Liberties - with Forcible Compulsion – Criminal Solicitation (if convicted as an adult for an offense committed on or after 6/8/2000)	A	X
9A.44.040	Rape 1 (if convicted as an adult for an offense committed on or after 6/8/2000)	A	XII
9A.28.020(3)(a)	Rape 1 – Criminal Attempt (if convicted as an adult for an offense committed on or after 6/8/2000)	A	XII
9A.28.030(2)	Rape 1 – Criminal Solicitation (if convicted as an adult for an offense committed on or after 6/8/2000)	A	XII
9A.44.050	Rape 2 (with Forcible Compulsion) (if convicted as an adult for an offense committed on or after 6/8/2000)	A	XI
9A.28.020(3)(a)	Rape 2 (with Forcible Compulsion) – Criminal Attempt (if convicted as an adult for an offense committed on or after 6/8/2000)	A	XI
9A.28.030(2)	Rape 2 (with Forcible Compulsion) – Criminal Solicitation (if convicted as an adult for an offense committed on or after 6/8/2000)	A	XI

INDEFINITE REGISTRATION			
Statute (RCW)	Offense	Class	Seriousness Level
9A.44.083	Child Molestation 1	A	X
9A.28.020(3)(a)	Child Molestation 1 – Criminal Attempt	A	X
9A.28.030(2)	Child Molestation 1 – Criminal Solicitation	A	X
9.68A.101	Promoting Commercial Sexual Abuse of a Minor	A	XII
9A.44.040	Rape 1 (for an offense committed prior to 6/8/2000)	A	XII
9A.28.020(3)(a)	Rape 1 – Criminal Attempt (for an offense committed prior to 6/8/2000)	A	XII
9A.28.030(2)	Rape 1 – Criminal Solicitation (for an offense committed prior to 6/8/2000)	A	XII
9A.44.050	Rape 2 (with Forcible Compulsion) (for an offense committed prior to 6/8/2000)	A	XI
9A.28.020(3)(a)	Rape 2 (with Forcible Compulsion) – Criminal Attempt (for an offense committed prior to 6/8/2000)	A	XI
9A.28.030(2)	Rape 2 (with Forcible Compulsion) – Criminal Solicitation (for an offense committed prior to 6/8/2000)	A	XI
9A.44.050	Rape 2 (without Forcible Compulsion)	A	XI
9A.28.020(3)(a)	Rape 2 (without Forcible Compulsion) – Criminal Attempt	A	XI
9A.28.030(2)	Rape 2 (without Forcible Compulsion) – Criminal Solicitation	A	XI
9A.44.073	Rape of a Child 1	A	XII
9A.28.020(3)(a)	Rape of a Child 1 – Criminal Attempt	A	XII
9A.28.030(2)	Rape of a Child 1 – Criminal Solicitation	A	XII
9A.44.076	Rape of a Child 2	A	XI
9A.28.020(3)(a)	Rape of a Child 2 – Criminal Attempt	A	XI
9A.28.030(2)	Rape of a Child 2 – Criminal Solicitation	A	XI
9A.40.100(1)	Trafficking 1, when violation of (1)(b)(ii); (1)(a)(i)(A)(III) or (IV); or (a)(i)(B)	A	XIV
Any sex offense or a kidnapping offense when the defendant already has one or more prior convictions for a sex offense or a kidnapping offense.			
Any Class A felony offense with a finding of sexual motivation under RCW 9.94A.835.			

15 YEAR REGISTRATION

Duty to register shall end 15 years after the last date of release from confinement, if any, (including full-time residential treatment) pursuant to the conviction, or entry of the judgment and sentence, if the person has spent 15 consecutive years in the community without being convicted of a disqualifying offense during that time period.

Statute (RCW)	Offense	Class	Seriousness Level
9A.44.086	Child Molestation 2	B	VII
9.68A.100	Commercial Sexual Abuse of a Minor	B	VIII
9A.44.160	Custodial Sexual Misconduct 1	B	VII
9.68A.050(1)	Dealing in Depictions of Minor Engaged in Sexually Explicit Conduct 1	B	VII
9.68A.050(2)	Dealing in Depictions of Minor Engaged in Sexually Explicit Conduct 2	B	V
9A.44.132(1)(b)	Failure to Register as a Sex Offender (Third or Subsequent Violation Committed on or after 6/10/2010)	B	II
9A.64.020(1)	Incest 1	B	VI
9A.44.100(1)(a)	Indecent Liberties - with Forcible Compulsion (for an offense committed prior to 6/8/2000)	B	X
9A.28.020(3)(a)	Indecent Liberties - with Forcible Compulsion – Criminal Attempt (for an offense committed prior to 6/8/2000)	B	X
9A.28.030(2)	Indecent Liberties - with Forcible Compulsion – Criminal Solicitation (for an offense committed prior to 6/8/2000)	B	X
9A.44.100(1)(b-c)	Indecent Liberties - without Forcible Compulsion	B	VII
9A.44.100(1)(d-f)	Indecent Liberties - without Forcible Compulsion	B	Unranked
9.68A.053(2)	Minor Dealing in Depictions of Another Minor Twelve Years or Younger Engaged in Sexually Explicit Conduct 1	B	Unranked
9.68A.053(3)	Minor Dealing in Depictions of Another Minor Twelve Years or Younger Engaged in Sexually Explicit Conduct 2	B	Unranked
9.68A.053(4)	Minor Financing or Selling Depictions of Another Minor Engaged in Sexually Explicit Conduct	B	Unranked
9.68A.070(1)	Possession of Depictions of Minor Engaged in Sexually Explicit Conduct 1	B	VI
9.68A.070(2)	Possession of Depictions of Minor Engaged in Sexually Explicit Conduct 2	B	IV
9A.88.070	Promoting Prostitution 1*	B	VIII
9.68A.060(1)	Sending, Bringing into the State Depictions of Minor Engaged in Sexually Explicit Conduct 1	B	VII
9.68A.060(2)	Sending, Bringing into the State Depictions of Minor Engaged in Sexually Explicit Conduct 2	B	V
9.68A.040	Sexual Exploitation of a Minor	B	IX
9.68A.075(1)	Viewing Depictions of Minor Engaged in Sexually Explicit Conduct 1	B	IV
9.68A.075(2)	Viewing Depictions of Minor Engaged in Sexually Explicit Conduct 2	B	Unranked

No prior convictions for a sex or kidnapping offense.

Any Class B felony offense with a finding of sexual motivation under RCW 9.94A.835.

Only subsequent violations of Promoting Prostitution 1 are considered registerable per RCW 9A.44.128.

10 YEAR REGISTRATION

Duty to register shall end ten years after the last date of release from confinement, if any, (including full-time residential treatment) pursuant to the conviction, or entry of the judgment and sentence, if the person has spent fifteen consecutive years in the community without being convicted of a disqualifying offense during that time period.

Statute (RCW)	Offense	Class	Seriousness Level
9A.44.089	Child Molestation 3	C	V
9.68A.090(2)	Communication with Minor for Immoral Purposes (Subsequent Violation or Prior Sex Offense Conviction)	C	III
9A.44.196	Criminal Trespass Against Children	C	Unranked
9A.44.170	Custodial Sexual Misconduct 2	C	V
9A.44.132(1)(a)	Failure to Register as a Sex Offender (Second Violation Committed on or after 6/10/2010)	C	II
9A.64.020(2)	Incest 2	C	V
9A.88.080	Promoting Prostitution 2*	C	III
9.68A.102	Promoting Travel for Commercial Sexual Abuse of a Minor	C	Unranked
9A.44.060	Rape 3	C	V
9A.44.079	Rape of a Child 3	C	VI
9A.44.093	Sexual Misconduct with a Minor 1	C	V
9A.44.105	Sexually Violating Human Remains	C	V
9.68A.075(2)	Viewing Depictions of Minor Engaged in Sexually Explicit Conduct 2	C	Unranked
9A.44.115	Voyeurism 1	C	II
Violation of RCW 9.68A.090			
Violation of RCW 9A.44.096			
Attempt, solicitation, or conspiracy to commit a Class C sex offense			

Only subsequent violations of Promoting Prostitution 2 are considered registerable per RCW 9A.44.128.

NONVIOLENT OFFENSES

Statute (RCW)	Offense	Class	Seriousness Level
9A.42.060	Abandonment of Dependent Person 1	B	IX
9A.42.070	Abandonment of Dependent Person 2	C	V
29A.84.680(1)	Absentee Voting Violation	C	Unranked
46.52.130(6)(b)	Abstracts of Driving Records – Intentional Misuse	C	Unranked
20.01.460(2)	Acting as Commission Merchant, Dealer, Cash Buyer without License	C	Unranked
9A.82.030	Advancing Money or Property for Extortionate Extension of Credit	B	V
69.52.030(3)	Advertising Imitation Controlled Substances	C	Unranked
46.37.660(2)(c)	Air Bag Diagnostic Systems	C	V
46.37.660(2)(b)	Air Bag Diagnostic Systems (Causing Bodily Injury or Death)	C	VII
46.37.660(1)(c)	Air Bag Replacement Requirements	C	V
46.37.660(1)(b)	Air Bag Replacement Requirements (Causing Bodily Injury or Death)	C	VII
30A.42.290(3)	Alien Bank or Bureau – Destroy or Secrete Records	B	Unranked
30A.42.290(2)	Alien Bank or Bureau – False Entry, Statements, etc.	B	Unranked
9.41.171	Alien Possession of a Firearm	C	Unranked
9.45.210	Altering Sample or Certificate of Assay	C	Unranked
9A.76.177	Amber Alert – Making False Statements to a Public Servant	C	Unranked
68.64.160	Anatomical Gift - Illegal Financial Gain	C	Unranked
68.64.150	Anatomical Gifts - Illegal Purchase or Sale	C	Unranked
16.52.205(2)	Animal Cruelty 1	C	Unranked
16.52.205(3)	Animal Cruelty 1 - Sexual Conduct or Contact	C	III
16.52.117(2)(a)	Animal Fighting	C	Unranked
16.52.117(2)(b)	Animal Fighting - Mutilation	B	Unranked
9A.36.031(1)(h)	Assault 3 of a Peace Officer with a Projectile Stun Gun	C	IV
9A.36.031(1)(a-g) & (i-j)	Assault 3, excluding Assault 3 of a Peace Officer with a Projectile Stun Gun	C	III
9A.36.041(3)	Assault 4 (Third Domestic Violence Offense)	C	IV
79A.60.060	Assault by Watercraft	B	IV
9A.36.140	Assault of a Child 3	C	III
9.05.030	Assembly of Saboteurs	B	Unranked
72.23.170	Assist Escape of Mental Patient	C	Unranked
46.61.024	Attempting to Elude Pursuing Police Vehicle	C	I
9A.76.170(3)(b)	Bail Jumping with Class A Felony	B	V
9A.76.170(3)(c)	Bail Jumping with Class B or C Felony	C	III

Statute (RCW)	Offense	Class	Seriousness Level
30A.12.100	Bank or Trust Company - Destroy or Secrete Records	B	Unranked
30A.12.090	Bank or Trust Company - False Entry, Statements, etc.	B	Unranked
30A.44.120	Bank or Trust Company - Receiving Deposits When Insolvent	B	Unranked
30A.44.110	Bank or Trust Company - Transfer of Assets Prior to Insolvency	B	Unranked
9A.64.010	Bigamy	C	Unranked
9A.72.100	Bribe Received by Witness	B	IV
9A.68.010	Bribery	B	VI
9A.72.090	Bribing a Witness	B	IV
9.46.155	Bribing to Obtain a License from Public Officials, Employees, Agents	C	Unranked
72.23.300	Bringing Narcotics, Liquor, or Weapons into State Institution or Grounds	B	Unranked
9.47.120	Bunco Steering	B	Unranked
9A.52.030	Burglary 2	B	III
46.87.260	Cab Card Forgery (Effective Until 7/1/2016)	B	Unranked
9.46.180	Causing Person to Violate Gambling Laws	B	Unranked
9.46.1961	Cheating 1	C	IV
9A.64.030(3)(b)	Child Buying	C	Unranked
49.12.410(2)	Child Labor Law Violation – Death/Disability	C	Unranked
9A.44.086	Child Molestation 2	B	VII
9A.44.089	Child Molestation 3	C	V
9A.64.030(3)(a)	Child Selling	C	Unranked
9A.48.120	Civil Disorder Training	B	VII
9A.40.110	Coercion of Involuntary Servitude	C	Unranked
9A.82.045	Collection of Unlawful Debt	C	Unranked
9A.68.060	Commercial Bribery	B	IV
77.15.500(3)(b)	Commercial Fishing without a License 1	C	II
9.68A.100	Commercial Sexual Abuse of a Minor	B	VIII
19.158.160	Commercial Telephone Solicitor Deception (Value of $250 or more)	C	Unranked
30A.04.240	Commingling of Funds or Securities	B	Unranked
21.30.140	Commodity Transaction Violation	B	Unranked
9.68A.090(2)	Communication with Minor for Immoral Purposes (Subsequent Violation or Prior Sex Offense Conviction)	C	III
9A.90.040	Computer Trespass 1	C	II
69.50.465	Conducting or Maintaining a Cannabis Club	C	Unranked
19.144.100(2)	Control of Real Property Resulting from Mortgage Fraud Activities	B	Unranked
69.50.415	Controlled Substance Homicide	B	DG-III
69.50.416	Controlled Substance Label Violation	C	Unranked

Statute (RCW)	Offense	Class	Seriousness Level
9.16.035(4)	Counterfeiting - Endanger Public Health or Safety	C	IV
9.16.035(3)	Counterfeiting – Third Conviction and Value $10,000 or more	C	II
69.50.4011(2)(a-b)	Create or Deliver a Counterfeit Controlled Substance – Schedule I or II Narcotic or Flunitrazepam or Methamphetamine	B	DG-II
69.50.4011(2)(c-e)	Create or Deliver a Counterfeit Controlled Substance – Schedule I-II Nonnarcotic, Schedule III-V Except Flunitrazepam or Methamphetamine	C	DG-II
46.87.260	Credential Forgery (Effective 7/1/2016)	B	Unranked
31.12.724(3)	Credit Union - Fraudulent Receipt of Credit Union Deposit	B	Unranked
31.12.724(2)	Credit Union - Transfer of Credit Union Assets Prior to Insolvency	B	Unranked
9.08.090	Crimes Against Animal Facilities	C	Unranked
9A.46.120	Criminal Gang Intimidation	C	III
9A.60.040	Criminal Impersonation 1	C	Unranked
9A.84.010(2)(b)	Criminal Mischief	C	Unranked
9A.42.020	Criminal Mistreatment 1	B	X
9A.42.030	Criminal Mistreatment 2	C	V
9A.82.160	Criminal Profiteering Lien after Service of Notice	C	Unranked
9.05.060(2)	Criminal Sabotage	B	Unranked
9A.44.196	Criminal Trespass Against Children	C	Unranked
9A.36.100	Custodial Assault	C	III
9A.40.060	Custodial Interference 1	C	Unranked
9A.40.070	Custodial Interference 2 (Subsequent Offense)	C	Unranked
9A.44.160	Custodial Sexual Misconduct 1	B	VII
9A.44.170	Custodial Sexual Misconduct 2	C	V
9A.90.120(2)(b)	Cyber Harassment	C	III
43.06.230	Damage Property or Cause Personal Injury after State of Emergency Proclaimed	B	Unranked
16.08.100(2)	Dangerous Dog Attack (Subsequent Offense)	C	Unranked
16.08.100(3)	Dangerous Dog Attack Resulting in Severe Injury or Death	C	Unranked
9.68A.050(1)	Dealing in Depictions of Minor Engaged in Sexually Explicit Conduct 1	B	VII
9.68A.050(2)	Dealing in Depictions of Minor Engaged in Sexually Explicit Conduct 2	B	V
22.09.310	Dealing in Unauthorized Warehouse Receipts for Agricultural Commodities	C	Unranked
39.44.101	Defraud a Facsimile Signature on Bonds and Coupons	B	Unranked
87.03.200	Defraud Facsimile Signatures on Bonds and Coupons – Irrigation Districts	B	Unranked
19.110.120	Defraud or Provide Misleading or Untrue Documents Related to a Business Opportunity Sale	B	Unranked

Statute (RCW)	Offense	Class	Seriousness Level
9A.61.030	Defrauding a Public Utility 1	B	Unranked
9A.61.040	Defrauding a Public Utility 2	C	Unranked
19.48.110(1)(b)	Defrauding an Innkeeper (Value of $75 or more)	B	Unranked
69.50.401(2)(b)	Deliver or Possess with Intent to Deliver - Methamphetamine	B	DG-II
69.50.4012	Delivery of a Material in Lieu of a Controlled Substance	C	DG-II
9.41.110(8)	Delivery of Firearm by Dealer to Ineligible Person	C	Unranked
9.41.080	Delivery of Firearms to Ineligible Person	C	Unranked
69.52.030(2)	Delivery of Imitation Controlled Substance by Person 18 or Over to Person under 18	B	DG-III
35A.36.040	Designation of Bonds – Violation (Code Cities)	B	Unranked
35.36.040	Designation of Bonds – Violation (First Class Cities)	B	Unranked
27.44.040(1)	Destroying, Removing or Defacing Indian Graves	C	Unranked
68.60.040(1)	Destruction of Tomb, Plot, Marker, or Cemetery Property	C	Unranked
9.38.060	Digital Signatures Fraud	C	Unranked
9A.76.023(2)(a)	Disarming a Law Enforcement or Corrections Officer	C	Unranked
9A.76.023(2)(b)	Disarming a Law Enforcement or Corrections Officer and Firearm is Discharged	B	Unranked
9A.86.010	Disclosing Intimate Images	C	Unranked
19.110.075(2)	Disclosures Knowingly Not Provided at Sale of Business Opportunity (Violation of RCW 19.110.070)	B	Unranked
69.50.402	Dispensing Violation (VUCSA)	C	Unranked
82.26.190	Distributors and Retailer of Tobacco Products License Violation	C	Unranked
27.53.060	Disturbing Archaeological Resources or Site	C	Unranked
43.43.856	Divulging Confidential Investigative Information Pertaining to Organized Crime	B	Unranked
7.105.450, 10.99.040, 10.99.050, 26.09.300, 26.26B.050, or 26.52.070	Domestic Violence Court Order Violation	C	V
46.61.502(6)	Driving while under the Influence of Intoxicating Liquor or any Drug	B	IV
29A.84.270	Duplication of Name – Conspiracy to Mislead	B	Unranked
29A.84.320	Duplication of Names on Declaration of Candidacy	B	Unranked
29A.84.655	Election Officer Permits Repeat Vote	C	Unranked
29A.84.720	Election Officers – Violation	C	Unranked
29A.84.030	Election or Mail Ballot Violation	C	Unranked
19.300.020	Electronic Communication Devices – Illegal Scanning	C	Unranked
9A.90.060	Electronic Data Service Interference	C	II

Statute (RCW)	Offense	Class	Seriousness Level
9A.90.080	Electronic Data Tampering 1	C	II
9A.90.100	Electronic Data Theft	C	II
79A.60.090	Eluding a Law Enforcement Vessel	C	Unranked
18.39.350	Embalmers/Funeral Directors Violation	C	Unranked
43.08.140	Embezzlement by State Treasurer	B	Unranked
9A.42.100	Endangerment with a Controlled Substance	B	IV
46.80.020(b)	Engage in Business of Wrecking Vehicles without a License (Subsequent Offense)	C	Unranked
51.48.103(2)	Engaging in Business after Certificate of Coverage Revocation	C	Unranked
70.345.090	Engaging in Delivery Sales of Vapor Products without a License or Proper Shipping Documentation	C	Unranked
77.15.620(3)(b)	Engaging in Fish Dealing Activity Unlicensed 1	C	II
61.34.030	Equity Skimming	B	II
9.68.060	Erotic Material (Third or Subsequent Offense)	B	Unranked
9A.76.110	Escape 1	B	IV
9A.76.120	Escape 2	C	III
9A.76.130(3)(b)	Escape 3 (Third or Subsequent Offense)	C	Unranked
72.09.310	Escape from Community Custody	C	II
51.48.020(1)	Evading Industrial Insurance Premiums	C	Unranked
82.42.085	Evading the Collection of Aircraft Fuel Tax	C	Unranked
74.09.260	Excessive Charges, Payments	C	Unranked
48.06.190	Exhibiting False Accounts of Insurer	B	Unranked
9A.56.130	Extortion 2	C	III
9A.82.020	Extortionate Extension of Credit	B	V
9A.82.040	Extortionate Means to Collect Extensions of Credit	B	V
19.25.040(2)(a)	Failure to Disclose Origin of Certain Recordings (at least 100 Recordings or Subsequent Conviction)	B	Unranked
19.25.040(2)(b)	Failure to Disclose Origin of Certain Recordings (more than 10 but less than 100 Recordings)	C	Unranked
36.18.170	Failure to Pay Over Fees to County Treasurer	C	Unranked
9A.44.132(3)	Failure to Register as a Kidnapping Offender	C	Unranked
9A.44.132(1)(a)	Failure to Register as a Sex Offender (First Violation)	C	Unranked
9A.44.132(1)(a)	Failure to Register as a Sex Offender (Second Violation Committed on or after 6/10/2010)	C	II
9A.44.132(1)(b)	Failure to Register as a Sex Offender (Third or Subsequent Violation Committed on or after 6/10/2010)	B	II
19.146.050	Failure to Use a Trust Account	C	Unranked
19.142.080	Failure to Use a Trust Account or Furnish Bond for Health Studio	C	Unranked
38.42.050	False Affidavit under Service Member Civil Relief Act	C	Unranked
74.08.100	False Age and Residency Public Assistance Verification	B	Unranked

Statute (RCW)	Offense	Class	Seriousness Level
42.24.100	False Claim from Municipal Corporation (Charged as Perjury 2)	C	Unranked
42.17A.750	False Documents Registered with Public Disclosure Commission	C	Unranked
51.48.020(2)	False Information in Industrial Insurance Claim (Charged as Theft)		
48.30.230	False Insurance Claims (Value in Excess of $1,500)	C	Unranked
9.24.050	False Report of Corporation	B	Unranked
9A.84.040(2)(a)	False Reporting 1	B	VII
9A.84.040(2)(b)	False Reporting 2	C	III
74.09.230	False Statement for Medical Assistance	C	Unranked
69.43.080	False Statement in Report of Precursor Drugs	C	Unranked
9.38.015	False Statement of Identity to a Financial Institution – 3rd or Subsequent Offense	C	Unranked
51.48.270	False Statement or Concealing Information by Employee	C	Unranked
82.32.290(2)	False Statement to Department of Revenue	C	Unranked
19.230.300	False Statement, Misrepresentation or False Certification of Uniform Money Services Record	C	Unranked
41.26.062	False Statements or Records to Defraud Law Enforcement Officers and Firefighters Retirement System	B	Unranked
41.32.055(1)	False Statements or Records to Defraud Teachers Retirement System	B	Unranked
74.09.250	False Statements Regarding Institutions, Facilities	C	Unranked
46.12.750(1)	False Statements, Illegal Transfers, Alterations or Forgeries of Vehicle Title	B	Unranked
65.12.740	False Swearing - Registration of Land Title (Charged as Perjury)		
74.08.055(2)	False Verification for Welfare	B	I
26.20.030	Family Abandonment	C	Unranked
69.41.020	Forged Prescription - Legend Drug	B	DG-I
69.50.403	Forged Prescription for a Controlled Substance	C	DG-I
9A.60.020	Forgery	C	I
76.36.120	Forgery of Forest Product Mark	B	Unranked
65.12.760	Forgery of Registrar's Signature or Seal	B	Unranked
82.24.100	Forgery or Counterfeit Cigarette Tax Stamp	B	Unranked
19.100.210	Franchise Investment Protection Violation	B	Unranked
29A.84.711	Fraud in Certification of Nomination or Ballot	C	Unranked
9.45.170	Fraud in Liquor Warehouse Receipts	C	Unranked
9.45.124	Fraud in Measurement of Goods	B	Unranked
9.26A.110(3)	Fraud in Obtaining Telecommunications Services (Value Exceeds $250)	C	Unranked
67.24.010	Fraud in Sporting Contest	B	Unranked

Statute (RCW)	Offense	Class	Seriousness Level
9A.60.060	Fraudulent Creation or Revocation of Mental Health Advance Directive	C	I
76.48.141(1)(a)	Fraudulent Document as Specialized Forest Products Permit, Sales Invoice, Bill of Lading, etc.	C	Unranked
76.48.141(2)	Fraudulent Document for Specialized Forest Products Buyer	C	Unranked
9.45.270(3)	Fraudulent Filing of Vehicle Report of Sale (Value Exceeds $1,500)	B	Unranked
9.45.270(2)	Fraudulent Filing of Vehicle Report of Sale (Value Exceeds $250)	C	Unranked
9.24.020	Fraudulent Issue of Stock, Scrip, etc.	B	Unranked
48.102.160(3)	Fraudulent Life Insurance Settlement	B	Unranked
65.12.750	Fraudulent Procurement or False Entry on Land Title Registration	C	Unranked
76.48.141(1)(b)	Fraudulent Representation of Authority to Harvest Specialized Forest Products	C	Unranked
9.46.160	Gambling without License	B	Unranked
9.46.039	Greyhound Racing	B	Unranked
9A.46.020(2)(b)	Harassment	C	III
9A.76.200	Harming a Police Dog/Horse or an Accelerant Detection Dog	C	Unranked
9A.36.080	Hate Crime Offense	C	IV
28B.10.901(2)(b)	Hazing	C	III
48.80.030	Health Care False Claims	C	II
29A.84.620	Hindering or Bribing Voter	C	Unranked
46.52.020(4)(a)	Hit and Run - Death	B	IX
46.52.020(4)(b)	Hit and Run - Injury	C	IV
79A.60.200(3)	Hit and Run with Vessel - Injury Accident	C	IV
9.94.030	Holding Hostages or Interfering with Officer's Duty	B	Unranked
9.35.020(2)	Identity Theft 1	B	IV
9.35.020(3)	Identity Theft 2	C	II
69.41.040	Illegal Issuance of Legend Drug Prescription	B	Unranked
9.16.020	Imitating Lawful Brands with Intent	C	Unranked
19.146.235(9)	Impairing Mortgage Broker Investigation	B	Unranked
9.35.010	Improperly Obtaining Financial Information	C	II
9A.64.020(1)	Incest 1	B	VI
9A.64.020(2)	Incest 2	C	V
9A.88.010(2)(c)	Indecent Exposure to a Person Age 14 or Older (Subsequent Conviction or has Prior Sex Offense Conviction)	C	Unranked
9A.88.010(2)(c)	Indecent Exposure to a Person under Age 14 (Subsequent Sex Offense)	C	IV
9A.44.100(1)(b-c)	Indecent Liberties - without Forcible Compulsion	B	VII
9A.44.100(1)(d-f)	Indecent Liberties - without Forcible Compulsion	B	Unranked

Statute (RCW)	Offense	Class	Seriousness Level
9.45.126	Inducing Fraud in Measurement of Goods	B	Unranked
9A.82.070	Influencing Outcome of Sporting Event	C	IV
40.16.010	Injury to a Public Record	C	Unranked
40.16.020	Injury to and Misappropriation of Public Record by Officer	B	Unranked
88.08.050(1)	Injury to Lighthouses or United States Light	B	Unranked
9.24.030	Insolvent Bank Receiving Deposit	B	Unranked
48.06.030	Insurance Solicitation Permit Violation	B	Unranked
9.91.170(5)	Intentional Infliction, Injury or Death to a Dog Guide or Service Animal	C	Unranked
9.91.175(3)	Intentionally Injures, Disables or Causes Death of an On-Duty Search and Rescue Dog	C	Unranked
9.73.230	Intercepting, Transmitting or Recording Conversations Concerning Controlled Substances	C	Unranked
69.25.155(1)	Interference with Person Performing Official Duties	C	Unranked
69.25.155(2)	Interference with Person Performing Official Duties with a Deadly Weapon	B	Unranked
9A.72.160	Intimidating a Judge	B	VI
9A.72.130	Intimidating a Juror	B	VI
9A.76.180	Intimidating a Public Servant	B	III
9A.72.110	Intimidating a Witness	B	VI
70.74.275	Intimidation or Harassment with an Explosive	C	Unranked
9A.76.140	Introducing Contraband 1	B	VII
9A.76.150	Introducing Contraband 2	C	III
69.50.4015	Involving a Minor in Drug Dealing	C	DG-III
9A.60.070	Issuing a False Academic Credential	C	Unranked
16.52.320	Kill or Cause Substantial Harm with Malice to Livestock	C	Unranked
82.87.140	Knowingly Attempts to Evade Capital Gains Tax Payment	C	Unranked
9A.82.060(1)(b)	Leading Organized Crime - Inciting Criminal Profiteering	B	IX
46.70.021	Licensing Violation for Car Dealers or Manufacturers (Subsequent Violation)	C	Unranked
30A.12.120	Loan to Officer or Employee from Trust Fund	B	Unranked
67.70.130	Lottery Fraud	B	Unranked
9A.40.090	Luring of a Child or a Person with a Developmental Disability	C	Unranked
9A.56.370	Mail Theft	C	Unranked
9.47.090	Maintaining a Bucket Shop	C	Unranked
69.50.402(1)(f)	Maintaining a Dwelling or Place for Controlled Substances	C	DG-II
31.12.850(2)	Make a False Statement or Entry in Credit Union Books	C	Unranked
9.45.220	Making False Sample or Assay of Ore	C	Unranked

Statute (RCW)	Offense	Class	Seriousness Level
70.74.280(3)	Malicious Explosion of a Substance 3	B	X
81.60.070	Malicious Injury to Railroad Property	B	III
9A.48.070	Malicious Mischief 1	B	II
9A.48.080	Malicious Mischief 2	C	I
70.74.270(2)	Malicious Placement of an Explosive 2	B	IX
70.74.270(3)	Malicious Placement of an Explosive 3	B	VII
70.74.272(1)(a)	Malicious Placement of an Imitation Device 1	B	XII
70.74.272(1)(b)	Malicious Placement of an Imitation Device 2	C	VI
9.62.010(1)	Malicious Prosecution	C	Unranked
9.45.260	Malicious Sprinkler Contractor Work	C	Unranked
69.50.401(2)(b)	Manufacture Methamphetamine	B	DG-III
9.41.190	Manufacture of Untraceable Firearm with Intent to Sell	C	III
9.41.325	Manufacture or Assembly of an Undetectable Firearm or Untraceable Firearm	C	III
46.37.650(1)(c)	Manufacture or Import Counterfeit, Nonfunctional, Damaged, or Previously Deployed Air Bag	C	V
46.37.650(1)(b)	Manufacture or Import Counterfeit, Nonfunctional, Damaged, or Previously Deployed Air Bag (Causing Bodily Injury or Death)	C	VII
69.50.401(2)(b)	Manufacture, Deliver or Possess with Intent to Deliver - Amphetamine	B	DG-II
69.50.401(2)(c)	Manufacture, Deliver or Possess with Intent to Deliver - Cannabis	C	DG-I
69.50.401(2)(a)	Manufacture, Deliver or Possess with Intent to Deliver - Narcotics from Schedule I or II or Flunitrazepam from Schedule IV	B	DG-II
69.50.401(2)(c-e)	Manufacture, Deliver or Possess with Intent to Deliver - Narcotics from Schedule III, IV, or V or Nonnarcotics from Schedule I-V (except Cannabis, Amphetamine, Methamphetamine, or Flunitrazepam)	C	DG-II
69.52.030(1)	Manufacture, Distribute or Possess with Intent to Distribute an Imitation Controlled Substance	C	DG-II
70.74.022(1)	Manufacture, Purchase, Sell or Store Explosive Device without License	C	Unranked
46.20.0921(3)(a)	Manufacture, Sell or Deliver Forged Driver's License or Identicard	C	Unranked
82.24.570(2)	Manufacture, Sell or Possess Counterfeit Cigarettes	C	Unranked
82.24.570(3)	Manufacture, Sell or Possess Counterfeit Cigarettes (Subsequent Violation)	B	Unranked
69.51A.240	Medical Cannabis – Unlawful Actions	C	Unranked
78.44.330	Mineral Trespass	C	I
9.68A.053(2)	Minor Dealing in Depictions of Another Minor Twelve Years or Younger Engaged in Sexually Explicit Conduct 1	B	Unranked

Nonviolent Offenses

Statute (RCW)	Offense	Class	Seriousness Level
9.68A.053(3)	Minor Dealing in Depictions of Another Minor Twelve Years or Younger Engaged in Sexually Explicit Conduct 2	B	Unranked
9.68A.053(4)	Minor Financing or Selling Depictions of Another Minor Engaged in Sexually Explicit Conduct	B	Unranked
42.20.070	Misappropriating and Falsifying Accounts by Public Officer	B	Unranked
42.20.090	Misappropriating and Falsifying Accounts by Treasurer	C	Unranked
9.82.030	Misprision of Treason	C	Unranked
29A.08.740	Misuse of Registered Voter Data	C	Unranked
29A.84.150	Misuse or Alteration of Registration Database	C	Unranked
9.45.070	Mock Auction	C	Unranked
9A.83.020	Money Laundering	B	Unranked
19.144.080	Mortgage Fraud	B	III
32.04.110	Mutual Savings Bank - Conceal or Destroy Evidence	B	Unranked
32.04.100	Mutual Savings Bank - Falsify Savings Book, Document or Statement	B	Unranked
32.24.080	Mutual Savings Bank - Transfer Bank Assets after Insolvency	B	Unranked
46.37.675	Negligently Causing Death by Use of a Signal Preemption Device	B	VII
46.37.674	Negligently Causing Substantial Bodily Harm by Use of a Signal Preemption Device	B	III
9A.60.030	Obtaining Signature by Deception or Duress	C	Unranked
46.70.180(5)	Odometer Offense	C	Unranked
40.16.030	Offering False Instrument for Filing or Record	C	Unranked
68.50.140(3)	Opening Graves with Intent to Sell or Remove Personal Effects or Human Remains	C	Unranked
90.56.540	Operation of a Vessel while under the Influence of Intoxicating Liquor or Drugs	C	Unranked
9A.56.350(2)	Organized Retail Theft 1	B	III
9A.56.350(3)	Organized Retail Theft 2	C	II
69.50.406(2)	Over 18 and Deliver Narcotic from Schedule III, IV or V, or a Nonnarcotic, Except Flunitrazepam or Methamphetamine, from Schedule I-V to Someone under 18 and 3 Years Junior	B	DG-III
9.46.215	Ownership or Interest in Gambling Device	C	Unranked
69.30.085	Participation in Shellfish Operation or Activities while License is Denied, Revoked or Suspended	C	Unranked
74.09.240(2)	Paying or Offering Bribes, Kickbacks or Rebates	C	Unranked
9A.72.020	Perjury 1	B	V
9A.72.030	Perjury 2	C	III
9.94.070	Persistent Prison Misbehavior	C	V
82.32.290(4)	Phantomware Violation	C	Unranked

Statute (RCW)	Offense	Class	Seriousness Level
46.61.504(6)	Physical Control of a Vehicle while under the Influence of Intoxicating Liquor or any Drug	C	IV
69.40.030	Placing Poison or other Harmful Object or Substance in Food, Drinks, Medicine or Water	B	Unranked
69.40.020	Poison in Milk or Food Product	C	Unranked
69.50.418	Possess, Purchase, Deliver, Sell, or Possess with Intent to Sell a Tableting Machine or Encapsulating Machine	C	DG-II
9A.58.020	Possessing or Capturing Personal Identification Document	C	Unranked
7.105.460	Possession of a Firearm in Violation of an Extreme Risk Protection Order - 3rd or Subsequent Offense	C	Unranked
9A.56.310	Possession of a Stolen Firearm	B	V
9A.56.068	Possession of a Stolen Vehicle	B	II
9.94.041(2)	Possession of Controlled Substance by Prisoner (County or Local Facility)	C	Unranked
9.94.041(1)	Possession of Controlled Substance by Prisoner (State Facility)	C	Unranked
9.94.045	Possession of Controlled Substance in Prison by Non-prisoner	C	Unranked
9.68A.070(1)	Possession of Depictions of Minor Engaged in Sexually Explicit Conduct 1	B	VI
9.68A.070(2)	Possession of Depictions of Minor Engaged in Sexually Explicit Conduct 2	B	IV
69.50.440	Possession of Ephedrine, Pseudoephedrine or Anhydrous Ammonia with Intent to Manufacture Methamphetamine	B	DG-III
9.40.120	Possession of Incendiary Device	B	III
9.41.190	Possession of Machine Gun, Bump-fire Stock, Undetectable Firearm, or Short-Barreled Shotgun or Rifle	C	III
69.41.350	Possession of Steroids in Excess of 200 tablets or (8) 2cc Bottles without a Valid Prescription	C	Unranked
9A.56.380	Possession of Stolen Mail	C	Unranked
9A.56.150	Possession of Stolen Property 1 (other than Firearm or Motor Vehicle)	B	II
9A.56.160	Possession of Stolen Property 2 (other than Firearm or Motor Vehicle)	C	I
9.94.040(2)	Possession of Weapons by Prisoners (County or Local Facility)	C	Unranked
9.94.040(1)	Possession of Weapons by Prisoners (State Facility)	B	Unranked
9.94.043	Possession of Weapons in Prison by Non-prisoner	B	Unranked
9.94.010	Prison Riot	B	Unranked
9.46.220	Professional Gambling 1	B	Unranked
9.46.221	Professional Gambling 2	C	Unranked
9A.36.060	Promoting a Suicide Attempt	C	Unranked
67.08.015	Promoting Illegal Boxing, Martial Arts and Wrestling	C	Unranked

Statute (RCW)	Offense	Class	Seriousness Level
9.68.140	Promoting Pornography	C	Unranked
9A.88.070	Promoting Prostitution 1	B	VIII
9A.88.080	Promoting Prostitution 2	C	III
9.68A.102	Promoting Travel for Commercial Sexual Abuse of a Minor	C	Unranked
9A.88.085	Promoting Travel for Prostitution	C	Unranked
29A.84.311	Provides False Information or Conceals or Destroys Candidacy Declaration or Nominating Petition	C	Unranked
26.04.210	Providing False Statements in Affidavits for Marriage	C	Unranked
68.50.140(2)	Purchasing or Receiving Human Remains	C	Unranked
9A.44.060	Rape 3	C	V
9A.44.079	Rape of a Child 3	C	VI
74.09.240(1)	Receiving or Asking for Bribes, Kickbacks or Rebates	C	Unranked
9A.68.030	Receiving or Granting Unlawful Compensation	C	Unranked
81.60.080(2)	Receiving Stolen Railroad Property	C	Unranked
9A.48.040	Reckless Burning 1	C	I
90.56.530	Reckless Operation of a Tank Vessel	C	Unranked
19.110.075(2)	Registration Knowingly not Obtained Prior to Sale of Business Opportunity (Violation of RCW 19.110.050)	B	Unranked
70A.15.3150(3)	Releasing into Ambient Air Hazardous Air Pollutant	C	Unranked
46.12.560	Removal of Sticker on Vehicle Stating Previously Destroyed or Title 1 Loss	C	Unranked
68.50.140(4)	Removal, Disinterment or Mutilation of Human Remains	C	Unranked
68.60.050	Removes, Defaces or Destroys any Historic Grave	C	Unranked
29A.84.540	Removing a Ballot from a Voting Center or Ballot Drop Location	C	Unranked
68.50.140(1)	Removing Human Remains	C	Unranked
9.16.010	Removing Lawful Brands	C	Unranked
9A.76.070(2)(a)	Rendering Criminal Assistance 1	B	V
19.25.020(2)(a)	Reproduction of Sound Recording without Consent of Owner - Recording Fixed before 2/15/1972 (at least 1,000 Recordings or Subsequent Conviction)	B	Unranked
19.25.020(2)(b)	Reproduction of Sound Recording without Consent of Owner - Recording Fixed before 2/15/1972 (more than 100 but less than 1,000 Recordings)	C	Unranked
9A.68.020	Requesting Unlawful Compensation	C	Unranked
9A.52.025	Residential Burglary	B	IV
70.345.030	Retail Sales, Distribution or Delivery Sales of Vapor Products without a License	C	Unranked
9A.56.360(2)	Retail Theft with Special Circumstances 1	B	III
9A.56.360(3)	Retail Theft with Special Circumstances 2	C	II
9A.56.360(4)	Retail Theft with Special Circumstances 3	C	Unranked

Statute (RCW)	Offense	Class	Seriousness Level
81.60.080(1)	Sabotaging Rolling Stock	C	Unranked
69.41.030(2)(a)	Sale, Delivery or Possession with Intent to Sell Legend Drug without Prescription	B	Unranked
33.36.040	Savings and Loan Association - Making False Statement of Assets or Liabilities	C	Unranked
33.36.030	Savings and Loan Association - Preference in Case of Insolvency	C	Unranked
33.36.060	Savings and Loan Association - Suppressing, Secreting or Destroying Evidence or Records	C	Unranked
19.290.100	Scrap Processing, Recycling, or Supplying without a License (Second or Subsequent Offense)	C	II
19.60.067(2)	Second-hand Precious Metal Dealer Violations (Subsequent Violation)	C	Unranked
21.20.400	Securities Act Violation	B	III
46.20.0921(2)	Sell or Deliver a Stolen Driver's License or Identicard	C	Unranked
46.37.650(2)(b)	Sell, Install, or Reinstall Counterfeit, Nonfunctional, Damaged, or Previously Deployed Airbag	C	VII
46.37.650(2)(c)	Sell, Install, or Reinstall Counterfeit, Nonfunctional, Damaged, or Previously Deployed Airbag	C	V
27.44.040(2)	Selling Artifacts or Human Remains from Indian Graves	C	Unranked
69.50.410	Selling for Profit (Controlled or Counterfeit) any Controlled Substance in Schedule I	C	DG-III
48.160.080	Sells Guaranteed Asset Protection Waivers without Registration	B	Unranked
9.68A.060(1)	Sending, Bringing into the State Depictions of Minor Engaged in Sexually Explicit Conduct 1	B	VII
9.68A.060(2)	Sending, Bringing into the State Depictions of Minor Engaged in Sexually Explicit Conduct 2	B	V
9.68A.040	Sexual Exploitation of a Minor	B	IX
9A.44.093	Sexual Misconduct with a Minor 1	C	V
9A.44.105	Sexually Violating Human Remains	C	V
70.155.140	Shipping or Transporting Tobacco Products Ordered Through Mail or Internet	C	Unranked
82.38.270	Special Fuel Violations	C	Unranked
77.15.450(3)(b)	Spotlighting Big Game 1	C	I
9A.46.110	Stalking	B	V
67.70.160	State Lottery Violations Except Lottery Fraud and Unlicensed Lottery Activity	C	Unranked
30B.12.050	State Trust Company – False Entry, Conceal or Destroy Records	B	Unranked
30B.44B.110(2)	State Trust Company – Transfer of Assets	B	Unranked
9.45.020	Substitution of Child	B	Unranked
77.15.670(3)(b)	Suspension of Department Privileges 1	C	I
9A.56.070	Taking Motor Vehicle without Permission 1	B	V
9A.56.075	Taking Motor Vehicle without Permission 2	C	I

Statute (RCW)	Offense	Class	Seriousness Level
9A.72.120	Tampering with a Witness	C	III
29A.84.550	Tampering with Election Materials	C	Unranked
9.40.105	Tampering with Fire Alarm, Emergency Signal, or Fire-fighting Equipment with Intent to Commit Arson	B	Unranked
88.08.020	Tampering with Lights or Signals	B	Unranked
29A.84.560	Tampering with Voting Machine	C	Unranked
9.61.230(2)	Telephone Harassment (with Prior Harassment Conviction or Threat of Death)	C	III
9A.56.030	Theft 1 (Excluding Firearm and Motor Vehicle)	B	II
9A.56.040	Theft 2 (Excluding Firearm and Motor Vehicle)	C	I
9A.56.400(1)	Theft from a Vulnerable Adult 1	B	VI
9A.56.400(2)	Theft from a Vulnerable Adult 2	C	I
9A.56.300	Theft of a Firearm	B	VI
9A.56.065	Theft of a Motor Vehicle	B	II
69.55.010	Theft of Ammonia	C	VIII
9A.56.080	Theft of Livestock 1	B	IV
9A.56.083	Theft of Livestock 2	C	III
9A.56.096(5)(a)	Theft of Rental, Leased, Lease-purchased or Loaned Property (Valued at $5,000 or more)	B	II
9A.56.096(5)(b)	Theft of Rental, Leased, Lease-purchased or Loaned Property (Valued at $750 or more but less than $5,000)	C	I
9A.56.262	Theft of Telecommunication Service	C	Unranked
9A.56.340(2)	Theft with Intent to Resell 1	B	III
9A.56.340(3)	Theft with Intent to Resell 2	C	II
9A.36.090	Threats Against Governor or Family	C	Unranked
9.61.160	Threats to Bomb	B	IV
64.36.210	Timeshare Fraud	C	Unranked
64.36.020(5)(b)	Timeshare Registration Requirement Violation	C	Unranked
9A.68.040	Trading in Public Office	C	Unranked
9A.68.050	Trading in Special Influence	C	Unranked
48.30A.015	Trafficking in Insurance Claims (Subsequent Violation)	C	II
9A.82.050	Trafficking in Stolen Property 1	B	IV
9A.82.055	Trafficking in Stolen Property 2	C	III
48.17.063	Transaction of Insurance Business Beyond the Scope of Licensure (Violation of RCW 48.17.060)	B	I
9.08.076	Transferring a Stolen Pet Animal to a Research Institution by a USDA Licensed Dealer	C	Unranked
9.08.074	Transferring a Stolen Pet Animal to a Person who Previously Sold a Stolen Pet Animal to a Research Facility	C	Unranked
9.08.072	Transferring a Stolen Pet Animal to a Research Institution, not by a USDA Licensed Dealer – 2nd or Subsequent Offense	C	Unranked

Statute (RCW)	Offense	Class	Seriousness Level
9.46.240	Transmission or Receiving Gambling Information by Internet	C	Unranked
70A.300.100(1)(a)	Transport, Disposal or Export of Hazardous Waste that Places Another Person in Danger of Injury or Death	B	Unranked
70A.300.100(1)(b)	Transport, Disposal or Export of Hazardous Waste that Places Another Person's Property in Danger of Harm	C	Unranked
82.24.110(2)	Transportation of more than 10,000 Cigarettes without Proper Stamps	C	Unranked
68.60.040(3)	Transports Removed Human Remains, Opens a Grave or Removes Personal Effects from Grave	C	Unranked
9.91.150(1)	Tree Spiking	C	Unranked
9.02.120	Unauthorized Abortion	C	Unranked
68.44.060	Unauthorized Loans to Cemetery Authority	C	Unranked
29A.84.545	Unauthorized Removal of Paper Record from Electronic Voting Device	C	Unranked
9.26A.140(1)(a-c)	Unauthorized Sale or Procurement of Telephone Records	C	Unranked
39.62.040	Unauthorized Use of Public Official Facsimile Signature or Seal	B	Unranked
68.05.330	Unfair Practice of Funeral or Cemetery Board	C	Unranked
19.225.110	Uniform Athlete Agent Act Violation	C	Unranked
69.43.070(1)	Unlawful Delivery of Precursor Drug with Intent to Use	B	Unranked
9A.49.020	Unlawful Discharge of a Laser 1	C	Unranked
74.09.290	Unlawful Disclosure of Patient Records or DSHS Information	C	Unranked
9A.56.290(4)(a)	Unlawful Factoring of a Credit or Payment Card Transaction	C	II
9A.56.290(4)(b)	Unlawful Factoring of a Credit or Payment Card Transaction (Subsequent Violation)	B	IV
77.15.630(3)(b)	Unlawful Fish and Shellfish Catch Accounting 1	C	I
69.53.020	Unlawful Fortification of Building for Drug Purposes	C	Unranked
77.15.410(3)(b)	Unlawful Hunting of Big Game 1	C	III
9A.40.040	Unlawful Imprisonment	C	III
9A.56.060(4)	Unlawful Issuance of Checks or Drafts (Value Greater Than $750)	C	I
9A.56.264	Unlawful Manufacture of a Telecommunication Device	C	Unranked
77.140.060(3)	Unlawful Misbranding of Fish or Shellfish 1	C	III
51.48.280(2)	Unlawful Offer or Payment for Kickbacks, Bribes, or Rebates to any Person	C	Unranked
88.46.080(2)(b)	Unlawful Operation of a Covered Vessel (Subsequent Violation)	C	Unranked
90.56.300(2)(b)	Unlawful Operation of Onshore or Offshore Facility (Subsequent Conviction)	C	Unranked
77.15.570(2)	Unlawful Participation on Non-Indians in Indian Fishery	C	II
9.41.040(1)	Unlawful Possession of a Firearm 1	B	VII

Nonviolent Offenses

Statute (RCW)	Offense	Class	Seriousness Level
9.41.040(2)	Unlawful Possession of a Firearm 2	C	III
9A.56.320(3)	Unlawful Possession of a Personal Identification Device	C	I
9A.56.320(4)	Unlawful Possession of Fictitious Identification	C	I
9A.56.320(5)	Unlawful Possession of Instruments of Financial Fraud	C	I
9A.56.320(2)	Unlawful Possession of Payment Instruments	C	I
2.48.180	Unlawful Practice of Law (Subsequent Violation)	C	II
9.41.115	Unlawful Private Transfer of a Firearm (Subsequent Offense)	C	Unranked
9A.56.320(1)	Unlawful Production of Payment Instruments	C	I
77.15.650(3)(b)	Unlawful Purchase or Use of a License 1	C	II
69.43.070(2)	Unlawful Receipt of Precursor Drug with Intent to Use	B	Unranked
51.48.280(1)	Unlawful Receipt of Remuneration for Kickbacks, Bribes, or Rebates by any Person	C	Unranked
9.91.144	Unlawful Redemption of Food Stamps	C	I
77.15.250(2)(b)	Unlawful Releasing, Planting, Possessing or Placing Deleterious Exotic Wildlife	C	I
9A.56.266	Unlawful Sale of a Telecommunication Device	C	Unranked
9A.56.230	Unlawful Sale of Subscription Television Services	C	Unranked
46.12.750(3)	Unlawful Sale of Vehicle Certificate of Ownership	C	Unranked
18.64.046(7)	Unlawful Selling of Ephedrine, Pseudoephedrine or Phenylpropanolamine by a Wholesaler	C	Unranked
65.12.730	Unlawful Stealing or Carrying Away Certification of Land Registration (Charged as Theft)		
69.55.020	Unlawful Storage of Ammonia	C	VI
19.116.080(1)	Unlawful Subleasing of Motor Vehicle	C	Unranked
77.15.120(3)(b)	Unlawful Taking of Endangered Fish or Wildlife 1	C	III
77.15.770(2)	Unlawful Trade in Shark Fins 1	C	Unranked
77.15.260(3)(b)	Unlawful Trafficking in Fish, Shellfish or Wildlife 1	B	III
77.15.260(3)(a)	Unlawful Trafficking in Fish, Shellfish or Wildlife 2	C	II
9.91.142(1)	Unlawful Trafficking in Food Stamps	C	I
77.15.135(4)(d)	Unlawful Trafficking in Species with Extinction 1	C	Unranked
48.44.016(3)	Unlawful Transaction of Health Coverage as Health Care Service Contractor	B	IV
48.46.033(3)	Unlawful Transaction of Health Coverage as Health Maintenance Organization	B	IV
48.15.023(3)	Unlawful Transaction of Insurance Business	B	IV
19.116.080(2)	Unlawful Transfer of Ownership of Motor Vehicle	C	Unranked
77.15.530(4)	Unlawful Use of a Nondesignated Vessel	C	III
18.04.370(1)(b)	Unlawful Use of a Professional Title	C	Unranked
69.53.010	Unlawful Use of Building for Drug Purposes	C	DG-I
18.04.370(1)(c)	Unlawful Use of CPA Title after Suspension	C	Unranked
69.53.030	Unlawful Use of Fortified Building	C	Unranked

Statute (RCW)	Offense	Class	Seriousness Level
77.15.811	Unlawful Use of Invasive Species 1	C	Unranked
66.44.120(2)(b)	Unlawful Use of Liquor Board Seal (Third or Subsequent Offense)	C	Unranked
77.15.580(3)(b)	Unlawful Use of Net to Take Fish	C	I
9.46.037	Unlawful Wagers of a Sporting Event, Athletic Event, or Competition	C	Unranked
19.310.120	Unlawfully Engaging in Business as an Exchange Facilitator (RCW 19.310.100(1)-(9))	B	Unranked
82.24.500	Unlawfully Purchase, Sell, Consign or Distribute Cigarettes	C	Unranked
48.102.160(4)	Unlicensed Life Insurance Provider	B	Unranked
67.70.140	Unlicensed Lottery Activity	B	Unranked
48.17.063(2)	Unlicensed Practice as an Insurance Professional	B	IV
18.130.190(7)(b)	Unlicensed Practice of a Profession or Business (Subsequent Violation)	C	II
48.102.160(5)	Unlicensed Settlement Broker	B	Unranked
29A.84.660	Unqualified Person Voting	C	Unranked
29A.84.140	Unqualified Voting Registration	C	Unranked
9.41.360	Unsafe Storage of a Firearm	C	Unranked
19.210.040	Unused Property, Merchants –Prohibited Sales (Third or Subsequent Offense within 5 Years)	C	Unranked
46.37.673	Use of a Signal Preemption Device Resulting in Property Damage or less Substantial Bodily Harm	C	Unranked
9.26A.115	Use of Fraudulent Telecommunication Services	B	Unranked
9A.82.080(1),(2)	Use of Proceeds of Criminal Profiteering	B	IV
	Use of Proceeds of Criminal Profiteering – Attempt or Conspiracy	C	Unranked
19.25.030(2)(a)	Use of Recording of Live Performance without Consent of Owner (at least 1,000 Recordings or at least 100 Unauthorized Audiovisual Recordings or Subsequent Offense)	B	Unranked
19.25.030(2)(b)	Use of Recording of Live Performance without Consent of Owner (at least 100 but less than 1,000 Recordings or more than 10 but less than 100 Unauthorized Audiovisual Recording or Subsequent Offense)	C	Unranked
19.144.100(1)	Use or Investment of Proceeds from Mortgage Fraud Activities	B	Unranked
9A.52.095	Vehicle Prowl 1	C	I
9A.52.100(3)	Vehicle Prowling 2 (Third or Subsequent Offense)	C	IV
46.61.522(1)(c)	Vehicular Assault - Disregard for the Safety of Others	B	III
46.61.520(1)(c)	Vehicular Homicide - Disregard for the Safety of Others	A*	VII
9.68A.075(1)	Viewing Depictions of Minor Engaged in Sexually Explicit Conduct 1 (Effective 6/10/2010)	B	IV
9.68A.075(2)	Viewing Depictions of Minor Engaged in Sexually Explicit Conduct 2 (Effective 6/10/2010)	C	Unranked
77.15.550(3)(b)	Violating Commercial Fishing Area or Time 1	C	I

Statute (RCW)	Offense	Class	Seriousness Level
29A.84.230(1)	Violation by Signer – Initiative or Referendum with False Name	C	Unranked
29A.84.240(1)	Violations by Signers – Recall Petition with False Name	B	Unranked
9.46.190	Violations of Fraud or Deceit Regarding Gambling Activity	C	Unranked
29A.84.130	Voter Violation of Registration Law	C	Unranked
29A.84.650(1)	Voting Repeater – more than one Vote at any Election	C	Unranked
9A.44.115	Voyeurism 1	C	II
48.30.220	Willful Destruction, Injury, Secretion of Insured Property	C	Unranked
10.66.090	Willfully Disobeys an Off-limits Order (Subsequent Violation or Enters Protected Against Drug Trafficking Area)	C	Unranked

Vehicular Homicide – Disregard for the Safety of Others is defined as a Class A felony offense and appears to be a violent offense under RCW 9.94A.030. However, under State v. Stately, 152 Wn. App. 604, 216 P.3d 1102 (2009), it is not to be considered a violent offense.

UNRANKED OFFENSES

Statute (RCW)	Offense	Class	Seriousness Level
29A.84.680(1)	Absentee Voting Violation	C	Unranked
46.52.130(6)(b)	Abstracts of Driving Records – Intentional Misuse	C	Unranked
20.01.460(2)	Acting as Commission Merchant, Dealer, Cash Buyer without License	C	Unranked
69.52.030(3)	Advertising Imitation Controlled Substances	C	Unranked
30A.42.290(3)	Alien Bank or Bureau – Destroy or Secrete Records	B	Unranked
30A.42.290(2)	Alien Bank or Bureau – False Entry, Statements, etc.	B	Unranked
9.41.171	Alien Possession of a Firearm	C	Unranked
9.45.210	Altering Sample or Certificate of Assay	C	Unranked
9A.76.177	Amber Alert – Making False Statements to a Public Servant	C	Unranked
68.64.160	Anatomical Gift - Illegal Financial Gain	C	Unranked
68.64.150	Anatomical Gifts - Illegal Purchase or Sale	C	Unranked
16.52.205(2)	Animal Cruelty 1	C	Unranked
16.52.117(2)(a)	Animal Fighting	C	Unranked
16.52.117(2)(b)	Animal Fighting - Mutilation	B	Unranked
9.05.030	Assembly of Saboteurs	B	Unranked
72.23.170	Assist Escape of Mental Patient	C	Unranked
30A.12.100	Bank or Trust Company - Destroy or Secrete Records	B	Unranked
30A.12.090	Bank or Trust Company - False Entry, Statements, etc.	B	Unranked
30A.44.120	Bank or Trust Company - Receiving Deposits When Insolvent	B	Unranked
30A.44.110	Bank or Trust Company - Transfer of Assets Prior to Insolvency	B	Unranked
9A.64.010	Bigamy	C	Unranked
9.46.155	Bribing to Obtain a License from Public Officials, Employees, Agents	C	Unranked
72.23.300	Bringing Narcotics, Liquor, or Weapons into State Institution or Grounds	B	Unranked
9.47.120	Bunco Steering	B	Unranked
46.87.260	Cab Card Forgery (Effective Until 7/1/2016)	B	Unranked
9.46.180	Causing Person to Violate Gambling Laws	B	Unranked
9A.64.030(3)(b)	Child Buying	C	Unranked
49.12.410(2)	Child Labor Law Violation – Death/Disability	C	Unranked
9A.64.030(3)(a)	Child Selling	C	Unranked
70.245.200(2)	Coerce Patient to Request Life-ending Medication	A	Unranked
9A.40.110	Coercion of Involuntary Servitude	C	Unranked
9A.82.045	Collection of Unlawful Debt	C	Unranked

Statute (RCW)	Offense	Class	Seriousness Level
19.158.160	Commercial Telephone Solicitor Deception (Value of $250 or more)	C	Unranked
30A.04.240	Commingling of Funds or Securities	B	Unranked
21.30.140	Commodity Transaction Violation	B	Unranked
69.50.465	Conducting or Maintaining a Cannabis Club	C	Unranked
19.144.100(2)	Control of Real Property Resulting from Mortgage Fraud Activities	B	Unranked
69.50.416	Controlled Substance Label Violation	C	Unranked
46.87.260	Credential Forgery (Effective 7/1/2016)	B	Unranked
31.12.724(3)	Credit Union - Fraudulent Receipt of Credit Union Deposit	B	Unranked
31.12.724(2)	Credit Union - Transfer of Credit Union Assets Prior to Insolvency	B	Unranked
9.08.090	Crimes Against Animal Facilities	C	Unranked
9A.60.040	Criminal Impersonation 1	C	Unranked
9A.84.010(2)(b)	Criminal Mischief	C	Unranked
9A.82.160	Criminal Profiteering Lien after Service of Notice	C	Unranked
9.05.060(2)	Criminal Sabotage	B	Unranked
9A.44.196	Criminal Trespass Against Children	C	Unranked
9A.40.060	Custodial Interference 1	C	Unranked
9A.40.070	Custodial Interference 2 (Subsequent Offense)	C	Unranked
43.06.230	Damage Property or Cause Personal Injury after State of Emergency Proclaimed	B	Unranked
16.08.100(2)	Dangerous Dog Attack (Subsequent Offense)	C	Unranked
16.08.100(3)	Dangerous Dog Attack Resulting in Severe Injury or Death	C	Unranked
22.09.310	Dealing in Unauthorized Warehouse Receipts for Agricultural Commodities	C	Unranked
39.44.101	Defraud a Facsimile Signature on Bonds and Coupons	B	Unranked
87.03.200	Defraud Facsimile Signatures on Bonds and Coupons – Irrigation Districts	B	Unranked
19.110.120	Defraud or Provide Misleading or Untrue Documents Related to a Business Opportunity Sale	B	Unranked
9A.61.030	Defrauding a Public Utility 1	B	Unranked
9A.61.040	Defrauding a Public Utility 2	C	Unranked
19.48.110(1)(b)	Defrauding an Innkeeper (Value of $75 or more)	B	Unranked
9.41.110(8)	Delivery of Firearm by Dealer to Ineligible Person	C	Unranked
9.41.080	Delivery of Firearms to Ineligible Person	C	Unranked
35A.36.040	Designation of Bonds – Violation (Code Cities)	B	Unranked
35.36.040	Designation of Bonds – Violation (First Class Cities)	B	Unranked
27.44.040(1)	Destroying, Removing or Defacing Indian Graves	C	Unranked
68.60.040(1)	Destruction of Tomb, Plot, Marker, or Cemetery Property	C	Unranked

Statute (RCW)	Offense	Class	Seriousness Level
9.38.060	Digital Signatures Fraud	C	Unranked
9A.76.023(2)(a)	Disarming a Law Enforcement or Corrections Officer	C	Unranked
9A.76.023(2)(b)	Disarming a Law Enforcement or Corrections Officer and Firearm is Discharged	B	Unranked
9A.86.010	Disclosing Intimate Images	C	Unranked
19.110.075(2)	Disclosures Knowingly Not Provided at Sale of Business Opportunity (Violation of RCW 19.110.070)	B	Unranked
69.50.402	Dispensing Violation (VUCSA)	C	Unranked
82.26.190	Distributors and Retailer of Tobacco Products License Violation	C	Unranked
27.53.060	Disturbing Archaeological Resources or Site	C	Unranked
43.43.856	Divulging Confidential Investigative Information Pertaining to Organized Crime	B	Unranked
29A.84.270	Duplication of Name – Conspiracy to Mislead	B	Unranked
29A.84.320	Duplication of Names on Declaration of Candidacy	B	Unranked
29A.84.655	Election Officer Permits Repeat Vote	C	Unranked
29A.84.720	Election Officers – Violation	C	Unranked
29A.84.030	Election or Mail Ballot Violation	C	Unranked
19.300.020	Electronic Communication Devices – Illegal Scanning	C	Unranked
79A.60.090	Eluding a Law Enforcement Vessel	C	Unranked
18.39.350	Embalmers/Funeral Directors Violation	C	Unranked
43.08.140	Embezzlement by State Treasurer	B	Unranked
46.80.020(b)	Engage in Business of Wrecking Vehicles without a License (Subsequent Offense)	C	Unranked
51.48.103(2)	Engaging in Business after Certificate of Coverage Revocation	C	Unranked
70.345.090	Engaging in Delivery Sales of Vapor Products without a License or Proper Shipping Documentation	C	Unranked
9.68.060	Erotic Material (Third or Subsequent Offense)	B	Unranked
9A.76.130(3)(b)	Escape 3 (Third or Subsequent Offense)	C	Unranked
51.48.020(1)	Evading Industrial Insurance Premiums	C	Unranked
82.42.085	Evading the Collection of Aircraft Fuel Tax	C	Unranked
74.09.260	Excessive Charges, Payments	C	Unranked
48.06.190	Exhibiting False Accounts of Insurer	B	Unranked
19.25.040(2)(a)	Failure to Disclose Origin of Certain Recordings (at least 100 Recordings or Subsequent Conviction)	B	Unranked
19.25.040(2)(b)	Failure to Disclose Origin of Certain Recordings (more than 10 but less than 100 Recordings)	C	Unranked
36.18.170	Failure to Pay Over Fees to County Treasurer	C	Unranked
9A.44.132(3)	Failure to Register as a Kidnapping Offender	C	Unranked
9A.44.132(1)(a)	Failure to Register as a Sex Offender (First Violation)	C	Unranked
19.146.050	Failure to Use a Trust Account	C	Unranked

Statute (RCW)	Offense	Class	Seriousness Level
19.142.080	Failure to Use a Trust Account or Furnish Bond for Health Studio	C	Unranked
38.42.050	False Affidavit under Service Member Civil Relief Act	C	Unranked
74.08.100	False Age and Residency Public Assistance Verification	B	Unranked
42.24.100	False Claim from Municipal Corporation (Charged as Perjury 2)	C	Unranked
42.17A.750	False Documents Registered with Public Disclosure Commission	C	Unranked
48.30.230	False Insurance Claims (Value in Excess of $1,500)	C	Unranked
9.24.050	False Report of Corporation	B	Unranked
74.09.230	False Statement for Medical Assistance	C	Unranked
69.43.080	False Statement in Report of Precursor Drugs	C	Unranked
9.38.015	False Statement of Identity to a Financial Institution - 3rd or Subsequent Offense	C	Unranked
51.48.270	False Statement or Concealing Information by Employee	C	Unranked
82.32.290(2)	False Statement to Department of Revenue	C	Unranked
19.230.300	False Statement, Misrepresentation or False Certification of Uniform Money Services Record	C	Unranked
41.26.062	False Statements or Records to Defraud Law Enforcement Officers and Firefighters Retirement System	B	Unranked
41.32.055(1)	False Statements or Records to Defraud Teachers Retirement System	B	Unranked
74.09.250	False Statements Regarding Institutions, Facilities	C	Unranked
46.12.750(1)	False Statements, Illegal Transfers, Alterations or Forgeries of Vehicle Title	B	Unranked
26.20.030	Family Abandonment	C	Unranked
76.36.120	Forgery of Forest Product Mark	B	Unranked
65.12.760	Forgery of Registrar's Signature or Seal	B	Unranked
82.24.100	Forgery or Counterfeit Cigarette Tax Stamp	B	Unranked
70.245.200(1)	Forging Request for Medication	A	Unranked
19.100.210	Franchise Investment Protection Violation	B	Unranked
29A.84.711	Fraud in Certification of Nomination or Ballot	C	Unranked
9.45.170	Fraud in Liquor Warehouse Receipts	C	Unranked
9.45.124	Fraud in Measurement of Goods	B	Unranked
9.26A.110(3)	Fraud in Obtaining Telecommunications Services (Value Exceeds $250)	C	Unranked
67.24.010	Fraud in Sporting Contest	B	Unranked
76.48.141(1)(a)	Fraudulent Document as Specialized Forest Products Permit, Sales Invoice, Bill of Lading, etc.	C	Unranked
76.48.141(2)	Fraudulent Document for Specialized Forest Products Buyer	C	Unranked
9.45.270(3)	Fraudulent Filing of Vehicle Report of Sale (Value Exceeds $1,500)	B	Unranked

Statute (RCW)	Offense	Class	Seriousness Level
9.45.270(2)	Fraudulent Filing of Vehicle Report of Sale (Value Exceeds $250)	C	Unranked
9.24.020	Fraudulent Issue of Stock, Scrip, etc.	B	Unranked
48.102.160(3)	Fraudulent Life Insurance Settlement	B	Unranked
65.12.750	Fraudulent Procurement or False Entry on Land Title Registration	C	Unranked
76.48.141(1)(b)	Fraudulent Representation of Authority to Harvest Specialized Forest Products	C	Unranked
9.46.160	Gambling without License	B	Unranked
9.46.039	Greyhound Racing	B	Unranked
9A.76.200	Harming a Police Dog/Horse or an Accelerant Detection Dog	C	Unranked
29A.84.620	Hindering or Bribing Voter	C	Unranked
9.94.030	Holding Hostages or Interfering with Officer's Duty	B	Unranked
69.41.040	Illegal Issuance of Legend Drug Prescription	B	Unranked
9.16.020	Imitating Lawful Brands with Intent	C	Unranked
19.146.235(9)	Impairing Mortgage Broker Investigation	B	Unranked
9A.88.010(2)(c)	Indecent Exposure to a Person Age 14 or Older (Subsequent Conviction or has Prior Sex Offense Conviction)	C	Unranked
9A.44.100(1)(d-f)	Indecent Liberties - without Forcible Compulsion	B	Unranked
9.45.126	Inducing Fraud in Measurement of Goods	B	Unranked
40.16.010	Injury to a Public Record	C	Unranked
40.16.020	Injury to and Misappropriation of Public Record by Officer	B	Unranked
88.08.050(1)	Injury to Lighthouses or United States Light	B	Unranked
9.24.030	Insolvent Bank Receiving Deposit	B	Unranked
48.06.030	Insurance Solicitation Permit Violation	B	Unranked
9.91.170(5)	Intentional Infliction, Injury or Death to a Dog Guide or Service Animal	C	Unranked
9.91.175(3)	Intentionally Injures, Disables or Causes Death of an On-Duty Search and Rescue Dog	C	Unranked
9.73.230	Intercepting, Transmitting or Recording Conversations Concerning Controlled Substances	C	Unranked
69.25.155(1)	Interference with Person Performing Official Duties	C	Unranked
69.25.155(2)	Interference with Person Performing Official Duties with a Deadly Weapon	B	Unranked
70.74.275	Intimidation or Harassment with an Explosive	C	Unranked
9A.60.070	Issuing a False Academic Credential	C	Unranked
16.52.320	Kill or Cause Substantial Harm with Malice to Livestock	C	Unranked
82.87.140	Knowingly Attempts to Evade Capital Gains Tax Payment	C	Unranked
46.70.021	Licensing Violation for Car Dealers or Manufacturers (Subsequent Violation)	C	Unranked

Statute (RCW)	Offense	Class	Seriousness Level
30A.12.120	Loan to Officer or Employee from Trust Fund	B	Unranked
67.70.130	Lottery Fraud	B	Unranked
9A.40.090	Luring of a Child or a Person with a Developmental Disability	C	Unranked
9A.56.370	Mail Theft	C	Unranked
9.47.090	Maintaining a Bucket Shop	C	Unranked
31.12.850(2)	Make a False Statement or Entry in Credit Union Books	C	Unranked
9.45.220	Making False Sample or Assay of Ore	C	Unranked
9.62.010(1)	Malicious Prosecution	C	Unranked
9.45.260	Malicious Sprinkler Contractor Work	C	Unranked
70.74.022(1)	Manufacture, Purchase, Sell or Store Explosive Device without License	C	Unranked
46.20.0921(3)(a)	Manufacture, Sell or Deliver Forged Driver's License or Identicard	C	Unranked
82.24.570(2)	Manufacture, Sell or Possess Counterfeit Cigarettes	C	Unranked
82.24.570(3)	Manufacture, Sell or Possess Counterfeit Cigarettes (Subsequent Violation)	B	Unranked
69.51A.240	Medical Cannabis – Unlawful Actions	C	Unranked
9.68A.053(2)	Minor Dealing in Depictions of Another Minor Twelve Years or Younger Engaged in Sexually Explicit Conduct 1	B	Unranked
9.68A.053(3)	Minor Dealing in Depictions of Another Minor Twelve Years or Younger Engaged in Sexually Explicit Conduct 2	B	Unranked
9.68A.053(4)	Minor Financing or Selling Depictions of Another Minor Engaged in Sexually Explicit Conduct	B	Unranked
42.20.070	Misappropriating and Falsifying Accounts by Public Officer	B	Unranked
42.20.090	Misappropriating and Falsifying Accounts by Treasurer	C	Unranked
9.82.030	Misprision of Treason	C	Unranked
29A.08.740	Misuse of Registered Voter Data	C	Unranked
29A.84.150	Misuse or Alteration of Registration Database	C	Unranked
9.45.070	Mock Auction	C	Unranked
9A.83.020	Money Laundering	B	Unranked
32.04.110	Mutual Savings Bank - Conceal or Destroy Evidence	B	Unranked
32.04.100	Mutual Savings Bank - Falsify Savings Book, Document or Statement	B	Unranked
32.24.080	Mutual Savings Bank - Transfer Bank Assets after Insolvency	B	Unranked
9A.60.030	Obtaining Signature by Deception or Duress	C	Unranked
46.70.180(5)	Odometer Offense	C	Unranked
40.16.030	Offering False Instrument for Filing or Record	C	Unranked
68.50.140(3)	Opening Graves with Intent to Sell or Remove Personal Effects or Human Remains	C	Unranked

Statute (RCW)	Offense	Class	Seriousness Level
90.56.540	Operation of a Vessel while under the Influence of Intoxicating Liquor or Drugs	C	Unranked
9.46.215	Ownership or Interest in Gambling Device	C	Unranked
69.30.085	Participation in Shellfish Operation or Activities while License is Denied, Revoked or Suspended	C	Unranked
74.09.240(2)	Paying or Offering Bribes, Kickbacks or Rebates	C	Unranked
82.32.290(4)	Phantomware Violation	C	Unranked
69.40.030	Placing Poison or other Harmful Object or Substance in Food, Drinks, Medicine or Water	B	Unranked
69.40.020	Poison in Milk or Food Product	C	Unranked
9A.58.020	Possessing or Capturing Personal Identification Document	C	Unranked
7.105.460	Possession of a Firearm in Violation of an Extreme Risk Protection Order - 3rd or Subsequent Offense	C	Unranked
9.94.041(2)	Possession of Controlled Substance by Prisoner (County or Local Facility)	C	Unranked
9.94.041(1)	Possession of Controlled Substance by Prisoner (State Facility)	C	Unranked
9.94.045	Possession of Controlled Substance in Prison by Non-prisoner	C	Unranked
69.41.350	Possession of Steroids in Excess of 200 tablets or (8) 2cc Bottles without a Valid Prescription	C	Unranked
9A.56.380	Possession of Stolen Mail	C	Unranked
9.94.040(2)	Possession of Weapons by Prisoners (County or Local Facility)	C	Unranked
9.94.040(1)	Possession of Weapons by Prisoners (State Facility)	B	Unranked
9.94.043	Possession of Weapons in Prison by Non-prisoner	B	Unranked
9.94.010	Prison Riot	B	Unranked
9.46.220	Professional Gambling 1	B	Unranked
9.46.221	Professional Gambling 2	C	Unranked
9A.36.060	Promoting a Suicide Attempt	C	Unranked
67.08.015	Promoting Illegal Boxing, Martial Arts and Wrestling	C	Unranked
9.68.140	Promoting Pornography	C	Unranked
9.68A.102	Promoting Travel for Commercial Sexual Abuse of a Minor	C	Unranked
9A.88.085	Promoting Travel for Prostitution	C	Unranked
29A.84.311	Provides False Information or Conceals or Destroys Candidacy Declaration or Nominating Petition	C	Unranked
26.04.210	Providing False Statements in Affidavits for Marriage	C	Unranked
68.50.140(2)	Purchasing or Receiving Human Remains	C	Unranked
74.09.240(1)	Receiving or Asking for Bribes, Kickbacks or Rebates	C	Unranked
9A.68.030	Receiving or Granting Unlawful Compensation	C	Unranked
81.60.080(2)	Receiving Stolen Railroad Property	C	Unranked
90.56.530	Reckless Operation of a Tank Vessel	C	Unranked

Statute (RCW)	Offense	Class	Seriousness Level
19.110.075(2)	Registration Knowingly not Obtained Prior to Sale of Business Opportunity (Violation of RCW 19.110.050)	B	Unranked
70A.15.3150(3)	Releasing into Ambient Air Hazardous Air Pollutant	C	Unranked
46.12.560	Removal of Sticker on Vehicle Stating Previously Destroyed or Title 1 Loss	C	Unranked
68.50.140(4)	Removal, Disinterment or Mutilation of Human Remains	C	Unranked
68.60.050	Removes, Defaces or Destroys any Historic Grave	C	Unranked
29A.84.540	Removing a Ballot from a Voting Center or Ballot Drop Location	C	Unranked
68.50.140(1)	Removing Human Remains	C	Unranked
9.16.010	Removing Lawful Brands	C	Unranked
19.25.020(2)(a)	Reproduction of Sound Recording without Consent of Owner - Recording Fixed before 2/15/1972 (at least 1,000 Recordings or Subsequent Conviction)	B	Unranked
19.25.020(2)(b)	Reproduction of Sound Recording without Consent of Owner - Recording Fixed before 2/15/1972 (more than 100 but less than 1,000 Recordings)	C	Unranked
9A.68.020	Requesting Unlawful Compensation	C	Unranked
70.345.030	Retail Sales, Distribution or Delivery Sales of Vapor Products without a License	C	Unranked
9A.56.360(4)	Retail Theft with Special Circumstances 3	C	Unranked
81.60.080(1)	Sabotaging Rolling Stock	C	Unranked
69.41.030(2)(a)	Sale, Delivery or Possession with Intent to Sell Legend Drug without Prescription	B	Unranked
33.36.040	Savings and Loan Association - Making False Statement of Assets or Liabilities	C	Unranked
33.36.030	Savings and Loan Association - Preference in Case of Insolvency	C	Unranked
33.36.060	Savings and Loan Association - Suppressing, Secreting or Destroying Evidence or Records	C	Unranked
19.60.067(2)	Second-hand Precious Metal Dealer Violations (Subsequent Violation)	C	Unranked
46.20.0921(2)	Sell or Deliver a Stolen Driver's License or Identicard	C	Unranked
27.44.040(2)	Selling Artifacts or Human Remains from Indian Graves	C	Unranked
48.160.080	Sells Guaranteed Asset Protection Waivers without Registration	B	Unranked
70.155.140	Shipping or Transporting Tobacco Products Ordered Through Mail or Internet	C	Unranked
82.38.270	Special Fuel Violations	C	Unranked
67.70.160	State Lottery Violations Except Lottery Fraud and Unlicensed Lottery Activity	C	Unranked
30B.12.050	State Trust Company – False Entry, Conceal or Destroy Records	B	Unranked
30B.44B.110(2)	State Trust Company – Transfer of Assets	B	Unranked
9.45.020	Substitution of Child	B	Unranked
29A.84.550	Tampering with Election Materials	C	Unranked

Statute (RCW)	Offense	Class	Seriousness Level
9.40.105	Tampering with Fire Alarm, Emergency Signal, or Fire-fighting Equipment with Intent to Commit Arson	B	Unranked
88.08.020	Tampering with Lights or Signals	B	Unranked
29A.84.560	Tampering with Voting Machine	C	Unranked
9A.56.262	Theft of Telecommunication Service	C	Unranked
9A.36.090	Threats Against Governor or Family	C	Unranked
64.36.210	Timeshare Fraud	C	Unranked
64.36.020(5)(b)	Timeshare Registration Requirement Violation	C	Unranked
9A.68.040	Trading in Public Office	C	Unranked
9A.68.050	Trading in Special Influence	C	Unranked
9.08.076	Transferring a Stolen Pet Animal to a Research Institution by a USDA Licensed Dealer	C	Unranked
9.08.074	Transferring Stolen Pet Animal to a Person who Previously Sold a Stolen Pet Animal to a Research Facility	C	Unranked
9.08.072	Transferring Stolen Pet Animal to a Research Institution, not by a USDA Licensed Dealer -2nd or Subsequent Offense	C	Unranked
9.46.240	Transmission or Receiving Gambling Information by Internet	C	Unranked
70A.300.100(1)(a)	Transport, Disposal or Export of Hazardous Waste that Places Another Person in Danger of Injury or Death	B	Unranked
70A.300.100(1)(b)	Transport, Disposal or Export of Hazardous Waste that Places Another Person's Property in Danger of Harm	C	Unranked
82.24.110(2)	Transportation of more than 10,000 Cigarettes without Proper Stamps	C	Unranked
68.60.040(3)	Transports Removed Human Remains, Opens a Grave or Removes Personal Effects from Grave	C	Unranked
9.82.010	Treason	A	Unranked
9.91.150(1)	Tree Spiking	C	Unranked
9.02.120	Unauthorized Abortion	C	Unranked
68.44.060	Unauthorized Loans to Cemetery Authority	C	Unranked
29A.84.545	Unauthorized Removal of Paper Record from Electronic Voting Device	C	Unranked
9.26A.140(1)(a-c)	Unauthorized Sale or Procurement of Telephone Records	C	Unranked
39.62.040	Unauthorized Use of Public Official Facsimile Signature or Seal	B	Unranked
68.05.330	Unfair Practice of Funeral or Cemetery Board	C	Unranked
19.225.110	Uniform Athlete Agent Act Violation	C	Unranked
69.43.070(1)	Unlawful Delivery of Precursor Drug with Intent to Use	B	Unranked
9A.49.020	Unlawful Discharge of a Laser 1	C	Unranked
74.09.290	Unlawful Disclosure of Patient Records or DSHS Information	C	Unranked
69.53.020	Unlawful Fortification of Building for Drug Purposes	C	Unranked
9A.56.264	Unlawful Manufacture of a Telecommunication Device	C	Unranked

Statute (RCW)	Offense	Class	Seriousness Level
51.48.280(2)	Unlawful Offer or Payment for Kickbacks, Bribes, or Rebates to any Person	C	Unranked
88.46.080(2)(b)	Unlawful Operation of a Covered Vessel (Subsequent Violation)	C	Unranked
90.56.300(2)(b)	Unlawful Operation of Onshore or Offshore Facility (Subsequent Conviction)	C	Unranked
9.41.115	Unlawful Private Transfer of a Firearm (Subsequent Offense)	C	Unranked
69.43.070(2)	Unlawful Receipt of Precursor Drug with Intent to Use	B	Unranked
51.48.280(1)	Unlawful Receipt of Remuneration for Kickbacks, Bribes, or Rebates by any Person	C	Unranked
9A.56.266	Unlawful Sale of a Telecommunication Device	C	Unranked
9A.56.230	Unlawful Sale of Subscription Television Services	C	Unranked
46.12.750(3)	Unlawful Sale of Vehicle Certificate of Ownership	C	Unranked
18.64.046(7)	Unlawful Selling of Ephedrine, Pseudoephedrine or Phenylpropanolamine by a Wholesaler	C	Unranked
19.116.080(1)	Unlawful Subleasing of Motor Vehicle	C	Unranked
77.15.770(2)	Unlawful Trade in Shark Fins 1	C	Unranked
77.15.135(4)(d)	Unlawful Trafficking in Species with Extinction 1	C	Unranked
19.116.080(2)	Unlawful Transfer of Ownership of Motor Vehicle	C	Unranked
18.04.370(1)(b)	Unlawful Use of a Professional Title	C	Unranked
18.04.370(1)(c)	Unlawful Use of CPA Title after Suspension	C	Unranked
69.53.030	Unlawful Use of Fortified Building	C	Unranked
77.15.811	Unlawful Use of Invasive Species 1	C	Unranked
66.44.120(2)(b)	Unlawful Use of Liquor Board Seal (Third or Subsequent Offense)	C	Unranked
9.46.037	Unlawful Wagers of a Sporting Event, Athletic Event, or Competition	C	Unranked
19.310.120	Unlawfully Engaging in Business as an Exchange Facilitator (RCW 19.310.100(1)-(9))	B	Unranked
82.24.500	Unlawfully Purchase, Sell, Consign or Distribute Cigarettes	C	Unranked
48.102.160(4)	Unlicensed Life Insurance Provider	B	Unranked
67.70.140	Unlicensed Lottery Activity	B	Unranked
48.102.160(5)	Unlicensed Settlement Broker	B	Unranked
29A.84.660	Unqualified Person Voting	C	Unranked
29A.84.140	Unqualified Voting Registration	C	Unranked
9.41.360	Unsafe Storage of a Firearm	C	Unranked
19.210.040	Unused Property, Merchants –Prohibited Sales (Third or Subsequent Offense within 5 Years)	C	Unranked
46.37.673	Use of a Signal Preemption Device Resulting in Property Damage or less Substantial Bodily Harm	C	Unranked
9.26A.115	Use of Fraudulent Telecommunication Services	B	Unranked
9A.82.080(3)	Use of Proceeds of Criminal Profiteering – Attempt or Conspiracy	C	Unranked

Statute (RCW)	Offense	Class	Seriousness Level
19.25.030(2)(a)	Use of Recording of Live Performance without Consent of Owner (at least 1,000 Recordings or at least 100 Unauthorized Audiovisual Recordings or Subsequent Offense)	B	Unranked
19.25.030(2)(b)	Use of Recording of Live Performance without Consent of Owner (at least 100 but less than 1,000 Recordings or more than 10 but less than 100 Unauthorized Audiovisual Recording or Subsequent Offense)	C	Unranked
19.144.100(1)	Use or Investment of Proceeds from Mortgage Fraud Activities	B	Unranked
9.68A.075(2)	Viewing Depictions of Minor Engaged in Sexually Explicit Conduct 2 (Effective 6/10/2010)	C	Unranked
29A.84.230(1)	Violation by Signer – Initiative or Referendum with False Name	C	Unranked
29A.84.240(1)	Violations by Signers – Recall Petition with False Name	B	Unranked
9.46.190	Violations of Fraud or Deceit Regarding Gambling Activity	C	Unranked
29A.84.130	Voter Violation of Registration Law	C	Unranked
29A.84.650(1)	Voting Repeater – more than one Vote at any Election	C	Unranked
48.30.220	Willful Destruction, Injury, Secretion of Insured Property	C	Unranked
10.66.090	Willfully Disobeys an Off-limits Order (Subsequent Violation or Enters Protected Against Drug Trafficking Area)	C	Unranked

MANDATORY REMAND OFFENSES
RCW 10.64.025(2)

Statute (RCW)	Offense	Class	Seriousness Level
9A.44.083	Child Molestation 1	A	X
9A.44.086	Child Molestation 2	B	VII
9A.44.089	Child Molestation 3	C	V
9.68A.090(2)	Communication with Minor for Immoral Purposes (Subsequent Violation or Prior Sex Offense Conviction)	C	III
9A.64.020(1)	Incest 1	B	VI
9A.64.020(2)	Incest 2	C	V
9A.44.100(1)(a)	Indecent Liberties - with Forcible Compulsion	A	X
9A.44.100(1)(b-c)	Indecent Liberties - without Forcible Compulsion	B	VII
9A.44.100(1)(d-f)	Indecent Liberties - without Forcible Compulsion	B	Unranked
9A.40.090	Luring of a Child or a Person with a Developmental Disability	C	Unranked
9.68A.101	Promoting Commercial Sexual Abuse of a Minor	A	XII
9A.44.040	Rape 1	A	XII
9A.44.050	Rape 2	A	XI
9A.44.073	Rape of a Child 1	A	XII
9A.44.076	Rape of a Child 2	A	XI
9A.44.079	Rape of a Child 3	C	VI
9A.44.093	Sexual Misconduct with a Minor 1	C	V
9A.40.100(1)	Trafficking 1	A	XIV
9A.40.100(3)	Trafficking 2	A	XII

Any Class A or B felony with a finding of sexual motivation as defined in RCW 9.94A.030(48).

Any offense that is, under chapter 9A.28 RCW, a criminal attempt, solicitation, or conspiracy to commit one of these offenses.

FELONY INDEX BY OFFENSE

Statute (RCW)	Offense	Class	Seriousness Level
9A.42.060	Abandonment of Dependent Person 1	B	IX
9A.42.070	Abandonment of Dependent Person 2	C	V
29A.84.680(1)	Absentee Voting Violation	C	Unranked
46.52.130(6)(b)	Abstracts of Driving Records – Intentional Misuse	C	Unranked
20.01.460(2)	Acting as Commission Merchant, Dealer, Cash Buyer without License	C	Unranked
9A.82.030	Advancing Money or Property for Extortionate Extension of Credit	B	V
69.52.030(3)	Advertising Imitation Controlled Substances	C	Unranked
10.95.020	Aggravated Murder 1	A	XVI
46.37.660(2)(c)	Air Bag Diagnostic Systems	C	V
46.37.660(2)(b)	Air Bag Diagnostic Systems (Causing Bodily Injury or Death)	C	VII
46.37.660(1)(c)	Air Bag Replacement Requirements	C	V
46.37.660(1)(b)	Air Bag Replacement Requirements (Causing Bodily Injury or Death)	C	VII
30A.42.290(3)	Alien Bank or Bureau – Destroy or Secrete Records	B	Unranked
30A.42.290(2)	Alien Bank or Bureau – False Entry, Statements, etc.	B	Unranked
9.41.171	Alien Possession of a Firearm	C	Unranked
9.45.210	Altering Sample or Certificate of Assay	C	Unranked
9A.76.177	Amber Alert – Making False Statements to a Public Servant	C	Unranked
68.64.160	Anatomical Gift - Illegal Financial Gain	C	Unranked
68.64.150	Anatomical Gifts - Illegal Purchase or Sale	C	Unranked
16.52.205(2)	Animal Cruelty 1	C	Unranked
16.52.205(3)	Animal Cruelty 1 - Sexual Conduct or Contact	C	III
16.52.117(2)(a)	Animal Fighting	C	Unranked
16.52.117(2)(b)	Animal Fighting - Mutilation	B	Unranked
9A.48.020	Arson 1	A	VIII
9A.28.020(3)(a)	Arson 1 – Criminal Attempt	A	VIII
9A.28.030(2)	Arson 1 – Criminal Solicitation	A	VIII
9A.48.030	Arson 2	B	IV
9A.36.011	Assault 1	A	XII
9A.36.021(2)(a)	Assault 2	B	IV
9A.36.021(2)(b)	Assault 2 with a Finding of Sexual Motivation	A	IV
9A.36.031(1)(h)	Assault 3 of a Peace Officer with a Projectile Stun Gun	C	IV
9A.36.031(1)(a-g) & (i-j)	Assault 3, excluding Assault 3 of a Peace Officer with a Projectile Stun Gun	C	III

Statute (RCW)	Offense	Class	Seriousness Level
9A.36.041(3)	Assault 4 (Third Domestic Violence Offense)	C	IV
79A.60.060	Assault by Watercraft	B	IV
9A.36.120	Assault of a Child 1	A	XII
9A.36.130	Assault of a Child 2	B	IX
9A.36.140	Assault of a Child 3	C	III
9.05.030	Assembly of Saboteurs	B	Unranked
72.23.170	Assist Escape of Mental Patient	C	Unranked
46.61.024	Attempting to Elude Pursuing Police Vehicle	C	I
9A.76.170(3)(b)	Bail Jumping with Class A Felony	B	V
9A.76.170(3)(c)	Bail Jumping with Class B or C Felony	C	III
9A.76.170(3)(a)	Bail Jumping with Murder 1	A	VI
30A.12.100	Bank or Trust Company - Destroy or Secrete Records	B	Unranked
30A.12.090	Bank or Trust Company - False Entry, Statements, etc.	B	Unranked
30A.44.120	Bank or Trust Company - Receiving Deposits When Insolvent	B	Unranked
30A.44.110	Bank or Trust Company - Transfer of Assets Prior to Insolvency	B	Unranked
9A.64.010	Bigamy	C	Unranked
9A.72.100	Bribe Received by Witness	B	IV
9A.68.010	Bribery	B	VI
9A.72.090	Bribing a Witness	B	IV
9.46.155	Bribing to Obtain a License from Public Officials, Employees, Agents	C	Unranked
72.23.300	Bringing Narcotics, Liquor, or Weapons into State Institution or Grounds	B	Unranked
9.47.120	Bunco Steering	B	Unranked
9A.52.020	Burglary 1	A	VII
9A.52.030	Burglary 2	B	III
46.87.260	Cab Card Forgery (Effective Until 7/1/2016)	B	Unranked
9.46.180	Causing Person to Violate Gambling Laws	B	Unranked
9.46.1961	Cheating 1	C	IV
9A.64.030(3)(b)	Child Buying	C	Unranked
49.12.410(2)	Child Labor Law Violation – Death/Disability	C	Unranked
9A.44.083	Child Molestation 1	A	X
9A.28.020(3)(a)	Child Molestation 1 – Criminal Attempt	A	X
9A.28.030(2)	Child Molestation 1 – Criminal Solicitation	A	X
9A.44.086	Child Molestation 2	B	VII
9A.44.089	Child Molestation 3	C	V
9A.64.030(3)(a)	Child Selling	C	Unranked
9A.48.120	Civil Disorder Training	B	VII

Statute (RCW)	Offense	Class	Seriousness Level
70.245.200(2)	Coerce Patient to Request Life-ending Medication	A	Unranked
9A.40.110	Coercion of Involuntary Servitude	C	Unranked
9A.82.045	Collection of Unlawful Debt	C	Unranked
9A.68.060	Commercial Bribery	B	IV
77.15.500(3)(b)	Commercial Fishing without a License 1	C	II
9.68A.100	Commercial Sexual Abuse of a Minor	B	VIII
19.158.160	Commercial Telephone Solicitor Deception (Value of $250 or more)	C	Unranked
30A.04.240	Commingling of Funds or Securities	B	Unranked
21.30.140	Commodity Transaction Violation	B	Unranked
9.68A.090(2)	Communication with Minor for Immoral Purposes (Subsequent Violation or Prior Sex Offense Conviction)	C	III
9A.90.040	Computer Trespass 1	C	II
69.50.465	Conducting or Maintaining a Cannabis Club	C	Unranked
19.144.100(2)	Control of Real Property Resulting from Mortgage Fraud Activities	B	Unranked
69.50.415	Controlled Substance Homicide	B	DG-III
69.50.416	Controlled Substance Label Violation	C	Unranked
9.16.035(4)	Counterfeiting - Endanger Public Health or Safety	C	IV
9.16.035(3)	Counterfeiting – Third Conviction and Value $10,000 or more	C	II
69.50.4011(2)(a-b)	Create or Deliver Possess a Counterfeit Controlled Substance – Schedule I or II Narcotic or Flunitrazepam or Methamphetamine	B	DG-II
69.50.4011(2)(c-e)	Create or Deliver a Counterfeit Controlled Substance – Schedule I-II Nonnarcotic, Schedule III-V Except Flunitrazepam or Methamphetamine	C	DG-II
46.87.260	Credential Forgery (Effective 7/1/2016)	B	Unranked
31.12.724(3)	Credit Union - Fraudulent Receipt of Credit Union Deposit	B	Unranked
31.12.724(2)	Credit Union - Transfer of Credit Union Assets Prior to Insolvency	B	Unranked
9.08.090	Crimes Against Animal Facilities	C	Unranked
9A.46.120	Criminal Gang Intimidation	C	III
9A.60.040	Criminal Impersonation 1	C	Unranked
9A.84.010(2)(b)	Criminal Mischief	C	Unranked
9A.42.020	Criminal Mistreatment 1	B	X
9A.42.030	Criminal Mistreatment 2	C	V
9A.82.160	Criminal Profiteering Lien after Service of Notice	C	Unranked
9.05.060(2)	Criminal Sabotage	B	Unranked
9A.44.196	Criminal Trespass Against Children	C	Unranked
9A.36.100	Custodial Assault	C	III

Statute (RCW)	Offense	Class	Seriousness Level
9A.40.060	Custodial Interference 1	C	Unranked
9A.40.070	Custodial Interference 2 (Subsequent Offense)	C	Unranked
9A.44.160	Custodial Sexual Misconduct 1	B	VII
9A.44.170	Custodial Sexual Misconduct 2	C	V
9A.90.120(2)(b)	Cyber Harassment	C	III
43.06.230	Damage Property or Cause Personal Injury after State of Emergency Proclaimed	B	Unranked
16.08.100(2)	Dangerous Dog Attack (Subsequent Offense)	C	Unranked
16.08.100(3)	Dangerous Dog Attack Resulting in Severe Injury or Death	C	Unranked
9.68A.050(1)	Dealing in Depictions of Minor Engaged in Sexually Explicit Conduct 1	B	VII
9.68A.050(2)	Dealing in Depictions of Minor Engaged in Sexually Explicit Conduct 2	B	V
22.09.310	Dealing in Unauthorized Warehouse Receipts for Agricultural Commodities	C	Unranked
39.44.101	Defraud a Facsimile Signature on Bonds and Coupons	B	Unranked
87.03.200	Defraud Facsimile Signatures on Bonds and Coupons – Irrigation Districts	B	Unranked
19.110.120	Defraud or Provide Misleading or Untrue Documents Related to a Business Opportunity Sale	B	Unranked
9A.61.030	Defrauding a Public Utility 1	B	Unranked
9A.61.040	Defrauding a Public Utility 2	C	Unranked
19.48.110(1)(b)	Defrauding an Innkeeper (Value of $75 or more)	B	Unranked
69.50.401(2)(b)	Deliver or Possess with Intent to Deliver - Methamphetamine	B	DG-II
69.50.4012	Delivery of a Material in Lieu of a Controlled Substance	C	DG-II
9.41.110(8)	Delivery of Firearm by Dealer to Ineligible Person	C	Unranked
9.41.080	Delivery of Firearms to Ineligible Person	C	Unranked
69.52.030(2)	Delivery of Imitation Controlled Substance by Person 18 or Over to Person under 18	B	DG-III
35A.36.040	Designation of Bonds – Violation (Code Cities)	B	Unranked
35.36.040	Designation of Bonds – Violation (First Class Cities)	B	Unranked
27.44.040(1)	Destroying, Removing or Defacing Indian Graves	C	Unranked
68.60.040(1)	Destruction of Tomb, Plot, Marker, or Cemetery Property	C	Unranked
9.38.060	Digital Signatures Fraud	C	Unranked
9A.76.023(2)(a)	Disarming a Law Enforcement or Corrections Officer	C	Unranked
9A.76.023(2)(b)	Disarming a Law Enforcement or Corrections Officer and Firearm is Discharged	B	Unranked
9A.86.010	Disclosing Intimate Images	C	Unranked

Statute (RCW)	Offense	Class	Seriousness Level
19.110.075(2)	Disclosures Knowingly Not Provided at Sale of Business Opportunity (Violation of RCW 19.110.070)	B	Unranked
69.50.402	Dispensing Violation (VUCSA)	C	Unranked
82.26.190	Distributors and Retailer of Tobacco Products License Violation	C	Unranked
27.53.060	Disturbing Archaeological Resources or Site	C	Unranked
43.43.856	Divulging Confidential Investigative Information Pertaining to Organized Crime	B	Unranked
7.105.450, 10.99.040, 10.99.050, 26.09.300, 26.26B.050, or 26.52.070	Domestic Violence Court Order Violation	C	V
9A.36.045	Drive-by Shooting	B	VII
46.61.502(6)	Driving while under the Influence of Intoxicating Liquor or any Drug	B	IV
29A.84.270	Duplication of Name – Conspiracy to Mislead	B	Unranked
29A.84.320	Duplication of Names on Declaration of Candidacy	B	Unranked
29A.84.655	Election Officer Permits Repeat Vote	C	Unranked
29A.84.720	Election Officers – Violation	C	Unranked
29A.84.030	Election or Mail Ballot Violation	C	Unranked
19.300.020	Electronic Communication Devices – Illegal Scanning	C	Unranked
9A.90.060	Electronic Data Service Interference	C	II
9A.90.080	Electronic Data Tampering 1	C	II
9A.90.100	Electronic Data Theft	C	II
79A.60.090	Eluding a Law Enforcement Vessel	C	Unranked
18.39.350	Embalmers/Funeral Directors Violation	C	Unranked
43.08.140	Embezzlement by State Treasurer	B	Unranked
9A.42.100	Endangerment with a Controlled Substance	B	IV
46.80.020(b)	Engage in Business of Wrecking Vehicles without a License (Subsequent Offense)	C	Unranked
51.48.103(2)	Engaging in Business after Certificate of Coverage Revocation	C	Unranked
70.345.090	Engaging in Delivery Sales of Vapor Products without a License or Proper Shipping Documentation	C	Unranked
77.15.620(3)(b)	Engaging in Fish Dealing Activity Unlicensed 1	C	II
61.34.030	Equity Skimming	B	II
9.68.060	Erotic Material (Third or Subsequent Offense)	B	Unranked
9A.76.110	Escape 1	B	IV
9A.76.120	Escape 2	C	III
9A.76.130(3)(b)	Escape 3 (Third or Subsequent Offense)	C	Unranked

Statute (RCW)	Offense	Class	Seriousness Level
72.09.310	Escape from Community Custody	C	II
51.48.020(1)	Evading Industrial Insurance Premiums	C	Unranked
82.42.085	Evading the Collection of Aircraft Fuel Tax	C	Unranked
74.09.260	Excessive Charges, Payments	C	Unranked
48.06.190	Exhibiting False Accounts of Insurer	B	Unranked
70.74.180	Explosive Devices Prohibited	A	IX
9A.56.120	Extortion 1	B	V
9A.56.130	Extortion 2	C	III
9A.82.020	Extortionate Extension of Credit	B	V
9A.82.040	Extortionate Means to Collect Extensions of Credit	B	V
19.25.040(2)(a)	Failure to Disclose Origin of Certain Recordings (at least 100 Recordings or Subsequent Conviction)	B	Unranked
19.25.040(2)(b)	Failure to Disclose Origin of Certain Recordings (more than 10 but less than 100 Recordings)	C	Unranked
36.18.170	Failure to Pay Over Fees to County Treasurer	C	Unranked
9A.44.132(3)	Failure to Register as a Kidnapping Offender	C	Unranked
9A.44.132(1)(a)	Failure to Register as a Sex Offender (First Violation)	C	Unranked
9A.44.132(1)(a)	Failure to Register as a Sex Offender (Second Violation Committed on or after 6/10/2010)	C	II
9A.44.132(1)(b)	Failure to Register as a Sex Offender (Third or Subsequent Violation Committed on or after 6/10/2010)	B	II
19.146.050	Failure to Use a Trust Account	C	Unranked
19.142.080	Failure to Use a Trust Account or Furnish Bond for Health Studio	C	Unranked
38.42.050	False Affidavit under Service Member Civil Relief Act	C	Unranked
74.08.100	False Age and Residency Public Assistance Verification	B	Unranked
42.24.100	False Claim from Municipal Corporation (Charged as Perjury 2)	C	Unranked
42.17A.750	False Documents Registered with Public Disclosure Commission	C	Unranked
51.48.020(2)	False Information in Industrial Insurance Claim (Charged as Theft)		
48.30.230	False Insurance Claims (Value in Excess of $1,500)	C	Unranked
9.24.050	False Report of Corporation	B	Unranked
9A.84.040(2)(a)	False Reporting 1	B	VII
9A.84.040(2)(b)	False Reporting 2	C	III
74.09.230	False Statement for Medical Assistance	C	Unranked
69.43.080	False Statement in Report of Precursor Drugs	C	Unranked

Statute (RCW)	Offense	Class	Seriousness Level
9.38.015	False Statement of Identity to a Financial Institution - 3rd or Subsequent Offense	C	Unranked
51.48.270	False Statement or Concealing Information by Employee	C	Unranked
82.32.290(2)	False Statement to Department of Revenue	C	Unranked
19.230.300	False Statement, Misrepresentation or False Certification of Uniform Money Services Record	C	Unranked
41.26.062	False Statements or Records to Defraud Law Enforcement Officers and Firefighters Retirement System	B	Unranked
41.32.055(1)	False Statements or Records to Defraud Teachers Retirement System	B	Unranked
74.09.250	False Statements Regarding Institutions, Facilities	C	Unranked
46.12.750(1)	False Statements, Illegal Transfers, Alterations or Forgeries of Vehicle Title	B	Unranked
65.12.740	False Swearing - Registration of Land Title (Charged as Perjury)		
74.08.055(2)	False Verification for Welfare	B	I
26.20.030	Family Abandonment	C	Unranked
69.41.020	Forged Prescription - Legend Drug	B	DG-I
69.50.403	Forged Prescription for a Controlled Substance	C	DG-I
9A.60.020	Forgery	C	I
76.36.120	Forgery of Forest Product Mark	B	Unranked
65.12.760	Forgery of Registrar's Signature or Seal	B	Unranked
82.24.100	Forgery or Counterfeit Cigarette Tax Stamp	B	Unranked
70.245.200(1)	Forging Request for Medication	A	Unranked
19.100.210	Franchise Investment Protection Violation	B	Unranked
29A.84.711	Fraud in Certification of Nomination or Ballot	C	Unranked
9.45.170	Fraud in Liquor Warehouse Receipts	C	Unranked
9.45.124	Fraud in Measurement of Goods	B	Unranked
9.26A.110(3)	Fraud in Obtaining Telecommunications Services (Value Exceeds $250)	C	Unranked
67.24.010	Fraud in Sporting Contest	B	Unranked
9A.60.060	Fraudulent Creation or Revocation of Mental Health Advance Directive	C	I
76.48.141(1)(a)	Fraudulent Document as Specialized Forest Products Permit, Sales Invoice, Bill of Lading, etc.	C	Unranked
76.48.141(2)	Fraudulent Document for Specialized Forest Products Buyer	C	Unranked
9.45.270(3)	Fraudulent Filing of Vehicle Report of Sale (Value Exceeds $1,500)	B	Unranked
9.45.270(2)	Fraudulent Filing of Vehicle Report of Sale (Value Exceeds $250)	C	Unranked
9.24.020	Fraudulent Issue of Stock, Scrip, etc.	B	Unranked
48.102.160(3)	Fraudulent Life Insurance Settlement	B	Unranked

Statute (RCW)	Offense	Class	Seriousness Level
65.12.750	Fraudulent Procurement or False Entry on Land Title Registration	C	Unranked
76.48.141(1)(b)	Fraudulent Representation of Authority to Harvest Specialized Forest Products	C	Unranked
9.46.160	Gambling without License	B	Unranked
9.46.039	Greyhound Racing	B	Unranked
9A.46.020(2)(b)	Harassment	C	III
9A.76.200	Harming a Police Dog/Horse or an Accelerant Detection Dog	C	Unranked
9A.36.080	Hate Crime Offense	C	IV
28B.10.901(2)(b)	Hazing	C	III
48.80.030	Health Care False Claims	C	II
29A.84.620	Hindering or Bribing Voter	C	Unranked
46.52.020(4)(a)	Hit and Run - Death	B	IX
46.52.020(4)(b)	Hit and Run - Injury	C	IV
79A.60.200(3)	Hit and Run with Vessel - Injury Accident	C	IV
9.94.030	Holding Hostages or Interfering with Officer's Duty	B	Unranked
9A.32.055	Homicide by Abuse	A	XV
79A.60.050(1)(c)	Homicide by Watercraft - Disregard for the Safety of Others	A	VII
79A.60.050(1)(b)	Homicide by Watercraft – in a Reckless Manner	A	VIII
79A.60.050(1)(a)	Homicide by Watercraft – while under the Influence of Intoxicating Liquor or any Drug	A	IX
9.35.020(2)	Identity Theft 1	B	IV
9.35.020(3)	Identity Theft 2	C	II
69.41.040	Illegal Issuance of Legend Drug Prescription	B	Unranked
9.16.020	Imitating Lawful Brands with Intent	C	Unranked
19.146.235(9)	Impairing Mortgage Broker Investigation	B	Unranked
9.35.010	Improperly Obtaining Financial Information	C	II
9A.64.020(1)	Incest 1	B	VI
9A.64.020(2)	Incest 2	C	V
9A.88.010(2)(c)	Indecent Exposure to a Person Age 14 or Older (Subsequent Conviction or has Prior Sex Offense Conviction)	C	Unranked
9A.88.010(2)(c)	Indecent Exposure to a Person under Age 14 (Subsequent Sex Offense)	C	IV
9A.44.100(1)(a)	Indecent Liberties - with Forcible Compulsion	A	X
9A.28.020(3)(a)	Indecent Liberties - with Forcible Compulsion – Criminal Attempt	A	X
9A.28.030(2)	Indecent Liberties - with Forcible Compulsion – Criminal Solicitation	A	X
9A.44.100(1)(b-c)	Indecent Liberties - without Forcible Compulsion	B	VII
9A.44.100(1)(d-f)	Indecent Liberties - without Forcible Compulsion	B	Unranked

Statute (RCW)	Offense	Class	Seriousness Level
9.45.126	Inducing Fraud in Measurement of Goods	B	Unranked
9A.82.070	Influencing Outcome of Sporting Event	C	IV
40.16.010	Injury to a Public Record	C	Unranked
40.16.020	Injury to and Misappropriation of Public Record by Officer	B	Unranked
88.08.050(1)	Injury to Lighthouses or United States Light	B	Unranked
9.24.030	Insolvent Bank Receiving Deposit	B	Unranked
48.06.030	Insurance Solicitation Permit Violation	B	Unranked
9.91.170(5)	Intentional Infliction, Injury or Death to a Dog Guide or Service Animal	C	Unranked
9.91.175(3)	Intentionally Injures, Disables or Causes Death of an On-Duty Search and Rescue Dog	C	Unranked
9.73.230	Intercepting, Transmitting or Recording Conversations Concerning Controlled Substances	C	Unranked
69.25.155(1)	Interference with Person Performing Official Duties	C	Unranked
69.25.155(2)	Interference with Person Performing Official Duties with a Deadly Weapon	B	Unranked
9A.72.160	Intimidating a Judge	B	VI
9A.72.130	Intimidating a Juror	B	VI
9A.76.180	Intimidating a Public Servant	B	III
9A.72.110	Intimidating a Witness	B	VI
70.74.275	Intimidation or Harassment with an Explosive	C	Unranked
9A.76.140	Introducing Contraband 1	B	VII
9A.76.150	Introducing Contraband 2	C	III
69.50.4015	Involving a Minor in Drug Dealing	C	DG-III
9A.60.070	Issuing a False Academic Credential	C	Unranked
9A.40.020	Kidnapping 1	A	X
9A.40.030(3)(a)	Kidnapping 2	B	V
9A.40.030(3)(b)	Kidnapping 2 with a Finding of Sexual Motivation	A	V
16.52.320	Kill or Cause Substantial Harm with Malice to Livestock	C	Unranked
82.87.140	Knowingly Attempts to Evade Capital Gains Tax Payment	C	Unranked
9A.82.060(1)(b)	Leading Organized Crime - Inciting Criminal Profiteering	B	IX
9A.82.060(1)(a)	Leading Organized Crime – Organizing Criminal Profiteering	A	X
46.70.021	Licensing Violation for Car Dealers or Manufacturers (Subsequent Violation)	C	Unranked
30A.12.120	Loan to Officer or Employee from Trust Fund	B	Unranked
67.70.130	Lottery Fraud	B	Unranked
9A.40.090	Luring of a Child or a Person with a Developmental Disability	C	Unranked

Statute (RCW)	Offense	Class	Seriousness Level
9A.56.370	Mail Theft	C	Unranked
9.47.090	Maintaining a Bucket Shop	C	Unranked
69.50.402(1)(f)	Maintaining a Dwelling or Place for Controlled Substances	C	DG-II
31.12.850(2)	Make a False Statement or Entry in Credit Union Books	C	Unranked
9.45.220	Making False Sample or Assay of Ore	C	Unranked
70.74.280(1)	Malicious Explosion of a Substance 1	A	XV
70.74.280(2)	Malicious Explosion of a Substance 2	A	XIII
70.74.280(3)	Malicious Explosion of a Substance 3	B	X
81.60.070	Malicious Injury to Railroad Property	B	III
9A.48.070	Malicious Mischief 1	B	II
9A.48.080	Malicious Mischief 2	C	I
70.74.270(1)	Malicious Placement of an Explosive 1	A	XIII
70.74.270(2)	Malicious Placement of an Explosive 2	B	IX
70.74.270(3)	Malicious Placement of an Explosive 3	B	VII
70.74.272(1)(a)	Malicious Placement of an Imitation Device 1	B	XII
70.74.272(1)(b)	Malicious Placement of an Imitation Device 2	C	VI
9.62.010(1)	Malicious Prosecution	C	Unranked
9.45.260	Malicious Sprinkler Contractor Work	C	Unranked
9A.32.060	Manslaughter 1	A	XI
9A.32.070	Manslaughter 2	B	VIII
69.50.401(2)(b)	Manufacture Methamphetamine	B	DG-III
9.41.190	Manufacture of Untraceable Firearm with Intent to Sell	C	III
9.41.325	Manufacture or Assembly of an Undetectable Firearm or Untraceable Firearm	C	III
46.37.650(1)(c)	Manufacture or Import Counterfeit, Nonfunctional, Damaged, or Previously Deployed Air Bag	C	V
46.37.650(1)(b)	Manufacture or Import Counterfeit, Nonfunctional, Damaged, or Previously Deployed Air Bag (Causing Bodily Injury or Death)	C	VII
69.50.401(2)(b)	Manufacture, Deliver or Possess with Intent to Deliver - Amphetamine	B	DG-II
69.50.401(2)(c)	Manufacture, Deliver or Possess with Intent to Deliver - Cannabis	C	DG-I
69.50.401(2)(a)	Manufacture, Deliver or Possess with Intent to Deliver - Narcotics from Schedule I or II or Flunitrazepam from Schedule IV	B	DG-II
69.50.401(2)(c-e)	Manufacture, Deliver or Possess with Intent to Deliver - Narcotics from Schedule III, IV, or V or Nonnarcotics from Schedule I-V (except Cannabis, Amphetamine, Methamphetamine, or Flunitrazepam)	C	DG-II

Statute (RCW)	Offense	Class	Seriousness Level
69.52.030(1)	Manufacture, Distribute or Possess with Intent to Distribute an Imitation Controlled Substance	C	DG-II
70.74.022(1)	Manufacture, Purchase, Sell or Store Explosive Device without License	C	Unranked
46.20.0921(3)(a)	Manufacture, Sell or Deliver Forged Driver's License or Identicard	C	Unranked
82.24.570(2)	Manufacture, Sell or Possess Counterfeit Cigarettes	C	Unranked
82.24.570(3)	Manufacture, Sell or Possess Counterfeit Cigarettes (Subsequent Violation)	B	Unranked
69.51A.240	Medical Cannabis – Unlawful Actions	C	Unranked
78.44.330	Mineral Trespass	C	I
9.68A.053(2)	Minor Dealing in Depictions of Another Minor Twelve Years or Younger Engaged in Sexually Explicit Conduct 1	B	Unranked
9.68A.053(3)	Minor Dealing in Depictions of Another Minor Twelve Years or Younger Engaged in Sexually Explicit Conduct 2	B	Unranked
9.68A.053(4)	Minor Financing or Selling Depictions of Another Minor Engaged in Sexually Explicit Conduct	B	Unranked
42.20.070	Misappropriating and Falsifying Accounts by Public Officer	B	Unranked
42.20.090	Misappropriating and Falsifying Accounts by Treasurer	C	Unranked
9.82.030	Misprision of Treason	C	Unranked
29A.08.740	Misuse of Registered Voter Data	C	Unranked
29A.84.150	Misuse or Alteration of Registration Database	C	Unranked
9.45.070	Mock Auction	C	Unranked
9A.83.020	Money Laundering	B	Unranked
19.144.080	Mortgage Fraud	B	III
9A.32.030	Murder 1	A	XV
9A.28.020(3)(a)	Murder 1 – Criminal Attempt	A	XV
9A.28.040(3)(a)	Murder 1 - Criminal Conspiracy	A	XV
9A.28.030(2)	Murder 1 – Criminal Solicitation	A	XV
9A.32.050	Murder 2	A	XIV
9A.28.020(3)(a)	Murder 2 – Criminal Attempt	A	XIV
9A.28.030(2)	Murder 2 – Criminal Solicitation	A	XIV
32.04.110	Mutual Savings Bank - Conceal or Destroy Evidence	B	Unranked
32.04.100	Mutual Savings Bank - Falsify Savings Book, Document or Statement	B	Unranked
32.24.080	Mutual Savings Bank - Transfer Bank Assets after Insolvency	B	Unranked
46.37.675	Negligently Causing Death by Use of a Signal Preemption Device	B	VII

Statute (RCW)	Offense	Class	Seriousness Level
46.37.674	Negligently Causing Substantial Bodily Harm by Use of a Signal Preemption Device	B	III
9A.60.030	Obtaining Signature by Deception or Duress	C	Unranked
46.70.180(5)	Odometer Offense	C	Unranked
40.16.030	Offering False Instrument for Filing or Record	C	Unranked
68.50.140(3)	Opening Graves with Intent to Sell or Remove Personal Effects or Human Remains	C	Unranked
90.56.540	Operation of a Vessel while under the Influence of Intoxicating Liquor or Drugs	C	Unranked
9A.56.350(2)	Organized Retail Theft 1	B	III
9A.56.350(3)	Organized Retail Theft 2	C	II
69.50.406(1)	Over 18 and Deliver Heroin, Methamphetamine, a Narcotic from Schedule I or II, or Flunitrazepam from Schedule IV to Someone under 18	A	DG-III
69.50.406(2)	Over 18 and Deliver Narcotic from Schedule III, IV or V, or a Nonnarcotic, Except Flunitrazepam or Methamphetamine, from Schedule I-V to Someone under 18 and 3 Years Junior	B	DG-III
9.46.215	Ownership or Interest in Gambling Device	C	Unranked
69.30.085	Participation in Shellfish Operation or Activities while License is Denied, Revoked or Suspended	C	Unranked
74.09.240(2)	Paying or Offering Bribes, Kickbacks or Rebates	C	Unranked
9A.72.020	Perjury 1	B	V
9A.72.030	Perjury 2	C	III
9.94.070	Persistent Prison Misbehavior	C	V
82.32.290(4)	Phantomware Violation	C	Unranked
46.61.504(6)	Physical Control of a Vehicle while under the Influence of Intoxicating Liquor or any Drug	C	IV
69.40.030	Placing Poison or other Harmful Object or Substance in Food, Drinks, Medicine or Water	B	Unranked
69.40.020	Poison in Milk or Food Product	C	Unranked
69.50.418	Possess, Purchase, Deliver, Sell, or Possess with Intent to Sell a Tableting Machine or Encapsulating Machine	C	DG-II
9A.58.020	Possessing or Capturing Personal Identification Document	C	Unranked
7.105.460	Possession of a Firearm in Violation of an Extreme Risk Protection Order - 3rd or Subsequent Offense	C	Unranked
9A.56.310	Possession of a Stolen Firearm	B	V
9A.56.068	Possession of a Stolen Vehicle	B	II
9.94.041(2)	Possession of Controlled Substance by Prisoner (County or Local Facility)	C	Unranked
9.94.041(1)	Possession of Controlled Substance by Prisoner (State Facility)	C	Unranked

Statute (RCW)	Offense	Class	Seriousness Level
9.94.045	Possession of Controlled Substance in Prison by Non-prisoner	C	Unranked
9.68A.070(1)	Possession of Depictions of Minor Engaged in Sexually Explicit Conduct 1	B	VI
9.68A.070(2)	Possession of Depictions of Minor Engaged in Sexually Explicit Conduct 2	B	IV
69.50.440	Possession of Ephedrine, Pseudoephedrine or Anhydrous Ammonia with Intent to Manufacture Methamphetamine	B	DG-III
9.40.120	Possession of Incendiary Device	B	III
9.41.190	Possession of Machine Gun, Bump-fire Stock, Undetectable Firearm, or Short-Barreled Shotgun or Rifle	C	III
69.41.350	Possession of Steroids in Excess of 200 tablets or (8) 2cc Bottles without a Valid Prescription	C	Unranked
9A.56.380	Possession of Stolen Mail	C	Unranked
9A.56.150	Possession of Stolen Property 1 (other than Firearm or Motor Vehicle)	B	II
9A.56.160	Possession of Stolen Property 2 (other than Firearm or Motor Vehicle)	C	I
9.94.040(2)	Possession of Weapons by Prisoners (County or Local Facility)	C	Unranked
9.94.040(1)	Possession of Weapons by Prisoners (State Facility)	B	Unranked
9.94.043	Possession of Weapons in Prison by Non-prisoner	B	Unranked
9.94.010	Prison Riot	B	Unranked
9.46.220	Professional Gambling 1	B	Unranked
9.46.221	Professional Gambling 2	C	Unranked
9A.36.060	Promoting a Suicide Attempt	C	Unranked
9.68A.101	Promoting Commercial Sexual Abuse of a Minor	A	XII
67.08.015	Promoting Illegal Boxing, Martial Arts and Wrestling	C	Unranked
9.68.140	Promoting Pornography	C	Unranked
9A.88.070	Promoting Prostitution 1	B	VIII
9A.88.080	Promoting Prostitution 2	C	III
9.68A.102	Promoting Travel for Commercial Sexual Abuse of a Minor	C	Unranked
9A.88.085	Promoting Travel for Prostitution	C	Unranked
29A.84.311	Provides False Information or Conceals or Destroys Candidacy Declaration or Nominating Petition	C	Unranked
26.04.210	Providing False Statements in Affidavits for Marriage	C	Unranked
68.50.140(2)	Purchasing or Receiving Human Remains	C	Unranked
9A.44.040	Rape 1	A	XII
9A.28.020(3)(a)	Rape 1 – Criminal Attempt	A	XII

Statute (RCW)	Offense	Class	Seriousness Level
9A.28.030(2)	Rape 1 – Criminal Solicitation	A	XII
9A.44.050	Rape 2	A	XI
9A.28.020(3)(a)	Rape 2 – Criminal Attempt	A	XI
9A.28.030(2)	Rape 2 – Criminal Solicitation	A	XI
9A.44.060	Rape 3	C	V
9A.44.073	Rape of a Child 1	A	XII
9A.28.020(3)(a)	Rape of a Child 1 – Criminal Attempt	A	XII
9A.28.030(2)	Rape of a Child 1 – Criminal Solicitation	A	XII
9A.44.076	Rape of a Child 2	A	XI
9A.28.020(3)(a)	Rape of a Child 2 – Criminal Attempt	A	XI
9A.28.030(2)	Rape of a Child 2 – Criminal Solicitation	A	XI
9A.44.079	Rape of a Child 3	C	VI
74.09.240(1)	Receiving or Asking for Bribes, Kickbacks or Rebates	C	Unranked
9A.68.030	Receiving or Granting Unlawful Compensation	C	Unranked
81.60.080(2)	Receiving Stolen Railroad Property	C	Unranked
9A.48.040	Reckless Burning 1	C	I
90.56.530	Reckless Operation of a Tank Vessel	C	Unranked
19.110.075(2)	Registration Knowingly not Obtained Prior to Sale of Business Opportunity (Violation of RCW 19.110.050)	B	Unranked
70A.15.3150(3)	Releasing into Ambient Air Hazardous Air Pollutant	C	Unranked
46.12.560	Removal of Sticker on Vehicle Stating Previously Destroyed or Title 1 Loss	C	Unranked
68.50.140(4)	Removal, Disinterment or Mutilation of Human Remains	C	Unranked
68.60.050	Removes, Defaces or Destroys any Historic Grave	C	Unranked
29A.84.540	Removing a Ballot from a Voting Center or Ballot Drop Location	C	Unranked
68.50.140(1)	Removing Human Remains	C	Unranked
9.16.010	Removing Lawful Brands	C	Unranked
9A.76.070(2)(a)	Rendering Criminal Assistance 1	B	V
19.25.020(2)(a)	Reproduction of Sound Recording without Consent of Owner - Recording Fixed before 2/15/1972 (at least 1,000 Recordings or Subsequent Conviction)	B	Unranked
19.25.020(2)(b)	Reproduction of Sound Recording without Consent of Owner - Recording Fixed before 2/15/1972 (more than 100 but less than 1,000 Recordings)	C	Unranked
9A.68.020	Requesting Unlawful Compensation	C	Unranked
9A.52.025	Residential Burglary	B	IV

Statute (RCW)	Offense	Class	Seriousness Level
70.345.030	Retail Sales, Distribution or Delivery Sales of Vapor Products without a License	C	Unranked
9A.56.360(2)	Retail Theft with Special Circumstances 1	B	III
9A.56.360(3)	Retail Theft with Special Circumstances 2	C	II
9A.56.360(4)	Retail Theft with Special Circumstances 3	C	Unranked
9A.56.200	Robbery 1	A	IX
9A.56.210	Robbery 2	B	IV
81.60.080(1)	Sabotaging Rolling Stock	C	Unranked
69.41.030(2)(a)	Sale, Delivery or Possession with Intent to Sell Legend Drug without Prescription	B	Unranked
33.36.040	Savings and Loan Association - Making False Statement of Assets or Liabilities	C	Unranked
33.36.030	Savings and Loan Association - Preference in Case of Insolvency	C	Unranked
33.36.060	Savings and Loan Association - Suppressing, Secreting or Destroying Evidence or Records	C	Unranked
19.290.100	Scrap Processing, Recycling, or Supplying without a License (Second or Subsequent Offense)	C	II
19.60.067(2)	Second-hand Precious Metal Dealer Violations (Subsequent Violation)	C	Unranked
21.20.400	Securities Act Violation	B	III
46.20.0921(2)	Sell or Deliver a Stolen Driver's License or Identicard	C	Unranked
46.37.650(2)(b)	Sell, Install, or Reinstall Counterfeit, Nonfunctional, Damaged, or Previously Deployed Airbag	C	VII
46.37.650(2)(c)	Sell, Install, or Reinstall Counterfeit, Nonfunctional, Damaged, or Previously Deployed Airbag	C	V
27.44.040(2)	Selling Artifacts or Human Remains from Indian Graves	C	Unranked
69.50.410	Selling for Profit (Controlled or Counterfeit) any Controlled Substance in Schedule I	C	DG-III
48.160.080	Sells Guaranteed Asset Protection Waivers without Registration	B	Unranked
9.68A.060(1)	Sending, Bringing into the State Depictions of Minor Engaged in Sexually Explicit Conduct 1	B	VII
9.68A.060(2)	Sending, Bringing into the State Depictions of Minor Engaged in Sexually Explicit Conduct 2	B	V
9.68A.040	Sexual Exploitation of a Minor	B	IX
9A.44.093	Sexual Misconduct with a Minor 1	C	V
9A.44.105	Sexually Violating Human Remains	C	V
9A.76.115	Sexually Violent Predator Escape	A	X
70.155.140	Shipping or Transporting Tobacco Products Ordered Through Mail or Internet	C	Unranked
82.38.270	Special Fuel Violations	C	Unranked

Statute (RCW)	Offense	Class	Seriousness Level
77.15.450(3)(b)	Spotlighting Big Game 1	C	I
9A.46.110	Stalking	B	V
67.70.160	State Lottery Violations Except Lottery Fraud and Unlicensed Lottery Activity	C	Unranked
30B.12.050	State Trust Company – False Entry, Conceal or Destroy Records	B	Unranked
30B.44B.110(2)	State Trust Company – Transfer of Assets	B	Unranked
9.45.020	Substitution of Child	B	Unranked
77.15.670(3)(b)	Suspension of Department Privileges 1	C	I
9A.56.070	Taking Motor Vehicle without Permission 1	B	V
9A.56.075	Taking Motor Vehicle without Permission 2	C	I
9A.72.120	Tampering with a Witness	C	III
29A.84.550	Tampering with Election Materials	C	Unranked
9.40.105	Tampering with Fire Alarm, Emergency Signal, or Fire-fighting Equipment with Intent to Commit Arson	B	Unranked
88.08.020	Tampering with Lights or Signals	B	Unranked
29A.84.560	Tampering with Voting Machine	C	Unranked
9.61.230(2)	Telephone Harassment (with Prior Harassment Conviction or Threat of Death)	C	III
9A.56.030	Theft 1 (Excluding Firearm and Motor Vehicle)	B	II
9A.56.040	Theft 2 (Excluding Firearm and Motor Vehicle)	C	I
9A.56.400(1)	Theft from a Vulnerable Adult 1	B	VI
9A.56.400(2)	Theft from a Vulnerable Adult 2	C	I
9A.56.300	Theft of a Firearm	B	VI
9A.56.065	Theft of a Motor Vehicle	B	II
69.55.010	Theft of Ammonia	C	VIII
9A.56.080	Theft of Livestock 1	B	IV
9A.56.083	Theft of Livestock 2	C	III
9A.56.096(5)(a)	Theft of Rental, Leased, Lease-purchased or Loaned Property (Valued at $5,000 or more)	B	II
9A.56.096(5)(b)	Theft of Rental, Leased, Lease-purchased or Loaned Property (Valued at $750 or more but less than $5,000)	C	I
9A.56.262	Theft of Telecommunication Service	C	Unranked
9A.56.340(2)	Theft with Intent to Resell 1	B	III
9A.56.340(3)	Theft with Intent to Resell 2	C	II
9A.36.090	Threats Against Governor or Family	C	Unranked
9.61.160	Threats to Bomb	B	IV
64.36.210	Timeshare Fraud	C	Unranked
64.36.020(5)(b)	Timeshare Registration Requirement Violation	C	Unranked
9A.68.040	Trading in Public Office	C	Unranked

Statute (RCW)	Offense	Class	Seriousness Level
9A.68.050	Trading in Special Influence	C	Unranked
9A.40.100(1)	Trafficking 1	A	XIV
9A.40.100(3)	Trafficking 2	A	XII
48.30A.015	Trafficking in Insurance Claims (Subsequent Violation)	C	II
9A.82.050	Trafficking in Stolen Property 1	B	IV
9A.82.055	Trafficking in Stolen Property 2	C	III
48.17.063	Transaction of Insurance Business Beyond the Scope of Licensure (Violation of RCW 48.17.060)	B	I
9.08.076	Transferring a Stolen Pet Animal to a Research Institution by a USDA Licensed Dealer	C	Unranked
9.08.074	Transferring Stolen Pet Animal to a Person who Previously Sold a Stolen Pet Animal to a Research Facility	C	Unranked
9.08.072	Transferring Stolen Pet Animal to a Research Institution, not by a USDA Licensed Dealer -2nd or Subsequent Offense	C	Unranked
9.46.240	Transmission or Receiving Gambling Information by Internet	C	Unranked
70A.300.100(1)(a)	Transport, Disposal or Export of Hazardous Waste that Places Another Person in Danger of Injury or Death	B	Unranked
70A.300.100(1)(b)	Transport, Disposal or Export of Hazardous Waste that Places Another Person's Property in Danger of Harm	C	Unranked
82.24.110(2)	Transportation of more than 10,000 Cigarettes without Proper Stamps	C	Unranked
68.60.040(3)	Transports Removed Human Remains, Opens a Grave or Removes Personal Effects from Grave	C	Unranked
9.82.010	Treason	A	Unranked
9.91.150(1)	Tree Spiking	C	Unranked
9.02.120	Unauthorized Abortion	C	Unranked
68.44.060	Unauthorized Loans to Cemetery Authority	C	Unranked
29A.84.545	Unauthorized Removal of Paper Record from Electronic Voting Device	C	Unranked
9.26A.140(1)(a-c)	Unauthorized Sale or Procurement of Telephone Records	C	Unranked
39.62.040	Unauthorized Use of Public Official Facsimile Signature or Seal	B	Unranked
68.05.330	Unfair Practice of Funeral or Cemetery Board	C	Unranked
19.225.110	Uniform Athlete Agent Act Violation	C	Unranked
69.43.070(1)	Unlawful Delivery of Precursor Drug with Intent	B	Unranked
9A.49.020	Unlawful Discharge of a Laser 1	C	Unranked
74.09.290	Unlawful Disclosure of Patient Records or DSHS Information	C	Unranked

Statute (RCW)	Offense	Class	Seriousness Level
9A.56.290(4)(a)	Unlawful Factoring of a Credit or Payment Card Transaction	C	II
9A.56.290(4)(b)	Unlawful Factoring of a Credit or Payment Card Transaction (Subsequent Violation)	B	IV
77.15.630(3)(b)	Unlawful Fish and Shellfish Catch Accounting 1	C	I
69.53.020	Unlawful Fortification of Building for Drug Purposes	C	Unranked
77.15.410(3)(b)	Unlawful Hunting of Big Game 1	C	III
9A.40.040	Unlawful Imprisonment	C	III
9A.56.060(4)	Unlawful Issuance of Checks or Drafts (Value Greater Than $750)	C	I
9A.56.264	Unlawful Manufacture of a Telecommunication Device	C	Unranked
77.140.060(3)	Unlawful Misbranding of Fish or Shellfish 1	C	III
51.48.280(2)	Unlawful Offer or Payment for Kickbacks, Bribes, or Rebates to any Person	C	Unranked
88.46.080(2)(b)	Unlawful Operation of a Covered Vessel (Subsequent Violation)	C	Unranked
90.56.300(2)(b)	Unlawful Operation of Onshore or Offshore Facility (Subsequent Conviction)	C	Unranked
77.15.570(2)	Unlawful Participation on Non-Indians in Indian Fishery	C	II
9.41.040(1)	Unlawful Possession of a Firearm 1	B	VII
9.41.040(2)	Unlawful Possession of a Firearm 2	C	III
9A.56.320(3)	Unlawful Possession of a Personal Identification Device	C	I
9A.56.320(4)	Unlawful Possession of Fictitious Identification	C	I
9A.56.320(5)	Unlawful Possession of Instruments of Financial Fraud	C	I
9A.56.320(2)	Unlawful Possession of Payment Instruments	C	I
2.48.180	Unlawful Practice of Law (Subsequent Violation)	C	II
9.41.115	Unlawful Private Transfer of a Firearm (Subsequent Offense)	C	Unranked
9A.56.320(1)	Unlawful Production of Payment Instruments	C	I
77.15.650(3)(b)	Unlawful Purchase or Use of a License 1	C	II
69.43.070(2)	Unlawful Receipt of Precursor Drug with Intent to Use	B	Unranked
51.48.280(1)	Unlawful Receipt of Remuneration for Kickbacks, Bribes, or Rebates by any Person	C	Unranked
9.91.144	Unlawful Redemption of Food Stamps	C	I
77.15.250(2)(b)	Unlawful Releasing, Planting, Possessing or Placing Deleterious Exotic Wildlife	C	I
9A.56.266	Unlawful Sale of a Telecommunication Device	C	Unranked
9A.56.230	Unlawful Sale of Subscription Television Services	C	Unranked
46.12.750(3)	Unlawful Sale of Vehicle Certificate of Ownership	C	Unranked

Statute (RCW)	Offense	Class	Seriousness Level
18.64.046(7)	Unlawful Selling of Ephedrine, Pseudoephedrine or Phenylpropanolamine by a Wholesaler	C	Unranked
65.12.730	Unlawful Stealing or Carrying Away Certification of Land Registration (Charged as Theft)		
69.55.020	Unlawful Storage of Ammonia	C	VI
19.116.080(1)	Unlawful Subleasing of Motor Vehicle	C	Unranked
77.15.120(3)(b)	Unlawful Taking of Endangered Fish or Wildlife 1	C	III
77.15.770(2)	Unlawful Trade in Shark Fins 1	C	Unranked
77.15.260(3)(b)	Unlawful Trafficking Fish, Shellfish or Wildlife 1	B	III
77.15.260(3)(a)	Unlawful Trafficking Fish, Shellfish or Wildlife 2	C	II
9.91.142(1)	Unlawful Trafficking in Food Stamps	C	I
77.15.135(4)(d)	Unlawful Trafficking in Species with Extinction 1	C	Unranked
48.44.016(3)	Unlawful Transaction of Health Coverage as Health Care Service Contractor	B	IV
48.46.033(3)	Unlawful Transaction of Health Coverage as Health Maintenance Organization	B	IV
48.15.023(3)	Unlawful Transaction of Insurance Business	B	IV
19.116.080(2)	Unlawful Transfer of Ownership of Motor Vehicle	C	Unranked
77.15.530(4)	Unlawful Use of a Nondesignated Vessel	C	III
18.04.370(1)(b)	Unlawful Use of a Professional Title	C	Unranked
69.53.010	Unlawful Use of Building for Drug Purposes	C	DG-I
18.04.370(1)(c)	Unlawful Use of CPA Title after Suspension	C	Unranked
69.53.030	Unlawful Use of Fortified Building	C	Unranked
77.15.811	Unlawful Use of Invasive Species 1	C	Unranked
66.44.120(2)(b)	Unlawful Use of Liquor Board Seal (Third or Subsequent Offense)	C	Unranked
77.15.580(3)(b)	Unlawful Use of Net to Take Fish	C	I
9.46.037	Unlawful Wagers of a Sporting Event, Athletic Event, or Competition	C	Unranked
19.310.120	Unlawfully Engaging in Business as an Exchange Facilitator (RCW 19.310.100(1)-(9))	B	Unranked
82.24.500	Unlawfully Purchase, Sell, Consign or Distribute Cigarettes	C	Unranked
48.102.160(4)	Unlicensed Life Insurance Provider	B	Unranked
67.70.140	Unlicensed Lottery Activity	B	Unranked
48.17.063(2)	Unlicensed Practice as an Insurance Professional	B	IV
18.130.190(7)(b)	Unlicensed Practice of a Profession or Business (Subsequent Violation)	C	II
48.102.160(5)	Unlicensed Settlement Broker	B	Unranked
29A.84.660	Unqualified Person Voting	C	Unranked
29A.84.140	Unqualified Voting Registration	C	Unranked
9.41.360	Unsafe Storage of a Firearm	C	Unranked

Statute (RCW)	Offense	Class	Seriousness Level
19.210.040	Unused Property, Merchants –Prohibited Sales (Third or Subsequent Offense within 5 Years)	C	Unranked
9.41.225	Use of a Machine Gun or Bump-fire Stock in Commission of a Felony	A	VII
46.37.673	Use of a Signal Preemption Device Resulting in Property Damage or less Substantial Bodily Harm	C	Unranked
9.26A.115	Use of Fraudulent Telecommunication Services	B	Unranked
9A.82.080(1),(2)	Use of Proceeds of Criminal Profiteering	B	IV
9A.82.080(3)	Use of Proceeds of Criminal Profiteering – Attempt or Conspiracy	C	Unranked
19.25.030(2)(a)	Use of Recording of Live Performance without Consent of Owner (at least 1,000 Recordings or at least 100 Unauthorized Audiovisual Recordings or Subsequent Offense)	B	Unranked
19.25.030(2)(b)	Use of Recording of Live Performance without Consent of Owner (at least 100 but less than 1,000 Recordings or more than 10 but less than 100 Unauthorized Audiovisual Recording or Subsequent Offense)	C	Unranked
19.144.100(1)	Use or Investment of Proceeds from Mortgage Fraud Activities	B	Unranked
9A.52.095	Vehicle Prowl 1	C	I
9A.52.100(3)	Vehicle Prowling 2 (Third or Subsequent Offense)	C	IV
46.61.522(1)(c)	Vehicular Assault - Disregard for the Safety of Others	B	III
46.61.522(1)(a-b)	Vehicular Assault–Reckless Manner or under the Influence of Intoxicating Liquor or any Drug	B	IV
46.61.520(1)(c)	Vehicular Homicide - Disregard for the Safety of Others	A	VII
46.61.520(1)(b)	Vehicular Homicide – in a Reckless Manner	A	XI
46.61.520(1)(a)	Vehicular Homicide – while under the Influence of Intoxicating Liquor or any Drug	A	XI
9.68A.075(1)	Viewing Depictions of Minor Engaged in Sexually Explicit Conduct 1 (Effective 6/10/2010)	B	IV
9.68A.075(2)	Viewing Depictions of Minor Engaged in Sexually Explicit Conduct 2 (Effective 6/10/2010)	C	Unranked
77.15.550(3)(b)	Violating Commercial Fishing Area or Time 1	C	I
29A.84.230(1)	Violation by Signer – Initiative or Referendum with False Name	C	Unranked
29A.84.240(1)	Violations by Signers – Recall Petition with False Name	B	Unranked
9.46.190	Violations of Fraud or Deceit Regarding Gambling Activity	C	Unranked
29A.84.130	Voter Violation of Registration Law	C	Unranked
29A.84.650(1)	Voting Repeater – more than one Vote at any Election	C	Unranked
9A.44.115	Voyeurism 1	C	II

Statute (RCW)	Offense	Class	Seriousness Level
48.30.220	Willful Destruction, Injury, Secretion of Insured Property	C	Unranked
10.66.090	Willfully Disobeys an Off-limits Order (Subsequent Violation or Enters Protected Against Drug Trafficking Area)	C	Unranked

FELONY INDEX BY CLASSIFICATION

Statute (RCW)	Offense	Class	Seriousness Level
51.48.020(2)	False Information in Industrial Insurance Claim (Charged as Theft)		
65.12.740	False Swearing - Registration of Land Title (Charged as Perjury)		
65.12.730	Unlawful Stealing or Carrying Away Certification of Land Registration (Charged as Theft)		
10.95.020	Aggravated Murder 1	A	XVI
9A.48.020	Arson 1	A	VIII
9A.28.020(3)(a)	Arson 1 – Criminal Attempt	A	VIII
9A.28.030(2)	Arson 1 – Criminal Solicitation	A	VIII
9A.36.011	Assault 1	A	XII
9A.36.021(2)(b)	Assault 2 with a Finding of Sexual Motivation	A	IV
9A.36.120	Assault of a Child 1	A	XII
9A.76.170(3)(a)	Bail Jumping with Murder 1	A	VI
9A.52.020	Burglary 1	A	VII
9A.44.083	Child Molestation 1	A	X
9A.28.020(3)(a)	Child Molestation 1 – Criminal Attempt	A	X
9A.28.030(2)	Child Molestation 1 – Criminal Solicitation	A	X
70.245.200(2)	Coerce Patient to Request Life-ending Medication	A	Unranked
70.74.180	Explosive Devices Prohibited	A	IX
70.245.200(1)	Forging Request for Medication	A	Unranked
9A.32.055	Homicide by Abuse	A	XV
79A.60.050(1)(c)	Homicide by Watercraft - Disregard for the Safety of Others	A	VII
79A.60.050(1)(b)	Homicide by Watercraft – in a Reckless Manner	A	VIII
79A.60.050(1)(a)	Homicide by Watercraft – while under the Influence of Intoxicating Liquor or any Drug	A	IX
9A.44.100(1)(a)	Indecent Liberties - with Forcible Compulsion	A	X
9A.28.020(3)(a)	Indecent Liberties - with Forcible Compulsion – Criminal Attempt	A	X
9A.28.030(2)	Indecent Liberties - with Forcible Compulsion – Criminal Solicitation	A	X
9A.40.020	Kidnapping 1	A	X
9A.40.030(3)(b)	Kidnapping 2 with a Finding of Sexual Motivation	A	V
9A.82.060(1)(a)	Leading Organized Crime – Organizing Criminal Profiteering	A	X
70.74.280(1)	Malicious Explosion of a Substance 1	A	XV
70.74.280(2)	Malicious Explosion of a Substance 2	A	XIII
70.74.270(1)	Malicious Placement of an Explosive 1	A	XIII
9A.32.060	Manslaughter 1	A	XI
9A.32.030	Murder 1	A	XV

Statute (RCW)	Offense	Class	Seriousness Level
9A.28.020(3)(a)	Murder 1 – Criminal Attempt	A	XV
9A.28.040(3)(a)	Murder 1 - Criminal Conspiracy	A	XV
9A.28.030(2)	Murder 1 – Criminal Solicitation	A	XV
9A.32.050	Murder 2	A	XIV
9A.28.020(3)(a)	Murder 2 – Criminal Attempt	A	XIV
9A.28.030(2)	Murder 2 – Criminal Solicitation	A	XIV
69.50.406(1)	Over 18 and Deliver Heroin, Methamphetamine, a Narcotic from Schedule I or II, or Flunitrazepam from Schedule IV to Someone under 18	A	DG-III
9.68A.101	Promoting Commercial Sexual Abuse of a Minor	A	XII
9A.44.040	Rape 1	A	XII
9A.28.020(3)(a)	Rape 1 – Criminal Attempt	A	XII
9A.28.030(2)	Rape 1 – Criminal Solicitation	A	XII
9A.44.050	Rape 2	A	XI
9A.28.020(3)(a)	Rape 2 – Criminal Attempt	A	XI
9A.28.030(2)	Rape 2 – Criminal Solicitation	A	XI
9A.44.073	Rape of a Child 1	A	XII
9A.28.020(3)(a)	Rape of a Child 1 – Criminal Attempt	A	XII
9A.28.030(2)	Rape of a Child 1 – Criminal Solicitation	A	XII
9A.44.076	Rape of a Child 2	A	XI
9A.28.020(3)(a)	Rape of a Child 2 – Criminal Attempt	A	XI
9A.28.030(2)	Rape of a Child 2 – Criminal Solicitation	A	XI
9A.56.200	Robbery 1	A	IX
9A.76.115	Sexually Violent Predator Escape	A	X
9A.40.100(1)	Trafficking 1	A	XIV
9A.40.100(3)	Trafficking 2	A	XII
9.82.010	Treason	A	Unranked
9.41.225	Use of a Machine Gun or Bump-fire Stock in Commission of a Felony	A	VII
46.61.520(1)(c)	Vehicular Homicide - Disregard for the Safety of Others	A	VII
46.61.520(1)(b)	Vehicular Homicide – in a Reckless Manner	A	XI
46.61.520(1)(a)	Vehicular Homicide – while under the Influence of Intoxicating Liquor or any Drug	A	XI
9A.42.060	Abandonment of Dependent Person 1	B	IX
9A.82.030	Advancing Money or Property for Extortionate Extension of Credit	B	V
30A.42.290(3)	Alien Bank or Bureau – Destroy or Secrete Records	B	Unranked
30A.42.290(2)	Alien Bank or Bureau – False Entry, Statements, etc.	B	Unranked
16.52.117(2)(b)	Animal Fighting - Mutilation	B	Unranked
9A.48.030	Arson 2	B	IV

Statute (RCW)	Offense	Class	Seriousness Level
9A.36.021(2)(a)	Assault 2	B	IV
79A.60.060	Assault by Watercraft	B	IV
9A.36.130	Assault of a Child 2	B	IX
9.05.030	Assembly of Saboteurs	B	Unranked
9A.76.170(3)(b)	Bail Jumping with Class A Felony	B	V
30A.12.100	Bank or Trust Company - Destroy or Secrete Records	B	Unranked
30A.12.090	Bank or Trust Company - False Entry, Statements, etc.	B	Unranked
30A.44.120	Bank or Trust Company - Receiving Deposits When Insolvent	B	Unranked
30A.44.110	Bank or Trust Company - Transfer of Assets Prior to Insolvency	B	Unranked
9A.72.100	Bribe Received by Witness	B	IV
9A.68.010	Bribery	B	VI
9A.72.090	Bribing a Witness	B	IV
72.23.300	Bringing Narcotics, Liquor, or Weapons into State Institution or Grounds	B	Unranked
9.47.120	Bunco Steering	B	Unranked
9A.52.030	Burglary 2	B	III
46.87.260	Cab Card Forgery (Effective Until 7/1/2016)	B	Unranked
9.46.180	Causing Person to Violate Gambling Laws	B	Unranked
9A.44.086	Child Molestation 2	B	VII
9A.48.120	Civil Disorder Training	B	VII
9A.68.060	Commercial Bribery	B	IV
9.68A.100	Commercial Sexual Abuse of a Minor	B	VIII
30A.04.240	Commingling of Funds or Securities	B	Unranked
21.30.140	Commodity Transaction Violation	B	Unranked
19.144.100(2)	Control of Real Property Resulting from Mortgage Fraud Activities	B	Unranked
69.50.415	Controlled Substance Homicide	B	DG-III
69.50.4011(2)(a-b)	Create or Deliver a Counterfeit Controlled Substance – Schedule I or II Narcotic or Flunitrazepam or Methamphetamine	B	DG-II
46.87.260	Credential Forgery (Effective 7/1/2016)	B	Unranked
31.12.724(3)	Credit Union - Fraudulent Receipt of Credit Union Deposit	B	Unranked
31.12.724(2)	Credit Union - Transfer of Credit Union Assets Prior to Insolvency	B	Unranked
9A.42.020	Criminal Mistreatment 1	B	X
9.05.060(2)	Criminal Sabotage	B	Unranked
9A.44.160	Custodial Sexual Misconduct 1	B	VII
43.06.230	Damage Property or Cause Personal Injury after State of Emergency Proclaimed	B	Unranked

Statute (RCW)	Offense	Class	Seriousness Level
9.68A.050(1)	Dealing in Depictions of Minor Engaged in Sexually Explicit Conduct 1	B	VII
9.68A.050(2)	Dealing in Depictions of Minor Engaged in Sexually Explicit Conduct 2	B	V
39.44.101	Defraud a Facsimile Signature on Bonds and Coupons	B	Unranked
87.03.200	Defraud Facsimile Signatures on Bonds and Coupons – Irrigation Districts	B	Unranked
19.110.120	Defraud or Provide Misleading or Untrue Documents Related to a Business Opportunity Sale	B	Unranked
9A.61.030	Defrauding a Public Utility 1	B	Unranked
19.48.110(1)(b)	Defrauding an Innkeeper (Value of $75 or more)	B	Unranked
69.50.401(2)(b)	Deliver or Possess with Intent to Deliver - Methamphetamine	B	DG-II
69.52.030(2)	Delivery of Imitation Controlled Substance by Person 18 or Over to Person under 18	B	DG-III
35A.36.040	Designation of Bonds – Violation (Code Cities)	B	Unranked
35.36.040	Designation of Bonds – Violation (First Class Cities)	B	Unranked
9A.76.023(2)(b)	Disarming a Law Enforcement or Corrections Officer and Firearm is Discharged	B	Unranked
19.110.075(2)	Disclosures Knowingly Not Provided at Sale of Business Opportunity (Violation of RCW 19.110.070)	B	Unranked
43.43.856	Divulging Confidential Investigative Information Pertaining to Organized Crime	B	Unranked
9A.36.045	Drive-by Shooting	B	VII
46.61.502(6)	Driving while under the Influence of Intoxicating Liquor or any Drug	B	IV
29A.84.270	Duplication of Name – Conspiracy to Mislead	B	Unranked
29A.84.320	Duplication of Names on Declaration of Candidacy	B	Unranked
43.08.140	Embezzlement by State Treasurer	B	Unranked
9A.42.100	Endangerment with a Controlled Substance	B	IV
61.34.030	Equity Skimming	B	II
9.68.060	Erotic Material (Third or Subsequent Offense)	B	Unranked
9A.76.110	Escape 1	B	IV
48.06.190	Exhibiting False Accounts of Insurer	B	Unranked
9A.56.120	Extortion 1	B	V
9A.82.020	Extortionate Extension of Credit	B	V
9A.82.040	Extortionate Means to Collect Extensions of Credit	B	V
19.25.040(2)(a)	Failure to Disclose Origin of Certain Recordings (at least 100 Recordings or Subsequent Conviction)	B	Unranked
9A.44.132(1)(b)	Failure to Register as a Sex Offender (Third or Subsequent Violation Committed on or after 6/10/2010)	B	II

Statute (RCW)	Offense	Class	Seriousness Level
74.08.100	False Age and Residency Public Assistance Verification	B	Unranked
9.24.050	False Report of Corporation	B	Unranked
9A.84.040(2)(a)	False Reporting 1	B	VII
41.26.062	False Statements or Records to Defraud Law Enforcement Officers and Firefighters Retirement System	B	Unranked
41.32.055(1)	False Statements or Records to Defraud Teachers Retirement System	B	Unranked
46.12.750(1)	False Statements, Illegal Transfers, Alterations or Forgeries of Vehicle Title	B	Unranked
74.08.055(2)	False Verification for Welfare	B	I
69.41.020	Forged Prescription - Legend Drug	B	DG-I
76.36.120	Forgery of Forest Product Mark	B	Unranked
65.12.760	Forgery of Registrar's Signature or Seal	B	Unranked
82.24.100	Forgery or Counterfeit Cigarette Tax Stamp	B	Unranked
19.100.210	Franchise Investment Protection Violation	B	Unranked
9.45.124	Fraud in Measurement of Goods	B	Unranked
67.24.010	Fraud in Sporting Contest	B	Unranked
9.45.270(3)	Fraudulent Filing of Vehicle Report of Sale (Value Exceeds $1,500)	B	Unranked
9.24.020	Fraudulent Issue of Stock, Scrip, etc.	B	Unranked
48.102.160(3)	Fraudulent Life Insurance Settlement	B	Unranked
9.46.160	Gambling without License	B	Unranked
9.46.039	Greyhound Racing	B	Unranked
46.52.020(4)(a)	Hit and Run - Death	B	IX
9.94.030	Holding Hostages or Interfering with Officer's Duty	B	Unranked
9.35.020(2)	Identity Theft 1	B	IV
69.41.040	Illegal Issuance of Legend Drug Prescription	B	Unranked
19.146.235(9)	Impairing Mortgage Broker Investigation	B	Unranked
9A.64.020(1)	Incest 1	B	VI
9A.44.100(1)(b-c)	Indecent Liberties - without Forcible Compulsion	B	VII
9A.44.100(1)(d-f)	Indecent Liberties - without Forcible Compulsion	B	Unranked
9.45.126	Inducing Fraud in Measurement of Goods	B	Unranked
40.16.020	Injury to and Misappropriation of Public Record by Officer	B	Unranked
88.08.050(1)	Injury to Lighthouses or United States Light	B	Unranked
9.24.030	Insolvent Bank Receiving Deposit	B	Unranked
48.06.030	Insurance Solicitation Permit Violation	B	Unranked
69.25.155(2)	Interference with Person Performing Official Duties with a Deadly Weapon	B	Unranked
9A.72.160	Intimidating a Judge	B	VI

Statute (RCW)	Offense	Class	Seriousness Level
9A.72.130	Intimidating a Juror	B	VI
9A.76.180	Intimidating a Public Servant	B	III
9A.72.110	Intimidating a Witness	B	VI
9A.76.140	Introducing Contraband 1	B	VII
9A.40.030(3)(a)	Kidnapping 2	B	V
9A.82.060(1)(b)	Leading Organized Crime - Inciting Criminal Profiteering	B	IX
30A.12.120	Loan to Officer or Employee from Trust Fund	B	Unranked
67.70.130	Lottery Fraud	B	Unranked
70.74.280(3)	Malicious Explosion of a Substance 3	B	X
81.60.070	Malicious Injury to Railroad Property	B	III
9A.48.070	Malicious Mischief 1	B	II
70.74.270(2)	Malicious Placement of an Explosive 2	B	IX
70.74.270(3)	Malicious Placement of an Explosive 3	B	VII
70.74.272(1)(a)	Malicious Placement of an Imitation Device 1	B	XII
9A.32.070	Manslaughter 2	B	VIII
69.50.401(2)(b)	Manufacture Methamphetamine	B	DG-III
69.50.401(2)(b)	Manufacture, Deliver or Possess with Intent to Deliver - Amphetamine	B	DG-II
69.50.401(2)(a)	Manufacture, Deliver or Possess with Intent to Deliver - Narcotics from Schedule I or II or Flunitrazepam from Schedule IV	B	DG-II
82.24.570(3)	Manufacture, Sell or Possess Counterfeit Cigarettes (Subsequent Violation)	B	Unranked
9.68A.053(2)	Minor Dealing in Depictions of Another Minor Twelve Years or Younger Engaged in Sexually Explicit Conduct 1	B	Unranked
9.68A.053(3)	Minor Dealing in Depictions of Another Minor Twelve Years or Younger Engaged in Sexually Explicit Conduct 2	B	Unranked
9.68A.053(4)	Minor Financing or Selling Depictions of Another Minor Engaged in Sexually Explicit Conduct	B	Unranked
42.20.070	Misappropriating and Falsifying Accounts by Public Officer	B	Unranked
9A.83.020	Money Laundering	B	Unranked
19.144.080	Mortgage Fraud	B	III
32.04.110	Mutual Savings Bank - Conceal or Destroy Evidence	B	Unranked
32.04.100	Mutual Savings Bank - Falsify Savings Book, Document or Statement	B	Unranked
32.24.080	Mutual Savings Bank - Transfer Bank Assets after Insolvency	B	Unranked
46.37.675	Negligently Causing Death by Use of a Signal Preemption Device	B	VII
46.37.674	Negligently Causing Substantial Bodily Harm by Use of a Signal Preemption Device	B	III

Statute (RCW)	Offense	Class	Seriousness Level
9A.56.350(2)	Organized Retail Theft 1	B	III
69.50.406(2)	Over 18 and Deliver Narcotic from Schedule III, IV or V, or a Nonnarcotic, Except Flunitrazepam or Methamphetamine, from Schedule I-V to Someone under 18 and 3 Years Junior	B	DG-III
9A.72.020	Perjury 1	B	V
69.40.030	Placing Poison or other Harmful Object or Substance in Food, Drinks, Medicine or Water	B	Unranked
9A.56.310	Possession of a Stolen Firearm	B	V
9A.56.068	Possession of a Stolen Vehicle	B	II
9.68A.070(1)	Possession of Depictions of Minor Engaged in Sexually Explicit Conduct 1	B	VI
9.68A.070(2)	Possession of Depictions of Minor Engaged in Sexually Explicit Conduct 2	B	IV
69.50.440	Possession of Ephedrine, Pseudoephedrine or Anhydrous Ammonia with Intent to Manufacture Methamphetamine	B	DG-III
9.40.120	Possession of Incendiary Device	B	III
9A.56.150	Possession of Stolen Property 1 (other than Firearm or Motor Vehicle)	B	II
9.94.040(1)	Possession of Weapons by Prisoners (State Facility)	B	Unranked
9.94.043	Possession of Weapons in Prison by Non-prisoner	B	Unranked
9.94.010	Prison Riot	B	Unranked
9.46.220	Professional Gambling 1	B	Unranked
9A.88.070	Promoting Prostitution 1	B	VIII
19.110.075(2)	Registration Knowingly not Obtained Prior to Sale of Business Opportunity (Violation of RCW 19.110.050)	B	Unranked
9A.76.070(2)(a)	Rendering Criminal Assistance 1	B	V
19.25.020(2)(a)	Reproduction of Sound Recording without Consent of Owner - Recording Fixed before 2/15/1972 (at least 1,000 Recordings or Subsequent Conviction)	B	Unranked
9A.52.025	Residential Burglary	B	IV
9A.56.360(2)	Retail Theft with Special Circumstances 1	B	III
9A.56.210	Robbery 2	B	IV
69.41.030(2)(a)	Sale, Delivery or Possession with Intent to Sell Legend Drug without Prescription	B	Unranked
21.20.400	Securities Act Violation	B	III
48.160.080	Sells Guaranteed Asset Protection Waivers without Registration	B	Unranked
9.68A.060(1)	Sending, Bringing into the State Depictions of Minor Engaged in Sexually Explicit Conduct 1	B	VII
9.68A.060(2)	Sending, Bringing into the State Depictions of Minor Engaged in Sexually Explicit Conduct 2	B	V
9.68A.040	Sexual Exploitation of a Minor	B	IX

Statute (RCW)	Offense	Class	Seriousness Level
9A.46.110	Stalking	B	V
30B.12.050	State Trust Company – False Entry, Conceal or Destroy Records	B	Unranked
30B.44B.110(2)	State Trust Company – Transfer of Assets	B	Unranked
9.45.020	Substitution of Child	B	Unranked
9A.56.070	Taking Motor Vehicle without Permission 1	B	V
9.40.105	Tampering with Fire Alarm, Emergency Signal, or Fire-fighting Equipment with Intent to Commit Arson	B	Unranked
88.08.020	Tampering with Lights or Signals	B	Unranked
9A.56.030	Theft 1 (Excluding Firearm and Motor Vehicle)	B	II
9A.56.400(1)	Theft from a Vulnerable Adult 1	B	VI
9A.56.300	Theft of a Firearm	B	VI
9A.56.065	Theft of a Motor Vehicle	B	II
9A.56.080	Theft of Livestock 1	B	IV
9A.56.096(5)(a)	Theft of Rental, Leased, Lease-purchased or Loaned Property (Valued at $5,000 or more)	B	II
9A.56.340(2)	Theft with Intent to Resell 1	B	III
9.61.160	Threats to Bomb	B	IV
9A.82.050	Trafficking in Stolen Property 1	B	IV
48.17.063	Transaction of Insurance Business Beyond the Scope of Licensure (Violation of RCW 48.17.060)	B	I
70A.300.100(1)(a)	Transport, Disposal or Export of Hazardous Waste that Places Another Person in Danger of Injury or Death	B	Unranked
39.62.040	Unauthorized Use of Public Official Facsimile Signature or Seal	B	Unranked
69.43.070(1)	Unlawful Delivery of Precursor Drug with Intent to Use	B	Unranked
9A.56.290(4)(b)	Unlawful Factoring of a Credit or Payment Card Transaction (Subsequent Violation)	B	IV
9.41.040(1)	Unlawful Possession of a Firearm 1	B	VII
69.43.070(2)	Unlawful Receipt of Precursor Drug with Intent to Use	B	Unranked
77.15.260(3)(b)	Unlawful Trafficking in Fish, Shellfish or Wildlife 1	B	III
48.44.016(3)	Unlawful Transaction of Health Coverage as Health Care Service Contractor	B	IV
48.46.033(3)	Unlawful Transaction of Health Coverage as Health Maintenance Organization	B	IV
48.15.023(3)	Unlawful Transaction of Insurance Business	B	IV
19.310.120	Unlawfully Engaging in Business as an Exchange Facilitator (RCW 19.310.100(1)-(9))	B	Unranked
48.102.160(4)	Unlicensed Life Insurance Provider	B	Unranked
67.70.140	Unlicensed Lottery Activity	B	Unranked
48.17.063(2)	Unlicensed Practice as an Insurance Professional	B	IV

Statute (RCW)	Offense	Class	Seriousness Level
48.102.160(5)	Unlicensed Settlement Broker	B	Unranked
9.26A.115	Use of Fraudulent Telecommunication Services	B	Unranked
9A.82.080(1),(2)	Use of Proceeds of Criminal Profiteering	B	IV
19.25.030(2)(a)	Use of Recording of Live Performance without Consent of Owner (at least 1,000 Recordings or at least 100 Unauthorized Audiovisual Recordings or Subsequent Offense)	B	Unranked
19.144.100(1)	Use or Investment of Proceeds from Mortgage Fraud Activities	B	Unranked
46.61.522(1)(c)	Vehicular Assault - Disregard for the Safety of Others	B	III
46.61.522(1)(a-b)	Vehicular Assault – in a Reckless Manner or while under the Influence of Intoxicating Liquor or any Drug	B	IV
9.68A.075(1)	Viewing Depictions of Minor Engaged in Sexually Explicit Conduct 1 (Effective 6/10/2010)	B	IV
29A.84.240(1)	Violations by Signers – Recall Petition with False Name	B	Unranked
9A.42.070	Abandonment of Dependent Person 2	C	V
29A.84.680(1)	Absentee Voting Violation	C	Unranked
46.52.130(6)(b)	Abstracts of Driving Records – Intentional Misuse	C	Unranked
20.01.460(2)	Acting as Commission Merchant, Dealer, Cash Buyer without License	C	Unranked
69.52.030(3)	Advertising Imitation Controlled Substances	C	Unranked
46.37.660(2)(c)	Air Bag Diagnostic Systems	C	V
46.37.660(2)(b)	Air Bag Diagnostic Systems (Causing Bodily Injury or Death)	C	VII
46.37.660(1)(c)	Air Bag Replacement Requirements	C	V
46.37.660(1)(b)	Air Bag Replacement Requirements (Causing Bodily Injury or Death)	C	VII
9.41.171	Alien Possession of a Firearm	C	Unranked
9.45.210	Altering Sample or Certificate of Assay	C	Unranked
9A.76.177	Amber Alert – Making False Statements to a Public Servant	C	Unranked
68.64.160	Anatomical Gift - Illegal Financial Gain	C	Unranked
68.64.150	Anatomical Gifts - Illegal Purchase or Sale	C	Unranked
16.52.205(2)	Animal Cruelty 1	C	Unranked
16.52.205(3)	Animal Cruelty 1 - Sexual Conduct or Contact	C	III
16.52.117(2)(a)	Animal Fighting	C	Unranked
9A.36.031(1)(h)	Assault 3 of a Peace Officer with a Projectile Stun Gun	C	IV
9A.36.031(1)(a-g) & (i-j)	Assault 3, excluding Assault 3 of a Peace Officer with a Projectile Stun Gun	C	III
9A.36.041(3)	Assault 4 (Third Domestic Violence Offense)	C	IV
9A.36.140	Assault of a Child 3	C	III

Statute (RCW)	Offense	Class	Seriousness Level
72.23.170	Assist Escape of Mental Patient	C	Unranked
46.61.024	Attempting to Elude Pursuing Police Vehicle	C	I
9A.76.170(3)(c)	Bail Jumping with Class B or C Felony	C	III
9A.64.010	Bigamy	C	Unranked
9.46.155	Bribing to Obtain a License from Public Officials, Employees, Agents	C	Unranked
9.46.1961	Cheating 1	C	IV
9A.64.030(3)(b)	Child Buying	C	Unranked
49.12.410(2)	Child Labor Law Violation – Death/Disability	C	Unranked
9A.44.089	Child Molestation 3	C	V
9A.64.030(3)(a)	Child Selling	C	Unranked
9A.40.110	Coercion of Involuntary Servitude	C	Unranked
9A.82.045	Collection of Unlawful Debt	C	Unranked
77.15.500(3)(b)	Commercial Fishing without a License 1	C	II
19.158.160	Commercial Telephone Solicitor Deception (Value of $250 or more)	C	Unranked
9.68A.090(2)	Communication with Minor for Immoral Purposes (Subsequent Violation or Prior Sex Offense Conviction)	C	III
9A.90.040	Computer Trespass 1	C	II
69.50.465	Conducting or Maintaining a Cannabis Club	C	Unranked
69.50.416	Controlled Substance Label Violation	C	Unranked
9.16.035(4)	Counterfeiting - Endanger Public Health or Safety	C	IV
9.16.035(3)	Counterfeiting – Third Conviction and Value $10,000 or more	C	II
69.50.4011(2)(c-e)	Create or Deliver a Counterfeit Controlled Substance – Schedule I-II Nonnarcotic, Schedule III-V Except Flunitrazepam or Methamphetamine	C	DG-II
9.08.090	Crimes Against Animal Facilities	C	Unranked
9A.46.120	Criminal Gang Intimidation	C	III
9A.60.040	Criminal Impersonation 1	C	Unranked
9A.84.010(2)(b)	Criminal Mischief	C	Unranked
9A.42.030	Criminal Mistreatment 2	C	V
9A.82.160	Criminal Profiteering Lien after Service of Notice	C	Unranked
9A.44.196	Criminal Trespass Against Children	C	Unranked
9A.36.100	Custodial Assault	C	III
9A.40.060	Custodial Interference 1	C	Unranked
9A.40.070	Custodial Interference 2 (Subsequent Offense)	C	Unranked
9A.44.170	Custodial Sexual Misconduct 2	C	V
9A.90.120(2)(b)	Cyber Harassment	C	III
16.08.100(2)	Dangerous Dog Attack (Subsequent Offense)	C	Unranked

Statute (RCW)	Offense	Class	Seriousness Level
16.08.100(3)	Dangerous Dog Attack Resulting in Severe Injury or Death	C	Unranked
22.09.310	Dealing in Unauthorized Warehouse Receipts for Agricultural Commodities	C	Unranked
9A.61.040	Defrauding a Public Utility 2	C	Unranked
69.50.4012	Delivery of a Material in Lieu of a Controlled Substance	C	DG-II
9.41.110(8)	Delivery of Firearm by Dealer to Ineligible Person	C	Unranked
9.41.080	Delivery of Firearms to Ineligible Person	C	Unranked
27.44.040(1)	Destroying, Removing or Defacing Indian Graves	C	Unranked
68.60.040(1)	Destruction of Tomb, Plot, Marker, or Cemetery Property	C	Unranked
9.38.060	Digital Signatures Fraud	C	Unranked
9A.76.023(2)(a)	Disarming a Law Enforcement or Corrections Officer	C	Unranked
9A.86.010	Disclosing Intimate Images	C	Unranked
69.50.402	Dispensing Violation (VUCSA)	C	Unranked
82.26.190	Distributors and Retailer of Tobacco Products License Violation	C	Unranked
27.53.060	Disturbing Archaeological Resources or Site	C	Unranked
7.105.450, 10.99.040, 10.99.050, 26.09.300, 26.26B.050, or 26.52.070	Domestic Violence Court Order Violation	C	V
29A.84.655	Election Officer Permits Repeat Vote	C	Unranked
29A.84.720	Election Officers – Violation	C	Unranked
29A.84.030	Election or Mail Ballot Violation	C	Unranked
19.300.020	Electronic Communication Devices – Illegal Scanning	C	Unranked
9A.90.060	Electronic Data Service Interference	C	II
9A.90.080	Electronic Data Tampering 1	C	II
9A.90.100	Electronic Data Theft	C	II
79A.60.090	Eluding a Law Enforcement Vessel	C	Unranked
18.39.350	Embalmers/Funeral Directors Violation	C	Unranked
46.80.020(b)	Engage in Business of Wrecking Vehicles without a License (Subsequent Offense)	C	Unranked
51.48.103(2)	Engaging in Business after Certificate of Coverage Revocation	C	Unranked
70.345.090	Engaging in Delivery Sales of Vapor Products without a License or Proper Shipping Documentation	C	Unranked
77.15.620(3)(b)	Engaging in Fish Dealing Activity Unlicensed 1	C	II
9A.76.120	Escape 2	C	III

Statute (RCW)	Offense	Class	Seriousness Level
9A.76.130(3)(b)	Escape 3 (Third or Subsequent Offense)	C	Unranked
72.09.310	Escape from Community Custody	C	II
51.48.020(1)	Evading Industrial Insurance Premiums	C	Unranked
82.42.085	Evading the Collection of Aircraft Fuel Tax	C	Unranked
74.09.260	Excessive Charges, Payments	C	Unranked
9A.56.130	Extortion 2	C	III
19.25.040(2)(b)	Failure to Disclose Origin of Certain Recordings (more than 10 but less than 100 Recordings)	C	Unranked
36.18.170	Failure to Pay Over Fees to County Treasurer	C	Unranked
9A.44.132(3)	Failure to Register as a Kidnapping Offender	C	Unranked
9A.44.132(1)(a)	Failure to Register as a Sex Offender (First Violation)	C	Unranked
9A.44.132(1)(a)	Failure to Register as a Sex Offender (Second Violation Committed on or after 6/10/2010)	C	II
19.146.050	Failure to Use a Trust Account	C	Unranked
19.142.080	Failure to Use a Trust Account or Furnish Bond for Health Studio	C	Unranked
38.42.050	False Affidavit under Service Member Civil Relief Act	C	Unranked
42.24.100	False Claim from Municipal Corporation (Charged as Perjury 2)	C	Unranked
42.17A.750	False Documents Registered with Public Disclosure Commission	C	Unranked
48.30.230	False Insurance Claims (Value in Excess of $1,500)	C	Unranked
9A.84.040(2)(b)	False Reporting 2	C	III
74.09.230	False Statement for Medical Assistance	C	Unranked
69.43.080	False Statement in Report of Precursor Drugs	C	Unranked
9.38.015	False Statement of Identity to a Financial Institution - 3rd or Subsequent Offense	C	Unranked
51.48.270	False Statement or Concealing Information by Employee	C	Unranked
82.32.290(2)	False Statement to Department of Revenue	C	Unranked
19.230.300	False Statement, Misrepresentation or False Certification of Uniform Money Services Record	C	Unranked
74.09.250	False Statements Regarding Institutions, Facilities	C	Unranked
26.20.030	Family Abandonment	C	Unranked
69.50.403	Forged Prescription for a Controlled Substance	C	DG-I
9A.60.020	Forgery	C	I
29A.84.711	Fraud in Certification of Nomination or Ballot	C	Unranked
9.45.170	Fraud in Liquor Warehouse Receipts	C	Unranked
9.26A.110(3)	Fraud in Obtaining Telecommunications Services (Value Exceeds $250)	C	Unranked
9A.60.060	Fraudulent Creation or Revocation of Mental Health Advance Directive	C	I

Statute (RCW)	Offense	Class	Seriousness Level
76.48.141(1)(a)	Fraudulent Document as Specialized Forest Products Permit, Sales Invoice, Bill of Lading, etc.	C	Unranked
76.48.141(2)	Fraudulent Document for Specialized Forest Products Buyer	C	Unranked
9.45.270(2)	Fraudulent Filing of Vehicle Report of Sale (Value Exceeds $250)	C	Unranked
65.12.750	Fraudulent Procurement or False Entry on Land Title Registration	C	Unranked
76.48.141(1)(b)	Fraudulent Representation of Authority to Harvest Specialized Forest Products	C	Unranked
9A.46.020(2)(b)	Harassment	C	III
9A.76.200	Harming a Police Dog/Horse or an Accelerant Detection Dog	C	Unranked
9A.36.080	Hate Crime Offense	C	IV
28B.10.901(2)(b)	Hazing	C	III
48.80.030	Health Care False Claims	C	II
29A.84.620	Hindering or Bribing Voter	C	Unranked
46.52.020(4)(b)	Hit and Run - Injury	C	IV
79A.60.200(3)	Hit and Run with Vessel - Injury Accident	C	IV
9.35.020(3)	Identity Theft 2	C	II
9.16.020	Imitating Lawful Brands with Intent	C	Unranked
9.35.010	Improperly Obtaining Financial Information	C	II
9A.64.020(2)	Incest 2	C	V
9A.88.010(2)(c)	Indecent Exposure to a Person Age 14 or Older (Subsequent Conviction or has Prior Sex Offense Conviction)	C	Unranked
9A.88.010(2)(c)	Indecent Exposure to a Person under Age 14 (Subsequent Sex Offense)	C	IV
9A.82.070	Influencing Outcome of Sporting Event	C	IV
40.16.010	Injury to a Public Record	C	Unranked
9.91.170(5)	Intentional Infliction, Injury or Death to a Dog Guide or Service Animal	C	Unranked
9.91.175(3)	Intentionally Injures, Disables or Causes Death of an On-Duty Search and Rescue Dog	C	Unranked
9.73.230	Intercepting, Transmitting or Recording Conversations Concerning Controlled Substances	C	Unranked
69.25.155(1)	Interference with Person Performing Official Duties	C	Unranked
70.74.275	Intimidation or Harassment with an Explosive	C	Unranked
9A.76.150	Introducing Contraband 2	C	III
69.50.4015	Involving a Minor in Drug Dealing	C	DG-III
9A.60.070	Issuing a False Academic Credential	C	Unranked
16.52.320	Kill or Cause Substantial Harm with Malice to Livestock	C	Unranked
82.87.140	Knowingly Attempts to Evade Capital Gains Tax Payment	C	Unranked

Statute (RCW)	Offense	Class	Seriousness Level
46.70.021	Licensing Violation for Car Dealers or Manufacturers (Subsequent Violation)	C	Unranked
9A.40.090	Luring of a Child or a Person with a Developmental Disability	C	Unranked
9A.56.370	Mail Theft	C	Unranked
9.47.090	Maintaining a Bucket Shop	C	Unranked
69.50.402(1)(f)	Maintaining a Dwelling or Place for Controlled Substances	C	DG-II
31.12.850(2)	Make a False Statement or Entry in Credit Union Books	C	Unranked
9.45.220	Making False Sample or Assay of Ore	C	Unranked
9A.48.080	Malicious Mischief 2	C	I
70.74.272(1)(b)	Malicious Placement of an Imitation Device 2	C	VI
9.62.010(1)	Malicious Prosecution	C	Unranked
9.45.260	Malicious Sprinkler Contractor Work	C	Unranked
9.41.190	Manufacture of Untraceable Firearm with Intent to Sell	C	III
9.41.325	Manufacture or Assembly of an Undetectable Firearm or Untraceable Firearm	C	III
46.37.650(1)(c)	Manufacture or Import Counterfeit, Nonfunctional, Damaged, or Previously Deployed Air Bag	C	V
46.37.650(1)(b)	Manufacture or Import Counterfeit, Nonfunctional, Damaged, or Previously Deployed Air Bag (Causing Bodily Injury or Death)	C	VII
69.50.401(2)(c)	Manufacture, Deliver or Possess with Intent to Deliver - Cannabis	C	DG-I
69.50.401(2)(c-e)	Manufacture, Deliver or Possess with Intent to Deliver - Narcotics from Schedule III, IV, or V or Nonnarcotics from Schedule I-V (except Cannabis, Amphetamine, Methamphetamine, or Flunitrazepam)	C	DG-II
69.52.030(1)	Manufacture, Distribute or Possess with Intent to Distribute an Imitation Controlled Substance	C	DG-II
70.74.022(1)	Manufacture, Purchase, Sell or Store Explosive Device without License	C	Unranked
46.20.0921(3)(a)	Manufacture, Sell or Deliver Forged Driver's License or Identicard	C	Unranked
82.24.570(2)	Manufacture, Sell or Possess Counterfeit Cigarettes	C	Unranked
69.51A.240	Medical Cannabis – Unlawful Actions	C	Unranked
78.44.330	Mineral Trespass	C	I
42.20.090	Misappropriating and Falsifying Accounts by Treasurer	C	Unranked
9.82.030	Misprision of Treason	C	Unranked
29A.08.740	Misuse of Registered Voter Data	C	Unranked
29A.84.150	Misuse or Alteration of Registration Database	C	Unranked
9.45.070	Mock Auction	C	Unranked

Statute (RCW)	Offense	Class	Seriousness Level
9A.60.030	Obtaining Signature by Deception or Duress	C	Unranked
46.70.180(5)	Odometer Offense	C	Unranked
40.16.030	Offering False Instrument for Filing or Record	C	Unranked
68.50.140(3)	Opening Graves with Intent to Sell or Remove Personal Effects or Human Remains	C	Unranked
90.56.540	Operation of a Vessel while under the Influence of Intoxicating Liquor or Drugs	C	Unranked
9A.56.350(3)	Organized Retail Theft 2	C	II
9.46.215	Ownership or Interest in Gambling Device	C	Unranked
69.30.085	Participation in Shellfish Operation or Activities while License is Denied, Revoked or Suspended	C	Unranked
74.09.240(2)	Paying or Offering Bribes, Kickbacks or Rebates	C	Unranked
9A.72.030	Perjury 2	C	III
9.94.070	Persistent Prison Misbehavior	C	V
82.32.290(4)	Phantomware Violation	C	Unranked
46.61.504(6)	Physical Control of a Vehicle while under the Influence of Intoxicating Liquor or any Drug	C	IV
69.40.020	Poison in Milk or Food Product	C	Unranked
69.50.418	Possess, Purchase, Deliver, Sell, or Possess with Intent to Sell a Tableting Machine or Encapsulating Machine	C	DG-II
9A.58.020	Possessing or Capturing Personal Identification Document	C	Unranked
7.105.460	Possession of a Firearm in Violation of an Extreme Risk Protection Order - 3rd or Subsequent Offense	C	Unranked
9.94.041(2)	Possession of Controlled Substance by Prisoner (County or Local Facility)	C	Unranked
9.94.041(1)	Possession of Controlled Substance by Prisoner (State Facility)	C	Unranked
9.94.045	Possession of Controlled Substance in Prison by Non-prisoner	C	Unranked
9.41.190	Possession of Machine Gun, Bump-fire Stock, Undetectable Firearm, or Short-Barreled Shotgun or Rifle	C	III
69.41.350	Possession of Steroids in Excess of 200 tablets or (8) 2cc Bottles without a Valid Prescription	C	Unranked
9A.56.380	Possession of Stolen Mail	C	Unranked
9A.56.160	Possession of Stolen Property 2 (other than Firearm or Motor Vehicle)	C	I
9.94.040(2)	Possession of Weapons by Prisoners (County or Local Facility)	C	Unranked
9.46.221	Professional Gambling 2	C	Unranked
9A.36.060	Promoting a Suicide Attempt	C	Unranked
67.08.015	Promoting Illegal Boxing, Martial Arts and Wrestling	C	Unranked
9.68.140	Promoting Pornography	C	Unranked

Statute (RCW)	Offense	Class	Seriousness Level
9A.88.080	Promoting Prostitution 2	C	III
9.68A.102	Promoting Travel for Commercial Sexual Abuse of a Minor	C	Unranked
9A.88.085	Promoting Travel for Prostitution	C	Unranked
29A.84.311	Provides False Information or Conceals or Destroys Candidacy Declaration or Nominating Petition	C	Unranked
26.04.210	Providing False Statements in Affidavits for Marriage	C	Unranked
68.50.140(2)	Purchasing or Receiving Human Remains	C	Unranked
9A.44.060	Rape 3	C	V
9A.44.079	Rape of a Child 3	C	VI
74.09.240(1)	Receiving or Asking for Bribes, Kickbacks or Rebates	C	Unranked
9A.68.030	Receiving or Granting Unlawful Compensation	C	Unranked
81.60.080(2)	Receiving Stolen Railroad Property	C	Unranked
9A.48.040	Reckless Burning 1	C	I
90.56.530	Reckless Operation of a Tank Vessel	C	Unranked
70A.15.3150(3)	Releasing into Ambient Air Hazardous Air Pollutant	C	Unranked
46.12.560	Removal of Sticker on Vehicle Stating Previously Destroyed or Title 1 Loss	C	Unranked
68.50.140(4)	Removal, Disinterment or Mutilation of Human Remains	C	Unranked
68.60.050	Removes, Defaces or Destroys any Historic Grave	C	Unranked
29A.84.540	Removing a Ballot from a Voting Center or Ballot Drop Location	C	Unranked
68.50.140(1)	Removing Human Remains	C	Unranked
9.16.010	Removing Lawful Brands	C	Unranked
19.25.020(2)(b)	Reproduction of Sound Recording without Consent of Owner - Recording Fixed before 2/15/1972 (more than 100 but less than 1,000 Recordings)	C	Unranked
9A.68.020	Requesting Unlawful Compensation	C	Unranked
70.345.030	Retail Sales, Distribution or Delivery Sales of Vapor Products without a License	C	Unranked
9A.56.360(3)	Retail Theft with Special Circumstances 2	C	II
9A.56.360(4)	Retail Theft with Special Circumstances 3	C	Unranked
81.60.080(1)	Sabotaging Rolling Stock	C	Unranked
33.36.040	Savings and Loan Association - Making False Statement of Assets or Liabilities	C	Unranked
33.36.030	Savings and Loan Association - Preference in Case of Insolvency	C	Unranked
33.36.060	Savings and Loan Association - Suppressing, Secreting or Destroying Evidence or Records	C	Unranked
19.290.100	Scrap Processing, Recycling, or Supplying without a License (Second or Subsequent Offense)	C	II

Statute (RCW)	Offense	Class	Seriousness Level
19.60.067(2)	Second-hand Precious Metal Dealer Violations (Subsequent Violation)	C	Unranked
46.20.0921(2)	Sell or Deliver a Stolen Driver's License or Identicard	C	Unranked
46.37.650(2)(b)	Sell, Install, or Reinstall Counterfeit, Nonfunctional, Damaged, or Previously Deployed Airbag	C	VII
46.37.650(2)(c)	Sell, Install, or Reinstall Counterfeit, Nonfunctional, Damaged, or Previously Deployed Airbag	C	V
27.44.040(2)	Selling Artifacts or Human Remains from Indian Graves	C	Unranked
69.50.410	Selling for Profit (Controlled or Counterfeit) any Controlled Substance in Schedule I	C	DG-III
9A.44.093	Sexual Misconduct with a Minor 1	C	V
9A.44.105	Sexually Violating Human Remains	C	V
70.155.140	Shipping or Transporting Tobacco Products Ordered Through Mail or Internet	C	Unranked
82.38.270	Special Fuel Violations	C	Unranked
77.15.450(3)(b)	Spotlighting Big Game 1	C	I
67.70.160	State Lottery Violations Except Lottery Fraud and Unlicensed Lottery Activity	C	Unranked
77.15.670(3)(b)	Suspension of Department Privileges 1	C	I
9A.56.075	Taking Motor Vehicle without Permission 2	C	I
9A.72.120	Tampering with a Witness	C	III
29A.84.550	Tampering with Election Materials	C	Unranked
29A.84.560	Tampering with Voting Machine	C	Unranked
9.61.230(2)	Telephone Harassment (with Prior Harassment Conviction or Threat of Death)	C	III
9A.56.040	Theft 2 (Excluding Firearm and Motor Vehicle)	C	I
9A.56.400(2)	Theft from a Vulnerable Adult 2	C	I
69.55.010	Theft of Ammonia	C	VIII
9A.56.083	Theft of Livestock 2	C	III
9A.56.096(5)(b)	Theft of Rental, Leased, Lease-purchased or Loaned Property (Valued at $750 or more but less than $5,000)	C	I
9A.56.262	Theft of Telecommunication Service	C	Unranked
9A.56.340(3)	Theft with Intent to Resell 2	C	II
9A.36.090	Threats Against Governor or Family	C	Unranked
64.36.210	Timeshare Fraud	C	Unranked
64.36.020(5)(b)	Timeshare Registration Requirement Violation	C	Unranked
9A.68.040	Trading in Public Office	C	Unranked
9A.68.050	Trading in Special Influence	C	Unranked
48.30A.015	Trafficking in Insurance Claims (Subsequent Violation)	C	II
9A.82.055	Trafficking in Stolen Property 2	C	III

Statute (RCW)	Offense	Class	Seriousness Level
9.08.076	Transferring a Stolen Pet Animal to a Research Institution by a USDA Licensed Dealer	C	Unranked
9.08.074	Transferring Stolen Pet Animal to a Person who Previously Sold a Stolen Pet Animal to a Research Facility	C	Unranked
9.08.072	Transferring Stolen Pet Animal to a Research Institution, not by a USDA Licensed Dealer -2nd or Subsequent Offense	C	Unranked
9.46.240	Transmission or Receiving Gambling Information by Internet	C	Unranked
70A.300.100(1)(b)	Transport, Disposal or Export of Hazardous Waste that Places Another Person's Property in Danger of Harm	C	Unranked
82.24.110(2)	Transportation of more than 10,000 Cigarettes without Proper Stamps	C	Unranked
68.60.040(3)	Transports Removed Human Remains, Opens a Grave or Removes Personal Effects from Grave	C	Unranked
9.91.150(1)	Tree Spiking	C	Unranked
9.02.120	Unauthorized Abortion	C	Unranked
68.44.060	Unauthorized Loans to Cemetery Authority	C	Unranked
29A.84.545	Unauthorized Removal of Paper Record from Electronic Voting Device	C	Unranked
9.26A.140(1)(a),(b), or (c)	Unauthorized Sale or Procurement of Telephone Records	C	Unranked
68.05.330	Unfair Practice of Funeral or Cemetery Board	C	Unranked
19.225.110	Uniform Athlete Agent Act Violation	C	Unranked
9A.49.020	Unlawful Discharge of a Laser 1	C	Unranked
74.09.290	Unlawful Disclosure of Patient Records or DSHS Information	C	Unranked
9A.56.290(4)(a)	Unlawful Factoring of a Credit or Payment Card Transaction	C	II
77.15.630(3)(b)	Unlawful Fish and Shellfish Catch Accounting 1	C	I
69.53.020	Unlawful Fortification of Building for Drug Purposes	C	Unranked
77.15.410(3)(b)	Unlawful Hunting of Big Game 1	C	III
9A.40.040	Unlawful Imprisonment	C	III
9A.56.060(4)	Unlawful Issuance of Checks or Drafts (Value Greater Than $750)	C	I
9A.56.264	Unlawful Manufacture of a Telecommunication Device	C	Unranked
77.140.060(3)	Unlawful Misbranding of Fish or Shellfish 1	C	III
51.48.280(2)	Unlawful Offer or Payment for Kickbacks, Bribes, or Rebates to any Person	C	Unranked
88.46.080(2)(b)	Unlawful Operation of a Covered Vessel (Subsequent Violation)	C	Unranked
90.56.300(2)(b)	Unlawful Operation of Onshore or Offshore Facility (Subsequent Conviction)	C	Unranked

Statute (RCW)	Offense	Class	Seriousness Level
77.15.570(2)	Unlawful Participation on Non-Indians in Indian Fishery	C	II
9.41.040(2)	Unlawful Possession of a Firearm 2	C	III
9A.56.320(3)	Unlawful Possession of a Personal Identification Device	C	I
9A.56.320(4)	Unlawful Possession of Fictitious Identification	C	I
9A.56.320(5)	Unlawful Possession of Instruments of Financial Fraud	C	I
9A.56.320(2)	Unlawful Possession of Payment Instruments	C	I
2.48.180	Unlawful Practice of Law (Subsequent Violation)	C	II
9.41.115	Unlawful Private Transfer of a Firearm (Subsequent Offense)	C	Unranked
9A.56.320(1)	Unlawful Production of Payment Instruments	C	I
77.15.650(3)(b)	Unlawful Purchase or Use of a License 1	C	II
51.48.280(1)	Unlawful Receipt of Remuneration for Kickbacks, Bribes, or Rebates by any Person	C	Unranked
9.91.144	Unlawful Redemption of Food Stamps	C	I
77.15.250(2)(b)	Unlawful Releasing, Planting, Possessing or Placing Deleterious Exotic Wildlife	C	I
9A.56.266	Unlawful Sale of a Telecommunication Device	C	Unranked
9A.56.230	Unlawful Sale of Subscription Television Services	C	Unranked
46.12.750(3)	Unlawful Sale of Vehicle Certificate of Ownership	C	Unranked
18.64.046(7)	Unlawful Selling of Ephedrine, Pseudoephedrine or Phenylpropanolamine by a Wholesaler	C	Unranked
69.55.020	Unlawful Storage of Ammonia	C	VI
19.116.080(1)	Unlawful Subleasing of Motor Vehicle	C	Unranked
77.15.120(3)(b)	Unlawful Taking of Endangered Fish or Wildlife 1	C	III
77.15.770(2)	Unlawful Trade in Shark Fins 1	C	Unranked
77.15.260(3)(a)	Unlawful Trafficking in Fish, Shellfish or Wildlife 2	C	II
9.91.142(1)	Unlawful Trafficking in Food Stamps	C	I
77.15.135(4)(d)	Unlawful Trafficking in Species with Extinction 1	C	Unranked
19.116.080(2)	Unlawful Transfer of Ownership of Motor Vehicle	C	Unranked
77.15.530(4)	Unlawful Use of a Nondesignated Vessel	C	III
18.04.370(1)(b)	Unlawful Use of a Professional Title	C	Unranked
69.53.010	Unlawful Use of Building for Drug Purposes	C	DG-I
18.04.370(1)(c)	Unlawful Use of CPA Title after Suspension	C	Unranked
69.53.030	Unlawful Use of Fortified Building	C	Unranked
77.15.811	Unlawful Use of Invasive Species 1	C	Unranked
66.44.120(2)(b)	Unlawful Use of Liquor Board Seal (Third or Subsequent Offense)	C	Unranked
77.15.580(3)(b)	Unlawful Use of Net to Take Fish	C	I
9.46.037	Unlawful Wagers of a Sporting Event, Athletic Event, or Competition	C	Unranked

Statute (RCW)	Offense	Class	Seriousness Level
82.24.500	Unlawfully Purchase, Sell, Consign or Distribute Cigarettes	C	Unranked
18.130.190(7)(b)	Unlicensed Practice of a Profession or Business (Subsequent Violation)	C	II
29A.84.660	Unqualified Person Voting	C	Unranked
29A.84.140	Unqualified Voting Registration	C	Unranked
9.41.360	Unsafe Storage of a Firearm	C	Unranked
19.210.040	Unused Property, Merchants –Prohibited Sales (Third or Subsequent Offense within 5 Years)	C	Unranked
46.37.673	Use of a Signal Preemption Device Resulting in Property Damage or less Substantial Bodily Harm	C	Unranked
9A.82.080(3)	Use of Proceeds of Criminal Profiteering – Attempt or Conspiracy	C	Unranked
19.25.030(2)(b)	Use of Recording of Live Performance without Consent of Owner (at least 100 but less than 1,000 Recordings or more than 10 but less than 100 Unauthorized Audiovisual Recording or Subsequent Offense)	C	Unranked
9A.52.095	Vehicle Prowl 1	C	I
9A.52.100(3)	Vehicle Prowling 2 (Third or Subsequent Offense)	C	IV
9.68A.075(2)	Viewing Depictions of Minor Engaged in Sexually Explicit Conduct 2 (Effective 6/10/2010)	C	Unranked
77.15.550(3)(b)	Violating Commercial Fishing Area or Time 1	C	I
29A.84.230(1)	Violation by Signer – Initiative or Referendum with False Name	C	Unranked
9.46.190	Violations of Fraud or Deceit Regarding Gambling Activity	C	Unranked
29A.84.130	Voter Violation of Registration Law	C	Unranked
29A.84.650(1)	Voting Repeater – more than one Vote at any Election	C	Unranked
9A.44.115	Voyeurism 1	C	II
48.30.220	Willful Destruction, Injury, Secretion of Insured Property	C	Unranked
10.66.090	Willfully Disobeys an Off-limits Order (Subsequent Violation or Enters Protected Against Drug Trafficking Area)	C	Unranked

FELONY INDEX BY RCW

Statute (RCW)	Offense	Class	Seriousness Level
2.48.180	Unlawful Practice of Law (Subsequent Violation)	C	II
7.105.450*	Domestic Violence Court Order Violation	C	V
7.105.460	Possession of a Firearm in Violation of an Extreme Risk Protection Order - 3rd or Subsequent Offense	C	Unranked
9.02.120	Unauthorized Abortion	C	Unranked
9.05.030	Assembly of Saboteurs	B	Unranked
9.05.060(2)	Criminal Sabotage	B	Unranked
9.08.072	Transferring Stolen Pet Animal to a Research Institution, not by a USDA Licensed Dealer -2nd or Subsequent Offense	C	Unranked
9.08.074	Transferring Stolen Pet Animal to a Person who Previously Sold a Stolen Pet Animal to a Research Facility	C	Unranked
9.08.076	Transferring a Stolen Pet Animal to a Research Institution by a USDA Licensed Dealer	C	Unranked
9.08.090	Crimes Against Animal Facilities	C	Unranked
9.16.010	Removing Lawful Brands	C	Unranked
9.16.020	Imitating Lawful Brands with Intent	C	Unranked
9.16.035(3)	Counterfeiting – Third Conviction and Value $10,000 or more	C	II
9.16.035(4)	Counterfeiting - Endanger Public Health or Safety	C	IV
9.24.020	Fraudulent Issue of Stock, Scrip, etc.	B	Unranked
9.24.030	Insolvent Bank Receiving Deposit	B	Unranked
9.24.050	False Report of Corporation	B	Unranked
9.26A.110(3)	Fraud in Obtaining Telecommunications Services (Value Exceeds $250)	C	Unranked
9.26A.115	Use of Fraudulent Telecommunication Services	B	Unranked
9.26A.140(1)(a-c)	Unauthorized Sale or Procurement of Telephone Records	C	Unranked
9.35.010	Improperly Obtaining Financial Information	C	II
9.35.020(2)	Identity Theft 1	B	IV
9.35.020(3)	Identity Theft 2	C	II
9.38.015	False Statement of Identity to a Financial Institution - 3rd or Subsequent Offense	C	Unranked
9.38.060	Digital Signatures Fraud	C	Unranked
9.40.105	Tampering with Fire Alarm, Emergency Signal, or Fire-fighting Equipment with Intent to Commit Arson	B	Unranked
9.40.120	Possession of Incendiary Device	B	III
9.41.040(1)	Unlawful Possession of a Firearm 1	B	VII
9.41.040(2)	Unlawful Possession of a Firearm 2	C	III

Statute (RCW)	Offense	Class	Seriousness Level
9.41.080	Delivery of Firearms to Ineligible Person	C	Unranked
9.41.110(8)	Delivery of Firearm by Dealer to Ineligible Person	C	Unranked
9.41.115	Unlawful Private Transfer of a Firearm (Subsequent Offense)	C	Unranked
9.41.171	Alien Possession of a Firearm	C	Unranked
9.41.190	Manufacture of Untraceable Firearm with Intent to Sell	C	III
9.41.190	Possession of Machine Gun, Bump-fire Stock, Undetectable Firearm, or Short-Barreled Shotgun or Rifle	C	III
9.41.225	Use of a Machine Gun or Bump-fire Stock in Commission of a Felony	A	VII
9.41.325	Manufacture or Assembly of an Undetectable Firearm or Untraceable Firearm	C	III
9.41.360	Unsafe Storage of a Firearm	C	Unranked
9.45.020	Substitution of Child	B	Unranked
9.45.070	Mock Auction	C	Unranked
9.45.124	Fraud in Measurement of Goods	B	Unranked
9.45.126	Inducing Fraud in Measurement of Goods	B	Unranked
9.45.170	Fraud in Liquor Warehouse Receipts	C	Unranked
9.45.210	Altering Sample or Certificate of Assay	C	Unranked
9.45.220	Making False Sample or Assay of Ore	C	Unranked
9.45.260	Malicious Sprinkler Contractor Work	C	Unranked
9.45.270(2)	Fraudulent Filing of Vehicle Report of Sale (Value Exceeds $250)	C	Unranked
9.45.270(3)	Fraudulent Filing of Vehicle Report of Sale (Value Exceeds $1,500)	B	Unranked
9.46.037	Unlawful Wagers of a Sporting Event, Athletic Event, or Competition	C	Unranked
9.46.039	Greyhound Racing	B	Unranked
9.46.155	Bribing to Obtain a License from Public Officials, Employees, Agents	C	Unranked
9.46.160	Gambling without License	B	Unranked
9.46.180	Causing Person to Violate Gambling Laws	B	Unranked
9.46.190	Violations of Fraud or Deceit Regarding Gambling Activity	C	Unranked
9.46.1961	Cheating 1	C	IV
9.46.215	Ownership or Interest in Gambling Device	C	Unranked
9.46.220	Professional Gambling 1	B	Unranked
9.46.221	Professional Gambling 2	C	Unranked
9.46.240	Transmission or Receiving Gambling Information by Internet	C	Unranked
9.47.090	Maintaining a Bucket Shop	C	Unranked
9.47.120	Bunco Steering	B	Unranked
9.61.160	Threats to Bomb	B	IV

Statute (RCW)	Offense	Class	Seriousness Level
9.61.230(2)	Telephone Harassment (with Prior Harassment Conviction or Threat of Death)	C	III
9.62.010(1)	Malicious Prosecution	C	Unranked
9.68.060	Erotic Material (Third or Subsequent Offense)	B	Unranked
9.68.140	Promoting Pornography	C	Unranked
9.68A.040	Sexual Exploitation of a Minor	B	IX
9.68A.050(1)	Dealing in Depictions of Minor Engaged in Sexually Explicit Conduct 1	B	VII
9.68A.050(2)	Dealing in Depictions of Minor Engaged in Sexually Explicit Conduct 2	B	V
9.68A.053(2)	Minor Dealing in Depictions of Another Minor Twelve Years or Younger Engaged in Sexually Explicit Conduct 1	B	Unranked
9.68A.053(3)	Minor Dealing in Depictions of Another Minor Twelve Years or Younger Engaged in Sexually Explicit Conduct 2	B	Unranked
9.68A.053(4)	Minor Financing or Selling Depictions of Another Minor Engaged in Sexually Explicit Conduct	B	Unranked
9.68A.060(1)	Sending, Bringing into the State Depictions of Minor Engaged in Sexually Explicit Conduct 1	B	VII
9.68A.060(2)	Sending, Bringing into the State Depictions of Minor Engaged in Sexually Explicit Conduct 2	B	V
9.68A.070(1)	Possession of Depictions of Minor Engaged in Sexually Explicit Conduct 1	B	VI
9.68A.070(2)	Possession of Depictions of Minor Engaged in Sexually Explicit Conduct 2	B	IV
9.68A.075(1)	Viewing Depictions of Minor Engaged in Sexually Explicit Conduct 1 (Effective 6/10/2010)	B	IV
9.68A.075(2)	Viewing Depictions of Minor Engaged in Sexually Explicit Conduct 2 (Effective 6/10/2010)	C	Unranked
9.68A.090(2)	Communication with Minor for Immoral Purposes (Subsequent Violation or Prior Sex Offense Conviction)	C	III
9.68A.100	Commercial Sexual Abuse of a Minor	B	VIII
9.68A.101	Promoting Commercial Sexual Abuse of a Minor	A	XII
9.68A.102	Promoting Travel for Commercial Sexual Abuse of a Minor	C	Unranked
9.73.230	Intercepting, Transmitting or Recording Conversations Concerning Controlled Substances	C	Unranked
9.82.010	Treason	A	Unranked
9.82.030	Misprision of Treason	C	Unranked
9.91.142(1)	Unlawful Trafficking in Food Stamps	C	I
9.91.144	Unlawful Redemption of Food Stamps	C	I
9.91.150(1)	Tree Spiking	C	Unranked
9.91.170(5)	Intentional Infliction, Injury or Death to a Dog Guide or Service Animal	C	Unranked
9.91.175(3)	Intentionally Injures, Disables or Causes Death of an On-Duty Search and Rescue Dog	C	Unranked

Statute (RCW)	Offense	Class	Seriousness Level
9.94.010	Prison Riot	B	Unranked
9.94.030	Holding Hostages or Interfering with Officer's Duty	B	Unranked
9.94.040(1)	Possession of Weapons by Prisoners (State Facility)	B	Unranked
9.94.040(2)	Possession of Weapons by Prisoners (County or Local Facility)	C	Unranked
9.94.041(1)	Possession of Controlled Substance by Prisoner (State Facility)	C	Unranked
9.94.041(2)	Possession of Controlled Substance by Prisoner (County or Local Facility)	C	Unranked
9.94.043	Possession of Weapons in Prison by Non-prisoner	B	Unranked
9.94.045	Possession of Controlled Substance in Prison by Non-prisoner	C	Unranked
9.94.070	Persistent Prison Misbehavior	C	V
9A.28.020(3)(a)	Arson 1 – Criminal Attempt	A	VIII
9A.28.020(3)(a)	Child Molestation 1 – Criminal Attempt	A	X
9A.28.020(3)(a)	Indecent Liberties - with Forcible Compulsion – Criminal Attempt	A	X
9A.28.020(3)(a)	Murder 1 – Criminal Attempt	A	XV
9A.28.020(3)(a)	Murder 2 – Criminal Attempt	A	XIV
9A.28.020(3)(a)	Rape 1 – Criminal Attempt	A	XII
9A.28.020(3)(a)	Rape 2 – Criminal Attempt	A	XI
9A.28.020(3)(a)	Rape of a Child 1 – Criminal Attempt	A	XII
9A.28.020(3)(a)	Rape of a Child 2 – Criminal Attempt	A	XI
9A.28.030(2)	Arson 1 – Criminal Solicitation	A	VIII
9A.28.030(2)	Child Molestation 1 – Criminal Solicitation	A	X
9A.28.030(2)	Indecent Liberties - with Forcible Compulsion – Criminal Solicitation	A	X
9A.28.030(2)	Murder 1 – Criminal Solicitation	A	XV
9A.28.030(2)	Murder 2 – Criminal Solicitation	A	XIV
9A.28.030(2)	Rape 1 – Criminal Solicitation	A	XII
9A.28.030(2)	Rape 2 – Criminal Solicitation	A	XI
9A.28.030(2)	Rape of a Child 1 – Criminal Solicitation	A	XII
9A.28.030(2)	Rape of a Child 2 – Criminal Solicitation	A	XI
9A.28.040(3)(a)	Murder 1 - Criminal Conspiracy	A	XV
9A.32.030	Murder 1	A	XV
9A.32.050	Murder 2	A	XIV
9A.32.055	Homicide by Abuse	A	XV
9A.32.060	Manslaughter 1	A	XI
9A.32.070	Manslaughter 2	B	VIII
9A.36.011	Assault 1	A	XII
9A.36.021(2)(a)	Assault 2	B	IV
9A.36.021(2)(b)	Assault 2 with a Finding of Sexual Motivation	A	IV

Statute (RCW)	Offense	Class	Seriousness Level
9A.36.031(1)(a-g) & (i-j)	Assault 3, excluding Assault 3 of a Peace Officer with a Projectile Stun Gun	C	III
9A.36.031(1)(h)	Assault 3 of a Peace Officer with a Projectile Stun Gun	C	IV
9A.36.041(3)	Assault 4 (Third Domestic Violence Offense)	C	IV
9A.36.045	Drive-by Shooting	B	VII
9A.36.060	Promoting a Suicide Attempt	C	Unranked
9A.36.080	Hate Crime Offense	C	IV
9A.36.090	Threats Against Governor or Family	C	Unranked
9A.36.100	Custodial Assault	C	III
9A.36.120	Assault of a Child 1	A	XII
9A.36.130	Assault of a Child 2	B	IX
9A.36.140	Assault of a Child 3	C	III
9A.40.020	Kidnapping 1	A	X
9A.40.030(3)(a)	Kidnapping 2	B	V
9A.40.030(3)(b)	Kidnapping 2 with a Finding of Sexual Motivation	A	V
9A.40.040	Unlawful Imprisonment	C	III
9A.40.060	Custodial Interference 1	C	Unranked
9A.40.070	Custodial Interference 2 (Subsequent Offense)	C	Unranked
9A.40.090	Luring of a Child or a Person with a Developmental Disability	C	Unranked
9A.40.100(1)	Trafficking 1	A	XIV
9A.40.100(3)	Trafficking 2	A	XII
9A.40.110	Coercion of Involuntary Servitude	C	Unranked
9A.42.020	Criminal Mistreatment 1	B	X
9A.42.030	Criminal Mistreatment 2	C	V
9A.42.060	Abandonment of Dependent Person 1	B	IX
9A.42.070	Abandonment of Dependent Person 2	C	V
9A.42.100	Endangerment with a Controlled Substance	B	IV
9A.44.040	Rape 1	A	XII
9A.44.050	Rape 2	A	XI
9A.44.060	Rape 3	C	V
9A.44.073	Rape of a Child 1	A	XII
9A.44.076	Rape of a Child 2	A	XI
9A.44.079	Rape of a Child 3	C	VI
9A.44.083	Child Molestation 1	A	X
9A.44.086	Child Molestation 2	B	VII
9A.44.089	Child Molestation 3	C	V
9A.44.093	Sexual Misconduct with a Minor 1	C	V
9A.44.100(1)(a)	Indecent Liberties - with Forcible Compulsion	A	X
9A.44.100(1)(b-c)	Indecent Liberties - without Forcible Compulsion	B	VII

Statute (RCW)	Offense	Class	Seriousness Level
9A.44.100(1)(d-f)	Indecent Liberties - without Forcible Compulsion	B	Unranked
9A.44.105	Sexually Violating Human Remains	C	V
9A.44.115	Voyeurism 1	C	II
9A.44.132(1)(a)	Failure to Register as a Sex Offender (First Violation)	C	Unranked
9A.44.132(1)(a)	Failure to Register as a Sex Offender (Second Violation Committed on or after 6/10/2010)	C	II
9A.44.132(1)(b)	Failure to Register as a Sex Offender (Third or Subsequent Violation Committed on or after 6/10/2010)	B	II
9A.44.132(3)	Failure to Register as a Kidnapping Offender	C	Unranked
9A.44.160	Custodial Sexual Misconduct 1	B	VII
9A.44.170	Custodial Sexual Misconduct 2	C	V
9A.44.196	Criminal Trespass Against Children	C	Unranked
9A.46.020(2)(b)	Harassment	C	III
9A.46.110	Stalking	B	V
9A.46.120	Criminal Gang Intimidation	C	III
9A.48.020	Arson 1	A	VIII
9A.48.030	Arson 2	B	IV
9A.48.040	Reckless Burning 1	C	I
9A.48.070	Malicious Mischief 1	B	II
9A.48.080	Malicious Mischief 2	C	I
9A.48.120	Civil Disorder Training	B	VII
9A.49.020	Unlawful Discharge of a Laser 1	C	Unranked
9A.52.020	Burglary 1	A	VII
9A.52.025	Residential Burglary	B	IV
9A.52.030	Burglary 2	B	III
9A.52.095	Vehicle Prowl 1	C	I
9A.52.100(3)	Vehicle Prowling 2 (Third or Subsequent Offense)	C	IV
9A.56.030	Theft 1 (Excluding Firearm and Motor Vehicle)	B	II
9A.56.040	Theft 2 (Excluding Firearm and Motor Vehicle)	C	I
9A.56.060(4)	Unlawful Issuance of Checks or Drafts (Value Greater Than $750)	C	I
9A.56.065	Theft of a Motor Vehicle	B	II
9A.56.068	Possession of a Stolen Vehicle	B	II
9A.56.070	Taking Motor Vehicle without Permission 1	B	V
9A.56.075	Taking Motor Vehicle without Permission 2	C	I
9A.56.080	Theft of Livestock 1	B	IV
9A.56.083	Theft of Livestock 2	C	III
9A.56.096(5)(a)	Theft of Rental, Leased, Lease-purchased or Loaned Property (Valued at $5,000 or more)	B	II
9A.56.096(5)(b)	Theft of Rental, Leased, Lease-purchased or Loaned Property (Valued at $750 or more but less than $5,000)	C	I

Statute (RCW)	Offense	Class	Seriousness Level
9A.56.120	Extortion 1	B	V
9A.56.130	Extortion 2	C	III
9A.56.150	Possession of Stolen Property 1 (other than Firearm or Motor Vehicle)	B	II
9A.56.160	Possession of Stolen Property 2 (other than Firearm or Motor Vehicle)	C	I
9A.56.200	Robbery 1	A	IX
9A.56.210	Robbery 2	B	IV
9A.56.230	Unlawful Sale of Subscription Television Services	C	Unranked
9A.56.262	Theft of Telecommunication Service	C	Unranked
9A.56.264	Unlawful Manufacture of a Telecommunication Device	C	Unranked
9A.56.266	Unlawful Sale of a Telecommunication Device	C	Unranked
9A.56.290(4)(a)	Unlawful Factoring of a Credit or Payment Card Transaction	C	II
9A.56.290(4)(b)	Unlawful Factoring of a Credit or Payment Card Transaction (Subsequent Violation)	B	IV
9A.56.300	Theft of a Firearm	B	VI
9A.56.310	Possession of a Stolen Firearm	B	V
9A.56.320(1)	Unlawful Production of Payment Instruments	C	I
9A.56.320(2)	Unlawful Possession of Payment Instruments	C	I
9A.56.320(3)	Unlawful Possession of a Personal Identification Device	C	I
9A.56.320(4)	Unlawful Possession of Fictitious Identification	C	I
9A.56.320(5)	Unlawful Possession of Instruments of Financial Fraud	C	I
9A.56.340(2)	Theft with Intent to Resell 1	B	III
9A.56.340(3)	Theft with Intent to Resell 2	C	II
9A.56.350(2)	Organized Retail Theft 1	B	III
9A.56.350(3)	Organized Retail Theft 2	C	II
9A.56.360(2)	Retail Theft with Special Circumstances 1	B	III
9A.56.360(3)	Retail Theft with Special Circumstances 2	C	II
9A.56.360(4)	Retail Theft with Special Circumstances 3	C	Unranked
9A.56.370	Mail Theft	C	Unranked
9A.56.380	Possession of Stolen Mail	C	Unranked
9A.56.400(1)	Theft from a Vulnerable Adult 1	B	VI
9A.56.400(2)	Theft from a Vulnerable Adult 2	C	I
9A.58.020	Possessing or Capturing Personal Identification Document	C	Unranked
9A.60.020	Forgery	C	I
9A.60.030	Obtaining Signature by Deception or Duress	C	Unranked
9A.60.040	Criminal Impersonation 1	C	Unranked
9A.60.060	Fraudulent Creation or Revocation of Mental Health Advance Directive	C	I
9A.60.070	Issuing a False Academic Credential	C	Unranked

Statute (RCW)	Offense	Class	Seriousness Level
9A.61.030	Defrauding a Public Utility 1	B	Unranked
9A.61.040	Defrauding a Public Utility 2	C	Unranked
9A.64.010	Bigamy	C	Unranked
9A.64.020(1)	Incest 1	B	VI
9A.64.020(2)	Incest 2	C	V
9A.64.030(3)(a)	Child Selling	C	Unranked
9A.64.030(3)(b)	Child Buying	C	Unranked
9A.68.010	Bribery	B	VI
9A.68.020	Requesting Unlawful Compensation	C	Unranked
9A.68.030	Receiving or Granting Unlawful Compensation	C	Unranked
9A.68.040	Trading in Public Office	C	Unranked
9A.68.050	Trading in Special Influence	C	Unranked
9A.68.060	Commercial Bribery	B	IV
9A.72.020	Perjury 1	B	V
9A.72.030	Perjury 2	C	III
9A.72.090	Bribing a Witness	B	IV
9A.72.100	Bribe Received by Witness	B	IV
9A.72.110	Intimidating a Witness	B	VI
9A.72.120	Tampering with a Witness	C	III
9A.72.130	Intimidating a Juror	B	VI
9A.72.160	Intimidating a Judge	B	VI
9A.76.023(2)(a)	Disarming a Law Enforcement or Corrections Officer	C	Unranked
9A.76.023(2)(b)	Disarming a Law Enforcement or Corrections Officer and Firearm is Discharged	B	Unranked
9A.76.070(2)(a)	Rendering Criminal Assistance 1	B	V
9A.76.110	Escape 1	B	IV
9A.76.115	Sexually Violent Predator Escape	A	X
9A.76.120	Escape 2	C	III
9A.76.130(3)(b)	Escape 3 (Third or Subsequent Offense)	C	Unranked
9A.76.140	Introducing Contraband 1	B	VII
9A.76.150	Introducing Contraband 2	C	III
9A.76.170(3)(a)	Bail Jumping with Murder 1	A	VI
9A.76.170(3)(b)	Bail Jumping with Class A Felony	B	V
9A.76.170(3)(c)	Bail Jumping with Class B or C Felony	C	III
9A.76.177	Amber Alert – Making False Statements to a Public Servant	C	Unranked
9A.76.180	Intimidating a Public Servant	B	III
9A.76.200	Harming a Police Dog/Horse or an Accelerant Detection Dog	C	Unranked
9A.82.020	Extortionate Extension of Credit	B	V

Statute (RCW)	Offense	Class	Seriousness Level
9A.82.030	Advancing Money or Property for Extortionate Extension of Credit	B	V
9A.82.040	Extortionate Means to Collect Extensions of Credit	B	V
9A.82.045	Collection of Unlawful Debt	C	Unranked
9A.82.050	Trafficking in Stolen Property 1	B	IV
9A.82.055	Trafficking in Stolen Property 2	C	III
9A.82.060(1)(a)	Leading Organized Crime – Organizing Criminal Profiteering	A	X
9A.82.060(1)(b)	Leading Organized Crime - Inciting Criminal Profiteering	B	IX
9A.82.070	Influencing Outcome of Sporting Event	C	IV
9A.82.080(1),(2)	Use of Proceeds of Criminal Profiteering	B	IV
9A.82.080(3)	Use of Proceeds of Criminal Profiteering – Attempt or Conspiracy	C	Unranked
9A.82.160	Criminal Profiteering Lien after Service of Notice	C	Unranked
9A.83.020	Money Laundering	B	Unranked
9A.84.010(2)(b)	Criminal Mischief	C	Unranked
9A.84.040(2)(a)	False Reporting 1	B	VII
9A.84.040(2)(b)	False Reporting 2	C	III
9A.86.010	Disclosing Intimate Images	C	Unranked
9A.88.010(2)(c)	Indecent Exposure to a Person Age 14 or Older (Subsequent Conviction or has Prior Sex Offense Conviction)	C	Unranked
9A.88.010(2)(c)	Indecent Exposure to a Person under Age 14 (Subsequent Sex Offense)	C	IV
9A.88.070	Promoting Prostitution 1	B	VIII
9A.88.080	Promoting Prostitution 2	C	III
9A.88.085	Promoting Travel for Prostitution	C	Unranked
9A.90.040	Computer Trespass 1	C	II
9A.90.060	Electronic Data Service Interference	C	II
9A.90.080	Electronic Data Tampering 1	C	II
9A.90.100	Electronic Data Theft	C	II
9A.90.120(2)(b)	Cyber Harassment	C	III
10.66.090	Willfully Disobeys an Off-limits Order (Subsequent Violation or Enters Protected Against Drug Trafficking Area)	C	Unranked
10.95.020	Aggravated Murder 1	A	XVI
10.99.040	Domestic Violence Court Order Violation	C	V
10.99.050	Domestic Violence Court Order Violation	C	V
16.08.100(2)	Dangerous Dog Attack (Subsequent Offense)	C	Unranked
16.08.100(3)	Dangerous Dog Attack Resulting in Severe Injury or Death	C	Unranked
16.52.117(2)(a)	Animal Fighting	C	Unranked

Statute (RCW)	Offense	Class	Seriousness Level
16.52.117(2)(b)	Animal Fighting - Mutilation	B	Unranked
16.52.205(2)	Animal Cruelty 1	C	Unranked
16.52.205(3)	Animal Cruelty 1 - Sexual Conduct or Contact	C	III
16.52.320	Kill or Cause Substantial Harm with Malice to Livestock	C	Unranked
18.04.370(1)(b)	Unlawful Use of a Professional Title	C	Unranked
18.04.370(1)(c)	Unlawful Use of CPA Title after Suspension	C	Unranked
18.39.350	Embalmers/Funeral Directors Violation	C	Unranked
18.64.046(7)	Unlawful Selling of Ephedrine, Pseudoephedrine or Phenylpropanolamine by a Wholesaler	C	Unranked
18.130.190(7)(b)	Unlicensed Practice of a Profession or Business (Subsequent Violation)	C	II
19.25.020(2)(a)	Reproduction of Sound Recording without Consent of Owner - Recording Fixed before 2/15/1972 (at least 1,000 Recordings or Subsequent Conviction)	B	Unranked
19.25.020(2)(b)	Reproduction of Sound Recording without Consent of Owner - Recording Fixed before 2/15/1972 (more than 100 but less than 1,000 Recordings)	C	Unranked
19.25.030(2)(a)	Use of Recording of Live Performance without Consent of Owner (at least 1,000 Recordings or at least 100 Unauthorized Audiovisual Recordings or Subsequent Offense)	B	Unranked
19.25.030(2)(b)	Use of Recording of Live Performance without Consent of Owner (at least 100 but less than 1,000 Recordings or more than 10 but less than 100 Unauthorized Audiovisual Recording or Subsequent Offense)	C	Unranked
19.25.040(2)(a)	Failure to Disclose Origin of Certain Recordings (at least 100 Recordings or Subsequent Conviction)	B	Unranked
19.25.040(2)(b)	Failure to Disclose Origin of Certain Recordings (more than 10 but less than 100 Recordings)	C	Unranked
19.48.110(1)(b)	Defrauding an Innkeeper (Value of $75 or more)	B	Unranked
19.60.067(2)	Second-hand Precious Metal Dealer Violations (Subsequent Violation)	C	Unranked
19.100.210	Franchise Investment Protection Violation	B	Unranked
19.110.075(2)	Disclosures Knowingly Not Provided at Sale of Business Opportunity (Violation of RCW 19.110.070)	B	Unranked
19.110.075(2)	Registration Knowingly not Obtained Prior to Sale of Business Opportunity (Violation of RCW 19.110.050)	B	Unranked
19.110.120	Defraud or Provide Misleading or Untrue Documents Related to a Business Opportunity Sale	B	Unranked
19.116.080(1)	Unlawful Subleasing of Motor Vehicle	C	Unranked
19.116.080(2)	Unlawful Transfer of Ownership of Motor Vehicle	C	Unranked
19.142.080	Failure to Use a Trust Account or Furnish Bond for Health Studio	C	Unranked
19.144.080	Mortgage Fraud	B	III
19.144.100(1)	Use or Investment of Proceeds from Mortgage Fraud Activities	B	Unranked

Statute (RCW)	Offense	Class	Seriousness Level
19.144.100(2)	Control of Real Property Resulting from Mortgage Fraud Activities	B	Unranked
19.146.050	Failure to Use a Trust Account	C	Unranked
19.146.235(9)	Impairing Mortgage Broker Investigation	B	Unranked
19.158.160	Commercial Telephone Solicitor Deception (Value of $250 or more)	C	Unranked
19.210.040	Unused Property, Merchants –Prohibited Sales (Third or Subsequent Offense within 5 Years)	C	Unranked
19.225.110	Uniform Athlete Agent Act Violation	C	Unranked
19.230.300	False Statement, Misrepresentation or False Certification of Uniform Money Services Record	C	Unranked
19.290.100	Scrap Processing, Recycling, or Supplying without a License (Second or Subsequent Offense)	C	II
19.300.020	Electronic Communication Devices – Illegal Scanning	C	Unranked
19.310.120	Unlawfully Engaging in Business as an Exchange Facilitator (RCW 19.310.100(1)-(9))	B	Unranked
20.01.460(2)	Acting as Commission Merchant, Dealer, Cash Buyer without License	C	Unranked
21.20.400	Securities Act Violation	B	III
21.30.140	Commodity Transaction Violation	B	Unranked
22.09.310	Dealing in Unauthorized Warehouse Receipts for Agricultural Commodities	C	Unranked
26.04.210	Providing False Statements in Affidavits for Marriage	C	Unranked
26.09.300	Domestic Violence Court Order Violation	C	V
26.26B.050	Domestic Violence Court Order Violation	C	V
26.20.030	Family Abandonment	C	Unranked
26.52.070	Domestic Violence Court Order Violation	C	V
27.44.040(1)	Destroying, Removing or Defacing Indian Graves	C	Unranked
27.44.040(2)	Selling Artifacts or Human Remains from Indian Graves	C	Unranked
27.53.060	Disturbing Archaeological Resources or Site	C	Unranked
28B.10.901(2)(b)	Hazing	C	III
29A.08.740	Misuse of Registered Voter Data	C	Unranked
29A.84.030	Election or Mail Ballot Violation	C	Unranked
29A.84.130	Voter Violation of Registration Law	C	Unranked
29A.84.140	Unqualified Voting Registration	C	Unranked
29A.84.150	Misuse or Alteration of Registration Database	C	Unranked
29A.84.230(1)	Violation by Signer – Initiative or Referendum with False Name	C	Unranked
29A.84.240(1)	Violations by Signers – Recall Petition with False Name	B	Unranked
29A.84.270	Duplication of Name – Conspiracy to Mislead	B	Unranked
29A.84.311	Provides False Information or Conceals or Destroys Candidacy Declaration or Nominating Petition	C	Unranked
29A.84.320	Duplication of Names on Declaration of Candidacy	B	Unranked

Statute (RCW)	Offense	Class	Seriousness Level
29A.84.540	Removing a Ballot from a Voting Center or Ballot Drop Location	C	Unranked
29A.84.545	Unauthorized Removal of Paper Record from Electronic Voting Device	C	Unranked
29A.84.550	Tampering with Election Materials	C	Unranked
29A.84.560	Tampering with Voting Machine	C	Unranked
29A.84.620	Hindering or Bribing Voter	C	Unranked
29A.84.650(1)	Voting Repeater – more than one Vote at any Election	C	Unranked
29A.84.655	Election Officer Permits Repeat Vote	C	Unranked
29A.84.660	Unqualified Person Voting	C	Unranked
29A.84.680(1)	Absentee Voting Violation	C	Unranked
29A.84.711	Fraud in Certification of Nomination or Ballot	C	Unranked
29A.84.720	Election Officers – Violation	C	Unranked
30A.04.240	Commingling of Funds or Securities	B	Unranked
30A.12.090	Bank or Trust Company - False Entry, Statements, etc.	B	Unranked
30A.12.100	Bank or Trust Company - Destroy or Secrete Records	B	Unranked
30A.12.120	Loan to Officer or Employee from Trust Fund	B	Unranked
30A.42.290(2)	Alien Bank or Bureau – False Entry, Statements, etc.	B	Unranked
30A.42.290(3)	Alien Bank or Bureau – Destroy or Secrete Records	B	Unranked
30A.44.110	Bank or Trust Company - Transfer of Assets Prior to Insolvency	B	Unranked
30A.44.120	Bank or Trust Company - Receiving Deposits When Insolvent	B	Unranked
30B.12.050	State Trust Company – False Entry, Conceal or Destroy Records	B	Unranked
30B.44B.110(2)	State Trust Company – Transfer of Assets	B	Unranked
31.12.724(2)	Credit Union - Transfer of Credit Union Assets Prior to Insolvency	B	Unranked
31.12.724(3)	Credit Union - Fraudulent Receipt of Credit Union Deposit	B	Unranked
31.12.850(2)	Make a False Statement or Entry in Credit Union Books	C	Unranked
32.04.100	Mutual Savings Bank - Falsify Savings Book, Document or Statement	B	Unranked
32.04.110	Mutual Savings Bank - Conceal or Destroy Evidence	B	Unranked
32.24.080	Mutual Savings Bank - Transfer Bank Assets after Insolvency	B	Unranked
33.36.030	Savings and Loan Association - Preference in Case of Insolvency	C	Unranked
33.36.040	Savings and Loan Association - Making False Statement of Assets or Liabilities	C	Unranked
33.36.060	Savings and Loan Association - Suppressing, Secreting or Destroying Evidence or Records	C	Unranked
35.36.040	Designation of Bonds – Violation (First Class Cities)	B	Unranked
35A.36.040	Designation of Bonds – Violation (Code Cities)	B	Unranked

Statute (RCW)	Offense	Class	Seriousness Level
36.18.170	Failure to Pay Over Fees to County Treasurer	C	Unranked
38.42.050	False Affidavit under Service Member Civil Relief Act	C	Unranked
39.44.101	Defraud a Facsimile Signature on Bonds and Coupons	B	Unranked
39.62.040	Unauthorized Use of Public Official Facsimile Signature or Seal	B	Unranked
40.16.010	Injury to a Public Record	C	Unranked
40.16.020	Injury to and Misappropriation of Public Record by Officer	B	Unranked
40.16.030	Offering False Instrument for Filing or Record	C	Unranked
41.26.062	False Statements or Records to Defraud Law Enforcement Officers and Firefighters Retirement System	B	Unranked
41.32.055(1)	False Statements or Records to Defraud Teachers Retirement System	B	Unranked
42.17A.750	False Documents Registered with Public Disclosure Commission	C	Unranked
42.20.070	Misappropriating and Falsifying Accounts by Public Officer	B	Unranked
42.20.090	Misappropriating and Falsifying Accounts by Treasurer	C	Unranked
42.24.100	False Claim from Municipal Corporation (Charged as Perjury 2)	C	Unranked
43.06.230	Damage Property or Cause Personal Injury after State of Emergency Proclaimed	B	Unranked
43.08.140	Embezzlement by State Treasurer	B	Unranked
43.43.856	Divulging Confidential Investigative Information Pertaining to Organized Crime	B	Unranked
46.12.560	Removal of Sticker on Vehicle Stating Previously Destroyed or Title 1 Loss	C	Unranked
46.12.750(1)	False Statements, Illegal Transfers, Alterations or Forgeries of Vehicle Title	B	Unranked
46.12.750(3)	Unlawful Sale of Vehicle Certificate of Ownership	C	Unranked
46.20.0921(2)	Sell or Deliver a Stolen Driver's License or Identicard	C	Unranked
46.20.0921(3)(a)	Manufacture, Sell or Deliver Forged Driver's License or Identicard	C	Unranked
46.37.650(1)(b)	Manufacture or Import Counterfeit, Nonfunctional, Damaged, or Previously Deployed Air Bag (Causing Bodily Injury or Death)	C	VII
46.37.650(1)(c)	Manufacture or Import Counterfeit, Nonfunctional, Damaged, or Previously Deployed Air Bag	C	V
46.37.650(2)(b)	Sell, Install, or Reinstall Counterfeit, Nonfunctional, Damaged, or Previously Deployed Airbag	C	VII
46.37.650(2)(c)	Sell, Install, or Reinstall Counterfeit, Nonfunctional, Damaged, or Previously Deployed Airbag	C	V
46.37.660(1)(b)	Air Bag Replacement Requirements (Causing Bodily Injury or Death)	C	VII
46.37.660(1)(c)	Air Bag Replacement Requirements	C	V

Statute (RCW)	Offense	Class	Seriousness Level
46.37.660(2)(b)	Air Bag Diagnostic Systems (Causing Bodily Injury or Death)	C	VII
46.37.660(2)(c)	Air Bag Diagnostic Systems	C	V
46.37.673	Use of a Signal Preemption Device Resulting in Property Damage or less Substantial Bodily Harm	C	Unranked
46.37.674	Negligently Causing Substantial Bodily Harm by Use of a Signal Preemption Device	B	III
46.37.675	Negligently Causing Death by Use of a Signal Preemption Device	B	VII
46.52.020(4)(a)	Hit and Run - Death	B	IX
46.52.020(4)(b)	Hit and Run - Injury	C	IV
46.52.130(6)(b)	Abstracts of Driving Records – Intentional Misuse	C	Unranked
46.61.024	Attempting to Elude Pursuing Police Vehicle	C	I
46.61.502(6)	Driving while under the Influence of Intoxicating Liquor or any Drug	B	IV
46.61.504(6)	Physical Control of a Vehicle while under the Influence of Intoxicating Liquor or any Drug	C	IV
46.61.520(1)(a)	Vehicular Homicide – while under the Influence of Intoxicating Liquor or any Drug	A	XI
46.61.520(1)(b)	Vehicular Homicide – in a Reckless Manner	A	XI
46.61.520(1)(c)	Vehicular Homicide - Disregard for the Safety of Others	A	VII
46.61.522(1)(a-b)	Vehicular Assault – in a Reckless Manner or while under the Influence of Intoxicating Liquor or any Drug	B	IV
46.61.522(1)(c)	Vehicular Assault - Disregard for the Safety of Others	B	III
46.70.021	Licensing Violation for Car Dealers or Manufacturers (Subsequent Violation)	C	Unranked
46.70.180(5)	Odometer Offense	C	Unranked
46.80.020(b)	Engage in Business of Wrecking Vehicles without a License (Subsequent Offense)	C	Unranked
46.87.260	Cab Card Forgery (Effective Until 7/1/2016)	B	Unranked
46.87.260	Credential Forgery (Effective 7/1/2016)	B	Unranked
48.06.030	Insurance Solicitation Permit Violation	B	Unranked
48.06.190	Exhibiting False Accounts of Insurer	B	Unranked
48.15.023(3)	Unlawful Transaction of Insurance Business	B	IV
48.17.063	Transaction of Insurance Business Beyond the Scope of Licensure (Violation of RCW 48.17.060)	B	I
48.17.063(2)	Unlicensed Practice as an Insurance Professional	B	IV
48.30.220	Willful Destruction, Injury, Secretion of Insured Property	C	Unranked
48.30.230	False Insurance Claims (Value in Excess of $1,500)	C	Unranked
48.30A.015	Trafficking in Insurance Claims (Subsequent Violation)	C	II
48.44.016(3)	Unlawful Transaction of Health Coverage as Health Care Service Contractor	B	IV
48.46.033(3)	Unlawful Transaction of Health Coverage as Health Maintenance Organization	B	IV

Statute (RCW)	Offense	Class	Seriousness Level
48.80.030	Health Care False Claims	C	II
48.102.160(3)	Fraudulent Life Insurance Settlement	B	Unranked
48.102.160(4)	Unlicensed Life Insurance Provider	B	Unranked
48.102.160(5)	Unlicensed Settlement Broker	B	Unranked
48.160.080	Sells Guaranteed Asset Protection Waivers without Registration	B	Unranked
49.12.410(2)	Child Labor Law Violation – Death/Disability	C	Unranked
51.48.020(1)	Evading Industrial Insurance Premiums	C	Unranked
51.48.020(2)	False Information in Industrial Insurance Claim (Charged as Theft)		
51.48.103(2)	Engaging in Business after Certificate of Coverage Revocation	C	Unranked
51.48.270	False Statement or Concealing Information by Employee	C	Unranked
51.48.280(1)	Unlawful Receipt of Remuneration for Kickbacks, Bribes, or Rebates by any Person	C	Unranked
51.48.280(2)	Unlawful Offer or Payment for Kickbacks, Bribes, or Rebates to any Person	C	Unranked
61.34.030	Equity Skimming	B	II
64.36.020(5)(b)	Timeshare Registration Requirement Violation	C	Unranked
64.36.210	Timeshare Fraud	C	Unranked
65.12.730	Unlawful Stealing or Carrying Away Certification of Land Registration (Charged as Theft)		
65.12.740	False Swearing - Registration of Land Title (Charged as Perjury)		
65.12.750	Fraudulent Procurement or False Entry on Land Title Registration	C	Unranked
65.12.760	Forgery of Registrar's Signature or Seal	B	Unranked
66.44.120(2)(b)	Unlawful Use of Liquor Board Seal (Third or Subsequent Offense)	C	Unranked
67.08.015	Promoting Illegal Boxing, Martial Arts and Wrestling	C	Unranked
67.24.010	Fraud in Sporting Contest	B	Unranked
67.70.130	Lottery Fraud	B	Unranked
67.70.140	Unlicensed Lottery Activity	B	Unranked
67.70.160	State Lottery Violations Except Lottery Fraud and Unlicensed Lottery Activity	C	Unranked
68.05.330	Unfair Practice of Funeral or Cemetery Board	C	Unranked
68.44.060	Unauthorized Loans to Cemetery Authority	C	Unranked
68.50.140(1)	Removing Human Remains	C	Unranked
68.50.140(2)	Purchasing or Receiving Human Remains	C	Unranked
68.50.140(3)	Opening Graves with Intent to Sell or Remove Personal Effects or Human Remains	C	Unranked
68.50.140(4)	Removal, Disinterment or Mutilation of Human Remains	C	Unranked

Statute (RCW)	Offense	Class	Seriousness Level
68.60.040(1)	Destruction of Tomb, Plot, Marker, or Cemetery Property	C	Unranked
68.60.040(3)	Transports Removed Human Remains, Opens a Grave or Removes Personal Effects from Grave	C	Unranked
68.60.050	Removes, Defaces or Destroys any Historic Grave	C	Unranked
68.64.150	Anatomical Gifts - Illegal Purchase or Sale	C	Unranked
68.64.160	Anatomical Gift - Illegal Financial Gain	C	Unranked
69.25.155(1)	Interference with Person Performing Official Duties	C	Unranked
69.25.155(2)	Interference with Person Performing Official Duties with a Deadly Weapon	B	Unranked
69.30.085	Participation in Shellfish Operation or Activities while License is Denied, Revoked or Suspended	C	Unranked
69.40.020	Poison in Milk or Food Product	C	Unranked
69.40.030	Placing Poison or other Harmful Object or Substance in Food, Drinks, Medicine or Water	B	Unranked
69.41.020	Forged Prescription - Legend Drug	B	DG-I
69.41.030(2)(a)	Sale, Delivery or Possession with Intent to Sell Legend Drug without Prescription	B	Unranked
69.41.040	Illegal Issuance of Legend Drug Prescription	B	Unranked
69.41.350	Possession of Steroids in Excess of 200 tablets or (8) 2cc Bottles without a Valid Prescription	C	Unranked
69.43.070(1)	Unlawful Delivery of Precursor Drug with Intent to Use	B	Unranked
69.43.070(2)	Unlawful Receipt of Precursor Drug with Intent to Use	B	Unranked
69.43.080	False Statement in Report of Precursor Drugs	C	Unranked
69.50.401(2)(a)	Manufacture, Deliver or Possess with Intent to Deliver - Narcotics from Schedule I or II or Flunitrazepam from Schedule IV	B	DG-II
69.50.401(2)(b)	Deliver or Possess with Intent to Deliver - Methamphetamine	B	DG-II
69.50.401(2)(b)	Manufacture Methamphetamine	B	DG-III
69.50.401(2)(b)	Manufacture, Deliver or Possess with Intent to Deliver - Amphetamine	B	DG-II
69.50.401(2)(c)	Manufacture, Deliver or Possess with Intent to Deliver - Cannabis	C	DG-I
69.50.401(2)(c-e)	Manufacture, Deliver or Possess with Intent to Deliver - Narcotics from Schedule III, IV, or V or Nonnarcotics from Schedule I-V (except Cannabis, Amphetamine, Methamphetamine, or Flunitrazepam)	C	DG-II
69.50.4011(2)(a-b)	Create or Deliver a Counterfeit Controlled Substance – Schedule I or II Narcotic or Flunitrazepam or Methamphetamine	B	DG-II
69.50.4011(2)(c-e)	Create or Deliver a Counterfeit Controlled Substance – Schedule I-II Nonnarcotic, Schedule III-V Except Flunitrazepam or Methamphetamine	C	DG-II
69.50.4012	Delivery of a Material in Lieu of a Controlled Substance	C	DG-II
69.50.4015	Involving a Minor in Drug Dealing	C	DG-III

Statute (RCW)	Offense	Class	Seriousness Level
69.50.402	Dispensing Violation (VUCSA)	C	Unranked
69.50.402(1)(f)	Maintaining a Dwelling or Place for Controlled Substances	C	DG-II
69.50.403	Forged Prescription for a Controlled Substance	C	DG-I
69.50.406(1)	Over 18 and Deliver Heroin, Methamphetamine, a Narcotic from Schedule I or II, or Flunitrazepam from Schedule IV to Someone under 18	A	DG-III
69.50.406(2)	Over 18 and Deliver Narcotic from Schedule III, IV or V, or a Nonnarcotic, Except Flunitrazepam or Methamphetamine, from Schedule I-V to Someone under 18 and 3 Years Junior	B	DG-III
69.50.410	Selling for Profit (Controlled or Counterfeit) any Controlled Substance in Schedule I	C	DG-III
69.50.415	Controlled Substance Homicide	B	DG-III
69.50.416	Controlled Substance Label Violation	C	Unranked
69.50.418	Possess, Purchase, Deliver, Sell, or Possess with Intent to Sell a Tableting Machine or Encapsulating Machine	C	DG-II
69.50.440	Possession of Ephedrine, Pseudoephedrine or Anhydrous Ammonia with Intent to Manufacture Methamphetamine	B	DG-III
69.50.465	Conducting or Maintaining a Cannabis Club	C	Unranked
69.51A.240	Medical Cannabis – Unlawful Actions	C	Unranked
69.52.030(1)	Manufacture, Distribute or Possess with Intent to Distribute an Imitation Controlled Substance	C	DG-II
69.52.030(2)	Delivery of Imitation Controlled Substance by Person 18 or Over to Person under 18	B	DG-III
69.52.030(3)	Advertising Imitation Controlled Substances	C	Unranked
69.53.010	Unlawful Use of Building for Drug Purposes	C	DG-I
69.53.020	Unlawful Fortification of Building for Drug Purposes	C	Unranked
69.53.030	Unlawful Use of Fortified Building	C	Unranked
69.55.010	Theft of Ammonia	C	VIII
69.55.020	Unlawful Storage of Ammonia	C	VI
70.74.022(1)	Manufacture, Purchase, Sell or Store Explosive Device without License	C	Unranked
70.74.180	Explosive Devices Prohibited	A	IX
70.74.270(1)	Malicious Placement of an Explosive 1	A	XIII
70.74.270(2)	Malicious Placement of an Explosive 2	B	IX
70.74.270(3)	Malicious Placement of an Explosive 3	B	VII
70.74.272(1)(a)	Malicious Placement of an Imitation Device 1	B	XII
70.74.272(1)(b)	Malicious Placement of an Imitation Device 2	C	VI
70.74.275	Intimidation or Harassment with an Explosive	C	Unranked
70.74.280(1)	Malicious Explosion of a Substance 1	A	XV
70.74.280(2)	Malicious Explosion of a Substance 2	A	XIII
70.74.280(3)	Malicious Explosion of a Substance 3	B	X

Statute (RCW)	Offense	Class	Seriousness Level
70.155.140	Shipping or Transporting Tobacco Products Ordered Through Mail or Internet	C	Unranked
70.245.200(1)	Forging Request for Medication	A	Unranked
70.245.200(2)	Coerce Patient to Request Life-ending Medication	A	Unranked
70.345.030	Retail Sales, Distribution or Delivery Sales of Vapor Products without a License	C	Unranked
70.345.090	Engaging in Delivery Sales of Vapor Products without a License or Proper Shipping Documentation	C	Unranked
70A.15.3150(3)	Releasing into Ambient Air Hazardous Air Pollutant	C	Unranked
70A.300.100(1)(a)	Transport, Disposal or Export of Hazardous Waste that Places Another Person in Danger of Injury or Death	B	Unranked
70A.300.100(1)(b)	Transport, Disposal or Export of Hazardous Waste that Places Another Person's Property in Danger of Harm	C	Unranked
72.09.310	Escape from Community Custody	C	II
72.23.170	Assist Escape of Mental Patient	C	Unranked
72.23.300	Bringing Narcotics, Liquor, or Weapons into State Institution or Grounds	B	Unranked
74.08.055(2)	False Verification for Welfare	B	I
74.08.100	False Age and Residency Public Assistance Verification	B	Unranked
74.09.230	False Statement for Medical Assistance	C	Unranked
74.09.240(1)	Receiving or Asking for Bribes, Kickbacks or Rebates	C	Unranked
74.09.240(2)	Paying or Offering Bribes, Kickbacks or Rebates	C	Unranked
74.09.250	False Statements Regarding Institutions, Facilities	C	Unranked
74.09.260	Excessive Charges, Payments	C	Unranked
74.09.290	Unlawful Disclosure of Patient Records or DSHS Information	C	Unranked
76.36.120	Forgery of Forest Product Mark	B	Unranked
76.48.141(1)(a)	Fraudulent Document as Specialized Forest Products Permit, Sales Invoice, Bill of Lading, etc.	C	Unranked
76.48.141(1)(b)	Fraudulent Representation of Authority to Harvest Specialized Forest Products	C	Unranked
76.48.141(2)	Fraudulent Document for Specialized Forest Products Buyer	C	Unranked
77.15.120(3)(b)	Unlawful Taking of Endangered Fish or Wildlife 1	C	III
77.15.135(4)(d)	Unlawful Trafficking in Species with Extinction 1	C	Unranked
77.15.250(2)(b)	Unlawful Releasing, Planting, Possessing or Placing Deleterious Exotic Wildlife	C	I
77.15.260(3)(a)	Unlawful Trafficking in Fish, Shellfish or Wildlife 2	C	II
77.15.260(3)(b)	Unlawful Trafficking in Fish, Shellfish or Wildlife 1	B	III
77.15.410(3)(b)	Unlawful Hunting of Big Game 1	C	III
77.15.450(3)(b)	Spotlighting Big Game 1	C	I
77.15.500(3)(b)	Commercial Fishing without a License 1	C	II
77.15.530(4)	Unlawful Use of a Nondesignated Vessel	C	III
77.15.550(3)(b)	Violating Commercial Fishing Area or Time 1	C	I

Statute (RCW)	Offense	Class	Seriousness Level
77.15.570(2)	Unlawful Participation on Non-Indians in Indian Fishery	C	II
77.15.580(3)(b)	Unlawful Use of Net to Take Fish	C	I
77.15.620(3)(b)	Engaging in Fish Dealing Activity Unlicensed 1	C	II
77.15.630(3)(b)	Unlawful Fish and Shellfish Catch Accounting 1	C	I
77.15.650(3)(b)	Unlawful Purchase or Use of a License 1	C	II
77.15.670(3)(b)	Suspension of Department Privileges 1	C	I
77.15.770(2)	Unlawful Trade in Shark Fins 1	C	Unranked
77.15.811	Unlawful Use of Invasive Species 1	C	Unranked
77.140.060(3)	Unlawful Misbranding of Fish or Shellfish 1	C	III
78.44.330	Mineral Trespass	C	I
79A.60.050(1)(a)	Homicide by Watercraft – while under the Influence of Intoxicating Liquor or any Drug	A	IX
79A.60.050(1)(b)	Homicide by Watercraft – in a Reckless Manner	A	VIII
79A.60.050(1)(c)	Homicide by Watercraft - Disregard for the Safety of Others	A	VII
79A.60.060	Assault by Watercraft	B	IV
79A.60.090	Eluding a Law Enforcement Vessel	C	Unranked
79A.60.200(3)	Hit and Run with Vessel - Injury Accident	C	IV
81.60.070	Malicious Injury to Railroad Property	B	III
81.60.080(1)	Sabotaging Rolling Stock	C	Unranked
81.60.080(2)	Receiving Stolen Railroad Property	C	Unranked
82.24.100	Forgery or Counterfeit Cigarette Tax Stamp	B	Unranked
82.24.110(2)	Transportation of more than 10,000 Cigarettes without Proper Stamps	C	Unranked
82.24.500	Unlawfully Purchase, Sell, Consign or Distribute Cigarettes	C	Unranked
82.24.570(2)	Manufacture, Sell or Possess Counterfeit Cigarettes	C	Unranked
82.24.570(3)	Manufacture, Sell or Possess Counterfeit Cigarettes (Subsequent Violation)	B	Unranked
82.26.190	Distributors and Retailer of Tobacco Products License Violation	C	Unranked
82.32.290(2)	False Statement to Department of Revenue	C	Unranked
82.32.290(4)	Phantomware Violation	C	Unranked
82.38.270	Special Fuel Violations	C	Unranked
82.42.085	Evading the Collection of Aircraft Fuel Tax	C	Unranked
82.87.140	Knowingly Attempts to Evade Capital Gains Tax Payment	C	Unranked
87.03.200	Defraud Facsimile Signatures on Bonds and Coupons – Irrigation Districts	B	Unranked
88.08.020	Tampering with Lights or Signals	B	Unranked
88.08.050(1)	Injury to Lighthouses or United States Light	B	Unranked
88.46.080(2)(b)	Unlawful Operation of a Covered Vessel (Subsequent Violation)	C	Unranked

Statute (RCW)	Offense	Class	Seriousness Level
90.56.300(2)(b)	Unlawful Operation of Onshore or Offshore Facility (Subsequent Conviction)	C	Unranked
90.56.530	Reckless Operation of a Tank Vessel	C	Unranked
90.56.540	Operation of a Vessel while under the Influence of Intoxicating Liquor or Drugs	C	Unranked

*RCW 9.94A.515 lists some, but not all, of the offenses that are felonies punished under RCW 7.105.450(4) and (5), along with RCW 7.105.450 itself. For example, violations of 9A.40.104 and 9A.46.055 are felonies punishable under RCW 7.105.450 but they are not listed in RCW 9.94A.515. For purposes of this manual, the Caseload Forecast Council is presenting only those offenses listed in RCW 9.94A.515 at Seriousness Level V.

SECTION 5

QUICK REFERENCE SHEET

SENTENCING ALTERNATIVES
First-Time Offender Waiver (FTOW) (RCW 9.94A.650)

Eligibility

No prior conviction of a felony in this state, federal court, or another state; and

Never participated in a program of deferred prosecution for a felony.

Certain felony offenses are *not* eligible for a FTOW sentence.

Any offense classified as violent or sex under this chapter;

Manufacture, delivery, or possession with intent to manufacture or deliver a controlled substance classified in Schedule I or II that is a narcotic drug or flunitrazepam classified in Schedule IV;

Manufacture, delivery, or possession with intent to deliver a methamphetamine, its salts, isomers, and salts of its isomers as defined in RCW 69.50.206(d)(2);

Selling for profit of any controlled substance or counterfeit substance classified in Schedule I, RCW 69.50.204, except leaves and flowering tops of marihuana;

Felony driving while under the influence of intoxicating liquor or any drug; or

Felony physical control of a vehicle while under the influence of intoxicating liquor or any drug.

Sentencing

The court may waive the imposition of a sentence within the standard sentence range and impose a sentence which may include up to ninety days of confinement in a facility operated or utilized under contract by the county and a requirement that the person refrain from committing new offenses.

Community Custody

In 2011, the legislature reduced the duration of community custody for FTOW sentences.

Up to 6 months of community custody when treatment is not ordered;

Up to 12 months of community custody if treatment is ordered.

FTOW sentences are not eligible for the Supervision Compliance Credit established in RCW 9.94A.717. For further information on community custody conditions of an FTOW, see RCW 9.94A.703.

Parenting Sentencing Alternative (RCW 9.94A.655)

Eligibility

The high end of the standard sentence range for the current offense is greater than one year;

The individual has no prior or current conviction for a felony that is a sex offense, a serious violent offense, or a felony offense where the person was armed with a firearm or deadly weapon in the commission of the felony;

The individual has no current conviction for a violent offense;

The individual signs any release of information waivers required to allow information regarding current or prior child welfare cases to be shared with the Department and the court; and

The individual is:

(i) A parent with physical custody of a minor child;

(ii) An expectant parent;

(iii) A legal guardian of a minor child; or

(iv) A biological parent, adoptive parent, custodian, or stepparent with a proven, established, ongoing, and substantial relationship with a minor child that existed at the time of the offense.

Prior juvenile adjudications are not considered offenses when considering eligibility, expect for any sex offense, serious violent offense, or felony offense where the individual was armed with a firearm or deadly weapon in the commission of the offense.

In making its determination, the court may order the Department to complete a risk assessment report, including a family impact statement, or a chemical dependency screening report as provided in RCW 9.94A.500, prior to sentencing.

Open or prior child welfare cases or child abuse or neglect investigation:

If the person has an open child welfare case or child abuse or neglect investigation, the Department of Children, Youth, and Families (DCYF) or the tribal child welfare agency shall provide a report within seven business days. See RCW 9.94A.655(4)(a) for minimum requirements of the report.

Prior child welfare case: If there is a prior child welfare case with the DCYF or with a tribal child welfare agency, the Department will obtain information from the Children's Administration on the number and type of past substantiated referrals of abuse or neglect and report that information to the court.

Sentencing

Imposing the Parenting Sentencing Alternative:

The court shall waive imposition of a sentence within the standard sentence range and impose a sentence consisting of twelve months of community custody.

The court shall consider the criminal history when determining if the alternative is appropriate and must give great weight to the minor child's best interest.

When a Court Imposes a Sentence of Community Custody under this Section:

The court may impose conditions as provided in RCW 9.94A.703 and may impose other affirmative conditions as the court considers appropriate.

The Department may impose conditions as authorized in RCW 9.94A.704 that may include, but are not limited to:

- Parenting classes;
- Chemical dependency treatment;
- Mental health treatment;

- Vocational training;
- Change programs;
- Life skills classes.

The Department shall report to the court if any violations of sentence conditions occur.

Community Custody

The Department shall provide the court with quarterly progress reports regarding progress in required programming, treatment, and other supervision conditions. When an open child welfare case exists, the Department will seek to coordinate services with DCYF. Parenting Sentencing Alternative sentences are not eligible for the Supervision Compliance Credit established in RCW 9.94A.717.

Violations and Sanctions:

If a person is brought back to court, the court may modify the conditions of community custody or impose sanctions under RCW 9.94A.655(8)(d), including extending the length of participation in the program by not more than six months.

The court may a term of total confinement within the standard range of the current offense to be served at any time during the period of community custody (RCW 9.94A.655(8)(d)).

Drug Offender Sentencing Alternative (DOSA) (RCW 9.94A.660): Prison – Based Option (RCW 9.94A.662) or Residential-Based Treatment Option (RCW 9.94A.664)

Eligibility

A person is eligible for the Drug Offender Sentencing Alternative if:

The conviction is for a felony that is not a violent offense and the violation does not involve a sentence enhancement under RCW 9.94A.533(3) or (4);

The conviction is for a felony that is not a felony Driving while under the Influence of Intoxicating Liquor or any Drug (RCW 46.61.502(6)) or felony Physical Control of a Vehicle while under the Influence of Intoxicating Liquor or any Drug (RCW 46.61.504(6));

There are no current or prior convictions for a sex offense for which the person is currently or may be required to register as a sex offender;

There are no prior convictions in this state, and no prior convictions for an equivalent out-of-state or federal offense for the following offenses during the following time frames:

- Robbery in the Second Degree that did not involve the use of a firearm and was not reduced from Robbery in the First Degree within seven years before the conviction of the current offense; or

- Any other violent offense within ten years before the conviction of the of the current offense;

For a violation of the Uniform Controlled Substances Act under Chapter 69.50 RCW or a criminal solicitation to commit such a violation under Chapter 9A.28 RCW, the offense involved only a small quantity of the particular controlled substance as determined by the judge upon consideration of such factors as the weight, purity, packaging, sale price, and street value of the controlled substance;

The person has not been found by the United States attorney general to be subject to a deportation detainer or order and does not become subject to a deportation order during the period of the sentence;

The standard range meets certain qualifications:

- Prison-based option: the end of the standard sentence range for the current offense is greater than one year;
- Residential-based option: the midpoint of the standard range is 26 months or less; and

The person has not received a DOSA sentence in more than once in the prior ten years before the current offense.

Sentencing

If the sentencing court determines that the person is eligible for an alternative sentence under this section and that the alternative sentence is appropriate, the court shall:

- Waive imposition of a sentence within the standard sentence range; and
- Impose a sentence consisting of either a prison-based alternative or a residential substance use disorder treatment-based alternative.

To assist the court in making its determination, for defendants convicted of a felony offense in which domestic violence *was not* pleaded and proven, the court may order the Department to complete a risk assessment report, a substance use disorder screening report or both. For defendants convicted of a felony offense in which domestic violence *was* pleaded and proven, court is required to order the Department to complete a presentence investigation and a substance use disorder screening report, unless specifically waived. Refer to RCW 9.94A.500 for minimum requirements of both prison-based and residential treatment examinations.

Prison-based option will include a period of total confinement in a state facility for one-half the midpoint of the standard sentence range or 12 months, whichever is greater.

Community Custody

The court may bring anyone sentenced under this section back into court at any time on its own initiative to evaluate the progress in treatment or to determine if any violations of the conditions of the sentence have occurred.

If a person is brought back to court, the court may modify the conditions of the community custody or impose sanctions under RCW 9.94A.660(7)(c).

The court may order the person to serve a term of total confinement within the standard range of the current offense at any time during the period of community custody if violations of the conditions or requirements of the sentence occur or if the person is failing to make satisfactory progress in treatment (RCW 9.94A.660(7)(c)).

Prison-based option includes:

- A term of community custody equal to one-half of the midpoint of the standard sentence range;
- Appropriate substance use disorder treatment in a program approved by the Department of Health;
- For co-occurring drug and domestic violence cases, appropriate domestic violence treatment in a program by a state-certified domestic violence treatment provider;
- Crime-related prohibitions, including a condition not to use illegal controlled substances;
- A requirement to submit to urinalysis or other testing;
- Upon failure to complete or administrative termination from the program, a term of community custody pursuant to RCW 9.94A.701 is to be imposed.

Residential-based option includes:
- A term of community custody equal to one-half of the midpoint of the standard range or two years, whichever is greater;
- Entrance and remaining in residential chemical dependency treatment certified under Chapter 70.96A RCW for up to six months with treatment completion and continued care delivered in accordance with rules established by the Health Care Authority
- The sentence may include an indeterminate term of confinement of no more than thirty days in a county facility to facilitate direct transfer to a residential substance use disorder treatment facility.

DOSA sentences are not eligible for the Supervision Compliance Credit established in RCW 9.94A.717.

Special Sex Offender Sentencing Alternative (SSOSA) (RCW 9.94A.670)

Eligibility

A person is eligible for the Special Sex Offender Sentencing Alternative if:

The conviction is for a sex offense that is not:
- Serious violent offense
- Rape 2nd degree; and

The person has no prior:
- Convictions for a felony sex offense in this or any other state; and
- Adult conviction for a violent offense in the five years prior to the date the current offense was committed; and

The offense did not result in substantial bodily harm to the victim; and

There was an established relationship/connection to the victim other than that resulting from the crime; and

If the conviction results from a guilty plea, the person must voluntarily and affirmatively admit to committing all of the elements of the crime (Alford and Newton pleas are not eligible); and

The standard sentence range for the offense includes the possibility of confinement of less than 11 years.

If the court finds the person is eligible for SSOSA, it may order an examination to determine whether the person is amenable to treatment. After receipt of the reports, the court shall determine whether this alternative is appropriate. If the sentencing court determines that the person is eligible for an alternative sentence under this section and that the alternative sentence is appropriate, the court shall impose a sentence or minimum term (RCW 9.94A.507) within the standard range. If the sentencing imposed is less than 11 years, the court may suspend the execution of the sentence.

Suspended Sentence Confinement

The court must impose:

- A term of confinement up to 12 months or the maximum term within the standard range, whichever is less.

The court may impose:

- A term of confinement greater than 12 months or the maximum term within the standard range if an aggravating circumstance is present.

The court may order the person to serve all or part of the sentence in partial confinement.

SSOSA sentences are not eligible for earned release.

The court may revoke the suspended sentence at any time during the period of community custody and order execution of the sentence if:

- The person violated conditions of suspended sentence; or
- The court finds the person is failing to make satisfactory progress in treatment.

Suspended Sentencing Treatment

The court must impose outpatient or inpatient sex offender treatment for any period up to five years.

Suspended Sentence Community Custody

The court must impose:

- A term of community custody equal to the length of the suspended sentence, the length of the maximum term imposed per RCW 9.94A.507, or three years, whichever is greater; and
- Specific prohibitions and affirmative conditions related to precursor behaviors or activities.

Conditions of the suspended sentence may include one or more of the following:

- Crime-related prohibitions;
- Require the person to devote time to a specific employment or occupation;
- Remain within prescribed geographical boundaries and notify the court or community corrections officer prior to any address or employment change;
- Report as directed to the court and a community corrections officer;
- Pay all court-ordered legal financial obligations;
- Perform community restitution work; or

- Reimburse victim for any counseling costs as a result of the crime.

SSOSA sentences are not eligible for the Supervision Compliance Credit established in RCW 9.94A.717.

The Department may impose sanctions for a violation of a requirement that is not a condition of the suspended sentence.

For violations of the prohibited or affirmative conditions relating to precursor behaviors or activities, the Department shall:

- First violation
  * Impose sanctions per RCW 9.94A.633(1) or
  * Refer violation to the court and recommend revocation of suspended sentence
- Second violation – refer the violation to the court and recommend revocation of suspended sentence.

If the suspended sentence is revoked, all confinement time served during community custody shall be credited to the person.

Mental Health Sentencing Alternative (RCW 9.94A.695)

Eligibility

A person is eligible for the Mental Health Sentencing Alternative if:

The defendant has a conviction for a felony that is not a serious violent or sex offense;

The defendant is diagnosed with a serious mental illness recognized by the diagnostic manual in use by mental health professionals at the time of sentencing;

The judge has determined the defendant and community would benefit from supervision and treatment; and

The defendant is willing to participate in the sentencing alternative.

In making its determination as to whether the defendant has a serious mental illness, the court may rely on information including reports completed pursuant to chapters 71.05 and 10.77 RCW, or other mental health professional as defined in RCW 71.05.020, or other information or records related to mental health services. If insufficient information is available, the court may order an examination of the defendant.

The Department is required to provide a written report, in the form of a presentence investigation, to assist the court in its determination. The court may waive the report if sufficient information is available to the court to make the determination the defendant is eligible for the alternative.

The report must include:
- A proposed treatment plan for the defendant's mental illness, which mush include at a minimum:
  o The name and address of the treatment provider that has agreed to provide treatment to the defendant, including an intake evaluation, a psychiatric evaluation, and development of an individualized plan of treatment; and

- o An agreement by the treatment provider to monitor the progress of the defendant on the sentencing alternative and notify the Department and the court at any time during the duration of the order if reasonable efforts to engage the defendant fail to produce substantial and compliance with court-ordered treatment conditions;
- A proposed monitoring plan, including any requirements regarding living conditions lifestyle requirements, and monitoring by family members and others;
- Recommended crime-related prohibitions and affirmative conditions; and

Sentencing

Imposing the Mental Health Sentencing Alternative:

After consideration of all available information and determination if the defendant is eligible, the court shall consider whether the defendant and the community will benefit from the use of the alternative.

The court shall waive imposition of a sentence within the standard sentence range and impose a sentence consisting of between 12 and 24 months of community custody if the midpoint of the defendant's standard range is less than or equal to 36 months, or a term of community custody between 12 and 36 months if the midpoint of the defendant's standard range is longer than 36 months.

The actual length of community custody within the ranges is at the discretion of the court.

The court shall consider the victim's opinion whether the defendant should receive the sentencing alternative.

When a Court Imposes a Sentence of Community Custody under this Section:

The court shall impose conditions as provided in RCW 9.94A.703 that do not conflict with the section and may impose any additional conditions recommended by any of the written reports regarding the defendant.

The court shall impose specific treatment conditions:

- Meet with treatment providers and follow the recommendations provided in the individualized treatment plan as initially constituted or subsequently modified by the treatment provider;
- Take medications as prescribed, including monitoring of compliance with medication if needed; and
- Refrain from using alcohol and nonprescribed controlled substances if the defendant has a diagnosis of a substance use disorder. The court may order the Department to monitor for such use if the court prohibits the use of those substances;

Community Custody

The Department and the treatment provider shall each submit a written report informing the parties of the defendant's progress and compliance with treatment prior to scheduled progress hearings.

Violations and Sanctions:

Treatment issues arising during supervision shall be discussed collaboratively with the treatment provider, community corrections officer (CCO), and any representative of the person's medical assistance plan; and shall jointly determine intervention for violation of a treatment condition. The CCO shall have authority to address the violation independently if:

(a) The violation is safety related with respect to the defendant or others;

(b) The treatment violation consists of decompensation related to psychosis that presents a risk to the community or the defendant and cannot be mitigated by community interventions. The CCO may intervene with available resources such as a designated crisis responder; or

(c) The violation relates to a standard condition for supervision.

The court may schedule a review hearing at any time to evaluate the defendant's progress with treatment or to determine if any violations have occurred.

At the review hearing, the court may modify the terms of community custody or impose sanctions if the court finds that the conditions have been violated or that different or additional terms are in the best interest of the defendant.

The court may order the defendant to serve a term of total or partial confinement for violating the terms of community custody or failing to make satisfactory progress in treatment.

The court may schedule a termination hearing one month prior to the end of the defendant's community custody or may also be scheduled if the Department or the state reports that the defendant has violated the terms of community custody imposed by the court. At the hearing, the court may:

- Authorize the Department to terminate the defendant's community custody status on the expiration date; or

- Continue the hearing to a date before the expiration date of community custody, with or without modifying the conditions of community custody; or

- Revoke the sentencing alternative and impose a term of total or partial confinement within the standard range or impose an exceptional sentence below the standard sentence range if compelling reasons are found by the court or the parties agree to the downward departure. The defendant shall receive credit for time served while supervised in the community against any term of total confinement.

SENTENCING ENHANCEMENTS
Felony Traffic Enhancements

Vehicular Homicide while under the Influence of Intoxicating Liquor or any Drug (RCW 9.94A.533(7))

Enhancement duration of 24 months for each prior offense under RCW 46.61.5055 in a person's criminal history.

These prior offenses used to enhance a sentence do not count towards the person's criminal history score.

Shall be served in total confinement and shall run consecutive to all other sentencing provisions, including other impaired driving enhancements, for all offenses sentenced under this chapter.

Attempting to Elude a Police Vehicle (RCW 9.94A.533(11))

Resulting in the threat of physical injury or harm to one or more persons other than the defendant or the pursuing law enforcement officer.

Enhancement duration is 12 months and 1 day enhancement added to the standard range.

In order to obtain the enhancement, the State must file a special allegation and a judge or jury must find that it occurred beyond a reasonable doubt.

Minor Child (RCW 9.94A.533(13))

Applies to the following traffic offenses:
- Vehicular Homicide while under the Influence of Intoxicating Liquor or any Drug;
- Vehicular Assault while under the Influence of Intoxicating Liquor or any Drug;
- Any Felony Driving under the Influence; or
- Felony Physical Control under the Influence.

12-month enhancement for each child passenger under 16 in the defendant's vehicle.

Shall be served in total confinement and shall run consecutively to all other sentencing provisions.

The enhancement portion of the sentence is not eligible for earned release time.

If the minor child enhancement increases the sentence so that it would exceed the statutory maximum for the offense, the portion representing the enhancement may not be reduced.

Firearm and Deadly Weapon Enhancements

All felony offenses, except those listed in RCW 9.94A.533(3)(f) and 9.94A.533(4)(f), are eligible for weapon enhancements. RCW 9.94A.533(3) gives guidelines for firearm enhancements and RCW 9.94A.533(4) for deadly weapon enhancements.

Anytime a court makes a finding of fact or a jury returns a special verdict that the accused or accomplice was armed with a deadly weapon at the time of the commission of the crime, the court must apply the enhancement to the sentence.

Enhancements apply to both the accused and any accomplice(s).

All firearm and deadly weapon enhancements shall be served in total confinement and shall run consecutively to all other offenses included in the sentence.

The enhancement portion of the sentence is not eligible for earned release time.

This applies to anticipatory offenses, including attempts, conspiracies, and solicitations to commit a crime.

If the addition of a firearm enhancement increases the sentence so that it would exceed the statutory maximum for the offense, the portion of the sentence representing the enhancement may not be reduced. RCW 9.94A.599.

For the amounts of each enhancement and the applicable offenses by effective date, please go to the Deadly Weapon Enhancement scoring form under General Scoring Forms in Section 6.

Drug-Related Enhancements

Certain drug offenses are subject to enhancements when the offense takes place in a protected zone, in the presence of a child, or in a correctional facility.

Protected Zone (RCW 9.94A.533(6))

If a person is sentenced for committing certain drug offenses committed in a protected zone.

Committed in a protected zone include the following (RCW 69.50.435):

- Schools or school buses;
- 1,000 feet of a school bus route or a school ground perimeter;
- Public parks;
- Public transit vehicles or public transit stop shelter;
- Civic centers designated as a drug-free zone by the governing authority or 1,000 feet of the perimeter of the facility, if the local governing authority specifically designates the 1,000 foot perimeter;
- In a public housing project designated by a local governing authority as a drug-free zone.

Enhancement duration of 24 months is added to the standard sentence range for any ranked eligible offense.

Presence of a Child (RCW 9.94A.533(6))

Convicted of manufacture of methamphetamine or of the possession of ephedrine or pseudo-ephedrine with intent to manufacture; and

There was a special allegation proven that a person under the age of 18 years old was present in or upon the premises.

Enhancement duration is 24 months is added to the standard sentence range for any ranked eligible offense.

Correctional Facility (RCW 9.94A.533(5))

If the individual committing the crime or the accomplice committed certain violations of the VUCSA statute while in county or state correctional facility, an enhancement must be added to the presumptive range.

18-month enhancement for offenses under RCW 69.50.401(2)(a) or (b), 69.50.410:

- Manufacture, Possess w/Intent to Deliver Heroin or Cocaine;
- Manufacture, Deliver, Possess with Intent to Deliver Schedule I or II Narcotics (Except Heroin or Cocaine) or Flunitrazepam from Schedule IV;
- Selling for Profit (Controlled or Counterfeit) any Controlled Substance; Deliver or Possess with Intent to Deliver Methamphetamine;
- Manufacture of Methamphetamine; Manufacture, Deliver, Possess with Intent to Deliver Amphetamine.

15-month enhancement for offenses under RCW 69.50.401(c), (d) or (e):

- Manufacture, Deliver, Possess with Intent to Deliver Schedule III-V Narcotics or Schedule I-V Nonnarcotic (Except Cannabis, Amphetamine, Methamphetamine or Flunitrazepam);
- Manufacture, Deliver, Possess with Intent to Deliver Cannabis;

12-month enhancement for offenses under RCW 69.50.4013*:

- Possession of Controlled Substance that is either Heroin or Narcotics from Schedule I or II or Flunitrazepam from Schedule IV;
- Possession of Phencyclidine (PCP);
- Possession of a Controlled Substance that is a Narcotic from Schedule III-V or Nonnarcotic from Schedule I-V (Except Phencyclidine).
  The offense of Possession of a Controlled Substance is classified as a gross misdemeanor, and as such, does not qualify for a sentencing enhancement under the SRA.

Sex Offense Enhancements

Sexual Conduct in Return for a Fee (RCW 9.94A.533(9))

Anticipatory offenses receive the same enhancement as if completed.

Rape of a Child or Child Molestation in exchange for a fee with the victim if committed after July 22, 2007.

Duration of enhancement is 12 months.

If the person is being sentenced for more than one offense, the one-year enhancement must be added to the total period of total confinement for all offenses, regardless of which underlying offense is subject to the enhancement.

Anticipatory offenses receive same enhancement as if completed.

Sexual Motivation (RCW 9.94A.533(8))

This enhancement is applicable to any felony offense committed after July 1, 2006.

Anticipatory offenses receive same enhancement as if completed.

Enhancement duration:

- Class A = 24 months;
- Class B = 18 months;

- Class C = 12 months.

Prior sexual motivation (SM) enhancements: if the person has any prior SM enhancements after July 1, 2006, the subsequent SM enhancement duration is doubled.

The enhancement portion of the sentence is not eligible for earned release time.

If the addition of a SM enhancement increases the sentence so that it would exceed the statutory maximum for the offense, the portion of the sentence representing the enhancement may not be reduced.

SM enhancements shall run consecutively to all other sentencing provisions.

Law Enforcement Enhancement

Assault of law enforcement officer or other employee of a law enforcement agency (RCW 9.94A.533(12)).

Any person found guilty of assaulting a law enforcement officer, or other employee of a law enforcement agency who was performing his or her duties at the time of the assault

Duration of enhancement is 12 months.

In order to obtain the enhancement, the State must file a special allegation and a judge or jury must find that it occurred beyond a reasonable doubt.

Criminal Street Gang-Related Enhancement

Felony offense involving the compensation, threatening, or solicitation of a minor in order to involve that minor in the commission of a felony offense.

This enhancement increases the standard range sentence for the underlying crime.

When the State files a special allegation and proves that a felony offense involved the compensation, threatening, or solicitation of a minor in order to involve that minor in the commission of the felony offense, the standard range for that felony is determined by multiplying the grid range by 125%. RCW 9.94A.533(10)(a).

The enhancement does not apply to any criminal street gang-related felony for which involving a minor in the commission of the felony is already an element of the offense. RCW 9.94A.533(10)(b).

This enhancement is unavailable in the event that the prosecution gives notice that it will seek an exceptional sentence based on an aggravating factor under RCW 9.94A.535.

Robbery of a Pharmacy Enhancement

The robbery of a pharmacy special enhancement applies to convictions for First or Second Degree Robbery where a special allegation is pleaded and proven beyond a reasonable doubt that the defendant committed a robbery of a pharmacy. This enhancement adds an additional 12 months to the standard range (RCW 9.94A.533(14)).

Regardless of any sentencing enhancement provisions, if a person is being sentenced in adult court for a crime committed under age eighteen, the court has full discretion to depart from mandatory sentencing enhancements and to take the particular circumstances surrounding the defendant's youth into account.

COURT'S AUTHORITY TO ORDER COMMUNITY CUSTODY

Offense	Sentenced to a term of confinement for one year or less* See RCW 9.94A.702	Sentenced to the Department of Corrections* See RCW 9.94A.701
Sex offenses (see page 105)	Up to 12 months	36 months (if not sentenced under RCW 9.94A.507)
Violent offenses (see page 103)	Up to 12 months	18 months
A crime against a person under RCW 9.94A.411(2) (see page 112)	Up to 12 months	12 months
A felony offense under Chapter 69.50 or 69.52 RCW	Up to 12 months	12 months
A felony violation of RCW 9A.44.132(1)(a)(i), (Failure to Register as a Sex Offender, first conviction)	Up to 12 months	12 months
Serious violent offense (see page 102)		36 months
Offense involving the Unlawful Possession of a Firearm (RCW 9.41.040) where the person is a criminal street gang member/associate		12 months
Motor Vehicle Supervision Program: • Theft of a Motor Vehicle (RCW 9A.56.065), or attempt; • Possession of a Stolen Vehicle (RCW 9A.56.068), or attempt; • Taking a Motor Vehicle without Permission, first degree (RCW 9A.56.070); or • Taking a Motor Vehicle without Permission, second degree (RCW 9A.56.070).		6 to 12 months†

Community Custody – Sentencing Alternatives

For Community Custody for sentence alternatives (Drug Offender Sentencing Alternative, Special Sex Offender Sentencing Alternative, First-Time Offender Sentencing Alternative, Mental Health Sentencing Alternative, and Parenting Sentencing Alternative), see requirements under sentencing alternatives summary, beginning on page 215.

Supervision Compliance Credit – RCW 9.94A.717

Supervision Compliance Credit (SCC) is awarded to eligible individuals who are in compliance with supervision terms and are making progress towards the goals of their individualized supervision case plan, including: participation in specific targeted interventions, risk-related programming, or treatment; or completing steps towards specific targeted goals that enhance protective factors and stability, as determined by the Department. For each month in compliance with community custody as listed above, a person eligible for SCC that is supervised by DOC may earn SCC of ten days.

* The Department does not have authority to supervise all individuals with orders for community custody (RCW 9.94A.501).

† For those sentenced to community custody under these provisions, the sentence of incarceration may not exceed the midpoint of the standard range reduced by one-third the ordered term of community custody. RCW 9.94A.711 (Expires June 30, 2026).

SECTION 6

GENERAL FELONY SCORING FORMS

General scoring forms are provided in Section 6 and are followed by the individual offense scoring forms in Section 7. The General scoring forms include scoring sheets intended to assist in the calculation of offender scores and sentence ranges for offenses imposed with a deadly weapon enhancement, a sexual motivation finding or a domestic violence finding.

Individual offense scoring forms are arranged alphabetically in Section 7 and include forms for controlled substances, imitation controlled substances, and legend drug crimes. Please note that the scoring forms do not present sentencing options eligibility (*e.g.,* work release, work ethic camp). Please refer to Sentencing Alternatives in Section 5 of this manual for clarification of eligibility rules or conditions for each sentencing option.

In past manuals, if a sentence range extended past the statutory maximum of the offense, the sentence range was truncated and displayed an asterisk that referenced what the statutory maximum was. In this manual, the sentence range will still be truncated where available and display an asterisk. The corresponding asterisk will be next to the classification at the top of the page, *i.e.*, Class C*.

Per EHB 1324, for any offenses that are committed on or after July 23, 2023, convictions of juvenile adjudications are not included in the offender score unless the convictions were for Murder 1, Murder 2, or a Class A sex offense. The scoring forms have been updated to reflect this change. For any offenses committed prior to July 23, 2023, please refer to the scoring rules in place at that time of the offense for scoring of juvenile adjudications.

If offense was committed after July 23, 1995, with a firearm or other deadly weapon finding:

CLASS A FELONY	
First Deadly Weapon/Firearm Offense	
Firearm	5 years
Other Deadly Weapon	2 years
Subsequent Deadly Weapon/Firearm Offense	
Firearm	10 years
Other Deadly Weapon	4 years
CLASS B FELONY	
First Deadly Weapon/Firearm Offense	
Firearm	3 years
Other Deadly Weapon	1 years
Subsequent Deadly Weapon/Firearm Offense	
Firearm	6 years
Other Deadly Weapon	2 years
CLASS C FELONY	
First Deadly Weapon/Firearm Offense	
Firearm	18 months
Other Deadly Weapon	6 months
Subsequent Deadly Weapon/Firearm Offense	
Firearm	3 years
Other Deadly Weapon	1 year

Excluded offenses: Possession of a Machine gun, Possessing a Stolen Firearm, Drive-by Shooting, Theft of a Firearm, Unlawful Possession of a Firearm 1 and 2, Use of a Machine Gun in a felony.

To be sentenced to a subsequent deadly weapon finding, the offense in history with a deadly weapon finding must also have been committed after July 23, 1995.

If offense was committed after June 12, 1994, and before July 24, 1995, with a deadly weapon finding:

OFFENSES ELIGIBLE FOR A SPECIFIC DEADLY WEAPON ENHANCEMENT	
Kidnapping 1	
Rape 1	24 Months
Robbery 1	
Burglary 1	18 Months
Assault 2	
Assault of a Child 2	
Escape 1	
Kidnapping 2	
Burglary 2	
Drug offense	12 Months
Theft of Livestock 1	
Theft of Livestock 2	
Any Serious Violent or Violent Offense Not Listed Above	

The standard range may in no case exceed the statutory maximum.

STANDARD RANGE CALCULATION

Offender Score .... _____

Seriousness Level .... _____

	Low	to	High

STANDARD SENTENCE RANGE .... _____ ..... _____

DEADLY WEAPON ENHANCEMENT .... _____

	Low	to	High

STANDARD SENTENCE RANGE PLUS ENHANCEMENT.............. _____ ..... _____

✓   For anticipatory offenses, add the enhancement after reducing the standard sentence range.

General Nonviolent Offense where Domestic Violence has been Plead and Proven

NONVIOLENT
OFFENDER SCORING RCW 9.94A.525(21)

CURRENT OFFENSE BEING SCORED: ....

ADULT HISTORY:

Enter number of domestic violence felony convictions as listed below* .... _____ x 2 = _____

Enter number of <u>repetitive domestic violence offense</u> convictions (RCW 9.94A.030(42)) plead and proven after 8/1/11.. _____ x 1 = _____

Enter number of felony convictions .... _____ x 1 = _____

JUVENILE HISTORY:

Enter number of Murder 1, Murder 2, and Class A sex offense felony dispositions .... _____ x 1 = _____

OTHER CURRENT OFFENSES:

(Other current offenses that do not encompass the same conduct count in offender score)

Enter number of other domestic violence felony convictions as listed below* .... _____ x 2 = _____

Enter number of other <u>repetitive domestic violence offense</u> convictions plead and proven after 8/1/11.. _____ x 1 = _____

Enter number of other felony convictions .... _____ x 1 = _____

STATUS:

Was the offender on community custody on the date the current offense was committed? (if yes) _____ + 1 = _____

*   * If domestic violence was plead and proven after 8/1/2011 for the following felony offenses:*

Violation of a No-Contact Order, Violation of a Protection Order, Domestic Violence Harassment, Domestic Violence Stalking, Domestic Violence Burglary 1, Domestic Violence Kidnapping 1, Domestic Violence Kidnapping 2, Domestic Violence Unlawful Imprisonment, Domestic Violence Robbery 1, Domestic Violence Robbery 2, Domestic Violence Assault 1, Domestic Violence Assault 2, Domestic Violence Assault 3, Domestic Violence Arson 1, Domestic Violence Arson 2.

*   * If domestic violence was plead and proven after 7/23/17 for the following felony offenses:*

Assault of a Child 1, Assault of a Child 2, Assault of a Child 3, Criminal Mistreatment 1, Criminal Mistreatment 2.

STANDARD RANGE CALCULATION

Total the last column to get the **Offender Score** (Round down to the nearest whole number) .... = _____

Seriousness Level .... = _____

	Low	to	High

STANDARD SENTENCE RANGE .... _____ ..... _____

✓   For attempt, solicitation, conspiracy (RCW 9.94A.595) see page 54 or for gang-related felonies where the court found the offender involved a minor (RCW 9.94A.833) see page 227 for standard range adjustments.
✓   For deadly weapon enhancement, see page 233.
✓   For sentencing alternatives, see page 215.
✓   For community custody eligibility, see page 228.
✓   For any applicable enhancements other than deadly weapon enhancement, see page 224.

General Nonviolent/Sex Offense where Domestic Violence has been Plead and Proven

NONVIOLENT/SEX OFFENDER SCORING RCW 9.94A.525(17)

CURRENT OFFENSE BEING SCORED: ....

ADULT HISTORY:

Enter number of sex offense felony convictions .... _____ x 3 = _____

Enter number of domestic violence felony convictions as listed below* .... _____ x 2 = _____

Enter number of repetitive domestic violence offense convictions (RCW 9.94A.030(42)) plead and proven after 8/1/11 .... _____ x 1 = _____

Enter number of felony convictions .... _____ x 1 = _____

JUVENILE HISTORY:

Enter number of Class A sex offense felony dispositions .... _____ x 3 = _____

Enter number of Murder 1 and 2 dispositions .... _____ x 1 = _____

OTHER CURRENT OFFENSES:

(Other current offenses that do not encompass the same conduct count in offender score)

Enter number of other sex offense felony convictions .... _____ x 3 = _____

Enter number of other domestic violence felony convictions as listed below* .... _____ x 2 = _____

Enter number of other repetitive domestic violence offense convictions plead and proven after 8/1/11 .... _____ x 1 = _____

Enter number of other felony convictions .... _____ x 1 = _____

STATUS:

Was the offender on community custody on the date the current offense was committed? (if yes) _____ + 1 = _____

If domestic violence was plead and proven after 8/1/2011 for the following felony offenses:

Violation of a No-Contact Order, Violation of a Protection Order, Domestic Violence Harassment, Domestic Violence Stalking, Domestic Violence Burglary 1, Domestic Violence Kidnapping 1, Domestic Violence Kidnapping 2, Domestic Violence Unlawful Imprisonment, Domestic Violence Robbery 1, Domestic Violence Robbery 2, Domestic Violence Assault 1, Domestic Violence Assault 2, Domestic Violence Assault 3, Domestic Violence Arson 1, Domestic Violence Arson 2.

If domestic violence was plead and proven after 7/23/17 for the following felony offenses:

Assault of a Child 1, Assault of a Child 2, Assault of a Child 3, Criminal Mistreatment 1, Criminal Mistreatment 2.

STANDARD RANGE CALCULATION

Total the last column to get the **Offender Score** (Round down to the nearest whole number) .... = _____

Seriousness Level .... = _____

	Low	to	High

STANDARD SENTENCE RANGE .... _____ ..... _____

✓ For attempt, solicitation, conspiracy (RCW 9.94A.595) see page 54 or for gang-related felonies where the court found the offender involved a minor (RCW 9.94A.833) see page 227 for standard range adjustments.
✓ For deadly weapon enhancement, see page 233.
✓ For sentencing alternatives, see page 215.
✓ For community custody eligibility, see page 228.
✓ For any applicable enhancements other than deadly weapon enhancement, see page 224.
✓ If the offender is not a persistent offender and has a prior conviction for an offense listed in RCW 9.94A.030(37)(b), then the sentence is subject to the requirements of RCW 9.94A.507.

NONVIOLENT/SEX
OFFENDER SCORING RCW 9.94A.525(17)

CURRENT OFFENSE BEING SCORED: ....

ADULT HISTORY:

    Enter number of sex offense felony convictions .... _____ x 3 = _____

    Enter number of felony convictions .... _____ x 1 = _____

JUVENILE HISTORY:

    Enter number of Class A sex offense felony dispositions .... _____ x 3 = _____

    Enter number of Murder 1 and 2 dispositions .... _____ x 1 = _____

OTHER CURRENT OFFENSES:

(Other current offenses that do not encompass the same conduct count in offender score)

    Enter number of other sex offense felony convictions .... _____ x 3 = _____

    Enter number of other felony convictions .... _____ x 1 = _____

STATUS:

    Was the offender on community custody on the date the current offense was committed? (if yes) _____ + 1 = _____

STANDARD RANGE CALCULATION

Total the last column to get the **Offender Score** (Round down to the nearest whole number) .... _____

Seriousness Level .... _____

                                       Low   to   High

STANDARD SENTENCE RANGE .... _____ ..... _____

SEXUAL MOTIVATION ENHANCEMENT (Per Sexual Motivation Enhancement, page 226) .... _____

                                       Low   to   High

STANDARD SENTENCE RANGE PLUS ENHANCEMENT .... _____ ..... _____

✓ For attempt, solicitation, conspiracy (RCW 9.94A.595) see page 54 or for gang-related felonies where the court found the offender involved a minor (RCW 9.94A.833) see page 227 for standard range adjustments.

✓ For deadly weapon enhancement, see page 233.

✓ For sentencing alternatives, see page 215.

✓ For community custody eligibility, see page 228.

✓ For any applicable enhancements other than deadly weapon enhancement, see page 224.

✓ If the offender is not a persistent offender and has a <u>prior</u> conviction for an offense listed in RCW 9.94A.030(37)(b), then the sentence is subject to the requirements of RCW 9.94A.507.

General Nonviolent Drug Offense where Domestic Violence has been Plead and Proven

NONVIOLENT/DRUG
OFFENDER SCORING RCW 9.94A.525(21)

CURRENT OFFENSE BEING SCORED: ....

ADULT HISTORY:

Enter number of domestic violence felony convictions as listed below* .... _____ x 2 = _____

Enter number of repetitive domestic violence offense convictions (RCW 9.94A.030(42)) plead and proven after 8/1/11 .... _____ x 1 = _____

Does the offender have a prior sex or serious violent offense in history?

.... **YES,** Enter number of felony drug convictions _____ x 3 = _____

.... **NO,** Enter number of felony drug convictions _____ x 1 = _____

Enter number of felony convictions .... _____ x 1 = _____

JUVENILE HISTORY:

Enter number of Murder 1, Murder 2, and Class A sex offense felony dispositions .... _____ x 1 = _____

OTHER CURRENT OFFENSES:

(Other current offenses that do not encompass the same conduct count in offender score)

Enter number of other domestic violence felony convictions as listed below* .... _____ x 2 = _____

Enter number of other repetitive domestic violence offense convictions plead and proven after 8/1/11 .... _____ x 1 = _____

Does the offender have other prior sex or serious violent offense in history?

.... **YES,** Enter number of other felony drug convictions _____ x 3 = _____

.... **NO,** Enter number of other felony drug convictions _____ x 1 = _____

Enter number of other felony convictions .... _____ x 1 = _____

STATUS:

Was the offender on community custody on the date the current offense was committed? (if yes) _____ + 1 = _____

*If domestic violence was plead and proven after 8/1/2011 for the following felony offenses:

Violation of a No-Contact Order, Violation of a Protection Order, Domestic Violence Harassment, Domestic Violence Stalking, Domestic Violence Burglary 1, Domestic Violence Kidnapping 1, Domestic Violence Kidnapping 2, Domestic Violence Unlawful Imprisonment, Domestic Violence Robbery 1, Domestic Violence Robbery 2, Domestic Violence Assault 1, Domestic Violence Assault 2, Domestic Violence Assault 3, Domestic Violence Arson 1, Domestic Violence Arson 2.

*If domestic violence was plead and proven after 7/23/17 for the following felony offenses:

Assault of a Child 1, Assault of a Child 2, Assault of a Child 3, Criminal Mistreatment 1, Criminal Mistreatment 2.

STANDARD RANGE CALCULATION

Total the last column to get the **Offender Score** (Round down to the nearest whole number) .... = _____

Seriousness Level .... = _____

Low   to   High

STANDARD SENTENCE RANGE .... _____ ..... _____

✓ For attempt, solicitation, conspiracy (RCW 9.94A.595) see page 54 or for gang-related felonies where the court found the offender involved a minor (RCW 9.94A.833) see page 227 for standard range adjustments.
✓ For deadly weapon enhancement, see page 233.
✓ For sentencing alternatives, see page 215.
✓ For community custody eligibility, see page 228.
✓ For any applicable enhancements other than deadly weapon enhancement, see page 224.

General Nonviolent Drug Offense with a Sexual Motivation Finding
NONVIOLENT/DRUG/SEX
OFFENDER SCORING RCW 9.94A.525(17)

CURRENT OFFENSE BEING SCORED: ....

ADULT HISTORY:

Enter number of sex offense felony convictions .... _____ x 3 = _____

Does the offender have a prior sex or serious violent offense in history?

.... **YES,** Enter number of felony drug convictions _____ x 3 = _____

.... **NO,** Enter number of felony drug convictions _____ x 1 = _____

Enter number of felony convictions .... _____ x 1 = _____

JUVENILE HISTORY:

Enter number of Class A sex offense felony dispositions .... _____ x 3 = _____

Enter number of Murder 1 and 2 dispositions .... _____ x 1 = _____

OTHER CURRENT OFFENSES:

(Other current offenses that do not encompass the same conduct count in offender score)

Enter number of other sex offense felony convictions .... _____ x 3 = _____

Does the offender have other prior sex or serious violent offense in history?

.... **YES,** Enter number of other felony drug convictions _____ x 3 = _____

.... **NO,** Enter number of other felony drug convictions _____ x 1 = _____

Enter number of other felony convictions .... _____ x 1 = _____

STATUS:

Was the offender on community custody on the date the current offense was committed? (if yes) _____ + 1 = _____

STANDARD RANGE CALCULATION

Total the last column to get the **Offender Score** (Round down to the nearest whole number) .... _____

Seriousness Level .... _____

	Low	to	High

STANDARD SENTENCE RANGE .... _____ ..... _____

SEXUAL MOTIVATION ENHANCEMENT (Per Sexual Motivation Enhancement, page 226).................... _____

	Low	to	High

STANDARD SENTENCE RANGE PLUS ENHANCEMENT .... _____ ..... _____

✓   For attempt, solicitation, conspiracy (RCW 9.94A.595) see page 56 or for gang-related felonies where the court found the offender involved a minor (RCW 9.94A.833) see page 227 for standard range adjustments.
✓   For deadly weapon enhancement, see page 233.
✓   For sentencing alternatives, see page 215.
✓   For community custody eligibility, see page 228.
✓   For any applicable enhancements other than deadly weapon enhancement, see page 224.
✓   If the offender is not a persistent offender and has a prior conviction for an offense listed in RCW 9.94A.030(37)(b), then the sentence is subject to the requirements of RCW 9.94A.507.

General Serious Violent Offense where Domestic Violence has been Plead and Proven

SERIOUS VIOLENT
OFFENDER SCORING RCW 9.94A.525(21)

CURRENT OFFENSE BEING SCORED: ....

ADULT HISTORY:

Enter number of domestic violence felony convictions as listed below* .... _____ x 2 = _____

Enter number of <u>repetitive domestic violence offense</u> convictions (RCW 9.94A.030(42))
plead and proven after 8/1/11 .... _____ x 1 = _____

Enter number of serious violent felony convictions .... _____ x 3 = _____

Enter number of violent felony convictions .... _____ x 2 = _____

Enter number of nonviolent felony convictions .... _____ x 1 = _____

JUVENILE HISTORY:

Enter number of Murder 1, Murder 2, and Serious Violent sex offense felony dispositions .... _____ x 3 = _____

Enter number of Class A sex offense (not Serious Violent) felony dispositions .... _____ x 2 = _____

OTHER CURRENT OFFENSES:

(Other current offenses that do not encompass the same conduct count in offender score)

Enter number of other domestic violence felony convictions as listed below* .... _____ x 2 = _____

Enter number of other <u>repetitive domestic violence offense</u> convictions plead and
proven after 8/1/11 .... _____ x 1 = _____

Enter number of other violent felony convictions .... _____ x 2 = _____

Enter number of other nonviolent felony convictions .... _____ x 1 = _____

STATUS:

Was the offender on community custody on the date the current offense was committed?........... _____ + 1 = _____

*If domestic violence was plead and proven after 8/1/2011 for the following felony offenses:

Violation of a No-Contact Order, Violation of a Protection Order, Domestic Violence Harassment, Domestic Violence Stalking, Domestic Violence Burglary 1, Domestic Violence Kidnapping 1, Domestic Violence Kidnapping 2, Domestic Violence Unlawful Imprisonment, Domestic Violence Robbery 1, Domestic Violence Robbery 2, Domestic Violence Assault 1, Domestic Violence Assault 2, Domestic Violence Assault 3, Domestic Violence Arson 1, Domestic Violence Arson 2.

*If domestic violence was plead and proven after 7/23/17 for the following felony offenses:

Assault of a Child 1, Assault of a Child 2, Assault of a Child 3, Criminal Mistreatment 1, Criminal Mistreatment 2.

STANDARD RANGE CALCULATION

Total the last column to get the **Offender Score** (Round down to the nearest whole number) .... = _____

Seriousness Level .... = _____

	Low	to	High

STANDARD SENTENCE RANGE .... _____ ..... _____

✓ For attempt, solicitation, conspiracy (RCW 9.94A.595) see page 54 or for gang-related felonies where the court found the offender involved a minor (RCW 9.94A.833) see page 227 for standard range adjustments.
✓ For deadly weapon enhancement, see page 233.
✓ For sentencing alternatives, see page 215.
✓ For community custody eligibility, see page 228.
✓ For any applicable enhancements other than deadly weapon enhancement, see page 224.

General Serious Violent Sex Offense where Domestic Violence has been Plead and Proven

SERIOUS VIOLENT/SEX OFFENDER SCORING RCW 9.94A.525(17)

CURRENT OFFENSE BEING SCORED: ....

ADULT HISTORY:

Enter number of sex offense felony convictions .... _____ x 3 = _____

Enter number of domestic violence felony convictions as listed below* .... _____ x 2 = _____

Enter number of <u>repetitive domestic violence offense</u> convictions (RCW 9.94A.030(42)) plead and proven after 8/1/11.. _____ x 1 = _____

Enter number of serious violent felony convictions .... _____ x 3 = _____

Enter number of violent felony convictions .... _____ x 2 = _____

Enter number of nonviolent felony convictions .... _____ x 1 = _____

JUVENILE HISTORY:

Enter number of Murder 1, Murder 2, and Class A sex offense felony dispositions .... _____ x 3 = _____

OTHER CURRENT OFFENSES:

(Other current offenses that do not encompass the same conduct count in offender score)

Enter number of other sex offense felony convictions .... _____ x 3 = _____

Enter number of other domestic violence felony convictions as listed below* .... _____ x 2 = _____

Enter number of other <u>repetitive domestic violence offense</u> convictions plead and proven after 8/1/11.. _____ x 1 = _____

Enter number of other violent felony convictions .... _____ x 2 = _____

Enter number of other nonviolent felony convictions .... _____ x 1 = _____

STATUS:

Was the offender on community custody on the date the current offense was committed? .... _____ + 1 = _____

If domestic violence was plead and proven after 8/1/2011 for the following felony offenses:

Violation of a No-Contact Order, Violation of a Protection Order, Domestic Violence Harassment, Domestic Violence Stalking, Domestic Violence Burglary 1, Domestic Violence Kidnapping 1, Domestic Violence Kidnapping 2, Domestic Violence Unlawful Imprisonment, Domestic Violence Robbery 1, Domestic Violence Robbery 2, Domestic Violence Assault 1, Domestic Violence Assault 2, Domestic Violence Assault 3, Domestic Violence Arson 1, Domestic Violence Arson 2.

If domestic violence was plead and proven after 7/23/17 for the following felony offenses:

Assault of a Child 1, Assault of a Child 2, Assault of a Child 3, Criminal Mistreatment 1, Criminal Mistreatment 2.

STANDARD RANGE CALCULATION

Total the last column to get the **Offender Score** (Round down to the nearest whole number) .... = _____

Seriousness Level .... = _____

	Low	to	High

STANDARD SENTENCE RANGE .... _____ ..... _____

✓ For attempt, solicitation, conspiracy (RCW 9.94A.595) see page 54 or for gang-related felonies where the court found the offender involved a minor (RCW 9.94A.833) see page 227 for standard range adjustments.
✓ For deadly weapon enhancement, see page 233.
✓ For sentencing alternatives, see page 215.
✓ For community custody eligibility, see page 228.
✓ For any applicable enhancements other than deadly weapon enhancement, see page 224.
✓ If the offender is not a persistent offender and has a <u>prior</u> conviction for an offense listed in RCW 9.94A.030(37)(b), then the sentence is subject to the requirements of RCW 9.94A.507.

SERIOUS VIOLENT/SEX
OFFENDER SCORING RCW 9.94A.525(17)

CURRENT OFFENSE BEING SCORED: ....

ADULT HISTORY:

Enter number of sex offense felony convictions .... _____ x 3 = _____

Enter number of serious violent felony convictions .... _____ x 3 = _____

Enter number of violent felony convictions .... _____ x 2 = _____

Enter number of nonviolent felony convictions .... _____ x 1 = _____

JUVENILE HISTORY:

Enter number of Murder 1, Murder 2, and Class A sex offense felony dispositions .... _____ x 3 = _____

OTHER CURRENT OFFENSES:

(Other current offenses that do not encompass the same conduct count in offender score)

Enter number of other sex offense felony convictions .... _____ x 3 = _____

Enter number of other violent felony convictions .... _____ x 2 = _____

Enter number of other nonviolent felony convictions .... _____ x 1 = _____

STATUS:

Was the offender on community custody on the date the current offense was committed?........... _____ + 1 = _____

STANDARD RANGE CALCULATION

Total the last column to get the **Offender Score** (Round down to the nearest whole number) .... _____

Seriousness Level .... _____

	Low	to	High

STANDARD SENTENCE RANGE .... _____ ..... _____

SEXUAL MOTIVATION ENHANCEMENT (Per Sexual Motivation Enhancement, page 226) .... _____

	Low	to	High

STANDARD SENTENCE RANGE PLUS ENHANCEMENT.............. _____ ..... _____

✓ For attempt, solicitation, conspiracy (RCW 9.94A.595) see page 54 or for gang-related felonies where the court found the offender involved a minor (RCW 9.94A.833) see page 227 for standard range adjustments.
✓ For deadly weapon enhancement, see page 233.
✓ For sentencing alternatives, see page 215.
✓ For community custody eligibility, see page 228.
✓ For any applicable enhancements other than deadly weapon enhancement, see page 224.
✓ If the offender is not a persistent offender and has a <u>prior</u> conviction for an offense listed in RCW 9.94A.030(37)(b), then the sentence is subject to the requirements of RCW 9.94A.507.

General Violent Offense where Domestic Violence has been Plead and Proven

VIOLENT
OFFENDER SCORING RCW 9.94A.525(21)

CURRENT OFFENSE BEING SCORED: ....

ADULT HISTORY:

Enter number of domestic violence felony convictions as listed below* .... _____ x 2 = _____

Enter number of <u>repetitive domestic violence offense</u> convictions (RCW 9.94A.030(42)) plead and proven after 8/1/11.. _____ x 1 = _____

Enter number of serious violent and violent felony convictions .... _____ x 2 = _____

Enter number of nonviolent felony convictions .... _____ x 1 = _____

JUVENILE HISTORY:

Enter number of Murder 1, Murder 2, and Class A sex offense felony dispositions .... _____ x 2 = _____

OTHER CURRENT OFFENSES:

(Other current offenses that do not encompass the same conduct count in offender score)

Enter number of other domestic violence felony convictions as listed below* .... _____ x 2 = _____

Enter number of <u>repetitive domestic violence offense</u> convictions plead and proven after 8/1/11... _____ x 1 = _____

Enter number of other serious violent and violent felony convictions .... _____ x 2 = _____

Enter number of other nonviolent felony convictions .... _____ x 1 = _____

STATUS:

Was the offender on community custody on the date the current offense was committed? .... _____ + 1 = _____

> *If domestic violence was plead and proven after 8/1/2011 for the following felony offenses:*
>
> *Violation of a No-Contact Order, Violation of a Protection Order, Domestic Violence Harassment, Domestic Violence Stalking, Domestic Violence Burglary 1, Domestic Violence Kidnapping 1, Domestic Violence Kidnapping 2, Domestic Violence Unlawful Imprisonment, Domestic Violence Robbery 1, Domestic Violence Robbery 2, Domestic Violence Assault 1, Domestic Violence Assault 2, Domestic Violence Assault 3, Domestic Violence Arson 1, Domestic Violence Arson 2.*
>
> *If domestic violence was plead and proven after 7/23/17 for the following felony offenses:*
>
> *Assault of a Child 1, Assault of a Child 2, Assault of a Child 3, Criminal Mistreatment 1, Criminal Mistreatment 2.*

STANDARD RANGE CALCULATION

Total the last column to get the **Offender Score** (Round down to the nearest whole number) .... = _____

Seriousness Level .... = _____

| | Low | to | High |

STANDARD SENTENCE RANGE .... _____ ..... _____

✓ For attempt, solicitation, conspiracy (RCW 9.94A.595) see page 54 or for gang-related felonies where the court found the offender involved a minor (RCW 9.94A.833) see page 227 for standard range adjustments.
✓ For deadly weapon enhancement, see page 233.
✓ For sentencing alternatives, see page 215.
✓ For community custody eligibility, see page 228.
✓ For any applicable enhancements other than deadly weapon enhancement, see page 224.

General Violent Sex Offense where Domestic Violence has been Plead and Proven

VIOLENT/SEX
OFFENDER SCORING RCW 9.94A.525(17)

CURRENT OFFENSE BEING SCORED: ....

ADULT HISTORY:

Enter number of sex offense felony convictions .... _____ x 3 = _____

Enter number of domestic violence felony convictions as listed below* .... _____ x 2 = _____

Enter number of repetitive domestic violence offense convictions (RCW 9.94A.030(42)) plead and proven after 8/1/11 .... _____ x 1 = _____

Enter number of serious violent and violent felony convictions .... _____ x 2 = _____

Enter number of nonviolent felony convictions .... _____ x 1 = _____

JUVENILE HISTORY:

Enter number of Class A sex offense felony dispositions .... _____ x 3 = _____

Enter number of Murder 1 and Murder 2 felony dispositions .... _____ x 2 = _____

OTHER CURRENT OFFENSES:

(Other current offenses that do not encompass the same conduct count in offender score)

Enter number of other sex offense felony convictions .... _____ x 3 = _____

Enter number of other domestic violence felony convictions as listed below* .... _____ x 2 = _____

Enter number of repetitive domestic violence offense convictions plead and proven after 8/1/11 .... _____ x 1 = _____

Enter number of other serious violent and violent felony convictions .... _____ x 2 = _____

Enter number of other nonviolent felony convictions .... _____ x 1 = _____

STATUS:

Was the offender on community custody on the date the current offense was committed?............ _____ + 1 = _____

If domestic violence was plead and proven after 8/1/2011 for the following felony offenses:

Violation of a No-Contact Order, Violation of a Protection Order, Domestic Violence Harassment, Domestic Violence Stalking, Domestic Violence Burglary 1, Domestic Violence Kidnapping 1, Domestic Violence Kidnapping 2, Domestic Violence Unlawful Imprisonment, Domestic Violence Robbery 1, Domestic Violence Robbery 2, Domestic Violence Assault 1, Domestic Violence Assault 2, Domestic Violence Assault 3, Domestic Violence Arson 1, Domestic Violence Arson 2.

If domestic violence was plead and proven after 7/23/17 for the following felony offenses:

Assault of a Child 1, Assault of a Child 2, Assault of a Child 3, Criminal Mistreatment 1, Criminal Mistreatment 2.

STANDARD RANGE CALCULATION

Total the last column to get the **Offender Score** (Round down to the nearest whole number) .... = _____

Seriousness Level .... = _____

	Low	to	High

STANDARD SENTENCE RANGE .... _____ ..... _____

✓ For attempt, solicitation, conspiracy (RCW 9.94A.595) see page 54 or for gang-related felonies where the court found the offender involved a minor (RCW 9.94A.833) see page 227 for standard range adjustments.
✓ For deadly weapon enhancement, see page 233.
✓ For sentencing alternatives, see page 215.
✓ For community custody eligibility, see page 228.
✓ For any applicable enhancements other than deadly weapon enhancement, see page 224.
✓ If the offender is not a persistent offender and has a prior conviction for an offense listed in RCW 9.94A.030(37)(b), then the sentence is subject to the requirements of RCW 9.94A.507.

VIOLENT/SEX
OFFENDER SCORING RCW 9.94A.525(17)

CURRENT OFFENSE BEING SCORED: ....

ADULT HISTORY:

    Enter number of sex offense felony convictions .... _____ x 3 = _____

    Enter number of serious violent and violent felony convictions .... _____ x 2 = _____

    Enter number of nonviolent felony convictions .... _____ x 1 = _____

JUVENILE HISTORY:

    Enter number of Class A sex offense felony dispositions .... _____ x 3 = _____

    Enter number of Murder 1 and Murder 2 felony dispositions .... _____ x 2 = _____

OTHER CURRENT OFFENSES:

(Other current offenses that do not encompass the same conduct count in offender score)

    Enter number of other sex offense felony convictions .... _____ x 3 = _____

    Enter number of other serious violent and violent felony convictions .... _____ x 2 = _____

    Enter number of other nonviolent felony convictions .... _____ x 1 = _____

STATUS:

    Was the offender on community custody on the date the current offense was committed? .... _____ + 1 = _____

STANDARD RANGE CALCULATION

Total the last column to get the **Offender Score** (Round down to the nearest whole number) .... _____

Seriousness Level .... _____

                                            Low   to   High

STANDARD SENTENCE RANGE .... _____ ..... _____

SEXUAL MOTIVATION ENHANCEMENT (Per Sexual Motivation Enhancement, page 226).................... _____

                                            Low   to   High

STANDARD SENTENCE RANGE PLUS ENHANCEMENT .... _____ ..... _____

✓   For attempt, solicitation, conspiracy (RCW 9.94A.595) see page 54 or for gang-related felonies where the court found the offender involved a minor (RCW 9.94A.833) see page 227 for standard range adjustments.

✓   For deadly weapon enhancement, see page 233.

✓   For sentencing alternatives, see page 215.

✓   For community custody eligibility, see page 228.

✓   For any applicable enhancements other than deadly weapon enhancement, see page 224.

✓   If the offender is not a persistent offender and has a <u>prior</u> conviction for an offense listed in RCW 9.94A.030(37)(b), then the sentence is subject to the requirements of RCW 9.94A.507.

General Burglary First Degree Offense where Domestic Violence has been Plead and Proven

VIOLENT
OFFENDER SCORING RCW 9.94A.525(21)

CURRENT OFFENSE BEING SCORED: ....

ADULT HISTORY:

Enter number of domestic violence felony convictions as listed below* .... _____ x 2 = _____

Enter number of <u>repetitive domestic violence offense</u> convictions (RCW 9.94A.030(42)) plead and proven after 8/1/11 .... _____ x 1 = _____

Enter number of Burglary 2 and Residential Burglary felony convictions .... _____ x 2 = _____

Enter number of serious violent and violent felony convictions .... _____ x 2 = _____

Enter number of nonviolent felony convictions .... _____ x 1 = _____

JUVENILE HISTORY:

Enter number of Murder 1, Murder 2, and Class A sex offense felony dispositions .... _____ x 2 = _____

OTHER CURRENT OFFENSES:

(Other current offenses that do not encompass the same conduct count in offender score)

Enter number of other domestic violence felony convictions as listed below* .... _____ x 2 = _____

Enter number of <u>repetitive domestic violence offense</u> convictions plead and proven after 8/1/11 .... _____ x 1 = _____

Enter number of Burglary 2 and Residential Burglary felony convictions .... _____ x 2 = _____

Enter number of other serious violent and violent felony convictions .... _____ x 2 = _____

Enter number of other nonviolent felony convictions .... _____ x 1 = _____

STATUS:

Was the offender on community custody on the date the current offense was committed? .... _____ + 1 = _____

If domestic violence was plead and proven after 8/1/2011 for the following felony offenses:

Violation of a No-Contact Order, Violation of a Protection Order, Domestic Violence Harassment, Domestic Violence Stalking, Domestic Violence Burglary 1, Domestic Violence Kidnapping 1, Domestic Violence Kidnapping 2, Domestic Violence Unlawful Imprisonment, Domestic Violence Robbery 1, Domestic Violence Robbery 2, Domestic Violence Assault 1, Domestic Violence Assault 2, Domestic Violence Assault 3, Domestic Violence Arson 1, Domestic Violence Arson 2.

If domestic violence was plead and proven after 7/23/17 for the following felony offenses:

Assault of a Child 1, Assault of a Child 2, Assault of a Child 3, Criminal Mistreatment 1, Criminal Mistreatment 2.

STANDARD RANGE CALCULATION

Total the last column to get the **Offender Score** (Round down to the nearest whole number) .... = _____

Seriousness Level .... = _____

	Low	to	High

STANDARD SENTENCE RANGE .... _____ ..... _____

✓ For attempt, solicitation, conspiracy (RCW 9.94A.595) see page 54 or for gang-related felonies where the court found the offender involved a minor (RCW 9.94A.833) see page 227 for standard range adjustments.
✓ For deadly weapon enhancement, see page 233.
✓ For sentencing alternatives, see page 215.
✓ For community custody eligibility, see page 228.
✓ For any applicable enhancements other than deadly weapon enhancement, see page 224.

General Burglary Second Degree or Residential Burglary Offense where Domestic Violence has been Plead and Proven

NONVIOLENT
OFFENDER SCORING RCW 9.94A.525(21)

CURRENT OFFENSE BEING SCORED: ....

ADULT HISTORY:

Enter number of domestic violence felony convictions as listed below* .... _____ x 2 = _____

Enter number of <u>repetitive domestic violence offense</u> convictions (RCW 9.94A.030(42)) plead and proven after 8/1/11... _____ x 1 = _____

Enter number of Burglary 1 felony convictions .... _____ x 2 = _____

Enter number of Burglary 2 and Residential Burglary felony convictions .... _____ x 2 = _____

Enter number of felony convictions .... _____ x 1 = _____

JUVENILE HISTORY:

Enter number of Murder 1, Murder 2, and Class A sex offense felony dispositions ..... _____ x 1 = _____

OTHER CURRENT OFFENSES:

(Other current offenses that do not encompass the same conduct count in offender score)

Enter number of other domestic violence felony convictions as listed below* .... _____ x 2 = _____

Enter number of other <u>repetitive domestic violence offense</u> convictions plead and proven after 8/1/11... _____ x 1 = _____

Enter number of Burglary 1 felony convictions .... _____ x 2 = _____

Enter number of Burglary 2 and Residential Burglary felony convictions .... _____ x 2 = _____

Enter number of other felony convictions .... _____ x 1 = _____

STATUS:

Was the offender on community custody on the date the current offense was committed? (if yes) _____ + 1 = _____

If domestic violence was plead and proven after 8/1/2011 for the following felony offenses:

Violation of a No-Contact Order, Violation of a Protection Order, Domestic Violence Harassment, Domestic Violence Stalking, Domestic Violence Burglary 1, Domestic Violence Kidnapping 1, Domestic Violence Kidnapping 2, Domestic Violence Unlawful Imprisonment, Domestic Violence Robbery 1, Domestic Violence Robbery 2, Domestic Violence Assault 1, Domestic Violence Assault 2, Domestic Violence Assault 3, Domestic Violence Arson 1, Domestic Violence Arson 2.

If domestic violence was plead and proven after 7/23/17 for the following felony offenses:

Assault of a Child 1, Assault of a Child 2, Assault of a Child 3, Criminal Mistreatment 1, Criminal Mistreatment 2.

STANDARD RANGE CALCULATION

Total the last column to get the **Offender Score** (Round down to the nearest whole number) .... = _____

Seriousness Level .... = _____

	Low	to	High

STANDARD SENTENCE RANGE .... _____ ..... _____

✓ For attempt, solicitation, conspiracy (RCW 9.94A.595) see page 54 or for gang-related felonies where the court found the offender involved a minor (RCW 9.94A.833) see page 227 for standard range adjustments.
✓ For deadly weapon enhancement, see page 233.
✓ For sentencing alternatives, see page 215.
✓ For community custody eligibility, see page 228.
✓ For any applicable enhancements other than deadly weapon enhancement, see page 224.

NONVIOLENT/SEX
OFFENDER SCORING RCW 9.94A.525(17)

CURRENT OFFENSE BEING SCORED: ....

ADULT HISTORY:

> Not scored

JUVENILE HISTORY:

> Not scored

OTHER CURRENT OFFENSES:

> Not scored

STATUS:

> Not scored

STANDARD RANGE CALCULATION

	Low	to	High
STANDARD SENTENCE RANGE	_____	.....	_____
SEXUAL MOTIVATION ENHANCEMENT (Per Sexual Motivation Enhancement, page 226)			_____
	Low	to	High
STANDARD SENTENCE RANGE PLUS ENHANCEMENT..............	_____	.....	_____

- ✓ For gang-related felonies where the court found the offender involved a minor (RCW 9.94A.833) see page 227 for standard range adjustment.
- ✓ For deadly weapon enhancement, see page 233.
- ✓ For sentencing alternatives, see page 215.
- ✓ For community custody eligibility, see page 228.
- ✓ For any applicable enhancements other than deadly weapon enhancement, see page 224.
- ✓ If the offender is not a persistent offender and has a prior conviction for an offense listed in RCW 9.94A.030(37)(b), then the sentence is subject to the requirements of RCW 9.94A.507.

SECTION 7

ALPHABETIZED FELONY SCORING FORMS

General scoring forms are provided in Section 6 and are followed by the individual offense scoring forms in Section 7. The individual offense scoring forms are arranged alphabetically and include forms for controlled substances, imitation controlled substances, and legend drug crimes. Please note that the scoring forms do not present sentencing options eligibility (*e.g.*, work release, Graduated Reentry Program). Please refer to Sentencing Alternatives in Section 5 of this manual for clarification of eligibility rules or conditions for each sentencing option.

In past manuals, if a sentence range extended past the statutory maximum of the offense, the sentence range was truncated and displayed an asterisk that referenced what the statutory maximum was. In this manual, the sentence range will still be truncated where available and display an asterisk. The corresponding asterisk will be next to the classification at the top of the page, *i.e.*, Class C*.

Per EHB 1324, for any offenses that are committed on or after July 23, 2023, convictions of juvenile adjudications are not included in the offender score unless the convictions were for Murder 1, Murder 2, or a Class A sex offense. The scoring forms have been updated to reflect this change. For any offenses committed prior to July 23, 2023, please refer to the scoring rules in place at that time of the offense for scoring of juvenile adjudications.

Abandonment of Dependent Person First Degree
RCW 9A.42.060
CLASS B* – NONVIOLENT
OFFENDER SCORING RCW 9.94A.525(7)

If it was found that this offense was committed with sexual motivation (RCW 9.94A.533(8)) on or after 7/1/2006, use the General Nonviolent Offense with a Sexual Motivation Finding scoring form on page 236.

If the present conviction is for a felony domestic violence offense where domestic violence was plead and proven, use the General Nonviolent Offense Where Domestic Violence Has Been Plead and Proven scoring form on page 234.

ADULT HISTORY:

Enter number of felony convictions .... _____ x 1 = _____

JUVENILE HISTORY:

Enter number of Murder 1, Murder 2, and Class A sex offense felony dispositions .... _____ x 1 = _____

OTHER CURRENT OFFENSES:

(Other current offenses that do not encompass the same conduct count in offender score)

Enter number of other felony convictions .... _____ x 1 = _____

STATUS:

Was the offender on community custody on the date the current offense was committed? (if yes) _____ + 1 = _____

Total the last column to get the **Offender Score** (Round down to the nearest whole number)......................... _____

SENTENCE RANGE DISPLAYED IS FOR A COMPLETED OFFENSE

FOR **ATTEMPT**, **SOLICITATION**, OR **CONSPIRACY** (RCW 9.94A.595, see page 54), THE SENTENCE RANGE **IS 75%** OF THE COMPLETED RANGE LISTED BELOW

	Offender Score									
	0	**1**	**2**	**3**	**4**	**5**	**6**	**7**	**8**	**9+**
LEVEL IX	36m	42m	47.5m	53.5m	59.5m	66m	89.5m	101.5m	114m	
	31 - 41	36 - 48	41 - 54	46 - 61	51 - 68	57 - 75	77 - 102	87 - 116	108 - 120*	120- 120*

* Class B felony offenses have a statutory maximum sentence of 120 months, see RCW 9A.20.021.

✓ For gang-related felonies where the court found the offender involved a minor (RCW 9.94A.833) see page 227 for standard range adjustments.
✓ For deadly weapon enhancement, see page 233.
✓ For sentencing alternatives, see page 215.
✓ For community custody eligibility, see page 228.
✓ For any applicable enhancements other than deadly weapon enhancement, see page 224.

Abandonment of Dependent Person Second Degree

RCW 9A.42.070
CLASS C* – NONVIOLENT
OFFENDER SCORING RCW 9.94A.525(7)

If it was found that this offense was committed with sexual motivation (RCW 9.94A.533(8)) on or after 7/1/2006, use the General Nonviolent Offense with a Sexual Motivation Finding scoring form on page 236.

If the present conviction is for a felony domestic violence offense where domestic violence was plead and proven, use the General Nonviolent Offense Where Domestic Violence Has Been Plead and Proven scoring form on page 234.

ADULT HISTORY:

Enter number of felony convictions .... _____ x 1 = _____

JUVENILE HISTORY:

Enter number of Murder 1, Murder 2, and Class A sex offense felony dispositions .... _____ x 1 = _____

OTHER CURRENT OFFENSES:

(Other current offenses that do not encompass the same conduct count in offender score)

Enter number of other felony convictions .... _____ x 1 = _____

STATUS:

Was the offender on community custody on the date the current offense was committed? (if yes) _____ + 1 = _____

Total the last column to get the **Offender Score** (Round down to the nearest whole number)......................... _____

SENTENCE RANGE

	Offender Score									
	0	**1**	**2**	**3**	**4**	**5**	**6**	**7**	**8**	**9+**
LEVEL V	9m	13m	15m	17.5m	25.5m	38m	47.5m	55.5m		
	6 - 12	12+ - 14	13 - 17	15 - 20	22 - 29	33 - 43	41 - 54	51 - 60*	60 - 60*	60 - 60*

* Class C felony offenses have a statutory maximum sentence of 60 months, see RCW 9A.20.021.

✓ For gang-related felonies where the court found the offender involved a minor (RCW 9.94A.833), see page 227 for standard range adjustment.
✓ For deadly weapon enhancement, see page 233.
✓ For sentencing alternatives, see page 215.
✓ For community custody eligibility, see page 228.
✓ For any applicable enhancements other than deadly weapon enhancement, see page 224.

Advancing Money or Property for Extortionate Extension of Credit

RCW 9A.82.030
CLASS B – NONVIOLENT
OFFENDER SCORING RCW 9.94A.525(7)

If it was found that this offense was committed with sexual motivation (RCW 9.94A.533(8)) on or after 7/1/2006, use the General Nonviolent Offense with a Sexual Motivation Finding scoring form on page 236.

If the present conviction is for a felony domestic violence offense where domestic violence was plead and proven, use the General Nonviolent Offense Where Domestic Violence Has Been Plead and Proven scoring form on page 234.

ADULT HISTORY:

    Enter number of felony convictions .... _____ x 1 = _____

JUVENILE HISTORY:

    Enter number of Murder 1, Murder 2, and Class A sex offense felony dispositions .... _____ x 1 = _____

OTHER CURRENT OFFENSES:

(Other current offenses that do not encompass the same conduct count in offender score)

    Enter number of other felony convictions .... _____ x 1 = _____

STATUS:

    Was the offender on community custody on the date the current offense was committed? (if yes) _____ + 1 = _____

Total the last column to get the **Offender Score** (Round down to the nearest whole number).......................... _____

SENTENCE RANGE DISPLAYED IS FOR A COMPLETED OFFENSE

FOR **ATTEMPT**, **SOLICITATION**, OR **CONSPIRACY** (RCW 9.94A.595, see page 54), THE SENTENCE RANGE **IS 75%** OF THE COMPLETED RANGE LISTED BELOW

	Offender Score									
	0	**1**	**2**	**3**	**4**	**5**	**6**	**7**	**8**	**9+**
LEVEL V	9m	13m	15m	17.5m	25.5m	38m	47.5m	59.5m	72m	84m
	6 - 12	12+ - 14	13 - 17	15 - 20	22 - 29	33 - 43	41 - 54	51 - 68	62 - 82	72 - 96

✓   For gang-related felonies where the court found the offender involved a minor (RCW 9.94A.833) see page 227 for standard range adjustments.
✓   For deadly weapon enhancement, see page 233.
✓   For sentencing alternatives, see page 215.
✓   For community custody eligibility, see page 228.
✓   For any applicable enhancements other than deadly weapon enhancement, see page 224.

Aggravated Murder First Degree

RCW 10.95.020 & RCW 10.95.030(1)
CLASS A – SERIOUS VIOLENT/CRIMES AGAINST PERSONS
OFFENDER SCORING

ADULT HISTORY:

Not scored

JUVENILE HISTORY:

Not scored

OTHER CURRENT OFFENSES:

Not scored

STATUS:

Not scored

SENTENCE RANGE

	Offender Score									
	0	1	2	3	4	5	6	7	8	9+
LEVEL XVI	Life sentence without parole/death penalty for offenders at or over the age of eighteen. For offenders under the age of eighteen, a term of twenty-five years to life.									

✓ A person found to be intellectually disabled under RCW 10.95.030 may in no case be sentenced to death (RCW 10.95.070).

✓ A person who was at least 16 years old but less than 18 years old shall be sentenced to a maximum term of life imprisonment and a minimum term of total confinement of no less than 25 years. A minimum term of life may be imposed, in which case the person will be ineligible for parole or early release. (In setting the minimum term, the court must take into account mitigating factors that account for the diminished culpability of youth as provided in *Miller v. Alabama*, 132 S. Ct. 2455 (2012)).

✓ A person who was younger than 16 years old shall be sentenced to a maximum term of life imprisonment and a minimum term of total confinement of 25 years.

Animal Cruelty First Degree Sexual Conduct or Contact

RCW 16.52.205(3)
CLASS C* – NONVIOLENT
OFFENDER SCORING RCW 9.94A.525(7)

If it was found that this offense was committed with sexual motivation (RCW 9.94A.533(8)) on or after 7/1/2006, use the General Nonviolent Offense with a Sexual Motivation Finding scoring form on page 236.

If the present conviction is for a felony domestic violence offense where domestic violence was plead and proven, use the General Nonviolent Offense Where Domestic Violence Has Been Plead and Proven scoring form on page 234.

ADULT HISTORY:

    Enter number of felony convictions .... _____ x 1 = _____

JUVENILE HISTORY:

    Enter number of Murder 1, Murder 2, and Class A sex offense felony dispositions .... _____ x 1 = _____

OTHER CURRENT OFFENSES:

(Other current offenses that do not encompass the same conduct count in offender score)

    Enter number of other felony convictions .... _____ x 1 = _____

STATUS:

    Was the offender on community custody on the date the current offense was committed? (if yes) _____ + 1 = _____

Total the last column to get the **Offender Score** (Round down to the nearest whole number).......................... _____

SENTENCE RANGE

	Offender Score									
	0	**1**	**2**	**3**	**4**	**5**	**6**	**7**	**8**	**9+**
LEVEL III	2m	5m	8m	11m	14m	19.5m	25.5m	38m	50m	55.5m
	1 - 3	3 - 8	4 - 12	9 - 12	12+ - 16	17 - 22	22 - 29	33 - 43	43 - 57	51 - 60*

    * Class C felony offenses have a statutory maximum sentence of 60 months, see RCW 9A.20.021.

✓   For gang-related felonies where the court found the offender involved a minor (RCW 9.94A.833), see page 227 for standard range adjustment.
✓   For deadly weapon enhancement, see page 233.
✓   For sentencing alternatives, see page 215.
✓   For community custody eligibility, see page 228.
✓   For any applicable enhancements other than deadly weapon enhancement, see page 224.

RCW 9A.48.020
CLASS A – VIOLENT/CRIMES AGAINST PERSONS
ATTEMPT/SOLICITATION = CLASS A - VIOLENT
CONSPIRACY = CLASS B* - VIOLENT
OFFENDER SCORING RCW 9.94A.525(8)

If it was found that this offense was committed with sexual motivation (RCW 9.94A.533(8)) on or after 7/1/2006, use the General Violent Offense with a Sexual Motivation Finding scoring form on page 244.

If the present conviction is for a felony domestic violence offense where domestic violence was plead and proven, use the General Violent Offense Where Domestic Violence Has Been Plead and Proven scoring form on page 242.

ADULT HISTORY:

Enter number of serious violent and violent felony convictions .... _____ x 2 = _____

Enter number of nonviolent felony convictions .... _____ x 1 = _____

JUVENILE HISTORY:

Enter number of Murder 1, Murder 2, and Class A sex offense felony dispositions .... _____ x 2 = _____

OTHER CURRENT OFFENSES:

(Other current offenses that do not encompass the same conduct count in offender score)

Enter number of other serious violent and violent felony convictions .... _____ x 2 = _____

Enter number of other nonviolent felony convictions .... _____ x 1 = _____

STATUS:

Was the offender on community custody on the date the current offense was committed? (if yes) _____ + 1 = _____

Total the last column to get the **Offender Score** (Round down to the nearest whole number)......................... _____

SENTENCE RANGE DISPLAYED IS FOR A COMPLETED OFFENSE

FOR **ATTEMPT**, **SOLICITATION**, OR **CONSPIRACY** (RCW 9.94A.595, see page 54), THE SENTENCE RANGE **IS 75%** OF THE COMPLETED RANGE LISTED BELOW

	Offender Score									
	0	**1**	**2**	**3**	**4**	**5**	**6**	**7**	**8**	**9+**
LEVEL VIII	24m	30m	36m	42m	47.5m	53.5m	78m	89.5m	101.5m	126m
	21 - 27	26 - 34	31 - 41	36 - 48	41 - 54	46 - 61	67 - 89	77 - 102	87 - 116	108 - 144

* Class B felony offenses have a statutory maximum sentence of 120 months, see RCW 9A.20.021.

✓ For gang-related felonies where the court found the offender involved a minor (RCW 9.94A.833), see page 227 for standard range adjustments.
✓ For deadly weapon enhancement, see page 233.
✓ For sentencing alternatives, see page 215.
✓ For community custody eligibility, see page 228.
✓ For any applicable enhancements other than deadly weapon enhancement, see page 224.

Arson Second Degree

RCW 9A.48.030
CLASS B – VIOLENT
OFFENDER SCORING RCW 9.94A.525(8)

If it was found that this offense was committed with sexual motivation (RCW 9.94A.533(8)) on or after 7/1/2006, use the General Violent Offense with a Sexual Motivation Finding scoring form on page 244.

If the present conviction is for a felony domestic violence offense where domestic violence was plead and proven, use the General Violent Offense Where Domestic Violence Has Been Plead and Proven scoring form on page 242.

ADULT HISTORY:

Enter number of serious violent and violent felony convictions .... _____ x 2 = _____

Enter number of nonviolent felony convictions .... _____ x 1 = _____

JUVENILE HISTORY:

Enter number of Murder 1, Murder 2, and Class A sex offense felony dispositions .... _____ x 2 = _____

OTHER CURRENT OFFENSES:

(Other current offenses that do not encompass the same conduct count in offender score)

Enter number of other serious violent and violent felony convictions .... _____ x 2 = _____

Enter number of other nonviolent felony convictions .... _____ x 1 = _____

STATUS:

Was the offender on community custody on the date the current offense was committed? (if yes) _____ + 1 = _____

Total the last column to get the **Offender Score** (Round down to the nearest whole number)......................... _____

SENTENCE RANGE DISPLAYED IS FOR A COMPLETED OFFENSE

FOR **ATTEMPT**, **SOLICITATION**, OR **CONSPIRACY** (RCW 9.94A.595, see page 54), THE SENTENCE RANGE **IS 75%** OF THE COMPLETED RANGE LISTED BELOW

Offender Score										
	0	**1**	**2**	**3**	**4**	**5**	**6**	**7**	**8**	**9+**
LEVEL IV	6m	9m	13m	15m	17.5m	25.5m	38m	50m	61.5m	73.5m
	3 - 9	6 - 12	12+ - 14	13 - 17	15 - 20	22 - 29	33 - 43	43 - 57	53 - 70	63 - 84

✓ For gang-related felonies where the court found the offender involved a minor (RCW 9.94A.833) see page 227 for standard range adjustments.
✓ For deadly weapon enhancement, see page 233.
✓ For sentencing alternatives, see page 215.
✓ For community custody eligibility, see page 228.
✓ For any applicable enhancements other than deadly weapon enhancement, see page 224.

RCW 9A.36.011
CLASS A – SERIOUS VIOLENT/CRIMES AGAINST PERSONS
OFFENDER SCORING RCW 9.94A.525(9)

If the present conviction is for a felony domestic violence offense where domestic violence was plead and proven, use the General Serious Violent Offense Where Domestic Violence Has Been Plead and Proven scoring form on page 239.

ADULT HISTORY:

Enter number of serious violent felony convictions .... _____ x 3 = _____

Enter number of violent felony convictions .... _____ x 2 = _____

Enter number of nonviolent felony convictions .... _____ x 1 = _____

JUVENILE HISTORY:

Enter number of Murder 1, Murder 2, and Serious Violent sex offense felony dispositions .... _____ x 3 = _____

Enter number of Class A sex offense (not Serious Violent) felony dispositions .... _____ x 2 = _____

OTHER CURRENT OFFENSES:

(Other current offenses that do not encompass the same conduct count in offender score)

Enter number of other violent felony convictions .... _____ x 2 = _____

Enter number of other nonviolent felony convictions .... _____ x 1 = _____

STATUS:

Was the offender on community custody on the date the current offense was committed? .... _____ + 1 = _____

Total the last column to get the **Offender Score** (Round down to the nearest whole number)........................ _____

SENTENCE RANGE DISPLAYED IS FOR A COMPLETED OFFENSE

FOR **ATTEMPT**, **SOLICITATION**, OR **CONSPIRACY** (RCW 9.94A.595, see page 54), THE SENTENCE RANGE **IS 75%** OF THE COMPLETED RANGE LISTED BELOW

	Offender Score									
	0	1	2	3	4	5	6	7	8	9+
LEVEL XII	108m	119m	129m	140m	150m	161m	189m	207m	243m	279m
	93 - 123	102 - 136	111 - 147	120 - 160	129 - 171	138 - 184	162 - 216	178 - 236	209 - 277	240 - 318

✓ For gang-related felonies where the court found the offender involved a minor (RCW 9.94A.833), see page 227 for standard range adjustments.
✓ For deadly weapon enhancement, see page 233.
✓ For sentencing alternatives, see page 215.
✓ For community custody eligibility, see page 228.
✓ For any applicable enhancements other than deadly weapon enhancement, see page 224.
✓ Multiple current serious violent offenses shall have consecutive sentences imposed per the rules of RCW 9.94A.589(1)(b).
✓ Statutory <u>minimum</u> sentence is 60 months (RCW 9.94A.540) if the offender used force or means likely to result in death or intended to kill the victim. The statutory minimum sentence shall not be varied or modified under RCW 9.94A.535.

RCW 9A.36.011
CLASS A – SERIOUS VIOLENT/SEX/CRIMES AGAINST PERSONS
OFFENDER SCORING RCW 9.94A.525(17)

ADULT HISTORY:

Enter number of sex offense felony convictions .... _____ x 3 = _____

Enter number of serious violent felony convictions .... _____ x 3 = _____

Enter number of violent felony convictions .... _____ x 2 = _____

Enter number of nonviolent felony convictions .... _____ x 1 = _____

JUVENILE HISTORY:

Enter number of Murder 1, Murder 2, and Class A sex offense felony dispositions .... _____ x 3 = _____

OTHER CURRENT OFFENSES:
(Other current offenses that do not encompass the same conduct count in offender score)

Enter number of other sex offense felony convictions .... _____ x 3 = _____

Enter number of other violent felony convictions .... _____ x 2 = _____

Enter number of other nonviolent felony convictions .... _____ x 1 = _____

STATUS:

Was the offender on community custody on the date the current offense was committed?............ _____ + 1 = _____

Total the last column to get the **Offender Score** (Round down to the nearest whole number)......................... _____

SENTENCE RANGE DISPLAYED IS FOR A COMPLETED OFFENSE

FOR **ATTEMPT**, **SOLICITATION**, OR **CONSPIRACY** (RCW 9.94A.595, see page 54), THE SENTENCE RANGE **IS 75%** OF THE COMPLETED RANGE LISTED BELOW

	Offender Score									
	0	**1**	**2**	**3**	**4**	**5**	**6**	**7**	**8**	**9+**
LEVEL XII	108m	119m	129m	140m	150m	161m	189m	207m	243m	279m
	93 - 123	102 - 136	111 - 147	120 - 160	129 - 171	138 - 184	162 - 216	178 - 236	209 - 277	240 - 318

SEXUAL MOTIVATION ENHANCEMENT (Per Sexual Motivation Enhancement, page 226) .... _____

Low   to   High

STANDARD SENTENCE RANGE PLUS ENHANCEMENT.............. _____ ..... _____

✓ For gang-related felonies where the court found the offender involved a minor (RCW 9.94A.833), see page 227 for standard range adjustments.
✓ For deadly weapon enhancement, see page 233.
✓ For sentencing alternatives, see page 215.
✓ For community custody eligibility, see page 228.
✓ For any applicable enhancements other than deadly weapon enhancement, see page 224.
✓ If the offender is not a persistent offender and the <u>current</u> offense is either a completed offense or a criminal attempt under RCW 9A.28.020 that was committed on or after 9/1/2001, then the offender is subject to the requirements under RCW 9.94A.507.
✓ If the offender is not a persistent offender and has a <u>prior</u> conviction for an offense listed in RCW 9.94A.030(37)(b), then the sentence is subject to the requirements of RCW 9.94A.507.
✓ Multiple current serious violent offenses shall have consecutive sentences imposed per the rules of RCW 9.94A.589(1)(b).
✓ Statutory minimum sentence is 60 months per RCW 9.94A.540 if the offender used force or means likely to result in death or intended to kill the victim. The statutory minimum sentence shall not be varied or modified under RCW 9.94A.535.

Assault Second Degree

RCW 9A.36.021(2)(a)
CLASS B – VIOLENT/CRIMES AGAINST PERSONS
OFFENDER SCORING RCW 9.94A.525(8)

If the present conviction is for a felony domestic violence offense where domestic violence was plead and proven, use the General Violent Offense Where Domestic Violence Has Been Plead and Proven scoring form on page 242.

ADULT HISTORY:

Enter number of serious violent and violent felony convictions .... _____ x 2 = _____

Enter number of nonviolent felony convictions .... _____ x 1 = _____

JUVENILE HISTORY:

Enter number of Murder 1, Murder 2, and Class A sex offense felony dispositions .... _____ x 2 = _____

OTHER CURRENT OFFENSES:

(Other current offenses that do not encompass the same conduct count in offender score)

Enter number of other serious violent and violent felony convictions .... _____ x 2 = _____

Enter number of other nonviolent felony convictions .... _____ x 1 = _____

STATUS:

Was the offender on community custody on the date the current offense was committed? .... _____ + 1 = _____

Total the last column to get the **Offender Score** (Round down to the nearest whole number) .... _____

SENTENCE RANGE DISPLAYED IS FOR A COMPLETED OFFENSE

FOR **ATTEMPT**, **SOLICITATION**, OR **CONSPIRACY** (RCW 9.94A.595, see page 54), THE SENTENCE RANGE **IS 75%** OF THE COMPLETED RANGE LISTED BELOW

Offender Score										
	0	**1**	**2**	**3**	**4**	**5**	**6**	**7**	**8**	**9+**
LEVEL IV	6m	9m	13m	15m	17.5m	25.5m	38m	50m	61.5m	73.5m
	3 - 9	6 - 12	12+ - 14	13 - 17	15 - 20	22 - 29	33 - 43	43 - 57	53 - 70	63 - 84

✓ For gang-related felonies where the court found the offender involved a minor (RCW 9.94A.833), see page 227 for standard range adjustments.
✓ For deadly weapon enhancement, see page 233.
✓ For sentencing alternatives, see page 215.
✓ For community custody eligibility, see page 228.
✓ For any applicable enhancements other than deadly weapon enhancement, see page 224.

RCW 9A.36.021(2)(b)
CLASS A – VIOLENT/SEX/CRIMES AGAINST PERSONS
OFFENDER SCORING RCW 9.94A.525(17)

ADULT HISTORY:

Enter number of sex offense felony convictions .... _____ x 3 = _____

Enter number of serious violent and violent felony convictions .... _____ x 2 = _____

Enter number of nonviolent felony convictions .... _____ x 1 = _____

JUVENILE HISTORY:

Enter number of Class A sex offense felony dispositions .... _____ x 3 = _____

Enter number of Murder 1 and Murder 2 felony dispositions .... _____ x 2 = _____

OTHER CURRENT OFFENSES:

(Other current offenses that do not encompass the same conduct count in offender score)

Enter number of other sex offense felony convictions .... _____ x 3 = _____

Enter number of other serious violent and violent felony convictions .... _____ x 2 = _____

Enter number of other nonviolent felony convictions .... _____ x 1 = _____

STATUS:

Was the offender on community custody on the date the current offense was committed?............ _____ + 1 = _____

Total the last column to get the **Offender Score** (Round down to the nearest whole number)......................... _____

SENTENCE RANGE DISPLAYED IS FOR A COMPLETED OFFENSE

FOR **ATTEMPT**, **SOLICITATION**, OR **CONSPIRACY** (RCW 9.94A.595, see page 54), THE SENTENCE RANGE **IS 75%** OF THE COMPLETED RANGE LISTED BELOW

Offender Score										
	0	**1**	**2**	**3**	**4**	**5**	**6**	**7**	**8**	**9+**
LEVEL IV	6m	9m	13m	15m	17.5m	25.5m	38m	50m	61.5m	73.5m
	3 - 9	6 - 12	12+ - 14	13 - 17	15 - 20	22 - 29	33 - 43	43 - 57	53 - 70	63 - 84

SEXUAL MOTIVATION ENHANCEMENT (Per Sexual Motivation Enhancement, page 226) .... _____

Low   to   High

STANDARD SENTENCE RANGE PLUS ENHANCEMENT............. _____ ..... _____

- ✓ For gang-related felonies where the court found the offender involved a minor (RCW 9.94A.833), see page 227 for standard range adjustments.
- ✓ For deadly weapon enhancement, see page 233.
- ✓ For sentencing alternatives, see page 215.
- ✓ For community custody eligibility, see page 228.
- ✓ For any applicable enhancements other than deadly weapon enhancement, see page 224.
- ✓ If the offender is not a persistent offender and the <u>current</u> offense is either a completed offense or a criminal attempt under RCW 9A.28.020 that was committed on or after 9/1/2001, then the offender is subject to the requirements under RCW 9.94A.507.
- ✓ If the offender is not a persistent offender and has a <u>prior</u> conviction for an offense listed in RCW 9.94A.030(37)(b), then the sentence is subject to the requirements of RCW 9.94A.507.

Assault Third Degree, excluding Assault 3 of a Peace Officer with a Projectile Stun Gun

RCW 9A.36.031(1)(a)-(g) & (i)-(j)
CLASS C* – NONVIOLENT/CRIMES AGAINST PERSONS
OFFENDER SCORING RCW 9.94A.525(7)

If it was found that this offense was committed with sexual motivation (RCW 9.94A.533(8)) on or after 7/1/2006, use the General Nonviolent Offense with a Sexual Motivation Finding scoring form on page 236.

If the present conviction is for a felony domestic violence offense where domestic violence was plead and proven, use the General Nonviolent Offense Where Domestic Violence Has Been Plead and Proven scoring form on page 234.

ADULT HISTORY:

    Enter number of felony convictions .... _____ x 1 = _____

JUVENILE HISTORY:

    Enter number of Murder 1, Murder 2, and Class A sex offense felony dispositions .... _____ x 1 = _____

OTHER CURRENT OFFENSES:

(Other current offenses that do not encompass the same conduct count in offender score)

    Enter number of other felony convictions .... _____ x 1 = _____

STATUS:

    Was the offender on community custody on the date the current offense was committed? .... _____ + 1 = _____

Total the last column to get the **Offender Score** (Round down to the nearest whole number) .... _____

SENTENCE RANGE

	Offender Score									
	0	**1**	**2**	**3**	**4**	**5**	**6**	**7**	**8**	**9+**
LEVEL III	2m	5m	8m	11m	14m	19.5m	25.5m	38m	50m	55.5m
	1 - 3	3 - 8	4 - 12	9 - 12	12+ - 16	17 - 22	22 - 29	33 - 43	43 - 57	51 - 60*

    * Class C felony offenses have a statutory maximum sentence of 60 months, see RCW 9A.20.021.

✓   For gang-related felonies where the court found the offender involved a minor (RCW 9.94A.833), see page 227 for standard range adjustment.
✓   For deadly weapon enhancement, see page 233.
✓   For sentencing alternatives, see page 215.
✓   For community custody eligibility, see page 228.
✓   For any applicable enhancements other than deadly weapon enhancement, see page 224.

Assault Third Degree of a Peace Officer with a Projectile Stun Gun

RCW 9A.36.031(1)(h)
CLASS C* – NONVIOLENT/CRIMES AGAINST PERSONS
OFFENDER SCORING RCW 9.94A.525(7)

If it was found that this offense was committed with sexual motivation (RCW 9.94A.533(8)) on or after 7/1/2006, use the General Nonviolent Offense with a Sexual Motivation Finding scoring form on page 236.

If the present conviction is for a felony domestic violence offense where domestic violence was plead and proven, use the General Nonviolent Offense Where Domestic Violence Has Been Plead and Proven scoring form on page 234.

ADULT HISTORY:

Enter number of felony convictions .... _____ x 1 = _____

JUVENILE HISTORY:

Enter number of Murder 1, Murder 2, and Class A sex offense felony dispositions .... _____ x 1 = _____

OTHER CURRENT OFFENSES:

(Other current offenses that do not encompass the same conduct count in offender score)

Enter number of other felony convictions .... _____ x 1 = _____

STATUS:

Was the offender on community custody on the date the current offense was committed?............ _____ + 1 = _____

Total the last column to get the **Offender Score** (Round down to the nearest whole number).......................... _____

SENTENCE RANGE

	Offender Score									
	0	**1**	**2**	**3**	**4**	**5**	**6**	**7**	**8**	**9+**
LEVEL IV	6m	9m	13m	15m	17.5m	25.5m	38m	50m	56.5m	
	3 - 9	6 - 12	12+ - 14	13 - 17	15 - 20	22 - 29	33 - 43	43 - 57	53 - 60*	60 - 60*

* Class C felony offenses have a statutory maximum sentence of 60 months, see RCW 9A.20.021.

✓ For gang-related felonies where the court found the offender involved a minor (RCW 9.94A.833), see page 227 for standard range adjustment.
✓ For deadly weapon enhancement, see page 233.
✓ For sentencing alternatives, see page 215.
✓ For community custody eligibility, see page 228.
✓ For any applicable enhancements other than deadly weapon enhancement, see page 224.

Assault by Watercraft

RCW 79A.60.060
CLASS B – NONVIOLENT
OFFENDER SCORING RCW 9.94A.525(12)

If it was found that this offense was committed with sexual motivation (RCW 9.94A.533(8)) on or after 7/1/2006, use the General Nonviolent Offense with a Sexual Motivation Finding scoring form on page 236.

If the present conviction is for a felony domestic violence offense where domestic violence was plead and proven, use the General Nonviolent Offense Where Domestic Violence Has Been Plead and Proven scoring form on page 234.

ADULT HISTORY:

Enter number of Homicide by Watercraft and Assault by Watercraft convictions .... _____ x 2 = _____

Enter number of Driving under the Influence of Intoxicating Liquor or any Drug and
Actual Physical Control of a Motor Vehicle while under the Influence of Intoxicating Liquor or any Drug and
Operation of a Vessel while under the Influence of Intoxicating Liquor or any Drug convictions _____ x 1 = _____

Enter number of felony convictions .... _____ x 1 = _____

JUVENILE HISTORY:

Enter number of Murder 1, Murder 2, and Class A sex offense felony dispositions .... _____ x ½ = _____

OTHER CURRENT OFFENSES:

(Other current offenses that do not encompass the same conduct count in offender score)

Enter number of other Homicide by Watercraft and Assault by Watercraft convictions .... _____ x 2 = _____

Enter number of Driving under the Influence of Intoxicating Liquor or any Drug and
Actual Physical Control of a Motor Vehicle while under the Influence of Intoxicating Liquor or any Drug and
Operation of a Vessel while under the Influence of Intoxicating Liquor or any Drug convictions _____ x 1 = _____

Enter number of other felony convictions .... _____ x 1 = _____

STATUS:

Was the offender on community custody on the date the current offense was committed? .... _____ + 1 = _____

Total the last column to get the **Offender Score** (Round down to the nearest whole number)........................ _____

SENTENCE RANGE DISPLAYED IS FOR A COMPLETED OFFENSE

FOR **ATTEMPT**, **SOLICITATION**, OR **CONSPIRACY** (RCW 9.94A.595, see page 54), THE SENTENCE RANGE **IS 75%** OF THE COMPLETED RANGE LISTED BELOW

	Offender Score									
	0	**1**	**2**	**3**	**4**	**5**	**6**	**7**	**8**	**9+**
LEVEL IV	6m	9m	13m	15m	17.5m	25.5m	38m	50m	61.5m	73.5m
	3 - 9	6 - 12	12+ - 14	13 - 17	15 - 20	22 - 29	33 - 43	43 - 57	53 - 70	63 - 84

✓ For gang-related felonies where the court found the offender involved a minor (RCW 9.94A.833), see page 227 for standard range adjustments.
✓ For deadly weapon enhancement, see page 233.
✓ For sentencing alternatives, see page 215.
✓ For community custody eligibility, see page 228.
✓ For any applicable enhancements other than deadly weapon enhancement, see page 224.

RCW 9A.36.120
CLASS A – SERIOUS VIOLENT/CRIMES AGAINST PERSONS
OFFENDER SCORING RCW 9.94A.525(9)

If the present conviction is for a felony domestic violence offense where domestic violence was plead and proven, use the General Serious Violent Offense Where Domestic Violence Has Been Plead and Proven scoring form on page 239.

ADULT HISTORY:

Enter number of serious violent felony convictions .... _____ x 3 = _____

Enter number of violent felony convictions .... _____ x 2 = _____

Enter number of nonviolent felony convictions .... _____ x 1 = _____

JUVENILE HISTORY:

Enter number of Murder 1, Murder 2, and Serious Violent sex offense felony dispositions .... _____ x 3 = _____

Enter number of Class A sex offense (not Serious Violent) felony dispositions .... _____ x 2 = _____

OTHER CURRENT OFFENSES:

(Other current offenses that do not encompass the same conduct count in offender score)

Enter number of other violent felony convictions .... _____ x 2 = _____

Enter number of other nonviolent felony convictions .... _____ x 1 = _____

STATUS:

Was the offender on community custody on the date the current offense was committed?............ _____ + 1 = _____

Total the last column to get the **Offender Score** (Round down to the nearest whole number).......................... _____

SENTENCE RANGE DISPLAYED IS FOR A COMPLETED OFFENSE

FOR **ATTEMPT**, **SOLICITATION**, OR **CONSPIRACY** (RCW 9.94A.595, see page 54), THE SENTENCE RANGE **IS 75%** OF THE COMPLETED RANGE LISTED BELOW

	Offender Score									
	0	**1**	**2**	**3**	**4**	**5**	**6**	**7**	**8**	**9+**
LEVEL XII	108m	119m	129m	140m	150m	161m	189m	207m	243m	279m
	93 - 123	102 - 136	111 - 147	120 - 160	129 - 171	138 - 184	162 - 216	178 - 236	209 - 277	240 - 318

✓ For gang-related felonies where the court found the offender involved a minor (RCW 9.94A.833), see page 227 for standard range adjustments.
✓ For deadly weapon enhancement, see page 233.
✓ For sentencing alternatives, see page 215.
✓ For community custody eligibility, see page 228.
✓ For any applicable enhancements other than deadly weapon enhancement, see page 224.
✓ Multiple current serious violent offenses shall have consecutive sentences imposed per the rules of RCW 9.94A.589(1)(b).
✓ Statutory minimum sentence is 60 months (RCW 9.94A.540) if the offender used force or means likely to result in death or intended to kill the victim. The statutory minimum sentence shall not be varied or modified under RCW 9.94A.535.

Assault of a Child First Degree with a Finding of Sexual Motivation
RCW 9A.36.120
CLASS A – SERIOUS VIOLENT/SEX/CRIMES AGAINST PERSONS
OFFENDER SCORING RCW 9.94A.525(17)

ADULT HISTORY:

Enter number of sex offense felony convictions .... _____ x 3 = _____

Enter number of serious violent and violent felony convictions .... _____ x 2 = _____

Enter number of nonviolent felony convictions .... _____ x 1 = _____

JUVENILE HISTORY:

Enter number of Murder 1, Murder 2, and Class A sex offense felony dispositions .... _____ x 3 = _____

OTHER CURRENT OFFENSES:

(Other current offenses that do not encompass the same conduct count in offender score)

Enter number of other sex offense felony convictions .... _____ x 3 = _____

Enter number of other serious violent and violent felony convictions .... _____ x 2 = _____

Enter number of other nonviolent felony convictions .... _____ x 1 = _____

STATUS:

Was the offender on community custody on the date the current offense was committed? .... _____ + 1 = _____

Total the last column to get the **Offender Score** (Round down to the nearest whole number)......................... _____

SENTENCE RANGE DISPLAYED IS FOR A COMPLETED OFFENSE

FOR **ATTEMPT**, **SOLICITATION**, OR **CONSPIRACY** (RCW 9.94A.595, see page 54), THE SENTENCE RANGE **IS 75%** OF THE COMPLETED RANGE LISTED BELOW

	Offender Score									
	0	**1**	**2**	**3**	**4**	**5**	**6**	**7**	**8**	**9+**
LEVEL XII	108m	119m	129m	140m	150m	161m	189m	207m	243m	279m
	93 - 123	102 - 136	111 - 147	120 - 160	129 - 171	138 - 184	162 - 216	178 - 236	209 - 277	240 - 318

SEXUAL MOTIVATION ENHANCEMENT (Per Sexual Motivation Enhancement, page 226).................... _____

                                                    Low   to   High

STANDARD SENTENCE RANGE PLUS ENHANCEMENT .... _____ ..... _____

- ✓ For gang-related felonies where the court found the offender involved a minor (RCW 9.94A.833), see page 227 for standard range adjustments.
- ✓ For deadly weapon enhancement, see page 233.
- ✓ For sentencing alternatives, see page 215.
- ✓ For community custody eligibility, see page 228.
- ✓ For any applicable enhancements other than deadly weapon enhancement, see page 224.
- ✓ If the offender is not a persistent offender and the current offense is either a completed offense or a criminal attempt under RCW 9A.28.020 that was committed on or after 9/1/2001, then the offender is subject to the requirements under RCW 9.94A.507.
- ✓ If the offender is not a persistent offender and has a prior conviction for an offense listed in RCW 9.94A.030(37)(b), then the sentence is subject to the requirements of RCW 9.94A.507.
- ✓ Multiple current serious violent offenses shall have consecutive sentences imposed per the rules of RCW 9.94A.589(1)(b).
- ✓ Statutory minimum sentence is 60 months per RCW 9.94A.540 if the offender used force or means likely to result in death or intended to kill the victim. The statutory minimum sentence shall not be varied or modified under RCW 9.94A.535.

RCW 9A.36.130
CLASS B* – VIOLENT/CRIMES AGAINST PERSONS
OFFENDER SCORING RCW 9.94A.525(8)

If the present conviction is for a felony domestic violence offense where domestic violence was plead and proven, use the General Violent Offense Where Domestic Violence Has Been Plead and Proven scoring form on page 242.

ADULT HISTORY:

Enter number of serious violent and violent felony convictions .... _____ x 2 = _____

Enter number of nonviolent felony convictions .... _____ x 1 = _____

JUVENILE HISTORY:

Enter number of Murder 1, Murder 2, and Class A sex offense felony dispositions .... _____ x 2 = _____

OTHER CURRENT OFFENSES:

(Other current offenses that do not encompass the same conduct count in offender score)

Enter number of other serious violent and violent felony convictions .... _____ x 2 = _____

Enter number of other nonviolent felony convictions .... _____ x 1 = _____

STATUS:

Was the offender on community custody on the date the current offense was committed?............ _____ + 1 = _____

Total the last column to get the **Offender Score** (Round down to the nearest whole number)......................... _____

SENTENCE RANGE DISPLAYED IS FOR A COMPLETED OFFENSE

FOR **ATTEMPT**, **SOLICITATION**, OR **CONSPIRACY** (RCW 9.94A.595, see page 54), THE SENTENCE RANGE **IS 75%** OF THE COMPLETED RANGE LISTED BELOW

	\multicolumn{10}{c}{Offender Score}									
	0	**1**	**2**	**3**	**4**	**5**	**6**	**7**	**8**	**9+**
LEVEL IX	36m	42m	47.5m	53.5m	59.5m	66m	89.5m	101.5m	114m	
	31 - 41	36 - 48	41 - 54	46 - 61	51 - 68	57 - 75	77 - 102	87 - 116	108 - 120*	120 - 120*

* Class B felony offenses have a statutory maximum sentence of 120 months, see RCW 9A.20.021.

✓ For gang-related felonies where the court found the offender involved a minor (RCW 9.94A.833), see page 227 for standard range adjustments.
✓ For deadly weapon enhancement, see page 233.
✓ For sentencing alternatives, see page 215.
✓ For community custody eligibility, see page 228.
✓ For any applicable enhancements other than deadly weapon enhancement, see page 224.

Assault of a Child Second Degree with a Finding of Sexual Motivation
RCW 9A.36.130
CLASS B* – VIOLENT/SEX/CRIMES AGAINST PERSONS
OFFENDER SCORING RCW 9.94A.525(17)

ADULT HISTORY:

Enter number of sex offense felony convictions	_____ x 3 =	_____
Enter number of serious violent felony convictions	_____ x 3 =	_____
Enter number of violent felony convictions	_____ x 2 =	_____
Enter number of nonviolent felony convictions	_____ x 1 =	_____

JUVENILE HISTORY:

Enter number of Class A sex offense felony dispositions	_____ x 3 =	_____
Enter number of Murder 1 and Murder 2 felony dispositions	_____ x 2 =	_____

OTHER CURRENT OFFENSES:

(Other current offenses that do not encompass the same conduct count in offender score)

Enter number of other sex offense felony convictions	_____ x 3 =	_____
Enter number of other violent felony convictions	_____ x 2 =	_____
Enter number of other nonviolent felony convictions	_____ x 1 =	_____

STATUS:

Was the offender on community custody on the date the current offense was committed?	_____ + 1 =	_____

Total the last column to get the **Offender Score** (Round down to the nearest whole number)......................... _____

SENTENCE RANGE DISPLAYED IS FOR A COMPLETED OFFENSE

FOR **ATTEMPT**, **SOLICITATION**, OR **CONSPIRACY** (RCW 9.94A.595, see page 54), THE SENTENCE RANGE **IS 75%** OF THE COMPLETED RANGE LISTED BELOW

	Offender Score									
	0	**1**	**2**	**3**	**4**	**5**	**6**	**7**	**8**	**9+**
LEVEL IX	36m	42m	47.5m	53.5m	59.5m	66m	89.5m	101.5m	114m	
	31 - 41	36 - 48	41 - 54	46 - 61	51 - 68	57 - 75	77 - 102	87 - 116	108 - 120*	120 - 120*

SEXUAL MOTIVATION ENHANCEMENT (Per Sexual Motivation Enhancement, page 226).................... _____

Low   to   High

STANDARD SENTENCE RANGE PLUS ENHANCEMENT .... _____ ..... _____

---

* Class B felony offenses have a statutory maximum sentence of 120 months, see RCW 9A.20.021.

✓ For gang-related felonies where the court found the offender involved a minor (RCW 9.94A.833), see page 227 for standard range adjustments.
✓ For deadly weapon enhancement, see page 233.
✓ For sentencing alternatives, see page 215.
✓ For community custody eligibility, see page 228.
✓ For any applicable enhancements other than deadly weapon enhancement, see page 224.
✓ If the offender is not a persistent offender and the <u>current</u> offense is either a completed offense or a criminal attempt under RCW 9A.28.020 that was committed on or after 9/1/2001, then the offender is subject to the requirements under RCW 9.94A.507.
✓ If the offender is not a persistent offender and has a <u>prior</u> conviction for an offense listed in RCW 9.94A.030(37)(b), then the sentence is subject to the requirements of RCW 9.94A.507.

RCW 9A.36.140
CLASS C* – NONVIOLENT/CRIMES AGAINST PERSONS
OFFENDER SCORING RCW 9.94A.525(7)

If it was found that this offense was committed with sexual motivation (RCW 9.94A.533(8)) on or after 7/1/2006, use the General Nonviolent Offense with a Sexual Motivation Finding scoring form on page 236.

If the present conviction is for a felony domestic violence offense where domestic violence was plead and proven, use the General Nonviolent Offense Where Domestic Violence Has Been Plead and Proven scoring form on page 234.

ADULT HISTORY:

Enter number of felony convictions .... _____ x 1 = _____

JUVENILE HISTORY:

Enter number of Murder 1, Murder 2, and Class A sex offense felony dispositions .... _____ x 1 = _____

OTHER CURRENT OFFENSES:

(Other current offenses that do not encompass the same conduct count in offender score)

Enter number of other felony convictions .... _____ x 1 = _____

STATUS:

Was the offender on community custody on the date the current offense was committed?............ _____ + 1 = _____

Total the last column to get the **Offender Score** (Round down to the nearest whole number).......................... _____

SENTENCE RANGE

	Offender Score									
	0	**1**	**2**	**3**	**4**	**5**	**6**	**7**	**8**	**9+**
LEVEL III	2m	5m	8m	11m	14m	19.5m	25.5m	38m	50m	55.5m
	1 - 3	3 - 8	4 - 12	9 - 12	12+ - 16	17 - 22	22 - 29	33 - 43	43 - 57	51 - 60*

* Class C felony offenses have a statutory maximum sentence of 60 months, see RCW 9A.20.021.

✓ For gang-related felonies where the court found the offender involved a minor (RCW 9.94A.833), see page 227 for standard range adjustment.
✓ For deadly weapon enhancement, see page 233.
✓ For sentencing alternatives, see page 215.
✓ For community custody eligibility, see page 228.
✓ For any applicable enhancements other than deadly weapon enhancement, see page 224.

Attempting to Elude Pursuing Police Vehicle

RCW 46.61.024
CLASS C – NONVIOLENT/FELONY TRAFFIC OFFENSE
OFFENDER SCORING RCW 9.94A.525(11)

ADULT HISTORY:

Enter number of Vehicular Homicide and Vehicular Assault convictions .... _____ x 2 = _____

Enter number of Operation of a Vessel while under the Influence of Intoxicating Liquor or any Drug felony convictions .... _____ x 1 = _____

Enter number of felony convictions .... _____ x 1 = _____

Enter number of Driving while under the Influence of Intoxicating Liquor or any Drug and Actual Physical Control while under the Influence of Intoxicating Liquor or any Drug and Reckless Driving and Hit-and-Run Attended Vehicle non-felony convictions .... _____ x 1 = _____

JUVENILE HISTORY:

Enter number of Murder 1, Murder 2, and Class A sex offense felony dispositions .... _____ x ½ = _____

OTHER CURRENT OFFENSES:

(Other current offenses that do not encompass the same conduct count in offender score)

Enter number of Vehicular Homicide and Vehicular Assault convictions .... _____ x 2 = _____

Enter number of other Operation of a Vessel while under the Influence of Intoxicating Liquor or any Drug felony convictions .... _____ x 1 = _____

Enter number of other felony convictions .... _____ x 1 = _____

Enter number of Driving while under the Influence of Intoxicating Liquor or any Drug and Actual Physical Control while under the Influence of Intoxicating Liquor or any Drug and Reckless Driving and Hit-and-Run Attended Vehicle non-felony convictions .... _____ x 1 = _____

STATUS:

Was the offender on community custody on the date the current offense was committed? .... _____ + 1 = _____

Total the last column to get the **Offender Score** (Round down to the nearest whole number) .... _____

SENTENCE RANGE

		Offender Score								
	0	**1**	**2**	**3**	**4**	**5**	**6**	**7**	**8**	**9+**
LEVEL I	0-60 days	0-90 days	3m 2 - 5	4m 2 - 6	5.5m 3 - 8	8m 4 - 12	13m 12+ - 14	16m 14 - 18	19.5m 17 - 22	25.5m 22 - 29

✓ For gang-related felonies where the court found the offender involved a minor (RCW 9.94A.833), see page 227 for standard range adjustment.
✓ For deadly weapon enhancement, see page 233.
✓ For sentencing alternatives, see page 215.
✓ For community custody eligibility, see page 228.
✓ For any applicable enhancements other than deadly weapon enhancement, see page 224.
✓ If the conviction includes a finding by special allegation of 'endangering one or more persons' under RCW 9.94A.834, add 12 months and 1 day to the entire standard sentencing range for the current offense. Effective 06/12/2008.

Bail Jumping with Class A Felony

RCW 9A.76.170(3)(b)
CLASS B – NONVIOLENT
OFFENDER SCORING RCW 9.94A.525(7)

If it was found that this offense was committed with sexual motivation (RCW 9.94A.533(8)) on or after 7/1/2006, use the General Nonviolent Offense with a Sexual Motivation Finding scoring form on page 236.

If the present conviction is for a felony domestic violence offense where domestic violence was plead and proven, use the General Nonviolent Offense Where Domestic Violence Has Been Plead and Proven scoring form on page 234.

ADULT HISTORY:

    Enter number of felony convictions .... _____ x 1 = _____

JUVENILE HISTORY:

    Enter number of Murder 1, Murder 2, and Class A sex offense felony dispositions .... _____ x 1 = _____

OTHER CURRENT OFFENSES:

(Other current offenses that do not encompass the same conduct count in offender score)

    Enter number of other felony convictions .... _____ x 1 = _____

STATUS:

    Was the offender on community custody on the date the current offense was committed?............ _____ + 1 = _____

Total the last column to get the **Offender Score** (Round down to the nearest whole number)......................... _____

SENTENCE RANGE DISPLAYED IS FOR A COMPLETED OFFENSE

FOR **ATTEMPT**, **SOLICITATION**, OR **CONSPIRACY** (RCW 9.94A.595, see page 54), THE SENTENCE RANGE **IS 75%** OF THE COMPLETED RANGE LISTED BELOW

Offender Score										
	0	**1**	**2**	**3**	**4**	**5**	**6**	**7**	**8**	**9+**
LEVEL V	9m	13m	15m	17.5m	25.5m	38m	47.5m	59.5m	72m	84m
	6 - 12	12+ - 14	13 - 17	15 - 20	22 - 29	33 - 43	41 - 54	51 - 68	62 - 82	72 - 96

✓   For gang-related felonies where the court found the offender involved a minor (RCW 9.94A.833), see page 227 for standard range adjustments.
✓   For deadly weapon enhancement, see page 233.
✓   For sentencing alternatives, see page 215.
✓   For community custody eligibility, see page 228.
✓   For any applicable enhancements other than deadly weapon enhancement, see page 224.

Bail Jumping with Class B or C Felony

RCW 9A.76.170(3)(c)
CLASS C* – NONVIOLENT
OFFENDER SCORING RCW 9.94A.525(7)

If it was found that this offense was committed with sexual motivation (RCW 9.94A.533(8)) on or after 7/1/2006, use the General Nonviolent Offense with a Sexual Motivation Finding scoring form on page 236.

If the present conviction is for a felony domestic violence offense where domestic violence was plead and proven, use the General Nonviolent Offense Where Domestic Violence Has Been Plead and Proven scoring form on page 234.

ADULT HISTORY:

    Enter number of felony convictions .... _____ x 1 = _____

JUVENILE HISTORY:

    Enter number of Murder 1, Murder 2, and Class A sex offense felony dispositions .... _____ x 1 = _____

OTHER CURRENT OFFENSES:

(Other current offenses that do not encompass the same conduct count in offender score)

    Enter number of other felony convictions .... _____ x 1 = _____

STATUS:

    Was the offender on community custody on the date the current offense was committed? .... _____ + 1 = _____

Total the last column to get the **Offender Score** (Round down to the nearest whole number)........................ _____

SENTENCE RANGE

	Offender Score									
	0	**1**	**2**	**3**	**4**	**5**	**6**	**7**	**8**	**9+**
LEVEL III	2m	5m	8m	11m	14m	19.5m	25.5m	38m	50m	55.5m
	1 - 3	3 - 8	4 - 12	9 - 12	12+ - 16	17 - 22	22 - 29	33 - 43	43 - 57	51 - 60*

    * Class C felony offenses have a statutory maximum sentence of 60 months, see RCW 9A.20.021.

✓   For gang-related felonies where the court found the offender involved a minor (RCW 9.94A.833), see page 227 for standard range adjustment.
✓   For deadly weapon enhancement, see page 233.
✓   For sentencing alternatives, see page 215.
✓   For community custody eligibility, see page 228.
✓   For any applicable enhancements other than deadly weapon enhancement, see page 224.

RCW 9A.76.170(3)(a)
CLASS A – VIOLENT
OFFENDER SCORING RCW 9.94A.525(8)

If it was found that this offense was committed with sexual motivation (RCW 9.94A.533(8)) on or after 7/1/2006, use the General Violent Offense with a Sexual Motivation Finding scoring form on page 244.

If the present conviction is for a felony domestic violence offense where domestic violence was plead and proven, use the General Violent Offense Where Domestic Violence Has Been Plead and Proven scoring form on page 242.

ADULT HISTORY:

Enter number of serious violent and violent felony convictions .... _____ x 2 = _____

Enter number of nonviolent felony convictions .... _____ x 1 = _____

JUVENILE HISTORY:

Enter number of Murder 1, Murder 2, and Class A sex offense felony dispositions .... _____ x 2 = _____

OTHER CURRENT OFFENSES:

(Other current offenses that do not encompass the same conduct count in offender score)

Enter number of other serious violent and violent felony convictions .... _____ x 2 = _____

Enter number of other nonviolent felony convictions .... _____ x 1 = _____

STATUS:

Was the offender on community custody on the date the current offense was committed?........... _____ + 1 = _____

Total the last column to get the **Offender Score** (Round down to the nearest whole number)......................... _____

SENTENCE RANGE DISPLAYED IS FOR A COMPLETED OFFENSE

FOR **ATTEMPT**, **SOLICITATION**, OR **CONSPIRACY** (RCW 9.94A.595, see page 54), THE SENTENCE RANGE **IS 75%** OF THE COMPLETED RANGE LISTED BELOW

Offender Score										
	0	**1**	**2**	**3**	**4**	**5**	**6**	**7**	**8**	**9+**
LEVEL VI	13m	17.5m	24m	30m	36m	42m	53.5m	66m	78m	89.5m
	12+ - 14	15 - 20	21 - 27	26 - 34	31 - 41	36 - 48	46 - 61	57 - 75	67 - 89	77 - 102

✓ For gang-related felonies where the court found the offender involved a minor (RCW 9.94A.833), see page 227 for standard range adjustments.
✓ For deadly weapon enhancement, see page 233.
✓ For sentencing alternatives, see page 215.
✓ For community custody eligibility, see page 228.
✓ For any applicable enhancements other than deadly weapon enhancement, see page 224.

Bribe Received by Witness, Bribing a Witness
RCW 9A.72.100 & 9A.72.090
CLASS B – NONVIOLENT
OFFENDER SCORING RCW 9.94A.525(7)

If it was found that this offense was committed with sexual motivation (RCW 9.94A.533(8)) on or after 7/1/2006, use the General Nonviolent Offense with a Sexual Motivation Finding scoring form on page 236.

If the present conviction is for a felony domestic violence offense where domestic violence was plead and proven, use the General Nonviolent Offense Where Domestic Violence Has Been Plead and Proven scoring form on page 234.

ADULT HISTORY:

    Enter number of felony convictions .... _____ x 1 = _____

JUVENILE HISTORY:

    Enter number of Murder 1, Murder 2, and Class A sex offense felony dispositions .... _____ x 1 = _____

OTHER CURRENT OFFENSES:

(Other current offenses that do not encompass the same conduct count in offender score)

    Enter number of other felony convictions .... _____ x 1 = _____

STATUS:

    Was the offender on community custody on the date the current offense was committed? .... _____ + 1 = _____

Total the last column to get the **Offender Score** (Round down to the nearest whole number) .... _____

SENTENCE RANGE DISPLAYED IS FOR A COMPLETED OFFENSE

FOR **ATTEMPT**, **SOLICITATION**, OR **CONSPIRACY** (RCW 9.94A.595, see page 54), THE SENTENCE RANGE **IS 75%** OF THE COMPLETED RANGE LISTED BELOW

Offender Score										
	0	**1**	**2**	**3**	**4**	**5**	**6**	**7**	**8**	**9+**
LEVEL IV	6m	9m	13m	15m	17.5m	25.5m	38m	50m	61.5m	73.5m
	3 - 9	6 - 12	12+ - 14	13 - 17	15 - 20	22 - 29	33 - 43	43 - 57	53 - 70	63 - 84

✓   For gang-related felonies where the court found the offender involved a minor (RCW 9.94A.833), see page 227 for standard range adjustments.
✓   For deadly weapon enhancement, see page 233.
✓   For sentencing alternatives, see page 215.
✓   For community custody eligibility, see page 228.
✓   For any applicable enhancements other than deadly weapon enhancement, see page 224.

RCW 9A.68.010
CLASS B – NONVIOLENT
OFFENDER SCORING RCW 9.94A.525(7)

If it was found that this offense was committed with sexual motivation (RCW 9.94A.533(8)) on or after 7/1/2006, use the General Nonviolent Offense with a Sexual Motivation Finding scoring form on page 236.

If the present conviction is for a felony domestic violence offense where domestic violence was plead and proven, use the General Nonviolent Offense Where Domestic Violence Has Been Plead and Proven scoring form on page 234.

ADULT HISTORY:

Enter number of felony convictions .... _____ x 1 = _____

JUVENILE HISTORY:

Enter number of Murder 1, Murder 2, and Class A sex offense felony dispositions .... _____ x 1 = _____

OTHER CURRENT OFFENSES:

(Other current offenses that do not encompass the same conduct count in offender score)

Enter number of other felony convictions .... _____ x 1 = _____

STATUS:

Was the offender on community custody on the date the current offense was committed?............ _____ + 1 = _____

Total the last column to get the **Offender Score** (Round down to the nearest whole number).......................... _____

SENTENCE RANGE DISPLAYED IS FOR A COMPLETED OFFENSE

FOR **ATTEMPT**, **SOLICITATION**, OR **CONSPIRACY** (RCW 9.94A.595, see page 54), THE SENTENCE RANGE **IS 75%** OF THE COMPLETED RANGE LISTED BELOW

	Offender Score									
	0	1	2	3	4	5	6	7	8	9+
LEVEL VI	13m	17.5m	24m	30m	36m	42m	53.5m	66m	78m	89.5m
	12+ - 14	15 - 20	21 - 27	26 - 34	31 - 41	36 - 48	46 - 61	57 - 75	67 - 89	77 - 102

✓   For gang-related felonies where the court found the offender involved a minor (RCW 9.94A.833), see page 227 for standard range adjustments.
✓   For deadly weapon enhancement, see page 233.
✓   For sentencing alternatives, see page 215.
✓   For community custody eligibility, see page 228.
✓   For any applicable enhancements other than deadly weapon enhancement, see page 224.

Burglary First Degree

RCW 9A.52.020
CLASS A – VIOLENT/CRIMES AGAINST PERSONS
OFFENDER SCORING RCW 9.94A.525(10)

If the present conviction is for a felony domestic violence offense where domestic violence was plead and proven, use the General Burglary 1 Offense Where Domestic Violence Has Been Plead and Proven scoring form on page 245.

ADULT HISTORY:

Enter number of serious violent and violent felony convictions .... _____ x 2 = _____

Enter number of Burglary 2 and Residential Burglary felony convictions .... _____ x 2 = _____

Enter number of nonviolent felony convictions .... _____ x 1 = _____

JUVENILE HISTORY:

Enter number of Murder 1, Murder 2, and Class A sex offense felony dispositions .... _____ x 2 = _____

OTHER CURRENT OFFENSES:

(Other current offenses that do not encompass the same conduct count in offender score)

Enter number of other serious violent and violent felony convictions .... _____ x 2 = _____

Enter number of other Burglary 2 and Residential Burglary felony convictions .... _____ x 2 = _____

Enter number of other nonviolent felony convictions .... _____ x 1 = _____

STATUS:

Was the offender on community custody on the date the current offense was committed? .... _____ + 1 = _____

Total the last column to get the **Offender Score** (Round down to the nearest whole number)........................ _____

SENTENCE RANGE DISPLAYED IS FOR A COMPLETED OFFENSE

FOR **ATTEMPT**, **SOLICITATION**, OR **CONSPIRACY** (RCW 9.94A.595, see page 54), THE SENTENCE RANGE **IS 75%** OF THE COMPLETED RANGE LISTED BELOW

	Offender Score									
	0	**1**	**2**	**3**	**4**	**5**	**6**	**7**	**8**	**9+**
LEVEL VII	17.5m	24m	30m	36m	42m	47.5m	66m	78m	89.5m	101.5m
	15 - 20	21 - 27	26 - 34	31 - 41	36 - 48	41 - 54	57 - 75	67 - 89	77 - 102	87 - 116

✓ For gang-related felonies where the court found the offender involved a minor (RCW 9.94A.833), see page 227 for standard range adjustments.
✓ For deadly weapon enhancement, see page 233.
✓ For sentencing alternatives, see page 215.
✓ For community custody eligibility, see page 228.
✓ For any applicable enhancements other than deadly weapon enhancement, see page 224.

RCW 9A.52.020
CLASS A – VIOLENT/SEX/CRIMES AGAINST PERSONS
OFFENDER SCORING RCW 9.94A.525(17)

ADULT HISTORY:

Enter number of sex offense felony convictions .... _____ x 3 = _____

Enter number of serious violent and violent felony convictions .... _____ x 2 = _____

Enter number of Burglary 2 and Residential Burglary felony convictions .... _____ x 2 = _____

Enter number of nonviolent felony convictions .... _____ x 1 = _____

JUVENILE HISTORY:

Enter number of Class A sex offense felony dispositions .... _____ x 3 = _____

Enter number of Murder 1 and Murder 2 felony dispositions .... _____ x 2 = _____

OTHER CURRENT OFFENSES:

(Other current offenses that do not encompass the same conduct count in offender score)

Enter number of other sex offense felony convictions .... _____ x 3 = _____

Enter number of other serious violent and violent felony convictions .... _____ x 2 = _____

Enter number of other Burglary 2 and Residential Burglary felony convictions .... _____ x 2 = _____

Enter number of other nonviolent felony convictions .... _____ x 1 = _____

STATUS:

Was the offender on community custody on the date the current offense was committed?........... _____ + 1 = _____

Total the last column to get the **Offender Score** (Round down to the nearest whole number)......................... _____

SENTENCE RANGE DISPLAYED IS FOR A COMPLETED OFFENSE

FOR **ATTEMPT**, **SOLICITATION**, OR **CONSPIRACY** (RCW 9.94A.595, see page 54), THE SENTENCE RANGE **IS 75%** OF THE COMPLETED RANGE LISTED BELOW

Offender Score										
	0	**1**	**2**	**3**	**4**	**5**	**6**	**7**	**8**	**9+**
LEVEL VII	17.5m	24m	30m	36m	42m	47.5m	66m	78m	89.5m	101.5m
	15 - 20	21 - 27	26 - 34	31 - 41	36 - 48	41 - 54	57 - 75	67 - 89	77 - 102	87 - 116

SEXUAL MOTIVATION ENHANCEMENT (Per Sexual Motivation Enhancement, page 226) .... _____

Low   to   High

STANDARD SENTENCE RANGE PLUS ENHANCEMENT............. _____ ..... _____

✓   For gang-related felonies where the court found the offender involved a minor (RCW 9.94A.833), see page 227 for standard range adjustments.
✓   For deadly weapon enhancement, see page 233.
✓   For sentencing alternatives, see page 215.
✓   For community custody eligibility, see page 228.
✓   For any applicable enhancements other than deadly weapon enhancement, see page 224.
✓   If the offender is not a persistent offender and the <u>current</u> offense is either a completed offense or a criminal attempt under RCW 9A.28.020 that was committed on or after 9/1/2001, then the offender is subject to the requirements under RCW 9.94A.507.
✓   If the offender is not a persistent offender and has a <u>prior</u> conviction for an offense listed in RCW 9.94A.030(37)(b), then the sentence is subject to the requirements of RCW 9.94A.507.

Burglary Second Degree
RCW 9A.52.030
CLASS B – NONVIOLENT
OFFENDER SCORING RCW 9.94A.525(16)

If the present conviction is for a felony domestic violence offense where domestic violence was plead and proven, use the General Burglary Second Degree or Residential Burglary Offense Where Domestic Violence Has Been Plead and Proven scoring form on page 246.

ADULT HISTORY:

Enter number of Burglary 1 felony convictions .... _____ x 2 = _____

Enter number of Burglary 2 and Residential Burglary felony convictions .... _____ x 2 = _____

Enter number of felony convictions .... _____ x 1 = _____

JUVENILE HISTORY:

Enter number of Murder 1, Murder 2, and Class A sex offense felony dispositions .... _____ x 1 = _____

OTHER CURRENT OFFENSES:

(Other current offenses that do not encompass the same conduct count in offender score)

Enter number of other Burglary 1 felony convictions .... _____ x 2 = _____

Enter number of other Burglary 2 and Residential Burglary felony convictions .... _____ x 2 = _____

Enter number of other felony convictions .... _____ x 1 = _____

STATUS:

Was the offender on community custody on the date the current offense was committed? .... _____ + 1 = _____

Total the last column to get the **Offender Score** (Round down to the nearest whole number) .... _____

SENTENCE RANGE DISPLAYED IS FOR A COMPLETED OFFENSE

FOR **ATTEMPT**, **SOLICITATION**, OR **CONSPIRACY** (RCW 9.94A.595, see page 54), THE SENTENCE RANGE **IS 75%** OF THE COMPLETED RANGE LISTED BELOW

	Offender Score									
	0	**1**	**2**	**3**	**4**	**5**	**6**	**7**	**8**	**9+**
LEVEL III	2m	5m	8m	11m	14m	19.5m	25.5m	38m	50m	59.5m
	1 - 3	3 - 8	4 - 12	9 - 12	12+ - 16	17 - 22	22 - 29	33 - 43	43 - 57	51 - 68

✓ For gang-related felonies where the court found the offender involved a minor (RCW 9.94A.833), see page 227 for standard range adjustments.
✓ For deadly weapon enhancement, see page 233.
✓ For sentencing alternatives, see page 215.
✓ For community custody eligibility, see page 228.
✓ For any applicable enhancements other than deadly weapon enhancement, see page 224.

RCW 9A.52.030
CLASS B – NONVIOLENT/SEX
OFFENDER SCORING RCW 9.94A.525(17)

ADULT HISTORY:

Enter number of sex offense felony convictions .... _____ x 3 = _____

Enter number of Burglary 1 felony convictions .... _____ x 2 = _____

Enter number of Burglary 2 and Residential Burglary felony convictions .... _____ x 2 = _____

Enter number of felony convictions .... _____ x 1 = _____

JUVENILE HISTORY:

Enter number of Class A sex offense felony dispositions .... _____ x 3 = _____

Enter number of Murder 1 and Murder 2 felony dispositions .... _____ x 1 = _____

OTHER CURRENT OFFENSES:

(Other current offenses that do not encompass the same conduct count in offender score)

Enter number of other sex offense felony convictions .... _____ x 3 = _____

Enter number of other Burglary 1 felony convictions .... _____ x 2 = _____

Enter number of other Burglary 2 and Residential Burglary felony convictions .... _____ x 2 = _____

Enter number of other felony convictions .... _____ x 1 = _____

STATUS:

Was the offender on community custody on the date the current offense was committed?............ _____ + 1 = _____

Total the last column to get the **Offender Score** (Round down to the nearest whole number)......................... _____

SENTENCE RANGE DISPLAYED IS FOR A COMPLETED OFFENSE

FOR **ATTEMPT**, **SOLICITATION**, OR **CONSPIRACY** (RCW 9.94A.595, see page 54), THE SENTENCE RANGE **IS 75%** OF THE COMPLETED RANGE LISTED BELOW

Offender Score									
0	**1**	**2**	**3**	**4**	**5**	**6**	**7**	**8**	**9+**
2m	5m	8m	11m	14m	19.5m	25.5m	38m	50m	59.5m
1 - 3	3 - 8	4 - 12	9 - 12	12+ - 16	17 - 22	22 - 29	33 - 43	43 - 57	51 - 68

(LEVEL III)

SEXUAL MOTIVATION ENHANCEMENT (Per Sexual Motivation Enhancement, page 226) .... _____

                                                              Low   to   High

STANDARD SENTENCE RANGE PLUS ENHANCEMENT.............. _____ ..... _____

✓ For gang-related felonies where the court found the offender involved a minor (RCW 9.94A.833), see page 227 for standard range adjustments.
✓ For deadly weapon enhancement, see page 233.
✓ For sentencing alternatives, see page 215.
✓ For community custody eligibility, see page 228.
✓ For any applicable enhancements other than deadly weapon enhancement, see page 224.
✓ If the offender is not a persistent offender and has a prior conviction for an offense listed in RCW 9.94A.030(37)(b), then the sentence is subject to the requirements of RCW 9.94A.507.

Cheating First Degree

RCW 9.46.1961
CLASS C* – NONVIOLENT
OFFENDER SCORING RCW 9.94A.525(7)

If it was found that this offense was committed with sexual motivation (RCW 9.94A.533(8)) on or after 7/1/2006, use the General Nonviolent Offense with a Sexual Motivation Finding scoring form on page 236.

If the present conviction is for a felony domestic violence offense where domestic violence was plead and proven, use the General Nonviolent Offense Where Domestic Violence Has Been Plead and Proven scoring form on page 234.

ADULT HISTORY:

Enter number of felony convictions .... _____ x 1 = _____

JUVENILE HISTORY:

Enter number of Murder 1, Murder 2, and Class A sex offense felony dispositions .... _____ x 1 = _____

OTHER CURRENT OFFENSES:

(Other current offenses that do not encompass the same conduct count in offender score)

Enter number of other felony convictions .... _____ x 1 = _____

STATUS:

Was the offender on community custody on the date the current offense was committed? (if yes) _____ + 1 = _____

Total the last column to get the **Offender Score** (Round down to the nearest whole number) .... _____

SENTENCE RANGE

	Offender Score									
	0	1	2	3	4	5	6	7	8	9+
LEVEL IV	6m	9m	13m	15m	17.5m	25.5m	38m	50m	56.5m	
	3 - 9	6 - 12	12+ - 14	13 - 17	15 - 20	22 - 29	33 - 43	43 - 57	53 - 60*	60 - 60*

* Class C felony offenses have a statutory maximum sentence of 60 months, see RCW 9A.20.021.

✓ For gang-related felonies where the court found the offender involved a minor (RCW 9.94A.833), see page 227 for standard range adjustment.
✓ For deadly weapon enhancement, see page 233.
✓ For sentencing alternatives, see page 215.
✓ For community custody eligibility, see page 228.
✓ For any applicable enhancements other than deadly weapon enhancement, see page 224.

Child Molestation First Degree, Completed or Attempt

RCW 9A.44.083
CLASS A – VIOLENT/SEX/CRIMES AGAINST PERSONS
ATTEMPT = CLASS A - VIOLENT/SEX
OFFENDER SCORING RCW 9.94A.525(17)

If the present conviction is for a felony domestic violence offense where domestic violence was plead and proven, use the General Violent/Sex Offense Where Domestic Violence Has Been Plead and Proven scoring form on page 243.

ADULT HISTORY:

Enter number of sex offense felony convictions .... ______ x 3 = ______

Enter number of serious violent and violent felony convictions .... ______ x 2 = ______

Enter number of nonviolent felony convictions .... ______ x 1 = ______

JUVENILE HISTORY:

Enter number of Class A sex offense felony dispositions .... ______ x 3 = ______

Enter number of Murder 1 and Murder 2 felony dispositions .... ______ x 2 = ______

OTHER CURRENT OFFENSES:

(Other current offenses that do not encompass the same conduct count in offender score)

Enter number of other sex offense felony convictions .... ______ x 3 = ______

Enter number of other serious violent and violent felony convictions .... ______ x 2 = ______

Enter number of other nonviolent felony convictions .... ______ x 1 = ______

STATUS:

Was the offender on community custody on the date the current offense was committed?.......... ______ + 1 = ______

Total the last column to get the **Offender Score** (Round down to the nearest whole number).......... ______

SENTENCE RANGE DISPLAYED IS FOR A COMPLETED OFFENSE

FOR **ATTEMPT**, **SOLICITATION**, OR **CONSPIRACY** (RCW 9.94A.595, see page 54), THE SENTENCE RANGE **IS 75%** OF THE COMPLETED RANGE LISTED BELOW

	Offender Score									
	0	1	2	3	4	5	6	7	8	9+
LEVEL X	59.5m 51 - 68	66m 57 - 75	72m 62 - 82	78m 67 - 89	84m 72 - 96	89.5m 77 - 102	114m 98 - 130	126m 108 - 144	150m 129 - 171	173.5m 149 - 198

- ✓ For gang-related felonies where the court found the offender involved a minor (RCW 9.94A.833), see page 227 for standard range adjustments.
- ✓ For deadly weapon enhancement, see page 233.
- ✓ For sentencing alternatives, see page 215.
- ✓ For community custody eligibility, see page 228.
- ✓ For any applicable enhancements other than deadly weapon enhancement, see page 224.
- ✓ If the offender is older than 17 years of age and is not a persistent offender and the current offense was committed on or after 9/1/2001, then the offender is subject to the requirements under RCW 9.94A.507.
- ✓ If the offender engaged the victim in sexual conduct in exchange for a fee, an additional 12 months shall be added to the standard sentence range (RCW 9.94A.533(9)).
- ✓ Per RCW 9.94A.507(3)(c)(ii), excluding attempt convictions, the minimum term shall be either the maximum of the standard sentence range for the offense or 25 years, whichever is greater, for a finding that the offense was **predatory**.
- ✓ If the offender is older than 17 years of age and is not a persistent offender and has a prior conviction for an offense listed in RCW 9.94A.030(37)(b), then the sentence is subject to the requirements of RCW 9.94A.507.

Child Molestation First Degree, Solicitation
RCW 9A.44.083
CLASS A – VIOLENT/SEX
OFFENDER SCORING RCW 9.94A.525(17)

If the present conviction is for a felony domestic violence offense where domestic violence was plead and proven, use the General Violent/Sex Offense Where Domestic Violence Has Been Plead and Proven scoring form on page 243.

ADULT HISTORY:

Enter number of sex offense felony convictions .... _____ x 3 = _____

Enter number of serious violent and violent felony convictions .... _____ x 2 = _____

Enter number of nonviolent felony convictions .... _____ x 1 = _____

JUVENILE HISTORY:

Enter number of Class A sex offense felony dispositions .... _____ x 3 = _____

Enter number of Murder 1 and Murder 2 felony dispositions .... _____ x 2 = _____

OTHER CURRENT OFFENSES:

(Other current offenses that do not encompass the same conduct count in offender score)

Enter number of other sex offense felony convictions .... _____ x 3 = _____

Enter number of other serious violent and violent felony convictions .... _____ x 2 = _____

Enter number of other nonviolent felony convictions .... _____ x 1 = _____

STATUS:

Was the offender on community custody on the date the current offense was committed? .... _____ + 1 = _____

Total the last column to get the **Offender Score** (Round down to the nearest whole number) .... _____

SENTENCE RANGE DISPLAYED IS FOR A COMPLETED OFFENSE

FOR **ATTEMPT**, **SOLICITATION**, OR **CONSPIRACY** (RCW 9.94A.595, see page 54), THE SENTENCE RANGE **IS 75%** OF THE COMPLETED RANGE LISTED BELOW

	Offender Score									
	0	**1**	**2**	**3**	**4**	**5**	**6**	**7**	**8**	**9+**
LEVEL X	59.5m	66m	72m	78m	84m	89.5m	114m	126m	150m	173.5m
	51 - 68	57 - 75	62 - 82	67 - 89	72 - 96	77 - 102	98 - 130	108 - 144	129 - 171	149 - 198

✓ For gang-related felonies where the court found the offender involved a minor (RCW 9.94A.833), see page 227 for standard range adjustments.

✓ For deadly weapon enhancement, see page 233.

✓ For sentencing alternatives, see page 215.

✓ For community custody eligibility, see page 228.

✓ For any applicable enhancements other than deadly weapon enhancement, see page 224.

✓ If the offender engaged the victim in sexual conduct in exchange for a fee, an additional 12 months shall be added to the standard sentence range (RCW 9.94A.533(9)).

✓ If the offender is older than 17 years of age and is not a persistent offender and has a prior conviction for an offense listed in RCW 9.94A.030(37)(b), then the sentence is subject to the requirements of RCW 9.94A.507.

RCW 9A.44.083
CLASS B* – VIOLENT/SEX
OFFENDER SCORING RCW 9.94A.525(17)

If the present conviction is for a felony domestic violence offense where domestic violence was plead and proven, use the General Violent/Sex Offense Where Domestic Violence Has Been Plead and Proven scoring form on page 243.

ADULT HISTORY:

Enter number of sex offense felony convictions .... _____ x 3 = _____

Enter number of serious violent and violent felony convictions .... _____ x 2 = _____

Enter number of nonviolent felony convictions .... _____ x 1 = _____

JUVENILE HISTORY:

Enter number of Class A sex offense felony dispositions .... _____ x 3 = _____

Enter number of Murder 1 and Murder 2 felony dispositions .... _____ x 2 = _____

OTHER CURRENT OFFENSES:

(Other current offenses that do not encompass the same conduct count in offender score)

Enter number of other sex offense felony convictions .... _____ x 3 = _____

Enter number of other serious violent and violent felony convictions .... _____ x 2 = _____

Enter number of other nonviolent felony convictions .... _____ x 1 = _____

STATUS:

Was the offender on community custody on the date the current offense was committed?............ _____ + 1 = _____

Total the last column to get the **Offender Score** (Round down to the nearest whole number)......................... _____

SENTENCE RANGE DISPLAYED IS FOR A COMPLETED OFFENSE

FOR **ATTEMPT**, **SOLICITATION**, OR **CONSPIRACY** (RCW 9.94A.595, see page 54), THE SENTENCE RANGE **IS 75%** OF THE COMPLETED RANGE LISTED BELOW

Offender Score										
	0	**1**	**2**	**3**	**4**	**5**	**6**	**7**	**8**	**9+**
LEVEL X	59.5m	66m	72m	78m	84m	89.5m	109m	114m		
	51 - 68	57 - 75	62 - 82	67 - 89	72 - 96	77 - 102	98 - 120*	108 - 120*	120 - 120*	120 - 120*

*Class B felony offenses have a statutory maximum sentence of 120 months, see RCW 9A.20.021.

✓ For gang-related felonies where the court found the offender involved a minor (RCW 9.94A.833), see page 227 for standard range adjustments.
✓ For deadly weapon enhancement, see page 233.
✓ For sentencing alternatives, see page 215.
✓ For community custody eligibility, see page 228.
✓ For any applicable enhancements other than deadly weapon enhancement, see page 224.
✓ If the offender is older than 17 years of age and is not a persistent offender and has a prior conviction for an offense listed in RCW 9.94A.030(37)(b), then the sentence is subject to the requirements of RCW 9.94A.507.
✓ If the offender engaged the victim in sexual conduct in exchange for a fee, an additional 12 months shall be added to the standard sentence range (RCW 9.94A.533(9)).

RCW 9A.44.086
CLASS B – NONVIOLENT/SEX/CRIMES AGAINST PERSONS
OFFENDER SCORING RCW 9.94A.525(17)

If the present conviction is for a felony domestic violence offense where domestic violence was plead and proven, use the General Nonviolent/Sex Offense Where Domestic Violence Has Been Plead and Proven scoring form on page 235.

ADULT HISTORY:

Enter number of sex offense felony convictions .... _____ x 3 = _____

Enter number of felony convictions .... _____ x 1 = _____

JUVENILE HISTORY:

Enter number of Class A sex offense felony dispositions .... _____ x 3 = _____

Enter number of Murder 1 and Murder 2 felony dispositions .... _____ x 1 = _____

OTHER CURRENT OFFENSES:

(Other current offenses that do not encompass the same conduct count in offender score)

Enter number of other sex offense felony convictions .... _____ x 3 = _____

Enter number of other felony convictions .... _____ x 1 = _____

STATUS:

Was the offender on community custody on the date the current offense was committed? .... _____ + 1 = _____

Total the last column to get the **Offender Score** (Round down to the nearest whole number)......................... _____

SENTENCE RANGE DISPLAYED IS FOR A COMPLETED OFFENSE

FOR **ATTEMPT**, **SOLICITATION**, OR **CONSPIRACY** (RCW 9.94A.595, see page 54), THE SENTENCE RANGE **IS 75%** OF THE COMPLETED RANGE LISTED BELOW

	Offender Score									
	0	**1**	**2**	**3**	**4**	**5**	**6**	**7**	**8**	**9+**
LEVEL VII	17.5m	24m	30m	36m	42m	47.5m	66m	78m	89.5m	101.5m
	15 - 20	21 - 27	26 - 34	31 - 41	36 - 48	41 - 54	57 - 75	67 - 89	77 - 102	87 - 116

✓ For gang-related felonies where the court found the offender involved a minor (RCW 9.94A.833), see page 227 for standard range adjustments.
✓ For deadly weapon enhancement, see page 233.
✓ For sentencing alternatives, see page 215.
✓ For community custody eligibility, see page 228.
✓ For any applicable enhancements other than deadly weapon enhancement, see page 224.
✓ If the offender is not a persistent offender and has a prior conviction for an offense listed in RCW 9.94A.030(37)(b), then the sentence is subject to the requirements of RCW 9.94A.507.
✓ If the offender engaged the victim in sexual conduct in exchange for a fee, an additional 12 months shall be added to the standard sentence range (RCW 9.94A.533(9)).

Child Molestation Third Degree
RCW 9A.44.089
CLASS C* – NONVIOLENT/SEX/CRIMES AGAINST PERSONS
OFFENDER SCORING RCW 9.94A.525(17)

If the present conviction is for a felony domestic violence offense where domestic violence was plead and proven, use the General Nonviolent/Sex Offense Where Domestic Violence Has Been Plead and Proven scoring form on page 235.

ADULT HISTORY:

Enter number of sex offense felony convictions .... _____ x 3 = _____

Enter number of felony convictions .... _____ x 1 = _____

JUVENILE HISTORY:

Enter number of Class A sex offense felony dispositions .... _____ x 3 = _____

Enter number of Murder 1 and Murder 2 felony dispositions .... _____ x 1 = _____

OTHER CURRENT OFFENSES:

(Other current offenses that do not encompass the same conduct count in offender score)

Enter number of other sex offense felony convictions .... _____ x 3 = _____

Enter number of other felony convictions .... _____ x 1 = _____

STATUS:

Was the offender on community custody on the date the current offense was committed?............ _____ + 1 = _____

Total the last column to get the **Offender Score** (Round down to the nearest whole number).......................... _____

SENTENCE RANGE

	Offender Score									
	0	**1**	**2**	**3**	**4**	**5**	**6**	**7**	**8**	**9+**
LEVEL V	9m	13m	15m	17.5m	25.5m	38m	47.5m	55.5m		
	6 - 12	12+ - 14	13 - 17	15 - 20	22 - 29	33 - 43	41 - 54	51 - 60*	60 - 60*	60 - 60*

* Class C felony offenses have a statutory maximum sentence of 60 months, see RCW 9A.20.021.

✓ For gang-related felonies where the court found the offender involved a minor (RCW 9.94A.833), see page 227 for standard range adjustment.
✓ For deadly weapon enhancement, see page 233.
✓ For sentencing alternatives, see page 215.
✓ For community custody eligibility, see page 228.
✓ For any applicable enhancements other than deadly weapon enhancement, see page 224.
✓ If the offender is not a persistent offender and has a prior conviction for an offense listed in RCW 9.94A.030(37)(b), then the sentence is subject to the requirements of RCW 9.94A.507.
✓ If the offender engaged the victim in sexual conduct in exchange for a fee, an additional 12 months shall be added to the standard sentence range (RCW 9.94A.533(9)).

RCW 9A.48.120
CLASS B – NONVIOLENT
OFFENDER SCORING RCW 9.94A.525(7)

If it was found that this offense was committed with sexual motivation (RCW 9.94A.533(8)) on or after 7/1/2006, use the General Nonviolent Offense with a Sexual Motivation Finding scoring form on page 236.

If the present conviction is for a felony domestic violence offense where domestic violence was plead and proven, use the General Nonviolent Offense Where Domestic Violence Has Been Plead and Proven scoring form on page 234.

ADULT HISTORY:

    Enter number of felony convictions .... _____ x 1 = _____

JUVENILE HISTORY:

    Enter number of Murder 1, Murder 2, and Class A sex offense felony dispositions .... _____ x 1 = _____

OTHER CURRENT OFFENSES:

(Other current offenses that do not encompass the same conduct count in offender score)

    Enter number of other felony convictions .... _____ x 1 = _____

STATUS:

    Was the offender on community custody on the date the current offense was committed? (if yes) _____ + 1 = _____

Total the last column to get the **Offender Score** (Round down to the nearest whole number)......................... _____

SENTENCE RANGE DISPLAYED IS FOR A COMPLETED OFFENSE

FOR **ATTEMPT**, **SOLICITATION**, OR **CONSPIRACY** (RCW 9.94A.595, see page 54), THE SENTENCE RANGE **IS 75%** OF THE COMPLETED RANGE LISTED BELOW

Offender Score										
	0	**1**	**2**	**3**	**4**	**5**	**6**	**7**	**8**	**9+**
LEVEL VII	17.5m	24m	30m	36m	42m	47.5m	66m	78m	89.5m	101.5m
	15 - 20	21 - 27	26 - 34	31 - 41	36 - 48	41 - 54	57 - 75	67 - 89	77 - 102	87 - 116

✓   For gang-related felonies where the court found the offender involved a minor (RCW 9.94A.833), see page 227 for standard range adjustments.
✓   For deadly weapon enhancement, see page 233.
✓   For sentencing alternatives, see page 215.
✓   For community custody eligibility, see page 228.
✓   For any applicable enhancements other than deadly weapon enhancement, see page 224.

Commercial Bribery

RCW 9A.68.060
CLASS B – NONVIOLENT
OFFENDER SCORING RCW 9.94A.525(7)

If it was found that this offense was committed with sexual motivation (RCW 9.94A.533(8)) on or after 7/1/2006, use the General Nonviolent Offense with a Sexual Motivation Finding scoring form on page 236.

If the present conviction is for a felony domestic violence offense where domestic violence was plead and proven, use the General Nonviolent Offense Where Domestic Violence Has Been Plead and Proven scoring form on page 234.

ADULT HISTORY:

    Enter number of felony convictions .... _____ x 1 = _____

JUVENILE HISTORY:

    Enter number of Murder 1, Murder 2, and Class A sex offense felony dispositions .... _____ x 1 = _____

OTHER CURRENT OFFENSES:

(Other current offenses that do not encompass the same conduct count in offender score)

    Enter number of other felony convictions .... _____ x 1 = _____

STATUS:

    Was the offender on community custody on the date the current offense was committed? (if yes) _____ + 1 = _____

Total the last column to get the **Offender Score** (Round down to the nearest whole number).......................... _____

SENTENCE RANGE DISPLAYED IS FOR A COMPLETED OFFENSE

FOR **ATTEMPT**, **SOLICITATION**, OR **CONSPIRACY** (RCW 9.94A.595, see page 54), THE SENTENCE RANGE **IS 75%** OF THE COMPLETED RANGE LISTED BELOW

Offender Score									
	0	**1**	**2**	**3**	**4**	**5**	**6**	**7**	**8**	**9+**
LEVEL IV	6m	9m	13m	15m	17.5m	25.5m	38m	50m	61.5m	73.5m
	3 - 9	6 - 12	12+ - 14	13 - 17	15 - 20	22 - 29	33 - 43	43 - 57	53 - 70	63 - 84

✓ For gang-related felonies where the court found the offender involved a minor (RCW 9.94A.833), see page 227 for standard range adjustments.
✓ For deadly weapon enhancement, see page 233.
✓ For sentencing alternatives, see page 215.
✓ For community custody eligibility, see page 228.
✓ For any applicable enhancements other than deadly weapon enhancement, see page 224.

Commercial Sexual Abuse of a Minor

RCW 9.68A.100
CLASS B* – NONVIOLENT/SEX
OFFENDER SCORING RCW 9.94A.525(17)

If the present conviction is for a felony domestic violence offense where domestic violence was plead and proven, use the General Nonviolent/Sex Offense Where Domestic Violence Has Been Plead and Proven scoring form on page 235.

ADULT HISTORY:

Enter number of sex offense felony convictions .... _____ x 3 = _____

Enter number of felony convictions .... _____ x 1 = _____

JUVENILE HISTORY:

Enter number of Class A sex offense felony dispositions .... _____ x 3 = _____

Enter number of Murder 1 and Murder 2 felony dispositions .... _____ x 1 = _____

OTHER CURRENT OFFENSES:

(Other current offenses that do not encompass the same conduct count in offender score)

Enter number of other sex offense felony convictions .... _____ x 3 = _____

Enter number of other felony convictions .... _____ x 1 = _____

STATUS:

Was the offender on community custody on the date the current offense was committed? (if yes) _____ + 1 = _____

Total the last column to get the **Offender Score** (Round down to the nearest whole number)......................... _____

SENTENCE RANGE DISPLAYED IS FOR A COMPLETED OFFENSE

FOR **ATTEMPT**, **SOLICITATION**, OR **CONSPIRACY** (RCW 9.94A.595, see page 54), THE SENTENCE RANGE **IS 75%** OF THE COMPLETED RANGE LISTED BELOW

	Offender Score									
	0	**1**	**2**	**3**	**4**	**5**	**6**	**7**	**8**	**9+**
LEVEL VIII	24m	30m	36m	42m	47.5m	53.5m	78m	89.5m	101.5m	114m
	21 - 27	26 - 34	31 - 41	36 - 48	41 - 54	46 - 61	67 - 89	77 - 102	87 - 116	108 - 120*

* Class B felony offenses have a statutory maximum sentence of 120 months, see RCW 9A.20.021.

✓   For gang-related felonies where the court found the offender involved a minor (RCW 9.94A.833), see page 227 for standard range adjustments.

✓   For deadly weapon enhancement, see page 233.

✓   For sentencing alternatives, see page 215.

✓   For community custody eligibility, see page 228.

✓   For any applicable enhancements other than deadly weapon enhancement, see page 224.

✓   If the offender is not a persistent offender and has a <u>prior</u> conviction for an offense listed in RCW 9.94A.030(3)(b), then the sentence is subject to the requirements of RCW 9.94A.507.

Communication with a Minor for Immoral Purposes Subsequent Violation or Prior Sex Offense Conviction

RCW 9.68A.090(2)
CLASS C* – NONVIOLENT/SEX/CRIMES AGAINST PERSONS
OFFENDER SCORING RCW 9.94A.525(17)

If the present conviction is for a felony domestic violence offense where domestic violence was plead and proven, use the General Nonviolent/Sex Offense Where Domestic Violence Has Been Plead and Proven scoring form on page 235.

ADULT HISTORY:

Enter number of sex offense felony convictions .... _____ x 3 = _____

Enter number of felony convictions .... _____ x 1 = _____

JUVENILE HISTORY:

Enter number of Class A sex offense felony dispositions .... _____ x 3 = _____

Enter number of Murder 1 and Murder 2 felony dispositions .... _____ x 1 = _____

OTHER CURRENT OFFENSES:

(Other current offenses that do not encompass the same conduct count in offender score)

Enter number of other sex offense felony convictions .... _____ x 3 = _____

Enter number of other felony convictions .... _____ x 1 = _____

STATUS:

Was the offender on community custody on the date the current offense was committed? (if yes) _____ + 1 = _____

Total the last column to get the **Offender Score** (Round down to the nearest whole number)......................... _____

SENTENCE RANGE

	Offender Score									
	0	**1**	**2**	**3**	**4**	**5**	**6**	**7**	**8**	**9+**
LEVEL III	2m	5m	8m	11m	14m	19.5m	25.5m	38m	50m	55.5m
	1 - 3	3 - 8	4 - 12	9 - 12	12+ - 16	17 - 22	22 - 29	33 - 43	43 - 57	51 - 60*

* Class C felony offenses have a statutory maximum sentence of 60 months, see RCW 9A.20.021.

✓ For gang-related felonies where the court found the offender involved a minor (RCW 9.94A.833), see page 227 for standard range adjustment.
✓ For deadly weapon enhancement, see page 233.
✓ For sentencing alternatives, see page 215.
✓ For community custody eligibility, see page 228.
✓ For any applicable enhancements other than deadly weapon enhancement, see page 224.
✓ If the offender is not a persistent offender and has a <u>prior</u> conviction for an offense listed in RCW 9.94A.030(37)(b), then the sentence is subject to the requirements of RCW 9.94A.507.

Computer Trespass First Degree
RCW 9A.90.040
CLASS C – NONVIOLENT
OFFENDER SCORING RCW 9.94A.525(7)

If it was found that this offense was committed with sexual motivation (RCW 9.94A.533(8)) on or after 7/1/2006, use the General Nonviolent Offense with a Sexual Motivation Finding scoring form on page 236.

If the present conviction is for a felony domestic violence offense where domestic violence was plead and proven, use the General Nonviolent Offense Where Domestic Violence Has Been Plead and Proven scoring form on page 234.

ADULT HISTORY:

    Enter number of felony convictions .... _____ x 1 = _____

JUVENILE HISTORY:

    Enter number of Murder 1, Murder 2, and Class A sex offense felony dispositions .... _____ x 1 = _____

OTHER CURRENT OFFENSES:

(Other current offenses that do not encompass the same conduct count in offender score)

    Enter number of other felony convictions .... _____ x 1 = _____

STATUS:

    Was the offender on community custody on the date the current offense was committed? (if yes) _____ + 1 = _____

Total the last column to get the **Offender Score** (Round down to the nearest whole number)......................... _____

SENTENCE RANGE

		Offender Score									
		0	1	2	3	4	5	6	7	8	9+
LEVEL II			4m	6m	8m	13m	16m	19.5m	25.5m	38m	50m
	0-90 days	2 - 6	3 - 9	4 - 12	12+ - 14	14 - 18	17 - 22	22 - 29	33 - 43	43 - 57

✓   For gang-related felonies where the court found the offender involved a minor (RCW 9.94A.833), see page 227 for standard range adjustment.
✓   For deadly weapon enhancement, see page 233.
✓   For sentencing alternatives, see page 215.
✓   For community custody eligibility, see page 228.
✓   For any applicable enhancements other than deadly weapon enhancement, see page 224.

Controlled Substance Homicide

RCW 69.50.415
CLASS B – NONVIOLENT/DRUG
OFFENDER SCORING RCW 9.94A.525(13)

If it was found that this offense was committed with sexual motivation (RCW 9.94A.533(8)) on or after 7/1/2006, use the General Drug Offense with a Sexual Motivation Finding scoring form on page 238.

If the present conviction is for a felony domestic violence offense where domestic violence was plead and proven, use the General Drug Offense Where Domestic Violence Has Been Plead and Proven scoring form on page 237.

ADULT HISTORY:

Does the offender have a prior sex or serious violent offense in history?

.... **YES,** Enter number of felony drug convictions _____ x 3 = _____

....**NO,** Enter number of felony drug convictions _____ x 1 = _____

Enter number of felony convictions .... _____ x 1 = _____

JUVENILE HISTORY:

Enter number of Murder 1, Murder 2, and Class A sex offense felony dispositions .... _____ x 1 = _____

OTHER CURRENT OFFENSES:

(Other current offenses that do not encompass the same conduct count in offender score)

Does the offender have other prior sex or serious violent offense in history?

.... **YES,** Enter number of other felony drug convictions _____ x 3 = _____

....**NO,** Enter number of other felony drug convictions _____ x 1 = _____

Enter number of other felony convictions .... _____ x 1 = _____

STATUS:

Was the offender on community custody on the date the current offense was committed? (if yes) _____ + 1 = _____

Total the last column to get the **Offender Score** (Round down to the nearest whole number)......................... _____

SENTENCE RANGE – DRUG

	Offender Score		
	0 to 2	**3 to 5**	**6 to 9+**
LEVEL III	59.5m	84m	110m
	51 - 68	68+ - 100	100+ - 120

✓ For attempt, solicitation or conspiracy drug felonies see page 56, or for gang-related felonies where the court found the offender involved a minor (RCW 9.94A.833), see page 227 for standard range adjustments.
✓ Per RCW 9.94A.518, any felony offense under chapter 69.50 RCW with a deadly weapon special verdict under RCW 9.94A.602 becomes a level III offense.
✓ For deadly weapon enhancement, see page 233.
✓ For sentencing alternatives, see page 215.
✓ For community custody eligibility, see page 228.
✓ For any applicable enhancements other than deadly weapon enhancement, see page 224.
✓ Per RCW 69.50.408, the statutory maximum for a subsequent conviction under chapter 69.50 RCW is 240 months.

Counterfeiting - Third Conviction, Manufacture/Production of Items with Counterfeit Marks, or Value $10,000 or more

RCW 9.16.035(3)
CLASS C– NONVIOLENT
OFFENDER SCORING RCW 9.94A.525(7)

If it was found that this offense was committed with sexual motivation (RCW 9.94A.533(8)) on or after 7/1/2006, use the General Nonviolent Offense with a Sexual Motivation Finding scoring form on page 236.

If the present conviction is for a felony domestic violence offense where domestic violence was plead and proven, use the General Nonviolent Offense Where Domestic Violence Has Been Plead and Proven scoring form on page 234.

ADULT HISTORY:

    Enter number of felony convictions .... _____ x 1 = _____

JUVENILE HISTORY:

    Enter number of Murder 1, Murder 2, and Class A sex offense felony dispositions .... _____ x 1 = _____

OTHER CURRENT OFFENSES:

(Other current offenses that do not encompass the same conduct count in offender score)

    Enter number of other felony convictions .... _____ x 1 = _____

STATUS:

    Was the offender on community custody on the date the current offense was committed? (if yes) _____ + 1 = _____

Total the last column to get the **Offender Score** (Round down to the nearest whole number)........................ _____

SENTENCE RANGE

	Offender Score									
	0	**1**	**2**	**3**	**4**	**5**	**6**	**7**	**8**	**9+**
LEVEL II	0-90 days	4m 2 - 6	6m 3 - 9	8m 4 - 12	13m 12+ - 14	16m 14 - 18	19.5m 17 - 22	25.5m 22 - 29	38m 33 - 43	50m 43 - 57

✓   For gang-related felonies where the court found the offender involved a minor (RCW 9.94A.833), see page 227 for standard range adjustment.
✓   For deadly weapon enhancement, see page 233.
✓   For sentencing alternatives, see page 215.
✓   For community custody eligibility, see page 228.
✓   For any applicable enhancements other than deadly weapon enhancement, see page 224.

Counterfeiting - Endanger Public Health or Safety

RCW 9.16.035(4)
CLASS C* – NONVIOLENT/CRIMES AGAINST PERSONS
OFFENDER SCORING RCW 9.94A.525(7)

If it was found that this offense was committed with sexual motivation (RCW 9.94A.533(8)) on or after 7/1/2006, use the General Nonviolent Offense with a Sexual Motivation Finding scoring form on page 236.

If the present conviction is for a felony domestic violence offense where domestic violence was plead and proven, use the General Nonviolent Offense Where Domestic Violence Has Been Plead and Proven scoring form on page 234.

ADULT HISTORY:

Enter number of felony convictions .... ________x 1 = __________

JUVENILE HISTORY:

Enter number of Murder 1, Murder 2, and Class A sex offense felony dispositions .... ________x 1 = __________

OTHER CURRENT OFFENSES:

(Other current offenses that do not encompass the same conduct count in offender score)

Enter number of other felony convictions .... ________x 1 = __________

STATUS:

Was the offender on community custody on the date the current offense was committed? (if yes) ________+ 1 = __________

Total the last column to get the **Offender Score** (Round down to the nearest whole number).......................... __________

SENTENCE RANGE

	Offender Score									
	0	1	2	3	4	5	6	7	8	9+
LEVEL IV	6m 3 - 9	9m 6 - 12	13m 12+ - 14	15m 13 - 17	17.5m 15 - 20	25.5m 22 - 29	38m 33 - 43	50m 43 - 57	56.5m 53 - 60*	60 - 60*

* Class C felony offenses have a statutory maximum sentence of 60 months, see RCW 9A.20.021.

- ✓ For gang-related felonies where the court found the offender involved a minor (RCW 9.94A.833), see page 227 for standard range adjustment.
- ✓ For deadly weapon enhancement, see page 233.
- ✓ For sentencing alternatives, see page 215.
- ✓ For community custody eligibility, see page 228.
- ✓ For any applicable enhancements other than deadly weapon enhancement, see page 224.

Create or Deliver a Counterfeit Controlled Substance
Schedule I or II Narcotic or Flunitrazepam or Methamphetamine
RCW 69.50.4011(2)(a-b)
CLASS B – NONVIOLENT/DRUG
OFFENDER SCORING RCW 9.94A.525(13)

If it was found that this offense was committed with sexual motivation (RCW 9.94A.533(8)) on or after 7/1/2006, use the General Drug Offense with a Sexual Motivation Finding scoring form on page 238.

If the present conviction is for a felony domestic violence offense where domestic violence was plead and proven, use the General Drug Offense Where Domestic Violence Has Been Plead and Proven scoring form on page 237.

ADULT HISTORY:

Does the offender have a prior sex or serious violent offense in history?

.... **YES,** Enter number of felony drug convictions _____ x 3 = _____

.... **NO,** Enter number of felony drug convictions _____ x 1 = _____

Enter number of felony convictions .... _____ x 1 = _____

JUVENILE HISTORY:

Enter number of Murder 1, Murder 2, and Class A sex offense felony dispositions .... _____ x 1 = _____

OTHER CURRENT OFFENSES:

(Other current offenses that do not encompass the same conduct count in offender score)

Does the offender have other prior sex or serious violent offense in history?

.... **YES,** Enter number of other felony drug convictions _____ x 3 = _____

.... **NO,** Enter number of other felony drug convictions _____ x 1 = _____

Enter number of other felony convictions .... _____ x 1 = _____

STATUS:

Was the offender on community custody on the date the current offense was committed? (if yes) _____ + 1 = _____

Total the last column to get the **Offender Score** (Round down to the nearest whole number)......................... _____

SENTENCE RANGE – DRUG

	Offender Score		
	0 to 2	**3 to 5**	**6 to 9+**
LEVEL II	16m	40m	90m
	12+ - 20	20+ - 60	60+ - 120

✓ For attempt, solicitation or conspiracy drug felonies see page 56, or for gang-related felonies where the court found the offender involved a minor (RCW 9.94A.833), see page 227 for standard range adjustments.

✓ Per RCW 9.94A.518, any felony offense under chapter 69.50 RCW with a deadly weapon special verdict under RCW 9.94A.602 becomes a level III offense.

✓ For deadly weapon enhancement, see page 233.

✓ For sentencing alternatives, see page 215.

✓ For community custody eligibility, see page 228.

✓ For any applicable enhancements other than deadly weapon enhancement, see page 224.

✓ Per RCW 69.50.408, the statutory maximum for a subsequent conviction under chapter 69.50 RCW is 240 months.

Create or Deliver a Counterfeit Controlled Substance
Schedule I-II Nonnarcotic, Schedule III-V except Flunitrazepam or Methamphetamine

RCW 69.50.4011(2)(c-e)
CLASS C* – NONVIOLENT/DRUG
OFFENDER SCORING RCW 9.94A.525(13)

If it was found that this offense was committed with sexual motivation (RCW 9.94A.533(8)) on or after 7/1/2006, use the General Drug Offense with a Sexual Motivation Finding scoring form on page 238.

If the present conviction is for a felony domestic violence offense where domestic violence was plead and proven, use the General Drug Offense Where Domestic Violence Has Been Plead and Proven scoring form on page 237.

ADULT HISTORY:

Does the offender have a prior sex or serious violent offense in history?

.... **YES,** Enter number of felony drug convictions _____ x 3 = _____

....**NO,** Enter number of felony drug convictions _____ x 1 = _____

Enter number of felony convictions .... _____ x 1 = _____

JUVENILE HISTORY:

Enter number of Murder 1, Murder 2, and Class A sex offense felony dispositions .... _____ x 1 = _____

OTHER CURRENT OFFENSES:

(Other current offenses that do not encompass the same conduct count in offender score)

Does the offender have other prior sex or serious violent offense in history?

.... **YES,** Enter number of other felony drug convictions _____ x 3 = _____

....**NO,** Enter number of other felony drug convictions _____ x 1 = _____

Enter number of other felony convictions .... _____ x 1 = _____

STATUS:

Was the offender on community custody on the date the current offense was committed? (if yes) _____ + 1 = _____

Total the last column to get the **Offender Score** (Round down to the nearest whole number).......................... _____

SENTENCE RANGE – DRUG

	Offender Score		
	0 to 2	**3 to 5**	**6 to 9+**
LEVEL II	16m 12+ - 20	40m 20+ - 60	60 - 60*

* Class C felony offenses have a statutory maximum sentence of 60 months, see RCW 9A.20.021.

✓ For gang-related felonies where the court found the offender involved a minor (RCW 9.94A.833), see page 227 for standard range adjustments.
✓ Per RCW 9.94A.518, any felony offense under chapter 69.50 RCW with a deadly weapon special verdict under RCW 9.94A.602 becomes a level III offense.
✓ For deadly weapon enhancement, see page 233.
✓ For sentencing alternatives, see page 215.
✓ For community custody eligibility, see page 228.
✓ For any applicable enhancements other than deadly weapon enhancement, see page 224.
✓ Per RCW 69.50.408, the statutory maximum for a subsequent conviction under chapter 69.50 RCW is 120 months.

RCW 9A.46.120
CLASS C* – NONVIOLENT
OFFENDER SCORING RCW 9.94A.525(7)

If it was found that this offense was committed with sexual motivation (RCW 9.94A.533(8)) on or after 7/1/2006, use the General Nonviolent Offense with a Sexual Motivation Finding scoring form on page 236.

If the present conviction is for a felony domestic violence offense where domestic violence was plead and proven, use the General Nonviolent Offense Where Domestic Violence Has Been Plead and Proven scoring form on page 234.

ADULT HISTORY:

Enter number of felony convictions .... _____ x 1 = _____

JUVENILE HISTORY:

Enter number of Murder 1, Murder 2, and Class A sex offense felony dispositions .... _____ x 1 = _____

OTHER CURRENT OFFENSES:

(Other current offenses that do not encompass the same conduct count in offender score)

Enter number of other felony convictions .... _____ x 1 = _____

STATUS:

Was the offender on community custody on the date the current offense was committed? (if yes) _____ + 1 = _____

Total the last column to get the **Offender Score** (Round down to the nearest whole number)......................... _____

SENTENCE RANGE

	Offender Score									
	0	**1**	**2**	**3**	**4**	**5**	**6**	**7**	**8**	**9+**
LEVEL III	2m	5m	8m	11m	14m	19.5m	25.5m	38m	50m	55.5m
	1 - 3	3 - 8	4 - 12	9 - 12	12+ - 16	17 - 22	22 - 29	33 - 43	43 - 57	51 - 60*

* Class C felony offenses have a statutory maximum sentence of 60 months, see RCW 9A.20.021.

✓ For gang-related felonies where the court found the offender involved a minor (RCW 9.94A.833), see page 227 for standard range adjustment.
✓ For deadly weapon enhancement, see page 233.
✓ For sentencing alternatives, see page 215.
✓ For community custody eligibility, see page 228.
✓ For any applicable enhancements other than deadly weapon enhancement, see page 224.

RCW 9A.42.020
CLASS B* – NONVIOLENT/CRIMES AGAINST PERSONS
OFFENDER SCORING RCW 9.94A.525(7)

If it was found that this offense was committed with sexual motivation (RCW 9.94A.533(8)) on or after 7/1/2006, use the General Nonviolent Offense with a Sexual Motivation Finding scoring form on page 236.

If the present conviction is for a felony domestic violence offense where domestic violence was plead and proven, use the General Nonviolent Offense Where Domestic Violence Has Been Plead and Proven scoring form on page 234.

ADULT HISTORY:

    Enter number of felony convictions .... _____ x 1 = _____

JUVENILE HISTORY:

    Enter number of Murder 1, Murder 2, and Class A sex offense felony dispositions .... _____ x 1 = _____

OTHER CURRENT OFFENSES:

(Other current offenses that do not encompass the same conduct count in offender score)

    Enter number of other felony convictions .... _____ x 1 = _____

STATUS:

    Was the offender on community custody on the date the current offense was committed? (if yes) _____ + 1 = _____

Total the last column to get the **Offender Score** (Round down to the nearest whole number).......................... _____

SENTENCE RANGE DISPLAYED IS FOR A COMPLETED OFFENSE

FOR **ATTEMPT**, **SOLICITATION**, OR **CONSPIRACY** (RCW 9.94A.595, see page 54), THE SENTENCE RANGE **IS 75%** OF THE COMPLETED RANGE LISTED BELOW

Offender Score										
	0	**1**	**2**	**3**	**4**	**5**	**6**	**7**	**8**	**9+**
LEVEL X	59.5m 51 - 68	66m 57 - 75	72m 62 - 82	78m 67 - 89	84m 72 - 96	89.5m 77 - 102	109m 98 - 120*	120 - 120*	120 - 120*	120 - 120*

    * Class B felony offenses have a statutory maximum sentence of 120 months, see RCW 9A.20.021.

✓   For gang-related felonies where the court found the offender involved a minor (RCW 9.94A.833), see page 227 for standard range adjustments.
✓   For deadly weapon enhancement, see page 233.
✓   For sentencing alternatives, see page 215.
✓   For community custody eligibility, see page 228.
✓   For any applicable enhancements other than deadly weapon enhancement, see page 224.

Criminal Mistreatment Second Degree

RCW 9A.42.030
CLASS C* – NONVIOLENT/CRIMES AGAINST PERSONS
OFFENDER SCORING RCW 9.94A.525(7)

If it was found that this offense was committed with sexual motivation (RCW 9.94A.533(8)) on or after 7/1/2006, use the General Nonviolent Offense with a Sexual Motivation Finding scoring form on page 236.

If the present conviction is for a felony domestic violence offense where domestic violence was plead and proven, use the General Nonviolent Offense Where Domestic Violence Has Been Plead and Proven scoring form on page 234.

ADULT HISTORY:

    Enter number of felony convictions .... _____ x 1 = _____

JUVENILE HISTORY:

    Enter number of Murder 1, Murder 2, and Class A sex offense felony dispositions .... _____ x 1 = _____

OTHER CURRENT OFFENSES:

(Other current offenses that do not encompass the same conduct count in offender score)

    Enter number of other felony convictions .... _____ x 1 = _____

STATUS:

    Was the offender on community custody on the date the current offense was committed? (if yes) _____ + 1 = _____

Total the last column to get the **Offender Score** (Round down to the nearest whole number)......................... _____

SENTENCE RANGE

	Offender Score									
	0	**1**	**2**	**3**	**4**	**5**	**6**	**7**	**8**	**9+**
LEVEL V	9m	13m	15m	17.5m	25.5m	38m	47.5m	55.5m		
	6 - 12	12+ - 14	13 - 17	15 - 20	22 - 29	33 - 43	41 - 54	51 - 60*	60 - 60*	60 - 60*

    * Class C felony offenses have a statutory maximum sentence of 60 months, see RCW 9A.20.021.

✓   For gang-related felonies where the court found the offender involved a minor (RCW 9.94A.833), see page 227 for standard range adjustment.
✓   For deadly weapon enhancement, see page 233.
✓   For sentencing alternatives, see page 215.
✓   For community custody eligibility, see page 228.
✓   For any applicable enhancements other than deadly weapon enhancement, see page 224.

RCW 9A.36.100
CLASS C* – NONVIOLENT/CRIMES AGAINST PERSONS
OFFENDER SCORING RCW 9.94A.525(7)

If it was found that this offense was committed with sexual motivation (RCW 9.94A.533(8)) on or after 7/1/2006, use the General Nonviolent Offense with a Sexual Motivation Finding scoring form on page 236.

If the present conviction is for a felony domestic violence offense where domestic violence was plead and proven, use the General Nonviolent Offense Where Domestic Violence Has Been Plead and Proven scoring form on page 234.

ADULT HISTORY:

Enter number of felony convictions .... _____ x 1 = _____

JUVENILE HISTORY:

Enter number of Murder 1, Murder 2, and Class A sex offense felony dispositions .... _____ x 1 = _____

OTHER CURRENT OFFENSES:

(Other current offenses that do not encompass the same conduct count in offender score)

Enter number of other felony convictions .... _____ x 1 = _____

STATUS:

Was the offender on community custody on the date the current offense was committed? (if yes) _____ + 1 = _____

Total the last column to get the **Offender Score** (Round down to the nearest whole number)......................... _____

SENTENCE RANGE

	Offender Score									
	0	1	2	3	4	5	6	7	8	9+
LEVEL III	2m	5m	8m	11m	14m	19.5m	25.5m	38m	50m	55.5m
	1 - 3	3 - 8	4 - 12	9 - 12	12+ - 16	17 - 22	22 - 29	33 - 43	43 - 57	51 - 60*

* Class C felony offenses have a statutory maximum sentence of 60 months, see RCW 9A.20.021.

✓ For gang-related felonies where the court found the offender involved a minor (RCW 9.94A.833), see page 227 for standard range adjustment.
✓ For deadly weapon enhancement, see page 233.
✓ For sentencing alternatives, see page 215.
✓ For community custody eligibility, see page 228.
✓ For any applicable enhancements other than deadly weapon enhancement, see page 224.

Custodial Sexual Misconduct First Degree

RCW 9A.44.160
CLASS B – NONVIOLENT/SEX
OFFENDER SCORING RCW 9.94A.525(17)

If the present conviction is for a felony domestic violence offense where domestic violence was plead and proven, use the General Nonviolent/Sex Offense Where Domestic Violence Has Been Plead and Proven scoring form on page 235.

ADULT HISTORY:

Enter number of sex offense felony convictions .... _____ x 3 = _____

Enter number of felony convictions .... _____ x 1 = _____

JUVENILE HISTORY:

Enter number of Class A sex offense felony dispositions .... _____ x 3 = _____

Enter number of Murder 1 and Murder 2 felony dispositions .... _____ x 1 = _____

OTHER CURRENT OFFENSES:

(Other current offenses that do not encompass the same conduct count in offender score)

Enter number of other sex offense felony convictions .... _____ x 3 = _____

Enter number of other felony convictions .... _____ x 1 = _____

STATUS:

Was the offender on community custody on the date the current offense was committed? (if yes) _____ + 1 = _____

Total the last column to get the **Offender Score** (Round down to the nearest whole number)......................... _____

SENTENCE RANGE DISPLAYED IS FOR A COMPLETED OFFENSE

FOR **ATTEMPT**, **SOLICITATION**, OR **CONSPIRACY** (RCW 9.94A.595, see page 54), THE SENTENCE RANGE **IS 75%** OF THE COMPLETED RANGE LISTED BELOW

	Offender Score									
	0	**1**	**2**	**3**	**4**	**5**	**6**	**7**	**8**	**9+**
LEVEL VII	17.5m	24m	30m	36m	42m	47.5m	66m	78m	89.5m	101.5m
	15 - 20	21 - 27	26 - 34	31 - 41	36 - 48	41 - 54	57 - 75	67 - 89	77 - 102	87 - 116

✓ For gang-related felonies where the court found the offender involved a minor (RCW 9.94A.833), see page 227 for standard range adjustment.
✓ For deadly weapon enhancement, see page 233.
✓ For sentencing alternatives, see page 215.
✓ For community custody eligibility, see page 228.
✓ For any applicable enhancements other than deadly weapon enhancement, see page 224.
✓ If the offender is not a persistent offender and has a <u>prior</u> conviction for an offense listed in RCW 9.94A.030(37)(b), then the sentence is subject to the requirements of RCW 9.94A.507.

Custodial Sexual Misconduct Second Degree

RCW 9A.44.070
CLASS C* – NONVIOLENT/SEX
OFFENDER SCORING RCW 9.94A.525(17)

If the present conviction is for a felony domestic violence offense where domestic violence was plead and proven, use the General Nonviolent/Sex Offense Where Domestic Violence Has Been Plead and Proven scoring form on page 235.

ADULT HISTORY:

Enter number of sex offense felony convictions .... _____ x 3 = _____

Enter number of felony convictions .... _____ x 1 = _____

JUVENILE HISTORY:

Enter number of Class A sex offense felony dispositions .... _____ x 3 = _____

Enter number of Murder 1 and Murder 2 felony dispositions .... _____ x 1 = _____

OTHER CURRENT OFFENSES:

(Other current offenses that do not encompass the same conduct count in offender score)

Enter number of sex offense felony convictions .... _____ x 3 = _____

Enter number of other felony convictions .... _____ x 1 = _____

STATUS:

Was the offender on community custody on the date the current offense was committed? (if yes) _____ + 1 = _____

Total the last column to get the **Offender Score** (Round down to the nearest whole number).......................... _____

SENTENCE RANGE

	Offender Score									
	0	**1**	**2**	**3**	**4**	**5**	**6**	**7**	**8**	**9+**
LEVEL V	9m	13m	15m	17.5m	25.5m	38m	47.5m	55.5m		
	6 - 12	12+ - 14	13 - 17	15 - 20	22 - 29	33 - 43	41 - 54	51 - 60*	60 - 60*	60 - 60*

* Class C felony offenses have a statutory maximum sentence of 60 months, see RCW 9A.20.021.

✓ For gang-related felonies where the court found the offender involved a minor (RCW 9.94A.833), see page 227 for standard range adjustment.
✓ For deadly weapon enhancement, see page 233.
✓ For sentencing alternatives, see page 215.
✓ For community custody eligibility, see page 228.
✓ For any applicable enhancements other than deadly weapon enhancement, see page 224.
✓ If the offender is not a persistent offender and has a <u>prior</u> conviction for an offense listed in RCW 9.94A.030(37)(b), then the sentence is subject to the requirements of RCW 9.94A.507.

RCW 9A.90.120(2)(b)
CLASS C* – NONVIOLENT
OFFENDER SCORING RCW 9.94A.525(7)

If it was found that this offense was committed with sexual motivation (RCW 9.94A.533(8)) on or after 7/1/2006, use the General Nonviolent Offense with a Sexual Motivation Finding scoring form on page 236.

If the present conviction is for a felony domestic violence offense where domestic violence was plead and proven, use the General Nonviolent Offense Where Domestic Violence Has Been Plead and Proven scoring form on page 234.

ADULT HISTORY:

Enter number of felony convictions .... _____ x 1 = _____

JUVENILE HISTORY:

Enter number of Murder 1, Murder 2, and Class A sex offense felony dispositions .... _____ x 1 = _____

OTHER CURRENT OFFENSES:

(Other current offenses that do not encompass the same conduct count in offender score)

Enter number of other felony convictions .... _____ x 1 = _____

STATUS:

Was the offender on community custody on the date the current offense was committed? (if yes) _____ + 1 = _____

Total the last column to get the **Offender Score** (Round down to the nearest whole number)........................ _____

SENTENCE RANGE

	Offender Score									
	0	**1**	**2**	**3**	**4**	**5**	**6**	**7**	**8**	**9+**
LEVEL III	2m	5m	8m	11m	14m	19.5m	25.5m	38m	50m	55.5m
	1 - 3	3 - 8	4 - 12	9 - 12	12+ - 16	17 - 22	22 - 29	33 - 43	43 - 57	51 - 60*

* Class C felony offenses have a statutory maximum sentence of 60 months, see RCW 9A.20.021.

✓ For gang-related felonies where the court found the offender involved a minor (RCW 9.94A.833), see page 227 for standard range adjustment.
✓ For deadly weapon enhancement, see page 233.
✓ For sentencing alternatives, see page 215.
✓ For community custody eligibility, see page 228.
✓ For any applicable enhancements other than deadly weapon enhancement, see page 224.

Dealing in Depictions of a Minor Engaged in Sexually Explicit Conduct First Degree
RCW 9.68A.050(1)
CLASS B – NONVIOLENT/SEX
OFFENDER SCORING RCW 9.94A.525(17)

If the present conviction is for a felony domestic violence offense where domestic violence was plead and proven, use the General Nonviolent/Sex Offense Where Domestic Violence Has Been Plead and Proven scoring form on page 235.

ADULT HISTORY:

Enter number of sex offense felony convictions .... _____ x 3 = _____

Enter number of felony convictions .... _____ x 1 = _____

JUVENILE HISTORY:

Enter number of Class A sex offense felony dispositions .... _____ x 3 = _____

Enter number of Murder 1 and Murder 2 felony dispositions .... _____ x 1 = _____

OTHER CURRENT OFFENSES:
(Other current offenses that do not encompass the same conduct count in offender score)

Enter number of other sex offense felony convictions .... _____ x 3 = _____

Enter number of other felony convictions .... _____ x 1 = _____

STATUS:

Was the offender on community custody on the date the current offense was committed? (if yes) _____ + 1 = _____

Total the last column to get the **Offender Score** (Round down to the nearest whole number).......................... _____

SENTENCE RANGE DISPLAYED IS FOR A COMPLETED OFFENSE

FOR **ATTEMPT**, **SOLICITATION**, OR **CONSPIRACY** (RCW 9.94A.595, see page 54), THE SENTENCE RANGE **IS 75%** OF THE COMPLETED RANGE LISTED BELOW

	Offender Score									
	0	**1**	**2**	**3**	**4**	**5**	**6**	**7**	**8**	**9+**
LEVEL VII	17.5m	24m	30m	36m	42m	47.5m	66m	78m	89.5m	101.5m
	15 - 20	21 - 27	26 - 34	31 - 41	36 - 48	41 - 54	57 - 75	67 - 89	77 - 102	87 - 116

✓ For gang-related felonies where the court found the offender involved a minor (RCW 9.94A.833), see page 227 for standard range adjustments.
✓ For deadly weapon enhancement, see page 233.
✓ For sentencing alternatives, see page 215.
✓ For community custody eligibility, see page 228.
✓ For any applicable enhancements other than deadly weapon enhancement, see page 224.
✓ If the offender is not a persistent offender and has a <u>prior</u> conviction for an offense listed in RCW 9.94A.030(37)(b), then the sentence is subject to the requirements of RCW 9.94A.507.

Dealing in Depictions of a Minor Engaged in Sexually Explicit Conduct Second Degree

RCW 9.68A.050(2)
CLASS B – NONVIOLENT/SEX
OFFENDER SCORING RCW 9.94A.525(17)

If the present conviction is for a felony domestic violence offense where domestic violence was plead and proven, use the General Nonviolent/Sex Offense Where Domestic Violence Has Been Plead and Proven scoring form on page 235.

ADULT HISTORY:

Enter number of sex offense felony convictions .... _____ x 3 = _____

Enter number of felony convictions .... _____ x 1 = _____

JUVENILE HISTORY:

Enter number of Class A sex offense felony dispositions .... _____ x 3 = _____

Enter number of Murder 1 and Murder 2 felony dispositions .... _____ x 1 = _____

OTHER CURRENT OFFENSES:

(Other current offenses that do not encompass the same conduct count in offender score)

Enter number of other sex offense felony convictions .... _____ x 3 = _____

Enter number of other felony convictions .... _____ x 1 = _____

STATUS:

Was the offender on community custody on the date the current offense was committed? (if yes) _____ + 1 = _____

Total the last column to get the **Offender Score** (Round down to the nearest whole number)........................ _____

SENTENCE RANGE DISPLAYED IS FOR A COMPLETED OFFENSE

FOR **ATTEMPT**, **SOLICITATION**, OR **CONSPIRACY** (RCW 9.94A.595, see page 54), THE SENTENCE RANGE **IS 75%** OF THE COMPLETED RANGE LISTED BELOW

Offender Score										
	0	**1**	**2**	**3**	**4**	**5**	**6**	**7**	**8**	**9+**
LEVEL V	9m	13m	15m	17.5m	25.5m	38m	47.5m	59.5m	72m	84m
	6 - 12	12+ - 14	13 - 17	15 - 20	22 - 29	33 - 43	41 - 54	51 - 68	62 - 82	72 - 96

✓ For gang-related felonies where the court found the offender involved a minor (RCW 9.94A.833), see page 227 for standard range adjustment.
✓ For deadly weapon enhancement, see page 233.
✓ For sentencing alternatives, see page 215.
✓ For community custody eligibility, see page 228.
✓ For any applicable enhancements other than deadly weapon enhancement, see page 224.
✓ If the offender is not a persistent offender and has a prior conviction for an offense listed in RCW 9.94A.030(37)(b), then the sentence is subject to the requirements of RCW 9.94A.507.

Deliver or Possess with Intent to Deliver Methamphetamine
RCW 69.50.401(2)(b)
CLASS B – NONVIOLENT/DRUG
OFFENDER SCORING RCW 9.94A.525(13)

If it was found that this offense was committed with sexual motivation (RCW 9.94A.533(8)) on or after 7/1/2006, use the General Drug Offense with a Sexual Motivation Finding scoring form on page 238.

If the present conviction is for a felony domestic violence offense where domestic violence was plead and proven, use the General Drug Offense Where Domestic Violence Has Been Plead and Proven scoring form on page 237.

ADULT HISTORY:

Does the offender have a prior sex or serious violent offense in history?

.... **YES,** Enter number of felony drug convictions _____ x 3 = _____

.... **NO,** Enter number of felony drug convictions _____ x 1 = _____

Enter number of felony convictions .... _____ x 1 = _____

JUVENILE HISTORY:

Enter number of Murder 1, Murder 2, and Class A sex offense felony dispositions .... _____ x 1 = _____

OTHER CURRENT OFFENSES:

(Other current offenses that do not encompass the same conduct count in offender score)

Does the offender have other prior sex or serious violent offense in history?

.... **YES,** Enter number of other felony drug convictions _____ x 3 = _____

.... **NO,** Enter number of other felony drug convictions _____ x 1 = _____

Enter number of other felony convictions .... _____ x 1 = _____

STATUS:

Was the offender on community custody on the date the current offense was committed? (if yes) _____ + 1 = _____

Total the last column to get the **Offender Score** (Round down to the nearest whole number)......................... _____

SENTENCE RANGE – DRUG

	Offender Score		
	0 to 2	**3 to 5**	**6 to 9+**
LEVEL II	16m	40m	90m
	12+ - 20	20+ - 60	60+ - 120

✓   For attempt, solicitation or conspiracy drug felonies see page 56, or for gang-related felonies where the court found the offender involved a minor (RCW 9.94A.833), see page 227 for standard range adjustments.
✓   Per RCW 9.94A.518, any felony offense under chapter 69.50 RCW with a deadly weapon special verdict under RCW 9.94A.602 becomes a level III offense.
✓   For deadly weapon enhancement, see page 233.
✓   For sentencing alternatives, see page 215.
✓   For community custody eligibility, see page 228.
✓   For any applicable enhancements other than deadly weapon enhancement, see page 224.
✓   Per RCW 69.50.408, the statutory maximum for a subsequent conviction under chapter 69.50 RCW is 240 months.
✓   Per RCW 69.50.435, if the offense occurred within a protected zone, 24 months shall be added to the standard range and the statutory maximum is 240 months.

Delivery of Imitation Controlled Substance
by Person 18 or over to Person under 18

RCW 69.52.030(2)
CLASS B – NONVIOLENT
OFFENDER SCORING RCW 9.94A.525(7)

If it was found that this offense was committed with sexual motivation (RCW 9.94A.533(8)) on or after 7/1/2006, use the General Nonviolent Offense with a Sexual Motivation Finding scoring form on page 236.

If the present conviction is for a felony domestic violence offense where domestic violence was plead and proven, use the General Nonviolent Offense Where Domestic Violence Has Been Plead and Proven scoring form on page 234.

ADULT HISTORY:

    Enter number of felony convictions .... _____ x 1 = _____

JUVENILE HISTORY:

    Enter number of Murder 1, Murder 2, and Class A sex offense felony dispositions .... _____ x 1 = _____

OTHER CURRENT OFFENSES:

(Other current offenses that do not encompass the same conduct count in offender score)

    Enter number of other felony convictions .... _____ x 1 = _____

STATUS:

    Was the offender on community custody on the date the current offense was committed? (if yes) _____ + 1 = _____

Total the last column to get the **Offender Score** (Round down to the nearest whole number)......................... _____

SENTENCE RANGE – DRUG

	Offender Score		
	0 to 2	**3 to 5**	**6 to 9+**
LEVEL III	59.5m	84m	110m
	51 - 68	68+ - 100	100+ - 120

✓   For attempt, solicitation, conspiracy (RCW 9.94A.595) see page 54 or for gang-related felonies where the court found the offender involved a minor (RCW 9.94A.833), see page 227 for standard range adjustments.
✓   For deadly weapon enhancement, see page 233.
✓   For sentencing alternatives, see page 215.
✓   For community custody eligibility, see page 228.
✓   For any applicable enhancements other than deadly weapon enhancement, see page 224.

RCW 69.50.4012
CLASS C* – NONVIOLENT/DRUG
OFFENDER SCORING RCW 9.94A.525(13)

If it was found that this offense was committed with sexual motivation (RCW 9.94A.533(8)) on or after 7/1/2006, use the General Drug Offense with a Sexual Motivation Finding scoring form on page 238.

If the present conviction is for a felony domestic violence offense where domestic violence was plead and proven, use the General Drug Offense Where Domestic Violence Has Been Plead and Proven scoring form on page 237.

ADULT HISTORY:

Does the offender have a prior sex or serious violent offense in history?

.... **YES,** Enter number of felony drug convictions _____ x 3 = _____

....**NO,** Enter number of felony drug convictions _____ x 1 = _____

Enter number of felony convictions .... _____ x 1 = _____

JUVENILE HISTORY:

Enter number of Murder 1, Murder 2, and Class A sex offense felony dispositions .... _____ x 1 = _____

OTHER CURRENT OFFENSES:

(Other current offenses that do not encompass the same conduct count in offender score)

Does the offender have other prior sex or serious violent offense in history?

.... **YES,** Enter number of other felony drug convictions _____ x 3 = _____

....**NO,** Enter number of other felony drug convictions _____ x 1 = _____

Enter number of other felony convictions .... _____ x 1 = _____

STATUS:

Was the offender on community custody on the date the current offense was committed? (if yes) _____ + 1 = _____

Total the last column to get the **Offender Score** (Round down to the nearest whole number)......................... _____

SENTENCE RANGE – DRUG

	Offender Score		
	0 to 2	**3 to 5**	**6 to 9+**
LEVEL II	16m	40m	
	12+ - 20	20+ - 60	60 - 60*

* Class C felony offenses have a statutory maximum sentence of 60 months, see RCW 9A.20.021.

✓ For gang-related felonies where the court found the offender involved a minor (RCW 9.94A.833), see page 227 for standard range adjustments.
✓ Per RCW 9.94A.518, any felony offense under chapter 69.50 RCW with a deadly weapon special verdict under RCW 9.94A.602 becomes a level III offense.
✓ For deadly weapon enhancement, see page 233.
✓ For sentencing alternatives, see page 215.
✓ For community custody eligibility, see page 228.
✓ For any applicable enhancements other than deadly weapon enhancement, see page 224.
✓ Per RCW 69.50.408, the statutory maximum for a subsequent conviction under chapter 69.50 RCW is 120 months.

Domestic Violence Court Order Violation
RCWs 7.105.450, 10.99.040, 10.99.050, 26.09.300, 26.26B.050 or 26.52.070
CLASS C* – NONVIOLENT/CRIMES AGAINST PERSONS
OFFENDER SCORING RCW 9.94A.525(21)

If it was found that this offense was committed with sexual motivation (RCW 9.94A.533(8)) on or after 7/1/2006, use the General Nonviolent Offense with a Sexual Motivation Finding scoring form on page 236.

If the present conviction is for a felony domestic violence offense where domestic violence was plead and proven, the General Drug Offense Where Domestic Violence Has Been Plead and Proven scoring form on page 237 may be used as an alternative to this scoring form.

ADULT HISTORY:

Enter number of domestic violence (DV) felony convictions as listed below when the present

conviction is for a felony DV offense where DV was plead and proven* .... _____ x 2 = _____

    Enter number of repetitive DV offense convictions (RCW 9.94A.030(42))
    plead and proven after 8/1/11 when the present conviction is for a felony DV offense where

    DV was plead and proven* .... _____ x 1 = _____

    Enter number of other felony convictions .... _____ x 1 = _____

JUVENILE HISTORY:

    Enter number of Murder 1, Murder 2, and Class A sex offense felony dispositions .... _____ x 1 = _____

OTHER CURRENT OFFENSES:

(Other current offenses that do not encompass the same conduct count in offender score)

Enter number of other DV felony convictions as listed below when the present

conviction is for a felony DV offense where DV was plead and proven* .... _____ x 2 = _____

    Enter number of repetitive DV offense convictions (RCW 9.94A.030(42))
    plead and proven after 8/1/11 when the present conviction is for a felony DV offense where

    DV was plead and proven* .... _____ x 1 = _____

    Enter number of other felony convictions .... _____ x 1 = _____

STATUS:

    Was the offender on community custody on the date the current offense was committed? (if yes) _____ + 1 = _____

    If domestic violence was plead and proven after 8/1/2011 for the following felony offenses:

    Violation of a No-Contact Order, Violation of a Protection Order, Domestic Violence Harassment, Domestic Violence Stalking, Domestic Violence Burglary 1, Domestic Violence Kidnapping 1, Domestic Violence Kidnapping 2, Domestic Violence Unlawful Imprisonment, Domestic Violence Robbery 1, Domestic Violence Robbery 2, Domestic Violence Assault 1, Domestic Violence Assault 2, Domestic Violence Assault 3, Domestic Violence Arson 1, Domestic Violence Arson 2.

    * *If domestic violence was plead and proven after 7/23/17 for the following felony offenses:*

    Assault of a Child 1, Assault of a Child 2, Assault of a Child 3, Criminal Mistreatment 1, Criminal Mistreatment 2.

Total the last column to get the **Offender Score** (Round down to the nearest whole number)......................... _____

SENTENCE RANGE

	Offender Score									
	0	**1**	**2**	**3**	**4**	**5**	**6**	**7**	**8**	**9+**
LEVEL V	9m	13m	15m	17.5m	25.5m	38m	47.5m	55.5m		
	6 - 12	12+ - 14	13 - 17	15 - 20	22 - 29	33 - 43	41 - 54	51 - 60*	60 - 60*	60 - 60*

    * Class C felony offenses have a statutory maximum sentence of 60 months, see RCW 9A.20.021.

✓   For gang-related felonies where the court found the offender involved a minor (RCW 9.94A.833), see page 227 for standard range adjustment.
✓   For deadly weapon enhancement, see page 233.
✓   For sentencing alternatives, see page 215.
✓   For community custody eligibility, see page 228.
✓   For any applicable enhancements other than deadly weapon enhancement, see page 224.

RCW 9A.36.045
CLASS B – VIOLENT
OFFENDER SCORING RCW 9.94A.525(8)

If it was found that this offense was committed with sexual motivation (RCW 9.94A.533(8)) on or after 7/1/2006, use the General Violent Offense with a Sexual Motivation Finding scoring form on page 244.

If the present conviction is for a felony domestic violence offense where domestic violence was plead and proven, use the General Violent Offense Where Domestic Violence Has Been Plead and Proven scoring form on page 242.

ADULT HISTORY:

Enter number of serious violent and violent felony convictions .... _____ x 2 = _____

Enter number of nonviolent felony convictions .... _____ x 1 = _____

JUVENILE HISTORY:

Enter number of Murder 1, Murder 2, and Class A sex offense felony dispositions .... _____ x 2 = _____

OTHER CURRENT OFFENSES:

(Other current offenses that do not encompass the same conduct count in offender score)

Enter number of other serious violent and violent felony convictions .... _____ x 2 = _____

Enter number of other nonviolent felony convictions .... _____ x 1 = _____

STATUS:

Was the offender on community custody on the date the current offense was committed? (if yes) _____ + 1 = _____

Total the last column to get the **Offender Score** (Round down to the nearest whole number).......................... _____

SENTENCE RANGE DISPLAYED IS FOR A COMPLETED OFFENSE

FOR **ATTEMPT**, **SOLICITATION**, OR **CONSPIRACY** (RCW 9.94A.595, see page 54), THE SENTENCE RANGE **IS 75%** OF THE COMPLETED RANGE LISTED BELOW

	Offender Score									
	0	**1**	**2**	**3**	**4**	**5**	**6**	**7**	**8**	**9+**
LEVEL VII	17.5m	24m	30m	36m	42m	47.5m	66m	78m	89.5m	101.5m
	15 - 20	21 - 27	26 - 34	31 - 41	36 - 48	41 - 54	57 - 75	67 - 89	77 - 102	87 - 116

✓ For gang-related felonies where the court found the offender involved a minor (RCW 9.94A.833), see page 227 for standard range adjustments.
✓ For deadly weapon enhancement, see page 233.
✓ For sentencing alternatives, see page 215.
✓ For community custody eligibility, see page 228.
✓ For any applicable enhancements other than deadly weapon enhancement, see page 224.

Driving while under the Influence of Intoxicating Liquor or any Drug
RCW 46.61.502(6)
CLASS B – NONVIOLENT/TRAFFIC OFFENSE/CRIMES AGAINST PERSONS
OFFENDER SCORING RCW 9.94A.525(11)

ADULT HISTORY:

Enter number of Vehicular Homicide and Vehicular Assault felony convictions .... _____ x 2 = _____

Enter number of Operation of a Vessel while under the Influence of Intoxicating Liquor or any Drug felony convictions .... _____ x 1 = _____

Enter number of felony convictions .... _____ x 1 = _____

Enter number of Driving while under the Influence of Intoxicating Liquor or any Drug and Actual Physical Control while under the Influence of Intoxicating Liquor or any Drug and Reckless Driving and Hit-and-Run Attended Vehicle <u>non-felony</u> convictions .... _____ x 1 = _____

JUVENILE HISTORY:

Enter number of Murder 1, Murder 2, and Class A sex offense felony dispositions .... _____ x ½ = _____

OTHER CURRENT OFFENSES:

(Other current offenses that do not encompass the same conduct count in offender score)

Enter number of Vehicular Homicide and Vehicular Assault convictions .... _____ x 2 = _____

Enter number of other Operation of a Vessel while under the Influence of Intoxicating Liquor or any Drug felony convictions .... _____ x 1 = _____

Enter number of other felony convictions .... _____ x 1 = _____

Enter number of Driving while under the Influence of Intoxicating Liquor or any Drug and Actual Physical Control while under the Influence of Intoxicating Liquor or any Drug and Reckless Driving and Hit-and-Run Attended Vehicle <u>non-felony</u> convictions .... _____ x 1 = _____

STATUS:

Was the offender on community custody on the date the current offense was committed? (if yes) _____ + 1 = _____

Total the last column to get the **Offender Score** (Round down to the nearest whole number)........................ _____

SENTENCE RANGE DISPLAYED IS FOR A COMPLETED OFFENSE

FOR **ATTEMPT**, **SOLICITATION**, OR **CONSPIRACY** (RCW 9.94A.595, see page 54), THE SENTENCE RANGE **IS 75%** OF THE COMPLETED RANGE LISTED BELOW

	Offender Score									
	0	**1**	**2**	**3**	**4**	**5**	**6**	**7**	**8**	**9+**
LEVEL IV	6m	9m	13m	15m	17.5m	25.5m	38m	50m	61.5m	73.5m
	3 - 9	6 - 12	12+ - 14	13 - 17	15 - 20	22 - 29	33 - 43	43 - 57	53 - 70	63 - 84

✓ For gang-related felonies where the court found the offender involved a minor (RCW 9.94A.833), see page 227 for standard range adjustments.
✓ For deadly weapon enhancement, see page 233.
✓ For sentencing alternatives, see page 215.
✓ For community custody eligibility, see page 228.
✓ For any applicable enhancements other than deadly weapon enhancement, see page 224.
✓ For consecutive/concurrent provisions, see page 62.

Endangerment with a Controlled Substance
RCW 9A.42.100
CLASS B – NONVIOLENT
OFFENDER SCORING RCW 9.94A.525(7)

If it was found that this offense was committed with sexual motivation (RCW 9.94A.533(8)) on or after 7/1/2006, use the General Nonviolent Offense with a Sexual Motivation Finding scoring form on page 236.

If the present conviction is for a felony domestic violence offense where domestic violence was plead and proven, use the General Nonviolent Offense Where Domestic Violence Has Been Plead and Proven scoring form on page 234.

ADULT HISTORY:

Enter number of felony convictions .... _____ x 1 = _____

JUVENILE HISTORY:

Enter number of Murder 1, Murder 2, and Class A sex offense felony dispositions .... _____ x 1 = _____

OTHER CURRENT OFFENSES:

(Other current offenses that do not encompass the same conduct count in offender score)

Enter number of other felony convictions .... _____ x 1 = _____

STATUS:

Was the offender on community custody on the date the current offense was committed? (if yes) _____ + 1 = _____

Total the last column to get the **Offender Score** (Round down to the nearest whole number).......................... _____

SENTENCE RANGE DISPLAYED IS FOR A COMPLETED OFFENSE

FOR **ATTEMPT**, **SOLICITATION**, OR **CONSPIRACY** (RCW 9.94A.595, see page 54), THE SENTENCE RANGE **IS 75%** OF THE COMPLETED RANGE LISTED BELOW

Offender Score										
	0	**1**	**2**	**3**	**4**	**5**	**6**	**7**	**8**	**9+**
LEVEL IV	6m	9m	13m	15m	17.5m	25.5m	38m	50m	61.5m	73.5m
	3 - 9	6 - 12	12+ - 14	13 - 17	15 - 20	22 - 29	33 - 43	43 - 57	53 - 70	63 - 84

✓ For gang-related felonies where the court found the offender involved a minor (RCW 9.94A.833), see page 227 for standard range adjustments.
✓ For deadly weapon enhancement, see page 233.
✓ For sentencing alternatives, see page 215.
✓ For community custody eligibility, see page 228.
✓ For any applicable enhancements other than deadly weapon enhancement, see page 224.

RCW 9A.76.110
CLASS B – NONVIOLENT
OFFENDER SCORING RCW 9.94A.525(15)

If it was found that this offense was committed with sexual motivation (RCW 9.94A.533(8)) on or after 7/1/2006, use the General Nonviolent Offense with a Sexual Motivation Finding scoring form on page 236.

If the present conviction is for a felony domestic violence offense where domestic violence was plead and proven, use the General Nonviolent Offense Where Domestic Violence Has Been Plead and Proven scoring form on page 234.

ADULT HISTORY:

Enter number of felony convictions .... _____ x 1 = _____

JUVENILE HISTORY:

Enter number Murder 1, Murder 2, and Class A sex offense felony dispositions .... _____ x ½ = _____

OTHER CURRENT OFFENSES:

(Other current offenses that do not encompass the same conduct count in offender score)

Enter number of other felony convictions .... _____ x 1 = _____

STATUS:

Was the offender on community custody on the date the current offense was committed? (if yes) _____ + 1 = _____

Total the last column to get the **Offender Score** (Round down to the nearest whole number)........................ _____

SENTENCE RANGE DISPLAYED IS FOR A COMPLETED OFFENSE

FOR **ATTEMPT**, **SOLICITATION**, OR **CONSPIRACY** (RCW 9.94A.595, see page 54), THE SENTENCE RANGE **IS 75%** OF THE COMPLETED RANGE LISTED BELOW

Offender Score										
	0	**1**	**2**	**3**	**4**	**5**	**6**	**7**	**8**	**9+**
LEVEL IV	6m	9m	13m	15m	17.5m	25.5m	38m	50m	61.5m	73.5m
	3 - 9	6 - 12	12+ - 14	13 - 17	15 - 20	22 - 29	33 - 43	43 - 57	53 - 70	63 - 84

✓ For gang-related felonies where the court found the offender involved a minor (RCW 9.94A.833), see page 227 for standard range adjustments.
✓ For deadly weapon enhancement, see page 233.
✓ For sentencing alternatives, see page 215.
✓ For community custody eligibility, see page 228.
✓ For any applicable enhancements other than deadly weapon enhancement, see page 224.

Escape Second Degree
RCW 9A.76.120
CLASS C* – NONVIOLENT
OFFENDER SCORING RCW 9.94A.525(15)

If it was found that this offense was committed with sexual motivation (RCW 9.94A.533(8)) on or after 7/1/2006, use the General Nonviolent Offense with a Sexual Motivation Finding scoring form on page 236.

If the present conviction is for a felony domestic violence offense where domestic violence was plead and proven, use the General Nonviolent Offense Where Domestic Violence Has Been Plead and Proven scoring form on page 234.

ADULT HISTORY:

    Enter number of felony convictions .... _____ x 1 = _____

JUVENILE HISTORY:

    Enter number Murder 1, Murder 2, and Class A sex offense felony dispositions .... _____ x ½ = _____

OTHER CURRENT OFFENSES:

(Other current offenses that do not encompass the same conduct count in offender score)

    Enter number of other felony convictions .... _____ x 1 = _____

STATUS:

    Was the offender on community custody on the date the current offense was committed? (if yes) _____ + 1 = _____

Total the last column to get the **Offender Score** (Round down to the nearest whole number).......................... _____

SENTENCE RANGE

	Offender Score									
	0	**1**	**2**	**3**	**4**	**5**	**6**	**7**	**8**	**9+**
LEVEL III	2m	5m	8m	11m	14m	19.5m	25.5m	38m	50m	55.5m
	1 - 3	3 - 8	4 - 12	9 - 12	12+ - 16	17 - 22	22 - 29	33 - 43	43 - 57	51 - 60*

    * Class C felony offenses have a statutory maximum sentence of 60 months, see RCW 9A.20.021.

✓   For gang-related felonies where the court found the offender involved a minor (RCW 9.94A.833), see page 227 for standard range adjustment.
✓   For deadly weapon enhancement, see page 233.
✓   For sentencing alternatives, see page 215.
✓   For community custody eligibility, see page 228.
✓   For any applicable enhancements other than deadly weapon enhancement, see page 224.

Escape from Community Custody

RCW 72.09.310
CLASS C – NONVIOLENT
OFFENDER SCORING RCW 9.94A.525(14)

If it was found that this offense was committed with sexual motivation (RCW 9.94A.533(8)) on or after 7/1/2006, use the General Nonviolent Offense with a Sexual Motivation Finding scoring form on page 236.

If the present conviction is for a felony domestic violence offense where domestic violence was plead and proven, use the General Nonviolent Offense Where Domestic Violence Has Been Plead and Proven scoring form on page 234.

ADULT HISTORY:

Enter number of Escape 1, Escape 2, Willful Failure to Return from Furlough,

Willful Failure to Return from Work Release and Escape from Community Custody convictions   _____ x 1 = _____

OTHER CURRENT OFFENSES:

(Other current offenses that do not encompass the same conduct count in offender score)

Enter number of Escape 1, Escape 2, Willful Failure to Return from Furlough,

Willful Failure to Return from Work Release and Escape from Community Custody convictions   _____ x 1 = _____

Total the last column to get the **Offender Score** (Round down to the nearest whole number)......................... _____

SENTENCE RANGE

	Offender Score									
	0	1	2	3	4	5	6	7	8	9+
LEVEL II		4m	6m	8m	13m	16m	19.5m	25.5m	38m	50m
	0-90 days	2 - 6	3 - 9	4 - 12	12+ - 14	14 - 18	17 - 22	22 - 29	33 - 43	43 - 57

✓ For gang-related felonies where the court found the offender involved a minor (RCW 9.94A.833), see page 227 for standard range adjustment.
✓ For deadly weapon enhancement, see page 233.
✓ For sentencing alternatives, see page 215.
✓ For community custody eligibility, see page 228.
✓ For any applicable enhancements other than deadly weapon enhancement, see page 224.

RCW 70.74.180
CLASS A – VIOLENT
OFFENDER SCORING RCW 9.94A.525(8)

If it was found that this offense was committed with sexual motivation (RCW 9.94A.533(8)) on or after 7/1/2006, use the General Violent Offense with a Sexual Motivation Finding scoring form on page 244.

If the present conviction is for a felony domestic violence offense where domestic violence was plead and proven, use the General Violent Offense Where Domestic Violence Has Been Plead and Proven scoring form on page 242.

ADULT HISTORY:

Enter number of serious violent and violent felony convictions .... _____ x 2 = _____

Enter number of nonviolent felony convictions .... _____ x 1 = _____

JUVENILE HISTORY:

Enter number of Murder 1, Murder 2, and Class A sex offense felony dispositions .... _____ x 2 = _____

OTHER CURRENT OFFENSES:

(Other current offenses that do not encompass the same conduct count in offender score)

Enter number of other serious violent and violent felony convictions .... _____ x 2 = _____

Enter number of other felony convictions .... _____ x 1 = _____

STATUS:

Was the offender on community custody on the date the current offense was committed? (if yes) _____ + 1 = _____

Total the last column to get the **Offender Score** (Round down to the nearest whole number)......................... _____

SENTENCE RANGE DISPLAYED IS FOR A COMPLETED OFFENSE

FOR **ATTEMPT**, **SOLICITATION**, OR **CONSPIRACY** (RCW 9.94A.595, see page 54), THE SENTENCE RANGE **IS 75%** OF THE COMPLETED RANGE LISTED BELOW

	Offender Score									
	0	**1**	**2**	**3**	**4**	**5**	**6**	**7**	**8**	**9+**
LEVEL IX	36m	42m	47.5m	53.5m	59.5m	66m	89.5m	101.5m	126m	150m
	31 - 41	36 - 48	41 - 54	46 - 61	51 - 68	57 - 75	77 - 102	87 - 116	108 - 144	129 - 171

✓ For gang-related felonies where the court found the offender involved a minor (RCW 9.94A.833), see page 227 for standard range adjustments.
✓ For deadly weapon enhancement, see page 233.
✓ For sentencing alternatives, see page 215.
✓ For community custody eligibility, see page 228.
✓ For any applicable enhancements other than deadly weapon enhancement, see page 224.

RCW 9A.56.120
CLASS B – VIOLENT/CRIMES AGAINST PERSONS
OFFENDER SCORING RCW 9.94A.525(8)

If it was found that this offense was committed with sexual motivation (RCW 9.94A.533(8)) on or after 7/1/2006, use the General Violent Offense with a Sexual Motivation Finding scoring form on page 244.

If the present conviction is for a felony domestic violence offense where domestic violence was plead and proven, use the General Violent Offense Where Domestic Violence Has Been Plead and Proven scoring form on page 242.

ADULT HISTORY:

Enter number of serious violent and violent felony convictions .... _____ x 2 = _____

Enter number of nonviolent felony convictions .... _____ x 1 = _____

JUVENILE HISTORY:

Enter number of Murder 1, Murder 2, and Class A sex offense felony dispositions .... _____ x 2 = _____

OTHER CURRENT OFFENSES:

(Other current offenses that do not encompass the same conduct count in offender score)

Enter number of other serious violent and violent felony convictions .... _____ x 2 = _____

Enter number of other felony convictions .... _____ x 1 = _____

STATUS:

Was the offender on community custody on the date the current offense was committed? (if yes) _____ + 1 = _____

Total the last column to get the **Offender Score** (Round down to the nearest whole number)........................ _____

SENTENCE RANGE DISPLAYED IS FOR A COMPLETED OFFENSE

FOR **ATTEMPT**, **SOLICITATION**, OR **CONSPIRACY** (RCW 9.94A.595, see page 54), THE SENTENCE RANGE **IS 75%** OF THE COMPLETED RANGE LISTED BELOW

Offender Score										
	0	**1**	**2**	**3**	**4**	**5**	**6**	**7**	**8**	**9+**
LEVEL V	9m	13m	15m	17.5m	25.5m	38m	47.5m	59.5m	72m	84m
	6 - 12	12+ - 14	13 - 17	15 - 20	22 - 29	33 - 43	41 - 54	51 - 68	62 - 82	72 - 96

✓ For gang-related felonies where the court found the offender involved a minor (RCW 9.94A.833), see page 227 for standard range adjustments.
✓ For deadly weapon enhancement, see page 233.
✓ For sentencing alternatives, see page 215.
✓ For community custody eligibility, see page 228.
✓ For any applicable enhancements other than deadly weapon enhancement, see page 224.

RCW 9A.56.130
CLASS C* – NONVIOLENT/CRIMES AGAINST PERSONS
OFFENDER SCORING RCW 9.94A.525(7)

If it was found that this offense was committed with sexual motivation (RCW 9.94A.533(8)) on or after 7/1/2006, use the General Nonviolent Offense with a Sexual Motivation Finding scoring form on page 236.

If the present conviction is for a felony domestic violence offense where domestic violence was plead and proven, use the General Nonviolent Offense Where Domestic Violence Has Been Plead and Proven scoring form on page 234.

ADULT HISTORY:

    Enter number of felony convictions .... _____ x 1 = _____

JUVENILE HISTORY:

    Enter number of Murder 1, Murder 2, and Class A sex offense felony dispositions .... _____ x 1 = _____

OTHER CURRENT OFFENSES:

(Other current offenses that do not encompass the same conduct count in offender score)

    Enter number of other felony convictions .... _____ x 1 = _____

STATUS:

    Was the offender on community custody on the date the current offense was committed? (if yes) _____ + 1 = _____

Total the last column to get the **Offender Score** (Round down to the nearest whole number).......................... _____

SENTENCE RANGE

	Offender Score									
	0	**1**	**2**	**3**	**4**	**5**	**6**	**7**	**8**	**9+**
LEVEL III	2m	5m	8m	11m	14m	19.5m	25.5m	38m	50m	55.5m
	1 - 3	3 - 8	4 - 12	9 - 12	12+ - 16	17 - 22	22 - 29	33 - 43	43 - 57	51 - 60*

    * Class C felony offenses have a statutory maximum sentence of 60 months, see RCW 9A.20.021.

✓   For gang-related felonies where the court found the offender involved a minor (RCW 9.94A.833), see page 227 for standard range adjustment.
✓   For deadly weapon enhancement, see page 233.
✓   For sentencing alternatives, see page 215.
✓   For community custody eligibility, see page 228.
✓   For any applicable enhancements other than deadly weapon enhancement, see page 224.

Extortionate Extension of Credit, Use of Extortionate Means
to Collect Extensions of Credit

RCW 9A.82.020 & RCW 9A.82.040
CLASS B – NONVIOLENT
OFFENDER SCORING RCW 9.94A.525(7)

If it was found that this offense was committed with sexual motivation (RCW 9.94A.533(8)) on or after 7/1/2006, use the General Nonviolent Offense with a Sexual Motivation Finding scoring form on page 236.

If the present conviction is for a felony domestic violence offense where domestic violence was plead and proven, use the General Nonviolent Offense Where Domestic Violence Has Been Plead and Proven scoring form on page 234.

ADULT HISTORY:

    Enter number of felony convictions .... _____ x 1 = _____

JUVENILE HISTORY:

    Enter number of Murder 1, Murder 2, and Class A sex offense felony dispositions .... _____ x 1 = _____

OTHER CURRENT OFFENSES:

(Other current offenses that do not encompass the same conduct count in offender score)

    Enter number of other felony convictions .... _____ x 1 = _____

STATUS:

    Was the offender on community custody on the date the current offense was committed? (if yes) _____ + 1 = _____

Total the last column to get the **Offender Score** (Round down to the nearest whole number)......................... _____

SENTENCE RANGE DISPLAYED IS FOR A COMPLETED OFFENSE

FOR **ATTEMPT**, **SOLICITATION**, OR **CONSPIRACY** (RCW 9.94A.595, see page 54), THE SENTENCE RANGE **IS 75%** OF THE COMPLETED RANGE LISTED BELOW

Offender Score										
	0	**1**	**2**	**3**	**4**	**5**	**6**	**7**	**8**	**9+**
LEVEL V	9m	13m	15m	17.5m	25.5m	38m	47.5m	59.5m	72m	84m
	6 - 12	12+ - 14	13 - 17	15 - 20	22 - 29	33 - 43	41 - 54	51 - 68	62 - 82	72 - 96

✓   For gang-related felonies where the court found the offender involved a minor (RCW 9.94A.833), see page 227 for standard range adjustments.
✓   For deadly weapon enhancement, see page 233.
✓   For sentencing alternatives, see page 215.
✓   For community custody eligibility, see page 228.
✓   For any applicable enhancements other than deadly weapon enhancement, see page 224.

RCW 9A.44.132(1)(a)
CLASS C – NONVIOLENT/SEX
OFFENDER SCORING RCW 9.94A.525(18)

If the present conviction is for a felony domestic violence offense where domestic violence was plead and proven, use the General Nonviolent/Sex Offense Where Domestic Violence Has Been Plead and Proven scoring form on page 235.

ADULT HISTORY:

Enter number of sex offense felony convictions .... _____ x 3 = _____

Enter number of Failure to Register as a Sex Offender* felony convictions .... _____ x 1 = _____

Enter number of felony convictions .... _____ x 1 = _____

JUVENILE HISTORY:

Enter number of Class A sex offense felony dispositions .... _____ x 3 = _____

Enter number of Murder 1 and Murder 2 felony dispositions .... _____ x 1 = _____

OTHER CURRENT OFFENSES:

(Other current offenses that do not encompass the same conduct count in offender score)

Enter number of other sex offense felony convictions .... _____ x 3 = _____

Enter number of other Failure to Register as a Sex Offender* felony dispositions .... _____ x 1 = _____

Enter number of other felony convictions .... _____ x 1 = _____

STATUS:

Was the offender on community custody on the date the current offense was committed?........... _____ + 1 = _____

Total the last column to get the **Offender Score** (Round down to the nearest whole number) .... _____

SENTENCE RANGE

		Offender Score									
		0	1	2	3	4	5	6	7	8	9+
LEVEL II	0-90 days		4m 2 - 6	6m 3 - 9	8m 4 - 12	13m 12+ - 14	16m 14 - 18	19.5m 17 - 22	25.5m 22 - 29	38m 33 - 43	50m 43 - 57

✓ For gang-related felonies where the court found the offender involved a minor (RCW 9.94A.833), see page 227 for standard range adjustments.
✓ For deadly weapon enhancement, see page 233.
✓ For sentencing alternatives, see page 215.
✓ For community custody eligibility, see page 228.
✓ For any applicable enhancements other than deadly weapon enhancement, see page 224.

NOTE: In 2008 it was noted that Failure to Register as a Sex Offender would become a Class B offense as of ninety days sine die 2010 Legislative Session. The statute was changed before this could take effect.

---

* The first violation of Failure to Register as a Sex Offender (unranked level and Class C felony) is <u>NOT</u> a sex offense per RCW 9.94A.030(47).

Failure to Register as a Sex Offender Third or Subsequent Violation Committed on or after 6/10/2010

RCW 9A.44.132(1)(b)
CLASS B – NONVIOLENT/SEX
OFFENDER SCORING RCW 9.94A.525(18)

If the present conviction is for a felony domestic violence offense where domestic violence was plead and proven, use the General Nonviolent/Sex Offense Where Domestic Violence Has Been Plead and Proven scoring form on page 235.

ADULT HISTORY:

Enter number of sex offense felony convictions .... _____ x 3 = _____

Enter number of Failure to Register as a Sex Offender* felony convictions .... _____ x 1 = _____

Enter number of felony convictions .... _____ x 1 = _____

JUVENILE HISTORY:

Enter number of Class A sex offense felony dispositions .... _____ x 3 = _____

Enter number of Murder 1 and Murder 2 felony dispositions .... _____ x 1 = _____

OTHER CURRENT OFFENSES:

(Other current offenses that do not encompass the same conduct count in offender score)

Enter number of other sex offense felony convictions .... _____ x 3 = _____

Enter number of other Failure to Register as a Sex Offender* felony dispositions .... _____ x 1 = _____

Enter number of other felony convictions .... _____ x 1 = _____

STATUS:

Was the offender on community custody on the date the current offense was committed? .... _____ + 1 = _____

Total the last column to get the **Offender Score** (Round down to the nearest whole number)........ _____

SENTENCE RANGE DISPLAYED IS FOR A COMPLETED OFFENSE

FOR **ATTEMPT**, **SOLICITATION**, OR **CONSPIRACY** (RCW 9.94A.595, see page 54), THE SENTENCE RANGE **IS 75%** OF THE COMPLETED RANGE LISTED BELOW

	Offender Score									
	0	1	2	3	4	5	6	7	8	9+
LEVEL II	0-90 days	4m 2 - 6	6m 3 - 9	8m 4 - 12	13m 12+ - 14	16m 14 - 18	19.5m 17 - 22	25.5m 22 - 29	38m 33 - 43	50m 43 - 57

- ✓ For gang-related felonies where the court found the offender involved a minor (RCW 9.94A.833), see page 227 for standard range adjustments.
- ✓ For deadly weapon enhancement, see page 233.
- ✓ For sentencing alternatives, see page 215.
- ✓ For community custody eligibility, see page 228.
- ✓ For any applicable enhancements other than deadly weapon enhancement, see page 224.

NOTE: In 2008 it was noted that Failure to Register as a Sex Offender would become a Class B offense as of ninety days sine die 2010 Legislative Session. The statute was changed before this could take effect.

* The first violation of Failure to Register as a Sex Offender (unranked level and Class C felony) is NOT a sex offense per RCW 9.94A.030(47).

False Reporting First Degree

RCW 9A.84.040(2)(a)
CLASS B – NONVIOLENT
OFFENDER SCORING RCW 9.94A.525(7)

If it was found that this offense was committed with sexual motivation (RCW 9.94A.533(8)) on or after 7/1/2006, use the General Nonviolent Offense with a Sexual Motivation Finding scoring form on page 236.

If the present conviction is for a felony domestic violence offense where domestic violence was plead and proven, use the General Nonviolent Offense Where Domestic Violence Has Been Plead and Proven scoring form on page 234.

ADULT HISTORY:

Enter number of felony convictions .... _____ x 1 = _____

JUVENILE HISTORY:

Enter number of Murder 1, Murder 2, and Class A sex offense felony dispositions .... _____ x 1 = _____

OTHER CURRENT OFFENSES:

(Other current offenses that do not encompass the same conduct count in offender score)

Enter number of other felony convictions .... _____ x 1 = _____

STATUS:

Was the offender on community custody on the date the current offense was committed? (if yes) _____ + 1 = _____

Total the last column to get the **Offender Score** (Round down to the nearest whole number)......................... _____

SENTENCE RANGE DISPLAYED IS FOR A COMPLETED OFFENSE

FOR **ATTEMPT**, **SOLICITATION**, OR **CONSPIRACY** (RCW 9.94A.595, see page 54), THE SENTENCE RANGE **IS 75%** OF THE COMPLETED RANGE LISTED BELOW

	Offender Score									
	0	1	2	3	4	5	6	7	8	9+
LEVEL VII	17.5m	24m	30m	36m	42m	47.5m	66m	78m	89.5m	101.5m
	15 - 20	21 - 27	26 - 34	31 - 41	36 - 48	41 - 54	57 - 75	67 - 89	77 - 102	87 - 116

✓ For gang-related felonies where the court found the offender involved a minor (RCW 9.94A.833), see page 227 for standard range adjustments.
✓ For deadly weapon enhancement, see page 233.
✓ For sentencing alternatives, see page 215.
✓ For community custody eligibility, see page 228.
✓ For any applicable enhancements other than deadly weapon enhancement, see page 224.

False Reporting Second Degree

RCW 9A.84.040(2)(b)
CLASS C* – NONVIOLENT
OFFENDER SCORING RCW 9.94A.525(7)

If it was found that this offense was committed with sexual motivation (RCW 9.94A.533(8)) on or after 7/1/2006, use the General Nonviolent Offense with a Sexual Motivation Finding scoring form on page 236.

If the present conviction is for a felony domestic violence offense where domestic violence was plead and proven, use the General Nonviolent Offense Where Domestic Violence Has Been Plead and Proven scoring form on page 234.

ADULT HISTORY:

    Enter number of felony convictions .... _____ x 1 = _____

JUVENILE HISTORY:

    Enter number of Murder 1, Murder 2, and Class A sex offense felony dispositions .... _____ x 1 = _____

OTHER CURRENT OFFENSES:

(Other current offenses that do not encompass the same conduct count in offender score)

    Enter number of other felony convictions .... _____ x 1 = _____

STATUS:

    Was the offender on community custody on the date the current offense was committed? (if yes) _____ + 1 = _____

Total the last column to get the **Offender Score** (Round down to the nearest whole number) .... _____

SENTENCE RANGE

	Offender Score									
	0	**1**	**2**	**3**	**4**	**5**	**6**	**7**	**8**	**9+**
LEVEL III	2m	5m	8m	11m	14m	19.5m	25.5m	38m	50m	55.5m
	1 - 3	3 - 8	4 - 12	9 - 12	12+ - 16	17 - 22	22 - 29	33 - 43	43 - 57	51 - 60*

    * Class C felony offenses have a statutory maximum sentence of 60 months, see RCW 9A.20.021.

✓   For gang-related felonies where the court found the offender involved a minor (RCW 9.94A.833), see page 227 for standard range adjustment.
✓   For deadly weapon enhancement, see page 233.
✓   For sentencing alternatives, see page 215.
✓   For community custody eligibility, see page 228.
✓   For any applicable enhancements other than deadly weapon enhancement, see page 224.

False Verification for Welfare

RCW 74.08.055(2)
CLASS B – NONVIOLENT
OFFENDER SCORING RCW 9.94A.525(7)

If it was found that this offense was committed with sexual motivation (RCW 9.94A.533(8)) on or after 7/1/2006, use the General Nonviolent Offense with a Sexual Motivation Finding scoring form on page 236.

If the present conviction is for a felony domestic violence offense where domestic violence was plead and proven, use the General Nonviolent Offense Where Domestic Violence Has Been Plead and Proven scoring form on page 234.

ADULT HISTORY:

    Enter number of felony convictions .... _____ x 1 = _____

JUVENILE HISTORY:

    Enter number of Murder 1, Murder 2, and Class A sex offense felony dispositions .... _____ x 1 = _____

OTHER CURRENT OFFENSES:

(Other current offenses that do not encompass the same conduct count in offender score)

    Enter number of other felony convictions .... _____ x 1 = _____

STATUS:

    Was the offender on community custody on the date the current offense was committed? (if yes) _____ + 1 = _____

Total the last column to get the **Offender Score** (Round down to the nearest whole number).......................... _____

SENTENCE RANGE DISPLAYED IS FOR A COMPLETED OFFENSE

FOR **ATTEMPT**, **SOLICITATION**, OR **CONSPIRACY** (RCW 9.94A.595, see page 54), THE SENTENCE RANGE **IS 75%** OF THE COMPLETED RANGE LISTED BELOW

	Offender Score									
	0	**1**	**2**	**3**	**4**	**5**	**6**	**7**	**8**	**9+**
LEVEL I			3m	4m	5.5m	8m	13m	16m	19.5m	25.5m
	0-60 days	0-90 days	2 - 5	2 - 6	3 - 8	4 - 12	12+ - 14	14 - 18	17 - 22	22 - 29

✓   For gang-related felonies where the court found the offender involved a minor (RCW 9.94A.833), see page 227 for standard range adjustments.
✓   For deadly weapon enhancement, see page 233.
✓   For sentencing alternatives, see page 215.
✓   For community custody eligibility, see page 228.
✓   For any applicable enhancements other than deadly weapon enhancement, see page 224.

Forged Prescription Legend Drug

RCW 69.41.020
CLASS B – NONVIOLENT
OFFENDER SCORING RCW 9.94A.525(7)

If it was found that this offense was committed with sexual motivation (RCW 9.94A.533(8)) on or after 7/1/2006, use the General Nonviolent Offense with a Sexual Motivation Finding scoring form on page 236.

If the present conviction is for a felony domestic violence offense where domestic violence was plead and proven, use the General Nonviolent Offense Where Domestic Violence Has Been Plead and Proven scoring form on page 234.

ADULT HISTORY:

Enter number of felony convictions .... _____ x 1 = _____

JUVENILE HISTORY:

Enter number of Murder 1, Murder 2, and Class A sex offense felony dispositions .... _____ x 1 = _____

OTHER CURRENT OFFENSES:

(Other current offenses that do not encompass the same conduct count in offender score)

Enter number of other felony convictions .... _____ x 1 = _____

STATUS:

Was the offender on community custody on the date the current offense was committed? (if yes) _____ + 1 = _____

Total the last column to get the **Offender Score** (Round down to the nearest whole number)........................ _____

SENTENCE RANGE – DRUG

	Offender Score		
	0 to 2	**3 to 5**	**6 to 9+**
LEVEL I	3m	12m	18m
	0 - 6	6+ - 18	12+ - 24

✓   For attempt, solicitation, conspiracy (RCW 9.94A.595) see page 54 or for gang-related felonies where the court found the offender involved a minor (RCW 9.94A.833), see page 227 for standard range adjustments.
✓   For deadly weapon enhancement, see page 233.
✓   For sentencing alternatives, see page 215.
✓   For community custody eligibility, see page 228.
✓   For any applicable enhancements other than deadly weapon enhancement, see page 224.

Forged Prescription for a Controlled Substance

RCW 69.50.403
CLASS C – NONVIOLENT
OFFENDER SCORING RCW 9.94A.525(7)

If it was found that this offense was committed with sexual motivation (RCW 9.94A.533(8)) on or after 7/1/2006, use the General Nonviolent Offense with a Sexual Motivation Finding scoring form on page 236.

If the present conviction is for a felony domestic violence offense where domestic violence was plead and proven, use the General Nonviolent Offense Where Domestic Violence Has Been Plead and Proven scoring form on page 234.

ADULT HISTORY:

   Enter number of felony convictions .... _____ x 1 = _____

JUVENILE HISTORY:

   Enter number of Murder 1, Murder 2, and Class A sex offense felony dispositions .... _____ x 1 = _____

OTHER CURRENT OFFENSES:

(Other current offenses that do not encompass the same conduct count in offender score)

   Enter number of other felony convictions .... _____ x 1 = _____

STATUS:

   Was the offender on community custody on the date the current offense was committed? (if yes) _____ + 1 = _____

Total the last column to get the **Offender Score** (Round down to the nearest whole number).......................... _____

SENTENCE RANGE - DRUG

	Offender Score		
	0 to 2	3 to 5	6 to 9+
LEVEL I	3m	12m	18m
	0 - 6	6+ - 18	12+ - 24

- ✓ For gang-related felonies where the court found the offender involved a minor (RCW 9.94A.833), see page 227 for standard range adjustments.
- ✓ Per RCW 9.94A.518, any felony offense under chapter 69.50 RCW with a deadly weapon special verdict under RCW 9.94A.602 becomes a level III offense.
- ✓ For deadly weapon enhancement, see page 233.
- ✓ For sentencing alternatives, see page 215.
- ✓ For community custody eligibility, see page 228.
- ✓ For any applicable enhancements other than deadly weapon enhancement, see page 224.
- ✓ Per RCW 69.50.408, the statutory maximum for a subsequent conviction under Chapter 69.50 RCW is 48 months.

Forgery

RCW 9A.60.020
CLASS C – NONVIOLENT
OFFENDER SCORING RCW 9.94A.525(7)

If it was found that this offense was committed with sexual motivation (RCW 9.94A.533(8)) on or after 7/1/2006, use the General Nonviolent Offense with a Sexual Motivation Finding scoring form on page 236.

If the present conviction is for a felony domestic violence offense where domestic violence was plead and proven, use the General Nonviolent Offense Where Domestic Violence Has Been Plead and Proven scoring form on page 234.

ADULT HISTORY:

    Enter number of felony convictions .... _____ x 1 = _____

JUVENILE HISTORY:

    Enter number of Murder 1, Murder 2, and Class A sex offense felony dispositions .... _____ x 1 = _____

OTHER CURRENT OFFENSES:

(Other current offenses that do not encompass the same conduct count in offender score)

    Enter number of other felony convictions .... _____ x 1 = _____

STATUS:

    Was the offender on community custody on the date the current offense was committed? (if yes) _____ + 1 = _____

Total the last column to get the **Offender Score** (Round down to the nearest whole number)........................ _____

SENTENCE RANGE

	Offender Score									
	0	1	2	3	4	5	6	7	8	9+
LEVEL I	0-60 days	0-90 days	3m 2 - 5	4m 2 - 6	5.5m 3 - 8	8m 4 - 12	13m 12+ - 14	16m 14 - 18	19.5m 17 - 22	25.5m 22 - 29

✓ For gang-related felonies where the court found the offender involved a minor (RCW 9.94A.833), see page 227 for standard range adjustment.
✓ For deadly weapon enhancement, see page 233.
✓ For sentencing alternatives, see page 215.
✓ For community custody eligibility, see page 228.
✓ For any applicable enhancements other than deadly weapon enhancement, see page 224.

RCW 9A.46.020(2)(b)
CLASS C* – NONVIOLENT
OFFENDER SCORING RCW 9.94A.525(7)

If it was found that this offense was committed with sexual motivation (RCW 9.94A.533(8)) on or after 7/1/2006, use the General Nonviolent Offense with a Sexual Motivation Finding scoring form on page 236.

If the present conviction is for a felony domestic violence offense where domestic violence was plead and proven, use the General Nonviolent Offense Where Domestic Violence Has Been Plead and Proven scoring form on page 234.

ADULT HISTORY:

    Enter number of felony convictions .... _____ x 1 = _____

JUVENILE HISTORY:

    Enter number of Murder 1, Murder 2, and Class A sex offense felony dispositions .... _____ x 1 = _____

OTHER CURRENT OFFENSES:

(Other current offenses that do not encompass the same conduct count in offender score)

    Enter number of other felony convictions .... _____ x 1 = _____

STATUS:

    Was the offender on community custody on the date the current offense was committed? (if yes) _____ + 1 = _____

Total the last column to get the **Offender Score** (Round down to the nearest whole number).......................... _____

SENTENCE RANGE

	Offender Score									
	0	**1**	**2**	**3**	**4**	**5**	**6**	**7**	**8**	**9+**
LEVEL III	2m	5m	8m	11m	14m	19.5m	25.5m	38m	50m	55.5m
	1 - 3	3 - 8	4 - 12	9 - 12	12+ - 16	17 - 22	22 - 29	33 - 43	43 - 57	51 - 60*

* Class C felony offenses have a statutory maximum sentence of 60 months, see RCW 9A.20.021.

✓   For gang-related felonies where the court found the offender involved a minor (RCW 9.94A.833), see page 227 for standard range adjustment.
✓   For deadly weapon enhancement, see page 233.
✓   For sentencing alternatives, see page 215.
✓   For community custody eligibility, see page 228.
✓   For any applicable enhancements other than deadly weapon enhancement, see page 224.

RCW 9A.36.080
CLASS C* – NONVIOLENT/CRIMES AGAINST PERSONS
OFFENDER SCORING RCW 9.94A.525(7)

If it was found that this offense was committed with sexual motivation (RCW 9.94A.533(8)) on or after 7/1/2006, use the General Nonviolent Offense with a Sexual Motivation Finding scoring form on page 236.

If the present conviction is for a felony domestic violence offense where domestic violence was plead and proven, use the General Nonviolent Offense Where Domestic Violence Has Been Plead and Proven scoring form on page 234.

ADULT HISTORY:

Enter number of felony convictions .... _____ x 1 = _____

JUVENILE HISTORY:

Enter number of Murder 1, Murder 2, and Class A sex offense felony dispositions .... _____ x 1 = _____

OTHER CURRENT OFFENSES:

(Other current offenses that do not encompass the same conduct count in offender score)

Enter number of other felony convictions .... _____ x 1 = _____

STATUS:

Was the offender on community custody on the date the current offense was committed? (if yes) _____ + 1 = _____

Total the last column to get the **Offender Score** (Round down to the nearest whole number)......................... _____

SENTENCE RANGE

	Offender Score									
	0	**1**	**2**	**3**	**4**	**5**	**6**	**7**	**8**	**9+**
LEVEL IV	6m	9m	13m	15m	17.5m	25.5m	38m	50m	56.5m	
	3 - 9	6 - 12	12+ - 14	13 - 17	15 - 20	22 - 29	33 - 43	43 - 57	53 - 60*	60 - 60*

* Class C felony offenses have a statutory maximum sentence of 60 months, see RCW 9A.20.021.

✓ For gang-related felonies where the court found the offender involved a minor (RCW 9.94A.833), see page 227 for standard range adjustment.
✓ For deadly weapon enhancement, see page 233.
✓ For sentencing alternatives, see page 215.
✓ For community custody eligibility, see page 228.
✓ For any applicable enhancements other than deadly weapon enhancement, see page 224.

Hazing

RCW 28B.10.901(2)(b)
CLASS C* – NONVIOLENT/CRIMES AGAINST PERSONS
OFFENDER SCORING RCW 9.94A.525(7)

If it was found that this offense was committed with sexual motivation (RCW 9.94A.533(8)) on or after 7/1/2006, use the General Nonviolent Offense with a Sexual Motivation Finding scoring form on page 236.

If the present conviction is for a felony domestic violence offense where domestic violence was plead and proven, use the General Nonviolent Offense Where Domestic Violence Has Been Plead and Proven scoring form on page 234.

ADULT HISTORY:

Enter number of felony convictions .... _____ x 1 = _____

JUVENILE HISTORY:

Enter number of Murder 1, Murder 2, and Class A sex offense felony dispositions .... _____ x 1 = _____

OTHER CURRENT OFFENSES:

(Other current offenses that do not encompass the same conduct count in offender score)

Enter number of other felony convictions .... _____ x 1 = _____

STATUS:

Was the offender on community custody on the date the current offense was committed? (if yes) _____ + 1 = _____

Total the last column to get the **Offender Score** (Round down to the nearest whole number).......................... _____

SENTENCE RANGE

	Offender Score									
	0	**1**	**2**	**3**	**4**	**5**	**6**	**7**	**8**	**9+**
LEVEL III	2m	5m	8m	11m	14m	19.5m	25.5m	38m	50m	55.5m
	1 - 3	3 - 8	4 - 12	9 - 12	12+ - 16	17 - 22	22 - 29	33 - 43	43 - 57	51 - 60*

* Class C felony offenses have a statutory maximum sentence of 60 months, see RCW 9A.20.021.

✓ For gang-related felonies where the court found the offender involved a minor (RCW 9.94A.833), see page 227 for standard range adjustment.
✓ For deadly weapon enhancement, see page 233.
✓ For sentencing alternatives, see page 215.
✓ For community custody eligibility, see page 228.
✓ For any applicable enhancements other than deadly weapon enhancement, see page 224.

RCW 48.80.030
CLASS C – NONVIOLENT
OFFENDER SCORING RCW 9.94A.525(7)

If it was found that this offense was committed with sexual motivation (RCW 9.94A.533(8)) on or after 7/1/2006, use the General Nonviolent Offense with a Sexual Motivation Finding scoring form on page 236.

If the present conviction is for a felony domestic violence offense where domestic violence was plead and proven, use the General Nonviolent Offense Where Domestic Violence Has Been Plead and Proven scoring form on page 234.

ADULT HISTORY:

Enter number of felony convictions .... _____ x 1 = _____

JUVENILE HISTORY:

Enter number of Murder 1, Murder 2, and Class A sex offense felony dispositions .... _____ x 1 = _____

OTHER CURRENT OFFENSES:

(Other current offenses that do not encompass the same conduct count in offender score)

Enter number of other felony convictions .... _____ x 1 = _____

STATUS:

Was the offender on community custody on the date the current offense was committed? (if yes) _____ + 1 = _____

Total the last column to get the **Offender Score** (Round down to the nearest whole number)......................... _____

SENTENCE RANGE

		0	1	2	3	4	5	6	7	8	9+
	Offender Score										
LEVEL II		4m	6m	8m	13m	16m	19.5m	25.5m	38m	50m
	0-90 days	2 - 6	3 - 9	4 - 12	12+ - 14	14 - 18	17 - 22	22 - 29	33 - 43	43 - 57

✓ For gang-related felonies where the court found the offender involved a minor (RCW 9.94A.833), see page 227 for standard range adjustment.
✓ For deadly weapon enhancement, see page 233.
✓ For sentencing alternatives, see page 215.
✓ For community custody eligibility, see page 228.
✓ For any applicable enhancements other than deadly weapon enhancement, see page 224.

RCW 46.52.020(4)(a)
CLASS B* – NONVIOLENT/TRAFFIC OFFENSE
OFFENDER SCORING RCW 9.94A.525(11)

ADULT HISTORY:

Enter number of Vehicular Homicide and Vehicular Assault felony convictions .... _____ x 2 = _____

Enter number of Operation of a Vessel while under the Influence of Intoxicating Liquor or any Drug felony convictions .... _____ x 1 = _____

Enter number of felony convictions .... _____ x 1 = _____

Enter number of Driving while under the Influence of Intoxicating Liquor or any Drug and Actual Physical Control while under the Influence of Intoxicating Liquor or any Drug and Reckless Driving and Hit-and-Run Attended Vehicle <u>non-felony</u> convictions .... _____ x 1 = _____

JUVENILE HISTORY:

Enter number of Murder 1, Murder 2, and Class A sex offense felony dispositions .... _____ x ½ = _____

OTHER CURRENT OFFENSES:

(Other current offenses that do not encompass the same conduct count in offender score)

Enter number of Vehicular Homicide and Vehicular Assault convictions .... _____ x 2 = _____

Enter number of other Operation of a Vessel while under the Influence of Intoxicating Liquor or any Drug felony convictions .... _____ x 1 = _____

Enter number of other felony convictions .... _____ x 1 = _____

Enter number of Driving while under the Influence of Intoxicating Liquor or any Drug and Actual Physical Control while under the Influence of Intoxicating Liquor or any Drug and Reckless Driving and Hit-and-Run Attended Vehicle <u>non-felony</u> convictions .... _____ x 1 = _____

STATUS:

Was the offender on community custody on the date the current offense was committed? (if yes) _____ + 1 = _____

Total the last column to get the **Offender Score** (Round down to the nearest whole number)......................... _____

SENTENCE RANGE DISPLAYED IS FOR A COMPLETED OFFENSE

FOR **ATTEMPT**, **SOLICITATION**, OR **CONSPIRACY** (RCW 9.94A.595, see page 54), THE SENTENCE RANGE **IS 75%** OF THE COMPLETED RANGE LISTED BELOW

Offender Score										
	0	1	2	3	4	5	6	7	8	9+
LEVEL IX	36m	42m	47.5m	53.5m	59.5m	66m	89.5m	101.5m	114m	
	31 - 41	36 - 48	41 - 54	46 - 61	51 - 68	57 - 75	77 - 102	87 - 116	108 - 120*	120 - 120*

* Class B felony offenses have a statutory maximum sentence of 120 months, see RCW 9A.20.021.

✓ For gang-related felonies where the court found the offender involved a minor (RCW 9.94A.833), see page 227 for standard range adjustments.
✓ For deadly weapon enhancement, see page 233.
✓ For sentencing alternatives, see page 215.
✓ For community custody eligibility, see page 228.
✓ For any applicable enhancements other than deadly weapon enhancement, see page 224.

RCW 46.52.020(4)(b)
CLASS C* – NONVIOLENT/TRAFFIC OFFENSE
OFFENDER SCORING RCW 9.94A.525(11)

ADULT HISTORY:

Enter number of Vehicular Homicide and Vehicular Assault felony convictions .... _____ x 2 = _____

Enter number of Operation of a Vessel while under the Influence of Intoxicating Liquor or

any Drug felony convictions .... _____ x 1 = _____

Enter number of felony convictions .... _____ x 1 = _____

Enter number of Driving while under the Influence of Intoxicating Liquor or any Drug and
Actual Physical Control while under the Influence of Intoxicating Liquor or any Drug and
Reckless Driving and Hit-and-Run Attended Vehicle <u>non-felony</u> convictions .... _____ x 1 = _____

JUVENILE HISTORY:

Enter number of Murder 1, Murder 2, and Class A sex offense felony dispositions ..... _____ x ½ = _____

OTHER CURRENT OFFENSES:

(Other current offenses that do not encompass the same conduct count in offender score)

Enter number of Vehicular Homicide and Vehicular Assault convictions .... _____ x 2 = _____

Enter number of other Operation of a Vessel while under the Influence of Intoxicating Liquor
or any Drug felony convictions .... _____ x 1 = _____

Enter number of other felony convictions .... _____ x 1 = _____

Enter number of Driving while under the Influence of Intoxicating Liquor or any Drug and
Actual Physical Control while under the Influence of Intoxicating Liquor or any Drug and
Reckless Driving and Hit-and-Run Attended Vehicle <u>non-felony</u> convictions .... _____ x 1 = _____

STATUS:

Was the offender on community custody on the date the current offense was committed? (if yes) _____ + 1 = _____

Total the last column to get the **Offender Score** (Round down to the nearest whole number)........................ _____

SENTENCE RANGE

					Offender Score					
	0	**1**	**2**	**3**	**4**	**5**	**6**	**7**	**8**	**9+**
LEVEL IV	6m	9m	13m	15m	17.5m	25.5m	38m	50m	56.5m	
	3 - 9	6 - 12	12+ - 14	13 - 17	15 - 20	22 - 29	33 - 43	43 - 57	53 - 60*	60 - 60*

* Class C felony offenses have a statutory maximum sentence of 60 months, see RCW 9A.20.021.

✓ For gang-related felonies where the court found the offender involved a minor (RCW 9.94A.833), see page 227 for standard range adjustment.
✓ For deadly weapon enhancement, see page 233.
✓ For sentencing alternatives, see page 215.
✓ For community custody eligibility, see page 228.
✓ For any applicable enhancements other than deadly weapon enhancement, see page 224.

RCW 79A.60.200(3)
CLASS C* – NONVIOLENT
OFFENDER SCORING RCW 9.94A.525(7)

If it was found that this offense was committed with sexual motivation (RCW 9.94A.533(8)) on or after 7/1/2006, use the General Nonviolent Offense with a Sexual Motivation Finding scoring form on page 236.

If the present conviction is for a felony domestic violence offense where domestic violence was plead and proven, use the General Nonviolent Offense Where Domestic Violence Has Been Plead and Proven scoring form on page 234.

ADULT HISTORY:

Enter number of felony convictions .... _____ x 1 = _____

JUVENILE HISTORY:

Enter number of Murder 1, Murder 2, and Class A sex offense felony dispositions .... _____ x 1 = _____

OTHER CURRENT OFFENSES:

(Other current offenses that do not encompass the same conduct count in offender score)

Enter number of other felony convictions .... _____ x 1 = _____

STATUS:

Was the offender on community custody on the date the current offense was committed? (if yes) _____ + 1 = _____

Total the last column to get the **Offender Score** (Round down to the nearest whole number).......................... _____

SENTENCE RANGE

	Offender Score									
	0	**1**	**2**	**3**	**4**	**5**	**6**	**7**	**8**	**9+**
LEVEL IV	6m	9m	13m	15m	17.5m	25.5m	38m	50m	56.5m	
	3 - 9	6 - 12	12+ - 14	13 - 17	15 - 20	22 - 29	33 - 43	43 - 57	53 - 60*	60 - 60*

* Class C felony offenses have a statutory maximum sentence of 60 months, see RCW 9A.20.021.

✓ For gang-related felonies where the court found the offender involved a minor (RCW 9.94A.833), see page 227 for standard range adjustment.
✓ For deadly weapon enhancement, see page 233.
✓ For sentencing alternatives, see page 215.
✓ For community custody eligibility, see page 228.
✓ For any applicable enhancements other than deadly weapon enhancement, see page 224.

RCW 9A.32.055
CLASS A – SERIOUS VIOLENT
OFFENDER SCORING RCW 9.94A.525(9)

If the present conviction is for a felony domestic violence offense where domestic violence was plead and proven, use the General Serious Violent Offense Where Domestic Violence Has Been Plead and Proven scoring form on page 239.

ADULT HISTORY:

Enter number of serious violent felony convictions .... _____ x 3 = _____

Enter number of violent felony convictions .... _____ x 2 = _____

Enter number of nonviolent felony convictions .... _____ x 1 = _____

JUVENILE HISTORY:

Enter number of Murder 1, Murder 2, and Serious Violent sex offense felony dispositions .... _____ x 3 = _____

Enter number of Class A sex offense (not Serious Violent) felony dispositions .... _____ x 2 = _____

OTHER CURRENT OFFENSES:

(Other current offenses that do not encompass the same conduct count in offender score)

Enter number of other violent felony convictions .... _____ x 2 = _____

Enter number of other nonviolent felony convictions .... _____ x 1 = _____

STATUS:

Was the offender on community custody on the date the current offense was committed? .... _____ + 1 = _____

Total the last column to get the **Offender Score** (Round down to the nearest whole number)................. _____

SENTENCE RANGE DISPLAYED IS FOR A COMPLETED OFFENSE

FOR **ATTEMPT**, **SOLICITATION**, OR **CONSPIRACY** (RCW 9.94A.595, see page 54), THE SENTENCE RANGE **IS 75%** OF THE COMPLETED RANGE LISTED BELOW

Offender Score										
	0	**1**	**2**	**3**	**4**	**5**	**6**	**7**	**8**	**9+**
LEVEL XV	280m	291.5m	304m	316m	327.5m	339.5m	364m	394m	431.5m	479.5m
	240 - 320	250 - 333	261 - 347	271 - 361	281 - 374	291 - 388	312 - 416	338 - 450	370 - 493	411 - 548

✓ For gang-related felonies where the court found the offender involved a minor (RCW 9.94A.833), see page 227 for standard range adjustments.
✓ For deadly weapon enhancement, see page 233.
✓ For sentencing alternatives, see page 215.
✓ For community custody eligibility, see page 228.
✓ For any applicable enhancements other than deadly weapon enhancement, see page 224.
✓ Multiple current serious violent offenses shall have consecutive sentences imposed per the rules of RCW 9.94A.589(1)(b).

ADULT HISTORY:

Enter number of sex offense felony convictions .... _____ x 3 = _____

Enter number of serious violent felony convictions .... _____ x 3 = _____

Enter number of violent felony convictions .... _____ x 2 = _____

Enter number of nonviolent felony convictions .... _____ x 1 = _____

JUVENILE HISTORY:

Enter number of Murder 1, Murder 2, and Class A sex offense felony dispositions .... _____ x 3 = _____

OTHER CURRENT OFFENSES:

(Other current offenses that do not encompass the same conduct count in offender score)

Enter number of other sex offense felony convictions .... _____ x 3 = _____

Enter number of other violent felony convictions .... _____ x 2 = _____

Enter number of other nonviolent felony convictions .... _____ x 1 = _____

STATUS:

Was the offender on community custody on the date the current offense was committed?............ _____ + 1 = _____

Total the last column to get the **Offender Score** (Round down to the nearest whole number) .... _____

SENTENCE RANGE DISPLAYED IS FOR A COMPLETED OFFENSE

FOR **ATTEMPT**, **SOLICITATION**, OR **CONSPIRACY** (RCW 9.94A.595, see page 54), THE SENTENCE RANGE **IS 75%** OF THE COMPLETED RANGE LISTED BELOW

Offender Score									
0	**1**	**2**	**3**	**4**	**5**	**6**	**7**	**8**	**9+**
LEVEL XV 280m 240 - 320	291.5m 250 - 333	304m 261 - 347	316m 271 - 361	327.5m 281 - 374	339.5m 291 - 388	364m 312 - 416	394m 338 - 450	431.5m 370 - 493	479.5m 411 - 548

SEXUAL MOTIVATION ENHANCEMENT (Per Sexual Motivation Enhancement, page 226) .... _____

Low   to   High

STANDARD SENTENCE RANGE PLUS ENHANCEMENT.............. _____ ..... _____

✓ For gang-related felonies where the court found the offender involved a minor (RCW 9.94A.833), see page 227 for standard range adjustments.
✓ For deadly weapon enhancement, see page 233.
✓ For sentencing alternatives, see page 215.
✓ For community custody eligibility, see page 228.
✓ For any applicable enhancements other than deadly weapon enhancement, see page 224.
✓ If the offender is not a persistent offender and the current offense is either a completed offense or a criminal attempt under RCW 9A.28.020 that was committed on or after 9/1/2001, then the offender is subject to the requirements under RCW 9.94A.507.
✓ If the offender is not a persistent offender and has a prior conviction for an offense listed in RCW 9.94A.030(37)(b), then the sentence is subject to the requirements of RCW 9.94A.507.
✓ Multiple current serious violent offenses shall have consecutive sentences imposed per the rules of RCW 9.94A.589(1)(b).

Homicide by Watercraft while under the Influence of Intoxicating Liquor or any Drug

RCW 79A.60.050(1)(a)
CLASS A – VIOLENT
OFFENDER SCORING RCW 9.94A.525(12)

If it was found that this offense was committed with sexual motivation (RCW 9.94A.533(8)) on or after 7/1/2006, use the General Violent Offense with a Sexual Motivation Finding scoring form on page 244.

If the present conviction is for a felony domestic violence offense where domestic violence was plead and proven, use the General Violent Offense Where Domestic Violence Has Been Plead and Proven scoring form on page 242.

ADULT HISTORY:

Enter number of Homicide by Watercraft and Assault by Watercraft felony convictions .... _____ x 2 = _____

Enter number of Driving under the Influence of Intoxicating Liquor or any Drug and Actual Physical Control of a Vehicle while under the Influence of Intoxicating Liquor or any Drug and Operation of a Vessel while under the Influence of Intoxicating Liquor or any Drug convictions .... _____ x 1 = _____

Enter number of felony convictions .... _____ x 1 = _____

JUVENILE HISTORY:

Enter number of Murder 1, Murder 2, and Class A sex offense felony dispositions .... _____ x ½ = _____

OTHER CURRENT OFFENSES:

(Other current offenses that do not encompass the same conduct count in offender score)

Enter number of other Homicide by Watercraft and Assault by Watercraft felony convictions .... _____ x 2 = _____

Enter number of Driving under the Influence of Intoxicating Liquor or any Drug and Actual Physical Control of a Vehicle while under the Influence of Intoxicating Liquor or any Drug and Operation of a Vessel while under the Influence of Intoxicating Liquor or any Drug convictions .... _____ x 1 = _____

Enter number of other felony convictions .... _____ x 1 = _____

STATUS:

Was the offender on community custody on the date the current offense was committed? (if yes) _____ + 1 = _____

Total the last column to get the **Offender Score** (Round down to the nearest whole number)......................... _____

SENTENCE RANGE DISPLAYED IS FOR A COMPLETED OFFENSE

FOR **ATTEMPT**, **SOLICITATION**, OR **CONSPIRACY** (RCW 9.94A.595, see page 54), THE SENTENCE RANGE **IS 75%** OF THE COMPLETED RANGE LISTED BELOW

	Offender Score									
	0	**1**	**2**	**3**	**4**	**5**	**6**	**7**	**8**	**9+**
LEVEL IX	36m	42m	47.5m	53.5m	59.5m	66m	89.5m	101.5m	126m	150m
	31 - 41	36 - 48	41 - 54	46 - 61	51 - 68	57 - 75	77 - 102	87 - 116	108 - 144	129 - 171

✓ For gang-related felonies where the court found the offender involved a minor (RCW 9.94A.833), see page 227 for standard range adjustments.
✓ For deadly weapon enhancement, see page 233.
✓ For sentencing alternatives, see page 215.
✓ For community custody eligibility, see page 228.
✓ For any applicable enhancements other than deadly weapon enhancement, see page 224.

RCW 79A.60.050(1)(c)
CLASS A – VIOLENT
OFFENDER SCORING RCW 9.94A.525(12)

If it was found that this offense was committed with sexual motivation (RCW 9.94A.533(8)) on or after 7/1/2006, use the General Violent Offense with a Sexual Motivation Finding scoring form on page 244.

If the present conviction is for a felony domestic violence offense where domestic violence was plead and proven, use the General Violent Offense Where Domestic Violence Has Been Plead and Proven scoring form on page 242.

ADULT HISTORY:

Enter number of Homicide by Watercraft and Assault by Watercraft felony convictions .... _____ x 2 = _____

Enter number of Driving under the Influence of Intoxicating Liquor or any Drug and Actual Physical Control of a Vehicle while under the Influence of Intoxicating Liquor or any Drug and Operation of a Vessel while under the Influence of Intoxicating Liquor or any Drug convictions .... _____ x 1 = _____

Enter number of felony convictions .... _____ x 1 = _____

JUVENILE HISTORY:

Enter number of Murder 1, Murder 2, and Class A sex offense felony dispositions .... _____ x ½ = _____

OTHER CURRENT OFFENSES:

(Other current offenses that do not encompass the same conduct count in offender score)

Enter number of other Homicide by Watercraft and Assault by Watercraft felony convictions .... _____ x 2 = _____

Enter number of Driving under the Influence of Intoxicating Liquor or any Drug and Actual Physical Control of a Vehicle while under the Influence of Intoxicating Liquor or any Drug and Operation of a Vessel while under the Influence of Intoxicating Liquor or any Drug convictions .... _____ x 1 = _____

Enter number of other felony convictions .... _____ x 1 = _____

STATUS:

Was the offender on community custody on the date the current offense was committed? (if yes) _____ + 1 = _____

Total the last column to get the **Offender Score** (Round down to the nearest whole number).......................... _____

SENTENCE RANGE DISPLAYED IS FOR A COMPLETED OFFENSE

FOR **ATTEMPT**, **SOLICITATION**, OR **CONSPIRACY** (RCW 9.94A.595, see page 54), THE SENTENCE RANGE **IS 75%** OF THE COMPLETED RANGE LISTED BELOW

	Offender Score									
	0	**1**	**2**	**3**	**4**	**5**	**6**	**7**	**8**	**9+**
LEVEL VII	17.5m	24m	30m	36m	42m	47.5m	66m	78m	89.5m	101.5m
	15 - 20	21 - 27	26 - 34	31 - 41	36 - 48	41 - 54	57 - 75	67 - 89	77 - 102	87 - 116

✓ For gang-related felonies where the court found the offender involved a minor (RCW 9.94A.833), see page 227 for standard range adjustments.
✓ For deadly weapon enhancement, see page 233.
✓ For sentencing alternatives, see page 215.
✓ For community custody eligibility, see page 228.
✓ For any applicable enhancements other than deadly weapon enhancement, see page 224.

RCW 79A.60.050(1)(b)
CLASS A – VIOLENT
OFFENDER SCORING RCW 9.94A.525(12)

If it was found that this offense was committed with sexual motivation (RCW 9.94A.533(8)) on or after 7/1/2006, use the General Violent Offense with a Sexual Motivation Finding scoring form on page 244.

If the present conviction is for a felony domestic violence offense where domestic violence was plead and proven, use the General Violent Offense Where Domestic Violence Has Been Plead and Proven scoring form on page 242.

ADULT HISTORY:

Enter number of Homicide by Watercraft and Assault by Watercraft felony convictions .... _____ x 2 = _____

Enter number of Driving under the Influence of Intoxicating Liquor or any Drug and Actual Physical Control of a Vehicle while under the Influence of Intoxicating Liquor or any Drug and Operation of a Vessel while under the Influence of Intoxicating Liquor or any Drug convictions .... _____ x 1 = _____

Enter number of felony convictions .... _____ x 1 = _____

JUVENILE HISTORY:

Enter number of Murder 1, Murder 2, and Class A sex offense felony dispositions .... _____ x ½ = _____

OTHER CURRENT OFFENSES:

(Other current offenses that do not encompass the same conduct count in offender score)

Enter number of other Homicide by Watercraft and Assault by Watercraft felony convictions .... _____ x 2 = _____

Enter number of Driving under the Influence of Intoxicating Liquor or any Drug and Actual Physical Control of a Vehicle while under the Influence of Intoxicating Liquor or any Drug and Operation of a Vessel while under the Influence of Intoxicating Liquor or any Drug convictions .... _____ x 1 = _____

Enter number of other felony convictions .... _____ x 1 = _____

STATUS:

Was the offender on community custody on the date the current offense was committed? (if yes) _____ + 1 = _____

Total the last column to get the **Offender Score** (Round down to the nearest whole number) .... _____

SENTENCE RANGE DISPLAYED IS FOR A COMPLETED OFFENSE

FOR **ATTEMPT**, **SOLICITATION**, OR **CONSPIRACY** (RCW 9.94A.595, see page 54), THE SENTENCE RANGE **IS 75%** OF THE COMPLETED RANGE LISTED BELOW

	Offender Score									
	0	1	2	3	4	5	6	7	8	9+
LEVEL VIII	24m	30m	36m	42m	47.5m	53.5m	78m	89.5m	101.5m	126m
	21 - 27	26 - 34	31 - 41	36 - 48	41 - 54	46 - 61	67 - 89	77 - 102	87 - 116	108 - 144

✓ For gang-related felonies where the court found the offender involved a minor (RCW 9.94A.833), see page 227 for standard range adjustments.
✓ For deadly weapon enhancement, see page 233.
✓ For sentencing alternatives, see page 215.
✓ For community custody eligibility, see page 228.
✓ For any applicable enhancements other than deadly weapon enhancement, see page 224.

RCW 9.35.020(2)
CLASS B – NONVIOLENT/CRIMES AGAINST PERSONS
OFFENDER SCORING RCW 9.94A.525(7)

If it was found that this offense was committed with sexual motivation (RCW 9.94A.533(8)) on or after 7/1/2006, use the General Nonviolent Offense with a Sexual Motivation Finding scoring form on page 236.

If the present conviction is for a felony domestic violence offense where domestic violence was plead and proven, use the General Nonviolent Offense Where Domestic Violence Has Been Plead and Proven scoring form on page 234.

ADULT HISTORY:

Enter number of felony convictions .... _____ x 1 = _____

JUVENILE HISTORY:

Enter number of Murder 1, Murder 2, and Class A sex offense felony dispositions .... _____ x 1 = _____

OTHER CURRENT OFFENSES:

(Other current offenses that do not encompass the same conduct count in offender score)

Enter number of other felony convictions .... _____ x 1 = _____

STATUS:

Was the offender on community custody on the date the current offense was committed? (if yes) _____ + 1 = _____

Total the last column to get the **Offender Score** (Round down to the nearest whole number)......................... _____

SENTENCE RANGE DISPLAYED IS FOR A COMPLETED OFFENSE

FOR **ATTEMPT**, **SOLICITATION**, OR **CONSPIRACY** (RCW 9.94A.595, see page 54), THE SENTENCE RANGE **IS 75%** OF THE COMPLETED RANGE LISTED BELOW

	Offender Score									
	0	**1**	**2**	**3**	**4**	**5**	**6**	**7**	**8**	**9+**
LEVEL IV	6m	9m	13m	15m	17.5m	25.5m	38m	50m	61.5m	73.5m
	3 - 9	6 - 12	12+ - 14	13 - 17	15 - 20	22 - 29	33 - 43	43 - 57	53 - 70	63 - 84

✓ For gang-related felonies where the court found the offender involved a minor (RCW 9.94A.833), see page 227 for standard range adjustments.
✓ For deadly weapon enhancement, see page 233.
✓ For sentencing alternatives, see page 215.
✓ For community custody eligibility, see page 228.
✓ For any applicable enhancements other than deadly weapon enhancement, see page 224.

Identity Theft Second Degree
RCW 9.35.020(3)
CLASS C – NONVIOLENT/CRIMES AGAINST PERSONS
OFFENDER SCORING RCW 9.94A.525(7)

If it was found that this offense was committed with sexual motivation (RCW 9.94A.533(8)) on or after 7/1/2006, use the General Nonviolent Offense with a Sexual Motivation Finding scoring form on page 236.

If the present conviction is for a felony domestic violence offense where domestic violence was plead and proven, use the General Nonviolent Offense Where Domestic Violence Has Been Plead and Proven scoring form on page 234.

ADULT HISTORY:

Enter number of felony convictions .... _____ x 1 = _____

JUVENILE HISTORY:

Enter number of Murder 1, Murder 2, and Class A sex offense felony dispositions .... _____ x 1 = _____

OTHER CURRENT OFFENSES:

(Other current offenses that do not encompass the same conduct count in offender score)

Enter number of other felony convictions .... _____ x 1 = _____

STATUS:

Was the offender on community custody on the date the current offense was committed? (if yes) _____ + 1 = _____

Total the last column to get the **Offender Score** (Round down to the nearest whole number)......................... _____

SENTENCE RANGE

	Offender Score									
	0	1	2	3	4	5	6	7	8	9+
LEVEL II		4m	6m	8m	13m	16m	19.5m	25.5m	38m	50m
	0-90 days	2 - 6	3 - 9	4 - 12	12+ - 14	14 - 18	17 - 22	22 - 29	33 - 43	43 - 57

✓ For gang-related felonies where the court found the offender involved a minor (RCW 9.94A.833), see page 227 for standard range adjustment.
✓ For deadly weapon enhancement, see page 233.
✓ For sentencing alternatives, see page 215.
✓ For community custody eligibility, see page 228.
✓ For any applicable enhancements other than deadly weapon enhancement, see page 224.

RCW 9.35.010
CLASS C – NONVIOLENT
OFFENDER SCORING RCW 9.94A.525(7)

If it was found that this offense was committed with sexual motivation (RCW 9.94A.533(8)) on or after 7/1/2006, use the General Nonviolent Offense with a Sexual Motivation Finding scoring form on page 236.

If the present conviction is for a felony domestic violence offense where domestic violence was plead and proven, use the General Nonviolent Offense Where Domestic Violence Has Been Plead and Proven scoring form on page 234.

ADULT HISTORY:

Enter number of felony convictions .... _____ x 1 = _____

JUVENILE HISTORY:

Enter number of Murder 1, Murder 2, and Class A sex offense felony dispositions .... _____ x 1 = _____

OTHER CURRENT OFFENSES:

(Other current offenses that do not encompass the same conduct count in offender score)

Enter number of other felony convictions .... _____ x 1 = _____

STATUS:

Was the offender on community custody on the date the current offense was committed? (if yes) _____ + 1 = _____

Total the last column to get the **Offender Score** (Round down to the nearest whole number).......................... _____

SENTENCE RANGE

	Offender Score									
	0	**1**	**2**	**3**	**4**	**5**	**6**	**7**	**8**	**9+**
LEVEL II		4m	6m	8m	13m	16m	19.5m	25.5m	38m	50m
	0-90 days	2 - 6	3 - 9	4 - 12	12+ - 14	14 - 18	17 - 22	22 - 29	33 - 43	43 - 57

✓ For gang-related felonies where the court found the offender involved a minor (RCW 9.94A.833), see page 227 for standard range adjustment.
✓ For deadly weapon enhancement, see page 233.
✓ For sentencing alternatives, see page 215.
✓ For community custody eligibility, see page 228.
✓ For any applicable enhancements other than deadly weapon enhancement, see page 224.

Incest First Degree

RCW 9A.64.020(1)
CLASS B – NONVIOLENT/SEX/CRIMES AGAINST PERSONS
OFFENDER SCORING RCW 9.94A.525(17)

If the present conviction is for a felony domestic violence offense where domestic violence was plead and proven, use the General Nonviolent/Sex Offense Where Domestic Violence Has Been Plead and Proven scoring form on page 235.

ADULT HISTORY:

Enter number of sex offense felony convictions .... _____ x 3 = _____

Enter number of felony convictions .... _____ x 1 = _____

JUVENILE HISTORY:

Enter number of Class A sex offense felony dispositions .... _____ x 3 = _____

Enter number of Murder 1 and Murder 2 felony dispositions .... _____ x 1 = _____

OTHER CURRENT OFFENSES:

(Other current offenses that do not encompass the same conduct count in offender score)

Enter number of other sex offense felony convictions .... _____ x 3 = _____

Enter number of other felony convictions .... _____ x 1 = _____

STATUS:

Was the offender on community custody on the date the current offense was committed? (if yes) _____ + 1 = _____

Total the last column to get the **Offender Score** (Round down to the nearest whole number)......................... _____

SENTENCE RANGE DISPLAYED IS FOR A COMPLETED OFFENSE

FOR **ATTEMPT**, **SOLICITATION**, OR **CONSPIRACY** (RCW 9.94A.595, see page 54), THE SENTENCE RANGE **IS 75%** OF THE COMPLETED RANGE LISTED BELOW

	Offender Score									
	0	**1**	**2**	**3**	**4**	**5**	**6**	**7**	**8**	**9+**
LEVEL VI	13m	17.5m	24m	30m	36m	42m	53.5m	66m	78m	89.5m
	12+ - 14	15 - 20	21 - 27	26 - 34	31 - 41	36 - 48	46 - 61	57 - 75	67 - 89	77 - 102

- ✓ For gang-related felonies where the court found the offender involved a minor (RCW 9.94A.833), see page 227 for standard range adjustments.
- ✓ For deadly weapon enhancement, see page 233.
- ✓ For sentencing alternatives, see page 215.
- ✓ For community custody eligibility, see page 228.
- ✓ For any applicable enhancements other than deadly weapon enhancement, see page 224.
- ✓ If the offender is not a persistent offender and has a prior conviction for an offense listed in RCW 9.94A.030(37)(b), then the sentence is subject to the requirements of RCW 9.94A.507.

Incest Second Degree

RCW 9A.64.020(2)
CLASS C* – NONVIOLENT/SEX/CRIMES AGAINST PERSONS
OFFENDER SCORING RCW 9.94A.525(17)

If the present conviction is for a felony domestic violence offense where domestic violence was plead and proven, use the General Nonviolent/Sex Offense Where Domestic Violence Has Been Plead and Proven scoring form on page 235.

ADULT HISTORY:

    Enter number of sex offense felony convictions .... _____ x 3 = _____

    Enter number of felony convictions .... _____ x 1 = _____

JUVENILE HISTORY:

    Enter number of Class A sex offense felony dispositions .... _____ x 3 = _____

    Enter number of Murder 1 and Murder 2 felony dispositions .... _____ x 1 = _____

OTHER CURRENT OFFENSES:

(Other current offenses that do not encompass the same conduct count in offender score)

    Enter number of other sex offense felony convictions .... _____ x 3 = _____

    Enter number of other felony convictions .... _____ x 1 = _____

STATUS:

    Was the offender on community custody on the date the current offense was committed? (if yes) _____ + 1 = _____

Total the last column to get the **Offender Score** (Round down to the nearest whole number)......................... _____

SENTENCE RANGE

	Offender Score									
	0	**1**	**2**	**3**	**4**	**5**	**6**	**7**	**8**	**9+**
LEVEL V	9m	13m	15m	17.5m	25.5m	38m	47.5m	55.5m		
	6 - 12	12+ - 14	13 - 17	15 - 20	22 - 29	33 - 43	41 - 54	51 - 60*	60 - 60*	60 - 60*

    * Class C felony offenses have a statutory maximum sentence of 60 months, see RCW 9A.20.021.

✓   For gang-related felonies where the court found the offender involved a minor (RCW 9.94A.833), see page 227 for standard range adjustment.
✓   For deadly weapon enhancement, see page 233.
✓   For sentencing alternatives, see page 215.
✓   For community custody eligibility, see page 228.
✓   For any applicable enhancements other than deadly weapon enhancement, see page 224.
✓   If the offender is not a persistent offender and has a prior conviction for an offense listed in RCW 9.94A.030(37)(b), then the sentence is subject to the requirements of RCW 9.94A.507.

Indecent Exposure to a Person under Age 14, Subsequent Sex Offense Conviction

RCW 9A.88.010(2)(c)
CLASS C* – NONVIOLENT
OFFENDER SCORING RCW 9.94A.525(7)

If it was found that this offense was committed with sexual motivation (RCW 9.94A.533(8)) on or after 7/1/2006, use the General Nonviolent Offense with a Sexual Motivation Finding scoring form on page 236.

ADULT HISTORY:

  Enter number of felony convictions .... _____ x 1 = _____

JUVENILE HISTORY:

  Enter number of Murder 1, Murder 2, and Class A sex offense felony dispositions .... _____ x 1 = _____

OTHER CURRENT OFFENSES:

(Other current offenses that do not encompass the same conduct count in offender score)

  Enter number of other felony convictions .... _____ x 1 = _____

STATUS:

  Was the offender on community custody on the date the current offense was committed? (if yes) _____ + 1 = _____

Total the last column to get the **Offender Score** (Round down to the nearest whole number)......................... _____

SENTENCE RANGE

	Offender Score									
	0	**1**	**2**	**3**	**4**	**5**	**6**	**7**	**8**	**9+**
LEVEL IV	6m	9m	13m	15m	17.5m	25.5m	38m	50m	56.5m	
	3 - 9	6 - 12	12+ - 14	13 - 17	15 - 20	22 - 29	33 - 43	43 - 57	53 - 60*	60 - 60*

  * Class C felony offenses have a statutory maximum sentence of 60 months, see RCW 9A.20.021.

✓ For gang-related felonies where the court found the offender involved a minor (RCW 9.94A.833), see page 227 for standard range adjustment.
✓ For deadly weapon enhancement, see page 233.
✓ For sentencing alternatives, see page 215.
✓ For community custody eligibility, see page 228.
✓ For any applicable enhancements other than deadly weapon enhancement, see page 224.

Indecent Liberties with Forcible Compulsion, Completed or Attempt
RCW 9A.44.100(1)(a)
CLASS A – VIOLENT/SEX/CRIMES AGAINST PERSONS
ATTEMPT = CLASS A – VIOLENT/SEX
OFFENDER SCORING RCW 9.94A.525(17)

If the present conviction is for a felony domestic violence offense where domestic violence was plead and proven, use the General Violent/Sex Offense Where Domestic Violence Has Been Plead and Proven scoring form on page 243.

ADULT HISTORY:

Enter number of sex offense felony convictions .... _____ x 3 = _____

Enter number of serious violent and violent felony convictions .... _____ x 2 = _____

Enter number of nonviolent felony convictions .... _____ x 1 = _____

JUVENILE HISTORY:

Enter number of Class A sex offense felony dispositions .... _____ x 3 = _____

Enter number of Murder 1 and Murder 2 felony dispositions .... _____ x 2 = _____

OTHER CURRENT OFFENSES:

(Other current offenses that do not encompass the same conduct count in offender score)

Enter number of other sex offense felony convictions .... _____ x 3 = _____

Enter number of other serious violent and violent felony convictions .... _____ x 2 = _____

Enter number of other nonviolent felony convictions .... _____ x 1 = _____

STATUS:

Was the offender on community custody on the date the current offense was committed? (if yes) _____ + 1 = _____

Total the last column to get the **Offender Score** (Round down to the nearest whole number)......................... _____

SENTENCE RANGE DISPLAYED IS FOR A COMPLETED OFFENSE

FOR **ATTEMPT**, **SOLICITATION**, OR **CONSPIRACY** (RCW 9.94A.595, see page 54), THE SENTENCE RANGE **IS 75%** OF THE COMPLETED RANGE LISTED BELOW

	Offender Score									
	0	**1**	**2**	**3**	**4**	**5**	**6**	**7**	**8**	**9+**
LEVEL X	59.5m	66m	72m	78m	84m	89.5m	114m	126m	150m	173.5m
	51 - 68	57 - 75	62 - 82	67 - 89	72 - 96	77 - 102	98 - 130	108 - 144	129 - 171	149 - 198

✓ For gang-related felonies where the court found the offender involved a minor (RCW 9.94A.833), see page 227 for standard range adjustments.
✓ For deadly weapon enhancement, see page 233.
✓ For sentencing alternatives, see page 215.
✓ For community custody eligibility, see page 228.
✓ For any applicable enhancements other than deadly weapon enhancement, see page 224.
✓ If the offender is not a persistent offender and the current offense was committed on or after 9/1/2001, then the offender is subject to the requirements under RCW 9.94A.507.
✓ Per RCW 9.94A.507 (3)(c)(ii), excluding convictions for an attempt, the minimum term shall be either the maximum of the standard sentence range for the offense or 25 years, whichever is greater, for a finding that the victim was under the age of 15 at the time of the offense under RCW 9.94A.837 or found to be a person with a developmental disability or mental disorder, a frail elder or vulnerable adult at the time of the offense under RCW 9.94A.838.

Indecent Liberties with Forcible Compulsion, Solicitation or Conspiracy

RCW 9A.44.100(1)(a)
VIOLENT/SEX
SOLICITATION = CLASS A
CONSPIRACY = CLASS B*
OFFENDER SCORING RCW 9.94A.525(17)

If the present conviction is for a felony domestic violence offense where domestic violence was plead and proven, use the General Violent/Sex Offense Where Domestic Violence Has Been Plead and Proven scoring form on page 243.

ADULT HISTORY:

Enter number of sex offense felony convictions .... _____ x 3 = _____

Enter number of serious violent and violent felony convictions .... _____ x 2 = _____

Enter number of nonviolent felony convictions .... _____ x 1 = _____

JUVENILE HISTORY:

Enter number of Class A sex offense felony dispositions .... _____ x 3 = _____

Enter number of Murder 1 and Murder 2 felony dispositions .... _____ x 2 = _____

OTHER CURRENT OFFENSES:

(Other current offenses that do not encompass the same conduct count in offender score)

Enter number of other sex offense felony convictions .... _____ x 3 = _____

Enter number of other serious violent and violent felony convictions .... _____ x 2 = _____

Enter number of other nonviolent felony convictions .... _____ x 1 = _____

STATUS:

Was the offender on community custody on the date the current offense was committed? (if yes) _____ + 1 = _____

Total the last column to get the **Offender Score** (Round down to the nearest whole number) .... _____

SENTENCE RANGE DISPLAYED IS FOR A COMPLETED OFFENSE

FOR **ATTEMPT**, **SOLICITATION**, OR **CONSPIRACY** (RCW 9.94A.595, see page 54), THE SENTENCE RANGE **IS 75%** OF THE COMPLETED RANGE LISTED BELOW

Offender Score										
	0	**1**	**2**	**3**	**4**	**5**	**6**	**7**	**8**	**9+**
LEVEL X	59.5m	66m	72m	78m	84m	89.5m	114m	126m	150m	173.5m
	51 - 68	57 - 75	62 - 82	67 - 89	72 - 96	77 - 102	98 - 130	108 - 144	129 - 171	149 - 198

* Class B felony offenses have a statutory maximum sentence of 120 months, see RCW 9A.20.021.

✓ For gang-related felonies where the court found the offender involved a minor (RCW 9.94A.833), see page 227 for standard range adjustments.
✓ For deadly weapon enhancement, see page 233.
✓ For sentencing alternatives, see page 215.
✓ For community custody eligibility, see page 228.
✓ For any applicable enhancements other than deadly weapon enhancement, see page 224.
✓ If the offender is not a persistent offender and has a prior conviction for an offense listed in RCW 9.94A.030(37)(b), then the sentence is subject to the requirements of RCW 9.94A.507.

Indecent Liberties without Forcible Compulsion

RCW 9A.44.100(1)(b) and (c)
CLASS B – NONVIOLENT/SEX/CRIMES AGAINST PERSONS
OFFENDER SCORING RCW 9.94A.525(17)

If the present conviction is for a felony domestic violence offense where domestic violence was plead and proven, use the General Nonviolent/Sex Offense Where Domestic Violence Has Been Plead and Proven scoring form on page 235.

ADULT HISTORY:

Enter number of sex offense felony convictions .... _____ x 3 = _____

Enter number of nonviolent felony convictions .... _____ x 1 = _____

JUVENILE HISTORY:

Enter number of Class A sex offense felony dispositions .... _____ x 3 = _____

Enter number of Murder 1 and Murder 2 felony dispositions .... _____ x 1 = _____

OTHER CURRENT OFFENSES:

(Other current offenses that do not encompass the same conduct count in offender score)

Enter number of other sex offense felony convictions .... _____ x 3 = _____

Enter number of other nonviolent felony convictions .... _____ x 1 = _____

STATUS:

Was the offender on community custody on the date the current offense was committed? (if yes) _____ + 1 = _____

Total the last column to get the **Offender Score** (Round down to the nearest whole number).......................... _____

SENTENCE RANGE DISPLAYED IS FOR A COMPLETED OFFENSE

FOR **ATTEMPT**, **SOLICITATION**, OR **CONSPIRACY** (RCW 9.94A.595, see page 54), THE SENTENCE RANGE **IS 75%** OF THE COMPLETED RANGE LISTED BELOW

Offender Score										
	0	**1**	**2**	**3**	**4**	**5**	**6**	**7**	**8**	**9+**
LEVEL VII	17.5m	24m	30m	36m	42m	47.5m	66m	78m	89.5m	101.5m
	15 - 20	21 - 27	26 - 34	31 - 41	36 - 48	41 - 54	57 - 75	67 - 89	77 - 102	87 - 116

✓ For gang-related felonies where the court found the offender involved a minor (RCW 9.94A.833), see page 227 for standard range adjustments.
✓ For deadly weapon enhancement, see page 233.
✓ For sentencing alternatives, see page 215.
✓ For community custody eligibility, see page 228.
✓ For any applicable enhancements other than deadly weapon enhancement, see page 224.
✓ If the offender is not a persistent offender and has a prior conviction for an offense listed in RCW 9.94A.030(37)(b), then the sentence is subject to the requirements of RCW 9.94A.507.

RCW 9A.82.070
CLASS C* – NONVIOLENT
OFFENDER SCORING RCW 9.94A.525(7)

If it was found that this offense was committed with sexual motivation (RCW 9.94A.533(8)) on or after 7/1/2006, use the General Nonviolent Offense with a Sexual Motivation Finding scoring form on page 236.

If the present conviction is for a felony domestic violence offense where domestic violence was plead and proven, use the General Nonviolent Offense Where Domestic Violence Has Been Plead and Proven scoring form on page 234.

ADULT HISTORY:

Enter number of felony convictions .... _____ x 1 = _____

JUVENILE HISTORY:

Enter number of Murder 1, Murder 2, and Class A sex offense felony dispositions .... _____ x 1 = _____

OTHER CURRENT OFFENSES:

(Other current offenses that do not encompass the same conduct count in offender score)

Enter number of other felony convictions .... _____ x 1 = _____

STATUS:

Was the offender on community custody on the date the current offense was committed? (if yes) _____ + 1 = _____

Total the last column to get the **Offender Score** (Round down to the nearest whole number)

SENTENCE RANGE

	Offender Score									
	0	**1**	**2**	**3**	**4**	**5**	**6**	**7**	**8**	**9+**
LEVEL IV	6m	9m	13m	15m	17.5m	25.5m	38m	50m	56.5m	
	3 - 9	6 - 12	12+ - 14	13 - 17	15 - 20	22 - 29	33 - 43	43 - 57	53 - 60*	60 - 60*

* Class C felony offenses have a statutory maximum sentence of 60 months, see RCW 9A.20.021.

✓ For gang-related felonies where the court found the offender involved a minor (RCW 9.94A.833), see page 227 for standard range adjustment.
✓ For deadly weapon enhancement, see page 233.
✓ For sentencing alternatives, see page 215.
✓ For community custody eligibility, see page 228.
✓ For any applicable enhancements other than deadly weapon enhancement, see page 224.

RCW 9A.72.160
CLASS B – NONVIOLENT
OFFENDER SCORING RCW 9.94A.525(7)

If it was found that this offense was committed with sexual motivation (RCW 9.94A.533(8)) on or after 7/1/2006, use the General Nonviolent Offense with a Sexual Motivation Finding scoring form on page 236.

If the present conviction is for a felony domestic violence offense where domestic violence was plead and proven, use the General Nonviolent Offense Where Domestic Violence Has Been Plead and Proven scoring form on page 234.

ADULT HISTORY:

Enter number of felony convictions .... _____ x 1 = _____

JUVENILE HISTORY:

Enter number of Murder 1, Murder 2, and Class A sex offense felony dispositions .... _____ x 1 = _____

OTHER CURRENT OFFENSES:

(Other current offenses that do not encompass the same conduct count in offender score)

Enter number of other felony convictions .... _____ x 1 = _____

STATUS:

Was the offender on community custody on the date the current offense was committed? (if yes) _____ + 1 = _____

Total the last column to get the **Offender Score** (Round down to the nearest whole number).......................... _____

SENTENCE RANGE DISPLAYED IS FOR A COMPLETED OFFENSE

FOR **ATTEMPT**, **SOLICITATION**, OR **CONSPIRACY** (RCW 9.94A.595, see page 54), THE SENTENCE RANGE **IS 75%** OF THE COMPLETED RANGE LISTED BELOW

Offender Score									
0	**1**	**2**	**3**	**4**	**5**	**6**	**7**	**8**	**9+**

	0	1	2	3	4	5	6	7	8	9+
LEVEL VI	13m	17.5m	24m	30m	36m	42m	53.5m	66m	78m	89.5m
	12+ - 14	15 - 20	21 - 27	26 - 34	31 - 41	36 - 48	46 - 61	57 - 75	67 - 89	77 - 102

✓ For gang-related felonies where the court found the offender involved a minor (RCW 9.94A.833), see page 227 for standard range adjustments.
✓ For deadly weapon enhancement, see page 233.
✓ For sentencing alternatives, see page 215.
✓ For community custody eligibility, see page 228.
✓ For any applicable enhancements other than deadly weapon enhancement, see page 224.

RCW 9A.72.130 & RCW 9A.72.110
CLASS B – NONVIOLENT/CRIMES AGAINST PERSONS
OFFENDER SCORING RCW 9.94A.525(7)

If it was found that this offense was committed with sexual motivation (RCW 9.94A.533(8)) on or after 7/1/2006, use the General Nonviolent Offense with a Sexual Motivation Finding scoring form on page 236.

If the present conviction is for a felony domestic violence offense where domestic violence was plead and proven, use the General Nonviolent Offense Where Domestic Violence Has Been Plead and Proven scoring form on page 234.

ADULT HISTORY:

Enter number of felony convictions .... _____ x 1 = _____

JUVENILE HISTORY:

Enter number of Murder 1, Murder 2, and Class A sex offense felony dispositions .... _____ x 1 = _____

OTHER CURRENT OFFENSES:

(Other current offenses that do not encompass the same conduct count in offender score)

Enter number of other felony convictions .... _____ x 1 = _____

STATUS:

Was the offender on community custody on the date the current offense was committed? (if yes) _____ + 1 = _____

Total the last column to get the **Offender Score** (Round down to the nearest whole number)......................... _____

SENTENCE RANGE DISPLAYED IS FOR A COMPLETED OFFENSE

FOR **ATTEMPT**, **SOLICITATION**, OR **CONSPIRACY** (RCW 9.94A.595, see page 54), THE SENTENCE RANGE **IS 75%** OF THE COMPLETED RANGE LISTED BELOW

	Offender Score									
	0	**1**	**2**	**3**	**4**	**5**	**6**	**7**	**8**	**9+**
LEVEL VI	13m	17.5m	24m	30m	36m	42m	53.5m	66m	78m	89.5m
	12+ - 14	15 - 20	21 - 27	26 - 34	31 - 41	36 - 48	46 - 61	57 - 75	67 - 89	77 - 102

✓ For gang-related felonies where the court found the offender involved a minor (RCW 9.94A.833), see page 227 for standard range adjustments.
✓ For deadly weapon enhancement, see page 233.
✓ For sentencing alternatives, see page 215.
✓ For community custody eligibility, see page 228.
✓ For any applicable enhancements other than deadly weapon enhancement, see page 224.

Intimidating a Public Servant
RCW 9A.76.180
CLASS B – NONVIOLENT/CRIMES AGAINST PERSONS
OFFENDER SCORING RCW 9.94A.525(7)

If it was found that this offense was committed with sexual motivation (RCW 9.94A.533(8)) on or after 7/1/2006, use the General Nonviolent Offense with a Sexual Motivation Finding scoring form on page 236.

If the present conviction is for a felony domestic violence offense where domestic violence was plead and proven, use the General Nonviolent Offense Where Domestic Violence Has Been Plead and Proven scoring form on page 234.

ADULT HISTORY:

Enter number of felony convictions .... _____ x 1 = _____

JUVENILE HISTORY:

Enter number of Murder 1, Murder 2, and Class A sex offense felony dispositions .... _____ x 1 = _____

OTHER CURRENT OFFENSES:

(Other current offenses that do not encompass the same conduct count in offender score)

Enter number of other felony convictions .... _____ x 1 = _____

STATUS:

Was the offender on community custody on the date the current offense was committed? (if yes) _____ + 1 = _____

Total the last column to get the **Offender Score** (Round down to the nearest whole number)......................... _____

SENTENCE RANGE DISPLAYED IS FOR A COMPLETED OFFENSE

FOR **ATTEMPT**, **SOLICITATION**, OR **CONSPIRACY** (RCW 9.94A.595, see page 54), THE SENTENCE RANGE **IS 75%** OF THE COMPLETED RANGE LISTED BELOW

Offender Score										
	0	**1**	**2**	**3**	**4**	**5**	**6**	**7**	**8**	**9+**
LEVEL III	2m	5m	8m	11m	14m	19.5m	25.5m	38m	50m	59.5m
	1 - 3	3 - 8	4 - 12	9 - 12	12+ - 16	17 - 22	22 - 29	33 - 43	43 - 57	51 - 68

✓ For gang-related felonies where the court found the offender involved a minor (RCW 9.94A.833), see page 227 for standard range adjustments.
✓ For deadly weapon enhancement, see page 233.
✓ For sentencing alternatives, see page 215.
✓ For community custody eligibility, see page 228.
✓ For any applicable enhancements other than deadly weapon enhancement, see page 224.

RCW 9A.76.140
CLASS B – NONVIOLENT
OFFENDER SCORING RCW 9.94A.525(7)

If it was found that this offense was committed with sexual motivation (RCW 9.94A.533(8)) on or after 7/1/2006, use the General Nonviolent Offense with a Sexual Motivation Finding scoring form on page 236.

If the present conviction is for a felony domestic violence offense where domestic violence was plead and proven, use the General Nonviolent Offense Where Domestic Violence Has Been Plead and Proven scoring form on page 234.

ADULT HISTORY:

    Enter number of felony convictions .... _____ x 1 = _____

JUVENILE HISTORY:

    Enter number of Murder 1, Murder 2, and Class A sex offense felony dispositions .... _____ x 1 = _____

OTHER CURRENT OFFENSES:

(Other current offenses that do not encompass the same conduct count in offender score)

    Enter number of other felony convictions .... _____ x 1 = _____

STATUS:

    Was the offender on community custody on the date the current offense was committed? (if yes) _____ + 1 = _____

Total the last column to get the **Offender Score** (Round down to the nearest whole number)......................... _____

SENTENCE RANGE DISPLAYED IS FOR A COMPLETED OFFENSE

FOR **ATTEMPT**, **SOLICITATION**, OR **CONSPIRACY** (RCW 9.94A.595, see page 54), THE SENTENCE RANGE **IS 75%** OF THE COMPLETED RANGE LISTED BELOW

Offender Score										
	0	**1**	**2**	**3**	**4**	**5**	**6**	**7**	**8**	**9+**
LEVEL VII	17.5m	24m	30m	36m	42m	47.5m	66m	78m	89.5m	101.5m
	15 - 20	21 - 27	26 - 34	31 - 41	36 - 48	41 - 54	57 - 75	67 - 89	77 - 102	87 - 116

✓   For gang-related felonies where the court found the offender involved a minor (RCW 9.94A.833), see page 227 for standard range adjustments.
✓   For deadly weapon enhancement, see page 233.
✓   For sentencing alternatives, see page 215.
✓   For community custody eligibility, see page 228.
✓   For any applicable enhancements other than deadly weapon enhancement, see page 224.

RCW 9A.76.150
CLASS C* – NONVIOLENT
OFFENDER SCORING RCW 9.94A.525(7)

If it was found that this offense was committed with sexual motivation (RCW 9.94A.533(8)) on or after 7/1/2006, use the General Nonviolent Offense with a Sexual Motivation Finding scoring form on page 236.

If the present conviction is for a felony domestic violence offense where domestic violence was plead and proven, use the General Nonviolent Offense Where Domestic Violence Has Been Plead and Proven scoring form on page 234.

ADULT HISTORY:

Enter number of felony convictions .... _____ x 1 = _____

JUVENILE HISTORY:

Enter number of Murder 1, Murder 2, and Class A sex offense felony dispositions .... _____ x 1 = _____

OTHER CURRENT OFFENSES:

(Other current offenses that do not encompass the same conduct count in offender score)

Enter number of other felony convictions .... _____ x 1 = _____

STATUS:

Was the offender on community custody on the date the current offense was committed? (if yes) _____ + 1 = _____

Total the last column to get the **Offender Score** (Round down to the nearest whole number)........................... _____

SENTENCE RANGE

	Offender Score									
	0	**1**	**2**	**3**	**4**	**5**	**6**	**7**	**8**	**9+**
LEVEL III	2m	5m	8m	11m	14m	19.5m	25.5m	38m	50m	55.5m
	1 - 3	3 - 8	4 - 12	9 - 12	12+ - 16	17 - 22	22 - 29	33 - 43	43 - 57	51 - 60*

* Class C felony offenses have a statutory maximum sentence of 60 months, see RCW 9A.20.021.

✓ For gang-related felonies where the court found the offender involved a minor (RCW 9.94A.833), see page 227 for standard range adjustment.
✓ For deadly weapon enhancement, see page 233.
✓ For sentencing alternatives, see page 215.
✓ For community custody eligibility, see page 228.
✓ For any applicable enhancements other than deadly weapon enhancement, see page 224.

Involving a Minor in Drug Dealing
RCW 69.50.4015
CLASS C* – NONVIOLENT/DRUG
OFFENDER SCORING RCW 9.94A.525(13)

If it was found that this offense was committed with sexual motivation (RCW 9.94A.533(8)) on or after 7/1/2006, use the General Drug Offense with a Sexual Motivation Finding scoring form on page 238.

If the present conviction is for a felony domestic violence offense where domestic violence was plead and proven, use the General Drug Offense Where Domestic Violence Has Been Plead and Proven scoring form on page 237.

ADULT HISTORY:

Does the offender have a prior sex or serious violent offense in history?

.... **YES,** Enter number of felony drug convictions _____ x 3 = _____

.... **NO,** Enter number of felony drug convictions _____ x 1 = _____

Enter number of felony convictions .... _____ x 1 = _____

JUVENILE HISTORY:

Enter number of Murder 1, Murder 2, and Class A sex offense felony dispositions .... _____ x 1 = _____

OTHER CURRENT OFFENSES:

(Other current offenses that do not encompass the same conduct count in offender score)

Does the offender have other prior sex or serious violent offense in history?

.... **YES,** Enter number of other felony drug convictions _____ x 3 = _____

.... **NO,** Enter number of other felony drug convictions _____ x 1 = _____

Enter number of other felony convictions .... _____ x 1 = _____

STATUS:

Was the offender on community custody on the date the current offense was committed? (if yes) _____ + 1 = _____

Total the last column to get the **Offender Score** (Round down to the nearest whole number)........................ _____

SENTENCE RANGE – DRUG

	Offender Score		
	0 to 2	3 to 5	6 to 9+
LEVEL III	55.5m 51 - 60*	60 - 60*	60 - 60*

* Class C felony offenses have a statutory maximum sentence of 60 months, see RCW 9A.20.021.

✓ For gang-related felonies where the court found the offender involved a minor (RCW 9.94A.833), see page 227 for standard range adjustments.
✓ Per RCW 9.94A.518, any felony offense under chapter 69.50 RCW with a deadly weapon special verdict under RCW 9.94A.602 becomes a level III offense.
✓ For deadly weapon enhancement, see page 233.
✓ For sentencing alternatives, see page 215.
✓ For community custody eligibility, see page 228.
✓ For any applicable enhancements other than deadly weapon enhancement, see page 224.
✓ Per RCW 69.50.408, the statutory maximum for a subsequent conviction under chapter 69.50 RCW is 120 months.

Kidnapping First Degree

RCW 9A.40.020
CLASS A – SERIOUS VIOLENT/CRIMES AGAINST PERSONS
OFFENDER SCORING RCW 9.94A.525(9)

If the present conviction is for a felony domestic violence offense where domestic violence was plead and proven, use the General Serious Violent Offense Where Domestic Violence Has Been Plead and Proven scoring form on page 239.

ADULT HISTORY:

Enter number of serious violent felony convictions .... _____ x 3 = _____

Enter number of violent felony convictions .... _____ x 2 = _____

Enter number of nonviolent felony convictions .... _____ x 1 = _____

JUVENILE HISTORY:

Enter number of Murder 1, Murder 2, and Serious Violent sex offense felony dispositions .... _____ x 3 = _____

Enter number of Class A sex offense (not Serious Violent) felony dispositions .... _____ x 2 = _____

OTHER CURRENT OFFENSES:

(Other current offenses that do not encompass the same conduct count in offender score)

Enter number of other violent felony convictions .... _____ x 2 = _____

Enter number of other nonviolent felony convictions .... _____ x 1 = _____

STATUS:

Was the offender on community custody on the date the current offense was committed?............ _____ + 1 = _____

Total the last column to get the **Offender Score** (Round down to the nearest whole number) .... _____

SENTENCE RANGE DISPLAYED IS FOR A COMPLETED OFFENSE

FOR **ATTEMPT**, **SOLICITATION**, OR **CONSPIRACY** (RCW 9.94A.595, see page 54), THE SENTENCE RANGE **IS 75%** OF THE COMPLETED RANGE LISTED BELOW

Offender Score										
	0	**1**	**2**	**3**	**4**	**5**	**6**	**7**	**8**	**9+**
LEVEL X	59.5m	66m	72m	78m	84m	89.5m	114m	126m	150m	173.5m
	51 - 68	57 - 75	62 - 82	67 - 89	72 - 96	77 - 102	98 - 130	108 - 144	129 - 171	149 - 198

✓ For gang-related felonies where the court found the offender involved a minor (RCW 9.94A.833), see page 227 for standard range adjustments.
✓ For deadly weapon enhancement, see page 233.
✓ For sentencing alternatives, see page 215.
✓ For community custody eligibility, see page 228.
✓ For any applicable enhancements other than deadly weapon enhancement, see page 224.
✓ Multiple current serious violent offenses shall have consecutive sentences imposed per the rules of RCW 9.94A.589(1)(b).

Kidnapping First Degree with a Finding of Sexual Motivation, Completed or Attempt
RCW 9A.40.020
CLASS A – SERIOUS VIOLENT/SEX/CRIMES AGAINST PERSONS
ATTEMPT = CLASS B* – SERIOUS VIOLENT/SEX
OFFENDER SCORING RCW 9.94A.525(17)

ADULT HISTORY:

    Enter number of sex offense felony convictions .... _____ x 3 = _____

    Enter number of serious violent felony convictions .... _____ x 3 = _____

    Enter number of violent felony convictions .... _____ x 2 = _____

    Enter number of nonviolent felony convictions .... _____ x 1 = _____

JUVENILE HISTORY:

    Enter number of Murder 1, Murder 2, and Class A sex offense felony dispositions .... _____ x 3 = _____

OTHER CURRENT OFFENSES:

(Other current offenses that do not encompass the same conduct count in offender score)

    Enter number of other sex offense felony convictions .... _____ x 3 = _____

    Enter number of other violent felony convictions .... _____ x 2 = _____

    Enter number of other nonviolent felony convictions .... _____ x 1 = _____

STATUS:

    Was the offender on community custody on the date the current offense was committed? .... _____ + 1 = _____

Total the last column to get the **Offender Score** (Round down to the nearest whole number).................. _____

SENTENCE RANGE DISPLAYED IS FOR A COMPLETED OFFENSE

FOR **ATTEMPT**, **SOLICITATION**, OR **CONSPIRACY** (RCW 9.94A.595, see page 54), THE SENTENCE RANGE **IS 75%** OF THE COMPLETED RANGE LISTED BELOW

Offender Score										
	0	**1**	**2**	**3**	**4**	**5**	**6**	**7**	**8**	**9+**
LEVEL X	59.5m	66m	72m	78m	84m	89.5m	114m	126m	150m	173.5m
	51 - 68	57 - 75	62 - 82	67 - 89	72 - 96	77 - 102	98 - 130	108 - 144	129 - 171	149 - 198

SEXUAL MOTIVATION ENHANCEMENT (Per Sexual Motivation Enhancement, page 226).................... _____

                                          Low   to   High

STANDARD SENTENCE RANGE PLUS ENHANCEMENT .... _____ ..... _____

* Class B felony offenses have a statutory maximum sentence of 120 months, see RCW 9A.20.021.

✓ For gang-related felonies where the court found the offender involved a minor (RCW 9.94A.833), see page 227 for standard range adjustments.
✓ For deadly weapon enhancement, see page 233.
✓ For sentencing alternatives, see page 215.
✓ For community custody eligibility, see page 228.
✓ For any applicable enhancements other than deadly weapon enhancement, see page 224.
✓ Multiple current serious violent offenses shall have consecutive sentences imposed per the rules of RCW 9.94A.589(1)(b).
✓ If the offender is not a persistent offender and the current offense was committed on or after 9/1/2001, then the offender is subject to the requirements under RCW 9.94A.507.
✓ Per RCW 9.94A.507(3)(c)(ii), excluding convictions for an attempt, the minimum term shall be either the maximum of the standard sentence range for the offense or 25 years, whichever is greater, for a finding that the victim was under the age of 15 at the time of the offense under RCW 9.94A.837 or found to be a person with a development disability or mental disorder, or a frail elder or vulnerable adult at the time of the offense under RCW 9.94A.838.

Kidnapping First Degree with a Finding of Sexual Motivation, Solicitation or Conspiracy

RCW 9A.40.020
SERIOUS VIOLENT/SEX
SOLICITATION/CONSPIRACY = CLASS B*
OFFENDER SCORING RCW 9.94A.525(17)

ADULT HISTORY:

Enter number of sex offense felony convictions .... _____ x 3 = _____

Enter number of serious violent felony convictions .... _____ x 3 = _____

Enter number of violent felony convictions .... _____ x 2 = _____

Enter number of nonviolent felony convictions .... _____ x 1 = _____

JUVENILE HISTORY:

Enter number of Murder 1, Murder 2, and Class A sex offense felony dispositions .... _____ x 3 = _____

OTHER CURRENT OFFENSES:

(Other current offenses that do not encompass the same conduct count in offender score)

Enter number of other sex offense felony convictions .... _____ x 3 = _____

Enter number of other violent felony convictions .... _____ x 2 = _____

Enter number of other nonviolent felony convictions .... _____ x 1 = _____

STATUS:

Was the offender on community custody on the date the current offense was committed?............ _____ + 1 = _____

Total the last column to get the **Offender Score** (Round down to the nearest whole number) .... _____

SENTENCE RANGE DISPLAYED IS FOR A COMPLETED OFFENSE

FOR **ATTEMPT**, **SOLICITATION**, OR **CONSPIRACY** (RCW 9.94A.595, see page 54), THE SENTENCE RANGE **IS 75%** OF THE COMPLETED RANGE LISTED BELOW

	Offender Score									
	0	**1**	**2**	**3**	**4**	**5**	**6**	**7**	**8**	**9+**
LEVEL X	59.5m	66m	72m	78m	84m	89.5m	114m	114m		
	51 - 68	57 - 75	62 - 82	67 - 89	72 - 96	77 - 102	98 - 130	108 - 120*	120 - 120*	120 - 120*

SEXUAL MOTIVATION ENHANCEMENT (Per Sexual Motivation Enhancement, page 226) .... _____

Low   to   High

STANDARD SENTENCE RANGE PLUS ENHANCEMENT.............. _____ ..... _____

* Class B felony offenses have a statutory maximum sentence of 120 months, see RCW 9A.20.021.

✓ For gang-related felonies where the court found the offender involved a minor (RCW 9.94A.833), see page 227 for standard range adjustments.
✓ For deadly weapon enhancement, see page 233.
✓ For sentencing alternatives, see page 215.
✓ For community custody eligibility, see page 228.
✓ For any applicable enhancements other than deadly weapon enhancement, see page 224.
✓ Multiple current serious violent offenses shall have consecutive sentences imposed per the rules of RCW 9.94A.589(1)(b).
✓ If the offender is not a persistent offender and has a prior conviction for an offense listed in RCW 9.94A.030(37)(b), then the sentence is subject to the requirements of RCW 9.94A.507.

Kidnapping Second Degree

RCW 9A.40.030(3)(a)
CLASS B – VIOLENT/CRIMES AGAINST PERSONS
OFFENDER SCORING RCW 9.94A.525(8)

If the present conviction is for a felony domestic violence offense where domestic violence was plead and proven, use the General Violent Offense Where Domestic Violence Has Been Plead and Proven scoring form on page 242.

ADULT HISTORY:

Enter number of serious violent and violent felony convictions .... _____ x 2 = _____

Enter number of nonviolent felony convictions .... _____ x 1 = _____

JUVENILE HISTORY:

Enter number of Murder 1, Murder 2, and Class A sex offense felony dispositions .... _____ x 2 = _____

OTHER CURRENT OFFENSES:

(Other current offenses that do not encompass the same conduct count in offender score)

Enter number of other serious violent and violent felony convictions .... _____ x 2 = _____

Enter number of other nonviolent felony convictions .... _____ x 1 = _____

STATUS:

Was the offender on community custody on the date the current offense was committed? (if yes) _____ + 1 = _____

Total the last column to get the **Offender Score** (Round down to the nearest whole number).......................... _____

SENTENCE RANGE DISPLAYED IS FOR A COMPLETED OFFENSE

FOR **ATTEMPT**, **SOLICITATION**, OR **CONSPIRACY** (RCW 9.94A.595, see page 54), THE SENTENCE RANGE **IS 75%** OF THE COMPLETED RANGE LISTED BELOW

Offender Score									
0	**1**	**2**	**3**	**4**	**5**	**6**	**7**	**8**	**9+**
9m	13m	15m	17.5m	25.5m	38m	47.5m	59.5m	72m	84m
6 - 12	12+ - 14	13 - 17	15 - 20	22 - 29	33 - 43	41 - 54	51 - 68	62 - 82	72 - 96

LEVEL V

✓ For gang-related felonies where the court found the offender involved a minor (RCW 9.94A.833), see page 227 for standard range adjustments.
✓ For deadly weapon enhancement, see page 233.
✓ For sentencing alternatives, see page 215.
✓ For community custody eligibility, see page 228.
✓ For any applicable enhancements other than deadly weapon enhancement, see page 224.

Kidnapping Second Degree with a Finding of Sexual Motivation, Completed or Attempt

RCW 9A.40.030(3)(b)
CLASS A – VIOLENT/SEX/CRIMES AGAINST PERSONS
ATTEMPT = CLASS B - VIOLENT/SEX
OFFENDER SCORING RCW 9.94A.525(17)

ADULT HISTORY:

Enter number of sex offense felony convictions .... _____ x 3 = _____

Enter number of serious violent and violent felony convictions .... _____ x 2 = _____

Enter number of nonviolent felony convictions .... _____ x 1 = _____

JUVENILE HISTORY:

Enter number of Class A sex offense felony dispositions .... _____ x 3 = _____

Enter number of Murder 1 and Murder 2 felony dispositions .... _____ x 2 = _____

OTHER CURRENT OFFENSES:

(Other current offenses that do not encompass the same conduct count in offender score)

Enter number of other sex offense felony dispositions .... _____ x 3 = _____

Enter number of other serious violent and violent felony convictions .... _____ x 2 = _____

Enter number of other nonviolent felony convictions .... _____ x 1 = _____

STATUS:

Was the offender on community custody on the date the current offense was committed? (if yes) _____ + 1 = _____

Total the last column to get the **Offender Score** (Round down to the nearest whole number)......................... _____

SENTENCE RANGE DISPLAYED IS FOR A COMPLETED OFFENSE

FOR **ATTEMPT**, **SOLICITATION**, OR **CONSPIRACY** (RCW 9.94A.595, see page 54), THE SENTENCE RANGE **IS 75%** OF THE COMPLETED RANGE LISTED BELOW

	Offender Score									
	0	**1**	**2**	**3**	**4**	**5**	**6**	**7**	**8**	**9+**
LEVEL V	9m	13m	15m	17.5m	25.5m	38m	47.5m	59.5m	72m	84m
	6 - 12	12+ - 14	13 - 17	15 - 20	22 - 29	33 - 43	41 - 54	51 - 68	62 - 82	72 - 96

SEXUAL MOTIVATION ENHANCEMENT (Per Sexual Motivation Enhancement, page 226) .... _____

                                              Low   to   High

STANDARD SENTENCE RANGE PLUS ENHANCEMENT.............. _____ ..... _____

✓ For gang-related felonies where the court found the offender involved a minor (RCW 9.94A.833), see page 227 for standard range adjustments.
✓ For deadly weapon enhancement, see page 233.
✓ For sentencing alternatives, see page 215.
✓ For community custody eligibility, see page 228.
✓ For any applicable enhancements other than deadly weapon enhancement, see page 224.
✓ If the offender is not a persistent offender and the <u>current</u> offense was committed on or after 9/1/2001, then the offender is subject to the requirements under RCW 9.94A.507.

Kidnapping Second Degree with a Finding of Sexual Motivation, Solicitation or Conspiracy

RCW 9A.40.030(3)(b)
VIOLENT/SEX
SOLICITATION/CONSPIRACY = CLASS B
OFFENDER SCORING RCW 9.94A.525(17)

ADULT HISTORY:

Enter number of sex offense felony convictions .... _____ x 3 = _____

Enter number of serious violent and violent felony convictions .... _____ x 2 = _____

Enter number of nonviolent felony convictions .... _____ x 1 = _____

JUVENILE HISTORY:

Enter number of Class A sex offense felony dispositions .... _____ x 3 = _____

Enter number of Murder 1 and Murder 2 felony dispositions .... _____ x 2 = _____

OTHER CURRENT OFFENSES:

(Other current offenses that do not encompass the same conduct count in offender score)

Enter number of other sex offense felony dispositions .... _____ x 3 = _____

Enter number of other serious violent and violent felony convictions .... _____ x 2 = _____

Enter number of other nonviolent felony convictions .... _____ x 1 = _____

STATUS:

Was the offender on community custody on the date the current offense was committed? (if yes) _____ + 1 = _____

Total the last column to get the **Offender Score** (Round down to the nearest whole number) .... _____

SENTENCE RANGE DISPLAYED IS FOR A COMPLETED OFFENSE

FOR **ATTEMPT**, **SOLICITATION**, OR **CONSPIRACY** (RCW 9.94A.595, see page 54), THE SENTENCE RANGE **IS 75%** OF THE COMPLETED RANGE LISTED BELOW

Offender Score										
	0	**1**	**2**	**3**	**4**	**5**	**6**	**7**	**8**	**9+**
LEVEL V	9m	13m	15m	17.5m	25.5m	38m	47.5m	59.5m	72m	84m
	6 - 12	12+ - 14	13 - 17	15 - 20	22 - 29	33 - 43	41 - 54	51 - 68	62 - 82	72 - 96

SEXUAL MOTIVATION ENHANCEMENT (Per Sexual Motivation Enhancement, page 226) .... _____

Low   to   High

STANDARD SENTENCE RANGE PLUS ENHANCEMENT .... _____ ..... _____

✓ For gang-related felonies where the court found the offender involved a minor (RCW 9.94A.833), see page 227 for standard range adjustments.
✓ For deadly weapon enhancement, see page 233.
✓ For sentencing alternatives, see page 215.
✓ For community custody eligibility, see page 228.
✓ For any applicable enhancements other than deadly weapon enhancement, see page 224.
✓ If the offender is not a persistent offender and has a prior conviction for an offense listed in RCW 9.94A.030(37)(b), then the sentence is subject to the requirements of RCW 9.94A.507.

Leading Organized Crime - Inciting Criminal Profiteering
RCW 9A.82.060(1)(b)
CLASS B* – NONVIOLENT
OFFENDER SCORING RCW 9.94A.525(7)

If it was found that this offense was committed with sexual motivation (RCW 9.94A.533(8)) on or after 7/1/2006, use the General Nonviolent Offense with a Sexual Motivation Finding scoring form on page 236.

If the present conviction is for a felony domestic violence offense where domestic violence was plead and proven, use the General Nonviolent Offense Where Domestic Violence Has Been Plead and Proven scoring form on page 234.

ADULT HISTORY:

Enter number of felony convictions .... _____ x 1 = _____

JUVENILE HISTORY:

Enter number of Murder 1, Murder 2, and Class A sex offense felony dispositions .... _____ x 1 = _____

OTHER CURRENT OFFENSES:

(Other current offenses that do not encompass the same conduct count in offender score)

Enter number of other felony convictions .... _____ x 1 = _____

STATUS:

Was the offender on community custody on the date the current offense was committed? (if yes) _____ + 1 = _____

Total the last column to get the **Offender Score** (Round down to the nearest whole number)......................... _____

SENTENCE RANGE DISPLAYED IS FOR A COMPLETED OFFENSE

FOR **ATTEMPT**, **SOLICITATION**, OR **CONSPIRACY** (RCW 9.94A.595, see page 54), THE SENTENCE RANGE **IS 75%** OF THE COMPLETED RANGE LISTED BELOW

	Offender Score									
	0	1	2	3	4	5	6	7	8	9+
LEVEL IX	36m	42m	47.5m	53.5m	59.5m	66m	89.5m	101.5m	114m	
	31 - 41	36 - 48	41 - 54	46 - 61	51 - 68	57 - 75	77 - 102	87 - 116	108 - 120*	120- 120*

* Class B felony offenses have a statutory maximum sentence of 120 months, see RCW 9A.20.021.

✓ For gang-related felonies where the court found the offender involved a minor (RCW 9.94A.833), see page 227 for standard range adjustments.
✓ For deadly weapon enhancement, see page 233.
✓ For sentencing alternatives, see page 215.
✓ For community custody eligibility, see page 228.
✓ For any applicable enhancements other than deadly weapon enhancement, see page 224.

RCW 9A.82.060(1)(a)
CLASS A – VIOLENT
OFFENDER SCORING RCW 9.94A.525(8)

If it was found that this offense was committed with sexual motivation (RCW 9.94A.533(8)) on or after 7/1/2006, use the General Violent Offense with a Sexual Motivation Finding scoring form on page 244.

If the present conviction is for a felony domestic violence offense where domestic violence was plead and proven, use the General Violent Offense Where Domestic Violence Has Been Plead and Proven scoring form on page 242.

ADULT HISTORY:

Enter number of serious violent and violent felony convictions .... _____ x 2 = _____

Enter number of nonviolent felony convictions .... _____ x 1 = _____

JUVENILE HISTORY:

Enter number of Murder 1, Murder 2, and Class A sex offense felony dispositions .... _____ x 2 = _____

OTHER CURRENT OFFENSES:

(Other current offenses that do not encompass the same conduct count in offender score)

Enter number of Murder 1, Murder 2, and Class A sex offense felony dispositions .... _____ x 2 = _____

STATUS:

Was the offender on community custody on the date the current offense was committed? (if yes) _____ + 1 = _____

Total the last column to get the **Offender Score** (Round down to the nearest whole number) .... _____

SENTENCE RANGE DISPLAYED IS FOR A COMPLETED OFFENSE

FOR **ATTEMPT**, **SOLICITATION**, OR **CONSPIRACY** (RCW 9.94A.595, see page 54), THE SENTENCE RANGE **IS 75%** OF THE COMPLETED RANGE LISTED BELOW

Offender Score										
	0	**1**	**2**	**3**	**4**	**5**	**6**	**7**	**8**	**9+**
LEVEL X	59.5m	66m	72m	78m	84m	89.5m	114m	126m	150m	173.5m
	51 - 68	57 - 75	62 - 82	67 - 89	72 - 96	77 - 102	98 - 130	108 - 144	129 - 171	149 - 198

✓ For gang-related felonies where the court found the offender involved a minor (RCW 9.94A.833), see page 227 for standard range adjustments.
✓ For deadly weapon enhancement, see page 233.
✓ For sentencing alternatives, see page 215.
✓ For community custody eligibility, see page 228.
✓ For any applicable enhancements other than deadly weapon enhancement, see page 224.

RCW 69.50.402
CLASS C* – NONVIOLENT/DRUG
OFFENDER SCORING RCW 9.94A.525(13)

If it was found that this offense was committed with sexual motivation (RCW 9.94A.533(8)) on or after 7/1/2006, use the General Drug Offense with a Sexual Motivation Finding scoring form on page 238.

If the present conviction is for a felony domestic violence offense where domestic violence was plead and proven, use the General Drug Offense Where Domestic Violence Has Been Plead and Proven scoring form on page 237.

ADULT HISTORY:

Does the offender have a prior sex or serious violent offense in history?

.... **YES,** Enter number of felony drug convictions _____ x 3 = _____

.... **NO,** Enter number of felony drug convictions _____ x 1 = _____

Enter number of felony convictions .... _____ x 1 = _____

JUVENILE HISTORY:

Enter number of Murder 1, Murder 2, and Class A sex offense felony dispositions .... _____ x 1 = _____

OTHER CURRENT OFFENSES:

(Other current offenses that do not encompass the same conduct count in offender score)

Does the offender have other prior sex or serious violent offense in history?

.... **YES,** Enter number of other felony drug convictions _____ x 3 = _____

.... **NO,** Enter number of other felony drug convictions _____ x 1 = _____

Enter number of other felony convictions .... _____ x 1 = _____

STATUS:

Was the offender on community custody on the date the current offense was committed? (if yes) _____ + 1 = _____

Total the last column to get the **Offender Score** (Round down to the nearest whole number)......................... _____

SENTENCE RANGE – DRUG

	Offender Score		
	0 to 2	**3 to 5**	**6 to 9+**
LEVEL II	16m 12+ - 20	22m 20+ - 24*	24*

* Per RCW 69.50.402, any person who violates this section may be imprisoned for not more than 24 months

✓   For gang-related felonies where the court found the offender involved a minor (RCW 9.94A.833), see page 227 for standard range adjustments.
✓   Per RCW 9.94A.518, any felony offense under chapter 69.50 RCW with a deadly weapon special verdict under RCW 9.94A.602 becomes a level III offense.
✓   For deadly weapon enhancement, see page 233.
✓   For sentencing alternatives, see page 215.
✓   For community custody eligibility, see page 228.
✓   For any applicable enhancements other than deadly weapon enhancement, see page 224.
✓   Per RCW 69.50.408, the statutory maximum for a subsequent conviction under chapter 69.50 RCW is 48 months.

RCW 69.50.402
CLASS C* – NONVIOLENT/DRUG
OFFENDER SCORING RCW 9.94A.525(13)

If it was found that this offense was committed with sexual motivation (RCW 9.94A.533(8)) on or after 7/1/2006, use the General Drug Offense with a Sexual Motivation Finding scoring form on page 238.

If the present conviction is for a felony domestic violence offense where domestic violence was plead and proven, use the General Drug Offense Where Domestic Violence Has Been Plead and Proven scoring form on page 237.

ADULT HISTORY:

Does the offender have a prior sex or serious violent offense in history?

.... **YES,** Enter number of felony drug convictions _____ x 3 = _____

.... **NO,** Enter number of felony drug convictions _____ x 1 = _____

Enter number of felony convictions .... _____ x 1 = _____

JUVENILE HISTORY:

Enter number of Murder 1, Murder 2, and Class A sex offense felony dispositions .... _____ x 1 = _____

OTHER CURRENT OFFENSES:

(Other current offenses that do not encompass the same conduct count in offender score)

Does the offender have other prior sex or serious violent offense in history?

.... **YES,** Enter number of other felony drug convictions _____ x 3 = _____

.... **NO,** Enter number of other felony drug convictions _____ x 1 = _____

Enter number of other felony convictions .... _____ x 1 = _____

STATUS:

Was the offender on community custody on the date the current offense was committed? (if yes) _____ + 1 = _____

Total the last column to get the **Offender Score** (Round down to the nearest whole number)........................ _____

SENTENCE RANGE – DRUG

	Offender Score		
	0 to 2	**3 to 5**	**6 to 9+**
LEVEL II	16m	34m	
	12+ - 20	20+ - 48*	48*

* Per RCW 69.50.408, the statutory maximum for a subsequent conviction under chapter 69.50 RCW is 48 months.

✓ For gang-related felonies where the court found the offender involved a minor (RCW 9.94A.833), see page 227 for standard range adjustments.
✓ Per RCW 9.94A.518, any felony offense under chapter 69.50 RCW with a deadly weapon special verdict under RCW 9.94A.602 becomes a level III offense.
✓ For deadly weapon enhancement, see page 233.
✓ For sentencing alternatives, see page 215.
✓ For community custody eligibility, see page 228.
✓ For any applicable enhancements other than deadly weapon enhancement, see page 224.

RCW 70.74.280(1)
CLASS A – VIOLENT
OFFENDER SCORING RCW 9.94A.525(8)

If it was found that this offense was committed with sexual motivation (RCW 9.94A.533(8)) on or after 7/1/2006, use the General Violent Offense with a Sexual Motivation Finding scoring form on page 244.

If the present conviction is for a felony domestic violence offense where domestic violence was plead and proven, use the General Violent Offense Where Domestic Violence Has Been Plead and Proven scoring form on page 242.

ADULT HISTORY:

Enter number of serious violent and violent felony convictions .... _____ x 2 = _____

Enter number of nonviolent felony convictions .... _____ x 1 = _____

JUVENILE HISTORY:

Enter number of Murder 1, Murder 2, and Class A sex offense felony dispositions .... _____ x 2 = _____

OTHER CURRENT OFFENSES:

(Other current offenses that do not encompass the same conduct count in offender score)

Enter number of other serious violent and violent felony convictions .... _____ x 2 = _____

Enter number of other nonviolent felony convictions .... _____ x 1 = _____

STATUS:

Was the offender on community custody on the date the current offense was committed? (if yes) _____ + 1 = _____

Total the last column to get the **Offender Score** (Round down to the nearest whole number)......................... _____

SENTENCE RANGE DISPLAYED IS FOR A COMPLETED OFFENSE

FOR **ATTEMPT**, **SOLICITATION**, OR **CONSPIRACY** (RCW 9.94A.595, see page 54), THE SENTENCE RANGE **IS 75%** OF THE COMPLETED RANGE LISTED BELOW

	Offender Score									
	0	**1**	**2**	**3**	**4**	**5**	**6**	**7**	**8**	**9+**
LEVEL XV	280m	291.5m	304m	316m	327.5m	339.5m	364m	394m	431.5m	479.5m
	240 - 320	250 - 333	261 - 347	271 - 361	281 - 374	291 - 388	312 - 416	338 - 450	370 - 493	411 - 548

✓ For gang-related felonies where the court found the offender involved a minor (RCW 9.94A.833), see page 227 for standard range adjustments.
✓ For deadly weapon enhancement, see page 233.
✓ For sentencing alternatives, see page 215.
✓ For community custody eligibility, see page 228.
✓ For any applicable enhancements other than deadly weapon enhancement, see page 224.

Malicious Explosion of a Substance Second Degree

RCW 70.74.280(2)
CLASS A – VIOLENT
OFFENDER SCORING RCW 9.94A.525(8)

If it was found that this offense was committed with sexual motivation (RCW 9.94A.533(8)) on or after 7/1/2006, use the General Violent Offense with a Sexual Motivation Finding scoring form on page 244.

If the present conviction is for a felony domestic violence offense where domestic violence was plead and proven, use the General Violent Offense Where Domestic Violence Has Been Plead and Proven scoring form on page 242.

ADULT HISTORY:

Enter number of serious violent and violent felony convictions .... _____ x 2 = _____

Enter number of nonviolent felony convictions .... _____ x 1 = _____

JUVENILE HISTORY:

Enter number of Murder 1, Murder 2, and Class A sex offense felony dispositions .... _____ x 2 = _____

OTHER CURRENT OFFENSES:

(Other current offenses that do not encompass the same conduct count in offender score)

Enter number of other serious violent and violent felony convictions .... _____ x 2 = _____

Enter number of other nonviolent felony convictions .... _____ x 1 = _____

STATUS:

Was the offender on community custody on the date the current offense was committed? (if yes) _____ + 1 = _____

Total the last column to get the **Offender Score** (Round down to the nearest whole number)......................... _____

SENTENCE RANGE DISPLAYED IS FOR A COMPLETED OFFENSE

FOR **ATTEMPT**, **SOLICITATION**, OR **CONSPIRACY** (RCW 9.94A.595, see page 54), THE SENTENCE RANGE **IS 75%** OF THE COMPLETED RANGE LISTED BELOW

	Offender Score									
	0	1	2	3	4	5	6	7	8	9+
LEVEL XIII	143.5m	156m	168m	179.5m	192m	204m	227.5m	252m	299.5m	347.5m
	123 - 164	134 - 178	144 - 192	154 - 205	165 - 219	175 - 233	195 - 260	216 - 288	257 - 342	298 - 397

✓ For gang-related felonies where the court found the offender involved a minor (RCW 9.94A.833), see page 227 for standard range adjustments.
✓ For deadly weapon enhancement, see page 233.
✓ For sentencing alternatives, see page 215.
✓ For community custody eligibility, see page 228.
✓ For any applicable enhancements other than deadly weapon enhancement, see page 224.

RCW 70.74.280(3)
CLASS B* – NONVIOLENT
OFFENDER SCORING RCW 9.94A.525(7)

If it was found that this offense was committed with sexual motivation (RCW 9.94A.533(8)) on or after 7/1/2006, use the General Nonviolent Offense with a Sexual Motivation Finding scoring form on page 236.

If the present conviction is for a felony domestic violence offense where domestic violence was plead and proven, use the General Nonviolent Offense Where Domestic Violence Has Been Plead and Proven scoring form on page 234.

ADULT HISTORY:

Enter number of felony convictions .... _____ x 1 = _____

JUVENILE HISTORY:

Enter number of Murder 1, Murder 2, and Class A sex offense felony dispositions .... _____ x 1 = _____

OTHER CURRENT OFFENSES:

(Other current offenses that do not encompass the same conduct count in offender score)

Enter number of other felony convictions .... _____ x 1 = _____

STATUS:

Was the offender on community custody on the date the current offense was committed? (if yes) _____ + 1 = _____

Total the last column to get the **Offender Score** (Round down to the nearest whole number)......................... _____

SENTENCE RANGE DISPLAYED IS FOR A COMPLETED OFFENSE

FOR **ATTEMPT**, **SOLICITATION**, OR **CONSPIRACY** (RCW 9.94A.595, see page 54), THE SENTENCE RANGE **IS 75%** OF THE COMPLETED RANGE LISTED BELOW

	Offender Score									
	0	1	2	3	4	5	6	7	8	9+
LEVEL X	59.5m	66m	72m	78m	84m	89.5m	109m	114m		
	51 - 68	57 - 75	62 - 82	67 - 89	72 - 96	77 - 102	98 - 120*	108 - 120*	120 - 120*	120 - 120*

* Class B felony offenses have a statutory maximum sentence of 120 months, see RCW 9A.20.021.

✓ For gang-related felonies where the court found the offender involved a minor (RCW 9.94A.833), see page 227 for standard range adjustments.
✓ For deadly weapon enhancement, see page 233.
✓ For sentencing alternatives, see page 215.
✓ For community custody eligibility, see page 228.
✓ For any applicable enhancements other than deadly weapon enhancement, see page 224.

RCW 81.60.070
CLASS B – NONVIOLENT
OFFENDER SCORING RCW 9.94A.525(7)

If it was found that this offense was committed with sexual motivation (RCW 9.94A.533(8)) on or after 7/1/2006, use the General Nonviolent Offense with a Sexual Motivation Finding scoring form on page 236.

If the present conviction is for a felony domestic violence offense where domestic violence was plead and proven, use the General Nonviolent Offense Where Domestic Violence Has Been Plead and Proven scoring form on page 234.

ADULT HISTORY:

Enter number of felony convictions .... _____ x 1 = _____

JUVENILE HISTORY:

Enter number of Murder 1, Murder 2, and Class A sex offense felony dispositions .... _____ x 1 = _____

OTHER CURRENT OFFENSES:

(Other current offenses that do not encompass the same conduct count in offender score)

Enter number of other felony convictions .... _____ x 1 = _____

STATUS:

Was the offender on community custody on the date the current offense was committed? (if yes) _____ + 1 = _____

Total the last column to get the **Offender Score** (Round down to the nearest whole number)......................... _____

SENTENCE RANGE DISPLAYED IS FOR A COMPLETED OFFENSE

FOR **ATTEMPT**, **SOLICITATION**, OR **CONSPIRACY** (RCW 9.94A.595, see page 54), THE SENTENCE RANGE **IS 75%** OF THE COMPLETED RANGE LISTED BELOW

Offender Score									
0	**1**	**2**	**3**	**4**	**5**	**6**	**7**	**8**	**9+**
2m	5m	8m	11m	14m	19.5m	25.5m	38m	50m	59.5m
1 - 3	3 - 8	4 - 12	9 - 12	12+ - 16	17 - 22	22 - 29	33 - 43	43 - 57	51 - 68

(row label: **LEVEL III**)

✓ For gang-related felonies where the court found the offender involved a minor (RCW 9.94A.833), see page 227 for standard range adjustments.
✓ For deadly weapon enhancement, see page 233.
✓ For sentencing alternatives, see page 215.
✓ For community custody eligibility, see page 228.
✓ For any applicable enhancements other than deadly weapon enhancement, see page 224.

Malicious Mischief First Degree

RCW 9A.48.070
CLASS B – NONVIOLENT
OFFENDER SCORING RCW 9.94A.525(7)

If it was found that this offense was committed with sexual motivation (RCW 9.94A.533(8)) on or after 7/1/2006, use the General Nonviolent Offense with a Sexual Motivation Finding scoring form on page 236.

If the present conviction is for a felony domestic violence offense where domestic violence was plead and proven, use the General Nonviolent Offense Where Domestic Violence Has Been Plead and Proven scoring form on page 234.

ADULT HISTORY:

Enter number of felony convictions .... _____ x 1 = _____

JUVENILE HISTORY:

Enter number of Murder 1, Murder 2, and Class A sex offense felony dispositions .... _____ x 1 = _____

OTHER CURRENT OFFENSES:

(Other current offenses that do not encompass the same conduct count in offender score)

Enter number of other felony convictions .... _____ x 1 = _____

STATUS:

Was the offender on community custody on the date the current offense was committed? (if yes) _____ + 1 = _____

Total the last column to get the **Offender Score** (Round down to the nearest whole number).......................... _____

SENTENCE RANGE DISPLAYED IS FOR A COMPLETED OFFENSE

FOR **ATTEMPT**, **SOLICITATION**, OR **CONSPIRACY** (RCW 9.94A.595, see page 54), THE SENTENCE RANGE **IS 75%** OF THE COMPLETED RANGE LISTED BELOW

		Offender Score								
		0	1	2	3	4	5	6	7	8	9+
LEVEL II			4m	6m	8m	13m	16m	19.5m	25.5m	38m	50m
	0-90 days	2 - 6	3 - 9	4 - 12	12+ - 14	14 - 18	17 - 22	22 - 29	33 - 43	43 - 57

✓ For gang-related felonies where the court found the offender involved a minor (RCW 9.94A.833), see page 227 for standard range adjustments.
✓ For deadly weapon enhancement, see page 233.
✓ For sentencing alternatives, see page 215.
✓ For community custody eligibility, see page 228.
✓ For any applicable enhancements other than deadly weapon enhancement, see page 224.

RCW 9A.48.080
CLASS C – NONVIOLENT
OFFENDER SCORING RCW 9.94A.525(7)

If it was found that this offense was committed with sexual motivation (RCW 9.94A.533(8)) on or after 7/1/2006, use the General Nonviolent Offense with a Sexual Motivation Finding scoring form on page 236.

If the present conviction is for a felony domestic violence offense where domestic violence was plead and proven, use the General Nonviolent Offense Where Domestic Violence Has Been Plead and Proven scoring form on page 234.

ADULT HISTORY:

　　Enter number of felony convictions .... _____ x 1 = _____

JUVENILE HISTORY:

　　Enter number of Murder 1, Murder 2, and Class A sex offense felony dispositions .... _____ x 1 = _____

OTHER CURRENT OFFENSES:

(Other current offenses that do not encompass the same conduct count in offender score)

　　Enter number of other felony convictions .... _____ x 1 = _____

STATUS:

　　Was the offender on community custody on the date the current offense was committed? (if yes) _____ + 1 = _____

Total the last column to get the **Offender Score** (Round down to the nearest whole number)........................ _____

SENTENCE RANGE

	Offender Score									
	0	**1**	**2**	**3**	**4**	**5**	**6**	**7**	**8**	**9+**
LEVEL I	0-60 days	0-90 days	3m 2 - 5	4m 2 - 6	5.5m 3 - 8	8m 4 - 12	13m 12+ - 14	16m 14 - 18	19.5m 17 - 22	25.5m 22 - 29

✓　For gang-related felonies where the court found the offender involved a minor (RCW 9.94A.833), see page 227 for standard range adjustment.
✓　For deadly weapon enhancement, see page 233.
✓　For sentencing alternatives, see page 215.
✓　For community custody eligibility, see page 228.
✓　For any applicable enhancements other than deadly weapon enhancement, see page 224.

Malicious Placement of an Explosive First Degree

RCW 70.74.270(1)
CLASS A – VIOLENT
OFFENDER SCORING RCW 9.94A.525(8)

If it was found that this offense was committed with sexual motivation (RCW 9.94A.533(8)) on or after 7/1/2006, use the General Violent Offense with a Sexual Motivation Finding scoring form on page 244.

If the present conviction is for a felony domestic violence offense where domestic violence was plead and proven, use the General Violent Offense Where Domestic Violence Has Been Plead and Proven scoring form on page 242.

ADULT HISTORY:

    Enter number of serious violent and violent felony convictions .... _____ x 2 = _____

    Enter number of nonviolent felony convictions .... _____ x 1 = _____

JUVENILE HISTORY:

    Enter number of Murder 1, Murder 2, and Class A sex offense felony dispositions .... _____ x 2 = _____

OTHER CURRENT OFFENSES:

(Other current offenses that do not encompass the same conduct count in offender score)

    Enter number of other serious violent and violent felony convictions .... _____ x 2 = _____

    Enter number of other nonviolent felony convictions .... _____ x 1 = _____

STATUS:

    Was the offender on community custody on the date the current offense was committed? (if yes) _____ + 1 = _____

Total the last column to get the **Offender Score** (Round down to the nearest whole number).......................... _____

SENTENCE RANGE DISPLAYED IS FOR A COMPLETED OFFENSE

FOR **ATTEMPT**, **SOLICITATION**, OR **CONSPIRACY** (RCW 9.94A.595, see page 54), THE SENTENCE RANGE **IS 75%** OF THE COMPLETED RANGE LISTED BELOW

	Offender Score									
	0	**1**	**2**	**3**	**4**	**5**	**6**	**7**	**8**	**9+**
LEVEL XIII	143.5m	156m	168m	179.5m	192m	204m	227.5m	252m	299.5m	347.5m
	123 - 164	134 - 178	144 - 192	154 - 205	165 - 219	175 - 233	195 - 260	216 - 288	257 - 342	298 - 397

✓   For gang-related felonies where the court found the offender involved a minor (RCW 9.94A.833), see page 227 for standard range adjustments.
✓   For deadly weapon enhancement, see page 233.
✓   For sentencing alternatives, see page 215.
✓   For community custody eligibility, see page 228.
✓   For any applicable enhancements other than deadly weapon enhancement, see page 224.

RCW 70.74.270(2)
CLASS B* – NONVIOLENT
OFFENDER SCORING RCW 9.94A.525(7)

If it was found that this offense was committed with sexual motivation (RCW 9.94A.533(8)) on or after 7/1/2006, use the General Nonviolent Offense with a Sexual Motivation Finding scoring form on page 236.

If the present conviction is for a felony domestic violence offense where domestic violence was plead and proven, use the General Nonviolent Offense Where Domestic Violence Has Been Plead and Proven scoring form on page 234.

ADULT HISTORY:

    Enter number of felony convictions .... _____ x 1 = _____

JUVENILE HISTORY:

    Enter number of Murder 1, Murder 2, and Class A sex offense felony dispositions .... _____ x 1 = _____

OTHER CURRENT OFFENSES:

(Other current offenses that do not encompass the same conduct count in offender score)

    Enter number of other felony convictions .... _____ x 1 = _____

STATUS:

    Was the offender on community custody on the date the current offense was committed? (if yes) _____ + 1 = _____

Total the last column to get the **Offender Score** (Round down to the nearest whole number)......................... _____

SENTENCE RANGE DISPLAYED IS FOR A COMPLETED OFFENSE

FOR **ATTEMPT**, **SOLICITATION**, OR **CONSPIRACY** (RCW 9.94A.595, see page 54), THE SENTENCE RANGE **IS 75%** OF THE COMPLETED RANGE LISTED BELOW

	Offender Score									
	0	**1**	**2**	**3**	**4**	**5**	**6**	**7**	**8**	**9+**
LEVEL IX	36m	42m	47.5m	53.5m	59.5m	66m	89.5m	101.5m	114m	
	31 - 41	36 - 48	41 - 54	46 - 61	51 - 68	57 - 75	77 - 102	87 - 116	108 - 120*	120 - 120*

    * Class B felony offenses have a statutory maximum sentence of 120 months, see RCW 9A.20.021.

✓   For gang-related felonies where the court found the offender involved a minor (RCW 9.94A.833), see page 227 for standard range adjustments.
✓   For deadly weapon enhancement, see page 233.
✓   For sentencing alternatives, see page 215.
✓   For community custody eligibility, see page 228.
✓   For any applicable enhancements other than deadly weapon enhancement, see page 224.

Malicious Placement of an Explosive Third Degree
RCW 70.74.270(3)
CLASS B – NONVIOLENT
OFFENDER SCORING RCW 9.94A.525(7)

If it was found that this offense was committed with sexual motivation (RCW 9.94A.533(8)) on or after 7/1/2006, use the General Nonviolent Offense with a Sexual Motivation Finding scoring form on page 236.

If the present conviction is for a felony domestic violence offense where domestic violence was plead and proven, use the General Nonviolent Offense Where Domestic Violence Has Been Plead and Proven scoring form on page 234.

ADULT HISTORY:

Enter number of felony convictions .... _____ x 1 = _____

JUVENILE HISTORY:

Enter number of Murder 1, Murder 2, and Class A sex offense felony dispositions .... _____ x 1 = _____

OTHER CURRENT OFFENSES:

(Other current offenses that do not encompass the same conduct count in offender score)

Enter number of other felony convictions .... _____ x 1 = _____

STATUS:

Was the offender on community custody on the date the current offense was committed? (if yes) _____ + 1 = _____

Total the last column to get the **Offender Score** (Round down to the nearest whole number)........................... _____

SENTENCE RANGE DISPLAYED IS FOR A COMPLETED OFFENSE

FOR **ATTEMPT**, **SOLICITATION**, OR **CONSPIRACY** (RCW 9.94A.595, see page 54), THE SENTENCE RANGE **IS 75%** OF THE COMPLETED RANGE LISTED BELOW

	Offender Score									
	0	**1**	**2**	**3**	**4**	**5**	**6**	**7**	**8**	**9+**
LEVEL VII	17.5m	24m	30m	36m	42m	47.5m	66m	78m	89.5m	101.5m
	15 - 20	21 - 27	26 - 34	31 - 41	36 - 48	41 - 54	57 - 75	67 - 89	77 - 102	87 - 116

✓ For gang-related felonies where the court found the offender involved a minor (RCW 9.94A.833), see page 227 for standard range adjustments.
✓ For deadly weapon enhancement, see page 233.
✓ For sentencing alternatives, see page 215.
✓ For community custody eligibility, see page 228.
✓ For any applicable enhancements other than deadly weapon enhancement, see page 224.

Malicious Placement of an Imitation Device First Degree

RCW 70.74.272(1)(a)
CLASS B* – NONVIOLENT
OFFENDER SCORING RCW 9.94A.525(7)

If it was found that this offense was committed with sexual motivation (RCW 9.94A.533(8)) on or after 7/1/2006, use the General Nonviolent Offense with a Sexual Motivation Finding scoring form on page 236.

If the present conviction is for a felony domestic violence offense where domestic violence was plead and proven, use the General Nonviolent Offense Where Domestic Violence Has Been Plead and Proven scoring form on page 234.

ADULT HISTORY:

Enter number of felony convictions .... _____ x 1 = _____

JUVENILE HISTORY:

Enter number of Murder 1, Murder 2, and Class A sex offense felony dispositions .... _____ x 1 = _____

OTHER CURRENT OFFENSES:

(Other current offenses that do not encompass the same conduct count in offender score)

Enter number of other felony convictions .... _____ x 1 = _____

STATUS:

Was the offender on community custody on the date the current offense was committed? (if yes) _____ + 1 = _____

Total the last column to get the **Offender Score** (Round down to the nearest whole number)......................... _____

SENTENCE RANGE DISPLAYED IS FOR A COMPLETED OFFENSE

FOR **ATTEMPT**, **SOLICITATION**, OR **CONSPIRACY** (RCW 9.94A.595, see page 54), THE SENTENCE RANGE **IS 75%** OF THE COMPLETED RANGE LISTED BELOW

	Offender Score									
	0	1	2	3	4	5	6	7	8	9+
LEVEL XII	106.5m	111m	115.5m							
	93 - 120*	102 - 120*	111 - 120*	120 - 120*	120 - 120*	120 - 120*	120 - 120*	120 - 120*	120 - 120*	120 - 120*

* Class B felony offenses have a statutory maximum sentence of 120 months, see RCW 9A.20.021.

✓ For gang-related felonies where the court found the offender involved a minor (RCW 9.94A.833), see page 227 for standard range adjustments.
✓ For deadly weapon enhancement, see page 233.
✓ For sentencing alternatives, see page 215.
✓ For community custody eligibility, see page 228.
✓ For any applicable enhancements other than deadly weapon enhancement, see page 224.

Malicious Placement of an Imitation Device Second Degree
RCW 70.74.272(1)(b)
CLASS C* – NONVIOLENT
OFFENDER SCORING RCW 9.94A.525(7)

If it was found that this offense was committed with sexual motivation (RCW 9.94A.533(8)) on or after 7/1/2006, use the General Nonviolent Offense with a Sexual Motivation Finding scoring form on page 236.

If the present conviction is for a felony domestic violence offense where domestic violence was plead and proven, use the General Nonviolent Offense Where Domestic Violence Has Been Plead and Proven scoring form on page 234.

ADULT HISTORY:

Enter number of felony convictions .... _____ x 1 = _____

JUVENILE HISTORY:

Enter number of Murder 1, Murder 2, and Class A sex offense felony dispositions .... _____ x 1 = _____

OTHER CURRENT OFFENSES:

(Other current offenses that do not encompass the same conduct count in offender score)

Enter number of other felony convictions .... _____ x 1 = _____

STATUS:

Was the offender on community custody on the date the current offense was committed? (if yes) _____ + 1 = _____

Total the last column to get the **Offender Score** (Round down to the nearest whole number).......................... _____

SENTENCE RANGE

	Offender Score									
	0	**1**	**2**	**3**	**4**	**5**	**6**	**7**	**8**	**9+**
LEVEL VI	13m	17.5m	24m	30m	36m	42m	53m	58.5m		
	12+ - 14	15 - 20	21 - 27	26 - 34	31 - 41	36 - 48	46 - 60*	57 - 60*	60 - 60*	60 - 60*

* Class C felony offenses have a statutory maximum sentence of 60 months, see RCW 9A.20.021.

✓ For gang-related felonies where the court found the offender involved a minor (RCW 9.94A.833), see page 227 for standard range adjustment.
✓ For deadly weapon enhancement, see page 233.
✓ For sentencing alternatives, see page 215.
✓ For community custody eligibility, see page 228.
✓ For any applicable enhancements other than deadly weapon enhancement, see page 224.

RCW 9A.32.060
CLASS A – SERIOUS VIOLENT/CRIMES AGAINST PERSONS
OFFENDER SCORING RCW 9.94A.525(9)

If it was found that this offense was committed with sexual motivation (RCW 9.94A.533(8)) on or after 7/1/2006, use the General Serious Violent Offense with a Sexual Motivation Finding scoring form on page 241.

If the present conviction is for a felony domestic violence offense where domestic violence was plead and proven, use the General Serious Violent Offense Where Domestic Violence Has Been Plead and Proven scoring form on page 239.

ADULT HISTORY:

    Enter number of serious violent felony convictions .... _____ x 3 = _____

    Enter number of violent felony convictions .... _____ x 2 = _____

    Enter number of nonviolent felony convictions .... _____ x 1 = _____

JUVENILE HISTORY:

    Enter number of Murder 1, Murder 2, and Serious Violent sex offense felony dispositions .... _____ x 3 = _____

    Enter number of Class A sex offense (not Serious Violent) felony dispositions .... _____ x 2 = _____

OTHER CURRENT OFFENSES:

(Other current offenses that do not encompass the same conduct count in offender score)

    Enter number of other violent felony convictions .... _____ x 2 = _____

    Enter number of other nonviolent felony convictions .... _____ x 1 = _____

STATUS:

    Was the offender on community custody on the date the current offense was committed? .... _____ + 1 = _____

Total the last column to get the **Offender Score** (Round down to the nearest whole number).................. _____

SENTENCE RANGE DISPLAYED IS FOR A COMPLETED OFFENSE

FOR **ATTEMPT**, **SOLICITATION**, OR **CONSPIRACY** (RCW 9.94A.595, see page 54), THE SENTENCE RANGE **IS 75%** OF THE COMPLETED RANGE LISTED BELOW

	Offender Score									
	0	**1**	**2**	**3**	**4**	**5**	**6**	**7**	**8**	**9+**
LEVEL XI	90m	100m	110m	119m	129m	139m	170m	185m	215m	245m
	78 - 102	86 - 114	95 - 125	102 - 136	111 - 147	120 - 158	146 - 194	159 - 211	185 - 245	210 - 280

✓   For gang-related felonies where the court found the offender involved a minor (RCW 9.94A.833), see page 227 for standard range adjustments.

✓   For deadly weapon enhancement, see page 233.

✓   For sentencing alternatives, see page 215.

✓   For community custody eligibility, see page 228.

✓   For any applicable enhancements other than deadly weapon enhancement, see page 224.

✓   Multiple current serious violent offenses shall have consecutive sentences imposed per the rules of RCW 9.94A.589(1)(b).

Manslaughter Second Degree

RCW 9A.32.070
CLASS B* – VIOLENT/CRIMES AGAINST PERSONS
OFFENDER SCORING RCW 9.94A.525(8)

If it was found that this offense was committed with sexual motivation (RCW 9.94A.533(8)) on or after 7/1/2006, use the General Violent Offense with a Sexual Motivation Finding scoring form on page 244.

If the present conviction is for a felony domestic violence offense where domestic violence was plead and proven, use the General Violent Offense Where Domestic Violence Has Been Plead and Proven scoring form on page 242.

ADULT HISTORY:

Enter number of serious violent and violent felony convictions .... _____ x 2 = _____

Enter number of nonviolent felony convictions .... _____ x 1 = _____

JUVENILE HISTORY:

Enter number of Murder 1, Murder 2, and Class A sex offense felony dispositions .... _____ x 2 = _____

OTHER CURRENT OFFENSES:

(Other current offenses that do not encompass the same conduct count in offender score)

Enter number of other serious violent and violent felony convictions .... _____ x 2 = _____

Enter number of other nonviolent felony convictions .... _____ x 1 = _____

STATUS:

Was the offender on community custody on the date the current offense was committed?............ _____ + 1 = _____

Total the last column to get the **Offender Score** (Round down to the nearest whole number) .... _____

SENTENCE RANGE DISPLAYED IS FOR A COMPLETED OFFENSE

FOR **ATTEMPT**, **SOLICITATION**, OR **CONSPIRACY** (RCW 9.94A.595, see page 54), THE SENTENCE RANGE **IS 75%** OF THE COMPLETED RANGE LISTED BELOW

Offender Score										
	0	**1**	**2**	**3**	**4**	**5**	**6**	**7**	**8**	**9+**
LEVEL VIII	24m	30m	36m	42m	47.5m	53.5m	78m	89.5m	101.5m	114m
	21 - 27	26 - 34	31 - 41	36 - 48	41 - 54	46 - 61	67 - 89	77 - 102	87 - 116	108 - 120*

* Class B felony offenses have a statutory maximum sentence of 120 months, see RCW 9A.20.021.

✓ For gang-related felonies where the court found the offender involved a minor (RCW 9.94A.833), see page 227 for standard range adjustments.
✓ For deadly weapon enhancement, see page 233.
✓ For sentencing alternatives, see page 215.
✓ For community custody eligibility, see page 228.
✓ For any applicable enhancements other than deadly weapon enhancement, see page 224.

Manufacture, Deliver or Possess with Intent to Deliver Amphetamine
RCW 69.50.401(2)(b)
CLASS B – NONVIOLENT/DRUG
OFFENDER SCORING RCW 9.94A.525(13)

If it was found that this offense was committed with sexual motivation (RCW 9.94A.533(8)) on or after 7/1/2006, use the General Drug Offense with a Sexual Motivation Finding scoring form on page 238.

If the present conviction is for a felony domestic violence offense where domestic violence was plead and proven, use the General Drug Offense Where Domestic Violence Has Been Plead and Proven scoring form on page 237.

ADULT HISTORY:

Does the offender have a prior sex or serious violent offense in history?

.... **YES,** Enter number of felony drug convictions _____ x 3 = _____

.... **NO,** Enter number of felony drug convictions _____ x 1 = _____

Enter number of felony convictions .... _____ x 1 = _____

JUVENILE HISTORY:

Enter number of Murder 1, Murder 2, and Class A sex offense felony dispositions .... _____ x 1 = _____

OTHER CURRENT OFFENSES:

(Other current offenses that do not encompass the same conduct count in offender score)

Does the offender have other prior sex or serious violent offense in history?

.... **YES,** Enter number of other felony drug convictions _____ x 3 = _____

.... **NO,** Enter number of other felony drug convictions _____ x 1 = _____

Enter number of other felony convictions .... _____ x 1 = _____

STATUS:

Was the offender on community custody on the date the current offense was committed? (if yes) _____ + 1 = _____

Total the last column to get the **Offender Score** (Round down to the nearest whole number)........................ _____

SENTENCE RANGE – DRUG

	Offender Score		
	0 to 2	**3 to 5**	**6 to 9+**
LEVEL II	16m 12+ - 20	40m 20+ - 60	90m 60+ - 120

✓ For attempt, solicitation or conspiracy drug felonies see page 56, or for gang-related felonies where the court found the offender involved a minor (RCW 9.94A.833), see page 227 for standard range adjustments.
✓ Per RCW 9.94A.518, any felony offense under chapter 69.50 RCW with a deadly weapon special verdict under RCW 9.94A.602 becomes a level III offense.
✓ For deadly weapon enhancement, see page 233.
✓ For sentencing alternatives, see page 215.
✓ For community custody eligibility, see page 228.
✓ For any applicable enhancements other than deadly weapon enhancement, see page 224.
✓ Per RCW 69.50.408, the statutory maximum for a subsequent conviction under chapter 69.50 RCW is 240 months.
✓ Per RCW 69.50.435, if the offense occurred within a protected zone, 24 months shall be added to the standard range and the statutory maximum will be 240 months.

RCW 69.50.401(2)(c)
CLASS C – NONVIOLENT/DRUG
OFFENDER SCORING RCW 9.94A.525(13)

If it was found that this offense was committed with sexual motivation (RCW 9.94A.533(8)) on or after 7/1/2006, use the General Drug Offense with a Sexual Motivation Finding scoring form on page 238.

If the present conviction is for a felony domestic violence offense where domestic violence was plead and proven, use the General Drug Offense Where Domestic Violence Has Been Plead and Proven scoring form on page 237.

ADULT HISTORY:

Does the offender have a prior sex or serious violent offense in history?

.... **YES,** Enter number of felony drug convictions _____ x 3 = _____

.... **NO,** Enter number of felony drug convictions _____ x 1 = _____

Enter number of felony convictions .... _____ x 1 = _____

JUVENILE HISTORY:

Enter number of Murder 1, Murder 2, and Class A sex offense felony dispositions .... _____ x 1 = _____

OTHER CURRENT OFFENSES:

(Other current offenses that do not encompass the same conduct count in offender score)

Does the offender have other prior sex or serious violent offense in history?

.... **YES,** Enter number of other felony drug convictions _____ x 3 = _____

.... **NO,** Enter number of other felony drug convictions _____ x 1 = _____

Enter number of other felony convictions .... _____ x 1 = _____

STATUS:

Was the offender on community custody on the date the current offense was committed? (if yes) _____ + 1 = _____

Total the last column to get the **Offender Score** (Round down to the nearest whole number) ....

SENTENCE RANGE – DRUG

	Offender Score		
	0 to 2	3 to 5	6 to 9+
LEVEL I	3m	12m	18m
	0 - 6	6+ - 18	12+ - 24

✓ For gang-related felonies where the court found the offender involved a minor (RCW 9.94A.833), see page 227 for standard range adjustments.
✓ Per RCW 9.94A.518, any felony offense under chapter 69.50 RCW with a deadly weapon special verdict under RCW 9.94A.602 becomes a level III offense.
✓ For deadly weapon enhancement, see page 233.
✓ For sentencing alternatives, see page 215.
✓ For community custody eligibility, see page 228.
✓ For any applicable enhancements other than deadly weapon enhancement, see page 224.
✓ Per RCW 69.50.408, the statutory maximum for a subsequent conviction under chapter 69.50 RCW is 120 months.
✓ Per RCW 69.50.435, if the offense occurred within a protected zone, 24 months shall be added to the standard range and the statutory maximum will be 120 months.

Manufacture, Deliver or Possess with Intent to Deliver Narcotics from Schedule I or II or Flunitrazepam from Schedule IV

RCW 69.50.401(2)(a)
CLASS B – NONVIOLENT/DRUG
OFFENDER SCORING RCW 9.94A.525(13)

If it was found that this offense was committed with sexual motivation (RCW 9.94A.533(8)) on or after 7/1/2006, use the General Drug Offense with a Sexual Motivation Finding scoring form on page 238.

If the present conviction is for a felony domestic violence offense where domestic violence was plead and proven, use the General Drug Offense Where Domestic Violence Has Been Plead and Proven scoring form on page 237.

ADULT HISTORY:

Does the offender have a prior sex or serious violent offense in history?

.... **YES,** Enter number of felony drug convictions _____ x 3 = _____

.... **NO,** Enter number of felony drug convictions _____ x 1 = _____

Enter number of felony convictions .... _____ x 1 = _____

JUVENILE HISTORY:

Enter number of Murder 1, Murder 2, and Class A sex offense felony dispositions .... _____ x 1 = _____

OTHER CURRENT OFFENSES:

(Other current offenses that do not encompass the same conduct count in offender score)

Does the offender have other prior sex or serious violent offense in history?

.... **YES,** Enter number of other felony drug convictions _____ x 3 = _____

.... **NO,** Enter number of other felony drug convictions _____ x 1 = _____

Enter number of other felony convictions .... _____ x 1 = _____

STATUS:

Was the offender on community custody on the date the current offense was committed? (if yes) _____ + 1 = _____

Total the last column to get the **Offender Score** (Round down to the nearest whole number)........................ _____

SENTENCE RANGE – DRUG

	Offender Score		
	0 to 2	3 to 5	6 to 9+
LEVEL II	16m	40m	90m
	12+ - 20	20+ - 60	60+ - 120

✓ For attempt, solicitation or conspiracy drug felonies see page 56, or for gang-related felonies where the court found the offender involved a minor (RCW 9.94A.833), see page 227 for standard range adjustments.
✓ Per RCW 9.94A.518, any felony offense under chapter 69.50 RCW with a deadly weapon special verdict under RCW 9.94A.602 becomes a level III offense.
✓ For deadly weapon enhancement, see page 233.
✓ For sentencing alternatives, see page 215.
✓ For community custody eligibility, see page 228.
✓ For any applicable enhancements other than deadly weapon enhancement, see page 224.
✓ Per RCW 69.50.408, the statutory maximum for a subsequent conviction under chapter 69.50 RCW is 240 months.
✓ Per RCW 69.50.435, if the offense occurred within a protected zone, 24 months shall be added to the standard range and the statutory maximum will be 240 months.

Manufacture, Deliver or Possess with Intent to Deliver Narcotics from Schedule III, IV or V or Nonnarcotics from Schedule I-V except Cannabis, Amphetamine, Methamphetamine or Flunitrazepam

RCW 69.50.401(2)(c-e)
CLASS C* – NONVIOLENT/DRUG
OFFENDER SCORING RCW 9.94A.525(13)

If it was found that this offense was committed with sexual motivation (RCW 9.94A.533(8)) on or after 7/1/2006, use the General Drug Offense with a Sexual Motivation Finding scoring form on page 238.

If the present conviction is for a felony domestic violence offense where domestic violence was plead and proven, use the General Drug Offense Where Domestic Violence Has Been Plead and Proven scoring form on page 237.

ADULT HISTORY:

Does the offender have a prior sex or serious violent offense in history?

.... **YES,** Enter number of felony drug convictions _____ x 3 = _____

....**NO,** Enter number of felony drug convictions _____ x 1 = _____

Enter number of felony convictions .... _____ x 1 = _____

JUVENILE HISTORY:

Enter number of Murder 1, Murder 2, and Class A sex offense felony dispositions .... _____ x 1 = _____

OTHER CURRENT OFFENSES:

(Other current offenses that do not encompass the same conduct count in offender score)

Does the offender have other prior sex or serious violent offense in history?

.... **YES,** Enter number of other felony drug convictions _____ x 3 = _____

....**NO,** Enter number of other felony drug convictions _____ x 1 = _____

Enter number of other felony convictions .... _____ x 1 = _____

STATUS:

Was the offender on community custody on the date the current offense was committed? (if yes) _____ + 1 = _____

Total the last column to get the **Offender Score** (Round down to the nearest whole number)......................... _____

SENTENCE RANGE – DRUG

	Offender Score		
	0 to 2	3 to 5	6 to 9+
LEVEL II	16m 12+ - 20	40m 20+ - 60	60 - 60*

* Class C felony offenses have a statutory maximum sentence of 60 months, see RCW 9A.20.021.

✓ For gang-related felonies where the court found the offender involved a minor (RCW 9.94A.833), see page 227 for standard range adjustments.
✓ Per RCW 9.94A.518, any felony offense under chapter 69.50 RCW with a deadly weapon special verdict under RCW 9.94A.602 becomes a level III offense.
✓ For deadly weapon enhancement, see page 233.
✓ For sentencing alternatives, see page 215.
✓ For community custody eligibility, see page 228.
✓ For any applicable enhancements other than deadly weapon enhancement, see page 224.
✓ Per RCW 69.50.408, the statutory maximum for a subsequent conviction under chapter 69.50 RCW is 120 months.
✓ Per RCW 69.50.435, if the offense occurred within a protected zone, 24 months shall be added to the standard range and the statutory maximum will be 120 months.

Manufacture, Distribute or Possess with Intent to Distribute an Imitation Controlled Substance

RCW 69.52.030(1)
CLASS C* – NONVIOLENT
OFFENDER SCORING RCW 9.94A.525(7)

If it was found that this offense was committed with sexual motivation (RCW 9.94A.533(8)) on or after 7/1/2006, use the General Nonviolent Offense with a Sexual Motivation Finding scoring form on page 236.

If the present conviction is for a felony domestic violence offense where domestic violence was plead and proven, use the General Nonviolent Offense Where Domestic Violence Has Been Plead and Proven scoring form on page 234.

ADULT HISTORY:

    Enter number of felony convictions .... _____ x 1 = _____

JUVENILE HISTORY:

    Enter number of Murder 1, Murder 2, and Class A sex offense felony dispositions .... _____ x 1 = _____

OTHER CURRENT OFFENSES:

(Other current offenses that do not encompass the same conduct count in offender score)

    Enter number of other felony convictions .... _____ x 1 = _____

STATUS:

    Was the offender on community custody on the date the current offense was committed? (if yes) _____ + 1 = _____

Total the last column to get the **Offender Score** (Round down to the nearest whole number) .... _____

SENTENCE RANGE – DRUG

	Offender Score		
	0 to 2	**3 to 5**	**6 to 9+**
LEVEL II	16m	40m	90m
	12+ - 20	20+ - 60	60* - 60*

* Class C felony offenses have a statutory maximum sentence of 60 months, see RCW 9A.20.021.

✓   For gang-related felonies where the court found the offender involved a minor (RCW 9.94A.833), see page 227 for standard range adjustments.
✓   For deadly weapon enhancement, see page 233.
✓   For sentencing alternatives, see page 215.
✓   For community custody eligibility, see page 228.
✓   For any applicable enhancements other than deadly weapon enhancement, see page 224.

Manufacture, Distribute or Possess with Intent to Distribute an Imitation Controlled Substance by a Person 18 or Older to a Person under 18

RCW 69.52.030(2)
CLASS B – NONVIOLENT
OFFENDER SCORING RCW 9.94A.525(7)

If it was found that this offense was committed with sexual motivation (RCW 9.94A.533(8)) on or after 7/1/2006, use the General Nonviolent Offense with a Sexual Motivation Finding scoring form on page 236.

If the present conviction is for a felony domestic violence offense where domestic violence was plead and proven, use the General Nonviolent Offense Where Domestic Violence Has Been Plead and Proven scoring form on page 234.

ADULT HISTORY:

    Enter number of felony convictions .... _____ x 1 = _____

JUVENILE HISTORY:

    Enter number of Murder 1, Murder 2, and Class A sex offense felony dispositions .... _____ x 1 = _____

OTHER CURRENT OFFENSES:

(Other current offenses that do not encompass the same conduct count in offender score)

    Enter number of other felony convictions .... _____ x 1 = _____

STATUS:

    Was the offender on community custody on the date the current offense was committed? (if yes) _____ + 1 = _____

Total the last column to get the **Offender Score** (Round down to the nearest whole number).......................... _____

SENTENCE RANGE – DRUG

	Offender Score		
	0 to 2	**3 to 5**	**6 to 9+**
LEVEL III	59.5m	84m	110m
	51 - 68	68+ - 100	100+ - 120

✓   For attempt, solicitation, conspiracy (RCW 9.94A.595) see page 54 or for gang-related felonies where the court found the offender involved a minor (RCW 9.94A.833), see page 227 for standard range adjustments.
✓   For deadly weapon enhancement, see page 233.
✓   For sentencing alternatives, see page 215.
✓   For community custody eligibility, see page 228.
✓   For any applicable enhancements other than deadly weapon enhancement, see page 224.

RCW 69.50.401(2)(b)
CLASS B – NONVIOLENT/DRUG
OFFENDER SCORING RCW 9.94A.525(13)

If it was found that this offense was committed with sexual motivation (RCW 9.94A.533(8)) on or after 7/1/2006, use the General Drug Offense with a Sexual Motivation Finding scoring form on page 238.

If the present conviction is for a felony domestic violence offense where domestic violence was plead and proven, use the General Drug Offense Where Domestic Violence Has Been Plead and Proven scoring form on page 237.

ADULT HISTORY:

Enter number of Manufacture Methamphetamine felony convictions .... _____ x 3 = _____

Does the offender have a prior sex or serious violent offense in history?

.... **YES,** Enter number of felony drug convictions _____ x 3 = _____

.... **NO,** Enter number of felony drug convictions _____ x 1 = _____

Enter number of felony convictions .... _____ x 1 = _____

JUVENILE HISTORY:

Enter number of Murder 1, Murder 2, and Class A sex offense felony dispositions .... _____ x 1 = _____

OTHER CURRENT OFFENSES:

(Other current offenses that do not encompass the same conduct count in offender score)

Enter number of other Manufacture Methamphetamine felony convictions .... _____ x 3 = _____

Does the offender have other prior sex or serious violent offense in history?

.... **YES,** Enter number of other felony drug convictions _____ x 3 = _____

.... **NO,** Enter number of other felony drug convictions _____ x 1 = _____

Enter number of other felony convictions .... _____ x 1 = _____

STATUS:

Was the offender on community custody on the date the current offense was committed? (if yes) _____ + 1 = _____

Total the last column to get the **Offender Score** (Round down to the nearest whole number)......................... _____

SENTENCE RANGE – DRUG

	Offender Score		
	0 to 2	**3 to 5**	**6 to 9+**
LEVEL III	59.5m	84m	110m
	51 - 68	68+ - 100	100+ - 120

✓ For attempt, solicitation or conspiracy drug felonies see page 56, or for gang-related felonies where the court found the offender involved a minor (RCW 9.94A.833), see page 227 for standard range adjustments.

✓ Per RCW 9.94A.518, any felony offense under chapter 69.50 RCW with a deadly weapon special verdict under RCW 9.94A.602 becomes a level III offense.

✓ For deadly weapon enhancement, see page 233.

✓ For sentencing alternatives, see page 215.

✓ For community custody eligibility, see page 228.

✓ For any applicable enhancements other than deadly weapon enhancement, see page 224.

✓ Per RCW 69.50.408, the statutory maximum for a subsequent conviction under chapter 69.50 RCW is 240 months.

✓ Per RCW 69.50.435, if the offense occurred within a protected zone, 24 months shall be added to the standard range and the statutory maximum will be 240 months.

✓ Per RCW 9.94A.827, if the offense is also a violation of Manufacture of Methamphetamine with a Child on Premise, 24 months shall be added to the standard range.

Mortgage Fraud

RCW 19.144.080
CLASS B – NONVIOLENT
OFFENDER SCORING RCW 9.94A.525(7)

If it was found that this offense was committed with sexual motivation (RCW 9.94A.533(8)) on or after 7/1/2006, use the General Nonviolent Offense with a Sexual Motivation Finding scoring form on page 236.

If the present conviction is for a felony domestic violence offense where domestic violence was plead and proven, use the General Nonviolent Offense Where Domestic Violence Has Been Plead and Proven scoring form on page 234.

ADULT HISTORY:

    Enter number of felony convictions .... _____ x 1 = _____

JUVENILE HISTORY:

    Enter number of Murder 1, Murder 2, and Class A sex offense felony dispositions .... _____ x 1 = _____

OTHER CURRENT OFFENSES:

(Other current offenses that do not encompass the same conduct count in offender score)

    Enter number of other felony convictions .... _____ x 1 = _____

STATUS:

    Was the offender on community custody on the date the current offense was committed? (if yes) _____ + 1 = _____

Total the last column to get the **Offender Score** (Round down to the nearest whole number).......................... _____

SENTENCE RANGE DISPLAYED IS FOR A COMPLETED OFFENSE

FOR **ATTEMPT**, **SOLICITATION**, OR **CONSPIRACY** (RCW 9.94A.595, see page 54), THE SENTENCE RANGE **IS 75%** OF THE COMPLETED RANGE LISTED BELOW

	Offender Score									
	0	**1**	**2**	**3**	**4**	**5**	**6**	**7**	**8**	**9+**
LEVEL III	2m	5m	8m	11m	14m	19.5m	25.5m	38m	50m	59.5m
	1 - 3	3 - 8	4 - 12	9 - 12	12+ - 16	17 - 22	22 - 29	33 - 43	43 - 57	51 - 68

✓   For gang-related felonies where the court found the offender involved a minor (RCW 9.94A.833), see page 227 for standard range adjustments.
✓   For deadly weapon enhancement, see page 233.
✓   For sentencing alternatives, see page 215.
✓   For community custody eligibility, see page 228.
✓   For any applicable enhancements other than deadly weapon enhancement, see page 224.

RCW 9A.32.030
CLASS A – SERIOUS VIOLENT/CRIMES AGAINST PERSONS
ATTEMPT/SOLICITATION/CONSPIRACY = CLASS A – SERIOUS VIOLENT
OFFENDER SCORING RCW 9.94A.525(9)

If the present conviction is for a felony domestic violence offense where domestic violence was plead and proven, use the General Serious Violent Offense Where Domestic Violence Has Been Plead and Proven scoring form on page 239.

ADULT HISTORY:

Enter number of serious violent felony convictions .... _____ x 3 = _____

Enter number of violent felony convictions .... _____ x 2 = _____

Enter number of nonviolent felony convictions .... _____ x 1 = _____

JUVENILE HISTORY:

Enter number of Murder 1, Murder 2, and Serious Violent sex offense felony dispositions .... _____ x 3 = _____

Enter number of Class A sex offense (not Serious Violent) felony dispositions .... _____ x 2 = _____

OTHER CURRENT OFFENSES:

(Other current offenses that do not encompass the same conduct count in offender score)

Enter number of other violent felony convictions .... _____ x 2 = _____

Enter number of other nonviolent felony convictions .... _____ x 1 = _____

STATUS:

Was the offender on community custody on the date the current offense was committed? .... _____ + 1 = _____

Total the last column to get the **Offender Score** (Round down to the nearest whole number).................. _____

SENTENCE RANGE DISPLAYED IS FOR A COMPLETED OFFENSE

FOR **ATTEMPT**, **SOLICITATION**, OR **CONSPIRACY** (RCW 9.94A.595, see page 54), THE SENTENCE RANGE **IS 75%** OF THE COMPLETED RANGE LISTED BELOW

	Offender Score									
	0	**1**	**2**	**3**	**4**	**5**	**6**	**7**	**8**	**9+**
LEVEL XV	280m	291.5m	304m	316m	327.5m	339.5m	364m	394m	431.5m	479.5m
	240 - 320	250 - 333	261 - 347	271 - 361	281 - 374	291 - 388	312 - 416	338 - 450	370 - 493	411 - 548

✓ For gang-related felonies where the court found the offender involved a minor (RCW 9.94A.833), see page 227 for standard range adjustments.
✓ For deadly weapon enhancement, see page 233.
✓ For sentencing alternatives, see page 215.
✓ For community custody eligibility, see page 228.
✓ For any applicable enhancements other than deadly weapon enhancement, see page 224.
✓ Multiple current serious violent offenses shall have consecutive sentences imposed per the rules of RCW 9.94A.589(1)(b).
✓ Excluding attempt, solicitation and conspiracy convictions, the statutory minimum sentence is 240 months (RCW 9.94A.540). The statutory minimum sentence shall not be varied or modified under RCW 9.94A.535.

Murder First Degree with a Finding of Sexual Motivation, Completed or Attempt
RCW 9A.32.030
CLASS A – SERIOUS VIOLENT/SEX/CRIMES AGAINST PERSONS
ATTEMPT = CLASS A – SERIOUS VIOLENT/SEX
OFFENDER SCORING RCW 9.94A.525(17)

ADULT HISTORY:

Enter number of sex offense felony convictions .... _____ x 3 = _____

Enter number of serious violent felony convictions .... _____ x 3 = _____

Enter number of violent felony convictions .... _____ x 2 = _____

Enter number of nonviolent felony convictions .... _____ x 1 = _____

JUVENILE HISTORY:

Enter number of Murder 1, Murder 2, and Class A sex offense felony dispositions .... _____ x 3 = _____

OTHER CURRENT OFFENSES:

(Other current offenses that do not encompass the same conduct count in offender score)

Enter number of other sex offense felony convictions .... _____ x 3 = _____

Enter number of other violent felony convictions .... _____ x 2 = _____

Enter number of other nonviolent felony convictions .... _____ x 1 = _____

STATUS:

Was the offender on community custody on the date the current offense was committed?............ _____ + 1 = _____

Total the last column to get the **Offender Score** (Round down to the nearest whole number) .... _____

SENTENCE RANGE DISPLAYED IS FOR A COMPLETED OFFENSE

FOR **ATTEMPT**, **SOLICITATION**, OR **CONSPIRACY** (RCW 9.94A.595, see page 54), THE SENTENCE RANGE **IS 75%** OF THE COMPLETED RANGE LISTED BELOW

	Offender Score									
	0	**1**	**2**	**3**	**4**	**5**	**6**	**7**	**8**	**9+**
LEVEL XV	280m	291.5m	304m	316m	327.5m	339.5m	364m	394m	431.5m	479.5m
	240 - 320	250 - 333	261 - 347	271 - 361	281 - 374	291 - 388	312 - 416	338 - 450	370 - 493	411 - 548

SEXUAL MOTIVATION ENHANCEMENT (Per Sexual Motivation Enhancement, page 226) .... _____

Low   to   High

STANDARD SENTENCE RANGE PLUS ENHANCEMENT.............. _____ ..... _____

- ✓ For gang-related felonies where the court found the offender involved a minor (RCW 9.94A.833), see page 227 for standard range adjustments.
- ✓ For deadly weapon enhancement, see page 233.
- ✓ For sentencing alternatives, see page 215.
- ✓ For community custody eligibility, see page 228.
- ✓ For any applicable enhancements other than deadly weapon enhancement, see page 224.
- ✓ If the offender is not a persistent offender and the current offense was committed on or after 9/1/2001, then the offender is subject to the requirements under RCW 9.94A.507.
- ✓ Multiple current serious violent offenses shall have consecutive sentences imposed per the rules of RCW 9.94A.589(1)(b).
- ✓ Excluding attempt convictions, the statutory minimum sentence is 240 months (RCW 9.94A.540). The statutory minimum sentence shall not be varied or modified under RCW 9.94A.535.

Murder First Degree with a Finding of Sexual Motivation, Solicitation or Conspiracy

RCW 9A.32.030
SERIOUS VIOLENT/SEX
SOLICITATION/CONSPIRACY = CLASS A
OFFENDER SCORING RCW 9.94A.525(17)

ADULT HISTORY:

Enter number of sex offense felony convictions .... _____ x 3 = _____

Enter number of serious violent felony convictions .... _____ x 3 = _____

Enter number of violent felony convictions .... _____ x 2 = _____

Enter number of nonviolent felony convictions .... _____ x 1 = _____

JUVENILE HISTORY:

Enter number of Murder 1, Murder 2, and Class A sex offense felony dispositions .... _____ x 3 = _____

OTHER CURRENT OFFENSES:

(Other current offenses that do not encompass the same conduct count in offender score)

Enter number of other sex offense felony convictions .... _____ x 3 = _____

Enter number of other violent felony convictions .... _____ x 2 = _____

Enter number of other nonviolent felony convictions .... _____ x 1 = _____

STATUS:

Was the offender on community custody on the date the current offense was committed? .... _____ + 1 = _____

Total the last column to get the **Offender Score** (Round down to the nearest whole number).................. _____

SENTENCE RANGE DISPLAYED IS FOR A COMPLETED OFFENSE

FOR **ATTEMPT**, **SOLICITATION**, OR **CONSPIRACY** (RCW 9.94A.595, see page 54), THE SENTENCE RANGE **IS 75%** OF THE COMPLETED RANGE LISTED BELOW

Offender Score										
	0	**1**	**2**	**3**	**4**	**5**	**6**	**7**	**8**	**9+**
LEVEL XV	280m	291.5m	304m	316m	327.5m	339.5m	364m	394m	431.5m	479.5m
	240 - 320	250 - 333	261 - 347	271 - 361	281 - 374	291 - 388	312 - 416	338 - 450	370 - 493	411 - 548

SEXUAL MOTIVATION ENHANCEMENT (Per Sexual Motivation Enhancement, page 226).................... _____

Low   to   High

STANDARD SENTENCE RANGE PLUS ENHANCEMENT .... _____ ..... _____

✓ For gang-related felonies where the court found the offender involved a minor (RCW 9.94A.833), see page 227 for standard range adjustments.
✓ For deadly weapon enhancement, see page 233.
✓ For sentencing alternatives, see page 215.
✓ For community custody eligibility, see page 228.
✓ For any applicable enhancements other than deadly weapon enhancement, see page 224.
✓ If the offender is not a persistent offender and has a prior conviction for an offense listed in RCW 9.94A.030(37)(b), then the sentence is subject to the requirements of RCW 9.94A.507.
✓ Multiple current serious violent offenses shall have consecutive sentences imposed per the rules of RCW 9.94A.589(1)(b).

RCW 9A.32.050
CLASS A – SERIOUS VIOLENT/CRIMES AGAINST PERSONS
ATTEMPT/SOLICITATION = CLASS A – SERIOUS VIOLENT
CONSPIRACY = CLASS B* – SERIOUS VIOLENT
OFFENDER SCORING RCW 9.94A.525(9)

If the present conviction is for a felony domestic violence offense where domestic violence was plead and proven, use the General Serious Violent Offense Where Domestic Violence Has Been Plead and Proven scoring form on page 239.

ADULT HISTORY:

Enter number of serious violent felony convictions .... _____ x 3 = _____

Enter number of violent felony convictions .... _____ x 2 = _____

Enter number of nonviolent felony convictions .... _____ x 1 = _____

JUVENILE HISTORY:

Enter number of Murder 1, Murder 2, and Serious Violent sex offense felony dispositions .... _____ x 3 = _____

Enter number of Class A sex offense (not Serious Violent) felony dispositions .... _____ x 2 = _____

OTHER CURRENT OFFENSES:

(Other current offenses that do not encompass the same conduct count in offender score)

Enter number of other violent felony convictions .... _____ x 2 = _____

Enter number of other nonviolent felony convictions .... _____ x 1 = _____

STATUS:

Was the offender on community custody on the date the current offense was committed?............ _____ + 1 = _____

Total the last column to get the **Offender Score** (Round down to the nearest whole number) .... _____

SENTENCE RANGE DISPLAYED IS FOR A COMPLETED OFFENSE

FOR **ATTEMPT**, **SOLICITATION**, OR **CONSPIRACY** (RCW 9.94A.595, see page 54), THE SENTENCE RANGE **IS 75%** OF THE COMPLETED RANGE LISTED BELOW

	Offender Score									
	0	**1**	**2**	**3**	**4**	**5**	**6**	**7**	**8**	**9+**
LEVEL XIV	171.5m	184m	194m	204m	215m	225m	245m	266m	307m	347.5m
	123 - 220	134 - 234	144 - 244	154 - 254	165 - 265	175 - 275	195 - 295	216 - 316	257 - 357	298 - 397

* Class B felony offenses have a statutory maximum sentence of 120 months, see RCW 9A.20.021.

✓ For gang-related felonies where the court found the offender involved a minor (RCW 9.94A.833), see page 227 for standard range adjustments.
✓ For deadly weapon enhancement, see page 233.
✓ For sentencing alternatives, see page 215.
✓ For community custody eligibility, see page 228.
✓ For any applicable enhancements other than deadly weapon enhancement, see page 224.
✓ Multiple current serious violent offenses shall have consecutive sentences imposed per the rules of RCW 9.94A.589(1)(b).

Murder Second Degree with a Finding of Sexual Motivation, Completed or Attempt
RCW 9A.32.050
CLASS A – SERIOUS VIOLENT/SEX/CRIMES AGAINST PERSONS
ATTEMPT = CLASS A – SERIOUS VIOLENT/SEX
OFFENDER SCORING RCW 9.94A.525(17)

ADULT HISTORY:

Enter number of sex offense felony convictions .... _____ x 3 = _____

Enter number of serious violent felony convictions .... _____ x 3 = _____

Enter number of violent felony convictions .... _____ x 2 = _____

Enter number of nonviolent felony convictions .... _____ x 1 = _____

JUVENILE HISTORY:

Enter number of Murder 1, Murder 2, and Class A sex offense felony dispositions .... _____ x 3 = _____

OTHER CURRENT OFFENSES:

(Other current offenses that do not encompass the same conduct count in offender score)

Enter number of other sex offense felony convictions .... _____ x 3 = _____

Enter number of other violent felony convictions .... _____ x 2 = _____

Enter number of other nonviolent felony convictions .... _____ x 1 = _____

STATUS:

Was the offender on community custody on the date the current offense was committed? .... _____ + 1 = _____

Total the last column to get the **Offender Score** (Round down to the nearest whole number).................. _____

SENTENCE RANGE DISPLAYED IS FOR A COMPLETED OFFENSE

FOR **ATTEMPT**, **SOLICITATION**, OR **CONSPIRACY** (RCW 9.94A.595, see page 54), THE SENTENCE RANGE **IS 75%** OF THE COMPLETED RANGE LISTED BELOW

Offender Score										
	0	**1**	**2**	**3**	**4**	**5**	**6**	**7**	**8**	**9+**
LEVEL XIV	171.5m	184m	194m	204m	215m	225m	245m	266m	307m	347.5m
	123 - 220	134 - 234	144 - 244	154 - 254	165 - 265	175 - 275	195 - 295	216 - 316	257 - 357	298 - 397

SEXUAL MOTIVATION ENHANCEMENT (Per Sexual Motivation Enhancement, page 226).................... _____

Low   to   High

STANDARD SENTENCE RANGE PLUS ENHANCEMENT .... _____ ..... _____

✓ For gang-related felonies where the court found the offender involved a minor (RCW 9.94A.833), see page 227 for standard range adjustments.
✓ For deadly weapon enhancement, see page 233.
✓ For sentencing alternatives, see page 215.
✓ For community custody eligibility, see page 228.
✓ For any applicable enhancements other than deadly weapon enhancement, see page 224.
✓ If the offender is not a persistent offender and the current offense was committed on or after 9/1/2001, then the offender is subject to the requirements under RCW 9.94A.507.
✓ Multiple current serious violent offenses shall have consecutive sentences imposed per the rules of RCW 9.94A.589(1)(b).

Murder Second Degree with a Finding of Sexual Motivation, Solicitation or Conspiracy

RCW 9A.32.050
SERIOUS VIOLENT/SEX
SOLICITATION = CLASS A
CONSPIRACY = CLASS B*
OFFENDER SCORING RCW 9.94A.525(17)

ADULT HISTORY:

Enter number of sex offense felony convictions .... _____ x 3 = _____

Enter number of serious violent felony convictions .... _____ x 3 = _____

Enter number of violent felony convictions .... _____ x 2 = _____

Enter number of nonviolent felony convictions .... _____ x 1 = _____

JUVENILE HISTORY:

Enter number of Murder 1, Murder 2, and Class A sex offense felony dispositions .... _____ x 3 = _____

OTHER CURRENT OFFENSES:

(Other current offenses that do not encompass the same conduct count in offender score)

Enter number of other sex offense felony convictions .... _____ x 3 = _____

Enter number of other violent felony convictions .... _____ x 2 = _____

Enter number of other nonviolent felony convictions .... _____ x 1 = _____

STATUS:

Was the offender on community custody on the date the current offense was committed?............ _____ + 1 = _____

Total the last column to get the **Offender Score** (Round down to the nearest whole number) .... _____

SENTENCE RANGE DISPLAYED IS FOR A COMPLETED OFFENSE

FOR **ATTEMPT**, **SOLICITATION**, OR **CONSPIRACY** (RCW 9.94A.595, see page 54), THE SENTENCE RANGE **IS 75%** OF THE COMPLETED RANGE LISTED BELOW

	Offender Score									
	0	**1**	**2**	**3**	**4**	**5**	**6**	**7**	**8**	**9+**
LEVEL XIV	171.5m	184m	194m	204m	215m	225m	245m	266m	307m	347.5m
	123 - 220	134 - 234	144 - 244	154 - 254	165 - 265	175 - 275	195 - 295	216 - 316	257 - 357	298 - 397

SEXUAL MOTIVATION ENHANCEMENT (Per Sexual Motivation Enhancement, page 226) .... _____

Low   to   High

STANDARD SENTENCE RANGE PLUS ENHANCEMENT............... _____ ..... _____

* Class B felony offenses have a statutory maximum sentence of 120 months, see RCW 9A.20.021.

✓ For gang-related felonies where the court found the offender involved a minor (RCW 9.94A.833), see page 227 for standard range adjustments.
✓ For deadly weapon enhancement, see page 233.
✓ For sentencing alternatives, see page 215.
✓ For community custody eligibility, see page 228.
✓ For any applicable enhancements other than deadly weapon enhancement, see page 224.
✓ Multiple current serious violent offenses shall have consecutive sentences imposed per the rules of RCW 9.94A.589(1)(b).
✓ If the offender is not a persistent offender and has a prior conviction for an offense listed in RCW 9.94A.030(37)(b), then the sentence is subject to the requirements of RCW 9.94A.507.

RCW 9A.56.350(2)
CLASS B – NONVIOLENT
OFFENDER SCORING RCW 9.94A.525(7)

If it was found that this offense was committed with sexual motivation (RCW 9.94A.533(8)) on or after 7/1/2006, use the General Nonviolent Offense with a Sexual Motivation Finding scoring form on page 236.

If the present conviction is for a felony domestic violence offense where domestic violence was plead and proven, use the General Nonviolent Offense Where Domestic Violence Has Been Plead and Proven scoring form on page 234.

ADULT HISTORY:

Enter number of felony convictions .... _____ x 1 = _____

JUVENILE HISTORY:

Enter number of Murder 1, Murder 2, and Class A sex offense felony dispositions .... _____ x 1 = _____

OTHER CURRENT OFFENSES:

(Other current offenses that do not encompass the same conduct count in offender score)

Enter number of other felony convictions .... _____ x 1 = _____

STATUS:

Was the offender on community custody on the date the current offense was committed? (if yes) _____ + 1 = _____

Total the last column to get the **Offender Score** (Round down to the nearest whole number) .... _____

SENTENCE RANGE DISPLAYED IS FOR A COMPLETED OFFENSE

FOR **ATTEMPT**, **SOLICITATION**, OR **CONSPIRACY** (RCW 9.94A.595, see page 54), THE SENTENCE RANGE **IS 75%** OF THE COMPLETED RANGE LISTED BELOW

Offender Score									
0	**1**	**2**	**3**	**4**	**5**	**6**	**7**	**8**	**9+**
LEVEL III 2m	5m	8m	11m	14m	19.5m	25.5m	38m	50m	59.5m
1 - 3	3 - 8	4 - 12	9 - 12	12+ - 16	17 - 22	22 - 29	33 - 43	43 - 57	51 - 68

✓ For gang-related felonies where the court found the offender involved a minor (RCW 9.94A.833), see page 227 for standard range adjustments.
✓ For deadly weapon enhancement, see page 233.
✓ For sentencing alternatives, see page 215.
✓ For community custody eligibility, see page 228.
✓ For any applicable enhancements other than deadly weapon enhancement, see page 224.

Organized Retail Theft Second Degree
RCW 9A.56.350(3)
CLASS C – NONVIOLENT
OFFENDER SCORING RCW 9.94A.525(7)

If it was found that this offense was committed with sexual motivation (RCW 9.94A.533(8)) on or after 7/1/2006, use the General Nonviolent Offense with a Sexual Motivation Finding scoring form on page 236.

If the present conviction is for a felony domestic violence offense where domestic violence was plead and proven, use the General Nonviolent Offense Where Domestic Violence Has Been Plead and Proven scoring form on page 234.

ADULT HISTORY:

Enter number of felony convictions .... _____ x 1 = _____

JUVENILE HISTORY:

Enter number of Murder 1, Murder 2, and Class A sex offense felony dispositions .... _____ x 1 = _____

OTHER CURRENT OFFENSES:

(Other current offenses that do not encompass the same conduct count in offender score)

Enter number of other felony convictions .... _____ x 1 = _____

STATU S:

Was the offender on community custody on the date the current offense was committed? (if yes) _____ + 1 = _____

Total the last column to get the **Offender Score** (Round down to the nearest whole number)......................... _____

SENTENCE RANGE

Offender Score										
	0	1	2	3	4	5	6	7	8	9+
LEVEL II		4m	6m	8m	13m	16m	19.5m	25.5m	38m	50m
	0-90 days	2 - 6	3 - 9	4 - 12	12+ - 14	14 - 18	17 - 22	22 - 29	33 - 43	43 - 57

✓ For gang-related felonies where the court found the offender involved a minor (RCW 9.94A.833), see page 227 for standard range adjustment.
✓ For deadly weapon enhancement, see page 233.
✓ For sentencing alternatives, see page 215.
✓ For community custody eligibility, see page 228.
✓ For any applicable enhancements other than deadly weapon enhancement, see page 224.

Over 18 and Deliver Heroin, Methamphetamine, a Narcotic from Schedule I or II or Flunitrazepam from Schedule IV to Someone under 18

RCW 69.50.406(1)
CLASS A – VIOLENT/DRUG
OFFENDER SCORING RCW 9.94A.525(13)

If it was found that this offense was committed with sexual motivation (RCW 9.94A.533(8)) on or after 7/1/2006, use the General Drug Offense with a Sexual Motivation Finding scoring form on page 238.

If the present conviction is for a felony domestic violence offense where domestic violence was plead and proven, use the General Drug Offense Where Domestic Violence Has Been Plead and Proven scoring form on page 237.

ADULT HISTORY:

Does the offender have a prior sex or serious violent offense in history?

.... **YES,** Enter number of felony drug convictions _____ x 3 = _____

.... **NO,** Enter number of felony drug convictions _____ x 1 = _____

Enter number of serious violent and violent felony convictions .... _____ x 2 = _____

Enter number of nonviolent felony convictions .... _____ x 1 = _____

JUVENILE HISTORY:

Enter number of Murder 1, Murder 2, and Class A sex offense felony dispositions .... _____ x 2 = _____

OTHER CURRENT OFFENSES:

(Other current offenses that do not encompass the same conduct count in offender score)

Does the offender have other prior sex or serious violent offense in history?

.... **YES,** Enter number of other felony drug convictions _____ x 3 = _____

.... **NO,** Enter number of other felony drug convictions _____ x 1 = _____

Enter number of other serious violent and violent felony convictions .... _____ x 2 = _____

Enter number of other nonviolent felony convictions .... _____ x 1 = _____

STATUS:

Was the offender on community custody on the date the current offense was committed? (if yes) _____ + 1 = _____

Total the last column to get the **Offender Score** (Round down to the nearest whole number) ....

SENTENCE RANGE – DRUG

	Offender Score		
	0 to 2	**3 to 5**	**6 to 9+**
LEVEL III	59.5m	84m	110m
	51 - 68	68+ - 100	100+ - 120

✓ For attempt, solicitation or conspiracy drug felonies see page 56, or for gang-related felonies where the court found the offender involved a minor (RCW 9.94A.833), see page 227 for standard range adjustments.
✓ Per RCW 9.94A.518, any felony offense under chapter 69.50 RCW with a deadly weapon special verdict under RCW 9.94A.602 becomes a level III offense.
✓ For deadly weapon enhancement, see page 233.
✓ For sentencing alternatives, see page 215.
✓ For community custody eligibility, see page 228.
✓ For any applicable enhancements other than deadly weapon enhancement, see page 224.
✓ Per RCW 69.50.408, the statutory maximum for a subsequent conviction under chapter 69.50 RCW is 240 months (based on RCW 69.50.406(1)).
✓ Per RCW 69.50.406(1), the current offense is punishable by a term of imprisonment up to 480 months, i.e., twice that authorized by RCW 69.50.401(2)(a) or (b).

Over 18 and Deliver Narcotic from Schedule III, IV, or V or a Nonnarcotic, Except Flunitrazepam or Methamphetamine from Schedule IV to Someone under 18 and 3 Years Junior

RCW 69.50.406(2)
CLASS B – NONVIOLENT/DRUG
OFFENDER SCORING RCW 9.94A.525(13)

If it was found that this offense was committed with sexual motivation (RCW 9.94A.533(8)) on or after 7/1/2006, use the General Drug Offense with a Sexual Motivation Finding scoring form on page 238.

If the present conviction is for a felony domestic violence offense where domestic violence was plead and proven, use the General Drug Offense Where Domestic Violence Has Been Plead and Proven scoring form on page 237.

ADULT HISTORY:

Does the offender have a prior sex or serious violent offense in history?

.... **YES,** Enter number of felony drug convictions _____ x 3 = _____

.... **NO,** Enter number of felony drug convictions _____ x 1 = _____

Enter number of felony convictions .... _____ x 1 = _____

JUVENILE HISTORY:

Enter number of Murder 1, Murder 2, and Class A sex offense felony dispositions .... _____ x 1 = _____

OTHER CURRENT OFFENSES:

(Other current offenses that do not encompass the same conduct count in offender score)

Does the offender have other prior sex or serious violent offense in history?

.... **YES,** Enter number of other felony drug convictions _____ x 3 = _____

.... **NO,** Enter number of other felony drug convictions _____ x 1 = _____

Enter number of other felony convictions .... _____ x 1 = _____

STATUS:

Was the offender on community custody on the date the current offense was committed? (if yes) _____ + 1 = _____

Total the last column to get the **Offender Score** (Round down to the nearest whole number)......................... _____

SENTENCE RANGE – DRUG

	Offender Score		
	0 to 2	3 to 5	6 to 9+
LEVEL III	59.5m 51 - 68	84m 68+ - 100	110m 100+ - 120

✓ For attempt, solicitation or conspiracy drug felonies see page 56, or for gang-related felonies where the court found the offender involved a minor (RCW 9.94A.833), see page 227 for standard range adjustments.
✓ Per RCW 9.94A.518, any felony offense under chapter 69.50 RCW with a deadly weapon special verdict under RCW 9.94A.602 becomes a level III offense.
✓ For deadly weapon enhancement, see page 233.
✓ For sentencing alternatives, see page 215.
✓ For community custody eligibility, see page 228.
✓ For any applicable enhancements other than deadly weapon enhancement, see page 224.
✓ Per RCW 69.50.408, the statutory maximum for a subsequent conviction under chapter 69-50 RCW is 240 months.
✓ Per RCW 69.50.406(1), the current offense is punishable by a term of imprisonment up to 120 months, i.e., twice that authorized by RCW 69.50.401(2)(c),(d) or (e).

Possess, Purchase, Deliver, Sell, or Possess with Intent to Sell a Tableting Machine or Encapsulating Machine

RCW 69.50.418
CLASS C* – NONVIOLENT/DRUG
OFFENDER SCORING RCW 9.94A.525(13)

If it was found that this offense was committed with sexual motivation (RCW 9.94A.533(8)) on or after 7/1/2006, use the General Drug Offense with a Sexual Motivation Finding scoring form on page 238.

If the present conviction is for a felony domestic violence offense where domestic violence was plead and proven, use the General Drug Offense Where Domestic Violence Has Been Plead and Proven scoring form on page 237.

ADULT HISTORY:

Does the offender have a prior sex or serious violent offense in history?

.... **YES,** Enter number of felony drug convictions _____ x 3 = _____

.... **NO,** Enter number of felony drug convictions _____ x 1 = _____

Enter number of felony convictions .... _____ x 1 = _____

JUVENILE HISTORY:

Enter number of Murder 1, Murder 2, and Class A sex offense felony dispositions .... _____ x 1 = _____

OTHER CURRENT OFFENSES:

(Other current offenses that do not encompass the same conduct count in offender score)

Does the offender have other prior sex or serious violent offense in history?

.... **YES,** Enter number of other felony drug convictions _____ x 3 = _____

.... **NO,** Enter number of other felony drug convictions _____ x 1 = _____

Enter number of other felony convictions .... _____ x 1 = _____

STATUS:

Was the offender on community custody on the date the current offense was committed? (if yes) _____ + 1 = _____

Total the last column to get the **Offender Score** (Round down to the nearest whole number)........................ _____

SENTENCE RANGE – DRUG

	Offender Score		
	0 to 2	**3 to 5**	**6 to 9+**
LEVEL II	16m	40m	
	12+ - 20	20+ - 60	60 - 60*

* Class C felony offenses have a statutory maximum sentence of 60 months, see RCW 9A.20.021.

✓ For gang-related felonies where the court found the offender involved a minor (RCW 9.94A.833), see page 227 for standard range adjustments.
✓ Per RCW 9.94A.518, any felony offense under chapter 69.50 RCW with a deadly weapon special verdict under RCW 9.94A.602 becomes a level III offense.
✓ For deadly weapon enhancement, see page 233.
✓ For sentencing alternatives, see page 215.
✓ For community custody eligibility, see page 228.
✓ For any applicable enhancements other than deadly weapon enhancement, see page 224.
✓ Per RCW 69.50.408, the statutory maximum for a subsequent conviction under chapter 69.50 RCW is 120 months.

Perjury First Degree

RCW 9A.72.020
CLASS B – NONVIOLENT
OFFENDER SCORING RCW 9.94A.525(7)

If it was found that this offense was committed with sexual motivation (RCW 9.94A.533(8)) on or after 7/1/2006, use the General Nonviolent Offense with a Sexual Motivation Finding scoring form on page 236.

If the present conviction is for a felony domestic violence offense where domestic violence was plead and proven, use the General Nonviolent Offense Where Domestic Violence Has Been Plead and Proven scoring form on page 234.

ADULT HISTORY:

Enter number of felony convictions .... _____ x 1 = _____

JUVENILE HISTORY:

Enter number of Murder 1, Murder 2, and Class A sex offense felony dispositions .... _____ x 1 = _____

OTHER CURRENT OFFENSES:

(Other current offenses that do not encompass the same conduct count in offender score)

Enter number of other felony convictions .... _____ x 1 = _____

STATUS:

Was the offender on community custody on the date the current offense was committed? (if yes) _____ + 1 = _____

Total the last column to get the **Offender Score** (Round down to the nearest whole number).......................... _____

SENTENCE RANGE DISPLAYED IS FOR A COMPLETED OFFENSE

FOR **ATTEMPT**, **SOLICITATION**, OR **CONSPIRACY** (RCW 9.94A.595, see page 54), THE SENTENCE RANGE **IS 75%** OF THE COMPLETED RANGE LISTED BELOW

	Offender Score									
	0	1	2	3	4	5	6	7	8	9+
LEVEL V	9m	13m	15m	17.5m	25.5m	38m	47.5m	59.5m	72m	84m
	6 - 12	12+ - 14	13 - 17	15 - 20	22 - 29	33 - 43	41 - 54	51 - 68	62 - 82	72 - 96

✓ For gang-related felonies where the court found the offender involved a minor (RCW 9.94A.833), see page 227 for standard range adjustments.
✓ For deadly weapon enhancement, see page 233.
✓ For sentencing alternatives, see page 215.
✓ For community custody eligibility, see page 228.
✓ For any applicable enhancements other than deadly weapon enhancement, see page 224.

Perjury Second Degree

RCW 9A.72.030
CLASS C* – NONVIOLENT
OFFENDER SCORING RCW 9.94A.525(7)

If it was found that this offense was committed with sexual motivation (RCW 9.94A.533(8)) on or after 7/1/2006, use the General Nonviolent Offense with a Sexual Motivation Finding scoring form on page 236.

If the present conviction is for a felony domestic violence offense where domestic violence was plead and proven, use the General Nonviolent Offense Where Domestic Violence Has Been Plead and Proven scoring form on page 234.

ADULT HISTORY:

    Enter number of felony convictions .... _____ x 1 = _____

JUVENILE HISTORY:

    Enter number of Murder 1, Murder 2, and Class A sex offense felony dispositions .... _____ x 1 = _____

OTHER CURRENT OFFENSES:

(Other current offenses that do not encompass the same conduct count in offender score)

    Enter number of other felony convictions .... _____ x 1 = _____

STATUS:

    Was the offender on community custody on the date the current offense was committed? (if yes) _____ + 1 = _____

Total the last column to get the **Offender Score** (Round down to the nearest whole number)......................... _____

SENTENCE RANGE

	Offender Score									
	0	**1**	**2**	**3**	**4**	**5**	**6**	**7**	**8**	**9+**
LEVEL III	2m	5m	8m	11m	14m	19.5m	25.5m	38m	50m	55.5m
	1 - 3	3 - 8	4 - 12	9 - 12	12+ - 16	17 - 22	22 - 29	33 - 43	43 - 57	51 - 60*

    * Class C felony offenses have a statutory maximum sentence of 60 months, see RCW 9A.20.021.

✓   For gang-related felonies where the court found the offender involved a minor (RCW 9.94A.833), see page 227 for standard range adjustment.
✓   For deadly weapon enhancement, see page 233.
✓   For sentencing alternatives, see page 215.
✓   For community custody eligibility, see page 228.
✓   For any applicable enhancements other than deadly weapon enhancement, see page 224.

RCW 9.94.070
CLASS C* – NONVIOLENT
OFFENDER SCORING RCW 9.94A.525(7)

If it was found that this offense was committed with sexual motivation (RCW 9.94A.533(8)) on or after 7/1/2006, use the General Nonviolent Offense with a Sexual Motivation Finding scoring form on page 236.

If the present conviction is for a felony domestic violence offense where domestic violence was plead and proven, use the General Nonviolent Offense Where Domestic Violence Has Been Plead and Proven scoring form on page 234.

ADULT HISTORY:

    Enter number of felony convictions .... _____ x 1 = _____

JUVENILE HISTORY:

    Enter number of Murder 1, Murder 2, and Class A sex offense felony dispositions .... _____ x 1 = _____

OTHER CURRENT OFFENSES:

(Other current offenses that do not encompass the same conduct count in offender score)

    Enter number of other felony convictions .... _____ x 1 = _____

STATUS:

    Was the offender on community custody on the date the current offense was committed? (if yes) _____ + 1 = _____

Total the last column to get the **Offender Score** (Round down to the nearest whole number)......................... _____

SENTENCE RANGE

	Offender Score									
	0	**1**	**2**	**3**	**4**	**5**	**6**	**7**	**8**	**9+**
LEVEL V	9m	13m	15m	17.5m	25.5m	38m	47.5m	55.5m		
	6 - 12	12+ - 14	13 - 17	15 - 20	22 - 29	33 - 43	41 - 54	51 - 60*	60 - 60*	60 - 60*

    * Class C felony offenses have a statutory maximum sentence of 60 months, see RCW 9A.20.021.

✓   For gang-related felonies where the court found the offender involved a minor (RCW 9.94A.833), see page 227 for standard range adjustment.
✓   For deadly weapon enhancement, see page 233.
✓   For sentencing alternatives, see page 215.
✓   For community custody eligibility, see page 228.
✓   For any applicable enhancements other than deadly weapon enhancement, see page 224.

Physical Control of a Vehicle while under the Influence
of Intoxicating Liquor or any Drug
RCW 46.61.504(6)
CLASS C* – NONVIOLENT/TRAFFIC OFFENSE/CRIMES AGAINST PERSONS
OFFENDER SCORING RCW 9.94A.525(11)

ADULT HISTORY:

Enter number of Vehicular Homicide and Vehicular Assault felony convictions .... _____ x 2 = _____

Enter number of Operation of a Vessel while under the Influence of Intoxicating Liquor
or any Drug felony convictions .... _____ x 1 = _____

Enter number of felony convictions .... _____ x 1 = _____

Enter number of Driving while under the Influence of Intoxicating Liquor or any Drug and
Actual Physical Control while under the Influence of Intoxicating Liquor or any Drug and
Reckless Driving and Hit-and-Run Attended Vehicle <u>non-felony</u> convictions .... _____ x 1 = _____

JUVENILE HISTORY:

Enter number of Murder 1, Murder 2, and Class A sex offense felony dispositions .... _____ x ½ = _____

OTHER CURRENT OFFENSES:

(Other current offenses that do not encompass the same conduct count in offender score)

Enter number of Vehicular Homicide and Vehicular Assault convictions .... _____ x 2 = _____

Enter number of other Operation of a Vessel while under the Influence of Intoxicating Liquor
or any Drug felony convictions .... _____ x 1 = _____

Enter number of other felony convictions .... _____ x 1 = _____

Enter number of Driving while under the Influence of Intoxicating Liquor or any Drug
and Actual Physical Control while under the Influence of Intoxicating Liquor or any Drug
and Reckless Driving and Hit-and-Run Attended Vehicle <u>non-felony</u> convictions .... _____ x 1 = _____

STATUS:

Was the offender on community custody on the date the current offense was committed? (if yes) _____ + 1 = _____

Total the last column to get the **Offender Score** (Round down to the nearest whole number)........................ _____

SENTENCE RANGE

	Offender Score									
	0	**1**	**2**	**3**	**4**	**5**	**6**	**7**	**8**	**9+**
LEVEL IV	6m	9m	13m	15m	17.5m	25.5m	38m	50m	56.5m	
	3 - 9	6 - 12	12+ - 14	13 - 17	15 - 20	22 - 29	33 - 43	43 - 57	53 - 60*	60 - 60*

* Class C felony offenses have a statutory maximum sentence of 60 months, see RCW 9A.20.021.

✓ For gang-related felonies where the court found the offender involved a minor (RCW 9.94A.833), see page 227 for standard range adjustments.
✓ For deadly weapon enhancement, see page 233.
✓ For sentencing alternatives, see page 215.
✓ For community custody eligibility, see page 228.
✓ For any applicable enhancements other than deadly weapon enhancement, see page 224.
✓ For consecutive/concurrent provisions, see page 62.

Possession of Depictions of Minor Engaged
in Sexually Explicit Conduct First Degree

RCW 9.68A.070(1)
CLASS B – NONVIOLENT/SEX
OFFENDER SCORING RCW 9.94A.525(17)

If the present conviction is for a felony domestic violence offense where domestic violence was plead and proven, use the General Nonviolent/Sex Offense Where Domestic Violence Has Been Plead and Proven scoring form on page 235.

ADULT HISTORY:

    Enter number of sex offense felony convictions .... _____ x 3 = _____

    Enter number of felony convictions .... _____ x 1 = _____

JUVENILE HISTORY:

    Enter number of Class A sex offense felony dispositions .... _____ x 3 = _____

    Enter number of Murder 1 and Murder 2 felony dispositions .... _____ x 1 = _____

OTHER CURRENT OFFENSES:

(Other current offenses that do not encompass the same conduct count in offender score)

    Enter number of sex offense felony convictions .... _____ x 3 = _____

    Enter number of other felony convictions .... _____ x 1 = _____

STATUS:

    Was the offender on community custody on the date the current offense was committed? (if yes) _____ + 1 = _____

Total the last column to get the **Offender Score** (Round down to the nearest whole number)......................... _____

SENTENCE RANGE DISPLAYED IS FOR A COMPLETED OFFENSE

FOR **ATTEMPT**, **SOLICITATION**, OR **CONSPIRACY** (RCW 9.94A.595, see page 54), THE SENTENCE RANGE **IS 75%** OF THE COMPLETED RANGE LISTED BELOW

	Offender Score									
	0	**1**	**2**	**3**	**4**	**5**	**6**	**7**	**8**	**9+**
LEVEL VI	13m	17.5m	24m	30m	36m	42m	53.5m	66m	78m	89.5m
	12+ - 14	15 - 20	21 - 27	26 - 34	31 - 41	36 - 48	46 - 61	57 - 75	67 - 89	77 - 102

✓   For gang-related felonies where the court found the offender involved a minor (RCW 9.94A.833), see page 227 for standard range adjustments.
✓   For deadly weapon enhancement, see page 233.
✓   For sentencing alternatives, see page 215.
✓   For community custody eligibility, see page 228.
✓   For any applicable enhancements other than deadly weapon enhancement, see page 224.
✓   If the offender is not a persistent offender and has a <u>prior</u> conviction for an offense listed in RCW 9.94A.030(37)(b), then the sentence is subject to the requirements of RCW 9.94A.507.

Possession of Depictions of Minor Engaged in Sexually Explicit Conduct Second Degree

RCW 9.68A.070(2)
CLASS B – NONVIOLENT/SEX
OFFENDER SCORING RCW 9.94A.525(17)

If the present conviction is for a felony domestic violence offense where domestic violence was plead and proven, use the General Nonviolent/Sex Offense Where Domestic Violence Has Been Plead and Proven scoring form on page 235.

ADULT HISTORY:

Enter number of sex offense felony convictions .... _____ x 3 = _____

Enter number of felony convictions .... _____ x 1 = _____

JUVENILE HISTORY:

Enter number of Class A sex offense felony dispositions .... _____ x 3 = _____

Enter number of Murder 1 and Murder 2 felony dispositions .... _____ x 1 = _____

OTHER CURRENT OFFENSES:

(Other current offenses that do not encompass the same conduct count in offender score)

Enter number of sex offense felony convictions .... _____ x 3 = _____

Enter number of other felony convictions .... _____ x 1 = _____

STATUS:

Was the offender on community custody on the date the current offense was committed? (if yes) _____ + 1 = _____

Total the last column to get the **Offender Score** (Round down to the nearest whole number) .... _____

S SENTENCE RANGE DISPLAYED IS FOR A COMPLETED OFFENSE

FOR **ATTEMPT**, **SOLICITATION**, OR **CONSPIRACY** (RCW 9.94A.595, see page 54), THE SENTENCE RANGE **IS 75%** OF THE COMPLETED RANGE LISTED BELOW

Offender Score										
	0	**1**	**2**	**3**	**4**	**5**	**6**	**7**	**8**	**9+**
LEVEL IV	6m	9m	13m	15m	17.5m	25.5m	38m	50m	61.5m	73.5m
	3 - 9	6 - 12	12+ - 14	13 - 17	15 - 20	22 - 29	33 - 43	43 - 57	53 - 70	63 - 84

✓ For gang-related felonies where the court found the offender involved a minor (RCW 9.94A.833), see page 227 for standard range adjustments.
✓ For deadly weapon enhancement, see page 233.
✓ For sentencing alternatives, see page 215.
✓ For community custody eligibility, see page 228.
✓ For any applicable enhancements other than deadly weapon enhancement, see page 224.
✓ If the offender is not a persistent offender and has a prior conviction for an offense listed in RCW 9.94A.030(37)(b), then the sentence is subject to the requirements of RCW 9.94A.507.

Possession of Ephedrine, Pseudoephedrine or Anhydrous Ammonia with Intent to Manufacture Methamphetamine

RCW 69.50.440
CLASS B – NONVIOLENT/DRUG
OFFENDER SCORING RCW 9.94A.525(13)

If it was found that this offense was committed with sexual motivation (RCW 9.94A.533(8)) on or after 7/1/2006, use the General Drug Offense with a Sexual Motivation Finding scoring form on page 238.

If the present conviction is for a felony domestic violence offense where domestic violence was plead and proven, use the General Drug Offense Where Domestic Violence Has Been Plead and Proven scoring form on page 237.

ADULT HISTORY:

Does the offender have a prior sex or serious violent offense in history?

.... **YES,** Enter number of felony drug convictions _____ x 3 = _____

.... **NO,** Enter number of felony drug convictions _____ x 1 = _____

Enter number of felony convictions .... _____ x 1 = _____

JUVENILE HISTORY:

Enter number of Murder 1, Murder 2, and Class A sex offense felony dispositions .... _____ x 1 = _____

OTHER CURRENT OFFENSES:

(Other current offenses that do not encompass the same conduct count in offender score)

Does the offender have other prior sex or serious violent offense in history?

.... **YES,** Enter number of other felony drug convictions _____ x 3 = _____

.... **NO,** Enter number of other felony drug convictions _____ x 1 = _____

Enter number of other felony convictions .... _____ x 1 = _____

STATUS:

Was the offender on community custody on the date the current offense was committed? (if yes) _____ + 1 = _____

Total the last column to get the **Offender Score** (Round down to the nearest whole number).......................... _____

SENTENCE RANGE – DRUG

	Offender Score		
	0 to 2	3 to 5	6 to 9+
LEVEL III	59.5m	84m	110m
	51 - 68	68+ - 100	100+ - 120

✓ For attempt, solicitation or conspiracy drug felonies see page 56, or for gang-related felonies where the court found the offender involved a minor (RCW 9.94A.833), see page 227 for standard range adjustments.
✓ Per RCW 9.94A.518, any felony offense under chapter 69.50 RCW with a deadly weapon special verdict under RCW 9.94A.602 becomes a level III offense.
✓ For deadly weapon enhancement, see page 233.
✓ For sentencing alternatives, see page 215.
✓ For community custody eligibility, see page 228.
✓ For any applicable enhancements other than deadly weapon enhancement, see page 224.
✓ Per RCW 69.50.408, the statutory maximum for a subsequent conviction under chapter 69.50 RCW is 240 months.

RCW 9.40.120
CLASS B – NONVIOLENT
OFFENDER SCORING RCW 9.94A.525(7)

If it was found that this offense was committed with sexual motivation (RCW 9.94A.533(8)) on or after 7/1/2006, use the General Nonviolent Offense with a Sexual Motivation Finding scoring form on page 236.

If the present conviction is for a felony domestic violence offense where domestic violence was plead and proven, use the General Nonviolent Offense Where Domestic Violence Has Been Plead and Proven scoring form on page 234.

ADULT HISTORY:

Enter number of felony convictions .... _____ x 1 = _____

JUVENILE HISTORY:

Enter number of Murder 1, Murder 2, and Class A sex offense felony dispositions .... _____ x 1 = _____

OTHER CURRENT OFFENSES:

(Other current offenses that do not encompass the same conduct count in offender score)

Enter number of other felony convictions .... _____ x 1 = _____

STATUS:

Was the offender on community custody on the date the current offense was committed? (if yes) _____ + 1 = _____

Total the last column to get the **Offender Score** (Round down to the nearest whole number)......................... _____

SENTENCE RANGE DISPLAYED IS FOR A COMPLETED OFFENSE

FOR **ATTEMPT**, **SOLICITATION**, OR **CONSPIRACY** (RCW 9.94A.595, see page 54), THE SENTENCE RANGE **IS 75%** OF THE COMPLETED RANGE LISTED BELOW

Offender Score									
0	**1**	**2**	**3**	**4**	**5**	**6**	**7**	**8**	**9+**
2m	5m	8m	11m	14m	19.5m	25.5m	38m	50m	59.5m
1 - 3	3 - 8	4 - 12	9 - 12	12+ - 16	17 - 22	22 - 29	33 - 43	43 - 57	51 - 68

(LEVEL III)

✓ For gang-related felonies where the court found the offender involved a minor (RCW 9.94A.833), see page 227 for standard range adjustments.
✓ For deadly weapon enhancement, see page 233.
✓ For sentencing alternatives, see page 215.
✓ For community custody eligibility, see page 228.
✓ For any applicable enhancements other than deadly weapon enhancement, see page 224.

Possession of Machine Gun, Bump-fire Stock, Undetectable Firearm, or Short-Barreled Shotgun or Rifle

RCW 9.41.190
CLASS C* – NONVIOLENT
OFFENDER SCORING RCW 9.94A.525(7)

If it was found that this offense was committed with sexual motivation (RCW 9.94A.533(8)) on or after 7/1/2006, use the General Nonviolent Offense with a Sexual Motivation Finding scoring form on page 236.

If the present conviction is for a felony domestic violence offense where domestic violence was plead and proven, use the General Nonviolent Offense Where Domestic Violence Has Been Plead and Proven scoring form on page 234.

ADULT HISTORY:

  Enter number of felony convictions .... _____ x 1 = _____

JUVENILE HISTORY:

  Enter number of Murder 1, Murder 2, and Class A sex offense felony dispositions .... _____ x 1 = _____

OTHER CURRENT OFFENSES:

(Other current offenses that do not encompass the same conduct count in offender score)

  Enter number of other felony convictions .... _____ x 1 = _____

STATUS:

  Was the offender on community custody on the date the current offense was committed? (if yes) _____ + 1 = _____

Total the last column to get the **Offender Score** (Round down to the nearest whole number).......................... _____

SENTENCE RANGE

	Offender Score									
	0	**1**	**2**	**3**	**4**	**5**	**6**	**7**	**8**	**9+**
LEVEL III	2m	5m	8m	11m	14m	19.5m	25.5m	38m	50m	55.5m
	1 - 3	3 - 8	4 - 12	9 - 12	12+ - 16	17 - 22	22 - 29	33 - 43	43 - 57	51 - 60*

  * Class C felony offenses have a statutory maximum sentence of 60 months, see RCW 9A.20.021.

✓　　For gang-related felonies where the court found the offender involved a minor (RCW 9.94A.833), see page 227 for standard range adjustment.
✓　　For sentencing alternatives, see page 215.
✓　　For community custody eligibility, see page 228.
✓　　For any applicable enhancements other than deadly weapon enhancement, see page 224.

RCW 9A.56.310
CLASS B – NONVIOLENT
OFFENDER SCORING RCW 9.94A.525(7)

If it was found that this offense was committed with sexual motivation (RCW 9.94A.533(8)) on or after 7/1/2006, use the General Nonviolent Offense with a Sexual Motivation Finding scoring form on page 236.

If the present conviction is for a felony domestic violence offense where domestic violence was plead and proven, use the General Nonviolent Offense Where Domestic Violence Has Been Plead and Proven scoring form on page 234.

ADULT HISTORY:

Enter number of felony convictions .... _____ x 1 = _____

JUVENILE HISTORY:

Enter number of Murder 1, Murder 2, and Class A sex offense felony dispositions .... _____ x 1 = _____

OTHER CURRENT OFFENSES:

(Other current offenses that do not encompass the same conduct count in offender score)

Enter number of other felony convictions .... _____ x 1 = _____

STATUS:

Was the offender on community custody on the date the current offense was committed? (if yes) _____ + 1 = _____

Total the last column to get the **Offender Score** (Round down to the nearest whole number)......................... _____

SENTENCE RANGE DISPLAYED IS FOR A COMPLETED OFFENSE

FOR **ATTEMPT**, **SOLICITATION**, OR **CONSPIRACY** (RCW 9.94A.595, see page 54), THE SENTENCE RANGE **IS 75%** OF THE COMPLETED RANGE LISTED BELOW

	Offender Score									
	0	**1**	**2**	**3**	**4**	**5**	**6**	**7**	**8**	**9+**
LEVEL V	9m	13m	15m	17.5m	25.5m	38m	47.5m	59.5m	72m	84m
	6 - 12	12+ - 14	13 - 17	15 - 20	22 - 29	33 - 43	41 - 54	51 - 68	62 - 82	72 - 96

✓ For gang-related felonies where the court found the offender involved a minor (RCW 9.94A.833), see page 227 for standard range adjustments.

✓ For sentencing alternatives, see page 215.

✓ For community custody eligibility, see page 228.

✓ For any applicable enhancements other than deadly weapon enhancement, see page 224.

✓ Each firearm possessed under this section is a separate offense.

✓ The offender shall be sentenced according to RCW 9.94A.589(1)(c) if the offender is convicted of Unlawful Possession of a Firearm 1 or 2 (RCW 9.41.040) and for felonies Theft of a Firearm or Possession of a Stolen Firearm, or both, as current offenses.

✓ If the present conviction is for Unlawful Possession of a Firearm 1 or 2 and felonies Theft of a Firearm or Possession of a Stolen Firearm, or both, charged under RCW 9.41.040, other current convictions for Unlawful Possession of a Firearm 1 or 2, Possession of a Stolen Firearm or Theft of a Firearm may not be included in the computation of the offender score per RCW 9.94A.589(1)(c). The offender will serve consecutive sentences for these particular offenses.

Possession of Stolen Property First Degree
other than a Firearm or Motor Vehicle

RCW 9A.56.150
CLASS B – NONVIOLENT
OFFENDER SCORING RCW 9.94A.525(7)

If it was found that this offense was committed with sexual motivation (RCW 9.94A.533(8)) on or after 7/1/2006, use the General Nonviolent Offense with a Sexual Motivation Finding scoring form on page 236.

If the present conviction is for a felony domestic violence offense where domestic violence was plead and proven, use the General Nonviolent Offense Where Domestic Violence Has Been Plead and Proven scoring form on page 234.

ADULT HISTORY:

Enter number of felony convictions .... _____ x 1 = _____

JUVENILE HISTORY:

Enter number of Murder 1, Murder 2, and Class A sex offense felony dispositions .... _____ x 1 = _____

OTHER CURRENT OFFENSES:

(Other current offenses that do not encompass the same conduct count in offender score)

Enter number of other felony convictions .... _____ x 1 = _____

STATUS:

Was the offender on community custody on the date the current offense was committed? (if yes) _____ + 1 = _____

Total the last column to get the **Offender Score** (Round down to the nearest whole number).......................... _____

SENTENCE RANGE DISPLAYED IS FOR A COMPLETED OFFENSE

FOR **ATTEMPT**, **SOLICITATION**, OR **CONSPIRACY** (RCW 9.94A.595, see page 54), THE SENTENCE RANGE **IS 75%** OF THE COMPLETED RANGE LISTED BELOW

Offender Score										
	0	**1**	**2**	**3**	**4**	**5**	**6**	**7**	**8**	**9+**
LEVEL II		4m	6m	8m	13m	16m	19.5m	25.5m	38m	50m
	0-90 days	2 - 6	3 - 9	4 - 12	12+ - 14	14 - 18	17 - 22	22 - 29	33 - 43	43 - 57

✓ For gang-related felonies where the court found the offender involved a minor (RCW 9.94A.833), see page 227 for standard range adjustments.
✓ For deadly weapon enhancement, see page 233.
✓ For sentencing alternatives, see page 215.
✓ For community custody eligibility, see page 228.
✓ For any applicable enhancements other than deadly weapon enhancement, see page 224.

Possession of Stolen Property Second Degree
other than a Firearm or Motor Vehicle
RCW 9A.56.160
CLASS C – NONVIOLENT
OFFENDER SCORING RCW 9.94A.525(7)

If it was found that this offense was committed with sexual motivation (RCW 9.94A.533(8)) on or after 7/1/2006, use the General Nonviolent Offense with a Sexual Motivation Finding scoring form on page 236.

If the present conviction is for a felony domestic violence offense where domestic violence was plead and proven, use the General Nonviolent Offense Where Domestic Violence Has Been Plead and Proven scoring form on page 234.

ADULT HISTORY:

Enter number of felony convictions .... _____ x 1 = _____

JUVENILE HISTORY:

Enter number of Murder 1, Murder 2, and Class A sex offense felony dispositions .... _____ x 1 = _____

OTHER CURRENT OFFENSES:

(Other current offenses that do not encompass the same conduct count in offender score)

Enter number of other felony convictions .... _____ x 1 = _____

STATUS:

Was the offender on community custody on the date the current offense was committed? (if yes) _____ + 1 = _____

Total the last column to get the **Offender Score** (Round down to the nearest whole number)........................ _____

SENTENCE RANGE

Offender Score										
	0	**1**	**2**	**3**	**4**	**5**	**6**	**7**	**8**	**9+**
LEVEL I			3m	4m	5.5m	8m	13m	16m	19.5m	25.5m
	0-60 days	0-90 days	2 - 5	2 - 6	3 - 8	4 - 12	12+ - 14	14 - 18	17 - 22	22 - 29

✓ For gang-related felonies where the court found the offender involved a minor (RCW 9.94A.833), see page 227 for standard range adjustment.
✓ For deadly weapon enhancement, see page 233.
✓ For sentencing alternatives, see page 215.
✓ For community custody eligibility, see page 228.
✓ For any applicable enhancements other than deadly weapon enhancement, see page 224.

Possession of a Stolen Vehicle

RCW 9A.56.068
CLASS B – NONVIOLENT
OFFENDER SCORING RCW 9.94A.525(20)

If it was found that this offense was committed with sexual motivation (RCW 9.94A.533(8)) on or after 7/1/2006, use the General Nonviolent Offense with a Sexual Motivation Finding scoring form on page 236.

If the present conviction is for a felony domestic violence offense where domestic violence was plead and proven, use the General Nonviolent Offense Where Domestic Violence Has Been Plead and Proven scoring form on page 234.

ADULT HISTORY:

Enter number of Theft of a Motor Vehicle, Theft 1 & 2 (of a Motor Vehicle),
Possession of Stolen Property 1 & 2 (of a Motor Vehicle), Possession of a Stolen Vehicle
and Taking a Motor Vehicle without Permission 1 & 2 felony convictions .... _____ x 3 = _____

Enter number of Vehicle Prowling 2 convictions .... _____ x 1 = _____

Enter number of felony convictions .... _____ x 1 = _____

JUVENILE HISTORY:

Enter number of Murder 1, Murder 2, and Class A sex offense felony dispositions .... _____ x 1 = _____

OTHER CURRENT OFFENSES:

(Other current offenses that do not encompass the same conduct count in offender score)

Enter number of other Theft of a Motor Vehicle, Theft 1 & 2 (of a Motor Vehicle),
Possession of Stolen Property 1 & 2 (of a Motor Vehicle), Possession of a Stolen Vehicle
and Taking a Motor Vehicle without Permission 1 & 2 felony convictions .... _____ x 3 = _____

Enter number of other Vehicle Prowling 2 convictions .... _____ x 1 = _____

Enter number of other felony convictions .... _____ x 1 = _____

STATUS:

Was the offender on community custody on the date the current offense was committed? (if yes) _____ + 1 = _____

Total the last column to get the **Offender Score** (Round down to the nearest whole number)......................... _____

SENTENCE RANGE DISPLAYED IS FOR A COMPLETED OFFENSE

FOR **ATTEMPT**, **SOLICITATION**, OR **CONSPIRACY** (RCW 9.94A.595, see page 54), THE SENTENCE RANGE **IS 75%** OF THE COMPLETED RANGE LISTED BELOW

	Offender Score									
	0	**1**	**2**	**3**	**4**	**5**	**6**	**7**	**8**	**9+**
LEVEL II		4m	6m	8m	13m	16m	19.5m	25.5m	38m	50m
	0-90 days	2 - 6	3 - 9	4 - 12	12+ - 14	14 - 18	17 - 22	22 - 29	33 - 43	43 - 57

✓ For gang-related felonies where the court found the offender involved a minor (RCW 9.94A.833), see page 227 for standard range adjustments.
✓ For deadly weapon enhancement, see page 233.
✓ For sentencing alternatives, see page 215.
✓ For community custody eligibility, see page 228.
✓ For any applicable enhancements other than deadly weapon enhancement, see page 224.

RCW 9.68A.101
CLASS A – VIOLENT/SEX
OFFENDER SCORING RCW 9.94A.525(17)

If the present conviction is for a felony domestic violence offense where domestic violence was plead and proven, use the General Violent/Sex Offense Where Domestic Violence Has Been Plead and Proven scoring form on page 243.

ADULT HISTORY:

Enter number of sex offense felony convictions .... _____ x 3 = _____

Enter number of serious violent and violent felony convictions .... _____ x 2 = _____

Enter number of nonviolent felony convictions .... _____ x 1 = _____

JUVENILE HISTORY:

Enter number of Class A sex offense felony dispositions .... _____ x 3 = _____

Enter number of Murder 1 and Murder 2 felony dispositions .... _____ x 2 = _____

OTHER CURRENT OFFENSES:

(Other current offenses that do not encompass the same conduct count in offender score)

Enter number of other sex offense felony convictions .... _____ x 3 = _____

Enter number of other serious violent and violent felony convictions .... _____ x 2 = _____

Enter number of other nonviolent felony convictions .... _____ x 1 = _____

STATUS:

Was the offender on community custody on the date the current offense was committed? .... _____ + 1 = _____

Total the last column to get the **Offender Score** (Round down to the nearest whole number).................. _____

SENTENCE RANGE DISPLAYED IS FOR A COMPLETED OFFENSE

FOR **ATTEMPT**, **SOLICITATION**, OR **CONSPIRACY** (RCW 9.94A.595, see page 54), THE SENTENCE RANGE **IS 75%** OF THE COMPLETED RANGE LISTED BELOW

	Offender Score									
	0	**1**	**2**	**3**	**4**	**5**	**6**	**7**	**8**	**9+**
LEVEL XII	108m	119m	129m	140m	150m	161m	189m	207m	243m	279m
	93 - 123	102 - 136	111 - 147	120 - 160	129 - 171	138 - 184	162 - 216	178 - 236	209 - 277	240 - 318

✓ For gang-related felonies where the court found the offender involved a minor (RCW 9.94A.833), see page 227 for standard range adjustments.
✓ For deadly weapon enhancement, see page 233.
✓ For sentencing alternatives, see page 215.
✓ For community custody eligibility, see page 228.
✓ For any applicable enhancements other than deadly weapon enhancement, see page 224.
✓ If the offender is not a persistent offender and has a <u>prior</u> conviction for an offense listed in RCW 9.94A.030(37)(b), then the sentence is subject to the requirements of RCW 9.94A.507.

RCW 9A.88.070
CLASS B* – NONVIOLENT/CRIMES AGAINST PERSONS
OFFENDER SCORING RCW 9.94A.525(7)

If it was found that this offense was committed with sexual motivation (RCW 9.94A.533(8)) on or after 7/1/2006, use the General Nonviolent Offense with a Sexual Motivation Finding scoring form on page 236.

If the present conviction is for a felony domestic violence offense where domestic violence was plead and proven, use the General Nonviolent Offense Where Domestic Violence Has Been Plead and Proven scoring form on page 234.

ADULT HISTORY:

Enter number of felony convictions .... _____ x 1 = _____

JUVENILE HISTORY:

Enter number of Murder 1, Murder 2, and Class A sex offense felony dispositions .... _____ x 1 = _____

OTHER CURRENT OFFENSES:

(Other current offenses that do not encompass the same conduct count in offender score)

Enter number of other felony convictions .... _____ x 1 = _____

STATUS:

Was the offender on community custody on the date the current offense was committed? (if yes) _____ + 1 = _____

Total the last column to get the **Offender Score** (Round down to the nearest whole number).......................... _____

SENTENCE RANGE DISPLAYED IS FOR A COMPLETED OFFENSE

FOR **ATTEMPT**, **SOLICITATION**, OR **CONSPIRACY** (RCW 9.94A.595, see page 54), THE SENTENCE RANGE **IS 75%** OF THE COMPLETED RANGE LISTED BELOW

	Offender Score									
	0	**1**	**2**	**3**	**4**	**5**	**6**	**7**	**8**	**9+**
LEVEL VIII	24m	30m	36m	42m	47.5m	53.5m	78m	89.5m	101.5m	114m
	21 - 27	26 - 34	31 - 41	36 - 48	41 - 54	46 - 61	67 - 89	77 - 102	87 - 116	108 - 120*

* Class B felony offenses have a statutory maximum sentence of 120 months, see RCW 9A.20.021.

✓ For gang-related felonies where the court found the offender involved a minor (RCW 9.94A.833), see page 227 for standard range adjustments.
✓ For deadly weapon enhancement, see page 233.
✓ For sentencing alternatives, see page 215.
✓ For community custody eligibility, see page 228.
✓ For any applicable enhancements other than deadly weapon enhancement, see page 224.

Promoting Prostitution Second Degree

RCW 9A.88.080
CLASS C* – NONVIOLENT
OFFENDER SCORING RCW 9.94A.525(7)

If it was found that this offense was committed with sexual motivation (RCW 9.94A.533(8)) on or after 7/1/2006, use the General Nonviolent Offense with a Sexual Motivation Finding scoring form on page 236.

If the present conviction is for a felony domestic violence offense where domestic violence was plead and proven, use the General Nonviolent Offense Where Domestic Violence Has Been Plead and Proven scoring form on page 234.

ADULT HISTORY:

Enter number of felony convictions .... _____ x 1 = _____

JUVENILE HISTORY:

Enter number of Murder 1, Murder 2, and Class A sex offense felony dispositions .... _____ x 1 = _____

OTHER CURRENT OFFENSES:

(Other current offenses that do not encompass the same conduct count in offender score)

Enter number of other felony convictions .... _____ x 1 = _____

STATUS:

Was the offender on community custody on the date the current offense was committed? (if yes) _____ + 1 = _____

Total the last column to get the **Offender Score** (Round down to the nearest whole number)......................... _____

SENTENCE RANGE

	Offender Score									
	0	**1**	**2**	**3**	**4**	**5**	**6**	**7**	**8**	**9+**
LEVEL III	2m	5m	8m	11m	14m	19.5m	25.5m	38m	50m	55.5m
	1 - 3	3 - 8	4 - 12	9 - 12	12+ - 16	17 - 22	22 - 29	33 - 43	43 - 57	51 - 60*

* Class C felony offenses have a statutory maximum sentence of 60 months, see RCW 9A.20.021.

✓ For gang-related felonies where the court found the offender involved a minor (RCW 9.94A.833), see page 227 for standard range adjustment.
✓ For deadly weapon enhancement, see page 233.
✓ For sentencing alternatives, see page 215.
✓ For community custody eligibility, see page 228.
✓ For any applicable enhancements other than deadly weapon enhancement, see page 224.

RCW 9A.44.040
CLASS A – SERIOUS VIOLENT/SEX/CRIMES AGAINST PERSONS
ATTEMPT = CLASS A - SERIOUS VIOLENT/SEX
OFFENDER SCORING RCW 9.94A.525(17)

If the present conviction is for a felony domestic violence offense where domestic violence was plead and proven, use the General Serious Violent/Sex Offense Where Domestic Violence Has Been Plead and Proven scoring form on page 240.

ADULT HISTORY:

Enter number of sex offense felony convictions .... _____ x 3 = _____

Enter number of serious violent felony convictions .... _____ x 3 = _____

Enter number of violent felony convictions .... _____ x 2 = _____

Enter number of nonviolent felony convictions .... _____ x 1 = _____

JUVENILE HISTORY:

Enter number of Murder 1, Murder 2, and Class A sex offense felony dispositions .... _____ x 3 = _____

OTHER CURRENT OFFENSES:

(Other current offenses that do not encompass the same conduct count in offender score)

Enter number of other sex offense felony convictions .... _____ x 3 = _____

Enter number of other violent felony convictions .... _____ x 2 = _____

Enter number of other nonviolent felony convictions .... _____ x 1 = _____

STATUS:

Was the offender on community custody on the date the current offense was committed?............ _____ + 1 = _____

Total the last column to get the **Offender Score** (Round down to the nearest whole number) .... _____

SENTENCE RANGE DISPLAYED IS FOR A COMPLETED OFFENSE

FOR **ATTEMPT**, **SOLICITATION**, OR **CONSPIRACY** (RCW 9.94A.595, see page 54), THE SENTENCE RANGE **IS 75%** OF THE COMPLETED RANGE LISTED BELOW

Offender Score									
0	**1**	**2**	**3**	**4**	**5**	**6**	**7**	**8**	**9+**
108m	119m	129m	140m	150m	161m	189m	207m	243m	279m
93 - 123	102 - 136	111 - 147	120 - 160	129 - 171	138 - 184	162 - 216	178 - 236	209 - 277	240 - 318

(Row label: **LEVEL XII**)

✓ For gang-related felonies where the court found the offender involved a minor (RCW 9.94A.833), see page 227 for standard range adjustments.
✓ For deadly weapon enhancement, see page 233.
✓ For sentencing alternatives, see page 215.
✓ For community custody eligibility, see page 228.
✓ For any applicable enhancements other than deadly weapon enhancement, see page 224.
✓ If the offender is not a persistent offender and the current offense was committed on or after 9/1/2001, then the offender is subject to the requirements under RCW 9.94A.507.
✓ Multiple current serious violent offenses shall have consecutive sentences imposed per the rules of RCW 9.94A.589(1)(b).
✓ Excluding convictions for attempt, the statutory minimum sentence is 60 months per RCW 9.94A.540 and is imposed under the rules of RCW 9.94A.507
✓ Per RCW 9.94A.507(3)(c)(ii), excluding convictions for attempt, the minimum term shall be either the maximum of the standard sentence range for the offense or 25 years, whichever is greater, for a finding that the victim was under the age of 15 at the time of the offense under RCW 9.94A.837 or found to be a person with a developmental disability or mental disorder, or a frail elder or vulnerable adult at the time of the offense under RCW 9.94A.838.

Rape First Degree, Solicitation or Conspiracy

RCW 9A.44.040
SERIOUS VIOLENT/SEX
SOLICITATION = CLASS A
CONSPIRACY = CLASS B*
OFFENDER SCORING RCW 9.94A.525(17)

If the present conviction is for a felony domestic violence offense where domestic violence was plead and proven, use the General Serious Violent/Sex Offense Where Domestic Violence Has Been Plead and Proven scoring form on page 240.

ADULT HISTORY:

Enter number of sex offense felony convictions .... _____ x 3 = _____

Enter number of serious violent felony convictions .... _____ x 3 = _____

Enter number of violent felony convictions .... _____ x 2 = _____

Enter number of nonviolent felony convictions .... _____ x 1 = _____

JUVENILE HISTORY:

Enter number of Murder 1, Murder 2, and Class A sex offense felony dispositions .... _____ x 3 = _____

OTHER CURRENT OFFENSES:

(Other current offenses that do not encompass the same conduct count in offender score)

Enter number of other sex offense felony convictions .... _____ x 3 = _____

Enter number of other violent felony convictions .... _____ x 2 = _____

Enter number of other nonviolent felony convictions .... _____ x 1 = _____

STATUS:

Was the offender on community custody on the date the current offense was committed? .... _____ + 1 = _____

Total the last column to get the **Offender Score** (Round down to the nearest whole number)................. _____

SENTENCE RANGE DISPLAYED IS FOR A COMPLETED OFFENSE

FOR **ATTEMPT**, **SOLICITATION**, OR **CONSPIRACY** (RCW 9.94A.595, see page 54), THE SENTENCE RANGE **IS 75%** OF THE COMPLETED RANGE LISTED BELOW

	Offender Score									
	0	1	2	3	4	5	6	7	8	9+
LEVEL XII	108m	119m	129m	140m	150m	161m	189m	207m	243m	279m
	93 - 123	102 - 136	111 - 147	120 - 160	129 - 171	138 - 184	162 - 216	178 - 236	209 - 277	240 - 318

* Class B felony offenses have a statutory maximum sentence of 120 months, see RCW 9A.20.021.

✓ For gang-related felonies where the court found the offender involved a minor (RCW 9.94A.833), see page 227 for standard range adjustments.
✓ For deadly weapon enhancement, see page 233.
✓ For sentencing alternatives, see page 215.
✓ For community custody eligibility, see page 228.
✓ For any applicable enhancements other than deadly weapon enhancement, see page 224.
✓ If the offender is not a persistent offender and has a prior conviction for an offense listed in RCW 9.94A.030(37)(b), then the sentence is subject to the requirements of RCW 9.94A.507.
✓ Multiple current serious violent offenses shall have consecutive sentences imposed per the rules of RCW 9.94A.589(1)(b).

Rape Second Degree, Completed or Attempt
RCW 9A.44.050
CLASS A – VIOLENT/SEX/CRIMES AGAINST PERSONS
ATTEMPT = CLASS A VIOLENT/SEX
OFFENDER SCORING RCW 9.94A.525(17)

If the present conviction is for a felony domestic violence offense where domestic violence was plead and proven, use the General Violent/Sex Offense Where Domestic Violence Has Been Plead and Proven scoring form on page 243.

ADULT HISTORY:

Enter number of sex offense felony convictions .... _____ x 3 = _____

Enter number of serious violent and violent felony convictions .... _____ x 2 = _____

Enter number of nonviolent felony convictions .... _____ x 1 = _____

JUVENILE HISTORY:

Enter number of Class A sex offense felony dispositions .... _____ x 3 = _____

Enter number of Murder 1 and Murder 2 felony dispositions .... _____ x 2 = _____

OTHER CURRENT OFFENSES:

(Other current offenses that do not encompass the same conduct count in offender score)

Enter number of other sex offense felony convictions .... _____ x 3 = _____

Enter number of other serious violent and violent felony convictions .... _____ x 2 = _____

Enter number of other nonviolent felony convictions .... _____ x 1 = _____

STATUS:

Was the offender on community custody on the date the current offense was committed?........... _____ + 1 = _____

Total the last column to get the **Offender Score** (Round down to the nearest whole number) .... _____

SENTENCE RANGE DISPLAYED IS FOR A COMPLETED OFFENSE

FOR **ATTEMPT**, **SOLICITATION**, OR **CONSPIRACY** (RCW 9.94A.595, see page 54), THE SENTENCE RANGE **IS 75%** OF THE COMPLETED RANGE LISTED BELOW

	Offender Score									
	0	**1**	**2**	**3**	**4**	**5**	**6**	**7**	**8**	**9+**
LEVEL XI	90m	100m	110m	119m	129m	139m	170m	185m	215m	245m
	78 - 102	86 - 114	95 - 125	102 - 136	111 - 147	120 - 158	146 - 194	159 - 211	185 - 245	210 - 280

✓ For gang-related felonies where the court found the offender involved a minor (RCW 9.94A.833), see page 227 for standard range adjustments.

✓ For deadly weapon enhancement, see page 233.

✓ For sentencing alternatives, see page 215.

✓ For community custody eligibility, see page 228.

✓ For any applicable enhancements other than deadly weapon enhancement, see page 224.

✓ If the offender is not a persistent offender and the current offense was committed on or after 9/1/2001, then the offender is subject to the requirements under RCW 9.94A.507.

✓ Per RCW 9.94A.507(3)(c)(ii), excluding convictions for attempt, the minimum term shall be either the maximum of the standard sentence range for the offense or 25 years, whichever is greater, for a finding that the victim was under the age of 15 at the time of the offense under RCW 9.94A.837.

✓ For Rape 2 with Forcible Compulsion: Per RCW 9.94A.507(3)(c)(ii), excluding convictions for attempt, the minimum term shall be either the maximum of the standard sentence range for the offense or 25 years, whichever is greater, for a finding that the victim found to be a person with a development disability or mental disorder, or a frail elder or vulnerable adult at the time of the offense under RCW 9.94A.838.

Rape Second Degree, Solicitation or Conspiracy

RCW 9A.44.050
VIOLENT/SEX
SOLICITATION = CLASS A
CONSPIRACY = CLASS B*
OFFENDER SCORING RCW 9.94A.525(17)

If the present conviction is for a felony domestic violence offense where domestic violence was plead and proven, use the General Violent/Sex Offense Where Domestic Violence Has Been Plead and Proven scoring form on page 243.

ADULT HISTORY:

Enter number of sex offense felony convictions .... _____ x 3 = _____

Enter number of serious violent and violent felony convictions .... _____ x 2 = _____

Enter number of nonviolent felony convictions .... _____ x 1 = _____

JUVENILE HISTORY:

Enter number of Class A sex offense felony dispositions .... _____ x 3 = _____

Enter number of Murder 1 and Murder 2 felony dispositions .... _____ x 2 = _____

OTHER CURRENT OFFENSES:

(Other current offenses that do not encompass the same conduct count in offender score)

Enter number of other sex offense felony convictions .... _____ x 3 = _____

Enter number of other serious violent and violent felony convictions .... _____ x 2 = _____

Enter number of other nonviolent felony convictions .... _____ x 1 = _____

STATUS:

Was the offender on community custody on the date the current offense was committed? .... _____ + 1 = _____

Total the last column to get the **Offender Score** (Round down to the nearest whole number).................. _____

SENTENCE RANGE DISPLAYED IS FOR A COMPLETED OFFENSE

FOR **ATTEMPT**, **SOLICITATION**, OR **CONSPIRACY** (RCW 9.94A.595, see page 54), THE SENTENCE RANGE **IS 75%** OF THE COMPLETED RANGE LISTED BELOW

	Offender Score									
	0	1	2	3	4	5	6	7	8	9+
LEVEL XI	90m	100m	110m	119m	129m	139m	170m	185m	215m	245m
	78 - 102	86 - 114	95 - 125	102 - 136	111 - 147	120 - 158	146 - 194	159 - 211	185 - 245	210 - 280

* Class B felony offenses have a statutory maximum sentence of 120 months, see RCW 9A.20.021.

✓ For gang-related felonies where the court found the offender involved a minor (RCW 9.94A.833), see page 227 for standard range adjustments.
✓ For deadly weapon enhancement, see page 233.
✓ For sentencing alternatives, see page 215.
✓ For community custody eligibility, see page 228.
✓ For any applicable enhancements other than deadly weapon enhancement, see page 224.
✓ If the offender is not a persistent offender and has a <u>prior</u> conviction for an offense listed in RCW 9.94A.030(37)(b), then the sentence is subject to the requirements of RCW 9.94A.507.

Rape Third Degree

RCW 9A.44.060
CLASS C* – NONVIOLENT/SEX/CRIMES AGAINST PERSONS
OFFENDER SCORING RCW 9.94A.525(17)

If the present conviction is for a felony domestic violence offense where domestic violence was plead and proven, use the General Nonviolent/Sex Offense Where Domestic Violence Has Been Plead and Proven scoring form on page 235.

ADULT HISTORY:

Enter number of sex offense felony convictions .... _____ x 3 = _____

Enter number of felony convictions .... _____ x 1 = _____

JUVENILE HISTORY:

Enter number of Class A sex offense felony dispositions .... _____ x 3 = _____

Enter number of Murder 1 and Murder 2 felony dispositions .... _____ x 1 = _____

OTHER CURRENT OFFENSES:

(Other current offenses that do not encompass the same conduct count in offender score)

Enter number of sex offense felony convictions .... _____ x 3 = _____

Enter number of other felony convictions .... _____ x 1 = _____

STATUS:

Was the offender on community custody on the date the current offense was committed? (if yes) _____ + 1 = _____

Total the last column to get the **Offender Score** (Round down to the nearest whole number).......................... _____

SENTENCE RANGE

	Offender Score									
	0	**1**	**2**	**3**	**4**	**5**	**6**	**7**	**8**	**9+**
LEVEL V	9m	13m	15m	17.5m	25.5m	38m	47.5m	55.5m		
	6 - 12	12+ - 14	13 - 17	15 - 20	22 - 29	33 - 43	41 - 54	51 - 60*	60 - 60*	60 - 60*

* Class C felony offenses have a statutory maximum sentence of 60 months, see RCW 9A.20.021.

✓ For gang-related felonies where the court found the offender involved a minor (RCW 9.94A.833), see page 227 for standard range adjustment.
✓ For deadly weapon enhancement, see page 233.
✓ For sentencing alternatives, see page 215.
✓ For community custody eligibility, see page 228.
✓ For any applicable enhancements other than deadly weapon enhancement, see page 224.
✓ If the offender is not a persistent offender and has a prior conviction for an offense listed in RCW 9.94A.030(37)(b), then the sentence is subject to the requirements of RCW 9.94A.507.

Rape of a Child First Degree, Completed or Attempt

RCW 9A.44.073
CLASS A – VIOLENT/SEX/CRIMES AGAINST PERSONS
ATTEMPT = CLASS A - VIOLENT/SEX
OFFENDER SCORING RCW 9.94A.525(17)

If the present conviction is for a felony domestic violence offense where domestic violence was plead and proven, use the General Violent/Sex Offense Where Domestic Violence Has Been Plead and Proven scoring form on page 243.

ADULT HISTORY:

Enter number of sex offense felony convictions .... _____ x 3 = _____

Enter number of serious violent and violent felony convictions .... _____ x 2 = _____

Enter number of nonviolent felony convictions .... _____ x 1 = _____

JUVENILE HISTORY:

Enter number of Class A sex offense felony dispositions .... _____ x 3 = _____

Enter number of Murder 1 and Murder 2 felony dispositions .... _____ x 2 = _____

OTHER CURRENT OFFENSES:

(Other current offenses that do not encompass the same conduct count in offender score)

Enter number of other sex offense felony convictions .... _____ x 3 = _____

Enter number of other serious violent and violent felony convictions .... _____ x 2 = _____

Enter number of other nonviolent felony convictions .... _____ x 1 = _____

STATUS:

Was the offender on community custody on the date the current offense was committed? .... _____ + 1 = _____

Total the last column to get the **Offender Score** (Round down to the nearest whole number)................. _____

SENTENCE RANGE DISPLAYED IS FOR A COMPLETED OFFENSE

FOR **ATTEMPT**, **SOLICITATION**, OR **CONSPIRACY** (RCW 9.94A.595, see page 54), THE SENTENCE RANGE **IS 75%** OF THE COMPLETED RANGE LISTED BELOW

Offender Score										
	0	**1**	**2**	**3**	**4**	**5**	**6**	**7**	**8**	**9+**
LEVEL XII	108m	119m	129m	140m	150m	161m	189m	207m	243m	279m
	93 - 123	102 - 136	111 - 147	120 - 160	129 - 171	138 - 184	162 - 216	178 - 236	209 - 277	240 - 318

✓ For gang-related felonies where the court found the offender involved a minor (RCW 9.94A.833), see page 227 for standard range adjustments.
✓ For deadly weapon enhancement, see page 233.
✓ For sentencing alternatives, see page 215.
✓ For community custody eligibility, see page 228.
✓ For any applicable enhancements other than deadly weapon enhancement, see page 224.
✓ If the offender is older than 17 years of age and is not a persistent offender and the current offense was committed on or after 9/1/2001, then the offender is subject to the requirements under RCW 9.94A.507.
✓ If the offender is older than 17 years of age and is not a persistent offender and has a prior conviction for an offense listed in RCW 9.94A.030(37)(b), then the sentence is subject to the requirements of RCW 9.94A.507.
✓ If the offender engaged the victim in sexual conduct in exchange for a fee, an additional 12 months shall be added to the standard sentence range (RCW 9.94A.533(9)).
✓ Per RCW 9.94A.507(3)(c)(ii), excluding convictions for attempt, the minimum term shall be either the maximum of the standard sentence range for the offense or 25 years, whichever is greater, for a finding that the offense was predatory under RCW 9.94A.836.

RCW 9A.44.073
VIOLENT/SEX
SOLICITATION = CLASS A
CONSPIRACY = CLASS B*
OFFENDER SCORING RCW 9.94A.525(17)

If the present conviction is for a felony domestic violence offense where domestic violence was plead and proven, use the General Violent/Sex Offense Where Domestic Violence Has Been Plead and Proven scoring form on page 243.

ADULT HISTORY:

Enter number of sex offense felony convictions .... _____ x 3 = _____

Enter number of serious violent and violent felony convictions .... _____ x 2 = _____

Enter number of nonviolent felony convictions .... _____ x 1 = _____

JUVENILE HISTORY:

Enter number of Class A sex offense felony dispositions .... _____ x 3 = _____

Enter number of Murder 1 and Murder 2 felony dispositions .... _____ x 2 = _____

OTHER CURRENT OFFENSES:

(Other current offenses that do not encompass the same conduct count in offender score)

Enter number of other sex offense felony convictions .... _____ x 3 = _____

Enter number of other serious violent and violent felony convictions .... _____ x 2 = _____

Enter number of other nonviolent felony convictions .... _____ x 1 = _____

STATUS:

Was the offender on community custody on the date the current offense was committed? .... _____ + 1 = _____

Total the last column to get the **Offender Score** (Round down to the nearest whole number) .... _____

SENTENCE RANGE DISPLAYED IS FOR A COMPLETED OFFENSE

FOR **ATTEMPT**, **SOLICITATION**, OR **CONSPIRACY** (RCW 9.94A.595, see page 54), THE SENTENCE RANGE **IS 75%** OF THE COMPLETED RANGE LISTED BELOW

Offender Score									
	0	1	2	3	4	5	6	7	8	9+
LEVEL XII	108m	119m	129m	140m	150m	161m	189m	207m	243m	279m
	93 - 123	102 - 136	111 - 147	120 - 160	129 - 171	138 - 184	162 - 216	178 - 236	209 - 277	240 - 318

* Class B felony offenses have a statutory maximum sentence of 120 months, see RCW 9A.20.021.

✓ For gang-related felonies where the court found the offender involved a minor (RCW 9.94A.833), see page 227 for standard range adjustments.
✓ For deadly weapon enhancement, see page 233.
✓ For sentencing alternatives, see page 215.
✓ For community custody eligibility, see page 228.
✓ For any applicable enhancements other than deadly weapon enhancement, see page 224.
✓ If the offender is not a persistent offender and has a prior conviction for an offense listed in RCW 9.94A.030(37)(b), then the sentence is subject to the requirements of RCW 9.94A.507.
✓ If the offender engaged the victim in sexual conduct in exchange for a fee, an additional 12 months shall be added to the standard sentence range (RCW 9.94A.533(9)).

RCW 9A.44.076
CLASS A – VIOLENT/SEX/CRIMES AGAINST PERSONS
ATTEMPT = CLASS A - VIOLENT/SEX
OFFENDER SCORING RCW 9.94A.525(17)

If the present conviction is for a felony domestic violence offense where domestic violence was plead and proven, use the General Violent/Sex Offense Where Domestic Violence Has Been Plead and Proven scoring form on page 243.

ADULT HISTORY:

Enter number of sex offense felony convictions .... _____ x 3 = _____

Enter number of serious violent and violent felony convictions .... _____ x 2 = _____

Enter number of nonviolent felony convictions .... _____ x 1 = _____

JUVENILE HISTORY:

Enter number of Class A sex offense felony dispositions .... _____ x 3 = _____

Enter number of Murder 1 and Murder 2 felony dispositions .... _____ x 2 = _____

OTHER CURRENT OFFENSES:

(Other current offenses that do not encompass the same conduct count in offender score)

Enter number of other sex offense felony convictions .... _____ x 3 = _____

Enter number of other serious violent and violent felony convictions .... _____ x 2 = _____

Enter number of other nonviolent felony convictions .... _____ x 1 = _____

STATUS:

Was the offender on community custody on the date the current offense was committed? .... _____ + 1 = _____

Total the last column to get the **Offender Score** (Round down to the nearest whole number).................. _____

SENTENCE RANGE DISPLAYED IS FOR A COMPLETED OFFENSE

FOR **ATTEMPT**, **SOLICITATION**, OR **CONSPIRACY** (RCW 9.94A.595, see page 54), THE SENTENCE RANGE **IS 75%** OF THE COMPLETED RANGE LISTED BELOW

Offender Score										
	0	**1**	**2**	**3**	**4**	**5**	**6**	**7**	**8**	**9+**
LEVEL XI	90m	100m	110m	119m	129m	139m	170m	185m	215m	245m
	78 - 102	86 - 114	95 - 125	102 - 136	111 - 147	120 - 158	146 - 194	159 - 211	185 - 245	210 - 280

✓ For gang-related felonies where the court found the offender involved a minor (RCW 9.94A.833), see page 227 for standard range adjustments.
✓ For deadly weapon enhancement, see page 233.
✓ For sentencing alternatives, see page 215.
✓ For community custody eligibility, see page 228.
✓ For any applicable enhancements other than deadly weapon enhancement, see page 224.
✓ If the offender is older than 17 years of age and is not a persistent offender and the current offense was committed on or after 9/1/2001, then the offender is subject to the requirements under RCW 9.94A.507.
✓ If the offender is older than 17 years of age and is not a persistent offender and has a prior conviction for an offense listed in RCW 9.94A.030(37)(b), then the sentence is subject to the requirements of RCW 9.94A.507.
✓ If the offender engaged the victim in sexual conduct in exchange for a fee, an additional 12 months shall be added to the standard sentence range (RCW 9.94A.533(9)).
✓ Per RCW 9.94A.507(3)(c)(ii), excluding convictions for attempt, the minimum term shall be either the maximum of the standard sentence range for the offense or 25 years, whichever is greater, for a finding that the offense was predatory under RCW 9.94A.836.

Rape of a Child Second Degree, Solicitation or Conspiracy

RCW 9A.44.076
VIOLENT/SEX
SOLICITATION = CLASS A
CONSPIRACY = CLASS B*
OFFENDER SCORING RCW 9.94A.525(17)

If the present conviction is for a felony domestic violence offense where domestic violence was plead and proven, use the General Violent/Sex Offense Where Domestic Violence Has Been Plead and Proven scoring form on page 243.

ADULT HISTORY:

Enter number of sex offense felony convictions .... _______ x 3 = _______
Enter number of serious violent and violent felony convictions .... _______ x 2 = _______
Enter number of nonviolent felony convictions .... _______ x 1 = _______

JUVENILE HISTORY:

Enter number of Class A sex offense felony dispositions .... _______ x 3 = _______
Enter number of Murder 1 and Murder 2 felony dispositions .... _______ x 2 = _______

OTHER CURRENT OFFENSES:

(Other current offenses that do not encompass the same conduct count in offender score)

Enter number of other sex offense felony convictions .... _______ x 3 = _______
Enter number of other serious violent and violent felony convictions .... _______ x 2 = _______
Enter number of other nonviolent felony convictions .... _______ x 1 = _______

STATUS:

Was the offender on community custody on the date the current offense was committed?.......... _______ + 1 = _______

Total the last column to get the **Offender Score** (Round down to the nearest whole number) .... _______

SENTENCE RANGE DISPLAYED IS FOR A COMPLETED OFFENSE

FOR **ATTEMPT**, **SOLICITATION**, OR **CONSPIRACY** (RCW 9.94A.595, see page 54), THE SENTENCE RANGE **IS 75%** OF THE COMPLETED RANGE LISTED BELOW

	Offender Score									
	0	1	2	3	4	5	6	7	8	9+
LEVEL XI	90m 78 - 102	100m 86 - 114	110m 95 - 125	119m 102 - 136	129m 111 - 147	139m 120 - 158	170m 146 - 194	185m 159 - 211	215m 185 - 245	245m 210 - 280

* Class B felony offenses have a statutory maximum sentence of 120 months, see RCW 9A.20.021.

- ✓ For gang-related felonies where the court found the offender involved a minor (RCW 9.94A.833), see page 227 for standard range adjustments.
- ✓ For deadly weapon enhancement, see page 233.
- ✓ For sentencing alternatives, see page 215.
- ✓ For community custody eligibility, see page 228.
- ✓ For any applicable enhancements other than deadly weapon enhancement, see page 224.
- ✓ If the offender is not a persistent offender and has a prior conviction for an offense listed in RCW 9.94A.030(37)(b), then the sentence is subject to the requirements of RCW 9.94A.507.
- ✓ If the offender engaged the victim in sexual conduct in exchange for a fee, an additional 12 months shall be added to the standard sentence range (RCW 9.94A.533(9)).

RCW 9A.44.079
CLASS C* – NONVIOLENT/SEX/CRIMES AGAINST PERSONS
OFFENDER SCORING RCW 9.94A.525(17)

If the present conviction is for a felony domestic violence offense where domestic violence was plead and proven, use the General Nonviolent/Sex Offense Where Domestic Violence Has Been Plead and Proven scoring form on page 235.

ADULT HISTORY:

Enter number of sex offense felony convictions .... _____ x 3 = _____

Enter number of felony convictions .... _____ x 1 = _____

JUVENILE HISTORY:

Enter number of Class A sex offense felony dispositions .... _____ x 3 = _____

Enter number of Murder 1 and Murder 2 felony dispositions .... _____ x 1 = _____

OTHER CURRENT OFFENSES:

(Other current offenses that do not encompass the same conduct count in offender score)

Enter number of sex offense felony convictions .... _____ x 3 = _____

Enter number of other felony convictions .... _____ x 1 = _____

STATUS:

Was the offender on community custody on the date the current offense was committed? (if yes) _____ + 1 = _____

Total the last column to get the **Offender Score** (Round down to the nearest whole number) .... _____

SENTENCE RANGE

	Offender Score									
	0	**1**	**2**	**3**	**4**	**5**	**6**	**7**	**8**	**9+**
LEVEL VI	13m	17.5m	24m	30m	36m	42m	53m	58.5m		
	12+ - 14	15 - 20	21 - 27	26 - 34	31 - 41	36 - 48	46 - 60*	57 - 60*	60 - 60*	60 - 60*

* Class C felony offenses have a statutory maximum sentence of 60 months, see RCW 9A.20.021.

✓ For gang-related felonies where the court found the offender involved a minor (RCW 9.94A.833), see page 227 for standard range adjustment.
✓ For deadly weapon enhancement, see page 233.
✓ For sentencing alternatives, see page 215.
✓ For community custody eligibility, see page 228.
✓ For any applicable enhancements other than deadly weapon enhancement, see page 224.
✓ If the offender is not a persistent offender and has a prior conviction for an offense listed in RCW 9.94A.030(37)(b), then the sentence is subject to the requirements of RCW 9.94A.507.
✓ If the offender engaged the victim in sexual conduct in exchange for a fee, an additional 12 months shall be added to the standard sentence range (RCW 9.94A.533(9)).

Reckless Burning First Degree

RCW 9A.48.040
CLASS C – NONVIOLENT
OFFENDER SCORING RCW 9.94A.525(7)

If it was found that this offense was committed with sexual motivation (RCW 9.94A.533(8)) on or after 7/1/2006, use the General Nonviolent Offense with a Sexual Motivation Finding scoring form on page 236.

If the present conviction is for a felony domestic violence offense where domestic violence was plead and proven, use the General Nonviolent Offense Where Domestic Violence Has Been Plead and Proven scoring form on page 234.

ADULT HISTORY:

    Enter number of felony convictions .... _____ x 1 = _____

JUVENILE HISTORY:

    Enter number of Murder 1, Murder 2, and Class A sex offense felony dispositions .... _____ x 1 = _____

OTHER CURRENT OFFENSES:

(Other current offenses that do not encompass the same conduct count in offender score)

    Enter number of other felony convictions .... _____ x 1 = _____

STATUS:

    Was the offender on community custody on the date the current offense was committed? (if yes) _____ + 1 = _____

Total the last column to get the **Offender Score** (Round down to the nearest whole number).......................... _____

SENTENCE RANGE

		Offender Score									
		0	1	2	3	4	5	6	7	8	9+
LEVEL I				3m	4m	5.5m	8m	13m	16m	19.5m	25.5m
		0-60 days	0-90 days	2 - 5	2 - 6	3 - 8	4 - 12	12+ - 14	14 - 18	17 - 22	22 - 29

✓   For gang-related felonies where the court found the offender involved a minor (RCW 9.94A.833), see page 227 for standard range adjustment.
✓   For deadly weapon enhancement, see page 233.
✓   For sentencing alternatives, see page 215.
✓   For community custody eligibility, see page 228.
✓   For any applicable enhancements other than deadly weapon enhancement, see page 224.

RCW 9A.76.070(2)(a)
CLASS B – NONVIOLENT
OFFENDER SCORING RCW 9.94A.525(7)

If it was found that this offense was committed with sexual motivation (RCW 9.94A.533(8)) on or after 7/1/2006, use the General Nonviolent Offense with a Sexual Motivation Finding scoring form on page 236.

If the present conviction is for a felony domestic violence offense where domestic violence was plead and proven, use the General Nonviolent Offense Where Domestic Violence Has Been Plead and Proven scoring form on page 234.

ADULT HISTORY:

Enter number of felony convictions .... _____ x 1 = _____

JUVENILE HISTORY:

Enter number of Murder 1, Murder 2, and Class A sex offense felony dispositions .... _____ x 1 = _____

OTHER CURRENT OFFENSES:

(Other current offenses that do not encompass the same conduct count in offender score)

Enter number of other felony convictions .... _____ x 1 = _____

STATUS:

Was the offender on community custody on the date the current offense was committed? (if yes) _____ + 1 = _____

Total the last column to get the **Offender Score** (Round down to the nearest whole number)......................... _____

SENTENCE RANGE DISPLAYED IS FOR A COMPLETED OFFENSE

FOR **ATTEMPT**, **SOLICITATION**, OR **CONSPIRACY** (RCW 9.94A.595, see page 54), THE SENTENCE RANGE **IS 75%** OF THE COMPLETED RANGE LISTED BELOW

Offender Score										
	0	**1**	**2**	**3**	**4**	**5**	**6**	**7**	**8**	**9+**
LEVEL V	9m	13m	15m	17.5m	25.5m	38m	47.5m	59.5m	72m	84m
	6 - 12	12+ - 14	13 - 17	15 - 20	22 - 29	33 - 43	41 - 54	51 - 68	62 - 82	72 - 96

✓ For gang-related felonies where the court found the offender involved a minor (RCW 9.94A.833), see page 227 for standard range adjustments.
✓ For deadly weapon enhancement, see page 233.
✓ For sentencing alternatives, see page 215.
✓ For community custody eligibility, see page 228.
✓ For any applicable enhancements other than deadly weapon enhancement, see page 224.

RCW 9A.52.025
CLASS B – NONVIOLENT
OFFENDER SCORING RCW 9.94A.525(16)

If the present conviction is for a felony domestic violence offense where domestic violence was plead and proven, use the General Burglary 2/Residential Burglary Offense Where Domestic Violence Has Been Plead and Proven scoring form on page 246.

ADULT HISTORY:

Enter number of Burglary 1 felony convictions .... _____ x 2 = _____

Enter number of Burglary 2 and Residential Burglary felony convictions .... _____ x 2 = _____

Enter number of felony convictions .... _____ x 1 = _____

JUVENILE HISTORY:

Enter number of Murder 1, Murder 2, and Class A sex offense felony dispositions .... _____ x 1 = _____

OTHER CURRENT OFFENSES:

(Other current offenses that do not encompass the same conduct count in offender score)

Enter number of other Burglary 1 felony convictions .... _____ x 2 = _____

Enter number of other Burglary 2 and Residential Burglary felony convictions .... _____ x 2 = _____

Enter number of other felony convictions .... _____ x 1 = _____

STATUS:

Was the offender on community custody on the date the current offense was committed?............ _____ + 1 = _____

Total the last column to get the **Offender Score** (Round down to the nearest whole number) .... _____

SENTENCE RANGE DISPLAYED IS FOR A COMPLETED OFFENSE

FOR **ATTEMPT**, **SOLICITATION**, OR **CONSPIRACY** (RCW 9.94A.595, see page 54), THE SENTENCE RANGE **IS 75%** OF THE COMPLETED RANGE LISTED BELOW

Offender Score										
	0	**1**	**2**	**3**	**4**	**5**	**6**	**7**	**8**	**9+**
LEVEL IV	6m	9m	13m	15m	17.5m	25.5m	38m	50m	61.5m	73.5m
	3 - 9	6 - 12	12+ - 14	13 - 17	15 - 20	22 - 29	33 - 43	43 - 57	53 - 70	63 - 84

✓ For gang-related felonies where the court found the offender involved a minor (RCW 9.94A.833), see page 227 for standard range adjustments.
✓ For deadly weapon enhancement, see page 233.
✓ For sentencing alternatives, see page 215.
✓ For community custody eligibility, see page 228.
✓ For any applicable enhancements other than deadly weapon enhancement, see page 224.

Residential Burglary with a Finding of Sexual Motivation
RCW 9A.52.025
CLASS B – NONVIOLENT/SEX
OFFENDER SCORING RCW 9.94A.525(17)

ADULT HISTORY:

Enter number of sex offense felony convictions .... _____ x 3 = _____

Enter number of Burglary 1 felony convictions .... _____ x 2 = _____

Enter number of Burglary 2 and Residential Burglary felony convictions .... _____ x 2 = _____

Enter number of felony convictions .... _____ x 1 = _____

JUVENILE HISTORY:

Enter number of Class A sex offense felony dispositions .... _____ x 3 = _____

Enter number of Murder 1 and Murder 2 felony dispositions .... _____ x 1 = _____

OTHER CURRENT OFFENSES:

(Other current offenses that do not encompass the same conduct count in offender score)

Enter number of other sex offense felony convictions .... _____ x 3 = _____

Enter number of other Burglary 1 felony convictions .... _____ x 2 = _____

Enter number of other Burglary 2 and Residential Burglary felony convictions .... _____ x 2 = _____

Enter number of other felony convictions .... _____ x 1 = _____

STATUS:

Was the offender on community custody on the date the current offense was committed? .... _____ + 1 = _____

Total the last column to get the **Offender Score** (Round down to the nearest whole number)................. _____

SENTENCE RANGE DISPLAYED IS FOR A COMPLETED OFFENSE

FOR **ATTEMPT**, **SOLICITATION**, OR **CONSPIRACY** (RCW 9.94A.595, see page 54), THE SENTENCE RANGE **IS 75%** OF THE COMPLETED RANGE LISTED BELOW

	0	1	2	3	4	5	6	7	8	9+
Offender Score										
LEVEL IV	6m	9m	13m	15m	17.5m	25.5m	38m	50m	61.5m	73.5m
	3 - 9	6 - 12	12+ - 14	13 - 17	15 - 20	22 - 29	33 - 43	43 - 57	53 - 70	63 - 84

SEXUAL MOTIVATION ENHANCEMENT (Per Sexual Motivation Enhancement, page 226).................... _____

Low   to   High

STANDARD SENTENCE RANGE PLUS ENHANCEMENT .... _____ ..... _____

✓ For gang-related felonies where the court found the offender involved a minor (RCW 9.94A.833), see page 227 for standard range adjustments.
✓ For deadly weapon enhancement, see page 233.
✓ For sentencing alternatives, see page 215.
✓ For community custody eligibility, see page 228.
✓ For any applicable enhancements other than deadly weapon enhancement, see page 224.
✓ If the offender is not a persistent offender and has a prior conviction for an offense listed in RCW 9.94A.030(37)(b), then the sentence is subject to the requirements of RCW 9.94A.507.

428   2023 Washington State Adult Sentencing Guidelines Manual, ver 20231115

Retail Theft with Special Circumstances First Degree

RCW 9A.56.360(2)
CLASS B – NONVIOLENT
OFFENDER SCORING RCW 9.94A.525(7)

If it was found that this offense was committed with sexual motivation (RCW 9.94A.533(8)) on or after 7/1/2006, use the General Nonviolent Offense with a Sexual Motivation Finding scoring form on page 236.

If the present conviction is for a felony domestic violence offense where domestic violence was plead and proven, use the General Nonviolent Offense Where Domestic Violence Has Been Plead and Proven scoring form on page 234.

ADULT HISTORY:

Enter number of felony convictions .... _____ x 1 = _____

JUVENILE HISTORY:

Enter number of Murder 1, Murder 2, and Class A sex offense felony dispositions .... _____ x 1 = _____

OTHER CURRENT OFFENSES:

(Other current offenses that do not encompass the same conduct count in offender score)

Enter number of other felony convictions .... _____ x 1 = _____

STATUS:

Was the offender on community custody on the date the current offense was committed? (if yes) _____ + 1 = _____

Total the last column to get the **Offender Score** (Round down to the nearest whole number).......................... _____

SENTENCE RANGE DISPLAYED IS FOR A COMPLETED OFFENSE

FOR **ATTEMPT**, **SOLICITATION**, OR **CONSPIRACY** (RCW 9.94A.595, see page 54), THE SENTENCE RANGE **IS 75%** OF THE COMPLETED RANGE LISTED BELOW

Offender Score										
	0	**1**	**2**	**3**	**4**	**5**	**6**	**7**	**8**	**9+**
LEVEL III	2m	5m	8m	11m	14m	19.5m	25.5m	38m	50m	59.5m
	1 - 3	3 - 8	4 - 12	9 - 12	12+ - 16	17 - 22	22 - 29	33 - 43	43 - 57	51 - 68

✓ For gang-related felonies where the court found the offender involved a minor (RCW 9.94A.833), see page 227 for standard range adjustments.
✓ For deadly weapon enhancement, see page 233.
✓ For sentencing alternatives, see page 215.
✓ For community custody eligibility, see page 228.
✓ For any applicable enhancements other than deadly weapon enhancement, see page 224.

Retail Theft with Special Circumstances Second Degree

RCW 9A.56.360(3)
CLASS C – NONVIOLENT
OFFENDER SCORING RCW 9.94A.525(7)

If it was found that this offense was committed with sexual motivation (RCW 9.94A.533(8)) on or after 7/1/2006, use the General Nonviolent Offense with a Sexual Motivation Finding scoring form on page 236.

If the present conviction is for a felony domestic violence offense where domestic violence was plead and proven, use the General Nonviolent Offense Where Domestic Violence Has Been Plead and Proven scoring form on page 234.

ADULT HISTORY:

    Enter number of felony convictions .... _____ x 1 = _____

JUVENILE HISTORY:

    Enter number of Murder 1, Murder 2, and Class A sex offense felony dispositions .... _____ x 1 = _____

OTHER CURRENT OFFENSES:

(Other current offenses that do not encompass the same conduct count in offender score)

    Enter number of other felony convictions .... _____ x 1 = _____

STATUS:

    Was the offender on community custody on the date the current offense was committed? (if yes) _____ + 1 = _____

Total the last column to get the **Offender Score** (Round down to the nearest whole number)........................ _____

SENTENCE RANGE

		Offender Score									
		0	**1**	**2**	**3**	**4**	**5**	**6**	**7**	**8**	**9+**
LEVEL II			4m	6m	8m	13m	16m	19.5m	25.5m	38m	50m
	0-90 days		2 - 6	3 - 9	4 - 12	12+ - 14	14 - 18	17 - 22	22 - 29	33 - 43	43 - 57

✓   For gang-related felonies where the court found the offender involved a minor (RCW 9.94A.833), see page 227 for standard range adjustment.
✓   For deadly weapon enhancement, see page 233.
✓   For sentencing alternatives, see page 215.
✓   For community custody eligibility, see page 228.
✓   For any applicable enhancements other than deadly weapon enhancement, see page 224.

Robbery First Degree
RCW 9A.56.200
CLASS A – VIOLENT/CRIMES AGAINST PERSONS
OFFENDER SCORING RCW 9.94A.525(8)

If it was found that this offense was committed with sexual motivation (RCW 9.94A.533(8)) on or after 7/1/2006, use the General Violent Offense with a Sexual Motivation Finding scoring form on page 244.

If the present conviction is for a felony domestic violence offense where domestic violence was plead and proven, use the General Violent Offense Where Domestic Violence Has Been Plead and Proven scoring form on page 242.

ADULT HISTORY:

    Enter number of serious violent and violent felony convictions .... _____ x 2 = _____

    Enter number of nonviolent felony convictions .... _____ x 1 = _____

JUVENILE HISTORY:

    Enter number of Murder 1, Murder 2, and Class A sex offense felony dispositions .... _____ x 2 = _____

OTHER CURRENT OFFENSES:

(Other current offenses that do not encompass the same conduct count in offender score)

    Enter number of other serious violent and violent felony convictions .... _____ x 2 = _____

    Enter number of other nonviolent felony convictions .... _____ x 1 = _____

STATUS:

    Was the offender on community custody on the date the current offense was committed?........... _____ + 1 = _____

Total the last column to get the **Offender Score** (Round down to the nearest whole number) .... _____

SENTENCE RANGE DISPLAYED IS FOR A COMPLETED OFFENSE

FOR **ATTEMPT**, **SOLICITATION**, OR **CONSPIRACY** (RCW 9.94A.595, see page 54), THE SENTENCE RANGE **IS 75%** OF THE COMPLETED RANGE LISTED BELOW

	Offender Score									
	0	**1**	**2**	**3**	**4**	**5**	**6**	**7**	**8**	**9+**
LEVEL IX	36m	42m	47.5m	53.5m	59.5m	66m	89.5m	101.5m	126m	150m
	31 - 41	36 - 48	41 - 54	46 - 61	51 - 68	57 - 75	77 - 102	87 - 116	108 - 144	129 - 171

✓   For gang-related felonies where the court found the offender involved a minor (RCW 9.94A.833), see page 227 for standard range adjustments.
✓   For deadly weapon enhancement, see page 233.
✓   For sentencing alternatives, see page 215.
✓   For community custody eligibility, see page 228.
✓   For any applicable enhancements other than deadly weapon enhancement, see page 224.

Robbery Second Degree

RCW 9A.56.210
CLASS B – VIOLENT/CRIMES AGAINST PERSONS
OFFENDER SCORING RCW 9.94A.525(8)

If it was found that this offense was committed with sexual motivation (RCW 9.94A.533(8)) on or after 7/1/2006, use the General Violent Offense with a Sexual Motivation Finding scoring form on page 244.

If the present conviction is for a felony domestic violence offense where domestic violence was plead and proven, use the General Violent Offense Where Domestic Violence Has Been Plead and Proven scoring form on page 242.

ADULT HISTORY:

Enter number of serious violent and violent felony convictions .... _____ x 2 = _____

Enter number of nonviolent felony convictions .... _____ x 1 = _____

JUVENILE HISTORY:

Enter number of Murder 1, Murder 2, and Class A sex offense felony dispositions .... _____ x 2 = _____

OTHER CURRENT OFFENSES:

(Other current offenses that do not encompass the same conduct count in offender score)

Enter number of other serious violent and violent felony convictions .... _____ x 2 = _____

Enter number of other nonviolent felony convictions .... _____ x 1 = _____

STATUS:

Was the offender on community custody on the date the current offense was committed? .... _____ + 1 = _____

Total the last column to get the **Offender Score** (Round down to the nearest whole number).................. _____

SENTENCE RANGE DISPLAYED IS FOR A COMPLETED OFFENSE

FOR **ATTEMPT**, **SOLICITATION**, OR **CONSPIRACY** (RCW 9.94A.595, see page 54), THE SENTENCE RANGE **IS 75%** OF THE COMPLETED RANGE LISTED BELOW

Offender Score									
0	**1**	**2**	**3**	**4**	**5**	**6**	**7**	**8**	**9+**
LEVEL IV 6m	9m	13m	15m	17.5m	25.5m	38m	50m	61.5m	73.5m
3 - 9	6 - 12	12+ - 14	13 - 17	15 - 20	22 - 29	33 - 43	43 - 57	53 - 70	63 - 84

✓ For gang-related felonies where the court found the offender involved a minor (RCW 9.94A.833), see page 227 for standard range adjustments.
✓ For deadly weapon enhancement, see page 233.
✓ For sentencing alternatives, see page 215.
✓ For community custody eligibility, see page 228.
✓ For any applicable enhancements other than deadly weapon enhancement, see page 224.

RCW 21.20.400
CLASS B – NONVIOLENT
OFFENDER SCORING RCW 9.94A.525(7)

If it was found that this offense was committed with sexual motivation (RCW 9.94A.533(8)) on or after 7/1/2006, use the General Nonviolent Offense with a Sexual Motivation Finding scoring form on page 236.

If the present conviction is for a felony domestic violence offense where domestic violence was plead and proven, use the General Nonviolent Offense Where Domestic Violence Has Been Plead and Proven scoring form on page 234.

ADULT HISTORY:

    Enter number of felony convictions .... _____ x 1 = _____

JUVENILE HISTORY:

    Enter number of Murder 1, Murder 2, and Class A sex offense felony dispositions .... _____ x 1 = _____

OTHER CURRENT OFFENSES:

(Other current offenses that do not encompass the same conduct count in offender score)

    Enter number of other felony convictions .... _____ x 1 = _____

STATUS:

    Was the offender on community custody on the date the current offense was committed? (if yes) _____ + 1 = _____

Total the last column to get the **Offender Score** (Round down to the nearest whole number).......................... _____

SENTENCE RANGE DISPLAYED IS FOR A COMPLETED OFFENSE

FOR **ATTEMPT**, **SOLICITATION**, OR **CONSPIRACY** (RCW 9.94A.595, see page 54), THE SENTENCE RANGE **IS 75%** OF THE COMPLETED RANGE LISTED BELOW

Offender Score									
	0	**1**	**2**	**3**	**4**	**5**	**6**	**7**	**8**	**9+**
LEVEL III	2m	5m	8m	11m	14m	19.5m	25.5m	38m	50m	59.5m
	1 - 3	3 - 8	4 - 12	9 - 12	12+ - 16	17 - 22	22 - 29	33 - 43	43 - 57	51 - 68

✓ For gang-related felonies where the court found the offender involved a minor (RCW 9.94A.833), see page 227 for standard range adjustments.
✓ For deadly weapon enhancement, see page 233.
✓ For sentencing alternatives, see page 215.
✓ For community custody eligibility, see page 228.
✓ For any applicable enhancements other than deadly weapon enhancement, see page 224.

Selling For Profit (Controlled or Counterfeit) any Controlled Substance in Schedule I
RCW 69.50.410
CLASS C* – NONVIOLENT/DRUG
OFFENDER SCORING RCW 9.94A.525(13)

If it was found that this offense was committed with sexual motivation (RCW 9.94A.533(8)) on or after 7/1/2006, use the General Drug Offense with a Sexual Motivation Finding scoring form on page 238.

If the present conviction is for a felony domestic violence offense where domestic violence was plead and proven, use the General Drug Offense Where Domestic Violence Has Been Plead and Proven scoring form on page 237.

ADULT HISTORY:

Does the offender have a prior sex or serious violent offense in history?

.... **YES,** Enter number of felony drug convictions _____ x 3 = _____

.... **NO,** Enter number of felony drug convictions _____ x 1 = _____

Enter number of felony convictions .... _____ x 1 = _____

JUVENILE HISTORY:

Enter number of Murder 1, Murder 2, and Class A sex offense felony dispositions .... _____ x 1 = _____

OTHER CURRENT OFFENSES:

(Other current offenses that do not encompass the same conduct count in offender score)

Does the offender have other prior sex or serious violent offense in history?

.... **YES,** Enter number of other felony drug convictions _____ x 3 = _____

.... **NO,** Enter number of other felony drug convictions _____ x 1 = _____

Enter number of other felony convictions .... _____ x 1 = _____

STATUS:

Was the offender on community custody on the date the current offense was committed? (if yes) _____ + 1 = _____

Total the last column to get the **Offender Score** (Round down to the nearest whole number)........................ _____

SENTENCE RANGE – DRUG

	Offender Score		
	0 to 2	3 to 5	6 to 9+
LEVEL III	55.5m 51 - 60*	60 - 60*	60 - 60*

* Class C felony offenses have a statutory maximum sentence of 60 months, see RCW 9A.20.021.

✓ For gang-related felonies where the court found the offender involved a minor (RCW 9.94A.833), see page 227 for standard range adjustments.
✓ Per RCW 9.94A.518, any felony offense under chapter 69.50 RCW with a deadly weapon special verdict under RCW 9.94A.602 becomes a level III offense.
✓ For deadly weapon enhancement, see page 233.
✓ For sentencing alternatives, see page 215.
✓ For community custody eligibility, see page 228.
✓ For any applicable enhancements other than deadly weapon enhancement, see page 224.
✓ Per RCW 69.50.408, the statutory maximum for a subsequent conviction under chapter 69.50 RCW is 120 months.
✓ Per RCW 69.50.435, if the offense occurred within a protected zone, 24 months shall be added to the standard range and the statutory maximum will be 120 months.
✓ Per RCW 69.50.410, subsequent convictions under RCW 69.50.410(1) shall receive a mandatory sentence of 5 years which shall not be suspended or deferred.
✓ Per RCW 69.50.410, if the violation involved selling heroin, a mandatory sentence of 2 years shall be imposed and shall not be suspended or deferred. A subsequent conviction of selling heroin shall receive a mandatory sentence of 10 years which shall not be suspended or deferred.

Sending, Bringing into the State Depictions of Minor Engaged in Sexually Explicit Conduct First Degree

RCW 9.68A.060(1)
CLASS B – NONVIOLENT/SEX
OFFENDER SCORING RCW 9.94A.525(17)

If the present conviction is for a felony domestic violence offense where domestic violence was plead and proven, use the General Nonviolent/Sex Offense Where Domestic Violence Has Been Plead and Proven scoring form on page 235.

ADULT HISTORY:

Enter number of sex offense felony convictions .... _____ x 3 = _____

Enter number of felony convictions .... _____ x 1 = _____

JUVENILE HISTORY:

Enter number of Class A sex offense felony dispositions .... _____ x 3 = _____

Enter number of Murder 1 and Murder 2 felony dispositions .... _____ x 1 = _____

OTHER CURRENT OFFENSES:

(Other current offenses that do not encompass the same conduct count in offender score)

Enter number of sex offense felony convictions .... _____ x 3 = _____

Enter number of other felony convictions .... _____ x 1 = _____

STATUS:

Was the offender on community custody on the date the current offense was committed? (if yes) _____ + 1 = _____

Total the last column to get the **Offender Score** (Round down to the nearest whole number)......................... _____

SENTENCE RANGE DISPLAYED IS FOR A COMPLETED OFFENSE

FOR **ATTEMPT**, **SOLICITATION**, OR **CONSPIRACY** (RCW 9.94A.595, see page 54), THE SENTENCE RANGE **IS 75%** OF THE COMPLETED RANGE LISTED BELOW

	Offender Score									
	0	1	2	3	4	5	6	7	8	9+
LEVEL VII	17.5m	24m	30m	36m	42m	47.5m	66m	78m	89.5m	101.5m
	15 - 20	21 - 27	26 - 34	31 - 41	36 - 48	41 - 54	57 - 75	67 - 89	77 - 102	87 - 116

✓ For gang-related felonies where the court found the offender involved a minor (RCW 9.94A.833), see page 227 for standard range adjustments.
✓ For deadly weapon enhancement, see page 233.
✓ For sentencing alternatives, see page 215.
✓ For community custody eligibility, see page 228.
✓ For any applicable enhancements other than deadly weapon enhancement, see page 224.
✓ If the offender is not a persistent offender and has a prior conviction for an offense listed in RCW 9.94A.030(37)(b), then the sentence is subject to the requirements of RCW 9.94A.507.

RCW 9.68A.060(2)
CLASS B – NONVIOLENT/SEX
OFFENDER SCORING RCW 9.94A.525(17)

If the present conviction is for a felony domestic violence offense where domestic violence was plead and proven, use the General Nonviolent/Sex Offense Where Domestic Violence Has Been Plead and Proven scoring form on page 235.

ADULT HISTORY:

Enter number of sex offense felony convictions .... _____ x 3 = _____

Enter number of felony convictions .... _____ x 1 = _____

JUVENILE HISTORY:

Enter number of Class A sex offense felony dispositions .... _____ x 3 =_____

Enter number of Murder 1 and Murder 2 felony dispositions .... _____ x 1 = _____

OTHER CURRENT OFFENSES:

(Other current offenses that do not encompass the same conduct count in offender score)

Enter number of sex offense felony convictions .... _____ x 3 = _____

Enter number of other felony convictions .... _____ x 1 = _____

STATUS:

Was the offender on community custody on the date the current offense was committed? (if yes) _____ + 1 = _____

Total the last column to get the **Offender Score** (Round down to the nearest whole number)........................ _____

SENTENCE RANGE DISPLAYED IS FOR A COMPLETED OFFENSE

FOR **ATTEMPT**, **SOLICITATION**, OR **CONSPIRACY** (RCW 9.94A.595, see page 54), THE SENTENCE RANGE **IS 75%** OF THE COMPLETED RANGE LISTED BELOW

Offender Score										
	0	**1**	**2**	**3**	**4**	**5**	**6**	**7**	**8**	**9+**
LEVEL V	9m	13m	15m	17.5m	25.5m	38m	47.5m	59.5m	72m	84m
	6 - 12	12+ - 14	13 - 17	15 - 20	22 - 29	33 - 43	41 - 54	51 - 68	62 - 82	72 - 96

✓ For gang-related felonies where the court found the offender involved a minor (RCW 9.94A.833), see page 227 for standard range adjustments.
✓ For deadly weapon enhancement, see page 233.
✓ For sentencing alternatives, see page 215.
✓ For community custody eligibility, see page 228.
✓ For any applicable enhancements other than deadly weapon enhancement, see page 224.
✓ If the offender is not a persistent offender and has a prior conviction for an offense listed in RCW 9.94A.030(37)(b), then the sentence is subject to the requirements of RCW 9.94A.507.

Sexual Exploitation of a Minor

RCW 9.68A.040
CLASS B* – NONVIOLENT/SEX
OFFENDER SCORING RCW 9.94A.525(17)

If the present conviction is for a felony domestic violence offense where domestic violence was plead and proven, use the General Nonviolent/Sex Offense Where Domestic Violence Has Been Plead and Proven scoring form on page 235.

ADULT HISTORY:

Enter number of sex offense felony convictions .... _____ x 3 = _____

Enter number of felony convictions .... _____ x 1 = _____

JUVENILE HISTORY:

Enter number of Class A sex offense felony dispositions .... _____ x 3 = _____

Enter number of Murder 1 and Murder 2 felony dispositions .... _____ x 1 = _____

OTHER CURRENT OFFENSES:

(Other current offenses that do not encompass the same conduct count in offender score)

Enter number of sex offense felony convictions .... _____ x 3 = _____

Enter number of other felony convictions .... _____ x 1 = _____

STATUS:

Was the offender on community custody on the date the current offense was committed? (if yes) _____ + 1 = _____

Total the last column to get the **Offender Score** (Round down to the nearest whole number)......................... _____

SENTENCE RANGE DISPLAYED IS FOR A COMPLETED OFFENSE

FOR **ATTEMPT**, **SOLICITATION**, OR **CONSPIRACY** (RCW 9.94A.595, see page 54), THE SENTENCE RANGE **IS 75%** OF THE COMPLETED RANGE LISTED BELOW

Offender Score									
0	**1**	**2**	**3**	**4**	**5**	**6**	**7**	**8**	**9+**
LEVEL IX 36m	42m	47.5m	53.5m	59.5m	66m	89.5m	101.5m	114m	
31 - 41	36 - 48	41 - 54	46 - 61	51 - 68	57 - 75	77 - 102	87 - 116	108 - 120*	120 - 120*

* Class B felony offenses have a statutory maximum sentence of 120 months, see RCW 9A.20.021.

✓ For gang-related felonies where the court found the offender involved a minor (RCW 9.94A.833), see page 227 for standard range adjustments.
✓ For deadly weapon enhancement, see page 233.
✓ For sentencing alternatives, see page 215.
✓ For community custody eligibility, see page 228.
✓ For any applicable enhancements other than deadly weapon enhancement, see page 224.
✓ If the offender is not a persistent offender and has a prior conviction for an offense listed in RCW 9.94A.030(37)(b), then the sentence is subject to the requirements of RCW 9.94A.507.

RCW 9A.44.093
CLASS C* – NONVIOLENT/SEX
OFFENDER SCORING RCW 9.94A.525(17)

If the present conviction is for a felony domestic violence offense where domestic violence was plead and proven, use the General Nonviolent/Sex Offense Where Domestic Violence Has Been Plead and Proven scoring form on page 235.

ADULT HISTORY:

    Enter number of sex offense felony convictions .... _____ x 3 = _____

    Enter number of felony convictions .... _____ x 1 = _____

JUVENILE HISTORY:

    Enter number of Class A sex offense felony dispositions .... _____ x 3 = _____

    Enter number of Murder 1 and Murder 2 felony dispositions .... _____ x 1 = _____

OTHER CURRENT OFFENSES:

(Other current offenses that do not encompass the same conduct count in offender score)

    Enter number of sex offense felony convictions .... _____ x 3 = _____

    Enter number of other felony convictions .... _____ x 1 = _____

STATUS:

    Was the offender on community custody on the date the current offense was committed? (if yes) _____ + 1 = _____

Total the last column to get the **Offender Score** (Round down to the nearest whole number)......................... _____

SENTENCE RANGE

	Offender Score									
	0	**1**	**2**	**3**	**4**	**5**	**6**	**7**	**8**	**9+**
LEVEL V	9m	13m	15m	17.5m	25.5m	38m	47.5m	55.5m		
	6 - 12	12+ - 14	13 - 17	15 - 20	22 - 29	33 - 43	41 - 54	51 - 60*	60 - 60*	60 - 60*

    * Class C felony offenses have a statutory maximum sentence of 60 months, see RCW 9A.20.021.

✓   For gang-related felonies where the court found the offender involved a minor (RCW 9.94A.833), see page 227 for standard range adjustment.

✓   For deadly weapon enhancement, see page 233.

✓   For sentencing alternatives, see page 215.

✓   For community custody eligibility, see page 228.

✓   For any applicable enhancements other than deadly weapon enhancement, see page 224.

✓   If the offender is not a persistent offender and has a prior conviction for an offense listed in RCW 9.94A.030(37)(b), then the sentence is subject to the requirements of RCW 9.94A.507.

RCW 9A.44.105
CLASS C* – NONVIOLENT/SEX
OFFENDER SCORING RCW 9.94A.525(17)

If the present conviction is for a felony domestic violence offense where domestic violence was plead and proven, use the General Nonviolent/Sex Offense Where Domestic Violence Has Been Plead and Proven scoring form on page 235.

ADULT HISTORY:

Enter number of sex offense felony convictions .... _____ x 3 = _____

Enter number of felony convictions .... _____ x 1 = _____

JUVENILE HISTORY:

Enter number of Class A sex offense felony dispositions .... _____ x 3 = _____

Enter number of Murder 1 and Murder 2 felony dispositions .... _____ x 1 = _____

OTHER CURRENT OFFENSES:

(Other current offenses that do not encompass the same conduct count in offender score)

Enter number of sex offense felony convictions .... _____ x 3 = _____

Enter number of other felony convictions .... _____ x 1 = _____

STATUS:

Was the offender on community custody on the date the current offense was committed? (if yes) _____ + 1 = _____

Total the last column to get the **Offender Score** (Round down to the nearest whole number)......................... _____

SENTENCE RANGE

	Offender Score									
	0	**1**	**2**	**3**	**4**	**5**	**6**	**7**	**8**	**9+**
LEVEL V	9m	13m	15m	17.5m	25.5m	38m	47.5m	55.5m		
	6 - 12	12+ - 14	13 - 17	15 - 20	22 - 29	33 - 43	41 - 54	51 - 60*	60 - 60*	60 - 60*

* Class C felony offenses have a statutory maximum sentence of 60 months, see RCW 9A.20.021.

✓ For gang-related felonies where the court found the offender involved a minor (RCW 9.94A.833), see page 227 for standard range adjustment.
✓ For deadly weapon enhancement, see page 233.
✓ For sentencing alternatives, see page 215.
✓ For community custody eligibility, see page 228.
✓ For any applicable enhancements other than deadly weapon enhancement, see page 224.
✓ If the offender is not a persistent offender and has a <u>prior</u> conviction for an offense listed in RCW 9.94A.030(37)(b), then the sentence is subject to the requirements of RCW 9.94A.507.

RCW 9A.76.115
CLASS A – VIOLENT
OFFENDER SCORING RCW 9.94A.525(8)

If it was found that this offense was committed with sexual motivation (RCW 9.94A.533(8)) on or after 7/1/2006, use the General Violent Offense with a Sexual Motivation Finding scoring form on page 244.

If the present conviction is for a felony domestic violence offense where domestic violence was plead and proven, use the General Violent Offense Where Domestic Violence Has Been Plead and Proven scoring form on page 242.

ADULT HISTORY:

Enter number of serious violent and violent felony convictions .... _____ x 2 = _____

Enter number of nonviolent felony convictions .... _____ x 1 = _____

JUVENILE HISTORY:

Enter number of Murder 1, Murder 2, and Class A sex offense felony dispositions .... _____ x 2 = _____

OTHER CURRENT OFFENSES:

(Other current offenses that do not encompass the same conduct count in offender score)

Enter number of other serious violent and violent felony convictions .... _____ x 2 = _____

Enter number of other nonviolent felony convictions .... _____ x 1 = _____

STATUS:

Was the offender on community custody on the date the current offense was committed? .... _____ + 1 = _____

Total the last column to get the **Offender Score** (Round down to the nearest whole number).................. _____

SENTENCE RANGE DISPLAYED IS FOR A COMPLETED OFFENSE

FOR **ATTEMPT**, **SOLICITATION**, OR **CONSPIRACY** (RCW 9.94A.595, see page 54), THE SENTENCE RANGE **IS 75%** OF THE COMPLETED RANGE LISTED BELOW

	Offender Score									
	0	**1**	**2**	**3**	**4**	**5**	**6**	**7**	**8**	**9+**
LEVEL X	59.5m	66m	72m	78m	84m	89.5m	114m	126m	150m	173.5m
	51 - 68	57 - 75	62 - 82	67 - 89	72 - 96	77 - 102	98 - 130	108 - 144	129 - 171	149 - 198

✓ For gang-related felonies where the court found the offender involved a minor (RCW 9.94A.833), see page 227 for standard range adjustments.
✓ For deadly weapon enhancement, see page 233.
✓ For sentencing alternatives, see page 215.
✓ For community custody eligibility, see page 228.
✓ For any applicable enhancements other than deadly weapon enhancement, see page 224.
✓ Statutory <u>minimum</u> sentence is 60 months per RCW 9.94A.540 and is imposed under the rules of RCW 9.94A.507

Stalking

RCW 9A.46.110
CLASS B – NONVIOLENT/CRIMES AGAINST PERSONS
OFFENDER SCORING RCW 9.94A.525(7)

If it was found that this offense was committed with sexual motivation (RCW 9.94A.533(8)) on or after 7/1/2006, use the General Nonviolent Offense with a Sexual Motivation Finding scoring form on page 236.

If the present conviction is for a felony domestic violence offense where domestic violence was plead and proven, use the General Nonviolent Offense Where Domestic Violence Has Been Plead and Proven scoring form on page 234.

ADULT HISTORY:

Enter number of felony convictions .... _____ x 1 = _____

JUVENILE HISTORY:

Enter number of Murder 1, Murder 2, and Class A sex offense felony dispositions .... _____ x 1 = _____

OTHER CURRENT OFFENSES:

(Other current offenses that do not encompass the same conduct count in offender score)

Enter number of other felony convictions .... _____ x 1 = _____

STATUS:

Was the offender on community custody on the date the current offense was committed? (if yes) _____ + 1 = _____

Total the last column to get the **Offender Score** (Round down to the nearest whole number)......................... _____

SENTENCE RANGE DISPLAYED IS FOR A COMPLETED OFFENSE

FOR **ATTEMPT**, **SOLICITATION**, OR **CONSPIRACY** (RCW 9.94A.595, see page 54), THE SENTENCE RANGE **IS 75%** OF THE COMPLETED RANGE LISTED BELOW

	Offender Score									
	0	**1**	**2**	**3**	**4**	**5**	**6**	**7**	**8**	**9+**
LEVEL V	9m	13m	15m	17.5m	25.5m	38m	47.5m	59.5m	72m	84m
	6 - 12	12+ - 14	13 - 17	15 - 20	22 - 29	33 - 43	41 - 54	51 - 68	62 - 82	72 - 96

✓   For gang-related felonies where the court found the offender involved a minor (RCW 9.94A.833), see page 227 for standard range adjustment.
✓   For deadly weapon enhancement, see page 233.
✓   For sentencing alternatives, see page 215.
✓   For community custody eligibility, see page 228.
✓   For any applicable enhancements other than deadly weapon enhancement, see page 224.

Taking Motor Vehicle without Permission First Degree

RCW 9A.56.070
CLASS B – NONVIOLENT
OFFENDER SCORING RCW 9.94A.525(20)

If it was found that this offense was committed with sexual motivation (RCW 9.94A.533(8)) on or after 7/1/2006, use the General Nonviolent Offense with a Sexual Motivation Finding scoring form on page 236.

If the present conviction is for a felony domestic violence offense where domestic violence was plead and proven, use the General Nonviolent Offense Where Domestic Violence Has Been Plead and Proven scoring form on page 234.

ADULT HISTORY:

Enter number of Theft of a Motor Vehicle, Theft 1 & 2 (of a Motor Vehicle), Possession of Stolen Property 1 & 2 (of a Motor Vehicle), Possession of a Stolen Vehicle and Taking a Motor Vehicle without Permission 1 & 2 felony convictions .... _____ x 3 = _____

Enter number of Vehicle Prowling 2 convictions .... _____ x 1 = _____

Enter number of felony convictions .... _____ x 1 = _____

JUVENILE HISTORY:

Enter number of Murder 1, Murder 2, and Class A sex offense felony dispositions .... _____ x 1 = _____

OTHER CURRENT OFFENSES:

(Other current offenses that do not encompass the same conduct count in offender score)

Enter number of other Theft of a Motor Vehicle, Theft 1 & 2 (of a Motor Vehicle), Possession of Stolen Property 1 & 2 (of a Motor Vehicle), Possession of a Stolen Vehicle and Taking a Motor Vehicle without Permission 1 & 2 felony convictions .... _____ x 3 = _____

Enter number of other Vehicle Prowling 2 convictions .... _____ x 1 = _____

Enter number of other felony convictions .... _____ x 1 = _____

STATUS:

Was the offender on community custody on the date the current offense was committed? (if yes) _____ + 1 = _____

Total the last column to get the **Offender Score** (Round down to the nearest whole number)........................ _____

SENTENCE RANGE DISPLAYED IS FOR A COMPLETED OFFENSE

FOR **ATTEMPT**, **SOLICITATION**, OR **CONSPIRACY** (RCW 9.94A.595, see page 54), THE SENTENCE RANGE **IS 75%** OF THE COMPLETED RANGE LISTED BELOW

	Offender Score									
	0	1	2	3	4	5	6	7	8	9+
LEVEL V	9m	13m	15m	17.5m	25.5m	38m	47.5m	59.5m	72m	84m
	6 - 12	12+ - 14	13 - 17	15 - 20	22 - 29	33 - 43	41 - 54	51 - 68	62 - 82	72 - 96

✓ For gang-related felonies where the court found the offender involved a minor (RCW 9.94A.833), see page 227 for standard range adjustments.
✓ For deadly weapon enhancement, see page 233.
✓ For sentencing alternatives, see page 215.
✓ For community custody eligibility, see page 228.
✓ For any applicable enhancements other than deadly weapon enhancement, see page 224.

Taking Motor Vehicle without Permission Second Degree
RCW 9A.56.075
CLASS C – NONVIOLENT
OFFENDER SCORING RCW 9.94A.525(20)

If it was found that this offense was committed with sexual motivation (RCW 9.94A.533(8)) on or after 7/1/2006, use the General Nonviolent Offense with a Sexual Motivation Finding scoring form on page 236.

If the present conviction is for a felony domestic violence offense where domestic violence was plead and proven, use the General Nonviolent Offense Where Domestic Violence Has Been Plead and Proven scoring form on page 234.

ADULT HISTORY:

Enter number of Theft of a Motor Vehicle, Theft 1 & 2 (of a Motor Vehicle), Possession of Stolen Property 1 & 2 (of a Motor Vehicle), Possession of a Stolen Vehicle and Taking a Motor Vehicle without Permission 1 & 2 felony convictions .... _____ x 3 = _____

Enter number of Vehicle Prowling 2 convictions .... _____ x 1 = _____

Enter number of felony convictions .... _____ x 1 = _____

JUVENILE HISTORY:

Enter number of Murder 1, Murder 2, and Class A sex offense felony dispositions .... _____ x 1 = _____

OTHER CURRENT OFFENSES:

(Other current offenses that do not encompass the same conduct count in offender score)

Enter number of other Theft of a Motor Vehicle, Theft 1 & 2 (of a Motor Vehicle), and Possession of Stolen Property 1 & 2 (of a Motor Vehicle), Possession of a Stolen Vehicle Taking a Motor Vehicle without Permission 1 & 2 felony convictions .... _____ x 3 = _____

Enter number of other Vehicle Prowling 2 convictions .... _____ x 1 = _____

Enter number of other felony convictions .... _____ x 1 = _____

STATUS:

Was the offender on community custody on the date the current offense was committed? (if yes) _____ + 1 = _____

Total the last column to get the **Offender Score** (Round down to the nearest whole number).......................... _____

SENTENCE RANGE

	Offender Score									
	0	**1**	**2**	**3**	**4**	**5**	**6**	**7**	**8**	**9+**
LEVEL I	0-60 days	0-90 days	3m 2 - 5	4m 2 - 6	5.5m 3 - 8	8m 4 - 12	13m 12+ - 14	16m 14 - 18	19.5m 17 - 22	25.5m 22 - 29

✓   For gang-related felonies where the court found the offender involved a minor (RCW 9.94A.833), see page 227 for standard range adjustment.
✓   For deadly weapon enhancement, see page 233.
✓   For sentencing alternatives, see page 215.
✓   For community custody eligibility, see page 228.
✓   For any applicable enhancements other than deadly weapon enhancement, see page 224.

RCW 9A.72.120
CLASS C* – NONVIOLENT
OFFENDER SCORING RCW 9.94A.525(7)

If it was found that this offense was committed with sexual motivation (RCW 9.94A.533(8)) on or after 7/1/2006, use the General Nonviolent Offense with a Sexual Motivation Finding scoring form on page 236.

If the present conviction is for a felony domestic violence offense where domestic violence was plead and proven, use the General Nonviolent Offense Where Domestic Violence Has Been Plead and Proven scoring form on page 234.

ADULT HISTORY:

Enter number of felony convictions .... _____ x 1 = _____

JUVENILE HISTORY:

Enter number of Murder 1, Murder 2, and Class A sex offense felony dispositions .... _____ x 1 = _____

OTHER CURRENT OFFENSES:

(Other current offenses that do not encompass the same conduct count in offender score)

Enter number of other felony convictions .... _____ x 1 = _____

STATUS:

Was the offender on community custody on the date the current offense was committed? (if yes) _____ + 1 = _____

Total the last column to get the **Offender Score** (Round down to the nearest whole number) .... _____

SENTENCE RANGE

	Offender Score									
	0	**1**	**2**	**3**	**4**	**5**	**6**	**7**	**8**	**9+**
LEVEL III	2m	5m	8m	11m	14m	19.5m	25.5m	38m	50m	55.5m
	1 - 3	3 - 8	4 - 12	9 - 12	12+ - 16	17 - 22	22 - 29	33 - 43	43 - 57	51 - 60*

* Class C felony offenses have a statutory maximum sentence of 60 months, see RCW 9A.20.021.

✓ For gang-related felonies where the court found the offender involved a minor (RCW 9.94A.833), see page 227 for standard range adjustment.
✓ For deadly weapon enhancement, see page 233.
✓ For sentencing alternatives, see page 215.
✓ For community custody eligibility, see page 228.
✓ For any applicable enhancements other than deadly weapon enhancement, see page 224.

Telephone Harassment with Prior Harassment Conviction
or Threat of Death
RCW 9.61.230(2)
CLASS C*– NONVIOLENT
OFFENDER SCORING RCW 9.94A.525(7)

If it was found that this offense was committed with sexual motivation (RCW 9.94A.533(8)) on or after 7/1/2006, use the General Nonviolent Offense with a Sexual Motivation Finding scoring form on page 236.

If the present conviction is for a felony domestic violence offense where domestic violence was plead and proven, use the General Nonviolent Offense Where Domestic Violence Has Been Plead and Proven scoring form on page 234.

ADULT HISTORY:

    Enter number of felony convictions .... _____ x 1 = _____

JUVENILE HISTORY:

    Enter number of Murder 1, Murder 2, and Class A sex offense felony dispositions .... _____ x 1 = _____

OTHER CURRENT OFFENSES:

(Other current offenses that do not encompass the same conduct count in offender score)

    Enter number of other felony convictions .... _____ x 1 = _____

STATUS:

    Was the offender on community custody on the date the current offense was committed? (if yes) _____ + 1 = _____

Total the last column to get the **Offender Score** (Round down to the nearest whole number)......................... _____

SENTENCE RANGE

	Offender Score									
	0	**1**	**2**	**3**	**4**	**5**	**6**	**7**	**8**	**9+**
LEVEL III	2m	5m	8m	11m	14m	19.5m	25.5m	38m	50m	55.5m
	1 - 3	3 - 8	4 - 12	9 - 12	12+ - 16	17 - 22	22 - 29	33 - 43	43 - 57	51 - 60*

* Class C felony offenses have a statutory maximum sentence of 60 months, see RCW 9A.20.021.

✓   For gang-related felonies where the court found the offender involved a minor (RCW 9.94A.833), see page 227 for standard range adjustment.
✓   For deadly weapon enhancement, see page 233.
✓   For sentencing alternatives, see page 215.
✓   For community custody eligibility, see page 228.
✓   For any applicable enhancements other than deadly weapon enhancement, see page 224.

Theft First Degree, excluding Firearm and Motor Vehicle

RCW 9A.56.030
CLASS B – NONVIOLENT
OFFENDER SCORING RCW 9.94A.525(7)

If it was found that this offense was committed with sexual motivation (RCW 9.94A.533(8)) on or after 7/1/2006, use the General Nonviolent Offense with a Sexual Motivation Finding scoring form on page 236.

If the present conviction is for a felony domestic violence offense where domestic violence was plead and proven, use the General Nonviolent Offense Where Domestic Violence Has Been Plead and Proven scoring form on page 234.

ADULT HISTORY:

Enter number of felony convictions .... _____ x 1 = _____

JUVENILE HISTORY:

Enter number of Murder 1, Murder 2, and Class A sex offense felony dispositions .... _____ x 1 = _____

OTHER CURRENT OFFENSES:

(Other current offenses that do not encompass the same conduct count in offender score)

Enter number of other felony convictions .... _____ x 1 = _____

STATUS:

Was the offender on community custody on the date the current offense was committed? (if yes) _____ + 1 = _____

Total the last column to get the **Offender Score** (Round down to the nearest whole number)......................... _____

SENTENCE RANGE DISPLAYED IS FOR A COMPLETED OFFENSE

FOR **ATTEMPT**, **SOLICITATION**, OR **CONSPIRACY** (RCW 9.94A.595, see page 54), THE SENTENCE RANGE **IS 75%** OF THE COMPLETED RANGE LISTED BELOW

		Offender Score									
		0	**1**	**2**	**3**	**4**	**5**	**6**	**7**	**8**	**9+**
LEVEL II			4m	6m	8m	13m	16m	19.5m	25.5m	38m	50m
	0-90 days		2 - 6	3 - 9	4 - 12	12+ - 14	14 - 18	17 - 22	22 - 29	33 - 43	43 - 57

✓ For gang-related felonies where the court found the offender involved a minor (RCW 9.94A.833), see page 227 for standard range adjustments.
✓ For deadly weapon enhancement, see page 233.
✓ For sentencing alternatives, see page 215.
✓ For community custody eligibility, see page 228.
✓ For any applicable enhancements other than deadly weapon enhancement, see page 224.

Theft Second Degree, excluding Firearm and Motor Vehicle

RCW 9A.56.040
CLASS C – NONVIOLENT
OFFENDER SCORING RCW 9.94A.525(7)

If it was found that this offense was committed with sexual motivation (RCW 9.94A.533(8)) on or after 7/1/2006, use the General Nonviolent Offense with a Sexual Motivation Finding scoring form on page 236.

If the present conviction is for a felony domestic violence offense where domestic violence was plead and proven, use the General Nonviolent Offense Where Domestic Violence Has Been Plead and Proven scoring form on page 234.

ADULT HISTORY:

Enter number of felony convictions .... _____ x 1 = _____

JUVENILE HISTORY:

Enter number of Murder 1, Murder 2, and Class A sex offense felony dispositions .... _____ x 1 = _____

OTHER CURRENT OFFENSES:

(Other current offenses that do not encompass the same conduct count in offender score)

Enter number of other felony convictions .... _____ x 1 = _____

STATUS:

Was the offender on community custody on the date the current offense was committed? (if yes) _____ + 1 = _____

Total the last column to get the **Offender Score** (Round down to the nearest whole number)......................... _____

SENTENCE RANGE

		Offender Score								
	0	**1**	**2**	**3**	**4**	**5**	**6**	**7**	**8**	**9+**
LEVEL I	0-60 days	0-90 days	3m 2 - 5	4m 2 - 6	5.5m 3 - 8	8m 4 - 12	13m 12+ - 14	16m 14 - 18	19.5m 17 - 22	25.5m 22 - 29

✓ For gang-related felonies where the court found the offender involved a minor (RCW 9.94A.833), see page 227 for standard range adjustment.
✓ For deadly weapon enhancement, see page 233.
✓ For sentencing alternatives, see page 215.
✓ For community custody eligibility, see page 228.
✓ For any applicable enhancements other than deadly weapon enhancement, see page 224.

Theft from a Vulnerable Adult First Degree

RCW 9A.56.400(1)
CLASS B – NONVIOLENT/CRIMES AGAINST PERSONS
OFFENDER SCORING RCW 9.94A.525 (7)

If it was found that this offense was committed with sexual motivation (RCW 9.94A.533(8)) on or after 7/1/2006, use the General Nonviolent Offense with a Sexual Motivation Finding scoring form on page 236.

If the present conviction is for a felony domestic violence offense where domestic violence was plead and proven, use the General Nonviolent Offense Where Domestic Violence Has Been Plead and Proven scoring form on page 234.

ADULT HISTORY:

Enter number of felony convictions .... _____ x 1 = _____

JUVENILE HISTORY:

Enter number of Murder 1, Murder 2, and Class A sex offense felony dispositions .... _____ x 1 = _____

OTHER CURRENT OFFENSES:

(Other current offenses that do not encompass the same conduct count in offender score)

Enter number of other felony convictions .... _____ x 1 = _____

STATUS:

Was the offender on community custody on the date the current offense was committed? (if yes) _____ + 1 = _____

Total the last column to get the **Offender Score** (Round down to the nearest whole number)........................ _____

SENTENCE RANGE DISPLAYED IS FOR A COMPLETED OFFENSE

FOR **ATTEMPT**, **SOLICITATION**, OR **CONSPIRACY** (RCW 9.94A.595, see page 54), THE SENTENCE RANGE **IS 75%** OF THE COMPLETED RANGE LISTED BELOW

Offender Score										
	0	1	2	3	4	5	6	7	8	9+
LEVEL VI	13m	17.5m	24m	30m	36m	42m	53.5m	66m	78m	89.5m
	12+ - 14	15 - 20	21 - 27	26 - 34	31 - 41	36 - 48	46 - 61	57 - 75	67 - 89	77 - 102

✓ For gang-related felonies where the court found the offender involved a minor (RCW 9.94A.833), see page 227 for standard range adjustments.
✓ For deadly weapon enhancement, see page 233.
✓ For sentencing alternatives, see page 215.
✓ For community custody eligibility, see page 228.
✓ For any applicable enhancements other than deadly weapon enhancement, see page 224.

Theft from a Vulnerable Adult Second Degree

RCW 9A.56.400(2)
CLASS C – NONVIOLENT/CRIMES AGAINST PERSONS
OFFENDER SCORING RCW 9.94A.525(7)

If it was found that this offense was committed with sexual motivation (RCW 9.94A.533(8)) on or after 7/1/2006, use the General Nonviolent Offense with a Sexual Motivation Finding scoring form on page 236.

If the present conviction is for a felony domestic violence offense where domestic violence was plead and proven, use the General Nonviolent Offense Where Domestic Violence Has Been Plead and Proven scoring form on page 234.

ADULT HISTORY:

    Enter number of felony convictions .... _____ x 1 = _____

JUVENILE HISTORY:

    Enter number of Murder 1, Murder 2, and Class A sex offense felony dispositions .... _____ x 1 = _____

OTHER CURRENT OFFENSES:

(Other current offenses that do not encompass the same conduct count in offender score)

    Enter number of other felony convictions .... _____ x 1 = _____

STATUS:

    Was the offender on community custody on the date the current offense was committed? (if yes) _____ + 1 = _____

Total the last column to get the **Offender Score** (Round down to the nearest whole number)......................... _____

SENTENCE RANGE

	Offender Score									
	0	**1**	**2**	**3**	**4**	**5**	**6**	**7**	**8**	**9+**
LEVEL I	0-60 days	0-90 days	3m 2 - 5	4m 2 - 6	5.5m 3 - 8	8m 4 - 12	13m 12+ - 14	16m 14 - 18	19.5m 17 - 22	25.5m 22 - 29

✓   For gang-related felonies where the court found the offender involved a minor (RCW 9.94A.833), see page 227 for standard range adjustment.
✓   For deadly weapon enhancement, see page 233.
✓   For sentencing alternatives, see page 215.
✓   For community custody eligibility, see page 228.
✓   For any applicable enhancements other than deadly weapon enhancement, see page 224.

Theft of Ammonia

RCW 69.55.010
CLASS C* – NONVIOLENT
OFFENDER SCORING RCW 9.94A.525(7)

If it was found that this offense was committed with sexual motivation (RCW 9.94A.533(8)) on or after 7/1/2006, use the General Nonviolent Offense with a Sexual Motivation Finding scoring form on page 236.

If the present conviction is for a felony domestic violence offense where domestic violence was plead and proven, use the General Nonviolent Offense Where Domestic Violence Has Been Plead and Proven scoring form on page 234.

ADULT HISTORY:

Enter number of felony convictions .... _____ x 1 = _____

JUVENILE HISTORY:

Enter number of Murder 1, Murder 2, and Class A sex offense felony dispositions .... _____ x 1 = _____

OTHER CURRENT OFFENSES:

(Other current offenses that do not encompass the same conduct count in offender score)

Enter number of other felony convictions .... _____ x 1 = _____

STATUS:

Was the offender on community custody on the date the current offense was committed? (if yes) _____ + 1 = _____

Total the last column to get the **Offender Score** (Round down to the nearest whole number)........................ _____

SENTENCE RANGE

	Offender Score									
	0	**1**	**2**	**3**	**4**	**5**	**6**	**7**	**8**	**9+**
LEVEL VIII	24m	30m	36m	42m	47.5m	53.m				
	21 - 27	26 - 34	31 - 41	36 - 48	41 - 54	46 - 60*	60 - 60*	60 - 60*	60 - 60*	60 - 60*

* Class C felony offenses have a statutory maximum sentence of 60 months, see RCW 9A.20.021.

✓ For gang-related felonies where the court found the offender involved a minor (RCW 9.94A.833), see page 227 for standard range adjustment.
✓ For deadly weapon enhancement, see page 233.
✓ For sentencing alternatives, see page 215.
✓ For community custody eligibility, see page 228.
✓ For any applicable enhancements other than deadly weapon enhancement, see page 224.

RCW 9A.56.300
CLASS B – NONVIOLENT
OFFENDER SCORING RCW 9.94A.525(7)

If it was found that this offense was committed with sexual motivation (RCW 9.94A.533(8)) on or after 7/1/2006, use the General Nonviolent Offense with a Sexual Motivation Finding scoring form on page 236.

If the present conviction is for a felony domestic violence offense where domestic violence was plead and proven, use the General Nonviolent Offense Where Domestic Violence Has Been Plead and Proven scoring form on page 234.

ADULT HISTORY:

    Enter number of felony convictions .... _____ x 1 = _____

JUVENILE HISTORY:

    Enter number of Murder 1, Murder 2, and Class A sex offense felony dispositions .... _____ x 1 = _____

OTHER CURRENT OFFENSES:

(Other current offenses that do not encompass the same conduct count in offender score)

    Enter number of other felony convictions .... _____ x 1 = _____

STATUS:

    Was the offender on community custody on the date the current offense was committed? (if yes) _____ + 1 = _____

Total the last column to get the **Offender Score** (Round down to the nearest whole number).......................... _____

SENTENCE RANGE DISPLAYED IS FOR A COMPLETED OFFENSE

FOR **ATTEMPT**, **SOLICITATION**, OR **CONSPIRACY** (RCW 9.94A.595, see page 54), THE SENTENCE RANGE **IS 75%** OF THE COMPLETED RANGE LISTED BELOW

	Offender Score									
	0	**1**	**2**	**3**	**4**	**5**	**6**	**7**	**8**	**9+**
LEVEL VI	13m	17.5m	24m	30m	36m	42m	53.5m	66m	78m	89.5m
	12+ - 14	15 - 20	21 - 27	26 - 34	31 - 41	36 - 48	46 - 61	57 - 75	67 - 89	77 - 102

✓   For gang-related felonies where the court found the offender involved a minor (RCW 9.94A.833), see page 227 for standard range adjustments.
✓   For deadly weapon enhancement, see page 233.
✓   For sentencing alternatives, see page 215.
✓   For community custody eligibility, see page 228.
✓   For any applicable enhancements other than deadly weapon enhancement, see page 224.
✓   Each firearm possessed under this section is a separate offense.
✓   The offender shall be sentenced according to RCW 9.94A.589(1)(c) if the offender is convicted of Unlawful Possession of a Firearm 1 or 2 (RCW 9.41.040) and for felonies Theft of a Firearm or Possession of a Stolen Firearm, or both, as current offenses.
✓   If the present conviction is for Unlawful Possession of a Firearm 1 or 2 and felonies Theft of a Firearm or Possession of a Stolen Firearm, or both, charged under RCW 9.41.040, other current convictions for Unlawful Possession of a Firearm 1 or 2, Possession of a Stolen Firearm or Theft of a Firearm may not be included in the computation of the offender score per RCW 9.94A.589(1)(c). The offender will serve consecutive sentences for these particular offenses.

Theft of Livestock First Degree

RCW 9A.56.080
CLASS B – NONVIOLENT
OFFENDER SCORING RCW 9.94A.525(7)

If it was found that this offense was committed with sexual motivation (RCW 9.94A.533(8)) on or after 7/1/2006, use the General Nonviolent Offense with a Sexual Motivation Finding scoring form on page 236.

If the present conviction is for a felony domestic violence offense where domestic violence was plead and proven, use the General Nonviolent Offense Where Domestic Violence Has Been Plead and Proven scoring form on page 234.

ADULT HISTORY:

    Enter number of felony convictions .... _____ x 1 = _____

JUVENILE HISTORY:

    Enter number of Murder 1, Murder 2, and Class A sex offense felony dispositions .... _____ x 1 = _____

OTHER CURRENT OFFENSES:

(Other current offenses that do not encompass the same conduct count in offender score)

    Enter number of other felony convictions .... _____ x 1 = _____

STATUS:

    Was the offender on community custody on the date the current offense was committed? (if yes) _____ + 1 = _____

Total the last column to get the **Offender Score** (Round down to the nearest whole number)......................... _____

SENTENCE RANGE DISPLAYED IS FOR A COMPLETED OFFENSE

FOR **ATTEMPT**, **SOLICITATION**, OR **CONSPIRACY** (RCW 9.94A.595, see page 54), THE SENTENCE RANGE **IS 75%** OF THE COMPLETED RANGE LISTED BELOW

	Offender Score									
	0	**1**	**2**	**3**	**4**	**5**	**6**	**7**	**8**	**9+**
LEVEL IV	6m	9m	13m	15m	17.5m	25.5m	38m	50m	61.5m	73.5m
	3 - 9	6 - 12	12+ - 14	13 - 17	15 - 20	22 - 29	33 - 43	43 - 57	53 - 70	63 - 84

✓   For gang-related felonies where the court found the offender involved a minor (RCW 9.94A.833), see page 227 for standard range adjustments.
✓   For deadly weapon enhancement, see page 233.
✓   For sentencing alternatives, see page 215.
✓   For community custody eligibility, see page 228.
✓   For any applicable enhancements other than deadly weapon enhancement, see page 224.
✓   Per RCW 9A.56.085, the convicting court shall order the person to pay the amount of $2,000 for each animal killed or possessed.

Theft of Livestock Second Degree

RCW 9A.56.083
CLASS C* – NONVIOLENT
OFFENDER SCORING RCW 9.94A.525(7)

If it was found that this offense was committed with sexual motivation (RCW 9.94A.533(8)) on or after 7/1/2006, use the General Nonviolent Offense with a Sexual Motivation Finding scoring form on page 236.

If the present conviction is for a felony domestic violence offense where domestic violence was plead and proven, use the General Nonviolent Offense Where Domestic Violence Has Been Plead and Proven scoring form on page 234.

ADULT HISTORY:

    Enter number of felony convictions .... _____ x 1 = _____

JUVENILE HISTORY:

    Enter number of Murder 1, Murder 2, and Class A sex offense felony dispositions .... _____ x 1 = _____

OTHER CURRENT OFFENSES:

(Other current offenses that do not encompass the same conduct count in offender score)

    Enter number of other felony convictions .... _____ x 1 = _____

STATUS:

    Was the offender on community custody on the date the current offense was committed? (if yes) _____ + 1 = _____

Total the last column to get the **Offender Score** (Round down to the nearest whole number)......................... _____

SENTENCE RANGE

	Offender Score									
	0	**1**	**2**	**3**	**4**	**5**	**6**	**7**	**8**	**9+**
LEVEL III	2m	5m	8m	11m	14m	19.5m	25.5m	38m	50m	55.5m
	1 - 3	3 - 8	4 - 12	9 - 12	12+ - 16	17 - 22	22 - 29	33 - 43	43 - 57	51 - 60*

    * Class C felony offenses have a statutory maximum sentence of 60 months, see RCW 9A.20.021.

✓   For gang-related felonies where the court found the offender involved a minor (RCW 9.94A.833), see page 227 for standard range adjustment.
✓   For deadly weapon enhancement, see page 233.
✓   For sentencing alternatives, see page 215.
✓   For community custody eligibility, see page 228.
✓   For any applicable enhancements other than deadly weapon enhancement, see page 224.
✓   Per RCW 9A.56.085, the convicting court shall order the person to pay the amount of $2,000 for each animal killed or possessed.

RCW 9A.56.065
CLASS B – NONVIOLENT
OFFENDER SCORING RCW 9.94A.525(20)

If it was found that this offense was committed with sexual motivation (RCW 9.94A.533(8)) on or after 7/1/2006, use the General Nonviolent Offense with a Sexual Motivation Finding scoring form on page 236.

If the present conviction is for a felony domestic violence offense where domestic violence was plead and proven, use the General Nonviolent Offense Where Domestic Violence Has Been Plead and Proven scoring form on page 234.

ADULT HISTORY:

Enter number of Theft of a Motor Vehicle, Theft 1 & 2 (of a Motor Vehicle),
Possession of Stolen Property 1 & 2 (of a Motor Vehicle), Possession of a Stolen Vehicle
and Taking a Motor Vehicle without Permission 1 & 2 felony convictions .... _____ x 3 = _____

Enter number of Vehicle Prowling 2 convictions .... _____ x 1 = _____

Enter number of felony convictions .... _____ x 1 = _____

JUVENILE HISTORY:

Enter number of Murder 1, Murder 2, and Class A sex offense felony dispositions .... _____ x 1 = _____

OTHER CURRENT OFFENSES:

(Other current offenses that do not encompass the same conduct count in offender score)

Enter number of other Theft of a Motor Vehicle, Theft 1 & 2 (of a Motor Vehicle),
Possession of Stolen Property 1 & 2 (of a Motor Vehicle), Possession of a Stolen Vehicle
and Taking a Motor Vehicle without Permission 1 & 2 felony convictions .... _____ x 3 = _____

Enter number of other Vehicle Prowling 2 convictions .... _____ x 1 = _____

Enter number of other felony convictions .... _____ x 1 = _____

STATUS:

Was the offender on community custody on the date the current offense was committed? (if yes) _____ + 1 = _____

Total the last column to get the **Offender Score** (Round down to the nearest whole number) .... _____

SENTENCE RANGE DISPLAYED IS FOR A COMPLETED OFFENSE

FOR **ATTEMPT**, **SOLICITATION**, OR **CONSPIRACY** (RCW 9.94A.595, see page 54), THE SENTENCE RANGE **IS 75%** OF THE COMPLETED RANGE LISTED BELOW

	Offender Score									
	0	**1**	**2**	**3**	**4**	**5**	**6**	**7**	**8**	**9+**
LEVEL II		4m	6m	8m	13m	16m	19.5m	25.5m	38m	50m
	0-90 days	2 - 6	3 - 9	4 - 12	12+ - 14	14 - 18	17 - 22	22 - 29	33 - 43	43 - 57

✓ For gang-related felonies where the court found the offender involved a minor (RCW 9.94A.833), see page 227 for standard range adjustments.
✓ For deadly weapon enhancement, see page 233.
✓ For sentencing alternatives, see page 215.
✓ For community custody eligibility, see page 228.
✓ For any applicable enhancements other than deadly weapon enhancement, see page 224.

Theft of Rental, Leased, Lease-Purchased or Loaned Property
Valued at $5,000 or more
RCW 9A.56.096(5)(a)
CLASS B – NONVIOLENT
OFFENDER SCORING RCW 9.94A.525(7)

If it was found that this offense was committed with sexual motivation (RCW 9.94A.533(8)) on or after 7/1/2006, use the General Nonviolent Offense with a Sexual Motivation Finding scoring form on page 236.

If the present conviction is for a felony domestic violence offense where domestic violence was plead and proven, use the General Nonviolent Offense Where Domestic Violence Has Been Plead and Proven scoring form on page 234.

ADULT HISTORY:

    Enter number of felony convictions .... _____ x 1 = _____

JUVENILE HISTORY:

    Enter number of Murder 1, Murder 2, and Class A sex offense felony dispositions .... _____ x 1 = _____

OTHER CURRENT OFFENSES:

(Other current offenses that do not encompass the same conduct count in offender score)

    Enter number of other felony convictions .... _____ x 1 = _____

STATUS:

    Was the offender on community custody on the date the current offense was committed? (if yes) _____ + 1 = _____

Total the last column to get the **Offender Score** (Round down to the nearest whole number)......................... _____

SENTENCE RANGE DISPLAYED IS FOR A COMPLETED OFFENSE

FOR **ATTEMPT**, **SOLICITATION**, OR **CONSPIRACY** (RCW 9.94A.595, see page 54), THE SENTENCE RANGE **IS 75%** OF THE COMPLETED RANGE LISTED BELOW

	0	1	2	3	4	5	6	7	8	9+
Offender Score										
LEVEL II		4m	6m	8m	13m	16m	19.5m	25.5m	38m	50m
	0-90 days	2 - 6	3 - 9	4 - 12	12+ - 14	14 - 18	17 - 22	22 - 29	33 - 43	43 - 57

- ✓ For gang-related felonies where the court found the offender involved a minor (RCW 9.94A.833), see page 227 for standard range adjustments.
- ✓ For deadly weapon enhancement, see page 233.
- ✓ For sentencing alternatives, see page 215.
- ✓ For community custody eligibility, see page 228.
- ✓ For any applicable enhancements other than deadly weapon enhancement, see page 224.

Theft of Rental, Leased, Lease-Purchased or Loaned Property
Valued at $750 or more but less than $5,000

RCW 9A.56.096(5)(b)
CLASS C – NONVIOLENT
OFFENDER SCORING RCW 9.94A.525(7)

If it was found that this offense was committed with sexual motivation (RCW 9.94A.533(8)) on or after 7/1/2006, use the General Nonviolent Offense with a Sexual Motivation Finding scoring form on page 236.

If the present conviction is for a felony domestic violence offense where domestic violence was plead and proven, use the General Nonviolent Offense Where Domestic Violence Has Been Plead and Proven scoring form on page 234.

ADULT HISTORY:

    Enter number of felony convictions .... _____ x 1 = _____

JUVENILE HISTORY:

    Enter number of Murder 1, Murder 2, and Class A sex offense felony dispositions .... _____ x 1 = _____

OTHER CURRENT OFFENSES:

(Other current offenses that do not encompass the same conduct count in offender score)

    Enter number of other felony convictions .... _____ x 1 = _____

STATUS:

    Was the offender on community custody on the date the current offense was committed? (if yes) _____ + 1 = _____

Total the last column to get the **Offender Score** (Round down to the nearest whole number) .... _____

SENTENCE RANGE

	Offender Score									
	0	**1**	**2**	**3**	**4**	**5**	**6**	**7**	**8**	**9+**
LEVEL I			3m	4m	5.5m	8m	13m	16m	19.5m	25.5m
	0-60 days	0-90 days	2 - 5	2 - 6	3 - 8	4 - 12	12+ - 14	14 - 18	17 - 22	22 - 29

✓ For gang-related felonies where the court found the offender involved a minor (RCW 9.94A.833), see page 227 for standard range adjustment.
✓ For deadly weapon enhancement, see page 233.
✓ For sentencing alternatives, see page 215.
✓ For community custody eligibility, see page 228.
✓ For any applicable enhancements other than deadly weapon enhancement, see page 224.

RCW 9A.56.340(2)
CLASS B – NONVIOLENT
OFFENDER SCORING RCW 9.94A.525(7)

If it was found that this offense was committed with sexual motivation (RCW 9.94A.533(8)) on or after 7/1/2006, use the General Nonviolent Offense with a Sexual Motivation Finding scoring form on page 236.

If the present conviction is for a felony domestic violence offense where domestic violence was plead and proven, use the General Nonviolent Offense Where Domestic Violence Has Been Plead and Proven scoring form on page 234.

ADULT HISTORY:

    Enter number of felony convictions .... _____ x 1 = _____

JUVENILE HISTORY:

    Enter number of Murder 1, Murder 2, and Class A sex offense felony dispositions .... _____ x 1 = _____

OTHER CURRENT OFFENSES:

(Other current offenses that do not encompass the same conduct count in offender score)

    Enter number of other felony convictions .... _____ x 1 = _____

STATUS:

    Was the offender on community custody on the date the current offense was committed? (if yes) _____ + 1 = _____

Total the last column to get the **Offender Score** (Round down to the nearest whole number) ....

SENTENCE RANGE DISPLAYED IS FOR A COMPLETED OFFENSE

FOR **ATTEMPT**, **SOLICITATION**, OR **CONSPIRACY** (RCW 9.94A.595, see page 54), THE SENTENCE RANGE **IS 75%** OF THE COMPLETED RANGE LISTED BELOW

Offender Score										
	0	1	2	3	4	5	6	7	8	9+
LEVEL III	2m	5m	8m	11m	14m	19.5m	25.5m	38m	50m	59.5m
	1 - 3	3 - 8	4 - 12	9 - 12	12+ - 16	17 - 22	22 - 29	33 - 43	43 - 57	51 - 68

✓   For gang-related felonies where the court found the offender involved a minor (RCW 9.94A.833), see page 227 for standard range adjustments.
✓   For deadly weapon enhancement, see page 233.
✓   For sentencing alternatives, see page 215.
✓   For community custody eligibility, see page 228.
✓   For any applicable enhancements other than deadly weapon enhancement, see page 224.

Theft with Intent to Resell Second Degree

RCW 9A.56.340(3)
CLASS C – NONVIOLENT
OFFENDER SCORING RCW 9.94A.525(7)

If it was found that this offense was committed with sexual motivation (RCW 9.94A.533(8)) on or after 7/1/2006, use the General Nonviolent Offense with a Sexual Motivation Finding scoring form on page 236.

If the present conviction is for a felony domestic violence offense where domestic violence was plead and proven, use the General Nonviolent Offense Where Domestic Violence Has Been Plead and Proven scoring form on page 234.

ADULT HISTORY:

    Enter number of felony convictions .... _____ x 1 = _____

JUVENILE HISTORY:

    Enter number of Murder 1, Murder 2, and Class A sex offense felony dispositions .... _____ x 1 = _____

OTHER CURRENT OFFENSES:

(Other current offenses that do not encompass the same conduct count in offender score)

    Enter number of other felony convictions .... _____ x 1 = _____

STATUS:

    Was the offender on community custody on the date the current offense was committed? (if yes) _____ + 1 = _____

Total the last column to get the **Offender Score** (Round down to the nearest whole number)......................... _____

SENTENCE RANGE

		0	1	2	3	4	5	6	7	8	9+
						Offender Score					
LEVEL II			4m	6m	8m	13m	16m	19.5m	25.5m	38m	50m
	0-90 days		2 - 6	3 - 9	4 - 12	12+ - 14	14 - 18	17 - 22	22 - 29	33 - 43	43 - 57

✓   For gang-related felonies where the court found the offender involved a minor (RCW 9.94A.833), see page 227 for standard range adjustments.

✓   For deadly weapon enhancement, see page 233.

✓   For sentencing alternatives, see page 215.

✓   For community custody eligibility, see page 228.

✓   For any applicable enhancements other than deadly weapon enhancement, see page 224.

RCW 9.61.160
CLASS B – NONVIOLENT/CRIMES AGAINST PERSONS (If Against Person)
OFFENDER SCORING RCW 9.94A.525(7)

If it was found that this offense was committed with sexual motivation (RCW 9.94A.533(8)) on or after 7/1/2006, use the General Nonviolent Offense with a Sexual Motivation Finding scoring form on page 236.

If the present conviction is for a felony domestic violence offense where domestic violence was plead and proven, use the General Nonviolent Offense Where Domestic Violence Has Been Plead and Proven scoring form on page 234.

ADULT HISTORY:

    Enter number of felony convictions .... _____ x 1 = _____

JUVENILE HISTORY:

    Enter number of Murder 1, Murder 2, and Class A sex offense felony dispositions .... _____ x 1 = _____

OTHER CURRENT OFFENSES:

(Other current offenses that do not encompass the same conduct count in offender score)

    Enter number of other felony convictions .... _____ x 1 = _____

STATUS:

    Was the offender on community custody on the date the current offense was committed? (if yes) _____ + 1 = _____

Total the last column to get the **Offender Score** (Round down to the nearest whole number).......................... _____

SENTENCE RANGE DISPLAYED IS FOR A COMPLETED OFFENSE

FOR **ATTEMPT**, **SOLICITATION**, OR **CONSPIRACY** (RCW 9.94A.595, see page 54), THE SENTENCE RANGE **IS 75%** OF THE COMPLETED RANGE LISTED BELOW

	Offender Score									
	0	**1**	**2**	**3**	**4**	**5**	**6**	**7**	**8**	**9+**
LEVEL IV	6m	9m	13m	15m	17.5m	25.5m	38m	50m	61.5m	73.5m
	3 - 9	6 - 12	12+ - 14	13 - 17	15 - 20	22 - 29	33 - 43	43 - 57	53 - 70	63 - 84

✓   For gang-related felonies where the court found the offender involved a minor (RCW 9.94A.833), see page 227 for standard range adjustments.
✓   For deadly weapon enhancement, see page 233.
✓   For sentencing alternatives, see page 215.
✓   For community custody eligibility, see page 228.
✓   For any applicable enhancements other than deadly weapon enhancement, see page 224.

RCW 48.30A.015
CLASS C – NONVIOLENT
OFFENDER SCORING RCW 9.94A.525(7)

If it was found that this offense was committed with sexual motivation (RCW 9.94A.533(8)) on or after 7/1/2006, use the General Nonviolent Offense with a Sexual Motivation Finding scoring form on page 236.

If the present conviction is for a felony domestic violence offense where domestic violence was plead and proven, use the General Nonviolent Offense Where Domestic Violence Has Been Plead and Proven scoring form on page 234.

ADULT HISTORY:

Enter number of felony convictions .... _____ x 1 = _____

JUVENILE HISTORY:

Enter number of Murder 1, Murder 2, and Class A sex offense felony dispositions .... _____ x 1 = _____

OTHER CURRENT OFFENSES:

(Other current offenses that do not encompass the same conduct count in offender score)

Enter number of other felony convictions .... _____ x 1 = _____

STATUS:

Was the offender on community custody on the date the current offense was committed? (if yes) _____ + 1 = _____

Total the last column to get the **Offender Score** (Round down to the nearest whole number) ....

SENTENCE RANGE

		Offender Score								
	0	**1**	**2**	**3**	**4**	**5**	**6**	**7**	**8**	**9+**
LEVEL II		4m	6m	8m	13m	16m	19.5m	25.5m	38m	50m
	0-90 days	2 - 6	3 - 9	4 - 12	12+ - 14	14 - 18	17 - 22	22 - 29	33 - 43	43 - 57

✓ For gang-related felonies where the court found the offender involved a minor (RCW 9.94A.833), see page 227 for standard range adjustment.
✓ For deadly weapon enhancement, see page 233.
✓ For sentencing alternatives, see page 215.
✓ For community custody eligibility, see page 228.
✓ For any applicable enhancements other than deadly weapon enhancement, see page 224.

RCW 9A.82.050
CLASS B – NONVIOLENT
OFFENDER SCORING RCW 9.94A.525(7)

If it was found that this offense was committed with sexual motivation (RCW 9.94A.533(8)) on or after 7/1/2006, use the General Nonviolent Offense with a Sexual Motivation Finding scoring form on page 236.

If the present conviction is for a felony domestic violence offense where domestic violence was plead and proven, use the General Nonviolent Offense Where Domestic Violence Has Been Plead and Proven scoring form on page 234.

ADULT HISTORY:

    Enter number of felony convictions .... _____ x 1 = _____

JUVENILE HISTORY:

    Enter number of Murder 1, Murder 2, and Class A sex offense felony dispositions .... _____ x 1 = _____

OTHER CURRENT OFFENSES:

(Other current offenses that do not encompass the same conduct count in offender score)

    Enter number of other felony convictions .... _____ x 1 = _____

STATUS:

    Was the offender on community custody on the date the current offense was committed? (if yes) _____ + 1 = _____

Total the last column to get the **Offender Score** (Round down to the nearest whole number).......................... _____

SENTENCE RANGE DISPLAYED IS FOR A COMPLETED OFFENSE

FOR **ATTEMPT**, **SOLICITATION**, OR **CONSPIRACY** (RCW 9.94A.595, see page 54), THE SENTENCE RANGE **IS 75%** OF THE COMPLETED RANGE LISTED BELOW

Offender Score										
	0	**1**	**2**	**3**	**4**	**5**	**6**	**7**	**8**	**9+**
LEVEL IV	6m	9m	13m	15m	17.5m	25.5m	38m	50m	61.5m	73.5m
	3 - 9	6 - 12	12+ - 14	13 - 17	15 - 20	22 - 29	33 - 43	43 - 57	53 - 70	63 - 84

✓ For gang-related felonies where the court found the offender involved a minor (RCW 9.94A.833), see page 227 for standard range adjustments.
✓ For deadly weapon enhancement, see page 233.
✓ For sentencing alternatives, see page 215.
✓ For community custody eligibility, see page 228.
✓ For any applicable enhancements other than deadly weapon enhancement, see page 224.

Trafficking in Stolen Property Second Degree
RCW 9A.82.055
CLASS C* – NONVIOLENT
OFFENDER SCORING RCW 9.94A.525(7)

If it was found that this offense was committed with sexual motivation (RCW 9.94A.533(8)) on or after 7/1/2006, use the General Nonviolent Offense with a Sexual Motivation Finding scoring form on page 236.

If the present conviction is for a felony domestic violence offense where domestic violence was plead and proven, use the General Nonviolent Offense Where Domestic Violence Has Been Plead and Proven scoring form on page 234.

ADULT HISTORY:

Enter number of felony convictions .... _____ x 1 = _____

JUVENILE HISTORY:

Enter number of Murder 1, Murder 2, and Class A sex offense felony dispositions .... _____ x 1 = _____

OTHER CURRENT OFFENSES:

(Other current offenses that do not encompass the same conduct count in offender score)

Enter number of other felony convictions .... _____ x 1 = _____

STATUS:

Was the offender on community custody on the date the current offense was committed? (if yes) _____ + 1 = _____

Total the last column to get the **Offender Score** (Round down to the nearest whole number)........................ _____

SENTENCE RANGE

| | Offender Score | | | | | | | | | |
	0	1	2	3	4	5	6	7	8	9+
LEVEL III	2m	5m	8m	11m	14m	19.5m	25.5m	38m	50m	55.5m
	1 - 3	3 - 8	4 - 12	9 - 12	12+ - 16	17 - 22	22 - 29	33 - 43	43 - 57	51 - 60*

* Class C felony offenses have a statutory maximum sentence of 60 months, see RCW 9A.20.021.

✓ For gang-related felonies where the court found the offender involved a minor (RCW 9.94A.833), see page 227 for standard range adjustment.
✓ For deadly weapon enhancement, see page 233.
✓ For sentencing alternatives, see page 215.
✓ For community custody eligibility, see page 228.
✓ For any applicable enhancements other than deadly weapon enhancement, see page 224.

Unlawful Factoring of a Credit or Payment Card Transaction

RCW 9A.56.290(4)(a)
CLASS C – NONVIOLENT
OFFENDER SCORING RCW 9.94A.525(7)

If it was found that this offense was committed with sexual motivation (RCW 9.94A.533(8)) on or after 7/1/2006, use the General Nonviolent Offense with a Sexual Motivation Finding scoring form on page 236.

If the present conviction is for a felony domestic violence offense where domestic violence was plead and proven, use the General Nonviolent Offense Where Domestic Violence Has Been Plead and Proven scoring form on page 234.

ADULT HISTORY:

Enter number of felony convictions .... _____ x 1 = _____

JUVENILE HISTORY:

Enter number of Murder 1, Murder 2, and Class A sex offense felony dispositions .... _____ x 1 = _____

OTHER CURRENT OFFENSES:

(Other current offenses that do not encompass the same conduct count in offender score)

Enter number of other felony convictions .... _____ x 1 = _____

STATUS:

Was the offender on community custody on the date the current offense was committed? (if yes) _____ + 1 = _____

Total the last column to get the **Offender Score** (Round down to the nearest whole number).......................... _____

SENTENCE RANGE

		0	1	2	3	4	5	6	7	8	9+
						Offender Score					
LEVEL II			4m	6m	8m	13m	16m	19.5m	25.5m	38m	50m
	0-90 days		2 - 6	3 - 9	4 - 12	12+ - 14	14 - 18	17 - 22	22 - 29	33 - 43	43 - 57

✓ For gang-related felonies where the court found the offender involved a minor (RCW 9.94A.833), see page 227 for standard range adjustment.
✓ For deadly weapon enhancement, see page 233.
✓ For sentencing alternatives, see page 215.
✓ For community custody eligibility, see page 228.
✓ For any applicable enhancements other than deadly weapon enhancement, see page 224.

Unlawful Factoring of a Credit or Payment Card Transaction
Subsequent Violation
RCW 9A.56.290(4)(b)
CLASS B – NONVIOLENT
OFFENDER SCORING RCW 9.94A.525(7)

If it was found that this offense was committed with sexual motivation (RCW 9.94A.533(8)) on or after 7/1/2006, use the General Nonviolent Offense with a Sexual Motivation Finding scoring form on page 236.

If the present conviction is for a felony domestic violence offense where domestic violence was plead and proven, use the General Nonviolent Offense Where Domestic Violence Has Been Plead and Proven scoring form on page 234.

ADULT HISTORY:

Enter number of felony convictions .... _____ x 1 = _____

JUVENILE HISTORY:

Enter number of Murder 1, Murder 2, and Class A sex offense felony dispositions .... _____ x 1 = _____

OTHER CURRENT OFFENSES:

(Other current offenses that do not encompass the same conduct count in offender score)

Enter number of other felony convictions .... _____ x 1 = _____

STATUS:

Was the offender on community custody on the date the current offense was committed? (if yes) _____ + 1 = _____

Total the last column to get the **Offender Score** (Round down to the nearest whole number)........................ _____

SENTENCE RANGE DISPLAYED IS FOR A COMPLETED OFFENSE

FOR **ATTEMPT**, **SOLICITATION**, OR **CONSPIRACY** (RCW 9.94A.595, see page 54), THE SENTENCE RANGE **IS 75%** OF THE COMPLETED RANGE LISTED BELOW

	Offender Score									
	0	**1**	**2**	**3**	**4**	**5**	**6**	**7**	**8**	**9+**
LEVEL IV	6m	9m	13m	15m	17.5m	25.5m	38m	50m	61.5m	73.5m
	3 - 9	6 - 12	12+ - 14	13 - 17	15 - 20	22 - 29	33 - 43	43 - 57	53 - 70	63 - 84

✓ For gang-related felonies where the court found the offender involved a minor (RCW 9.94A.833), see page 227 for standard range adjustments.
✓ For deadly weapon enhancement, see page 233.
✓ For sentencing alternatives, see page 215.
✓ For community custody eligibility, see page 228.
✓ For any applicable enhancements other than deadly weapon enhancement, see page 224.

RCW 9A.40.040
CLASS C* – NONVIOLENT/CRIMES AGAINST PERSONS
OFFENDER SCORING RCW 9.94A.525(7)

If it was found that this offense was committed with sexual motivation (RCW 9.94A.533(8)) on or after 7/1/2006, use the General Nonviolent Offense with a Sexual Motivation Finding scoring form on page 236.

If the present conviction is for a felony domestic violence offense where domestic violence was plead and proven, use the General Nonviolent Offense Where Domestic Violence Has Been Plead and Proven scoring form on page 234.

ADULT HISTORY:

Enter number of felony convictions .... _____ x 1 = _____

JUVENILE HISTORY:

Enter number of Murder 1, Murder 2, and Class A sex offense felony dispositions .... _____ x 1 = _____

OTHER CURRENT OFFENSES:

(Other current offenses that do not encompass the same conduct count in offender score)

Enter number of other felony convictions .... _____ x 1 = _____

STATUS:

Was the offender on community custody on the date the current offense was committed? (if yes) _____ + 1 = _____

Total the last column to get the **Offender Score** (Round down to the nearest whole number).......................... _____

SENTENCE RANGE

	Offender Score									
	0	**1**	**2**	**3**	**4**	**5**	**6**	**7**	**8**	**9+**
LEVEL III	2m	5m	8m	11m	14m	19.5m	25.5m	38m	50m	55.5m
	1 - 3	3 - 8	4 - 12	9 - 12	12+ - 16	17 - 22	22 - 29	33 - 43	43 - 57	51 - 60*

* Class C felony offenses have a statutory maximum sentence of 60 months, see RCW 9A.20.021.

✓ For gang-related felonies where the court found the offender involved a minor (RCW 9.94A.833), see page 227 for standard range adjustment.
✓ For deadly weapon enhancement, see page 233.
✓ For sentencing alternatives, see page 215.
✓ For community custody eligibility, see page 228.
✓ For any applicable enhancements other than deadly weapon enhancement, see page 224.

Unlawful Issuance of Checks or Drafts Value Greater than $750

RCW 9A.56.060(4)
CLASS C – NONVIOLENT
OFFENDER SCORING RCW 9.94A.525(7)

If it was found that this offense was committed with sexual motivation (RCW 9.94A.533(8)) on or after 7/1/2006, use the General Nonviolent Offense with a Sexual Motivation Finding scoring form on page 236.

If the present conviction is for a felony domestic violence offense where domestic violence was plead and proven, use the General Nonviolent Offense Where Domestic Violence Has Been Plead and Proven scoring form on page 234.

ADULT HISTORY:

    Enter number of felony convictions .... _____ x 1 = _____

JUVENILE HISTORY:

    Enter number of Murder 1, Murder 2, and Class A sex offense felony dispositions .... _____ x 1 = _____

OTHER CURRENT OFFENSES:

(Other current offenses that do not encompass the same conduct count in offender score)

    Enter number of other felony convictions .... _____ x 1 = _____

STATUS:

    Was the offender on community custody on the date the current offense was committed? (if yes) _____ + 1 = _____

Total the last column to get the **Offender Score** (Round down to the nearest whole number)......................... _____

SENTENCE RANGE

	Offender Score									
	0	**1**	**2**	**3**	**4**	**5**	**6**	**7**	**8**	**9+**
LEVEL I			3m	4m	5.5m	8m	13m	16m	19.5m	25.5m
	0-60 days	0-90 days	2 - 5	2 - 6	3 - 8	4 - 12	12+ - 14	14 - 18	17 - 22	22 - 29

✓   For gang-related felonies where the court found the offender involved a minor (RCW 9.94A.833), see page 227 for standard range adjustment.
✓   For deadly weapon enhancement, see page 233.
✓   For sentencing alternatives, see page 215.
✓   For community custody eligibility, see page 228.
✓   For any applicable enhancements other than deadly weapon enhancement, see page 224.

Unlawful Possession of Fictitious Identification,
Unlawful Possession of Instruments of Financial Fraud,
Unlawful Possession of Payment Instruments,
Unlawful Possession of a Personal Identification Device,
Unlawful Production of Payment Instruments

RCW 9A.56.320
CLASS C – NONVIOLENT
OFFENDER SCORING RCW 9.94A.525(7)

If it was found that this offense was committed with sexual motivation (RCW 9.94A.533(8)) on or after 7/1/2006, use the General Nonviolent Offense with a Sexual Motivation Finding scoring form on page 236.

If the present conviction is for a felony domestic violence offense where domestic violence was plead and proven, use the General Nonviolent Offense Where Domestic Violence Has Been Plead and Proven scoring form on page 234.

ADULT HISTORY:

Enter number of felony convictions .... _____ x 1 = _____

JUVENILE HISTORY:

Enter number of Murder 1, Murder 2, and Class A sex offense felony dispositions .... _____ x 1 = _____

OTHER CURRENT OFFENSES:

(Other current offenses that do not encompass the same conduct count in offender score)

Enter number of other felony convictions .... _____ x 1 = _____

STATUS:

Was the offender on community custody on the date the current offense was committed? (if yes) _____ + 1 = _____

Total the last column to get the **Offender Score** (Round down to the nearest whole number)......................... _____

SENTENCE RANGE

	Offender Score									
	0	**1**	**2**	**3**	**4**	**5**	**6**	**7**	**8**	**9+**
LEVEL I	0-60 days	0-90 days	3m 2 - 5	4m 2 - 6	5.5m 3 - 8	8m 4 - 12	13m 12+ - 14	16m 14 - 18	19.5m 17 - 22	25.5m 22 - 29

✓ For gang-related felonies where the court found the offender involved a minor (RCW 9.94A.833), see page 227 for standard range adjustment.
✓ For deadly weapon enhancement, see page 233.
✓ For sentencing alternatives, see page 215.
✓ For community custody eligibility, see page 228.
✓ For any applicable enhancements other than deadly weapon enhancement, see page 224.

RCW 9.41.040(1)
CLASS B – NONVIOLENT
OFFENDER SCORING RCW 9.94A.525(7)

If it was found that this offense was committed with sexual motivation (RCW 9.94A.533(8)) on or after 7/1/2006, use the General Nonviolent Offense with a Sexual Motivation Finding scoring form on page 236.

If the present conviction is for a felony domestic violence offense where domestic violence was plead and proven, use the General Nonviolent Offense Where Domestic Violence Has Been Plead and Proven scoring form on page 234.

ADULT HISTORY:

　　Enter number of felony convictions .... _____ x 1 = _____

JUVENILE HISTORY:

　　Enter number of Murder 1, Murder 2, and Class A sex offense felony dispositions .... _____ x 1 = _____

OTHER CURRENT OFFENSES:

(Other current offenses that do not encompass the same conduct count in offender score)

　　Enter number of other felony convictions .... _____ x 1 = _____

STATUS:

　　Was the offender on community custody on the date the current offense was committed? (if yes) _____ + 1 = _____

Total the last column to get the **Offender Score** (Round down to the nearest whole number)......................... _____

SENTENCE RANGE DISPLAYED IS FOR A COMPLETED OFFENSE

FOR **ATTEMPT**, **SOLICITATION**, OR **CONSPIRACY** (RCW 9.94A.595, see page 54), THE SENTENCE RANGE **IS 75%** OF THE COMPLETED RANGE LISTED BELOW

Offender Score									
0	**1**	**2**	**3**	**4**	**5**	**6**	**7**	**8**	**9+**
17.5m	24m	30m	36m	42m	47.5m	66m	78m	89.5m	101.5m
15 - 20	21 - 27	26 - 34	31 - 41	36 - 48	41 - 54	57 - 75	67 - 89	77 - 102	87 - 116

(**LEVEL VII**)

✓　For gang-related felonies where the court found the offender involved a minor (RCW 9.94A.833), see page 227 for standard range adjustments.

✓　For sentencing alternatives, see page 215.

✓　For community custody eligibility, see page 228.

✓　For any applicable enhancements other than deadly weapon enhancement, see page 224.

✓　Each firearm possessed under this section is a separate offense.

✓　The offender shall be sentenced according to RCW 9.94A.589(1)(c) if the offender is convicted of Unlawful Possession of a Firearm 1 or 2 (RCW 9.41.040) <u>and</u> for felonies Theft of a Firearm or Possession of a Stolen Firearm, or both, as current offenses.

✓　If the present conviction is for Unlawful Possession of a Firearm 1 or 2 <u>and</u> felonies Theft of a Firearm or Possession of a Stolen Firearm, or both, charged under RCW 9.41.040, other current convictions for Unlawful Possession of a Firearm 1 or 2, Possession of a Stolen Firearm or Theft of a Firearm may not be included in the computation of the offender score per RCW 9.94A.589(1)(c). The offender will serve consecutive sentences for these particular offenses.

Unlawful Possession of a Firearm Second Degree
RCW 9.41.040(2)
CLASS C* – NONVIOLENT
OFFENDER SCORING RCW 9.94A.525(7)

If it was found that this offense was committed with sexual motivation (RCW 9.94A.533(8)) on or after 7/1/2006, use the General Nonviolent Offense with a Sexual Motivation Finding scoring form on page 236.

ADULT HISTORY:

Enter number of felony convictions .... _____ x 1 = _____

JUVENILE HISTORY:

Enter number of Murder 1, Murder 2, and Class A sex offense felony dispositions .... _____ x 1 = _____

OTHER CURRENT OFFENSES:

(Other current offenses that do not encompass the same conduct count in offender score)

Enter number of other felony convictions .... _____ x 1 = _____

STATUS:

Was the offender on community custody on the date the current offense was committed? (if yes) _____ + 1 = _____

Total the last column to get the **Offender Score** (Round down to the nearest whole number).......................... _____

SENTENCE RANGE

	Offender Score									
	0	**1**	**2**	**3**	**4**	**5**	**6**	**7**	**8**	**9+**
LEVEL III	2m	5m	8m	11m	14m	19.5m	25.5m	38m	50m	55.5m
	1 - 3	3 - 8	4 - 12	9 - 12	12+ - 16	17 - 22	22 - 29	33 - 43	43 - 57	51 - 60*

* Class C felony offenses have a statutory maximum sentence of 60 months, see RCW 9A.20.021.

✓ For gang-related felonies where the court found the offender involved a minor (RCW 9.94A.833), see page 227 for standard range adjustment.
✓ For sentencing alternatives, see page 215.
✓ For community custody eligibility, see page 228.
✓ For any applicable enhancements other than deadly weapon enhancement, see page 224.
✓ Each firearm possessed under this section is a separate offense.
✓ The offender shall be sentenced according to RCW 9.94A.589(1)(c) if the offender is convicted of Unlawful Possession of a Firearm 1 or 2 (RCW 9.41.040) and for felonies Theft of a Firearm or Possession of a Stolen Firearm, or both, as current offenses.
✓ If the present conviction is for Unlawful Possession of a Firearm 1 or 2 and felonies Theft of a Firearm or Possession of a Stolen Firearm, or both, charged under RCW 9.41.040, other current convictions for Unlawful Possession of a Firearm 1 or 2, Possession of a Stolen Firearm or Theft of a Firearm may not be included in the computation of the offender score per RCW 9.94A.589(1)(c). The offender will serve consecutive sentences for these particular offenses.

RCW 2.48.180
CLASS C – NONVIOLENT
OFFENDER SCORING RCW 9.94A.525(7)

If it was found that this offense was committed with sexual motivation (RCW 9.94A.533(8)) on or after 7/1/2006, use the General Nonviolent Offense with a Sexual Motivation Finding scoring form on page 236.

If the present conviction is for a felony domestic violence offense where domestic violence was plead and proven, use the General Nonviolent Offense Where Domestic Violence Has Been Plead and Proven scoring form on page 234.

ADULT HISTORY:

Enter number of felony convictions .... _____ x 1 = _____

JUVENILE HISTORY:

Enter number of Murder 1, Murder 2, and Class A sex offense felony dispositions .... _____ x 1 = _____

OTHER CURRENT OFFENSES:

(Other current offenses that do not encompass the same conduct count in offender score)

Enter number of other felony convictions .... _____ x 1 = _____

STATUS:

Was the offender on community custody on the date the current offense was committed? (if yes) _____ + 1 = _____

Total the last column to get the **Offender Score** (Round down to the nearest whole number)........................ _____

SENTENCE RANGE

	Offender Score									
	0	**1**	**2**	**3**	**4**	**5**	**6**	**7**	**8**	**9+**
LEVEL II		4m	6m	8m	13m	16m	19.5m	25.5m	38m	50m
	0-90 days	2 - 6	3 - 9	4 - 12	12+ - 14	14 - 18	17 - 22	22 - 29	33 - 43	43 - 57

✓ For gang-related felonies where the court found the offender involved a minor (RCW 9.94A.833), see page 227 for standard range adjustments.
✓ For deadly weapon enhancement, see page 233.
✓ For sentencing alternatives, see page 215.
✓ For community custody eligibility, see page 228.
✓ For any applicable enhancements other than deadly weapon enhancement, see page 224.

Unlawful Storage of Ammonia

RCW 69.55.020
CLASS C* – NONVIOLENT
OFFENDER SCORING RCW 9.94A.525(7)

If it was found that this offense was committed with sexual motivation (RCW 9.94A.533(8)) on or after 7/1/2006, use the General Nonviolent Offense with a Sexual Motivation Finding scoring form on page 236.

If the present conviction is for a felony domestic violence offense where domestic violence was plead and proven, use the General Nonviolent Offense Where Domestic Violence Has Been Plead and Proven scoring form on page 234.

ADULT HISTORY:

　　Enter number of felony convictions .... _____ x 1 = _____

JUVENILE HISTORY:

　　Enter number of Murder 1, Murder 2, and Class A sex offense felony dispositions .... _____ x 1 = _____

OTHER CURRENT OFFENSES:

(Other current offenses that do not encompass the same conduct count in offender score)

　　Enter number of other felony convictions .... _____ x 1 = _____

STATUS:

　　Was the offender on community custody on the date the current offense was committed? (if yes) _____ + 1 = _____

Total the last column to get the **Offender Score** (Round down to the nearest whole number).......................... _____

SENTENCE RANGE

	Offender Score									
	0	**1**	**2**	**3**	**4**	**5**	**6**	**7**	**8**	**9+**
LEVEL VI	13m	17.5m	24m	30m	36m	42m	53m	58.5m		
	12+ - 14	15 - 20	21 - 27	26 - 34	31 - 41	36 - 48	46 - 60*	57 - 60*	60 - 60*	60 - 60*

* Class C felony offenses have a statutory maximum sentence of 60 months, see RCW 9A.20.021.

✓　For gang-related felonies where the court found the offender involved a minor (RCW 9.94A.833), see page 227 for standard range adjustment.
✓　For deadly weapon enhancement, see page 233.
✓　For sentencing alternatives, see page 215.
✓　For community custody eligibility, see page 228.
✓　For any applicable enhancements other than deadly weapon enhancement, see page 224.

Unlawful Use of Building for Drug Purposes
RCW 69.53.010
CLASS C – NONVIOLENT
OFFENDER SCORING RCW 9.94A.525(7)

If it was found that this offense was committed with sexual motivation (RCW 9.94A.533(8)) on or after 7/1/2006, use the General Nonviolent Offense with a Sexual Motivation Finding scoring form on page 236.

If the present conviction is for a felony domestic violence offense where domestic violence was plead and proven, use the General Nonviolent Offense Where Domestic Violence Has Been Plead and Proven scoring form on page 234.

ADULT HISTORY:

    Enter number of felony convictions .... _____ x 1 = _____

JUVENILE HISTORY:

    Enter number of Murder 1, Murder 2, and Class A sex offense felony dispositions .... _____ x 1 = _____

OTHER CURRENT OFFENSES:

(Other current offenses that do not encompass the same conduct count in offender score)

    Enter number of other felony convictions .... _____ x 1 = _____

STATUS:

    Was the offender on community custody on the date the current offense was committed? (if yes) _____ + 1 = _____

Total the last column to get the **Offender Score** (Round down to the nearest whole number) .... _____

SENTENCE RANGE - DRUG

	Offender Score		
	0 to 2	**3 to 5**	**6 to 9+**
LEVEL I	3m 0 - 6	12m 6+ - 18	18m 12+ - 24

✓ For gang-related felonies where the court found the offender involved a minor (RCW 9.94A.833), see page 227 for standard range adjustments.
✓ For deadly weapon enhancement, see page 233.
✓ For sentencing alternatives, see page 215.
✓ For community custody eligibility, see page 228.
✓ For any applicable enhancements other than deadly weapon enhancement, see page 224.

Unlawful Trafficking of Food Stamps, Unlawful Redemption of Food Stamps

RCW 9.91.142(1) & RCW 9.9A.144
CLASS C – NONVIOLENT
OFFENDER SCORING RCW 9.94A.525(7)

If it was found that this offense was committed with sexual motivation (RCW 9.94A.533(8)) on or after 7/1/2006, use the General Nonviolent Offense with a Sexual Motivation Finding scoring form on page 236.

If the present conviction is for a felony domestic violence offense where domestic violence was plead and proven, use the General Nonviolent Offense Where Domestic Violence Has Been Plead and Proven scoring form on page 234.

ADULT HISTORY:

    Enter number of felony convictions .... _____ x 1 = _____

JUVENILE HISTORY:

    Enter number of Murder 1, Murder 2, and Class A sex offense felony dispositions .... _____ x 1 = _____

OTHER CURRENT OFFENSES:

(Other current offenses that do not encompass the same conduct count in offender score)

    Enter number of other felony convictions .... _____ x 1 = _____

STATUS:

Was the offender on community custody on the date the current offense was committed? (if yes)...... _____ + 1 = _____

Total the last column to get the **Offender Score** (Round down to the nearest whole number).......................... _____

SENTENCE RANGE

	Offender Score									
	0	**1**	**2**	**3**	**4**	**5**	**6**	**7**	**8**	**9+**
LEVEL I			3m	4m	5.5m	8m	13m	16m	19.5m	25.5m
	0-60 days	0-90 days	2 - 5	2 - 6	3 - 8	4 - 12	12+ - 14	14 - 18	17 - 22	22 - 29

✓   For gang-related felonies where the court found the offender involved a minor (RCW 9.94A.833), see page 227 for standard range adjustment.
✓   For deadly weapon enhancement, see page 233.
✓   For sentencing alternatives, see page 215.
✓   For community custody eligibility, see page 228.
✓   For any applicable enhancements other than deadly weapon enhancement, see page 224.

RCW 18.130.190(7)(b)
CLASS C – NONVIOLENT
OFFENDER SCORING RCW 9.94A.525(7)

If it was found that this offense was committed with sexual motivation (RCW 9.94A.533(8)) on or after 7/1/2006, use the General Nonviolent Offense with a Sexual Motivation Finding scoring form on page 236.

If the present conviction is for a felony domestic violence offense where domestic violence was plead and proven, use the General Nonviolent Offense Where Domestic Violence Has Been Plead and Proven scoring form on page 234.

ADULT HISTORY:

Enter number of felony convictions .... _____ x 1 = _____

JUVENILE HISTORY:

Enter number of Murder 1, Murder 2, and Class A sex offense felony dispositions .... _____ x 1 = _____

OTHER CURRENT OFFENSES:

(Other current offenses that do not encompass the same conduct count in offender score)

Enter number of other felony convictions .... _____ x 1 = _____

STATUS:

Was the offender on community custody on the date the current offense was committed? (if yes) _____ + 1 = _____

Total the last column to get the **Offender Score** (Round down to the nearest whole number)........................ _____

SENTENCE RANGE

	Offender Score									
	0	**1**	**2**	**3**	**4**	**5**	**6**	**7**	**8**	**9+**
LEVEL II		4m	6m	8m	13m	16m	19.5m	25.5m	38m	50m
	0-90 days	2 - 6	3 - 9	4 - 12	12+ - 14	14 - 18	17 - 22	22 - 29	33 - 43	43 - 57

✓ For gang-related felonies where the court found the offender involved a minor (RCW 9.94A.833), see page 227 for standard range adjustment.
✓ For deadly weapon enhancement, see page 233.
✓ For sentencing alternatives, see page 215.
✓ For community custody eligibility, see page 228.
✓ For any applicable enhancements other than deadly weapon enhancement, see page 224.

Use of a Machine Gun in Commission of a Felony

RCW 9.41.225
CLASS A – VIOLENT
OFFENDER SCORING RCW 9.94A.525(8)

If it was found that this offense was committed with sexual motivation (RCW 9.94A.533(8)) on or after 7/1/2006, use the General Violent Offense with a Sexual Motivation Finding scoring form on page 244.

If the present conviction is for a felony domestic violence offense where domestic violence was plead and proven, use the General Violent Offense Where Domestic Violence Has Been Plead and Proven scoring form on page 242.

ADULT HISTORY:

Enter number of serious violent and violent felony convictions .... _____ x 2 = _____

Enter number of nonviolent felony convictions .... _____ x 1 = _____

JUVENILE HISTORY:

Enter number of Murder 1, Murder 2, and Class A sex offense felony dispositions .... _____ x 2 = _____

OTHER CURRENT OFFENSES:

(Other current offenses that do not encompass the same conduct count in offender score)

Enter number of other serious violent and violent felony convictions .... _____ x 2 = _____

Enter number of other nonviolent felony convictions .... _____ x 1 = _____

STATUS:

Was the offender on community custody on the date the current offense was committed? (if yes) _____ + 1 = _____

Total the last column to get the **Offender Score** (Round down to the nearest whole number)......................... _____

SENTENCE RANGE DISPLAYED IS FOR A COMPLETED OFFENSE

FOR **ATTEMPT**, **SOLICITATION**, OR **CONSPIRACY** (RCW 9.94A.595, see page 54), THE SENTENCE RANGE **IS 75%** OF THE COMPLETED RANGE LISTED BELOW

	Offender Score									
	0	**1**	**2**	**3**	**4**	**5**	**6**	**7**	**8**	**9+**
LEVEL VII	17.5m	24m	30m	36m	42m	47.5m	66m	78m	89.5m	101.5m
	15 - 20	21 - 27	26 - 34	31 - 41	36 - 48	41 - 54	57 - 75	67 - 89	77 - 102	87 - 116

✓ For gang-related felonies where the court found the offender involved a minor (RCW 9.94A.833), see page 227 for standard range adjustments.
✓ For sentencing alternatives, see page 215.
✓ For community custody eligibility, see page 228.
✓ For any applicable enhancements other than deadly weapon enhancement, see page 224.

Use of Proceeds of Criminal Profiteering, Completed or Solicitation

RCW 9A.82.080(1) & (2)
CLASS B – NONVIOLENT
OFFENDER SCORING RCW 9.94A.525(7)

If it was found that this offense was committed with sexual motivation (RCW 9.94A.533(8)) on or after 7/1/2006, use the General Nonviolent Offense with a Sexual Motivation Finding scoring form on page 236.

If the present conviction is for a felony domestic violence offense where domestic violence was plead and proven, use the General Nonviolent Offense Where Domestic Violence Has Been Plead and Proven scoring form on page 234.

ADULT HISTORY:

    Enter number of felony convictions .... _____ x 1 = _____

JUVENILE HISTORY:

    Enter number of Murder 1, Murder 2, and Class A sex offense felony dispositions .... _____ x 1 = _____

OTHER CURRENT OFFENSES:

(Other current offenses that do not encompass the same conduct count in offender score)

    Enter number of other felony convictions .... _____ x 1 = _____

STATUS:

    Was the offender on community custody on the date the current offense was committed? (if yes) _____ + 1 = _____

Total the last column to get the **Offender Score** (Round down to the nearest whole number)......................... _____

SENTENCE RANGE DISPLAYED IS FOR A COMPLETED OFFENSE

FOR **ATTEMPT**, **SOLICITATION**, OR **CONSPIRACY** (RCW 9.94A.595, see page 54), THE SENTENCE RANGE **IS 75%** OF THE COMPLETED RANGE LISTED BELOW

Offender Score									
0	**1**	**2**	**3**	**4**	**5**	**6**	**7**	**8**	**9+**
6m	9m	13m	15m	17.5m	25.5m	38m	50m	61.5m	73.5m
3 - 9	6 - 12	12+ - 14	13 - 17	15 - 20	22 - 29	33 - 43	43 - 57	53 - 70	63 - 84

(LEVEL IV)

✓ For gang-related felonies where the court found the offender involved a minor (RCW 9.94A.833), see page 227 for standard range adjustments.
✓ Knowingly attempting or conspiring to commit Use of Proceeds of Criminal Profiteering is an unranked felony (RCW 9A.82.080(3)), see page 58.
✓ For deadly weapon enhancement, see page 233.
✓ For sentencing alternatives, see page 215.
✓ For community custody eligibility, see page 228.
✓ For any applicable enhancements other than deadly weapon enhancement, see page 224.

Vehicle Prowl First Degree

RCW 9A.52.095
CLASS C – NONVIOLENT
OFFENDER SCORING RCW 9.94A.525(7)

If it was found that this offense was committed with sexual motivation (RCW 9.94A.533(8)) on or after 7/1/2006, use the General Nonviolent Offense with a Sexual Motivation Finding scoring form on page 236.

If the present conviction is for a felony domestic violence offense where domestic violence was plead and proven, use the General Nonviolent Offense Where Domestic Violence Has Been Plead and Proven scoring form on page 234.

ADULT HISTORY:

Enter number of felony convictions .... _____ x 1 = _____

JUVENILE HISTORY:

Enter number of Murder 1, Murder 2, and Class A sex offense felony dispositions .... _____ x 1 = _____

OTHER CURRENT OFFENSES:

(Other current offenses that do not encompass the same conduct count in offender score)

Enter number of other felony convictions .... _____ x 1 = _____

STATUS:

Was the offender on community custody on the date the current offense was committed? (if yes) _____ + 1 = _____

Total the last column to get the **Offender Score** (Round down to the nearest whole number).......................... _____

SENTENCE RANGE

		Offender Score								
	0	**1**	**2**	**3**	**4**	**5**	**6**	**7**	**8**	**9+**
LEVEL I			3m	4m	5.5m	8m	13m	16m	19.5m	25.5m
	0-60 days	0-90 days	2 - 5	2 - 6	3 - 8	4 - 12	12+ - 14	14 - 18	17 - 22	22 - 29

✓ For gang-related felonies where the court found the offender involved a minor (RCW 9.94A.833), see page 227 for standard range adjustment.
✓ For deadly weapon enhancement, see page 233.
✓ For sentencing alternatives, see page 215.
✓ For community custody eligibility, see page 228.
✓ For any applicable enhancements other than deadly weapon enhancement, see page 224.

Vehicle Prowling Second Degree (Third or Subsequent Offense)

RCW 9A.52.100(3)
CLASS C* – NONVIOLENT
OFFENDER SCORING RCW 9.94A.525(7)

If it was found that this offense was committed with sexual motivation (RCW 9.94A.533(8)) on or after 7/1/2006, use the General Nonviolent Offense with a Sexual Motivation Finding scoring form on page 236.

If the present conviction is for a felony domestic violence offense where domestic violence was plead and proven, use the General Nonviolent Offense Where Domestic Violence Has Been Plead and Proven scoring form on page 234.

ADULT HISTORY:

Enter number of felony convictions .... _____ x 1 = _____

JUVENILE HISTORY:

Enter number of Murder 1, Murder 2, and Class A sex offense felony dispositions .... _____ x 1 = _____

OTHER CURRENT OFFENSES:

(Other current offenses that do not encompass the same conduct count in offender score)

Enter number of other felony convictions .... _____ x 1 = _____

STATUS:

Was the offender on community custody on the date the current offense was committed? (if yes) _____ + 1 = _____

Total the last column to get the **Offender Score** (Round down to the nearest whole number)........................ _____

SENTENCE RANGE

	Offender Score									
	0	**1**	**2**	**3**	**4**	**5**	**6**	**7**	**8**	**9+**
LEVEL IV	6m	9m	13m	15m	17.5m	25.5m	38m	50m	56.5m	
	3 - 9	6 - 12	12+ - 14	13 - 17	15 - 20	22 - 29	33 - 43	43 - 57	53 - 60*	60 - 60*

* Class C felony offenses have a statutory maximum sentence of 60 months, see RCW 9A.20.021.

✓ For gang-related felonies where the court found the offender involved a minor (RCW 9.94A.833), see page 227 for standard range adjustment.
✓ For deadly weapon enhancement, see page 233.
✓ For sentencing alternatives, see page 215.
✓ For community custody eligibility, see page 228.
✓ For any applicable enhancements other than deadly weapon enhancement, see page 224.

Vehicular Assault Disregard for the Safety of Others

RCW 46.61.522(1)(c)
CLASS B – NONVIOLENT/TRAFFIC OFFENSE/CRIMES AGAINST PERSONS OFFENDER SCORING RCW 9.94A.525(11)

ADULT HISTORY:

Enter number of Vehicular Homicide and Vehicular Assault felony convictions .... _____ x 2 = _____

Enter number of Operation of a Vessel while under the Influence of Intoxicating Liquor or any Drug felony convictions .... _____ x 1 = _____

Enter number of felony convictions .... _____ x 1 = _____

Enter number of Driving while under the Influence of Intoxicating Liquor or any Drug and Actual Physical Control while under the Influence of Intoxicating Liquor or any Drug and Reckless Driving and Hit-and-Run Attended Vehicle <u>non-felony</u> convictions .... _____ x 1 = _____

JUVENILE HISTORY:

Enter number of Murder 1, Murder 2, and Class A sex offense felony dispositions .... _____ x ½ = _____

OTHER CURRENT OFFENSES:

(Other current offenses that do not encompass the same conduct count in offender score)

Enter number of Vehicular Homicide and Vehicular Assault convictions .... _____ x 2 = _____

Enter number of Operation of a Vessel while under the Influence of Intoxicating Liquor or any Drug felony convictions .... _____ x 1 = _____

Enter number of other felony convictions .... _____ x 1 = _____

Enter number of Driving while under the Influence of Intoxicating Liquor or any Drug and Actual Physical Control while under the Influence of Intoxicating Liquor or any Drug and Reckless Driving and Hit-and-Run Attended Vehicle <u>non-felony</u> convictions .... _____ x 1 = _____

STATUS:

Was the offender on community custody on the date the current offense was committed? (if yes) _____ + 1 = _____

Total the last column to get the **Offender Score** (Round down to the nearest whole number).......................... _____

SENTENCE RANGE DISPLAYED IS FOR A COMPLETED OFFENSE

FOR **ATTEMPT**, **SOLICITATION**, OR **CONSPIRACY** (RCW 9.94A.595, see page 54), THE SENTENCE RANGE **IS 75%** OF THE COMPLETED RANGE LISTED BELOW

	Offender Score									
	0	**1**	**2**	**3**	**4**	**5**	**6**	**7**	**8**	**9+**
LEVEL III	2m	5m	8m	11m	14m	19.5m	25.5m	38m	50m	59.5m
	1 - 3	3 - 8	4 - 12	9 - 12	12+ - 16	17 - 22	22 - 29	33 - 43	43 - 57	51 - 68

✓ For gang-related felonies where the court found the offender involved a minor (RCW 9.94A.833), see page 227 for standard range adjustments.
✓ For deadly weapon enhancement, see page 233.
✓ For sentencing alternatives, see page 215.
✓ For community custody eligibility, see page 228.
✓ For any applicable enhancements other than deadly weapon enhancement, see page 224.

Vehicular Assault in a Reckless Manner or while under the Influence of Intoxicating Liquor or any Drug

RCW 46.61.522(1)(a) & (b)
CLASS B – VIOLENT/TRAFFIC OFFENSE/CRIMES AGAINST PERSONS
OFFENDER SCORING RCW 9.94A.525(11)

ADULT HISTORY:

Enter number of Vehicular Homicide and Vehicular Assault felony convictions .... _____ x 2 = _____

Enter number of Operation of a Vessel while under the Influence of Intoxicating Liquor or any Drug felony convictions .... _____ x 1 = _____

Enter number of felony convictions .... _____ x 1 = _____

Enter number of Driving while under the Influence of Intoxicating Liquor or any Drug and Actual Physical Control while under the Influence of Intoxicating Liquor or any Drug and Reckless Driving and Hit-and-Run Attended Vehicle <u>non-felony</u> convictions .... _____ x 1 = _____

JUVENILE HISTORY:

Enter number of Murder 1, Murder 2, and Class A sex offense felony dispositions .... _____ x ½ = _____

OTHER CURRENT OFFENSES:

(Other current offenses that do not encompass the same conduct count in offender score)

Enter number of Vehicular Homicide and Vehicular Assault convictions..................................... _____ x 2 = _____

Enter number of Operation of a Vessel while under the Influence of Intoxicating Liquor or any Drug felony convictions .... _____ x 1 = _____

Enter number of other felony convictions .... _____ x 1 = _____

Enter number of Driving while under the Influence of Intoxicating Liquor or any Drug and Actual Physical Control while under the Influence of Intoxicating Liquor or any Drug and Reckless Driving and Hit-and-Run Attended Vehicle <u>non-felony</u> convictions .... _____ x 1 = _____

STATUS:

Was the offender on community custody on the date the current offense was committed? (if yes) _____ + 1 = _____

Total the last column to get the **Offender Score** (Round down to the nearest whole number)........................ _____

SENTENCE RANGE DISPLAYED IS FOR A COMPLETED OFFENSE

FOR **ATTEMPT**, **SOLICITATION**, OR **CONSPIRACY** (RCW 9.94A.595, see page 54), THE SENTENCE RANGE **IS 75%** OF THE COMPLETED RANGE LISTED BELOW

	Offender Score									
	0	**1**	**2**	**3**	**4**	**5**	**6**	**7**	**8**	**9+**
LEVEL IV	6m	9m	13m	15m	17.5m	25.5m	38m	50m	61.5m	73.5m
	3 - 9	6 - 12	12+ - 14	13 - 17	15 - 20	22 - 29	33 - 43	43 - 57	53 - 70	63 - 84

✓ For gang-related felonies where the court found the offender involved a minor (RCW 9.94A.833), see page 227 for standard range adjustments.
✓ For deadly weapon enhancement, see page 233.
✓ For sentencing alternatives, see page 215.
✓ For community custody eligibility, see page 228.
✓ For any applicable enhancements other than deadly weapon enhancement, see page 224.
✓ For consecutive/concurrent provisions, see page 62.

Vehicular Homicide – Disregard for the Safety of Others
RCW 46.61.520(1)(c)
CLASS A – NONVIOLENT*/TRAFFIC OFFENSE/CRIMES AGAINST PERSONS OFFENDER SCORING RCW 9.94A.525(11)

ADULT HISTORY:

Enter number of Vehicular Homicide and Vehicular Assault felony convictions .... _____ x 2 = _____

Enter number of Operation of a Vessel while under the Influence of Intoxicating Liquor or any Drug felony convictions .... _____ x 1 = _____

Enter number of felony convictions .... _____ x 1 = _____

Enter number of Driving while under the Influence of Intoxicating Liquor or any Drug and Actual Physical Control while under the Influence of Intoxicating Liquor or any Drug and Reckless Driving and Hit-and-Run Attended Vehicle non-felony convictions .... _____ x 1 = _____

JUVENILE HISTORY:

Enter number of Murder 1, Murder 2, and Class A sex offense felony dispositions .... _____ x ½ = _____

OTHER CURRENT OFFENSES:

(Other current offenses that do not encompass the same conduct count in offender score)

Enter number of Vehicular Homicide and Vehicular Assault convictions .... _____ x 2 = _____

Enter number of Operation of a Vessel while under the Influence of Intoxicating Liquor or any Drug felony convictions .... _____ x 1 = _____

Enter number of other felony convictions .... _____ x 1 = _____

Enter number of Driving while under the Influence of Intoxicating Liquor or any Drug and Actual Physical Control while under the Influence of Intoxicating Liquor or any Drug and Reckless Driving and Hit-and-Run Attended Vehicle non-felony convictions .... _____ x 1 = _____

STATUS:

Was the offender on community custody on the date the current offense was committed? (if yes) _____ + 1 = _____

Total the last column to get the **Offender Score** (Round down to the nearest whole number) .... _____

SENTENCE RANGE DISPLAYED IS FOR A COMPLETED OFFENSE

FOR **ATTEMPT**, **SOLICITATION**, OR **CONSPIRACY** (RCW 9.94A.595, see page 54), THE SENTENCE RANGE **IS 75%** OF THE COMPLETED RANGE LISTED BELOW

	Offender Score									
	0	**1**	**2**	**3**	**4**	**5**	**6**	**7**	**8**	**9+**
LEVEL VII	17.5m	24m	30m	36m	42m	47.5m	66m	78m	89.5m	101.5m
	15 - 20	21 - 27	26 - 34	31 - 41	36 - 48	41 - 54	57 - 75	67 - 89	77 - 102	87 - 116

✓ For gang-related felonies where the court found the offender involved a minor (RCW 9.94A.833), see page 227 for standard range adjustments.
✓ For deadly weapon enhancement, see page 233.
✓ For sentencing alternatives, see page 215.
✓ For community custody eligibility, see page 228.
✓ For any applicable enhancements other than deadly weapon enhancement, see page 224.

---

* Vehicular Homicide – Disregard for the Safety of Others is defined as a Class A felony offense and, therefore, appears to be a violent offense under RCW 9.94A.030. However, under *State v. Stately*, 152 Wn. App. 604, 216 P.3d 1102 (2009), it is not to be considered a violent offense.

Vehicular Homicide in a Reckless Manner

RCW 46.61.520(1)(b)
CLASS A – VIOLENT/TRAFFIC OFFENSE/CRIMES AGAINST PERSONS
OFFENDER SCORING RCW 9.94A.525(11)

ADULT HISTORY:

Enter number of Vehicular Homicide and Vehicular Assault felony convictions .... _____ x 2 = _____

Enter number of Operation of a Vessel while under the Influence of Intoxicating Liquor
or any Drug felony convictions .... _____ x 1 = _____

Enter number of felony convictions .... _____ x 1 = _____

Enter number of Driving while under the Influence of Intoxicating Liquor or any Drug
and Actual Physical Control while under the Influence of Intoxicating Liquor or any Drug
and Reckless Driving and Hit-and-Run Attended Vehicle non-felony convictions .... _____ x 1 = _____

JUVENILE HISTORY:

Enter number of Murder 1, Murder 2, and Class A sex offense felony dispositions .... _____ x ½ = _____

OTHER CURRENT OFFENSES:

(Other current offenses that do not encompass the same conduct count in offender score)

Enter number of Vehicular Homicide and Vehicular Assault convictions .... _____ x 2 = _____

Enter number of Operation of a Vessel while under the Influence of Intoxicating Liquor
or any Drug felony convictions .... _____ x 1 = _____

Enter number of other felony convictions .... _____ x 1 = _____

Enter number of Driving while under the Influence of Intoxicating Liquor or any Drug
and Actual Physical Control while under the Influence of Intoxicating Liquor or any Drug
and Reckless Driving and Hit-and-Run Attended Vehicle non-felony convictions .... _____ x 1 = _____

STATUS:

Was the offender on community custody on the date the current offense was committed? (if yes) _____ + 1 = _____

Total the last column to get the **Offender Score** (Round down to the nearest whole number)........................ _____

SENTENCE RANGE DISPLAYED IS FOR A COMPLETED OFFENSE

FOR **ATTEMPT**, **SOLICITATION**, OR **CONSPIRACY** (RCW 9.94A.595, see page 54), THE SENTENCE RANGE **IS 75%** OF THE COMPLETED RANGE LISTED BELOW

Offender Score										
	0	**1**	**2**	**3**	**4**	**5**	**6**	**7**	**8**	**9+**
LEVEL XI	90m	100m	110m	119m	129m	139m	170m	185m	215m	245m
	78 - 102	86 - 114	95 - 125	102 - 136	111 - 147	120 - 158	146 - 194	159 - 211	185 - 245	210 - 280

✓ For gang-related felonies where the court found the offender involved a minor (RCW 9.94A.833), see page 227 for standard range adjustments.
✓ For deadly weapon enhancement, see page 233.
✓ For sentencing alternatives, see page 215.
✓ For community custody eligibility, see page 228.
✓ For any applicable enhancements other than deadly weapon enhancement, see page 224.

Vehicular Homicide while under the Influence of Intoxicating Liquor or any Drug

RCW 46.61.520(1)(a)
CLASS A – VIOLENT/TRAFFIC OFFENSE/CRIMES AGAINST PERSONS
OFFENDER SCORING RCW 9.94A.525(11)

ADULT HISTORY:

Enter number of Vehicular Homicide and Vehicular Assault felony convictions .... _____ x 2 = _____

Enter number of Operation of a Vessel while under the Influence of Intoxicating Liquor or any Drug felony convictions .... _____ x 1 = _____

Enter number of felony convictions .... _____ x 1 = _____

Enter number of Driving while under the Influence of Intoxicating Liquor or any Drug and Actual Physical Control while under the Influence of Intoxicating Liquor or any Drug and Reckless Driving and Hit-and-Run Attended Vehicle non-felony convictions, except those which form the basis for an enhancement pursuant to RCW 46.61.520(2). .... _____ x 1 = _____

JUVENILE HISTORY:

Enter number of Murder 1, Murder 2, and Class A sex offense felony dispositions .... _____ x ½ = _____

OTHER CURRENT OFFENSES:

(Other current offenses that do not encompass the same conduct count in offender score)

Enter number of Vehicular Homicide and Vehicular Assault convictions .... _____ x 2 = _____

Enter number of Operation of a Vessel while under the Influence of Intoxicating Liquor or any Drug felony convictions .... _____ x 1 = _____

Enter number of other felony convictions .... _____ x 1 = _____

Enter number of Driving while under the Influence of Intoxicating Liquor or any Drug and Actual Physical Control while under the Influence of Intoxicating Liquor or any Drug and Reckless Driving and Hit-and-Run Attended Vehicle non-felony convictions, except those which form the basis for an enhancement pursuant to RCW 46.61.520(2). .... _____ x 1 = _____

STATUS:

Was the offender on community custody on the date the current offense was committed? (if yes) _____ + 1 = _____

Total the last column to get the **Offender Score** (Round down to the nearest whole number)......................... _____

SENTENCE RANGE DISPLAYED IS FOR A COMPLETED OFFENSE

FOR **ATTEMPT**, **SOLICITATION**, OR **CONSPIRACY** (RCW 9.94A.595, see page 54), THE SENTENCE RANGE **IS 75%** OF THE COMPLETED RANGE LISTED BELOW

Offender Score									
0	**1**	**2**	**3**	**4**	**5**	**6**	**7**	**8**	**9+**
LEVEL XI 90m	100m	110m	119m	129m	139m	170m	185m	215m	245m
78 - 102	86 - 114	95 - 125	102 - 136	111 - 147	120 - 158	146 - 194	159 - 211	185 - 245	210 - 280

✓ For gang-related felonies where the court found the offender involved a minor (RCW 9.94A.833), see page 227 for standard range adjustments.
✓ For deadly weapon enhancement, see page 233.
✓ For sentencing alternatives, see page 215.
✓ For community custody eligibility, see page 228.
✓ For any applicable enhancements other than deadly weapon enhancement, see page 224.
✓ An additional 24 months shall be added to the sentence for each prior offense as defined in RCW 46.61.5055.
✓ For consecutive/concurrent provisions, see page 62.

Viewing Depictions of Minor Engaged in Sexually Explicit Conduct
First Degree

RCW 9.68A.075(1)
CLASS B – NONVIOLENT/SEX
OFFENDER SCORING RCW 9.94A.525(17)

If the present conviction is for a felony domestic violence offense where domestic violence was plead and proven, use the General Nonviolent Offense Where Domestic Violence Has Been Plead and Proven scoring form on page 234.

ADULT HISTORY:

    Enter number of sex offense felony convictions .... _____ x 3 = _____

    Enter number of felony convictions .... _____ x 1 = _____

JUVENILE HISTORY:

    Enter number of Class A sex offense felony dispositions .... _____ x 3 = _____

    Enter number of Murder 1 and Murder 2 felony dispositions .... _____ x 1 = _____

OTHER CURRENT OFFENSES:

(Other current offenses that do not encompass the same conduct count in offender score)

    Enter number of other sex offense felony convictions .... _____ x 3 = _____

    Enter number of other felony convictions .... _____ x 1 = _____

STATUS:

    Was the offender on community custody on the date the current offense was committed? .... _____ + 1 = _____

Total the last column to get the **Offender Score** (Round down to the nearest whole number).................. _____

SENTENCE RANGE DISPLAYED IS FOR A COMPLETED OFFENSE

FOR **ATTEMPT**, **SOLICITATION**, OR **CONSPIRACY** (RCW 9.94A.595, see page 54), THE SENTENCE RANGE **IS 75%** OF THE COMPLETED RANGE LISTED BELOW

Offender Score										
	0	1	2	3	4	5	6	7	8	9+
LEVEL IV	6m	9m	13m	15m	17.5m	25.5m	38m	50m	61.5m	73.5m
	3 - 9	6 - 12	12+ - 14	13 - 17	15 - 20	22 - 29	33 - 43	43 - 57	53 - 70	63 - 84

✓   For gang-related felonies where the court found the offender involved a minor (RCW 9.94A.833), see page 227 for standard range adjustments.

✓   For deadly weapon enhancement, see page 233.

✓   For sentencing alternatives, see page 215.

✓   For community custody eligibility, see page 228.

✓   For any applicable enhancements other than deadly weapon enhancement, see page 224.

✓   If the offender is not a persistent offender and has a <u>prior</u> conviction for an offense listed in RCW 9.94A.030(37)(b), then the sentence is subject to the requirements of RCW 9.94A.507.

RCW 9A.44.115
CLASS C – NONVIOLENT/SEX
OFFENDER SCORING RCW 9.94A.525(17)

If the present conviction is for a felony domestic violence offense where domestic violence was plead and proven, use the General Nonviolent/Sex Offense Where Domestic Violence Has Been Plead and Proven scoring form on page 234.

ADULT HISTORY:

Enter number of sex offense felony convictions .... _____ x 3 = _____

Enter number of felony convictions .... _____ x 1 = _____

JUVENILE HISTORY:

Enter number of Class A sex offense felony dispositions .... _____ x 3 = _____

Enter number of Murder 1 and Murder 2 felony dispositions .... _____ x 1 = _____

OTHER CURRENT OFFENSES:

(Other current offenses that do not encompass the same conduct count in offender score)

Enter number of other sex offense felony convictions .... _____ x 3 = _____

Enter number of other felony convictions .... _____ x 1 = _____

STATUS:

Was the offender on community custody on the date the current offense was committed?............ _____ + 1 = _____

Total the last column to get the **Offender Score** (Round down to the nearest whole number) .... _____

SENTENCE RANGE

		0	1	2	3	4	5	6	7	8	9+
LEVEL II			4m	6m	8m	13m	16m	19.5m	25.5m	38m	50m
	0-90 days	2 - 6	3 - 9	4 - 12	12+ - 14	14 - 18	17 - 22	22 - 29	33 - 43	43 - 57

✓ For gang-related felonies where the court found the offender involved a minor (RCW 9.94A.833), see page 227 for standard range adjustment.
✓ For deadly weapon enhancement, see page 233.
✓ For sentencing alternatives, see page 215.
✓ For community custody eligibility, see page 228.
✓ For any applicable enhancements other than deadly weapon enhancement, see page 224.
✓ If the offender is not a persistent offender and has a prior conviction for an offense listed in RCW 9.94A.030(37)(b), then the sentence is subject to the requirements of RCW 9.94A.507.

Made in United States
Troutdale, OR
07/19/2024

21276126R00270